The Field

Sport history comprises a vast literature, covering sport from ancient to modern times, activities from aerobics to yachting, and themes such as race, class, gender and identity. Though the field is in good health, Douglas Booth argues that in comparison to most mainstream history, sport history has rarely been called upon to explain the foundations of its historical knowledge.

In *The Field: Truth and Fiction in Sport History*, Booth offers a comprehensive assessment of sport history as an academic discipline, exploring the diverse ways in which professional historians gather materials, construct and interrogate evidence and arguments, and present their stories about the sporting past.

- Part I examines theories of knowledge in sport history.
- Part II examines the construction and presentation of historical knowledge in sport history.

In advocating greater reflexivity and openness, *The Field* makes clear the need for a new rationale within sport history, and sets the agenda for the debate to come.

With a clear structure, sport-specific examples, summary tables and a glossary of terms, *The Field* provides students, teachers and researchers in sport history with an unparalleled resource to tackle issues that are fundamental to their subject.

Douglas Booth is Professor of Sport and Leisure Studies at the University of Waikato, New Zealand. He serves on the editorial boards of the *Journal of Sport History, Sport History Review* and *The International Journal of the History of Sport*.

He is a well-known, respected and prolific sport historian. His book *The Race Game: Politics and Sport in South Africa* (Frank Cass) won the 1998 North American Society for Sport History 'Book of the Year' award.

The Field

Truth and fiction in sport history

Douglas Booth

Routledge
Taylor & Francis Group

LONDON AND NEW YORK

First published 2005
by Routledge
2 Park Square, Milton Park, Abingdon, Oxon OX14 4RN

Simultaneously published in the USA and Canada
by Routledge
270 Madison Ave, New York, NY 10016

Routledge is an imprint of the Taylor & Francis Group

Typeset in Perpetua and Bell Gothic by
HWA Text and Data Management, Tunbridge Wells
Printed and bound in Great Britain by
TJ International Ltd, Padstow, Cornwall

British Library Cataloguing in Publication Data
A catalogue record for this book is available from the British Library

Library of Congress Cataloging-in-Publication Data
A catalog record for this book has been requested

ISBN 0–415–28227–6 (hbk)
ISBN 0–415–28228–4 (pbk)

To Colin Tatz and John Loy
Mentors without peer

Contents

Illustrations

Tables

Figure

Plates

Prologue

SOME KNOWLEDGE ABOUT THE ORIGINS OF, and influences on, this book may help readers understand my arguments and conclusions. My early research interests — apartheid sport and the sports boycott of South Africa, tensions between surfers and surf lifesavers on Australian beaches, and the olympic games and international relationships[1] — followed my academic background in politics, a discipline based on the principles of advocacy. When I began teaching a 200-level survey course on the history of sport at the University of Otago in the mid-1990s, I gave it a strong political flavour. The political dimension was less pronounced when I was teaching a 300-level course on the history of New Zealand sport. Politics underscored New Zealand's sporting relations with its great rugby rival South Africa, and especially that cataclysmic event in the nation's history, the 1981 Springbok rugby tour. However, the literature on these two subjects was, and remains, sparse and insufficient to support an upper level university course.[2] The paucity of literature in this area raised the question, what were historians of New Zealand sport studying in the second half of the 1990s? In fact, two key themes — the development of rugby as the national game and the marginalisation of women in local sporting culture — were potentially highly political. But most of the works on these subjects were either avowedly a-political histories or sociological treatises. From the perspective of a political advocate, this struck me as strange. What were the objectives of historians who shied from politics? Were these colleagues really writing history for its own sake? These simple questions launched my quest to discover how other professional historians of sport interpret their field and ply their craft.

It has not been an easy mission. As E. P. Thompson reminds us,

> the modes of historical writing are so diverse; the techniques employed by historians are so various; the themes of historical enquiry are so disparate; and, above all, the conclusions so controversial and so sharply contested within the profession, that it is difficult to adduce any disciplinary coherence.[3]

Indeed, like their colleagues throughout the discipline, historians of sport are reticent when it comes to explaining precisely how they deal with the past. Pressing for explanations often does not help. Those who do not scurry away typically refer and defer to Allen Guttmann's *From Ritual to Record* (1978), J. A. Mangan's *Athleticism in the Victorian and Edwardian Public School* (1981), Richard Holt's *Sport and the British* (1989) and Patricia Vertinsky's *The Eternally Wounded Woman* (1994).[4] These are held to be classic texts in sport history, the books by which sport historians measure and understand their field. Of course, describing these texts as classics does not explain why they enjoy this status. Pressing further may extract vague references to well-handled sources and eloquent writing. Very occasionally, someone might praise an author for the way they position themselves in relation to the evidence or the questions they propose. At this stage the more reflective might open up a little and concede that history is not as rigorous a discipline as it ought to be. Nonetheless, even the most candid practitioner is usually quick to add the caveat that if historians had to stop and explain, step by step, how they engaged with every single piece of evidence they would soon exhaust their readers' patience.[5]

Such replies are grist to critics, especially those working in other disciplines, who accuse historians of working in and promoting a discipline that they poorly understand.[6] Critics of historical practice – the philosophers, sociologists and literary theorists – are in fact the ones who offer the best insights into the nature and structure of history, and they are alerting growing numbers of practitioners to the inseparability of the philosophy of history and ordinary historical inquiry.[7] As Hayden White, an historian who works in the tradition of literary criticism, puts it, 'there can be no "proper history" which is not at the same time "philosophy of history"'.[8] Indeed, only after delving into this philosophy did I acquire the tools necessary to see and articulate the nature and structure of sport history.

Equipped with these tools, I learned that mainstream academic sport history has entered an accord with respect to ways of knowing and telling. The mainstream subscribes to analytical rigour within well-established conventions – '"getting the facts straight", consulting all the relevant source materials, providing adequate references, giving reliable summaries of factual minutiae, quoting accurately, ... ensuring quotations are not wrenched out of context, verifying the authenticity of texts and the accuracy of observations through "external and internal source criticism"', and keeping theory in the background.[9] The mainstream of sport history evinces virtually no interest in the cognitive status of studying the past; challenging questions about empiricist notions of certainty and veracity rarely surface. Rather, the field rests on the assumption – which has taken on rock-solid proportions – that there is a strong correspondence between words and the world, or between evidence and reality (whether an event, person, thing or process). For example, most historians of sport would assume that the archived minutes recording a meeting of olympic officials to discuss the merits of potential olympic host cities offers at least a reasonable account of the reality of those proceedings.

Yet, at the same time, the field of sport history accommodates a diversity of objectives and approaches. Evidence of this accommodation can be found by simply skimming the classic texts cited above, or, in a more contemporary vein, the last four winners of the North American Society for Sport History Book Award – Mike Huggins' *Flat Racing and British Society 1790–1914* (2000), Pamela Grundy's *Learning to Win: Sports, Education, and Social Change in Twentieth-Century North Carolina* (2001), Robert

Barney, Stephen Wenn and Scott Martyn, *Selling the Five Rings: The International Olympic Committee and the Rise of Olympic Commercialism* (2002), Daniel Nathan's *Saying It's So: A Cultural History of the Black Sox Scandal* (2003).[10] In each of these works the authors present a blend of 'intuition and empiricism, generalization and specificity, analysis and narrative, interpretation and explanation, creativity and reporting, objectivity and advocacy'.[11] Where Guttmann, Vertinsky, Huggins, Grundy and Nathan analyse, Mangan, Holt and Barney, Wenn and Martyn narrate; where Guttmann, Mangan, Holt, Huggins and Grundy generalise, Vertinsky, Nathan and Barney, Wenn and Martyn specify; where Guttmann, Vertinsky, Grundy and Nathan interpret, Mangan, Holt, Huggins and Barney, Wenn and Martyn explain; where Vertinsky and Nathan create, Holt and Barney, Wenn and Martyn report; where Vertinsky and Grundy advocate, Holt and Huggins detach; while Vertinsky and Nathan allow for intuition, Mangan and Huggins insist on rigorous empiricism; where Guttmann, Vertinsky, Grundy and Nathan abstract, Mangan, Huggins and Barney, Wenn and Martyn ply concrete and specific facts.

But do these different approaches fundamentally alter the epistemological foundations – the dominant ways of knowing and telling – in mainstream sport history? In order to answer this question, I discuss, analyse and evaluate the numerous ways that sport historians present their evidence and arguments, and I examine the assumptions about knowing and telling that underpin these different approaches. Thus, my objective in *The Field* is to unravel the epistemological and explanatory structures of sport history. While primarily an analytical exercise to distil and clarify the field, this text also carries a basic argument: the seemingly simple and straightforward decisions and judgements historians make about what is relevant evidence, and the ways they present that evidence, have consequences for how historians and their readers understand the past, the present and the relationship between the two.

My principal audience includes teachers, undergraduate and postgraduate students, and lecturers who are unfamiliar with the philosophy, theory and methods of history. Unfortunately, a lack of knowledge on these matters is not uncommon. In the case of sport history, this is partly due to the subject's primary location in departments of physical education, human movement or kinesiology that emphasise science and vocations (physical education teaching, sport management, sport coaching). These departments pay minimal attention to the humanities and the majority of sport historians work alone, often isolated from colleagues in the wider discipline. However, it is worth noting that sport historians are no more neglectful of philosophical and methodological questions than their colleagues who work in mainstream medieval history, religious history, political history or American history.[12] Indeed, it is not unfair to say that a great many historians 'study history without trying to understand it'![13] Nor does the language of philosophy, theory and methodology assist their study. Like all subject matter that deals with high levels of abstraction, the language is filled with jargon. To assist readers on this front, I provide a comprehensive introduction and overview (chapter 1), copious signposting, cross-referencing, summarising tables, a glossary and an index. I also endeavour to illustrate each abstract concept with at least one example from sport history.

I would not have completed this work without encouragement, ideas and resources offered by friends and colleagues. Thanks to Greg Anson, John Bale, Richard Cashman, Tim Chandler, Mike Cronin, John Dolan, Warwick Franks, Allen Guttmann, Gideon Haigh, Richard Holt, Brendan Hokowhitu, Donald Kyle, Tara Magdalinski, Malcolm

MacLean, Scott Martyn, Motohide Miyahara, Bill Murray, John O'Hara, Roberta Park, Steve Pope, Jay Scherer, Jaime Schultz, Andy Smith, Bob Stothart, Syndy Sydnor, Holly Thorpe, Patricia Vertinsky and Kevin Wamsley.

Five people played important roles in getting this project up and running and helping me see it through. John Loy first suggested I had a book in this material in 1998 after I presented a seminar on historiography to his graduate research class at the University of Otago. His words spurred me into action. Further encouragement came from Alan Metcalfe who graciously read and commented upon an early typology of sport historiography. As I began working, I discovered that my colleague and friend at the University of Queensland, Murray Phillips, had also found his way into historiography. Much more familiar with the current literature, he generously guided me to some key texts, notably works by Alun Munslow and Keith Jenkins; Munslow in particular exerts an enormous influence on this book. At the University of Otago I was also fortunate to befriend two philosophically progressive historians, Brian Moloughney and John Stenhouse. For a time they shared responsibility for teaching research methods to honours students in the Department of History and they introduced me to some major works on historiography and the philosophy of history.

Murray Phillips and Brian Moloughney also kindly read various chapters along the way, as did Stephen Hardy, Jeff Hill and Richard Pringle. All made valuable suggestions. Toni Bruce, Annemarie Jutel and Colin Tatz read the whole text. In addition to their intellectual insights, they offered sage editorial advice. My love and guide in all things, Gaye Booth, was always available to listen to my ideas. In addition to reading many drafts, she created the conditions that made completion of this book possible.

Chapter 1

An introduction to sport historiography

SPORT HISTORIANS HAVE NO DIFFICULTY recognising the content of their field. It includes any study of by-gone events, individuals, groups, practices and institutions with a sporting flavour. But ask historians of sport to formally define the objectives, assumptions, methods and forms of presentation of their field and they talk in vague terms about facts, narratives, context and theory. Ask them how their colleagues interpret the field and sport historians will likely refer to the prevailing themes of class, race and gender and their influence on the practice of sport in the past and present.[1] In other cases, they avoid the question and describe the sources of their own esoteric research, whether it be the biography of a deceased sport star, the leisure tastes of working-class coalminers in mid-Victorian Northumberland, women's intercollegiate basketball in the mid-West at the turn of the twentieth century, social changes experienced by Jewish-American sportswomen, or the culture of teenage Australian surfers in the 1960s. It is no surprise, therefore, that so many sport historians seem unsure of their field and its place in the discipline.

The Field analyses the philosophy and practice of a burgeoning subfield of academic history. It explores the questions sport historians ask, and discusses their approaches and techniques. The first substantial question is, how should I proceed? Nancy Struna suggested one model in her distinction between descriptive and analytical history.[2] According to her, historians will choose one of these two approaches, based on the type of questions they ask and the literature available to them. Likening descriptive history to a map, Struna said that just as 'a good map locates roads and landmarks', so good descriptive history locates 'a person, a trend, an event, or an organization in the past'.[3] Descriptive history reveals the variables of a specific topic, that is, the actors, social factors and structures identified in the secondary literature. Analytical history sets out to make sense of the detail. Analytical historians investigate how situations, events and phenomena came into being, they pose why questions (which focus on causes), and they examine changes across time. The analytical historian 'begins with

Table 1.1 Descriptive and analytical sport history

Description (Locates people and events in the past)		Analysis (Explains how or why something happened)	
Questions	Tools	Questions	Tools
• Where (was baseball first played?) • When (did the ancient Olympics cease?) • Who (founded the modern olympics?) • What (is the National Collegiate Athletic Association?)	• Gather sources • Interrogate sources • Verify sources	• How (did modern Western sports diffuse to Africa and Asia?) • Why (is the media less interested in women's sport?)	• Causation • Concepts • Comparisons • Contexts

the map (or description) of experiences, breaks apart and relates the constituents of those experiences, and ends with "making sense" of the entire scene'.[4] Table 1.1 provides a schematic representation of descriptive and analytical sport history, and identifies the different tools employed by the two approaches. Whereas gathering and verifying factual evidence is the principal method of descriptive history, analytical historians search for causes and build arguments around concepts, comparisons and contexts.

One variation on Struna's division of history into descriptive and analytical forms is to categorise the answers produced by these questions. Practitioners who ask where, when, who and what invariably focus on single points in the past, be they events, incidents or phenomena, and tend to highlight the actions of individuals or specific actors (clubs, organisations, groups, communities). This category might be called the still, or photographic, approach to history. By contrast, practitioners who ask how and why tend to conceptualise history as a process and emphasise social change and development. Abstract concepts, themes and patterns are usually elements of this approach. While Thompson found the photographic approach inadequate – every still is simultaneously a 'moment of being' and a 'moment of becoming', just as every 'historical moment is both a result of prior process and an index towards the direction of its future flow'[5] – it remains very much alive in sport history. Irrespective of Thompson's concerns, the still and process categories, represented schematically in Table 1.2, highlight additional differences in the way sport historians approach their work, particularly with respect to the incorporation of abstract structures.

As useful as these schemas might appear, they ignore fundamental epistemological differences in historical practice. These differences provide the foundations of *The Field*. In Part I, I investigate the general nature of historical knowledge using a framework developed by Alun Munslow. He discerns three basic models of historical inquiry. According to Munslow and his collaborator Keith Jenkins, 'no matter if history texts are written by economic or social or cultural historians; no matter what the period or specialisation; no matter if the writers are Marxist or liberals, feminists or reactionaries; no matter if they are overtly positioned or not, the most insightful and productive way of organising them all is to locate them as belonging to – having an orientation to – one of the following three genres: reconstructionist, constructionist or deconstructionist.'[6]

Table 1.2   Still and process approaches to sport history

Still (Point in the past)		Process (Change over time)	
Point	Orientation	Process	Orientation
• Event (1936 olympic games) • Incident (Australian v New Zealand 'under-arm bowling') • Phenomenon (cycling revolution)	• Agents (individuals, groups, communities) • Description • Context (concept free)	• Change (from traditional to modern sport) • Development (emergence of extreme sports) • Causation (diffusion of cricket)	• Concept (structures) • Themes • Context (concept driven)

Reconstructionism and constructionism dominate sport history. Disciples of these models privilege empirical methods, accept historical evidence as proof that they can recover the past, and insist that their forms of representation are transparent enough to ensure the objectivity of their observations. The key difference between reconstructionists and constructionists is the extent to which the latter embrace the concepts and theories of others as tools to propose and explain relationships between events. Reconstructionists oppose *a priori* knowledge on the grounds that it subjects historians to 'predetermined explanatory schemes' and reduces them to 'tailoring evidence'.[7] Sceptical of objective empirical history, deconstructionists view history 'as a constituted narrative' devoid of 'moral or intellectual certainty'.[8] Slow to penetrate sport history, deconstructionism poses some major challenges for reconstructionism which places inordinate confidence in the cognitive power of narratives that are held to emanate naturally from historical facts.

In Part II, I examine more explicit applications of historical knowledge in sport history under the heading 'explanatory paradigms'. An 'interactive structure of workable questions and the factual statements which are adduced to answer them',[9] an explanatory paradigm carries quite specific philosophical assumptions and constitutes the framework that historians use to orientate their arguments. I identify seven prominent explanatory paradigms in sport history: traditional narrative, advocacy, comparison, causation, social change, context and new culture. In *The Field* I analyse the strengths and weaknesses of these three models and seven paradigms. In the remainder of this introductory chapter I outline these models and explanatory paradigms as a prelude to deeper analysis in Parts I and II and clarify some of the issues that this approach raises.

Models

Historians disagree about much: the objectives of history, the meaning of facts, the construction of facts, methods of procedure, the role of theory, the basis of theory, the form of presentation. But they also agree that history is an evidence-based discipline, and that evidence imposes limits on interpretation.[10] I examine the philosophical and epistemological agreements and disagreements within sport history using Munslow's three models of historical inquiry. Sport history supports reconstructionists, constructionists and a lesser number of deconstructionists; each group conceptualises

Table 1.3 Models of history

	Reconstructionism	*Constructionism*	*Deconstructionism*
Objective	• Discover *the* (unique) past as it actually was (1)	• Interpret how, why, patterns and trends (2)	• Reflect on *a* (fragmented and partial) past (3)
Epistemology	• Delve into remnants of the past (historical materials) • Remnants of the past limit interpretations • Acknowledge relationship between distance and detachment (4) (spanning)		
	• Privilege empiricism • Accept historical remnants as proof that the past can be recovered • View the past as fixed • See the past as yielding knowledge about the development of the present • Regard the present as an unproblematic platform from which historians look back into the past • Iterative activity (5)		• Begins analysis with linguistic / discursive elements of historical materials • History both a narrative-linguistic aesthetic and an empirical-analytical craft • Holds the past as a slave to the present (6)
	• Objective discipline based on interrogation of sources • Facts frame interpretation • Content of the past determines the form of the narrative (i.e., narratives are transparent and preserve objectivity of the past) • Limits on interpretation imposed by institutional and professional conventions (7)	• Objectivity mediated by theory, concepts and evidence • *A priori* knowledge precedes facts • Limits on interpretation imposed by theory, concepts and evidence (8)	• Questions epistemological assumptions re: o relationship between reality and its description o truth-bearing statements o distinctions between fact and fiction o relationship between subjects and objects o accurate representations o power of concepts, theories and arguments to produce truth (9)
Presentation	• Narrative based • Concerns about style eliminate technical language • Narratives correspond with the past and the truth • Separates history and fiction • De-emphasises the text in favour of the world it purports to represent • Non-reflexive (10)	• Non-narrative based; often contains implicit narrative overlay • Concepts and theories engender technical language • Rejects narrative as a tool of explanation and context • Based on evidential arguments, models, logical propositions • Non-reflexive (11)	• Encourages diverse modes of presentation including fiction • Concepts and theories engender technical language • Narrative not epistemologically self-assured • Emphasises linguistic construction of sources, evidence and texts • Self-consciously reflexive (12)

Principal sources: Robert Berkhofer, *Beyond the Great Story* (1995), Louis Gottschalk, *Understanding History* (1969), Carolyn Hamilton *et al.* (eds), *Refiguring the Archive* (2002), Keith Jenkins and Alun Munslow, *The Nature of History Reader* (2004), Alun Munslow, *Reconstructing History* (1997).

history around a different set of objectives, epistemology and mode of presentation (see Table 1.3).

Reconstructionism

Operating under the assumption that they can discover the past as it really was, or as it actually happened (*wie es eigentlich gewesen*) (Table 1.3, box 1), reconstructionists promote history as a realist epistemology in which knowledge derives from empirical evidence and forensic research into primary sources (Table 1.3, boxes 5 and 7). Forensic research means interrogating, collaborating and contextualising sources to verify them as real and true (see Chapter 2). Reconstructionists maintain that history exists independently of the historian and that discovering the past is an objective process, uncontaminated by ideology. 'The historian is permitted only one attitude, that of impartial observer, unmoved equally by admiration or repugnance', argue reconstructionists, who insist that real historians are obliged to 'simply relate the facts' and to avoid dictating readers' responses.[11] Rejecting any notion that ideological considerations might influence their histories, reconstructionists are particularly vigilant of colleagues who mesh ideology with sources: this amounts to subjectivity and distorts history. Yves-Pierre Boulongne once accused 'feminist leagues', 'radical political groups' and the 'sporting-counter-society' of misconstruing Pierre de Coubertin, the founder of the International Olympic Committee (IOC), who the olympic historian said encouraged women and girls to partake in physical activity. These 'malicious detractors', Boulongne complained, 'abbreviate quotations' and remove evidence from its historical context.[12]

Narrative is the medium of reconstructionism which adherents assume is essentially transparent (Table 1.3, box 10). In evaluating good representations of sport history, reconstructionists gauge the structure, unity and coherence of the narrative. They place maximum emphasis on the narrative as a whole process and the way it informs the structure of the story, although they also assess relationships between individual statements and sources. Cross-examination of evidence involves interrogation of language to ascertain the tone and accuracy of sources, and to clarify what particular sources say and what they leave out. More specifically, interrogation entails questions about word usage, figures of speech and stylistic cadence, and the way that these articulate ideas and sympathies (see Chapter 4).[13] Reconstructionists maintain a strong vigilance over style and rhetoric in their sources, and especially in colleagues' texts. Style has 'enormous evidential value, both in getting and in giving evidence'; in contrast, rhetoric is a 'mechanical trick' associated with propaganda, poetics and oratory.[14] Yet, for all their talk about careful scrutiny of colleagues' language, reconstructionists rarely take their evaluations beyond banal observations about grace of expression and clarity of writing. Sport historians will be familiar with book reviewers who refer to 'wooden prose', 'mechanical prose', 'dull prose', 'hyperbolic prose', 'lively prose', 'sharp prose', 'witty prose', and every other conceivable type of prose. At the heart of these comments lies the trite notion that perfect prose is a recipe for the well-being of the field.[15]

Constructionism

Like reconstructionists, constructionists believe that empirical evidence provides the ultimate source of knowledge about the past. In this sense reconstructionism and constructionism are evidence-based, objectivist-inspired models in which historians aspire to build accurate, independent and truthful reconstructions of the past (Table 1.3, box 5). Both also distinguish the representation of history from fiction: history means attempting to discover what actually happened in the past. Where these models diverge is with respect to acceptance of *a priori* knowledge, particularly theory. Real historical phenomena, according to conservative reconstructionists, are unique configurations and one-off occurrences: history consists of the 'stories of ... individual lives or happenings, all seemingly individual and unrepeatable'.[16] Conservative reconstructionism – a form of methodological individualism emphasising human actions and intentions, or what sociologists call agency[17] – casts theory into the realm of speculation. Theory, argued Geoffrey Elton, 'infuses predestined meaning' into history by framing questions in such a manner that the answers elicit support for the theory.[18] In short, theory is antithetical to the objectives and practices of conservative reconstructionism.

Not all reconstructionists are averse to theory; not all reconstructionists consider the investigation of unique events as the 'litmus test' of historical knowledge. They acknowledge that historians also discern patterns of behaviour across time, societies and social groups, and that they categorise different forms of human action and place them into general moulds. Such approaches compel historians to think 'in terms of abstraction' and theory.[19] For example, collective identities such as nationalities, religions, occupational groups and social classes are invaluable and indispensable historical abstractions. While 'no two individuals are entirely alike', how they think and act in certain situations – as members of a sporting fraternity or fans of a national sporting team – will typically 'follow a highly regular pattern', even 'to the point where their response can be predicted'. Moreover, while theories alert historians to regularities and patterns, they can also reveal 'aspects which resist categorization and which give the event or the situation its unique qualities'.[20]

Constructionists deem theory integral to historical research (Table 1.3, box 8): 'The writer of history who desires to be more than a mere antiquarian must have a thorough *theoretical* training in those fields of inquiry with which his work is concerned'. While not denying that historians require an intimate and technical knowledge of their sources, Werner Sombart derided such attributes as the skills of the 'hodman'. 'Theoretical training alone makes the true historian', he believed.[21]

Constructionists claim that theory is fundamental in history for at least three reasons. First, the range and volume of evidence bearing on many historical problems is so large that historians cannot avoid selection, and theory is a critical tool. It provides frameworks and principles for selecting evidence and thus steers practitioners away from contradictions in their explanations. Second, theory brings to the fore interrelations between the components of human experiences at given times and in so doing enriches historical accounts. Third, as already mentioned, identifying historical patterns invariably involves some form of abstract thinking and connections to theoretical explanations and interpretations. Responding to the conservative reconstructionist charge that theory predetermines history, constructionists counter that theories enhance understanding and that historians cannot 'approach their evidence innocent of presupposition'.[22]

Where do sport historians sit in this debate between reconstructionism and constructionism over theory? The former position holds minimal sway but this does not mean that sport historians have embraced 'complex social science constructionism'.[23] On the contrary, sport historians have not employed the historical record to construct formal theories of sport, nor have they used it to apply, test or confirm theories. Indeed, sport historians have generally failed to cultivate in their students an awareness of theory, much less sharpen students' skills in the area.[24] Stephen Hardy probably comes closest to producing a formal theory of sport. At the heart of his work is the Sportgeist, the spirit of sport, consisting of four transhistorical values – physicality, competition, creativity and achievement. Each value begets its own set of tensions – between moderation and aggression, victory and fair play, freedom and regimen, and community and individual respectively – which 'connect sports to their historical surroundings'.[25] Hardy's Sportgeist falls well short of the positivist definition of a theory as a set of ordered propositions incorporated into a deductive system.[26] Far from proffering predictions about sport, Hardy places the meaning of sport at any historical conjuncture within 'three interrelated contexts: the Sportgeist, the sport structure and general structure'.[27]

The vast majority of sport historians utilise organising concepts, as distinct from fully fledged theories, to 'fine focus' their interpretations of the evidence.[28] Perhaps better recognised as classes of objects (for example, amateur sports and extreme sports), general notions (for example, hegemony and gender), themes (for example, urbanisation and democratisation), periods (for example, Victorian era and late capitalism) and constellations of interrelated traits (for example, sporting gentlemen and manliness), concepts abound in sport history. However, they remain descriptive labels and do not in themselves provide explanations for how something came about or changed. Nonetheless, by identifying recurrent features and patterns, concepts expose new realms of observation, enabling historians to move past the 'single instance' and to 'transcend immediate perceptions'.[29]

The proliferation of concepts in sport history raises the question, where do they come from? Most sport historians simply appropriate concepts from outside the field, too often without critical reflection or analysis.[30] John Hoberman is one exception. His concept of 'idealistic internationalisms' derives from a comparison of the Red Cross, the Boy Scout movement, the would-be international lingua franca Esperanto movement, and the Wagnerian and olympic movements.[31]

By examining 'analogies between historical instances', Hoberman follows Arthur Stinchcombe's recommendation for the invention of 'fruitful concepts'.[32] His idealistic internationalisms concept also fulfils Stinchcombe's notion of a 'profound concept': its invention emanates from 'comparison of [the] actions and sentiments' of the agents who create international movements.[33] (In this sense, Hoberman extols agency.) On the other hand, Hoberman's concept slips and slides. It is not clear how far he wants to extend the analogies between the movements that he asserts pursued an idealistic internationalism. Only the olympic movement appears as a twentieth century idealistic internationalism. The Red Cross, formed in 1863, hardly rates a mention, even in discussions of nineteenth-century internationalism; the Esperanto and Boy Scout movements receive scant attention in the interwar age of fascism and completely disappear from the discussion relating to the post-Second World War era. Indeed, idealistic internationalism becomes increasingly irrelevant to Hoberman's argument that in the second half of the twentieth century many transnational organisations became gathering points and havens for right-wing ideologues.

Stinchcombe and Norman Denzin regard concepts as the major units of theory; concepts define the shape and content of theory, especially when linked together.[34] The fact that Hoberman makes no attempt to link idealistic internationalisms to other concepts and thus develop a fully fledged theory is reflected in the title of his article: '*Toward* a Theory of Olympic Internationalism' (1995).

Deconstructionism

Deconstructionists have abandoned all pretexts of objectivity:[35] historical understanding involves unavoidable relativism (the belief that there are no overarching rules or procedures for precisely measuring bodies of knowledge, conceptual schemes or theories, and that without fixed benchmarks the only outcome can be difference and uncertainty.[36]) Thus, deconstructionists do not promote single interpretations of grand histories, for example, *the* history of women olympians. Rather, they examine different perspectives, for example, those of successful women olympians, women excluded from the olympics, black female olympians, Islamic female olympians, which they stress are partial and fragmented. In this sense, deconstructionists acknowledge that each group has its own unique history and faces its own struggles. Proceeding from the premise that nothing written can be read as a true meaning, deconstructionists attempt to discover the intentions of the author of each and every source or text. While reconstructionists claim that their process of interrogating or conversing with sources is tantamount to deconstruction, deconstructionists insist that the differences are substantial. According to deconstructionists, historians necessarily impose themselves on the reconstruction process and any notion that they can isolate themselves is erroneous.[37]

Deconstructionism deems interpretation an act of linguistic and literary creation (Table 1.3, box 12).[38] Historical material does not naturally organise, let alone write, narratives; nor are decisions about emplotments simple technical matters.[39] Hayden White, an historian who works in the tradition of literary criticism and who, more than any other scholar, has directed attention to the nature and role of historical narratives, argues that modes of emplotment involve ontological and epistemological choices. 'History as a plenum of documents that attest to the occurrence of events', writes White, 'can be put together in a number of different and equally plausible narrative accounts'. Moreover, these choices carry distinct ideological and political implications: historians and their readers may reach quite 'different conclusions' from these narratives 'about "what must be done" in the present'.[40] Sport historians have overwhelmingly ignored White's work, although Murray Phillips recently employed White's model to compare two sets of historical narratives about the Australian surf lifesaving movement. I examine Phillips' work more closely in Chapter 4. Phillips' analysis is profound; he clearly demonstrates the need for sport historians to familiarise themselves better with deconstructionism. This is all the more important as linguistic elements of deconstructionism diffuse from other quarters, notably cultural studies, into sport history. I take up some of these elements in Chapter 11.

Today, most sport historians work within a reconstructionist epistemology that Joyce Appleby, Lynn Hunt and Margaret Jacob label practical realism.[41] This form of epistemology acknowledges that a gap exists between words and reality. However, it does not consider the distance sufficient to abandon the search for truth; rarely are words arbitrarily connected to objects. For example, 'sport' may connote a range of behaviours and practices that have changed over time as different groups appropriated the term, but practical realists point to the fact that sport historians have built up a strong consensus about these meanings and their relevant contexts. Practical realism emphasises that historical facts derive from tangible material documents and hard supporting evidence. For example, the olympic charter, is a concrete document, separate from any language historians might use to describe it. Similarly, the charter limits the factual assertions that historians can extract from it and hence the interpretations they put forward. Practical realists concede that all histories begin from the personal interests and cultural attributes of the historian. They admit that no knowledge is neutral and that its production involves struggles between different interest groups. Nonetheless, they reject the view that historical narratives are forms of literature. Likewise, they dismiss the charge that constant reassessment of the past is proof that the field lacks objectivity: reassessment reflects attempts by successive generations to give new meaning to the past. I discuss practical realism further in Chapter 2.

Explanatory paradigms

More specific than a model, yet less prescriptive than a method, an explanatory paradigm is an 'interactive structure of workable questions and the factual statements which are adduced to answer them'.[42] Sport historians structure their arguments, or frame their questions and answers, within seven distinct explanatory paradigms: traditional narrative, advocacy, comparison, causation, social change, context and new culture (see Table 1.4, column 1). Of course, most historians embrace two or three paradigms, although the philosophical assumptions that undergird any one piece of work will determine the specific combination and range of paradigms in any one analysis. Generally speaking, the traditional narrative, advocacy and context explanatory paradigms fall within the ambit of reconstructionism, the comparison, causation and social change paradigms align with constructionism, and the new culture paradigm parallels deconstructionism. As shall become clear, the context, comparison and causation paradigms can also support the philosophies of both reconstructionism and constructionism (see Table 1.4, column 1).

Traditional narrative

The subject of vigorous debate, historians nonetheless agree that at the heart of narrative lies 'some sense of story' and that it is the overwhelmingly dominant form of representing the past.[43] Conservative reconstructionists assume a high degree of correspondence between narrative and the past, and promote the view that a narrative is simply the medium of their histories, the shape and structure of which closely resembles actual events in the past. In other words, reconstructionism holds that

Table 1.4   Explanatory paradigms in sport history

	Objectives	*Assumptions*
Traditional Narrative Reconstructionism	• Tells a story, through an authoritative work, for the story's sake • Emphasises sequence and consequence (i.e., causal relationships) • Suppresses historian's voice (especially personal pronouns, 'I') in favour of third-person narrative	• Past recoverable with evidence • Traditional representations are transparent and preserve the objectivity of observations • Texts are referential (refer to worlds outside their own linguistic systems) • Non-reflexive • Omniscience
Advocacy Reconstructionism	• Argues from the remnants of the past • Debunks myths by interrogating sources • Exposes motives of myth-makers	• Sources are the basis of truth • Historians' primary allegiance is to truth and the profession • Historians analogous to judges in courts of law • Historians must remove partisanship and demonstrate their objectivity
Comparison Reconstructionism Constructionism / Deconstructionism	• Metaphorical allusion: highlights commonalities • Systematic: seeks answers to specific questions • Post-binary: examines spaces between opposing cultural entities • Scientific: seeks universal laws	• Comparisons provide tools of explanation
Causation Reconstructionism / Constructionism	• Identifies the causes of events • Distinguishes between agents and structures as causal factors	• Motors of history either free agents or determining structures
Social change Reconstructionism / Constructionism	• Attributes change to accumulated modification • Theorises about change over time • Emphasises structural changes • Theorises about structures • Theorises relationships between structures, agents and culture	• Empirical generalisations refer to theoretical issues • History is a process
Context Reconstructionism / Constructionism	• Stresses interrelationships between part (sport) and whole (society) • Situates subject in the entirety of events to which it is bound	• Broader social, economic and political contexts 'legitimise' the study of sport • Broader social, economic and political contexts help interpret sport • Reconstructionists stress non-repetitive elements in network of relationships • Constructionists incorporate concepts (especially structures)
New Culture Deconstructionism	• Reveals how the processes that constitute texts also provide meaning for their producers and different audiences • Reveals the subtexts of topics explored • Emphasises multiple perspectives • Reflexive	• Sources are sites of intersecting meanings which receive diverse readings and interpretations • Texts read as structures of meaning • Texts constructed (textualised) by semiotic, social and cultural processes • Sources not concrete objects with fixed meanings • Narratives not epistemologically self-assured

narrative language is mimetic or referential, that is, unproblematic or, at the very least, adequate to the job of describing the past. Reconstructionists believe that an historical explanation materialises 'naturally from the archival raw data, its meaning offered as interpretation in the form of a story related explicitly, impersonally, transparently, and without resort to any of the devices used by writers of literary narratives, viz., imagery or figurative language'.[44] I look at examples of traditional narratives and their limitations in sport history in Chapter 4 of Part I. Although some practitioners still submit traditional narratives to academic sport history journals for review, it is fair to say that they have virtually disappeared from the field. On the other hand, narrative is making a resurgence under the auspices of the new culture paradigm among historians who hold that telling stories is the best way to understand the workings of a culture and the power relations in a society (see Chapter 11).

Advocacy

Reconstructionists charge advocates with undermining the objectivity of history and destroying the credibility of the historian as a 'neutral, or disinterested, judge' whose 'conclusions … display … judicial qualities of balance and evenhandedness'.[45] But as Robert Berkhofer reminds us, 'there is a difference between arguing *for* a point of view' and 'arguing *from* a point of view' (emphasis added), and by definition all historians are advocates for particular cases, stances, or interpretations.[46] However, in *The Field* I restrict the advocacy paradigm to those works that specifically debunk sporting myths by forensic interrogation of the evidence and examination of the motives and interests of myth-makers. The three best examples of the paradigm are the debunking of the myth that William Webb Ellis initiated the distinctive game of rugby, exposure of the false claim that Abner Doubleday invented baseball, and the revelation that ancient Greek Olympians were professional, rather than amateur, athletes.[47]

By channelling their energies into the interrogation of primary sources, advocate historians convey an air of judicial practice and imply that they are highly objective and non-partisan. But are advocate historians especially objective? A range of approaches and criteria are available to evaluate levels of partisanship and objectivity, and I apply one model, proposed by the historical sociologist Dennis Smith, to those sport historians who tackled the three great myths of sport and their claims that they were merely rummaging for the truth in the remnants of the past. Smith classifies advocates according to how they handle the relationship between involvement (the capacity to empathise with and evoke the situation of particular participants in specific historical situations) and detachment (the capacity to observe processes and relationships objectively, discounting political/moral commitments and emotion-laden responses).[48] His model affords some interesting conclusions and raises challenging questions for those historians who believe that they can escape their personal values and dispositions.

The advocacy paradigm raises another important question: why do some myths persist in the face of contrary evidence and the 'learned assaults' by intellectuals? In the case of sporting myths, is survival a case of credulous journalists and naïve fans, as reconstructonists imply? Or is it a case, as constructionists argue, that myths can serve important social functions? Recently several sport historians have analysed the way that sporting myths function to mediate social tensions and I also look at their work under the banner of the advocacy paradigm.[49]

Comparison

Although some conservative reconstructionists deem comparison 'wrong in principle', on the grounds that 'history is about unique entities' and that 'nothing in the past can be compared with anything else',[50] most historians agree that showing differences and similarities is integral to the gathering and presentation of historical evidence. As a method for distilling commonalities and sharpening distinctions between seemingly similar and parallel events and phenomena, comparison has proved invaluable and helped historians enhance their understanding and improve their classifications and categories.

Comparisons take a number of forms in sport history. Most comparisons in the field are simple allusions – to another person, place, event, practice or text. For example, to exemplify the rigid codes of conduct and peculiar masculinity associated with German pistol duelling in the late nineteenth century, Kevin McAleer compares it with British boxing.[51] Most historians use allusions to evoke sentiments and convey impressions rather than systematically build arguments, and the number of practitioners making systematic comparisons to argue specific cases or to offer an historical explanation or interpretation is quite small. I look at two examples by the African political scientist Ali Mazrui. His comparison of the influences of African traditions, Islamic thoughts and Western practices on contemporary sport in Africa is extremely insightful, while his comparison of boxer Muhammad Ali and former Ugandan president Idi Amin offers only limited perspectives on black masculinity.[52] Even fewer sport historians have used systematic comparison as a method to establish causal explanations. (I examine this latter form of comparison in Chapter 8 as part of the causation paradigm.)

I call the fourth form of comparison 'post-binary'. Grounded in deconstructionism, this form attempts to break down the tendency in Western thought to dichotomise natural and social phenomena, and to describe and define them in terms of oppositional characteristics and mutually opposed terms (for example, race – black and white – and gender – male and female). In post-binary comparisons the historian searches the space between oppositional entities for hybrid cultural forms. Several historians of sport, including Grant Farred, James Mills and Paul Dimeo, and John Hughson, have found some interesting ethnic adaptations to social environments via such post-binary comparisons.[53]

Causation

The centrality of causal reasoning and causal relationships in history is evident in the temporal sequencing of events in narrative presentations (that imply causation), and in the never-ending debates over whether agents or structures are the prime determinants of social outcomes. Yet, paradoxically, few historians consciously advocate causal explanations. Like their colleagues working in other areas of social history, sport historians remain divided between those who assign causality to agents – individuals, groups and organisations – acting in conscious pursuit of their goals, and those for whom the social and collective worlds of customs and laws variously rule, shape, order and structure (that is, cause) social outcomes. My focus in the causation paradigm is on those historians whose works examine agents as causes. I am particularly interested in the assumptions these historians make about agents and the types of events that they seek to explain. Generally, they assume the agent is free, conscious, responsible and motivated. The events that interest these historians are those where agents have waged political campaigns to bring about change, or those where the historian can easily apportion blame to agents for attempting to defend the status quo. Some of the richest examples in the field are women taking action 'to transcend practical and symbolic forms of oppression' in sport, especially in the 1920s and 1930s.[54] I leave the discussion of structural causality in sport history to the social change paradigm where structural causality has influenced many practitioners attempting to explain social changes in sport.

Social change

For some historians the prime purpose of the discipline is 'to understand the phenomenon of change over time'.[55] Fundamental differences between reconstructionists and constructionists emerge over the correct approach to social change. Reconstructionism typically proceeds by empirical investigation of particular actions, events and ideas rather than by abstract concepts and processes. Reconstructionists venturing into explanations of large-scale social change emphasise the accumulation of often small and gradual modifications which eventually reach a point that they agree denotes fundamental change. In sport history, reconstructionists describe modern sport as the coalescence of sporting and social modifications. These include the introduction of rules, umpires and administrative bodies, the construction of specialised and dedicated facilities (for example, pools, gymnasiums, fields), and the development of transport systems (especially rail which facilitated the movement of sporting teams and spectators), mass production (that lowered costs of sporting equipment and goods), and mass communication (notably penny newspapers that popularised sport).[56]

Constructionists have focused more attention on structural causality and the theoretical dimension of social change. Among constructionists real change emanates from new beliefs, values, norms, roles, practices and ways of doing things that differ from past forms and types and which, most importantly, have new structuring effects. For example, values and assumptions about the ideal woman changed in the second half of the nineteenth century and helped reshape or structure (that is, determine) ideas about sporting females; these ideas in turn translated into new patterns of behaviour. The notion of structuring effects derives from the concept of structure as a motor of history, but when we pose the question, how do structures change?, the answer depends entirely upon the historian's conceptualisation of structure and her or his understanding of the relationship between structure and human action. In the social change paradigm, I look at a range of theories of structural change and the particular problem of reductionism, of which so many of these theories are guilty.

Context

Nothing is more fundamental in the lexicon and methodology of history than context. Sport historians contextualise the remnants of the past and their evidence; they also contextualise sport, seeking to understand it in the circumstances of different places and different times. In this latter sense, I view context as primarily an interpretive paradigm.

Despite the importance of context as an aid to interpreting sport, 'historians rarely discuss what [this] involves'.[57] The general consensus is that context establishes patterns that share relationships beyond a temporal juxtaposition. Well-constructed contexts are successful, Thompson said, because they show a coherent and internally consistent set of relationships between all the parts in a cultural or social system; in contradistinction, many historical relationships are insignificant, 'muddled' and 'pretentious'.[58]

Of course, all contextualisations involve judgement about which events are significant and which are insignificant. However, in my analysis of context as a paradigm, I propose a model, based on Arthur Marwick's framework for analysing the Cultural Revolution in the 1960s, which I believe arguably removes at least some of the arbitrariness from the process and promotes a more systematic approach. The advantage of the model is that it opens to broader perspectives a vast range of phenomena which expose more general values and relationships.

Marwick's model comprises four principal components: major forces and constraints, events, human agents, and convergences and contingencies. Major forces and constraints (that is, structures) are of three main forms: structural (for example, geographical, demographic, economic and technological), ideological (for example, what is believed and can be believed, existing political and social philosophies), and institutional (for example, systems of government, justice, policing and voting, educational, religious and working-class organisations and the family). Events include those that have effects and consequences such as the Great Depression and the Second World War. Similarly, human agents also have effects and consequences. Politicians, presidents, prime ministers and protest movements comprise the more obvious human agents. Finally, convergences and contingencies refers to the interrelationships between events and human agents that generate unforeseen events and circumstances.[59]

It is not difficult to see these components collectively operating as a macro-context for any number of sporting phenomena and, indeed, many histories of sport attempt to capture these dimensions. I examine what I consider to be two exemplars: Elliot Gorn's account of gouging in the southern backwoods of North America from the late eighteenth century through the antebellum era, and Greg Ryan's study of New Zealand cricket.[60]

New culture

Sport history is currently undergoing a shift, with practitioners moving from the study of sport as a social practice towards the interpretation of sporting identities and cultures. A key focus of this so-called 'cultural turn' is the social and political power of language and the assumption that texts have 'no inherent or authentic meaning', rather they 'derive [their] effects from the power relationships in which [their] meaning is contested'.[61] Some sport historians working in the new culture paradigm have incorporated the 'techniques of literary and linguistic analysis' into their historical analyses as they attempt to 'lay bare *meaning* – its inscription in texts, its construction in terms of "otherness", its multidimensionality, and its relationship to the wider context of discourse'.[62] Indeed, in certain areas of sport history, notably the policing of female physicality, discourse analysis is already an orthodox method of interpretation, and is spreading into other areas such as the study of the olympics.[63]

In examining new culture as a paradigm in sport history, I look at the works of a group of sport historians (including John Bloom, Susan Cahn, John Hargreaves, Peter Mewett, Michael Oriard, Catriona Parratt, Synthia Sydnor and Patricia Vertinsky[64]) who treat sporting cultures as discursive formations and stress the relative autonomy of cultural practices. One interest of this group is the way language (for example, discourse, texts, narratives) helps constitute, transmit and transform sporting cultures. Practitioners of new culture also pay attention to the problems of the new culture paradigm, notably the attempts to break from master narratives, to restore people's actual experiences, to give voice to others, and to present subject matter in radically new ways.

Traditional narrative, advocacy, comparison, causation, social change, context and new culture are not the only paradigms in sport history but they are certainly the most prominent. Some readers might wonder about other possible paradigms such as a quantitative or statistical paradigm or a feminist paradigm. While quantitative research appears in economic, political and social history, in sport history quantitative expositions usually fall into the realm of 'elementary descriptive statistics' that 'identify the most important features of the data through rearrangement and presentation'.[65] Thus, I am not convinced that a quantitative paradigm warrants greater attention than traditional narrative. Feminism is a more complicated case.

Feminism has made an enormous contribution to sport history in at least four areas. First, it has helped write women's experiences into the field. Much of the early feminist-inspired scholarship analysed women as victims in the sporting world and looked at their exclusion from sporting practices.[66] But this focus quickly shifted to an examination of women as active agents empowering their own lives. Summing up the shift, Catriona Parratt praises the contribution of feminist historians who showed that middle-class women 'established enclaves' of 'support, solidarity and sisterhood' in male-dominated cultures of the late eighteenth and nineteenth centuries.[67] More recently feminist sport historians have turned their attention to examining gender and identity in sport.[68] Second, feminist historians have been at the fore in introducing traditionally unconventional sources – letters, diaries, memory and ephemera of various kinds[69] – into the field, and in legitimising the use of theory.[70] Third, feminists are key figures in the major interpretive paradigm in the field, new culture (see Chapter 11). Fourth, feminists have been prominent in demonstrating the contested nature of both sport and sport history.[71] In all these areas feminists have added to the common treasury of knowledge and interpretation in the field to the extent that it is now virtually unthinkable to ignore women when analysing sport.

Some scholars also argue the case for a feminist epistemology and have called for a new feminist way of knowing about the past and telling history.[72] As a general rule, feminists have proved more attuned to epistemological issues. Proponents of a feminist epistemology argue that it rests on a rejection of foundationalism – with its assumptions about the objective structure of reality and accessing reality via reason and sensory perception – and an acknowledgement that there are no general criteria for what constitutes knowledge, no single site of knowledge, no universal application of knowledge, and no unified viewpoints.[73] However, as Richard Mandell makes clear in his examination of sport criticism, an anti-foundational epistemology is not uniquely feminist and draws on a range of logical and political positions.[74] Some scholars do advocate the existence of a uniquely feminist epistemology. The French feminist theorist Julia Kristeva, for example, argues that there are distinct female and male affective rationalities and subjectivities based on time. In the case of the latter, women emphasise time as cyclic and recurrent, eternal and monumental, and governed essentially by rhythm; men stress the linearity of time as direction and teleology, departure and arrival, genetic growth and progression.[75] But how these might translate into a feminist historiography remains unclear. While sport sociologist Ann Hall has espoused the idea of a feminist epistemology, none of her examples of feminist method, particularly as they relate to oral testimony, are anti-foundational or gender specific in the same vein as Kristeva's gender subjectivities.[76] In short, feminist historians have not, in the words of Penelope Corfield, produced 'a new general interpretation [of the past or history] or, more ambitiously, a new epistemology. Instead, historians of gender share the same range of theoretical problems faced by other historians'. As she concludes, 'it is easier to call for a new epistemology than to create one'.[77]

On the basis of these debates, I prefer to view feminism as an organising concept that utilises a range of explanatory paradigms and that has traversed a number of epistemologies throughout its history. Currently, I see feminism as crossing constructionism and deconstructionism. While many of the assumptions of feminist history are compatible with deconstructionism, this is not true of all. 'One of the major premises of women's and feminist history has been that the inclusion of heretofore excluded subjects makes for a more true, more just, more "historical" history'. Rather than embracing such triumphal claims about the capacity of history, deconstructionists stress the 'unknowability of history in its totality'.[78]

In concluding this introduction to historical inquiry, I want to clarify some points and, in so doing, hopefully circumvent at least some criticisms.

Clarifications

The Field is not a review of the literature. I make no claim to have read every piece of academic literature in the field. As small as the history of sport may be, the volume of literature is vast and I doubt whether anyone today (with the possible exception of Allen Guttmann!) actually pores over every scholarly article or book. Nonetheless, as my bibliography testifies, I believe that I have captured the spectrum of sport history with respect to its structure. I do not intend my examples to be definitive; they are simply those with which I am familiar and I am sure that many readers will be able to substitute better examples to illustrate the same points. In many cases, I extract examples from larger pieces of work. Some historians may take affront at the categorisation of these examples and they could (mis)interpret my efforts as a criticism of an author's complete text or even the whole span of their work. They should not. My approach is to open every example to the scrutiny of contending models. For example, in praising Murray Phillips' deconstructionist approach to narrative, I also point out its limitations from reconstructionist and constructionist perspectives (see Chapter 4). Conversely, while the level of reflexivity shown by Douglas Hartmann is exemplary from a reconstructionist-constructionist perspective, it still falls short according to the criteria of deconstructionism (see Chapter 11).

Similarly, *The Field* does not categorise practitioners, much less assign them lifetime classifications according to the boxes in Tables 1.3 and 1.4. Some historians do work across a number of paradigms; I cite examples from C. L. R. James in the chapters dealing with comparison, context and new culture. Some even work with different models. Allen Guttmann's *From Ritual to Record* (1978) is classic constructionism; his *The Games Must Go On* (1984) is classic reconstructionism. In some cases, individual texts even support competing models; Eric Dunning and Kenneth Sheard's *Barbarians, Gentlemen and Players* (1979) is one example of reconstructionism and constructionism. It thus bears repeating that models, and especially paradigms, can be the simple function of the question that the historian asks, and any suggestion that my examples label practitioners and their collective works is manifestly wrong and misconstrues my objectives. On the other hand, I also recognise that categorisation and classification can force scholars to draw boundaries that in practice are often less sharp than they imply. Nonetheless, I stand by the basic premises of *The Field* that, despite different themes and sources, 'histories written from a particular "way of knowing" … have much in common', and that although some practitioners do transgress boundaries, they are 'relatively rare and … do not seriously invalidate [the] broad conceptions of how historians think and organise their work'.[79]

I do not advocate one model or one explanatory paradigm as superior to all others in all conditions. The relevance of a model or a paradigm depends entirely on the question the historian asks, and what answer she or he seeks. Some questions necessitate a careful gathering and interrogation of the remnants of the past.[80] Some questions demand the incorporation of abstract concepts such as structure.[81] In my own work to date, big picture, politically grounded questions have guided me towards constructionism and context. Nor do I try to reconcile different models or paradigms, although I do emphasise continuities and similarities more than discontinuities and differences. Unfortunately, the quite considerable (and unnecessary) hostility between disciples of respective models in the field means that likenesses are often ignored.

Finally, some readers may object to the inclusion of certain works or certain viewpoints on the grounds that the author or authors do not qualify as 'real' historians. Such objections usually stem from the more conservative ranks in the field whose criteria for affiliation are limited and limiting.

PART I

Models

IN PART I OF *THE FIELD* I examine the different foundations of knowledge that are called – in the often laboured language of analytical history – reconstructionism, constructionism and deconstructionism and their practice in sport history. These foundations include facts, evidence, objectivity, narrative, theory and interpretation. To start with, I trace the search for truth as the guiding principle of reconstructionist epistemology and practice (Chapter 2). Reconstructionist assumptions about historical truths have undergone a radical change over the last twenty years. Early reconstructionists promoted the notion that neutral, value-free, facts – gathered and collated from the remnants of human activity that they called sources – formed the basis of knowledge about the past. Today, all but the most conservative reconstructionists acknowledge that even innocuous and bland facts, such as dates of sporting events or sporting records, are ultimately prepositional and propositional statements that involve some degree of interpretation, and that history must incorporate judgements and viewpoints. Yet, despite shifts in philosophy and practice, reconstructionism remains firmly wedded to the use of historical materials as a means to secure objective knowledge about the past.

Historians have long debated the place of theory in their discipline (Chapter 3). Reconstructionists deem history as an a-theoretical practice. They see the historian's role as gathering sources, verifying their truthfulness, and arranging them in narratives; the incorporation of theory in this process merely distorts the craft of history. Constructionists insist that all historians use theory, or at least theoretical assumptions and concepts, either consciously or subconsciously, as a framework to select and interpret evidence. Theory, not validated sources, is the foundation of historical objectivity and the basis for understanding the past.

I then turn to narrative and non-narrative presentations of sport history (Chapter 4). Non-narrative presentations are usually laden with concepts, theories and explicit arguments, which are the hallmarks of constructionism. However, contemporary mainstream sport history tends to blur the distinction between narrative and non-narrative, with most presentations combining both forms. The pivotal debate over narrative is between reconstructionists and deconstructionists whose views provide the spectrum of opinion. The former assume that historical narratives flow 'naturally' from facts and sources, and that there is a high degree of correspondence between narrative and the past. By contrast, deconstructionists argue that historians create narratives independently of their sources or evidence. In other words, whereas reconstructionism propounds the view that sources shape narratives, deconstructionism maintains that historians mould evidence to fit their narratives.

Finally, I apply the different epistemological positions of reconstructionism and deconstructionism (with a brief foray into constructionism) to an analysis of four widely used categories of materials in sport history: official documents, documents of mass communication, oral testimony and visual sources (Chapter 5). I point to the different questions that the disciples of each model ask of these historical materials, and examine their respective assumptions, and the conclusions they draw, about the reliability of these materials.

The four chapters in Part I collectively show that sport history is becoming an increasingly interpretive practice. Contemporary practitioners make fewer epistemological claims to truth and objectivity than their past peers, and they are more likely to question the correspondence between remnants of the past and the presentation of the past. Yet, irrespective of which model they use, historians still hold the remnants of the past as the building blocks of historical practice.

Chapter 2

Facts, objectivity and interpretation

Truth in sport history

FACTS AND OBJECTIVITY are the knowledge base of reconstructionism, the dominant approach in sport history among those firmly committed to finding truths about the sporting past. 'It is the search for truth that must guide our labours', wrote Geoffrey Elton whose philosophy continues to guide the field.[1] However, if the search for truth prevails in history, reconstructionists have, over time, revised their understanding of the relationship between truth, facts and objectivity. As David Hackett Fischer reminded reconstructionists some time back, 'it is no easy matter to tell the truth, pure and simple, about past events; for historical truths are never pure, and rarely simple'. Indeed, he explained, 'the process of historical truth-telling itself is even more intricate than the truths which historians tell':

> Every true statement must be thrice true. It must be true to its evidence, true to itself, and true to other historical truths with which it is colligated. Moreover, a historian must not merely tell truths, but demonstrate their truthfulness as well. He is judged not simply by his veracity, but by his skill at verification.[2]

I begin this chapter by examining the shift in the meaning of facts from absolute, naturally occurring entities that reside in historical materials – and which are the converse of opinion, supposition and conjecture – to historical relevancies constructed by practitioners as they seek answers to specific questions. I then look at a revised approach to objectivity which stemmed from criticisms that historians are inextricably bound up with the construction of facts and that not even the most elaborate forensic tests of evidence will reduce the gap between historical materials and the interpretation of those materials. As Robert Berkhofer puts it, facts may be 'necessary' to 'produce a proper history', but they are 'not sufficient': 'facts do not determine an interpretation; rather all interpretations are underdetermined'.[3] Last, I investigate some recent thoughts about objectivity as proposed by a group of reconstructionists in their attempt to preserve history's status as a truth-finding discipline. I conclude with an outline of contemporary reconstructionism and a defence of the model in the face of criticisms from deconstructionist-leaning historians.

Questioning the facts

Early reconstructionism conceived of history as a simple practice. Disciples began by examining remnants of human activity – what Joyce Appleby, Lynn Hunt and Margaret Jacob call the 'detritus of past living'[4] – some of which they claimed to have discovered. They then extracted from those historical materials what they called 'facts', a term deemed synonymous with truth. From these facts, or truths, historians wrote their narratives – typically descriptions of what happened, with perhaps an explanation of why it happened. Reconstructionists, especially, praise their colleagues whose narratives or stories appeared to flow 'naturally' from the facts.[5] My analysis here is of early reconstructionism and its assumptions about facts and truths, and of the critiques launched by constructionists and proto-deconstructionists. As we shall see, these criticisms changed the notion of a fact in reconstructionism. What was previously a naturally occurring entity in the materials of the past now became a relevancy, that is, a truth-bearing statement pertinent to the question at hand.

Facts are the backbone of reconstructionism. But what is a fact? And how do reconstructionists use them? Followers of this model typically define facts as finite, permanent, fixed and transparent in their meaning,[6] although, given the indispensability of facts in this school, they have written surprisingly little on the subject. Bernard Whimpress is one of the few practitioners to discuss the centrality of facts in sport history. Reciting Australian cricketer Bill Lawry's batting record on the 1961 Australian tour of England (57 at Edgbaston, 130 and 1 at Lords, 28 and 28 at Leeds, 74 and 102 at Manchester, a duck at The Oval), Whimpress asserted that such facts inspire confidence in the understanding of the past. Echoing the view of the early descriptive approach to sport history (see Chapter 1), Whimpress drew an analogy between historical facts and maps (that provide 'a sense of place') and chronologies (that provide 'a sense of time').[7]

Long strings of factual statements – each one dutifully noted[8] – with some sort of conclusion tacked on, figure prominently in early sport history. Reconstructionists occasionally label these narratives as inductive histories, a term used to imply that the practitioner has drawn general conclusions directly from the facts.[9] The following account of women's golf in late nineteenth-century Canada (complete with the original note numbers) is a good example. 'It is difficult', the author began, 'to find mention of a golf club anywhere in Canada that did not have lady members in surprising numbers'.

> Probably the first women's golf club in the Dominion was the ladies' branch of the Royal Montreal Golf Club, formed in 1892.[78] The wife of George A. Drummond became the first president, and in addition to Mrs. Drummond, other ladies involved were: Mrs. H. V. Meredith, secretary; Mrs. W. Wallace Watson; Mrs. Halton; and Misses P. Young, A. Lamb, and A. Paterson.[79] The Montreal Club had moved to new premises at Dixie in 1896, after 'collisions with passing pedestrians were of such frequent occurrence that it was found

necessary to seek other grounds.'[80] The following year, no fewer than one hundred and fifty lady members 'built themselves a club-house adjoining that of their husbands and brothers at Dixie.'[81] … A Quebec Ladies Golf [Club] was also formed in 1892 or 1893; and the Ottawa Golf Club had '25 lady associate members' in 1894.[83] Four years later this total had risen to forty-eight ….[84] It was in 1896, too, that the Oshawa and Sherbrooke Golf Clubs came into being, and both had ladies' clubs attached within two years.[89] Also, by 1898, the Victoria Golf Club of British Columbia was 'nearly equally divided between the two sexes,' whilst at Hamilton in Ontario, the lady golf-club members actually outnumbered the men.[90] And at the Brantford Golf Club by the turn of the century, there were more female members than male, the reported figures being thirty-nine gentlemen and forty-eight ladies.[91]

By presenting these statements as a finite universe of transparent facts that require neither clarification nor elaboration, it is a simple matter for the author to conclude that 'feminine enthusiasm for the game was manifest through Canada …'.[10]

But what makes these statements facts? In large measure the factual properties derive from their origin in primary sources. A primary source is one with a direct link, in time and place, to the person, event, situation or culture under study. Secondary sources, in contradistinction, provide commentary on, or interpretations of, past events.[11] Reconstructionism ranks primary sources as the main repository of historical facts and as the basic building blocks of historical knowledge; in the words of Ronald Smith, 'effective histories' emanate only from 'mucking deeply in the primary source material'.[12] The primary sources in the extract above are a period book, four period magazines and two period newspapers; the secondary sources are a Master of Arts thesis and a general history of golf published in 1973.

Inductive or reconstructionist narrative histories have been subjected to loud and sharp criticisms. Fischer describes the process of induction as one where historians go 'a-wandering in the dark forest of the past, gathering facts like nuts and berries, until [they have] enough to make a general truth. Then [they] store up … general truths until [they have] the whole truth'.[13] R. G. Collingwood was more scathing. He called these forms of induction 'scissors-and-paste' history. According to Collingwood, facts in scissors-and-paste history are merely the minutiae flowing from historical materials.[14] Critics rebuked inductive historians for simply assuming a direct correspondence between their sources and the past, for failing to interrogate their sources with a view to verifying their truth content, and for shying from interpretation. Indeed, early reconstructionists took great pains to 'remain invisible' and to appear as the 'mere technicians or transmitters of knowledge' which they claimed was always revealed by their sources and never constructed by the historian.[15] Appleby, Hunt and Jacob capture well the mindset of these practitioners whom they describe as entering into a 'trance, clearing their minds, polishing the mind's mirror, and training it on the object of investigation'. In this state, historians 'simply brush aside' their own 'beliefs, values and interests … to allow the mirror to capture the reflection of [facts]'.[16] Last, critics admonish scissors-and-paste historians for not querying the subjective dimensions of their narratives or those present in their sources.[17]

Practitioners of induction did not passively retreat in the face of critics' claims. Defenders cited peer reviews, especially in academic journals, as the key sites at which historians confirm facts. An unwritten protocol in history directs book reviewers to check facts and highlight errors. Simon Milton, for example, finds a series of factual errors in *FIFA and the Contest for World Football*:

> Cameroon's opening match of the 1990 World Cup was against defending champions Argentina, not the hosts; Saudi Arabia faced Sweden, not Germany, in the second round of USA 1994; and Brazil faced and lost to Nigeria in the semi-final of the 1996 Olympic tournament, not the final.[18]

The insinuation here is that factual errors dilute readers' confidence in the reliability of a work. Andrew Moore agrees. In a blunt assessment of the *ABC of Rugby League*, he wrote, that 'when one brief entry, that on North Sydney [Rugby Club], contains two glaring errors, one is left with the impression that this volume is less than valuable.'[19]

Yet, supporters of inductionist-type histories confront a paradox: notwithstanding the apparent primacy of fact, practitioners rarely praise peers for getting the facts right.[20] (A reconstructionist might reply that facts are so obvious in historical material that only the grossly incompetent and wilfully dishonest err.[21] However, as I shall show in both this and subsequent chapters, the lengths to which historians go to prove facts, and the intensity with which they quarrel over them, illustrates the limitations of that argument.) Does this mean, then, that there is more to historical practice than simply discovering and/or identifying the facts of the past? Evidence from book reviews in academic journals informs us that factual accuracy is rarely the defining criterion on which historians judge each others' work.[22] Milton, for example, describes the 'surplus of historical mistakes' in *FIFA and the Contest for World Football* as merely 'irritating'.[23] So where does this leave the reconstructionist notion of facts as the self-evident truths upon which history rests?

Michael Postan implied that there is much more to history than collecting the facts when he argued that practitioners only gather those facts germane to their specific questions and that even so-called hard, or fast, facts are no more than relevancies. Within this conceptualisation every historical fact is a product of 'limited vision':

> If an historical 'event' can be defined as a past occurrence, ... then an historical fact is nothing more than one of the event's observed aspects. What makes it observable is its affinity to an interest uppermost in the observer's mind. This affinity impels the historian to focus [his or her] vision upon it; but to be able to focus the historian must also be prepared to neglect. Outside the facets of events within [his or her] focus, there must be other facets which [he or she does] not wish to observe, or even facets so far outside the range of ... professional vision as to be altogether outside the scope of historical study.[24]

Postan's views fused neatly with those of Edward Carr for whom the push for facts 'rests not on any quality in the facts themselves, but on an *a priori* decision of the historian'. Comparing historians to journalists who select and arrange the facts in order to influence opinion, Carr observed that 'the facts only speak when the historian calls on them'. Historians 'decide to which facts to give the floor, and in what order or context' and in this sense they are 'necessarily selective'. In Carr's opinion 'the belief in a hard core of historical facts existing objectively and independently of the interpretation of the historian is a preposterous fallacy'.[25] Indeed, the emergence of new complements of facts whenever sport historians turn their attention to a new problem or issue add weight to Postan's and Carr's arguments and direct our attention to the infinite composition of historical events and to the infinite choice of historical facts.[26] By Carr's reckoning then, historical facts are judgements about which historians agree; they are a function of whether other historians accept a particular incident or interpretation as 'valid and significant'.[27]

Those not persuaded by Postan and Carr, and convinced that indisputable facts exist, that is, that facts are more than 'constructions and interpretations of the past' framed by individual perspectives,[28] might consider the following statements taken from ostensibly factual histories of the legendary English cricketer William Gilbert Grace. Here I want to categorically demonstrate that even the simplest, most straightforward, of facts involve definitions, frameworks and concepts, all of which ultimately require some level of clarification while many others are contestable.

1 Grace was born 18 July 1848 and died 23 October 1915.
2 Grace scored 54,896 first-class runs.

Even these simple statements are not straightforward facts. Dates, for example, are defined by calendars, in this case the Gregorian calendar that was not a universal Western standard even in Grace's time. The Greeks, for example, used the Julian calendar to schedule the olympic games of 1896 from the 25 March to the 3 April (equating to the 6–15 April in the Gregorian calendar). Grace's tally of first-class runs varies according to the definition of a first-class match. Disagreement emerges here between figures produced by F. S. Ashley-Cooper for Wisden (the annual cricket almanac) in 1916 and the Association of Cricket Statisticians. The latter's definition reduces Grace's run tally to 54,211.

3 Grace was the founding father of modern cricket.
4 Grace was the king of nineteenth-century cricket and occupies an unassailable position in the history of sport.

The factual content of these two sentences resides in quite specific interpretive frameworks that derive their persuasive power from two metaphors – father and king (I discuss the centrality of metaphor in historical explanation in Chapter 4). Most rankings in sport focus on performances that rapidly lose their gloss as they are invariably surpassed. Not even Grace's 126th century, scored at the ripe old age of 56 in 1904, could earn him a place in one recent list of supreme twentieth-century British sporting achievements.

5 Grace was the best-known Englishman of his era.
6 Grace was instrumental in the establishment of Victorianism.
7 Grace embodied John Bull.

Even if the reader agrees with the description in the fifth sentence, acceptance of sentences six and seven mean subscribing to very specific ideological and class-based notions of Victorianism and English nationalism that tend to whitewash domestic class and political relationships. Both assertions rest on considerable theory (see Chapter 3). Furthermore, the John Bull allegory of English character is a caricature that has changed considerably over time, variously referring to an honest clothier, a gross and rather stupid figure, a prosperous citizen, and a jovial and honest farmer.

8 Grace aligned himself politically with Gentlemen (amateurs) against Players (professionals).
9 Grace was a notorious shamateur – a gentleman professional – whose expenses and appearance fees far exceeded the salaries earned by professional players.
10 Grace breached the amateur code which dictates that cricketers play for the love of the game.

Sentences eight to ten combine fact and opinion. The truth of Grace's hypocrisy in breaching the amateur code exists solely within the theoretical perspective of a pure amateur ideal that in practice rarely came to fruition. Moreover, it says nothing about the relationships between professional and amateur cricketers that were critical to the development of the game.[29]

Each of these sentences contains 'differing degrees of factuality depending on the proportion of empirical evidence and theory'.[30] Empirical evidence, however, is paramount and non-negotiable in the establishment of historical fact (although historians are not totally averse to treating silences as presumptive evidence and to reasoning from, and mounting arguments on the basis of, them.[31]) The final statement below is one that most academic sport historians would look at with scepticism without direct evidence:

11 Grace dreamed of cricket as the world game.

The varying degrees of interpretation and contextualisation in each of the other ten 'factual' sentences should alert even the most conservative reconstructionist to the artificiality and subjectivity of concrete statements that typically masquerade as facts; at the very least they should be persuaded that facts are not natural entities leaping at them from past materials. In the words of Keith Jenkins and Alun Munslow, 'facts are not bits of reality lying around in the past waiting to be picked up, polished and displayed. They are propositional statements about the nature of reality (past events under a description)'.[32]

The notion of a fact as something other than an incontrovertible fixed truth engendered enormous unease within reconstructionism. Among reconstructionists, the association of facts with interpretations and judgements not only undermined the foundations of truth upon which historical practice rests, but opened the door to ideologically and politically motivated practitioners who gathered selected facts that supported their political agendas (see Chapter 3). Yet, notwithstanding their discomfort, in formulating their replies to the Postans and Carrs, reconstructionists subtly shifted the focus of their craft away from gathering and reporting facts. The interrogation of historical material became the new paramount task of reconstructionists. And in an attempt to make their facts indisputable, reconstructionists increasingly referred them to in legalistic terms as evidence.[33] Espousing the modified reconstructionist doctrine, Keith Windschuttle conceded that the past does not advertise itself, and that the retrieval of facts is not one of merely extracting observations. Rather, discovering facts is a labour intensive activity that precludes practitioners from making prior decisions. Indeed, Windschuttle believes that historical evidence frequently forces practitioners to change their minds. When they 'go looking for evidence', he says, historians

> do not simply find the one thing they are looking for. Most will find many others that they have not anticipated. The result, more often than not, is that this unexpected evidence will suggest alternative arguments, interpretations and conclusions, and different problems to pursue.[34]

Windschuttle places colossal faith in the objectivity of historical materials. Objectivity, he asserts, exists in the creation and in the substance of historical material. Whether an eighteenth-century cricket bat, proclamations and laws banning men and women from swimming together in public pools, the diary of a mountaineer, a late-nineteenth-century film of a horserace, or police testimony presented to a court prosecuting men attending illegal dogfights, all these materials were created to serve contemporary wants, needs and goals, and not for the benefit of future historians. In this sense, they are untainted by foresight. Similarly, figures in cricket scorebooks, the poses adopted by members of a victorious football team for a photograph, or the relief images on a coin produced to commemorate a sporting festival, are fixed, irrespective of who might look at them later, their purposes for looking at them and their subsequent interpretations. Thus, Windschuttle concluded, historical analysis and interpretation are not open-ended: 'the evidence itself will restrict the purposes for which it can be used' and 'this is true even of those documents for which all historians agree that varying interpretations are possible. In these cases, the range of possibilities is always finite ...'.[35] However, I will argue that Windschuttle's claim about historical evidence setting limits on interpretation does not stand up to scrutiny.

Commited to finding the truth, mainstream reconstructionism turned to validating (or more correctly invalidating) historical evidence through what amounted to forensic-type examinations.[36] Such examinations became standard fare in reconstructionist methodology textbooks that invariably included multiple chapters on the subject. The critical question is, do these tests actually lead practitioners closer to historical truths? In order to answer this question, I now analyse a standard set of reconstructionist tests for verifying historical evidence.

Validating historical truths

In his primer of historical method, Louis Gottschalk defined historical facts as the 'credible' details derived 'directly or indirectly' from historical materials. According to him, historians validate or verify those details by interrogating (questioning) their materials. In practice, interrogation involves asking those who produced or created the historical materials or testimony (usually an author or a witness) questions like: was the witness *able* and *willing* to tell the truth, and did second-hand parties *accurately report* or *record* what primary witnesses said or observed? Interrogation also means searching for *independent corroboration*.[37] Reconstructionists typically see these and similar tests as forensic-type examinations that produce incontrovertible evidence. While space does not allow identification of the full range of tests needed to verify historical sources and arguments, I can apply a selection to several examples.[38] The objective here is simply to ascertain whether a rigorous examination of historical material is enough to establish the truth and shut the door on other possible interpretations, as Windschuttle claims.

Ability to tell the truth

Reconstructionism issues a standard set of questions for determining whether sources or witnesses are telling the truth:

- How close geographically and temporally was the witnesses to the event?
- How soon after the event did the witnesses record their observations, or provide their testimony to another party for recording?
- How competent were the witnesses, that is, what was their state of mental and physical health, age, and level of education, memory and narrative skills?

Following these lines of inquiry, Joan Patrick correctly challenged the reliability of three key sources widely cited in popular accounts of the events that led to the lifting of the bans on public bathing in daylight hours in Sydney. These are an article in the *Daily Telegraph* (Sydney) published on 7 January 1907, an account by P. W. Gledhill, a member of the Manly Historical Society published in his *Manly and Pittwater: Its Beauty and Progress* (1948), and another article in the *Manly Daily* (Manly, Sydney) newspaper that appeared on 28 July 1966. None of these sources, said Patrick, provides direct testimony; all were written well after municipal ordinances promulgated unrestricted daylight surfbathing hours in the summer of 1903–4. Patrick preferred the version given by the pioneer surfbather Arthur Lowe which she felt benefited from his personal involvement with the events. However, far from establishing the truth of Lowe's account, Patrick conceded that his reminiscences are those of 'a seventy-year-old man living in the 1950s nostalgic about a carefree past of endless summers'. Moreover, his story is 'disjointed, suggesting that it was written over a long period of time'.[39]

Patrick's work highlights two fundamental issues in historical interrogation. First, given that the 'toughest' questions in history are 'what is right?' and 'how do historians prove it is right?', interrogation tends to gravitate towards the easier approach, namely, identifying 'what is wrong with any given history'.[40] The second point is that reconstructionists usually express their judgements of competing interpretations of facts in terms of probabilities rather than absolute proofs.[41]

Willingness to tell the truth

The process of invalidating sources is even more conspicuous when practitioners set out to ascertain whether a witness or source was willing to tell the truth. Historians are especially tuned to witnesses who shade their testimony for personal motives, to please or displease another party, or who simply unconsciously colour their observations or thoughts with religious, social, economic, political, racial, national, regional and/or community nuances. Hence questions about motives and affiliations are mandatory in establishing the validity of a source.[42] Arthur Lowe's apparent desire to wear the crown of Australia's 'surfbathing pioneer' might explain his dismissal of popular accounts that attributed the lifting of the ban on daylight bathing to protests by the newspaper proprietor William Gocher. Lowe mocked Gocher, referring to him as a non-swimmer dressed in an oversized costume.[43] Florid literary styles typical of sporting programmes, souvenir brochures and media guides are prone to sacrificing the truth in the interests of pleasing organisers, sponsors and governing bodies. Dispensing with the prudent word, inconspicuous phrase, and the ifs and buts associated with precise discourse, the official souvenir programme for the opening ceremony of the 1956 olympic games in Melbourne eulogised the olympics as an international forum for peace and goodwill.[44] Even in the face of flagrant contradictory evidence, the desire to please can endure. Persisting with the popular view that the olympics are a forum for generating goodwill and peace, the official report of the 1956 games completely ignored moments of serious conflict. One salient example was the fracas in the water polo group final between Hungary and Russia which the *Argus* (Melbourne) labelled a 'kick, bite and gouge … session that would have done credit to an all-in wrestling match'.[45] (Three weeks before the games, Soviet tanks and troops brutally crushed a general strike by Hungarian workers in Budapest.) Indeed, in his foreword to the official report, the president of the 1956 games and prime minister of Australia, Robert Menzies, described his 'particular pleasure' in being able to 'record that no ill-will appeared'.[46]

In all these cases interrogation has facilitated the invalidation of sources on the grounds of factual inaccuracy and biased viewpoints. Yet, it has done so without offering a means by which to distil and synthesise validated facts for the 'best understanding of them'. Of course, the latter can only derive from the larger interpretation of events.[47]

Accurate reporting

Everyday people witness objects, events, happenings and incidents, and have feelings and express opinions and viewpoints about them. But these observations and opinions only become historical sources when they, or someone else – usually a relative, friend, student or journalist – record or preserve them. Reconstructionists correctly point out that the accurate recording of observations and testimony is no simple exercise, as different reports of the same event in newspapers continually reveal. Newspaper accounts of Jack Chalmers bringing shark attack victim Milton Coughlan ashore at Coogee Beach (Sydney) in 1922 offer conflicting details. According to the *Sunday Times* and *Sydney Morning Herald*, Coughlan's screams from the water alerted the crowd on the beach to his plight; the *Referee* and *Sun* also referred to screams, but stated that these came from shocked observers watching Coughlan from the balcony of the surf lifesaving clubhouse. The *Daily Telegraph*'s narrative, largely written through the eyes of Chalmers, made no mention of any screams. The *Sun*, *Sydney Morning Herald* and *Referee* said that in his haste to reach Coughlan, Chalmers slipped, fell and dazed himself on rocks before entering the water; no reference to Chalmers falling appears in the *Sunday Times* or *Daily Telegraph*. The *Sunday Times*, *Sydney Morning Herald* and *Referee* claimed Chalmers grabbed Coughlan while he was still in the jaws of the shark; the *Sun* and *Daily Telegraph* report the shark had already released Coughlan when Chalmers reached his patient.[48]

Clearly, some of these 'facts' are manifestly wrong, but which ones? To answer this question, forensically inclined reconstructionist historians pursue further questions while also seeking new sources, accounts and testimony.[49] Yet, in the context of a fear-inducing shark attack, the tragic death of a young surf lifesaver, Chalmers' heroics, and traumatised witnesses, one cannot escape the question: how important are these contested facts? Robert Berkhofer is surely right when he says that 'many genuine facts pertaining to a set of events or a period are not necessarily relevant to a given interpretation'.[50]

Independent corroboration

Irrespective of their confidence in a specific source, historians always seek additional corroboration. Preferably this comes from independent witnesses who have not influenced each other or been influenced by a common third-party. 'Unless the independence of the observers is established', Gottschalk said, 'agreement may be confirmation of a lie or of a mistake rather than corroboration of a fact'.[51] In an example of good corroboration, Joachim Rühl cites a diary entry (recorded by an indifferent observer) as evidence of poor jousting standards on the first day of a tournament at Westminster in 1501. (King Henry VII staged the tournament to honour the marriage of his eldest son Prince Arthur to Catherine of Aragon, the daughter of King Ferdinand II of Spain.) In the official report of the tournament, a herald praises the standard of the combatants: 'such a feld, and justs ryall, so noble and valiantly doon [as] have not ben sen ne herd'. But the check-list records a low standard among the jousters: in 57 charges, the challengers missed in 40 and the answerers in 42.[52] To evaluate which source was telling the truth, Rühl turns to an entry in Henry Machyn's diary as indirect evidence supporting the check-list. An undertaker by occupation, Machyn claimed no special interest in jousting but he does confirm that the judges and scorers sat closer to the tilt than any other court officials – so close that a piece of broken lance hit one judge.[53] Rühl believes that geographical proximity to the jousts increased the probability of the judges getting the facts right and he sees the diary entry as corroborating the check-list. Strictly speaking of course, corroborative evidence should also be subjected to the same forensic tests as primary evidence regarding the ability and willingness to tell the truth, and while Rühl confirms the ability of the judges to tell the truth (by virtue of their geographical proximity), he says nothing about their willingness to tell the truth. Rühl suggests that the judges were more likely to tell an unbiased truth by virtue of their function than would be the herald, who assumedly sang the combatants' praises in his role as a servant of the king.

As the preceding discussions imply, for the vast majority of historical questions, practitioners rarely find independent documents or more than one witness testifying to the same facts. For most historical questions – especially those pertaining to 'the emotions, ideals, interests, sensations, impressions, private opinions, attitudes, drives and motives of an individual' – there is only one source.[54] In these cases, where the evidence is known or knowable only by a single person, historians break the general rule of corroboration by an independent witness and look for other kinds of corroboration. This may include marrying opinions and professed interests with patterns of behaviour, the silence of other contemporary sources, or the more general credibility of a document. For example, journalist Ali Crombie points out that the willingness of John Coates (president of the Australian Olympic Committee and a key strategist for the Sydney Olympic Bid Committee) to violate the olympic spirit of fair play in lobbying on behalf of Sydney to host the 2000 olympic games, was consistent with other high-risk behaviour in his business, financial and political dealings.[55] (On the eve of the International Olympic Committee's (IOC) vote for the host city, Coates offered financial incentives to IOC members Charles Mukora and Francis Nyangweso, ostensibly to help develop sport in their home countries.[56]) Thus, Crombie employs a broader pattern of behaviour to 'corroborate' one action by Coates. Yet, even conclusions about Coates' behaviour based on firm evidence of one relationship with two IOC members raises issues. All relationships need a context, in this case within the olympic movement, and, as I shall show (Chapter 10), context leads historians further from their sources and closer to argument and interpretation.

In the final analysis, corroboration rarely, if ever, proves historical accounts. Catriona Parratt, for example, consulted an exhaustive array of sources to corroborate her account of Haxey Hood, a folk-football-type game played at Haxey village in north-west Lincolnshire. Among the sources she used to corroborate her description (based on personal observations of two Haxey Hoods, interviews with participants and spectators, and audio and visual recordings made while attending the events) are Jeremy Cooper's *A Fool's Game: The Ancient Tradition of the Haxey Hood* (1993) and W. B. Stonehouse's, *The History and Topography of the Isle of Axholme* (1839), and articles by Venetia Newell (1932), Mabel Peacock (1896), A. Pearson (1955) and Phillip Taylor (1932).[57] Clearly Parratt's reconstruction meets all reasonable standards of corroboration. However, it is still not enough. As I mentioned in the example of Rühl and the tournament cited above, absolute proof of something requires forensic examination of every piece of evidence. Parratt, like all historians, simply relies on the sheer weight of testimony or corroboration to increase the probability of reliability that does not, in the end, equate to absolute proof. In this sense, she is what all historians tend to be, advocates striving to build incontrovertible arguments (see Chapter 6).

All of these examples show that forensic examinations of the evidence do not reduce the gap between 'the records of the past' and 'the interpretation of those records'.[58] At least one historian of sport, Mark Golden, acknowledged this when he noted that historical records 'take on most meaning within a framework' and that 'different frameworks are always possible'.[59] While this position is classic constructionism, it is worth illustrating here with an example from Golden's own work: his analysis of Pindar's victory songs praising Olympians and their triumphs. Commissioned by victorious athletes or their families or friends, performed at celebrations in the champion's own community, and honouring the achievements of the victor, family members and his community, Pindar's odes seem self-explanatory in their objective: to present Olympic success as a 'public good, a benefaction from the victor upon the city' and thus fostering mutual amity and community.[60] But such an interpretation, Golden believes, derives from a specific vision of sport as a set of integrative relationships, and he prefers an alternative framework.[61] The 'discourse of difference' framework favoured by Golden views sport as an arena that creates and reinforces social divisions and hierarchies.[62] Obviously Pindar's songs of triumph remain fixed as records of the past in Golden's alternative framework. However, they led Golden to pose new questions and ultimately took on different meaning. Why, for example, did commemorative statues replace the epinician genre that all but vanished with Pindar's death? This 'change in fashion', Golden believes, 'needs more explanation' than the demise of a single poet.[63] It is in this context that the discourse of difference achieves salience.[64]

Golden's analysis helps to show that the preoccupation with facts and verification of historical materials will not secure factual authority, and will produce neither fundamental truths nor stable knowledge about the past.[65] When defined as irrefutable truths, historical facts are typically trivial – American Gertrude Ederle was the first woman to swim the English Channel, a swim she completed in 14 hours 30 minutes on 6 August 1926; Englishman Roger Bannister ran the first sub-four-minute mile on 6 May 1954. Moreover, as the example of William Gilbert Grace testifies, reducing the lives of sportspeople to sets of factual achievements leaves them absurdly incomplete.[66] The real truths of historical practice are that 'historical facts have no one-to-one relationship to historical interpretation, and vice versa' and that 'the same basic set of facts can support several points of view'.[67] In this sense, Postan was right: most historical facts are relevancies produced by practitioners in response to their specific questions.

Although forensic examination does little to produce historical truths, questioning evidence has helped establish one accepted principle of historical research: practitioners uncover more reliable information when the questions they ask of their sources are incidental to the purpose for which these remnants of human activity were originally created or functioned. In other words, reliability increases when historians employ historical materials in ways their producers or compilers could not possibly have foreseen or predicted.[68] In his work on interrogation, Gottschalk identified five sets of 'conditions favourable to truthfulness' in the absence of hard facts. First, indifferent witnesses are usually credible.[69] One example of this in sport might be found in a discussion of the captaincy of the New Zealand All Black rugby team. A fringe member of the national squad and fighting for a place in the 1998 team, Norm Hewitt claimed he was indifferent to Taine Randell's appointment as captain. Arguably his indifference spills over into a reliable assessment of Randell's leadership ability:

> I thought of Taine as a follower rather than a leader. ... he was head prefect material all right, but only because there would be a headmaster and other teachers around him. But All Black rugby isn't school. On the field, you've got to have the respect of your fellow players and you've got to have a real hard head. Taine wasn't that kind of leader.[70]

Although undoubtedly prejudiced by his low status in the New Zealand rugby players' hierarchy, Hewitt's assessment at least carried the credibility of a witness simultaneously close enough to, and far enough away from, Randell. (See also Chapter 6 for the example of Matthew Bloxam whose testimony supported claims that William Webb Ellis was the founder of rugby.)

Second, statements prejudicial to witnesses, their families and their causes are likely to be truthful.[71] Norm Hewitt, for example, admitted he was a 'thug' and a 'bully' during his school years.[72] Although historians rank volunteered confessions as 'excellent' forms of testimony, they also warn against confusing confessions with boasting or attempts to arouse self-pity.[73] Australian swimmer Dawn Fraser 'confessed' to being 'indolent at school' and to harbouring a 'contempt for authority'; but she cleverly weighs these claims against harsh treatment by swimming officials whom she casts as petty-minded and mean-spirited killjoys. Most commentators agree that Australian Swimming Union officials treated Fraser with undue harshness when they suspended her for ten years (later reduced to four) and denied her all rights to appeal.[74] However, by failing to reflect on her behaviour, Fraser's confession loses its effect and she remained, for at least one historian, the 'ugly Australian hero', a sportswoman who 'ignores the spirit behind the [rules]'.[75]

Third, matters of common knowledge, particularly those left unchallenged by contemporaries, generally contain high levels of reliability. In such instances, however, the historian must ensure that contemporaries knew of, and had every opportunity to contest the evidence.[76] The belief that sport contributes to the construction and reproduction of national identities has wide currency. Although many scholars question the significance of national identity – assigning it to relatively temporary and minor status behind more permanent gender, class, racial, familial and regional identities[77] – no one disputes the outpourings of national pride and sentiment when France won the World Soccer Cup in 1998 or when England won the World Rugby Cup in 2003. In both cases, national sentiment prevailed over other forms of identity, albeit temporarily, and its widespread acceptance amounts to reliable evidence of sport's ability to muster broad social consent.

Fourth, 'certain kinds of statements are both incidental and probable to such a degree that error or falsehood seems unlikely',[78] though not always in the manner expected. A plaque at Rugby School, England, proclaims William Webb Ellis the founder of rugby football in 1823. Erected in 1900, 77 years after Webb Ellis allegedly picked up the ball and ran with it, the accuracy of the wording on the plaque should immediately raise historians' suspicions. Apart from anything else, it extends all credibility to believe that a single act on a school ground could have instantaneously revolutionised a game especially when running with the ball had a long history in the traditional game of folk football. (The myth of rugby's origins is analysed in Chapter 6.) Nonetheless, as Gottschalk reminds us, 'even the boldest propaganda may be made to yield credible information'[79] and in this instance, it may at least be taken at face value as evidence that William Webb Ellis attended Rugby School and that boys played organised games at the school in the 1820s.

Last, actions and statements have a high degree of credibility when they are 'contrary to the witness's expectations or anticipations'.[80] Australian Rugby Union representative Paul Darveniza did not anticipate returning from the 1969 tour of South Africa as an opponent of sporting tours to the Republic. A medical student at a conformist university who played a deeply conservative sport, Darveniza received unparalleled hospitality on the tour from South African rugby officials who were determined to meet their guests' every need and whim. But his own observations and several incidents on the tour made him realise that sportspeople who toured apartheid South Africa were merely 'pawns in a bigger game of international politics'. Adding to Darveniza's credibility as a witness was his account of a 'secret' meeting with a Coloured woman (who he first met by chance on a flight from Cape Town to Durban) and her family in their township home during the tour; this account in turn assumes trustworthiness when corroborated with revelations that South African security police monitored his movements and warned the Australian tour managers that such behaviour should immediately cease.[81]

Gottschalk's five conditions of reliability also demonstrate another principle of historical practice, namely, that ingenuity and flair are prerequisites for grasping the full range of uses to which historical materials can be put.[82] Certainly social and cultural historians have become extremely adept at reading their sources with heightened sensitivity and creativity, and at finding in the remnants of the past evidence not seen by others or dismissed by them as unreliable (containing either lies or mistakes).[83] In their search for early barometers of football hooliganism as a social problem, Joseph Maguire and his colleagues found illumination in a comment by the Bishop of Liverpool in a 1939 edition of a religious magazine the *Liverpool Diocesan Review*. According to the Bishop, some spectators were over-stepping the 'limits of decent partisanship'. For Maguire the reliability of the Bishop's comments – the determination of which will always be hindered by the '[lack of] testimony from the accused' – is less relevant than the questions they raise about 'who decides, and by what criteria, whether specific forms of behaviour by particular groups in society … are … problematic'.[84] A small example, it nonetheless challenges Windschuttle's assertion above, that the range of interpretations open to historians is always finite.

Thus the mainstream of reconstructionism conceded the contingent nature of facts and recognised that a fact is 'merely a *contribution* to knowledge, immediately open to scrutiny, analysis and criticism' by peers.[85] Nonetheless, if reconstructionists abandoned notions of hard facts, they have remained firmly wedded to analysing and interpreting historical material. Not only do these materials make the past every bit as real as the present and provide the substance that distinguishes history from fiction, they underpin contemporary reconstructionist notions of historical objectivity.[86]

Reconstructionism and questions of objectivity

In the first edition of the *Journal of Sport History*, Marvin Eyler wrote that 'one cannot reflect long upon the question of truth in historical inquiry without coming to grips with a most important problem – that of objectivity'.[87] Like other problems in reconstructionism, such as facts and truths, objectivity has undergone radical reconceptualisation. Traditionally, reconstructionism defined history as 'objective', that is, free from personal perspective, without political agendas, and able to eliminate hindsight and present-centred approaches to the past.[88] However, such notions of objectivity were unsustainable once reconstructionists admitted that their facts assumed meaning only within specific interpretive frameworks. In the light of this recognition, reconstructionism tacitly transformed the meaning of objectivity. Today, objectivity calls 'attention to the intricate network of constraints (cognitive, ethical and institutional)' upon which practitioners rely to 'distinguish history from fiction, scholarship from propaganda, or good history from bad'.[89] I will explore one contemporary reconstructionist notion of objectivity. Proposed by Joyce Appleby, Lynn Hunt and Margaret Jacob, qualified objectivity comes complete with its own framework of knowledge or epistemology – practical realism.

Rather than looking at history as 'an objective compilation of facts', that is, 'the unqualified primacy of fact over interpretation', or as 'the subjective product of the mind of the historian',[90] practical realism advocates 'an interactive relationship between an inquiring subject and external object'.[91] The source of all historical knowledge, the inquiring subject, is a curious historian whose personal biases, values, emotions, and cultural preferences and privileges shape her or his questions, and who will also determine her or his own standards of objectivity in the examination of historical materials (external objects).[92] Unlike some deconstructionists, practical realists refuse to accept that the incorporation of subjectivity logically leads to total relativism. 'I entirely agree', concedes Miles Fairburn, 'that the ways we see the past are shaped by preconceptions and that as a result total objectivity is impossible to achieve'. However, 'that does not mean that we should not strive to be objective, nor that everything is entirely a matter of opinion'. 'Although it is impossible to know the "truth" about the social past in any absolute sense', Fairburn continues, under 'certain conditions' historians can make 'propositions' about the past that are 'reliable to varying degrees'.[93] And those conditions hinge upon external objects, the historical materials that yield evidence and concepts (see Chapter 3) and give historical writing its 'worth'.

As well as locating objectivity in external objects, practical realism also draws an important distinction between perspective and opinion. Perspective, of course, is widely held to confound historical practice.[94] When Bill Murray, for example, criticises the 'aristocratic' and 'old-world values' in Sir Derek Birley's three-volume history of British sport, he is actually slating the titled historian's perspective that disdains working-class sports and attitudes, and unashamedly celebrates 'the pounding of the turf, the cries of tally-ho, the grunts of amateur oarsmen heaving their way along the Thames, the puffing of amateur rugger chaps, … and, … the gentle applause of dignified cricket enthusiasts'.[95] Among practical realists, however, opinion is what exists within the mind's eye, and perspective 'refers to a point of view – literally, a point from which some thing, an object outside the mind is viewed'. Thus, the task of the historian is to interrogate each perspective for its accuracy and completeness.[96] Birley's history may be a narrow upper-class view of British sport history, but Murray's review does not prove that this translates into an inaccurate account.

Practical realists also warn historians not to 'discriminate [against] interpretations that rest on different assumptions'.[97] In their respective interpretations of amateurism in late nineteenth- and early twentieth-century America, Ronald Smith and Steve Pope employ two quite different concepts of amateurism. Smith treats it as an ideal code, Pope as a contradiction-laden practice. Not surprisingly these different concepts lead to radically different conclusions about amateurism in American sport.[98] From a practical realist standpoint, not even a deep delve into the historical sources will resolve the disparity between these two interpretations because the authors argue from completely different perspectives (one from ideal, the other from practice) which carry their own sets of evidence.[99]

Reconstructionists typically side-step discussions of epistemology; most confine themselves to historical practice which they claim marks out the field as a unique form of 'intellectual enterprise', with its own operating rules and principles guided by common sense empiricism.[100] The close relationship between historical material and practitioner in qualified objectivity is perfectly consistent with other reconstructionist definitions of historical practice as a process. Social historian of cycling Andrew Ritchie, for example, recently described history as a 'process of self-reasoning':

> By virtue of a life-time interest (call it chance or fate!) I was interested in this particular subject/subject area. I wanted to know more about it. My common

sense, and growing experience of library/archival research taught me gradually where I was most likely to find information about it. Effort and geographical access to good archival locations encouraged me in looking in these particular places. Growing skill at probing the source material, particularly newspapers and specialized periodicals, developed ways/techniques of tracking information, which increased my chances of finding relevant information. Through skilled detective work, reading widely in the extraordinary periodicals covering my field, and persistent surfing the web, I found others. As I researched and read, my already formed ideas and assumptions interacted with the nature of my findings to produce new patterns and arrangements of knowledge, suggestions, and ideas. Where I found good, primary source material, I could say with fair amount of certainty – 'This is what actually happened, or what was done or not done, and what was said'. All of these categories are the raw material from which data could be examined, conclusions proposed and history written about. Using my accumulated experience in the field/subject, I was able to begin to hazard a more complex picture of the relationship between action and result, between human intention and social result, between economic factors and real life, etc. But this analysis was of course dependent specifically on which aspects of my findings I chose to concentrate on, which also partly depended, of course, on the chance and effort of my original search.[101]

Similarly, Fischer calls history 'a process of *adductive* reasoning in the simple sense of adducing answers to specific questions', so that, irrespective of whether the question is 'general or specific', the historian achieves a 'satisfactory explanatory "fit"'.[102] In other words, historians achieve fits between aggregates of evidence and specific questions by framing their evidence in certain ways. (Explanatory fits, what Fischer calls paradigms, take a number of different forms; in Part II of *The Field* I identify and examine six different explanatory paradigms commonly found in sport history.)

Important omissions are apparent in these statements. Ritchie's commonsense version of historical practice, for example, excludes all accounts of methodology or theory. Apart from an unhelpful reference to 'chance or fate', Ritchie provides no explanation as to how or why he chose his topic. Nor does he nominate the criteria he uses to select, analyse and criticise his historical material, the sources, referents or veracity of his analytical concepts, or how he draws connections and relationships between his evidence.[103] Instead of answering these fundamental questions, Ritchie shelters in the skirts of 'the *methods* that social historians supposedly follow in their day-to-day examination of "evidence", beginning with their supposedly untheoretical attention to that evidence'.[104] I pursue these issues more fully in the following chapters.

Conclusion

Reconstructionists have continuously revised their notions of history and truth. Early practitioners believed that facts preceded interpretation, and assumed a faithful correspondence between evidence and knowledge of the past. They also believed that historians were objective, judicial and avoided *a priori* assumptions. One by one these pillars crumbled and led to an acknowledgement that history is a constantly shifting process of interpretation. 'The relation between facts and events is always open to negotiation, and reconceptualization', says Hayden White, 'not because the events change with time, but because we change our ways of conceptualizing them'. Moreover, White continues, 'if this is true of events, it is even more true of facts. We not only change our ideas of what the facts are of a given matter but our notions of what a fact might be, how facts are constructed, and what criteria should be used to assess the adequacy of a given array of facts to the events of which they purport to be descriptive'.[105] Of course, this is rarer for the practitioner working alone; very few individual historians change their ideas, their views of those ideas, or their conclusions.

Today, mainstream reconstructionism broadly accepts the 'provisional nature' of historical interpretations and concedes that absolute 'proof and truth do not exist in history'. Reconstructionists recognise that historical practice is a 'continuous process of discovering new evidence', and they are 'constantly recontextualising' that evidence and 'treating it with increasingly sophisticated mechanisms of analysis and conceptualisations'.[106] Where once Australian sport was used as evidence of the British Empire, today it constitutes evidence for interpretations deriving from globalisation and postcolonial frameworks.[107] Sport historian Nancy Struna captures the current reconstructionist perspective in a recent statement in *The International Journal of the History of Sport*:

> historians' faith in both *a* Truth and *the* truth of grand narratives has been supplanted by the realization that only smaller truths and narrower narratives are possible. No longer do many of us hold with traditional positivist claims about evidence, that it exists independently of the mind of the historian and that it does not change. We are quite able to distinguish between evidence and artefact (in whatever form) and willing to argue that while an artefact may not change, what the artefact is evidence of may change. We have also dispensed with any pretence to absolute objectivity and most predilections to predictability.[108]

These admissions notwithstanding, reconstructionists show no sign of abandoning their sources as the primary 'window on past reality'. While reconstructionists like Struna admit that new sources will always open new windows, they insist that the view beyond will always correspond to reality. In short, 'the ultimate claim of reconstructionism remains intact, that *the* past is knowable through [the remnants of the past]'.[109]

Reconstructionism can establish a reasonably satisfactory correspondence between sources and reality in simple cases such as the dates of a sporting figure's birth and death, or the statistical foundations of achievements. However, the accuracy of correspondence becomes more questionable when reconstructionists 'shift a gear to … interpretation', when, for example, they talk about the sports star as a national hero or national icon. 'It may be possible to demonstrate a strong, even probable correspondence between a single statement about the past and a single piece of evidence, sufficient to generate a factual statement', writes Alun Munslow. But any attempt to 'then translate this inductive "truth" to a whole historical interpretive narrative, so as to recover the past as it actually was', he cautions, 'is a flawed practice'.[110] While reconstructionists fear that removing certainties (truths) will render history irrelevant, obsolete and worthless, deconstructionists take a more positive view. Uncertainties, they suggest, are more encompassing and embracing than certainties that facilitate ideological colonisation of historical space by 'what is politically right, wrong, correct or incorrect'.[111] Michael Oriard illustrates this notion in his work on American football. He argues that the conflicts, contradictions and paradoxes within prevailing dominant value systems or ideologies such as amateurism that ultimately makes the game 'genuinely "democratic"'. Thus, while amateurs in the early twentieth century decried the abuses that professionalism introduced into football, the latter was a 'powerful force for democracy': the win-at-all-costs mentality of professionalism prompted the recruitment and subsidisation of 'the rugged sons of Italian and Polish and other despised immigrants who [would] build winning teams'.[112]

Reconstructionists believe that erasing the 'dividing line between evidence and its interpretation' ultimately opens the door to accepting 'any interpretation'. Deconstructionists reject this view. They insist that all interpretations 'have to be made with care and caution. … interpretations build on so many layers of interpretations that they have to be well grounded or they topple over. Meaning can only be reconstructed if the stories are grounded in relation to other evidence, other interpretations, other stories'.[113]

Finally, in their attempts to 'reduce a history text to a number of factual propositions about a past reality', reconstructionists 'overlooked the rest of the text as a multilayered form of representation' that includes the 'nature of the narrative organization or the rhetorical exposition'. 'Hunting for factual propositions', Berkhofer continues, 'not only masks the larger truthfulness about the past that historians say they seek; it also reduces the text to a series of sentences while neglecting its cumulative effect. Such an approach fails to look at a text as a totality whose sum is greater than its "factual" parts'.[114] I pursue these issues in subsequent chapters. In Chapter 3, for example, I examine the deconstructionist notion of facts as unstable 'linguistic entities' that are always 'subject to revision and further interpretation'. As Hayden White, following Roland Barthes, argues, 'the language used to describe a field of historical occurrences in effect constitutes the field itself and sets limits to the kinds of methods that can be used to analyse the events occurring within the field'.[115] Among reconstructionists, however, such notions suffer from 'linguistic determinism', that is, 'the reduction of the social and natural world to language and context to text'.[116]

Chapter 3

Facts, concepts and structures

Theory in sport history

THEORY IS A THORNY SUBJECT for historians. Conservative
reconstructionists maintain that history is an a-theoretical discipline. Geoffrey
Elton argues that 'theory directs the selection of evidence and infuses predestined
meaning into it. All questions are so framed as to produce support for the theory, and
all answers are predetermined by it.'[1]

Constructionists insist that theory is integral to historical practice. Writing in
1929, Werner Sombart insisted that 'the writer of history who desires to be more than
a mere antiquarian must have a thorough *theoretical* training in those fields of inquiry
with which his work is concerned'. This is not to deny that historians must 'have a
knowledge of sources and [the] ability to criticize them'. However, Sombart deems
these skills as belonging to the 'mere "hodman,"' the one who undertakes only 'menial'
tasks. 'Theoretical training makes the true historian', says Sombart adding his rail, 'no
theory – no history!'[2] Clouding the debate are imprecise definitions of theory. Whereas
the 'hard' or 'natural' scientists define theory as a formal arrangement of concepts
explaining a specific phenomenon,[3] historians accept theory as a 'framework of
interpretation' which sets out questions, directs practitioners to particular sources,
organises evidence and shapes explanations, and thereby gives 'impetus to an inquiry
and influences its outcomes'.[4] Certainly in sport history 'frameworks of interpretation'
rarely proceed beyond simple descriptions of systems or processes that barely justify
the theory label.

Here I present and evaluate the cases for and against the use of theory in sport
history as advocated by reconstructionists and constructionists. As Sombart's words
above reveal, the debates between reconstructionists and constructionists predate the
field of sport history. While these debates surface at conferences from time to time,
few sport historians have addressed them in print.[5] In rectifying this omission, I will
argue that both models have a place in sport history and both have legitimacy depending

on the questions the historian seeks to answer. At the same time, I posit that many of the criticisms of theory directed by reconstructionists miss their mark.

I begin by describing the general concerns expressed by reconstructionists about the intrusive nature of theory in history; I then turn to an examination of the constructionist case for theory. Evaluating the two perspectives is difficult: while constructionists repeatedly flounder when confronted with charges of factual inaccuracies and theoretical determinism, reconstructionists rarely acknowledge the rich contributions that theory has made to history. In the next two sections I investigate functionalism and structuralism as key theoretical concepts in sport history. These frameworks have dominated debates over the reliability of theory in sport history and in these sections I identify their strengths and weaknesses. Scientific language, and a fair dollop of jargon, further confuses the theory debate; ignoring social context and ideological content, the language of theory portrays unrealistic levels of objectivity and neutrality. Sociologist Jeffrey Alexander reminds us that theory is an ideological discourse with its own political history. Intellectuals produce theories 'in their search for meaning', he argues. Further, 'in response to continuing social change, generational shifts occur that can make the scientific and ideological efforts of earlier intellectual generations seem not only empirically implausible but psychologically shallow, politically irrelevant and morally obsolete'.[6] I delve into this notion in the final section, examining the social context and ideological contents of the few theories that have dominated sport history.

Reconstructionism: theory, agents, facts and concepts

Conservative reconstructionists deem theory antithetical to historical objectives and practice.[7] In their view, real history deals only with concrete detail: its sole objective is to describe and analyse causally connected events that produce unique configurations of the past. Capturing this notion, Michael Postan wrote that 'a phenomenon as it presents itself to an historian and is presented by him, is an individual occurrence':

> Its uniqueness is, of course, a counterpart of its concreteness. The particular position of an event in time and place will not combine with the particular assortment of its characteristics and will not fit into its accidental environment, except once and once only. To this extent history is made up ... of ... stories of lives, combinations of individual lives or happenings, all seemingly individual and unrepeatable.[8]

Central to the reconstructionist position is that human intentions and actions, referred to as human agency,[9] lie at the heart of history and that historical explanations rest on the motivations, goals, values and information available to agents. Critically, these drives, beliefs and knowledge constitute the intentions of individuals that cannot be subsumed under universal explanations of behaviour. Among conservative reconstructionists, universal explanations of behaviour – whether they are defined as generalisations, categories, concepts, models or theories – fuel speculation. Some reconstructionists have developed this line of thinking to argue against theory on logical grounds: general laws made from historical observations do not exhaust all known possibilities and therefore are beyond verification.[10]

Nor do conservative reconstructionists support the use of theory as an analytical tool to interpret the past. Geoffrey Elton has rallied reconstructionists here, pointing them to what he calls the artificial limits on interpretations that theory supposedly imposes. He warns that theory constitutes 'the first great threat to unprejudiced historical study' and 'threatens the virtue of history'. To these he adds another caution: 'once a man has subscribed to a general theory as the correct way to pursue historical truth he seems to be committed to perverting the past'.[11] Summing up the conservative reconstructionist position, renowned social historian E. P. Thompson referred to 'history' as an a-theoretical discipline. 'History', he said, 'is not a factory for the manufacture of Grand Theory, like some Concorde of the global air; nor is it an assembly-line for the production of midget theories in series. Nor yet is it some gigantic experimental station in which theory of foreign manufacture can be "applied", "tested" and "confirmed". That is not its business at all', Thompson continues. 'Its business is to recover, to "explain" and to "understand" its object: real history.'[12]

Conservative reconstructionism has been subject to vigorous attacks. The criticisms generally stem from concerns about its overly narrow focus. The goals of most people's agency are private and involve limited personal projects and small choices – pursuit of work, happy family relationships, entertaining and relaxing leisure activities[13] – that are so ordinary, mundane and common that they are of little interest to the overwhelming majority of historians. Indeed, as Thomas Haskell notes, the historian who worked solely in the tacitly shared social contexts of needs, opportunities, conventions and experiences would be thought 'daft'.[14] Historians concern themselves primarily with differences, exceptions, disruptions, abnormalities and tragedies; more often than not, these are the result of individuals banding together for collective goals.[15] It is the biographies of stars, especially those fallen from grace, and champion teams, the behaviour of unruly crowds, details of strikes and labour unrest, and the experiences of minority groups that occupy sport historians, rather than the lives of ordinary or average players, the conduct of peaceful spectators, the working relations between players and managers, or the experiences of social majorities.

Reconstructionists correctly retort that theory is often ill-equipped to explain the particulars of one-off events, differences and abnormalities. General laws, theories, explanatory schemes and the like may well identify the necessary or predisposing conditions for specific events, but they will not differentiate the precise weightings of the usually multitude of causes that precipitate particular – concrete and unique – historical events.[16] Exploitive labour relations offer a strong theoretical explanation for the worldwide proliferation of confrontational player unions from the late 1950s. However, this generalisation does not explain what precipitated the formation of specific militant unions like the Professional Footballers' Association in British soccer, the international Association of Tennis Professionals, the Victorian Football League Players Association in Australia, or the Professional Cricketers' Association of Australia. Nor does it explain the exact conditions that led to the radicalisation of the Major League Baseball Players Association in North America.[17]

Not all reconstructionists consider the investigation of unique events as the litmus test of historical knowledge. The majority recognise that individual and social behaviours recur as patterns. Indeed, many patterns in social life, such as the concentration of sporting facilities in urban areas or of young men in aggressive body-contact sports, 'obtrude at the level of humble reality' and in this sense are 'unavoidable'.[18] While it is true that 'no two individuals are entirely alike', how they think and act in certain situations – as members of a sporting fraternity, or fans celebrating the victory of their national sporting team – will typically 'follow a highly regular pattern', even 'to the point where their response can be predicted'. Moreover, from the reconstructionist perspective, historians sensitised to looking for regularities and patterns may, paradoxically, encounter 'aspects which resist categorization' and that reveal the 'unique qualities' in an event or situation.[19]

Patterns abound in sport history which practitioners quite legitimately classify or categorise. Sport historians identify classes of objects (for example, amateur sports, extreme sports), themes (for example, urbanisation, democratisation), periods (for example, Victorian era, late capitalism) and constellations of interrelated traits (for example, sporting gentlemen, manliness). Many of these have proved invaluable and indispensable to the field.[20] The categorisation or classification of patterns moves historians past the 'single instance' advocated by conservative reconstructionism, and encourages the 'transcendence of immediate perceptions',[21] abstraction, and the development of concepts, models and even theories.[22]

Like patterns, concepts abound in, and are integral components of, sport history. But few sport historians have discussed or analysed their nature.[23] Arthur Stinchcombe and Thompson offer two diverse reconstructionist views. The former asserted that valid concepts rest on foundations of facts. When historians 'do a good job of historical interpretation', said Stinchcombe, they think about the facts and use them to 'generate *historically specific general ideas*'. Facts, he continued, 'are good hard stones for honing ideas'.[24] (Stinchcombe's interest in facts derives from the way historians use them to '*improve* ideas' and make them 'more powerful', rather than from epistemological concerns about their truth or verifiability.[25]) Stinchcombe found too many irrelevant abstract concepts inserted into concrete historical situations and he believed that grand theorists erred by trying to invent concepts at the 'level of the large narrative of overall sequences'. The assumption that 'feudalism leads to the bourgeois revolution which leads to the proletarian revolution' amounts to 'reckless' theorising, Stinchcombe said, because it 'ignore[s] most of the facts in order to get its concepts going'.[26] The most 'fruitful' concepts, he argued, are 'invented' by historians who carefully examine the 'analogies between historical instances'. At the heart of his notion of concept lies the 'deep' analogy, that is, three or more equivalent relations among the elements of the class. More equivalent relations mean 'deeper' analogies[27] and, of course, greater attention to historical detail.

In contrast to Stinchcombe, who stressed concepts as formal constructions, Thompson highlighted their flexibility. In *The Poverty of Theory*, a polemic directed at the French philosopher and structural Marxist Louis Althusser, Thompson discusses historical concepts as special cases that 'display extreme elasticity and allow for great irregularity'. Although 'generalised by logic from many examples', historical concepts, Thompson explained:

> do not impose a rule, but … hasten and facilitate the interrogation of evidence, even though it is often found that each case departs, in this or that particular, from the rule. The evidence (and the real event) is not rule governed, and yet it could not be understood without the rule, to which it offers its own regularities.

Thompson saw historical concepts as being of a peculiar type. This may 'provoke impatience in some philosophers (and even sociologists) who consider that a concept with such elasticity is not a true concept, and a rule is not a rule unless the evidence conforms to it, and stands to attention in one place'. Nonetheless, Thompson held that historical concepts are 'appropriate' in two important senses. First, they facilitate the 'scrutiny of [historical] "facts" which, even in their moment of interrogation, change their form (or retain their form but change their "meanings"), or dissolve into other facts'. Second, historical concepts are fitting for the 'handling of evidence' that cannot be represented as a 'static' form and which only makes sense 'as manifestation or as contradiction'.[28]

John Hoberman's concept of 'idealistic internationalisms' affords an opportunity to explore the respective positions of Stinchcombe and Thompson. Hoberman constructed the formal concept from a comparison of the Red Cross, the Boy Scout movement, the would-be international lingua franca Esperanto movement, and the Wagnerian and olympic movements. He claims these movements maintained a 'core repertory of behaviors and orientations' that made them 'cohere as a distinct category of thematically interrelated organizations'. In addition to ideological opposition to Marxist internationalism, the principal values of these movements included gender segregation, 'a rhetoric of universal membership', 'an insistence on political neutrality', 'aristocratic affiliations', 'a professed interest in peacemaking or pacifism', 'the use of visual symbols such as flags and anthems', and 'anxieties about war'.[29]

Hoberman's concept led him to a particular conclusion about the relationship between these movements and Nazism: 'the dichotomy that most effectively separates twentieth-century internationalisms into opposing types is the difference between the Socialist and non-Socialist'. And this difference, more than any other, explains the 'willingness' of many idealistic internationalisms to do 'cultural business' with the Nazis during the age of fascism. Among the examples Hoberman cites of idealistic internationalisms accommodating fascism are the World Esperanto Federation's appointment of Cologne to host the world Esperanto congress in 1933, the IOC's selection of Berlin to stage the 1936 olympic games, and the continuation until 1938 of official relations between the Hitler Youth and the Boy Scouts. Fear of socialism was not the sole source of this accommodation. A code of chivalry and a shared enthusiasm for a masculinity inspired by physical and outdoor pursuits facilitated an 'ideological bonding' between many supporters of the IOC, scouting and Nazism.[30]

'Invented by careful comparison of [the] actions and sentiments' of the agents that comprise international movements, Hoberman's idealistic internationalisms fulfils Stinchcombe's notion of a 'profound concept'.[31] Yet, it also displays a troubling elasticity. Hoberman extends his analysis over three periods: prior to the First World War (the 'early internationalist period'), between the two world wars (the 'age of fascism') and since the Second World War (the 'age of transnational evangelism'). However, only the olympic movement appears as a twentieth-century idealistic internationalism. The Red Cross, formed in 1863, hardly rates a mention, even in discussions of nineteenth-century internationalism; the Esperanto and Boy Scout movements receive scant attention in the age of fascism and disappear from discussions in the age of transnational evangelism. Indeed, not only does idealistic internationalisms become increasingly irrelevant to Hoberman's argument but 'irregular' comparisons intrude. Describing the olympic movement after the Second World War as a 'refuge for the politically unsavoury', Hoberman draws parallels with Interpol and the World Medical Association.[32] Whether he considers these organisations idealistic is unclear. Such elasticity would not perturb Thompson for whom the primary objective of a concept is to handle the evidence in the best possible way at any one juncture rather than to preserve the integrity of the concept across time and space.

More problematic for Thompson would be Hoberman's penchant for jumping from broad generalisations about idealistic international groups to detailed accounts of the individuals who supposedly link these associations together. This penchant, Thompson said, undermines conceptual rigour.[33] For example, a generalisation about old Nazis and neo-fascists intermingling with traditional conservatives in the 'transnational political twilight' of the post-Second World War era is followed by a comprehensive account of IOC member Kim Un Yong. The analysis of Kim launches another concept: extreme right-wing 'doctrinal associations' in international sport. Hoberman uses comparison to underpin the notion of doctrinal association; he examines Kim and two other high ranking IOC members who also served as presidents of international sporting federations, Primo Nebiolo of the International Amateur Athletic Federation and João Havelange of the Fédération Internationale de Football Association (FIFA). But innuendo and conspiratorial undertones weaken this concept of doctrinal association. Nebiolo is 'scandal-plagued', while Havelange had alleged ties with the international arms trade.[34]

Notwithstanding conservative reconstructionism's emphasis on the study of unique or one-off events, history 'unavoidably depends' upon concepts (patterns, classes or categories of recurring phenomena). As Haskell puts it, historians 'throw' concepts

> into the unfathomable depths of the past. What we catch depends as much on the shape, weave and texture of our conceptual net as on what the sea contains. No doubt much eludes us, for beneath its tranquil surface the past contains things stranger than any surface-dweller can readily imagine. But any [concept] is better than none. Without a net we would catch nothing at all.[35]

The problem in sport history is not so much the rejection of concepts but the passive embrace of sociological, anthropological, philosophical and psychological concepts 'as if they were no more than harmless heuristic devices without any consequence beyond the meaning conveyed by the words themselves'.[36] In many respects, appropriating concepts is understandable. The distinguished British historian Herbert Butterfield argued that 'of all forms of mental activity the most difficult … is the art of handling the same bundle of data as before, but placing them in a new system of relations with one another and giving them a different framework'.[37] As I will show in subsequent sections, those who believe they can apply concepts at will or substitute 'loose commonsense' meanings for technical terms risk 'tumbling down all manner of slippery paths'.[38] At the very minimum, sport historians need to acknowledge the source of their concepts and the degree of rigour with which they intend to apply them.

Constructionism: formal concepts, structures and theory

Constructionists advocate and defend theory on at least three grounds. First, irrespective of how blatantly obvious an historical pattern may appear (for example, the absence of manual workers from amateur sports in the late nineteenth century), it will involve some form of abstract thinking (for example, working-class, amateurism). And abstraction translates into the development of concepts and theories.[39] Second, the range and volume of evidence bearing on many historical problems is so large that selection cannot be avoided. 'Material life', Fernand Braudel reminded us, 'appears first and foremost in the anecdotal form of thousands and thousands of diverse facts' and these need to be classified and 'put in order' to simplify historical explanation.[40] Theory is critical to this task, providing the frameworks and principles for the selection of evidence that will also help the historian circumvent contradictory results. Hooliganism is a well-documented phenomenon in English soccer, yet sport historians cannot agree on its nature and causes. Scholars have thus turned to theory for explanations. Even after interrogating reports of football hooliganism in the late nineteenth century and developing a six-fold typology of sources, Joseph Maguire and his colleagues struggled to comprehend the phenomenon. They subsequently examined the evidence through the lenses of 'existing substantive knowledge and theories about crime, deviance, leisure and working class youth'. Maguire is convinced that without this so-called dialogue between 'substantive detail' and 'theory' a satisfactory explanation (see below) would have eluded the team.[41]

Third, theories bring to the fore interrelations between the components of human experiences and in so doing they enrich historical accounts and explanations. A comparison of two accounts of disorderly crowds at sporting fixtures in the late nineteenth and early twentieth centuries illustrates this point. Whereas Wray Vamplew looks for the answers primarily within sport, focusing on the social composition and psychological attributes of sporting crowds, Maguire and his colleagues incorporate theories that take them beyond the obvious facts of sport. This leads them to the conclusion that spectator misconduct in the late Victorian era was more than a sporting issue. Rather, it was a manifestation of a 'perceived need' by 'increasingly anxious middle-class commentators' to resolve '"the great social problem of the age"', that is, to control every aspect of the working classes including their leisure.[42] Although an interesting and well-constructed piece of sport history, Vamplew's analysis is less satisfying than the theoretically richer and socially broader explanation proposed by Maguire and his collaborators.

As well as their support for theory, constructionists reject outright the conservative reconstructionist view that theory predetermines historians' findings.[43] Constructionists deny they are slaves to proving the accuracy of one over-arching theory. Rather, their theories are no more than 'concepts' that emerge from, and aid in the interpretation of, the evidence. Citing sociologist Norbert Elias, Maguire extolled the view that 'theoretical thinking retains its force ... only as long as it does not lose touch with the terra firma of empirical facts'.[44] Constructionists dismiss reconstructionists' claims to objectivity, insisting that 'it is impossible, even for the most stainless of reconstructionist historians, to approach their evidence innocent of presupposition'.[45] Reconstructionist Richard Holt, for example, admits that his 'own experience of playing sport' and his 'early memories of watching professional football' had an 'unavoidable influence' on his decision to privilege the 'emotional bonds sport creates between people' over the rational structures of sport, that is 'the significance of setting down rules and keeping records'.[46]

In a further refutation of reconstructionism, constructionists note that the reconstructionist formulation of simple hypotheses against which to test to the past is usually 'not just a preliminary assessment of a particular historical conjuncture in its own terms'. Experience shows, says John Tosh, that historical hypotheses 'reflect certain assumptions about the nature of society and of the historical process as a whole'; in other words, they 'amount to the application of *theory*'.[47] Reconstructionists typically emphasise the abilities, objectives, talents, experiences, choices and freedoms of individuals and play down social influences; constructionists tend to highlight the social and collective worlds of customs and laws that coerce, and impose constraints and restrictions on, individuals.

Today, many sport historians employ theory, particularly as a heuristic device, and the field dabbles across its spectrum.[48] Well into the 1980s, however, the number of sport historians with an interest in and understanding of theory remained sparse,[49] and the field generally subscribed to the reconstructionist notion that making explicit one's methodology, assumptions or theories constituted poor form.[50] But even in the early years, practitioners incorporating sport into holistic notions of society, or attempting to explain social change, often embraced theoretical assumptions, even if unwittingly or subconsciously.[51] (A tendency to connect sport to society is not just a logical outcome of practitioners conceptualising and theorising historical patterns; viewing sport as a part of the social totality gave sport historians an opportunity to counter charges levelled by peers that they engaged in trivial and not very scholarly pursuits.[52] It should be noted that a good number of practitioners examine the relationship between sport and society by putting the former into its broader social, economic and political context [see Chapter 10].)

The following sections scrutinise functionalism and structuralism as the primary theoretical concepts buttressing sport historians' ideas about the relationship between sport and society.[53] (Later I look at social change as an explanatory paradigm [see Chapter 9].) As well as providing the theoretical foundations of sport history for much of its existence, these two 'great traditions of sociological theorizing'[54] offer important insights into the general problems and strengths of theory in history.

Functionalism

Notions of function (referred to as functionalism) exist in sport history as general theoretical explanations of society and, more pervasively, as accounts of praxis or purposive actions by agents of sport. In the first instance, attempts to explain what they perceived as social stability in nineteenth-century North American cities led several historians to theorise about the role of sport in society. They found that sport functioned as a form of social cement in two senses. It provided social cohesion – inculcated a spirit of responsibility for, loyalty to, and solidarity in communities – and it redirected 'surplus energies and natural aggressions' that in congested, crime-plagued, stultifying urban environments might otherwise have fuelled crime and public disorder.[55] Ambiguous about the causes of sport, these theories typically portray it as an unintended consequence of the social system. More prevalent in sport history are references to actors' roles and activities (functions) in pursuit of their goals or objectives. Governments, for example, use sport to combat juvenile delinquency, train citizens for war, enhance leisure, improve health and promote international prestige. In a few instances, sport historians have alluded to the unintended consequences of these functions and in so doing invoke a form of functionalism. Reviewing the literature on the rise of sport in American cities, Stephen Hardy refers to the functions of urban-based voluntary sport clubs. Sports-minded people formed clubs to acquire playing space, construct clubhouses and storage facilities, purchase equipment, organise competitions and form regulatory bodies. Hardy notes that these activities (functions) had the unintended consequence of aiding the rise of modern, codified sport.[56] For the most part, sport historians have been lackadaisical in explaining precisely how they conceptualise function.[57] Thus in this section I outline the basic premises of functionalist theory, look at several examples of functionalism in sport history, and assess its intellectual contributions.

Using metaphors of the physical world to visualise human societies as wholes or totalities, functionalism conceives of society as an organism whose component parts (social patterns, activities) function to maintain relative stability or equilibrium and ensure its survival.[58] In one major form of functionalism, structural-functionalism, the components include structures defined as sets of observable roles and patterns of behaviour.[59] Functionalist analysis proceeds through two basis stages: 'identifying a social pattern' and 'explaining the persistence or the regularity of the pattern by establishing its consequences for the larger system of which it is a part'. Consequences are the essence of functional analysis. James Frey elucidates: functional analysis begins with 'the "effect" and works back to the "cause" in a sort of ex post facto fashion', with the 'ultimate goal' being to 'explain the role of each part in keeping a system in proper working order'.[60] In short, functionalism explains phenomena, events, actions and the like by reference to their consequences.

Notwithstanding the widespread appearance of functionalist thinking in sport history, perhaps as few as three practitioners have produced explicitly functionalist accounts of sport.[61] Robert Malcolmson is the best known. He employs functionalism to explain the recreational and sporting habits of the labouring classes in eighteenth-century and early nineteenth-century Britain. On the one hand, sport 'served to foster social cohesiveness and group unity'; on the other, it 'functioned as outlets' for licentious, aggressive and socially confrontational behaviours that, in the course of normal day-to-day life, were 'repressed'. Sports like football, cricket, boxing, running, wrestling and cudgelling illustrate the former. They afforded labouring men rare opportunities to 'perform publicly for the esteem of their peers' and they also 'left in their wake a reservoir of incidents which could be retrospectively enjoyed and discussed' and thus 'incorporated into the [group's] changing assessments of its own members'. Malcolmson lists smock races, common at wakes and other rural gatherings, and Shrovetide football in Derby as sites for the outlet of socially sanctioned aberrant behaviour. Conventional sexual proprieties evaporated at smock races with 'female competitors … encouraged to come lightly clad', while in Derby locals 'dusted' well-to-do spectators with bags of soot or powder.[62]

Functionalist theories of society have been widely criticised for being 'too abstract to account for the detail of history's vast panorama', teleological (that is, actions, phenomena, events and the like occur for the sake of their own goals), and tautological (that is, vacuous propositions that conflate causes and effects). Functionalist explanations in sport history typically gloss over disparities in sporting interests between different social and economic groups, exaggerate social stability and harmony, and ignore the inevitable losers and outsiders in local (community, regional, national) consensus-building initiatives.[63] Scarce on facts and frugal with context, Malcolmson's functionalist account of sport 'challenging conventional proprieties' raises more questions than it answers. Were the 'dusted' randomly selected or carefully targeted? Who received 'dustings' – magistrates, employers, merchants, elites, publicans, parsons, squires? Were the architects and executioners of 'dustings' one and the same? Did multiple 'dustings' occur at single events? How might historians assess the popularity of such non-verbal acts?[64]

Christopher Lloyd distinguishes strong from weak versions of functionalist explanations. The former contains causal mechanisms that, by offering at least contingent explanations, avoid the problem of teleology.[65] On this criterion, Malcolmson's explanation constitutes strong functionalism. The British class system in the eighteenth and early nineteenth centuries reproduced itself, in part, through the different sports pursued by each class. Playing strictly amongst themselves allowed the classes to distinguish themselves from each other and to coalesce as distinct entities. But why did the class system maintain labouring-class sports? This question is the key to finding the causal mechanisms by which the system functioned. Acts of defiance against authority figures, such as 'dusting' men-of-rank during Shrovetide football, provide important clues. Malcolmson suggests that expressions of hostility against the well-to-do articulated ordinary people's frustration with prevailing norms and constraints. For their part, the ruling classes sanctioned these acts as a relatively harmless safety valve for ordinary folk. Spatially and temporally delineated 'dustings' and the like posed no real threat to the established order which remained remarkably secure. Hence, the hostilities/safety valve ultimately helped preserve and maintain the class system.[66]

John Daly also includes a causal loop in his functionalist analysis of social cohesion in colonial South Australia. He maintains that weaker class antagonisms in the antipodean colony were an effect of community-based representative sporting teams. He argues that by including players from both the working and middle classes, community sports teams reduced class tensions and thus facilitated social cohesion in the colony. But where lies the causal connection in this relationship between social cohesion and community sports teams? According to Daly, adult suffrage provided one causal mechanism. To 'retain power', the gentry had to win working-class votes; this meant abandoning their 'aristocratic and aloof lifestyle' and ' "rubbing shoulders" with the common man' in an effort to 'earn' his 'respect'. And the most palatable place to do this was at the local football or cricket club.[67]

Weak versions of functionalism lack causal mechanisms. Weak functionalism accepts that 'if the unintended consequences are apparently beneficial for the system or apparently reinforce some process then they have meaning, or that there is some unknown but objective teleology within the system'.[68] Peter McIntosh adopts the former position in his reference to the signing of Jackie Robinson and other African Americans by major league baseball clubs. The 'infiltration' of African Americans into 'top level sport', McIntosh claimed, 'considerably reduced' the 'risk of [race] riots'.[69] Most functionalist-type explanations in sport history fall into the weak category by virtue of practitioners unwittingly giving agency to abstractions such as sport and society and assigning them functions and needs. Benjamin Rader's history of American sport emphasises the maintenance and equilibrium of society and insinuates that the latter is itself a goal. In his words, spectator sport constitutes one of the 'major pillars' of the twentieth century 'social order'. It 'replaced or supplemented the church, the family, the local community, subcommunities based upon status or ethnicity, and the older system of mutual class obligations as one of the sinews which held modern society together'.[70] Rader supplies no causal mechanism and implies that spectator sport is the product of processes operating according to a predetermined schedule. While his discussions of key components of spectator sport, notably television and its role in transforming sport into a popular pastime, contain empirically based assessments of intentional subjects, he implies that American society, an abstract concept, has needs and agency.

As a final criticism, tautologies define variables in terms of each other and so fail to separate cause and effect. Daly's explanations of class and gender divisions in colonial South Australian sport are tautological. In the case of gender, the division of sex roles in sport caused women from the lower orders to perform as auxiliaries (serve refreshments, wash laundry, raise funds, organise social events), while the need for women to undertake these tasks caused the division of sex roles.[71]

Typically incomplete and unsatisfying, functionalist explanations have, not surprisingly, waned in sport history. As we shall see, however, politics were as influential as scientific assessments in their demise. Interestingly some versions of structuralism lapse into functionalism. But for sport historians the removal of agency from extreme structuralism posed a greater problem. Although sport historians did not subscribe to extreme theories, the broader debates they incited in sport studies encouraged at least some practitioners to clarify their understanding of structure.

Structuralism

Sport historians commonly employ the term structure in a loosely theorised manner to describe patterns related to institutionalised or organised behaviour, that is, behaviour so ingrained that 'the options open to individuals thereafter are constrained' or structured.[72] (Notions of structure frequently evoke metaphors of buildings that hold people together.[73]) As soon as organisations and institutions enter historians' vocabulary, E. P. Thompson noted, they are 'talking about structure: and [they] are likely also to be talking about the ways in which human behaviour is ruled, shaped, ordered, limited and determined'.[74] While formal institutions such as the IOC and FIFA represent structures that impose limits on individuals even to the extent of oppressing them, they are also collectives endowed with agency; they have decision-making capabilities and they pursue goals that are formally stated and implemented in policies.

Historians also recognise abstract institutions, such as society and sport. Like formal institutions, abstract structures involve human interaction but, unlike formal institutions, they also exist outside the interactions of individuals.[75] The influence or weight of a crowd is a good example of an abstract structure:

> The great movements of enthusiasm, indignation, and pity in a crowd do not originate in any one of the particular individual consciousnesses. They come to each one of us from without and can carry us away in spite of ourselves. Of course, it may happen that, in abandoning myself to them unreservedly, I do not feel the pressure they exert upon me. But it is revealed as soon as I try to resist them. Let an individual attempt to oppose one of these collective manifestations, and the emotions that he denies will turn against him. Now, if this power of

external coercion asserts itself so clearly in cases of resistance, it must exist also in the first-mentioned cases, although we are unconscious of it.[76]

The critical point is that structures are objects of knowledge even though historians cannot attribute their properties to constituent individuals. Irrespective of its precise form, a cardinal principle of structuralism (theories of structures) is that crowds, societies and sport, for example, 'exist virtually independent of human behaviour'. Some versions take this principle to the logical conclusion that individuals have little autonomy or volition.[77] With respect to unruly crowds, their disorder cannot be blamed on isolated troublemakers and, from a policy perspective, the identification and removal of rabble-rousers will not resolve ill-behaviour because it is not the simple sum of individual actions.[78] Vamplew implicitly recognised this in his analysis of crowd unrest in sport when he observed that 'there was nothing that individual sports promoters, club committees, or boards of directors could do' and they 'concentrated on … the symptoms rather than the disease'.[79]

In the 1960s and 1970s social theorists typically approached abstract structures in one of two ways. The 'essentialist' or 'realist' approach conceptualised structure as a 'determining factor' underlying 'surface appearances'. According to this conceptualisation, 'everyday social experience … masks a … hidden reality which lies beneath the level of consciousness'.[80] The hidden reality constitutes a structure that typically endures, usually over long periods, and determines action independent of the will of human agents. 'Constructionist' approaches view structure as a 'regularity' emerging from the 'consequence[s] of human agency'. Here 'thinking and acting' men and women 'create structural arrangements', including 'the constraints which adhere in them'. Malcolm Waters elaborates: 'structure does indeed impinge upon and constrain each human individual and has the force of concrete reality, but its source and origin are within the sphere of human action – the whole structure has no greater reality than the sum of its constituent action components'.[81]

The essentialist approach to abstract structure, which emerged as a theoretical strand of sport sociology under the banner of structural Marxism, raised the hackles of sport historians for whom the removal of free thinking and acting agents violated a tenet of their discipline. Yet for all the condemnation, sport history benefited from an approach that alerted at least some practitioners to new patterns and areas of research – in particular social class, gender and race – and forced them to ask new questions about relations of power in sport.

Essentialist structures

Essentialist approaches to structure guided many European sociologists of sport in the 1970s, including Jean-Marie Brohm, Bero Rigauer and Gerhard Vinnai.[82] They were strongly influenced by the French social philosopher Louis Althusser. Following the German sociologist Karl Marx, Althusser recognised 'two structural components' in capitalist social formations:

> the infrastructure or economic base which combines forces of production with social relations of production, and the superstructure which itself has two 'levels'

or 'instances'. These are the politico-legal structure, which includes law and the state, and the ideological structure comprised of religious, ethical, legal and political orientations. This arrangement … may be considered analogous to a three-storey building in which the economic base is the ground floor, with political and ideological levels built upon the base. The analogy suggests: 'that the upper floors could not "stay up" (in the air) alone, if they did not rest precisely on their base'.[83]

Aware of the model's vulnerability to charges of economic determinism, Althusser proposed a relationship between the base and the superstructure unfolding in two directions:

> Going up, the base has the quality of 'determination in the last instance'. This does not mean that the economic base has the final say in a historical sense, but that it is the economic level which determines just how much autonomy might be found in the superstructure. … it imposes a 'complex unity' upon the 'totality'. Relationships of determination also apply in a downward direction in the structural edifice. First, the political and ideological levels are argued to exist in a state of 'relative autonomy'. These are said to be forms of autonomy which are in some sense 'allowed' by the economic base. They offer an illusion of freedom in the superstructure thus allowing the secret constraints of the economic arena to survive unchallenged. Second, the superstructure is said to engage in 'reciprocal action' towards the base. Here the state and ideological arrangements operate to keep the capitalist system going.[84]

Althusser identified the state as performing functions vital to the 'orderly operation' of capitalism. 'Repressive State Apparatuses' (police, courts, prisons, military) defended the interests of the capitalist class by checking strikes and protest movements, and 'Ideological State Apparatuses' (churches, schools, families, political parties, trade unions, media) established in the minds of individuals imaginary views about the conditions of existence. For example, ideological state apparatuses convince people that 'there is no alternative to capitalism, or that democracy is a genuine power sharing arrangement, or that individuals make real choices about the direction of their lives'.[85]

In Althusser's theory of capitalist social formations, structures operate 'independently' of the 'will of the participants'. Men and women are merely the representatives of their class, that is, their objective positions within the economic base; they are either workers (suppliers of labour and dependent upon wages) or capitalists (controllers of labour in the production process and owners of the means of production – land, tools, machinery, technology). As Althusser and his collaborator Etienne Balibar contended, 'the structure of the relations of production determines the *places* and *functions* occupied and adopted by the agents of production, who are never anything more than the occupants of these places, insofar as they are the "supports" (*Träger*) of these functions'.[86]

Structural Marxists conceptualise sport as an ideological state apparatus.[87] Sport functions as an ideology to preserve and perpetuate capitalist structures. It achieves this in three ways. First, 'sport celebrates capitalist values such as competition, discipline, hard work and achievement'. With respect to the latter, elite sport in particular is a form of work that similarly emphasises 'efficiency and maximum production'.[88] In the words of Pierre Laguillaumie, 'the champion is fabricated in the image of the worker and the track in the image of the factory. Athletic activity has become a form of production and takes on all the characteristics of industrial production'.[89] Second, sport 'retards the development of working class consciousness'. On the one hand, watching sport offers the working classes an 'emotional safety valve for the release of aggressive feelings which might otherwise be turned on the real class oppressors'. On the other, it 'provides a false sense of escape and functions as a compensatory mechanism to an alienated existence'.[90] Third, commercial sports such as professional boxing, horse-racing and motor sports are primarily 'profit maximizing business enterprise[s] in which investment functions to accumulate capital'. Sport also stimulates the accumulation of capital indirectly in other ways: providing a 'market for goods and services associated with it (sports-clothing and equipment, gambling, etc.)' and 'function[ing] as a sales adjunct ... through ... sponsorship and advertising'.[91]

I am not aware of any sport historian who has seriously entertained this structurally determined relationship between sport and society. Rather than adopting abstract notions of sport, most practitioners directed their attention to the process of sport (as evidenced in the plethora of studies examining 'the rise of ...') and in contextualising sport within broader social, economic and political conditions (which does not necessarily involve theory). In the eyes of sport historians, structural Marxists appeared more concerned with proving their theory than with empirical detail and factual accuracy about which they were 'overly cavalier'.[92] Dubbed 'correspondence theory', for the way it presented sport as a 'passive mirror' or 'completely determined product' of capitalism, this version of structural Marxism repeatedly faltered when confronted by historical evidence. The notion that sport socialises participants into 'reactionary political views' or that it *necessarily* ... discourages the development of an oppositional class consciousness within capitalism', appeared ludicrous to historians conversant with the workers sports movement (founded as 'a socialist alternative to bourgeois competitive sport') or the athletic revolution of the 1960s. It could not explain, for example, the experiences of heavyweight boxer Muhammed Ali who 'thumbed his nose' at the American 'government, military and the capitalist economy that supported them'.[93] Structural Marxist conceptualisations of the working class stereotyped a group that embraced 'a range of lived cultures'. Notwithstanding workers' common relationship with capital, historical investigations repeatedly showed that family, church, neighbourhood, locality and specific worker-employer relations also structured working class experiences.[94]

Sport historians found that rather than capitalist vehicles for the accumulation of wealth, most organised sport seeks only to 'break even, or to operate at least cost in order to remain financially viable'. Similarly, business interests often 'invest in sport for non-economic reasons: to gain prestige from being associated with a popular cultural activity, ... [as a] commitment to a life-style, and to exert social and cultural influence'.[95] Countering the correspondence position that the working classes are cultural dupes, Eric Hobsbawm maintained that manipulations by capitalists are most successful when they 'exploit practices which clearly meet a felt ... need'. And in the case of sport, 'tastes and fashions can be "created" only within very narrow limits; they have to be discovered before being exploited and shaped'.[96]

Thus, sport historians rebuffed essentialist approaches to structure that raised seemingly insurmountable problems for an evidence-based discipline. What constitutes evidence for the effects of structures? Could victims of structures provide valid accounts? And how do historians distinguish the effects of overlapping structures? How, for example, do historians separate the effects of capitalism and patriarchy on women's participation in sport?[97] Constructionist approaches to structure resolved some of these issues by introducing agents into the analysis but few sport historians bothered to explore the issues. Stephen Hardy was one exception.

Constructionist structures

Borrowing from sociologist Anthony Giddens, Hardy and the sport sociologist Alan Ingham defined structures as 'regularized relations of interdependence that contour and generate social practices'. Structures are 'constituted and transformed over time through social practices' and, critically, agency 'works in and through social structures. In Giddens' words, "social structures are both constituted by human agency, and yet at the same time are the very medium of this constitution"'.[98] Mainstream sociology and social history increasingly see this definition as the most feasible way to escape restrictive determinist concepts of structure.[99] Hardy later applied this definition of structure to an examination of four entrepreneurs who profoundly influenced American sport in the late nineteenth century and early twentieth century. In this article he showed how agency works in and through social structures. In their attempts to 'harness ... personal visions of the Sportgeist' – 'the spirit of sport' – these entrepreneurs 'cemented a new sport structure' (rules, tactics, organisations, facilities, records, equipment).[100]

As the 'founders of an industry of "providers", an interlocking network of rules committees, trade associations, manufacturers, retailers and professional experts', Henry Chadwick, Albert Spalding, James Sullivan and Senda Berenson developed and sold 'to the public *preformed* packages of play that included rules, equipment, and expert instructions'. In so doing, they transformed 'pastimes into organized, commercialized sports'. Yet, their agency had limits: 'it is one thing to fashion a game form', and quite 'another to control the spirit that people animate within the game form'. Chadwick *et al.* were less successful in employing the sport structure to 'spread a particular conception of the Sportgeist'. Spalding's 'standardization' of games, products and leagues 'lent force to a Sportgeist weighted towards regimen' but his actions 'set off other forces that frustrated his visions of a disciplined labor force'. In seeking 'star players as individual product endorsers', Spalding ironically nurtured a form of individualism that 'haunt[ed] professional sports in the forms of contract jumping and contract holdouts. Further, players who recognised their value in the market for goods created their own collectives to fight the magnates for higher wages'. In short, 'Spalding's empire in sporting goods fuelled a part of the Sportgeist that ran headlong against his own peculiar vision of the compliant athlete'.[101]

Hardy's incorporation of the Sportgeist and the sport structure into his examination of Spalding and other sport entrepreneurs is a brilliant example of a concept of structure contributing to historical analysis. No one should doubt that the Sportgeist and sport structure facilitate a much deeper understanding of late nineteenth century American sport entrepreneurship than would be the case had Hardy followed the conservative reconstructionist programme of treating Spalding and his colleagues as individual cases. The Sportgeist and sport structure help reveal the ways in which entrepreneurs shaped and ordered sport, and, in turn, the limitations and constraints that were imposed upon them.

Conceptualising the relationship between sport and society unavoidably involves theoretical considerations, a point that seems to have escaped many sport historians. Although theoretical notions of function (functionalism) and structure (structuralism) litter efforts to connect sport and society, many applications appear almost unwittingly; few practitioners apply these concepts, or indeed any concept, with rigour. Too often the end result is confusing. Conceptual precision and meticulousness, however, are not the sole drivers of theory which also carries an inescapable extra-scientific content.

Examining the extra-scientific contents of theory, sociologist Jeffrey Alexander identified a close relationship between the *Zeitgeist*, or spirit of the times, and the frameworks of interpretation that prevailed in post-Second World War America. Shifts in the *Zeitgeist* certainly explain better the emergence of new themes, explanations and theories in sport history than does the notion of practitioners abandoning earlier approaches under the weight of scientific critiques. I now look at the *Zeitgeists* of the early 1970s and 1980s that introduced new concepts and theories into sport history.

The politics of theory

According to Alexander, particular theories thrive and decline in certain *Zeitgeists*. Thus he assigns the popularity of functionalism in the 1940s, 1950s and early 1960s to extra-scientific ideological factors and the 'distinctive social characteristics' of postwar life in America. Amid increasing prosperity and suburban growth, American intellectuals and their audiences uncritically accepted functionalist assumptions about social stability, social uniformity and peaceful, incremental social change. Similarly, Alexander attributes the death of functionalism – which he says only died in the mid-1960s well after it had been 'scientifically invalidated' – to a new *Zeitgeist*. What 'pushed' functionalism 'over the edge', he continues, 'were not scientific alternatives in and of themselves'. The 'decisive' factor was

> the destruction of its ideological, discursive, and methodological core. The challenge that finally could not be met was existential. It emerged from new social movements that were increasingly espousing collective emancipation – peasant revolutions on a world-wide scale, black and Chicano national movements, indigenous people's rebellions, youth culture, hippies, rock music, and women's liberation.

These groups branded the West 'bureaucratic and repressive', and America 'capitalist, backward, greedy, anarchic, and impoverishing'.[102] I begin this section by examining the *Zeitgeist* that undermined functionalism in the 1960s and brought about a series of ideological twists that directly and indirectly influenced sport history over the following decades.

Alexander labels the *Zeitgeist* of the late 1960s as anti-modern.[103] Characterised in part by political activism in sport[104] and a new leisure movement,[105] the anti-modern *Zeitgeist* also moulded younger sport historians. 'Spurred' by political conditions within the sporting community and intellectual trends in social history, sport historians turned their attention to 'conservative groups' which they held to 'promote sport as a means of controlling social order'. 'Social control' and 'social order' occupied the 'most influential school of thought in American social history in the 1970s' and, not surprisingly, it penetrated some sport history.[106] Yet, for all their connotations of radicalism and moral and political disapproval, social control theories remained firmly within the ambit of functionalism. Adherents in sport history still searched for the relationship between sport and society within a functionalist framework. The only change was that 'plus signs' were turned into 'minuses'. As Gareth Stedman Jones argued, 'we may think of sport … as a healthy release for spontaneity and freedom …; or we may think of it as a diversionary use of leisure time reinforcing the alienated consciousness engendered by the workplace. But there is no challenge here to the functionalist analysis of sport'.[107]

The anti-modern *Zeitgeist* extended far beyond America and it undoubtedly helps explain structural Marxism's appeal to European sports scholars. Marxist historian Eric Hobsbawm described the insights as 'concentrated charges of intellectual explosive, designed to blow up crucial parts of the fortification of traditional history'. Ironically, the power of these insights lay in their simplicity. 'Those of us who recall our first encounters with [Marxism] may still bear witness to the immense liberating force of such simple discoveries', he observed.[108] Sport sociologist Richard Gruneau conceded that for all its overstatements and exaggerations, structural Marxism provided 'powerful' and 'penetrating' insights, especially into the ways sport reproduces many of the 'repressive constraints inherent in capitalism'.[109] Many of the scientific criticisms levelled at structural Marxism in the second half of the 1970s reappeared in the critiques of social order and social control theories. Historians working within the latter were accused of oversimplifying complex processes, ignoring agents, caricaturing and stereotyping the ruling classes, and reducing the working classes to cultural dupes. In the case of the latter, for example, critics had no trouble finding historical evidence of the lower classes defending and advancing their own interests.[110]

Raymond Williams provided left-leaning sport historians with the intellectual key to breaking what could be called a theoretical stalemate in the field. In *Marxism and Literature* (1977), Williams clarified the idea of hegemony in such a way that it appeared to include expressions of agency *and* account for the ongoing dominance of capitalist structures, while avoiding the problems of both functionalism (its teleology and tautologies) and structural Marxism (its reductionism and determinism).[111] Critics, of course, were quick to point out that hegemony did not quite fulfil all its promises. Jones, for example, observed that in many works hegemony operated in the same way as the 'functionalist notion of social control but with class terminology added'.[112] I examine hegemony in more detail later (see Chapter 10). The important point here is that hegemony theory emerged as the 'received critical view of sport.'[113] By the mid-1990s, nearly every issue of the major sport history journals contained an article using hegemony.[114] But just as the end of functionalism cannot be attributed to purely scientific factors, nor can the discipline's embrace of hegemony. Arguably, the appeal of hegemony to some sport historians derived from the emerging postmodern *Zeitgeist*.

Alexander traces the political background of the postmodern *Zeitgeist*. 'By the end of the 1970s', he writes,

the energy of the radical social movements of the preceding period had dissipated. Some of their demands became institutionalized; others were blocked by massive backlash movements that generated conservative publics and brought right-wing governments to power. Materialism replaced idealism among political influentials and surveys reported increasingly conservative views among young people and university students. Maoist ideologues … became anticommunist *nouveaux philosphes* and, some of them, neoconservatives. Yippies became yuppies. For many intellectuals who had matured during the radicalism of the 1960s and 1970s, these new developments brought unbearable disappointment.[115]

These disappointments gave birth to postmodernism. While the intellectual impact of postmodernism on sport history remains largely muted, I want to suggest here that the popularity of hegemony in sport history resonates with the politics of disappointment which is a feature of postmodernism.[116] (Of course, only careful empirical research into the thoughts and motives of those advocating hegemony theory will establish whether a true causal relationship exists.)

Alexander and Alex Callinicos analyse postmodernism as 'an ideology of intellectual disappointment', a 'reaction' to the apparent 'slipping away' of the 'collective radicalism' of the late 1960s and early 1970s.[117] This tone of pessimism appears in many historical analyses of sport where the authors blame the co-optation of oppositional or alternative sporting values on the objective structures of hegemonic capitalism or patriarchy. John Hargreaves, for example, observed that 'the achievement of hegemony over the working class' may have allowed members to indulge themselves in popular sports but 'this development signified also a degree of depoliticization within the working class which commercial interests were quick to exploit'.[118] The politics of pessimism is pronounced in discussions of masculine hegemony. Jan Cameron's views are typical. Notwithstanding the policy initiatives of both governments and sports controlling agencies to improve women's participation in sport, she believes that 'the hegemonic apparatus' will continue to keep women 'in their place' and 'well away from the locus of control and … the applause of the crowd'.[119]

In the debates over theory, reconstructionists highlight the (all too frequent) distortions that theory introduces into historical explanations, while constructionists point to the (well-evidenced) ability of theory to clarify and enrich historical accounts.[120] However, neither reconstructionists nor constructionists direct sufficient attention to the prevailing social conditions that generate specific theories. A delicious irony emerges here, one that will not be lost on those reconstructionists who have long pointed to the political biases in theory.

Conclusion

Accounts of events and situations within unique settings still comprise the bulk of work done in sport history. In this sense the majority of practitioners qualify as a-theoretical reconstructionists. This work is perfectly legitimate. All historians at some point in time ask questions about the facts of specific events and situations. But what detracts from so much of this scholarship is its incorporation of mind-numbing detail and trivia. Propagating this problem in the field, it should be noted, are reviewers whose works degenerate into nit-picking minutiae, that are, more often than not, irrelevant to the historical approach being applied. One reviewer of *Eddie Gilbert: The True Story of an Aboriginal Cricketing Legend*, for example, recently praised the authors for their rich source material, eloquent descriptions, and for identifying the full context of Gilbert's life in racist Australia – the latter being the prime aim of the book. He then chided them for committing factual errors pertaining to sport. Gilbert, this steadfast reviewer informed us, did not bowl outswingers, nor did umpire Orr call Jack Marsh for a no-ball, while the English fast bowler Harold Larwood came from Nottinghamshire and certainly not Lancashire![121]

Reconstructionism, however, is only one historical model. Even the mildest forms of comparison, categorisation and generalisation direct sport historians towards concept building, abstraction, theory and constructionism. This is particularly true among those practitioners who envision sport history as a form of social history; by definition, social history explores broad patterns of social relations, or social structures, rather than unique events or individual actions.

For their part, constructionists have refused to take seriously the criticisms levelled at them by reconstructionists. They continue to leave terms undefined and ambiguous, to oversimplify complex processes, and to obscure details. Not only are they 'insufficiently self-conscious as to their own conceptualizations',[122] they stretch others' concepts to fit their specific evidence, paying little attention to how concepts are built. In these contexts, the phrase 'poverty of theory' seems apt. This chapter has pointed to different concepts and theories enriching historical explanations in sport (for example, Hoberman's analysis of the olympic movement, the investigation by Maguire *et al.* into misconduct among football spectators, Hardy's discussion of sporting entrepreneurs). But against broader concerns it is not surprising that scepticism about the value of theory prevails.

Like Geoffrey Elton and Werner Sombart, reconstructionist- and constructionist-leaning sport historians continue to talk at cross-purposes; and the debate over theory as a source of distortion or enrichment will undoubtedly drag on. It need not be this way. Sport historians have an array of models and methods from which they can choose, and all have validity when used in their proper context. Marxist theories of labour relations may contribute little to the particular history of the operations of the Major League Baseball Players Association under the tutelage of Marvin Miller, but they are indispensable to an international history of labour relations in professional sport which, of necessity, will incorporate generalisations. Many of the antagonisms between reconstructionists and constructionists would disappear if practitioners spelled out their objectives, and were crystal clear about how far their particular evidence translated into generalisations across other contexts.

Chapter 4

Narratives, non-narratives and fiction

Presenting the sporting past

ALL HISTORIANS MUST PRESENT the past in some form or another and narrative is the most popular form of historical presentation. Indeed, I follow a narrative format in parts of *The Field*. A narrative is a coherent story comprising a series of sequential and consequential (that is, causal) relationships within a beginning, middle and end structure. Some reconstructionists even consider narrative to be synonymous with history.[1] Narratives also find their way into constructionist presentations of the past although usually in a secondary role overlying arguments grounded in both empiricism and concepts. Regardless of whether narrative takes a primary or secondary place in the presentation of the past, historians rarely discuss its nature or function.

Reconstructionists cast narratives as the uncomplicated medium of historical reports; they naturalise the story that constitutes the narrative as the past. Constructionists are wary of narratives; they challenge reconstructionist assumptions about the correspondence between narrative language and the actual objects and events being described. Nonetheless constructionists remain confident in their ability to ameliorate ambiguities of meaning in language. The key to constructionist clarity lies in the careful definition of terms, categories and concepts.[2] However, the traditional confidence in narrative faces a growing challenge from those who possess what Alun Munslow calls a 'deconstructive consciousness' and 'who think self-consciously about the nature and particular role of narrative' in history.[3] Deconstructionists believe that language plays a pivotal explanatory role in history. They argue that in the process of constructing the plots or story lines – be they romances, tragedies, comedies, satires or some combination – of their narratives, reconstructionists and constructionists impose meaning on the very sources and evidence that they purport to discover.[4]

This chapter analyses both narrative and non-narrative forms of presentations in sport history, and then presents a deconstructionist critique of traditional narrative forms based on Hayden White's work. Exploring the poetics of narrative, White concludes that historians create history rather than discover the past. Although very few historians of sport have engaged with White, his work introduces critical questions about the relationship between history and fiction, a subject receiving growing attention in the field and the focus of the final section. The debate between reconstructionism and deconstructionism frames much of my discussion. Focusing on these two extremes is, I believe, the best way to show the spectrum of approaches to narrative.

Narrative in reconstructionist thought

Narrative presentations abound in sport history. Recent examples include John Watterson's *College Football* (2000), Ronald Smith's *Play-by-Play* (2001), Charles Korr's *The End of Baseball As We Knew It* (2002), and two award-winning books Charles Alexander's *Breaking the Slump* (2002) and Robert Barney, Stephen Wenn and Scott Martyn's *Selling the Five Rings* (2002).[5] The authors of these texts all use narrative to present their respective historical research. Narratives are popular forms of presentation among reconstructionist sport historians because they offer ready access to the past.

Kenneth Gergen lists six central criteria of what he calls an 'intelligible' or 'well-formed' narrative: identification of a valued endpoint, selection of events (content) relevant to the endpoint, placement of events (content) in a linear or temporal sequence, the use of stable identities (agents or entities), establishment of causal linkages between events, and employment of demarcation signs.[6] Eric Dunning and Kenneth Sheard's account of the struggle between middle-class supporters of amateurism and working-class advocates for professionalism within the Rugby Football Union (RFU) late in the nineteenth century adheres to these criteria.

> Matters came to a head at the RFU General Meeting held in London on 20 September 1893, when J. A. Miller and M. Newsom of the Yorkshire Union proposed and seconded respectively 'that players be allowed compensation for *bona fide* loss of time'. The Rugby establishment learned of the Yorkshire intention some time prior to the AGM. They also learned that arrangements had been made to secure the attendance of a large Northern contingent. Thus forewarned, they formed an unofficial committee under the chairmanship of F. I. Currey, the Old Marlburian solicitor and President of the RFU from 1884-6. It met at the Sports Club, St James's Square, a club formed exclusively by and for public school old boys. The objects of the committee were to ensure that amateurs realized the seriousness of the threat posed to their interests and values by recent developments in the North and to secure a large turnout and united front at the forthcoming meeting. One of the first acts was to draft a circular 'over the names of about 70 prominent football men' appealing for support for the amateur principle and to send it to sympathetic clubs. At the same time H. E. Steed of Lennox RFC was directed to contact clubs known to be opposed to broken-time payments and to obtain proxy votes from those unable to send representatives. When the fateful day arrived, and after the Yorkshire motion had been put, William Cail of Northumberland, a manufacturer, export merchant and currently President of the RFU, and G. Rowland Hill, Hon. Secretary, proposed and seconded, respectively, the

following counter-motion: 'That this meeting, believing that the above principle is contrary to the true interest of the Game and its spirit, declines to sanction the same'. The counter-motion was carried 282 votes to 136. It is clear ... that [supporters of the Yorkshire motion] were caught out by these secret machinations of the Rugby establishment who had been spurred retroactively into achieving greater solidarity by the growing threat to their interests and values which they perceived in the industrial North.

Shortly after 20 September, a Special General Meeting of the RFU was held in order to alter the constitution. ... the object of the alterations 'was to crush any attempt to establish professional cells within the government machine'. Bye-law number one, for example, was made to declare that: '... the name of the Society shall be the "Rugby Football Union" and only clubs composed entirely of amateurs shall be eligible for membership ...'. In this way, the amateur principle, previously no more than an unwritten commitment of the Rugby establishment, became enshrined in the constitution of the RFU.[7]

The endpoint of this narrative – the constitutional amendment that enshrined amateur principles within the RFU – meets Gergen's prerequisite of a position loaded with value.[8]

'An intelligible story', writes Gergen, 'is one in which selected events serve to make the goal more or less probable, accessible, important, or vivid'.[9] In their account Dunning and Sheard identify two factors leading to the constitutional amendment (which in this narrative constitutes the endpoint or goal): news of the Yorkshire Union's proposal to compensate players for lost wages, and moves by the rugby establishment to defeat the northerners' compensation plans. The authors' language – 'the seriousness of the threat', 'sympathetic clubs', 'the fateful day', 'secret machinations' – draw in the reader, adding drama and excitement, thus making the endpoint not only more vivid, but also more valuable.

In a successful narrative the relevant events follow each other over time in a linear or temporal sequence.[10] Dunning and Sheard adopt this format. After describing the Yorkshire Union's plans, they report on the formation of an unofficial committee by the rugby establishment, the counter motion and vote at the general meeting, and finally the decisive constitutional amendment at the special general meeting. Chronological ordering is the means by which the narrator causally links events; each event emerges as 'a product of that which has preceded', another of Gergen's criteria for a credible narrative.[11] In their narrative Dunning and Sheard describe the establishment forming an unofficial committee to counter the Yorkshire Union's initiatives.

Additionally, the identities of actors in events fulfil an important role in the construction of narrative. As Gergen asserts, the characters (or objects) in an intelligible narrative 'possess a continuous or coherent identity across time. A given protagonist cannot felicitously serve as a villain at one moment and a hero in the next', he writes. 'Once defined by the story teller', he concludes, 'the individual (or entity) will tend to retain his/her identity or function within the story'.[12] In Dunning and Sheard's narrative, the Yorkshire Union and the rugby establishment hold to fixed positions. For example, the former is consistent in its advocacy of professional rugby and the latter in its support for amateurism.

Just as important are the literary devices that demarcate the narrative and indicate the progression of the story. The most obvious signs signal the beginning or end of a particular narrative.[13] Dunning and Sheard alert readers to the start of their narrative with the phrase 'matters came to head …' while the clause 'a Special General Meeting of the RFU was held to alter the constitution' warns readers that they are preparing to end their narrative. Dunning and Sheard also continually orientate their readers with transitional phrases such as 'one of the first acts', 'after the Yorkshire motion had been put' and 'shortly after the 20 September'.

Some philosophers of history, notably Wilhelm Dilthey, Frederick Olafson and David Carr, argue that narratives share a cognitive continuity with everyday life.[14] This so-called continuity thesis advances the notion that narrative structures, with their beginning, middle and end, parallel the ways in which people comprehend their own existence, or at least how they cast their personal histories and experiences as unfolding through time. This unfolding can be from hour to hour, as in Dunning and Sheard's account of the RFU's general meeting in September 1893; from day to day as in their account of the political crisis leading to the constitutional amendment; or over a natural lifespan as in a biography (see below). Of course, it is impossible to ignore the artifice and false open-endedness in those narratives where the author starts with the endpoint which they then use to direct readers 'back to the beginning from which the eventual outcome unwinds'.[15] Dunning and Sheard knew well before they constructed their narrative that the events of 20 September 1893 were decisive in the history of the RFU; by alerting readers to this at the beginning they also provide the starting point for the narrative and the issues around which their story unfolds.

Historians have largely ignored these philosophical issues, being more preoccupied with issues of factual accuracy, style and rhetoric in narratives. Founded upon concerns about the validity and accuracy of sources, early modern history 'retreated to the arid confines of empirical rigour'.[16] In this climate, the presentation of history frequently collapsed into strings of factual statements copied from different sources, a methodology R. G. Collingwood called 'scissors-and-paste' history. Such history, said Collingwood, begins with historians deciding what it is they want to know about, and then going 'in search of statements about it, oral or written, purporting to be made by actors in the events concerned, or by eyewitnesses of them, or by persons repeating what actors or eyewitnesses have told them, … and so on'. After locating relevant statements, historians 'excerpt' and 'incorporate' them into what they consider a suitable style, in their own history.[17] In this way the historical explanation 'emerges in a naturalistic fashion from the archival raw data, its meaning offered as interpretation in the form of a story related explicitly, impersonally, transparently, and without resort to any of the devices used by writers of literary narratives, viz., imagery or figurative language'.[18]

Scissors-and-paste narratives did not flood sport history and have all but disappeared.[19] However, reconstructionists continue to judge narratives on the basis of scissors-and-paste history. According to conservative reconstructionists, the 'most convincing' narratives are those possessing a 'structure, unity and/or coherence … in the intelligible and reasonable relationship established between individual statements and the sources'. In short, '"good history" … will contain a clear and up-front statement as to how the past actually was' and how the author 'got the story … straight' according to the sources.[20] Documentary film-maker Ken Burns' account of wrestling with a small section of narration in the fifth episode of the television documentary *Baseball* illustrates the reconstructionist's determination to get it right. An early draft included the lines 'by 1934 the world economy was in ruins. In Germany Adolf Hitler had come to power and instituted exclusionary laws against Jews based on Jim Crow laws in the United States'. 'It was', says Burns,

> a very incendiary bit of information .... I had voiced concern that ... somehow it could be misinterpreted – even though this was 1934, somehow Jim Crow was responsible for the Final Solution. Working with our consultants, we changed the sentence in several meaningful ways that I think softened the blow or helped to separate that. The final sentence, after we had gotten through with it, read: 'In 1934 the world economy was in ruins and fascism was on the rise. In Germany the National Socialists had come to power and begun to institute exclusionary laws against Jews based, in part, on Jim Crow laws in the United States'. So we made four significant changes in that sentence that make it less of a possibility that anyone could misinterpret our intentions.[21]

Concerns about factual accuracy also feed into issues of style among reconstructionists who deem ordinary language the best vehicle for preserving the integrity of historiography and for safeguarding facts against ideological contamination.[22] Similarly, reconstructionists refrain from inserting the personal 'I' in their narratives. They speak in the third person and deploy impersonal linguistic conventions to convey their neutrality and distance, and to elicit the 'seeming transparency [of] the past'.[23] As a general rule, however, reconstructionists regard style as an aesthetic feature rather than an analytical problem in narratives.

Reconstructionists exhort colleagues and peers to use plain, simple, jargon-free language. 'The flow of language', wrote Geoffrey Elton, 'must be simple, even ordinary, devoid of pompous obscurity. One of the chief tests of the quality of historical work lies in its readability.'[24] 'Clarity of exposition' and 'elegance of presentation' are J. A. Mangan's ambitions for sport history.[25] Historians have 'to remember ... the common denominator of speaking to a lot of people: you have to be a good writer, you have to be a good communicator', says Burns.[26] Richard Evans doubts whether many have learned the lesson. 'Most history books are hopelessly unreadable', he declares: 'few historians write competently' and 'fewer still display any real mastery of the language in which they publish their work.'[27] Elton concurs, lamenting the proliferation of 'clumsy and obscure' language.[28] A master wordsmith and fine craftsman of the English language, Mangan finds too much history of sport 'turgid and unclear'.[29] Ultimately, however, reconstructionists reduce style to a 'minor problem of presentation'.[30]

Reconstructionists acknowledge that language can pose problems for the historian but they maintain extreme confidence in their ability to navigate whatever problems language and narrative may present. Reconstructionists, of course, take inordinate care to contextualise and interpret language that is also 'a product of history'. As John Tosh reminds practitioners, 'old words pass out of currency, while others acquire new significance' and vigilance is required 'against reading modern meanings into the past'.[31] The very term sport has changed its meanings several times in the last two centuries. In the early nineteenth century it carried class connotations. By the early twentieth century sport was a moral construct; today it designates a physical contest within defined rules.[32]

Reconstructionists are also alert to ambiguities in language.[33] David Zang demonstrates his vigilance in two references to heavyweight boxer Muhammad Ali. In the first he raises doubts as to whether Ali's oft cited, 'I ain't got no quarrel with them Vietcong' comment in 1966, was the considered statement of a conscientious objector to the military draft or one made in 'exasperation'.[34] Likewise, Zang suggests that it was the tone of Ali's voice, 'not any philosophical thinking', that gave conviction to his retort to Congressman Robert Michel. When the Congressman from Illinois said that the boxer ' "will fight anyone but the Vietcong" ', Ali angrily answered, ' "there's one hell of a lot of difference in fighting in the ring and going to the War in Vietnam" '.[35]

Conservative reconstructionists' attempts to expunge style as an analytical issue in narrative floundered because they aspired to 'stylistic elegance, wit and aphorism'.[36] Moreover, these aspirations helped affirm the convergence of history and fiction.[37] However, before exploring this relationship, which resonates more closely with deconstructionism, I will look at non-narrative forms of presentation as found in constructionist histories.

Non-narrative historical presentations

Narrative receded as the preferred method of presentation after the Second World War under the combined influences of Marxism, the *Annales* school and social science methodology.[38] Particularly among social historians, the sequential, unilinear structure of traditional narratives seemed unable to capture the multifaceted political, cultural, social and economic nature of many events, or to deal with investigations into complex feelings, emotions, states of mind, behaviours, ideas, beliefs, values, symbols, rituals and customs. Nor did narrative seem appropriate when contextualising or explaining the past.[39] In each of these cases non-narrative forms of presentation seemed preferable.[40]

In his polemic against scissors-and-paste history, Collingwood – who Munslow labels a 'proto-deconstructionist'[41] – offers important clues into both the logic and structure of non-narrative histories. As previously noted, scissors-and-paste historians assume that the presentation of the past flows naturally from the sources. According to Collingwood, such presentations are the result of historians approaching their sources in a 'receptive spirit', that is, with the intention only of reporting what others have already said on a particular subject. By contrast, 'scientific' historians (to use Collingwood's terminology) look at the world around them, decide what it is that they want to know – or, more usually, what problem they want to solve – and formulate relevant questions that will guide them to an answer. While scissors-and-paste historians scour the sources for answers (and assume that the sources on any topic are both finite and verifiable by simple interrogations that validate either their truthfulness or falsity – see Chapters 2 and 5), scientific historians construct evidence. They start from the premise that every remnant of the past contains potential evidence and that the extraction of that evidence depends primarily on the questions historians ask of those remnants. In this sense, questions are the motors of history. As I showed in Chapter 2, the evidence often exists only in relation to a specific question. One corollary of this view is that historical conclusions can emerge even when the sources offer no formal supporting statements. In short, the scientific historian privileges evidence that derives from specific questions rather than banks of sources. The scientific historian continually asks where the evidence is, what it means and how it throws light on the subject.[42]

Non-narrative social histories typically break up the chronology and adopt a question-and-answer format with the answers based on reams of accumulated presumptive and corroborative evidence (see Chapter 2, note 31).[43] In the non-narrative format the links between actors, objects and entities are more diffuse, complex and perhaps even contradictory. Given its close association with social history, academic sport history also tends to follow this format.[44] In *The Games Ethic and Imperialism* (1986), for example, J. A. Mangan asks a range of questions about ethnocentricity, hegemony and patronage, ideals and idealism, educational values and aspirations, cultural assimilation, and adaptation in the Victorian and Edwardian eras. In one case, questions about the Sudan Political Service yield evidence of 'occupational self-patronage' among 'Oxford and Cambridge graduates with a public school and upper-middle-class background'.[45] Evidence collected by Mangan here includes statistical data about which public schools furnished the Sudan Political Service with recruits, the academic credentials of graduates working in the Service and the athletic prowess of Service recruits. Collectively, this data enables Mangan to make conclusions about the social traits, values and sporting backgrounds of Sudan Political Service personnel. One issue that historians face here is finding the balance between too much and too little evidence.[46]

Mangan's questions testify to the centrality of concepts in contemporary sport history and their place in framing questions about the sporting past and its presentation.[47] As I discussed in Chapter 3, concepts raise thorny questions about the nature of historical evidence. The issue here, however, is that historical concepts and empirically based historical evidence are usually situationally specific and bound up in complex arguments that lend themselves to non-narrative forms of presentation.

Yet, if the conceptual content in non-narrative forms of presentation suggests a close alignment with constructionism, the reality is that contemporary mainstream sport history does not sharply distinguish between narrative and non-narrative forms of presentation. In the words of Robert Berkhofer, 'there are usually argumentative elements in manifestly narrative histories and often some narrative elements in explicitly non-narrative histories'.[48] In his long narrative about American college football, John Watterson argues that officials have 'failed abysmally' to produce a game that conforms to 'the spirit and life of the university'. Brutality, chronic cheating, gambling and greed, he laments, have beset football throughout its history.[49] Mangan uses the demarcation signs and endpoint values of narrative to set the stage for his analysis of the Sudan branch of the Foreign Service and its role in the diffusion of British imperialism. He describes, for example, the conditions that led to the creation of the Sudan Political Service in 1899 and the domestic and international political climates in which it operated. These circumstances required a 'cadre of civilian administrators'; fortunately British officials found a ready supply of first-class recruits whose games ethic just happened to be a bulwark of imperialism.[50] It must be noted that Dunning and Sheard's narrative, dissected above, comes from an explicitly sociological approach to rugby. The authors claim that their approach 'differs from conventional history' by bringing 'sociological concepts explicitly to bear on the task of explanation' and by incorporating theoretical as well as empirical concerns.[51]

Even where historians 'eschew a manifest story', it is often the case that their 'arguments and larger contexts presume such a narrative as either partial or Great

Story'.[52] Richard Holt's *Sport and the British: A Modern History* (1989) is an example. Each of the five substantive chapters in the text pursues a distinct theme with its own set of arguments: cultural attitudes towards popular recreations in the eighteenth century, the theory and practice of amateurism, sport in urban working-class culture, sport as a tool of British imperialism, and professional sport. Yet, over these sets of arguments is a narrative of sporting development, a narrative that traces changes in the different recreations and sports and different ways of playing in Britain from the late eighteenth century onwards. Holt may abandon strict narrative but his text retains 'the general idea of sequence' following, in his words, 'a broad progression from the early nineteenth century to the present'.[53] It is this broad progression of change over time that gives Holt's *Sport and the British*, Mangan's *The Games Ethic and Imperialism*, and Dunning and Sheard's *Barbarians, Gentlemen and Players* their narrative quality.

Hayden White perhaps best captures the philosophical differences between traditional narrative and non-narrative analytical forms of historical presentation when he says that the former 'feigns to make the world speak itself and speak itself as a story', while the latter 'openly adopts a perspective that looks out on the world and reports it'.[54] White is also a leading proponent of the discontinuity perspective in narrative theory. While supporters of the continuity argument maintain that narratives are lived, opponents dismiss this position as 'a *hysteron proteron*'; they hold that 'stories are … told' and imposed on the past to produce artificial coherence. In Louis Mink's words, 'there are hopes, plans, battles and ideas, but only in retrospective stories are hopes unfulfilled, plans miscarried, battles decisive, and ideas seminal'.[55] Only in the story does Pierre de Coubertin found the modern olympics. The discontinuity argument lies at the heart of deconstructionism.

Deconstructionism: the poetics of narrative

Unlike reconstructionists and constructionists who assume a close correspondence between the past and its written form and content, deconstructionists consider history a 'precarious and speculative' craft and firmly implicate historians in the constitution of the past as history.[56] Far from viewing narratives as epistemologically self-assured, deconstructionists cast them into the realm of linguistic and literary creations.

I have noted on several occasions in this and preceding chapters that reconstructionists emphasise mastering the sources as the essential prerequisite for reconstructing the past. Among reconstructionists, the fragments of the past contain fixed meanings and those meanings flow naturally into historical narrative, hence the primacy of factual content in reconstructionist presentations. In contradistinction, deconstructionists maintain that historical presentations require the same 'imaginative powers and an eye for detail' as those practised by novelists and poets.[57] Ironically, the good style championed by reconstructionists, such as Kevin McAleer in his evocative and richly detailed description of insults that precipitated duels in late nineteenth-century Germany, lend the greatest support to deconstructionist claims that historical compositions simply do not flow naturally from the sorting of facts.

> A duel was only possible where there had been an insult … To merely touch another's person qualified as [an] … offense, and if at a masked ball you were

goosed by a tipsy soldier demanding a beer, the pinch that the Königsberg lawyer Ernst Borchert found himself in in 1896, a twenty-pace pistol duel with five exchanges was hardly an overreaction, though the rascal was dead by four. The violation of another's physical integrity was considered so reprehensible that even a threatened blow was regarded as an extreme offense, and so gentlemen would spare themselves the exertion by stating simply: 'Consider yourself slapped!' The seduction or lewd touching of one's wife, daughter, sister or other female dependent, could constitute a 'blow', and similar actions or words that jeopardized one's entire mortal being (as the phrase usually went) were also aggravated third-level insults, amenable only through bloodshed.[58]

The level of crafting in this paragraph is clear testimony to the range of choices about words, gaps and omissions, emplotments, figurative styles and arguments that historians face.[59] Moreover, culturally specific terms such as 'offence', 'rascal' and 'lewd touching' highlight the arbitrary nature of language which deconstructionists take as further evidence that historians impose their explanations on the past.[60]

Reconstructionists insist that they expunge imagination and fiction from their narratives but examples of their impositions intrude even in the blandest scissors-and-paste histories. Gerald Redmond's discussion of Canadian women's access to golf in the late nineteenth century is a good example. At one point he wrote, 'Lady members could use the links every morning except Saturday', and they could use the links 'Monday, Tuesday, Thursday and Friday afternoons'. This is not the only way that Redmond could have stated the facts concerning women's access. He could have said, 'women only had access to the links on the quiet mornings and afternoons'. It hardly needs to be said that the two presentations of the same facts connote quite different meanings. Redmond constructs a romantic overstatement of gender relations that ignores the power dispensations of dominance and subordination that prevailed in late nineteenth-century Canadian golf. Of course, the facts in a coherent narrative must be consistent with the endpoint which in Redmond's case amounts to a eulogy of the Scots who introduced golf to both sexes in Canada.[61] In order to preserve the coherence of his narrative, Redmond must eliminate any language, tone or plot that detracts from, contradicts or undermines this (desirable) endpoint.

However, the question still remains, how precisely, do reconstructionists, who claim to present history directly from validated primary sources, actually 'transform the "object" of study into a "subject" of a specifically historical discourse'?[62] Hayden White provides one answer in *Metahistory*, his text that professes a general theory of historical narrative.[63] *Metahistory* popularised the kinship of history, rhetoric, art and literature in mainstream history, although discussion of these relationships has only recently surfaced in sport history.

White's model of historical explanation consists of the deep structures of tropes – figures of speech used to create specific effects in the process of modifying or playing with the literal meaning of language – and three surface tiers: emplotment, argument and ideological implication. White argues that historians use tropes to prefigure their narratives (see Table 4.1). Summarising this poetic act which White calls troping, Keith Jenkins observes that historians, unlike scientists who have recourse to a precise 'technical language ... with specific terminological systems', must draw upon figurative language 'to make the unfamiliar (and ultimately unfathomable) past familiar'. Further, this figurative language 'works metaphorically' to transcribe meaning into ordinary language.[64] In short, through tropes historians 'seek to transform the unfamiliar realities of other places or times into metaphors that make the alien world familiar'.[65]

Sporting metaphors not only saturate the English language – 'it's not cricket' (it's not fair), 'playing with a straight bat', 'playing the game' (abiding by the spirit and letter of rules) – but they help us make sense of our own culture.[66] Pamela Grundy identifies sporting competition as the ultimate nineteenth-century American metaphor that both governed human action and blurred distinctions between athletics and society: 'sports took on the language of industry, with coaches speaking of "well-oiled machines" or of "clicking on all cylinders"', while 'politicians and business leaders began to describe their endeavors in terms of home runs, of fast breaks, and of hitting the line hard'.[67]

As a framework for characterising literary styles, White employs Roman Jacobson's typology of four tropes: metaphor, metonymy, synecdoche and irony. Each performs a particular rhetorical and, therefore, explanatory function:

> Irony, Metonymy, and Synecdoche are all kinds of Metaphor, but they differ from one another in the kinds of *reductions* or *integrations* they effect on the literal level of their meanings and by the kinds of illuminations they aim at on the figurative level. Metaphor is essentially *representational*, Metonymy is *reductionist*, Synecdoche is *integrative* and Irony is *negational*.[68]

Metonymy, synecdoche and irony figure throughout sport history narratives and non-narratives. W. F. Mandle reduces early Australian nationalism (whole) to the achievements of prominent sporting heroes (parts), including Phar Lap (a horse!) and cricketer Don Bradman, who, he says, rate more highly than any politician or artist.[69] Grant Jarvie's description of sport as 'a form of symbolic action which states the case for the nation itself' and as a source of 'shared memories' that help forge ideas about 'common destiny' is a classic statement of synecdochic consciousness.[70] Examples abound. David Andrews and Jeremy Howell refer to rugby nationalising the Welsh by speaking to them as a united nation and locating them in relationship to other nations. Rugby, they write,

> brings out the sparkle in a proud and historically downtrodden people. Feelings of joy and melancholia, pride and prejudice, community and memory, heritage and self-expression, politics and passion all come together as one, framed in a few moments of intense nationalistic fervor.[71]

Irony is the historical trajectory in Trevor Richards' recent history of New Zealand opposition to sporting ties with apartheid South Africa. Rather than sporting relations with apartheid South Africa nationalising New Zealanders, they fractured national consciousness, particularly in the 1970s and 1980s. For example, when the South African national rugby team visited in 1981 it faced mass protests. Opponents of the tour included large numbers of women – who voiced their opposition to the way rugby culture defined them as 'cleaners, cooks and comforters' – and Māori – who seized the protests to promote *te reo* (their own language) and indigenous sovereignty.[72]

Table 4.1   Hayden White's model of historical explanation

Trope	Emplotment	Argument	Ideological implication
Metaphor	Romantic	Formist	Anarchist
Metonymy	Tragic	Mechanistic	Radical
Synecdoche	Comic	Organicist	Conservative
Irony	Satirical	Contextualist	Liberal

Source: White, *Metahistory* (1973), p. 29.

If tropes preshape historians' descriptions and precede and prefigure their explanations, White believes that all narratives comprise a specific emplotment, argument and ideological implication. In each case White identifies four types, as shown in Table 4.1. Emplotment establishes the 'meaning' of a story by identifying its type.[73] Romantic-type histories 'unfold as a quest' on the part of an individual, a group or a nation; inevitably this quest, whether 'described as a journey [or] a struggle', ends with 'victory over adversity'. In a satirical history the historian portrays the agents/heroes or protagonists as 'inferior, captives of their world and destined to a life of obstacles and negation'. Tragic histories end in 'failure, defeat or death' with the heroes or protagonists 'eventually thwarted by fate or their tragic personality flaw'. In a comic emplotment 'the historian always hopes for at least a temporary victory over circumstance for the hero or protagonist through the process of reconciliation'.[74]

Formist arguments provide an explanation of what happens in the story by relating events, people or action according to the historian's notion of dispersion or integration.[75] A formist argument 'identifies the unique, atomistic or dispersive character of events, people and actions' from which the historian selects 'vivid individual events' as the basis of 'significant generalisations'. In contradistinction, the events or individuals in an organicist argument are 'components in a synthetic, integrative process' and are just one of many elements that 'make for complex historical change'. Mechanistic arguments tend towards reductionism by casting 'events, people and actions as subject to deterministic extra-historical laws'. Contextual arguments, which are 'moderately integrative', connect events, people and actions to others in 'webs of colligatory relationships within an era, or within a complex process of interconnected change'.[76] Of these four forms of explanation the formist and contextualist battle it out for orthodoxy.[77]

Finally, White's ideological implications designate the historian's 'general ideological preference' with respect to 'maintaining or changing the status quo, the direction that changes in the status quo ought to take, and the means of effecting such changes'. While conservative and liberal ideologies conceive of the 'fundamental structure of society [as] sound', they regard 'some change as inevitable'. This is 'most effective when particular parts, rather than *structural relationships*, of the totality are changed'.

Table 4.2 Locating Booth and Jaggard in Hayden White's model of historical explanation

Trope	Emplotment	Argument	Ideological Implication
Metaphor	Romantic (Jaggard)	Formist (Jaggard)	Anarchist
Metonymy (Jaggard)	Tragic (Booth)	Mechanistic	Radical (Booth)
Synecdoche (Booth)	Comic	Organicist	Conservative
Irony	Satirical	Contextualist (Booth / Jaggard)	Liberal (Jaggard)

Source: Phillips, 'Narrative in Sport History' (2002), p. 28 and p. 35.

More specifically, conservatives are highly 'suspicious of programmatic transformations'; they subscribe to the ' "natural" rhythm pace of change'. Liberals tend to view change 'through the analogy of adjustments, or "fine tunings", of a mechanism' and their preferred pace conforms to the 'social rhythms of parliamentary debates and educational processes'. Radicals and anarchists support 'structural transformations, the former in the interest of reconstituting society on new bases, the latter in the interest of abolishing "society" and substituting for it a "community" of individuals held together by a shared sense of their common "humanity" '.[78]

Virtually ignored by historians of sport, White's model has received its fullest attention in the field from Murray Phillips. He applied the model to an analysis of two bodies of work produced by Ed Jaggard and myself.[79] In numerous articles and books published in the 1990s, Jaggard and I debated the status of the Surf Life Saving Association (SLSA) in Australian history, the Association's institutional structure and the role of women in the lifesaving movement.[80] Rather than following the reconstructionist path of interrogating empirical evidence and context in the quest for the real past, Phillips analysed the 'literary construction of [our] respective historical narratives'.[81] Table 4.2 summarises Phillips' position.

According to Phillips, I use a synecdochic trope to prefigure my understanding of surf lifesaving. In other words, I integrate all the components of beach culture that collectively define SLSA's existence at different junctures. These components include the social construction of lifesavers' bodies, lifesavers' relationships to surfers, and different social and political struggles. By contrast, Jaggard's approach, says Phillips, is metonymic. Jaggard reduces the whole, surf-lifesaving, to a series of parts: women, humanitarians, surfer-hedonists, officials. He prioritises these parts which become the foundations for understanding the whole and for showing that lifesaving is not, and never was, a monolithic movement: not all lifesavers are highly disciplined nor the antithesis of surfer individualism. And Jaggard's metonymic approach allows him to find spaces for women within the masculine world of surf lifesaving.[82]

Phillips also identifies significant differences in the three surface dimensions of our respective narratives. In the case of plot, Phillips argues that Jaggard employs a romantic structure and that I utilise tragedy. Jaggard, says Phillips, argues that women overcame 'discrimination' to become actively involved in surf lifesaving and he emplots their increasing participation as a 'drama of the triumph of good over evil, of virtue over vice, of light over darkness'. Phillips finds no such 'heroic dimension' in my analysis. Although 'women work against their discrimination, the emphasis is on their pain, agony and suffering' – even after changes in official policy removed barriers to female membership. As Phillips' dramatically concludes his analysis, 'Booth's tortured souls are Jaggard's heroes'.[83]

Although Phillips finds some context in Jaggard's history, he argues that this is generally subordinate to a formist argument. For example, Jaggard highlights the surfboard riding interests of Adrian Curlewis, the long serving president of SLSA, to 'dispel the notion that the movement was essentially militaristic, authoritarian and conservative'. Most notably Jaggard 'reads a photo of Curlewis performing a headstand on a surfboard to … capture the apparently contradictory attitudes of thousands of other surf lifesavers towards their movement and surfing'. By contrast, my argument, according to Phillips, places the SLSA in the broader context of 'social movements or large social forces such as counterculture, the sexual revolution and hedonism'.[84]

Finally, Phillips sees major differences in the ideological positions of our histories: 'Jaggard's history favors a liberal ideology whereas Booth's history has radical ideological implications'. Jaggard comments on the numerous changes in surf lifesaving particularly with respect to administration, sponsorship, competition, technology and female membership. He describes these changes in great detail but most are 'fine-tuning' and adjustments to new policies and personnel within the institution rather than the surf lifesaving movement adapting to the broader social context. In Jaggard's history the pace of change follows the social rhythms of debate and policy amendments. On the other hand, Booth advocates 'structural transformations that would reconstitute the place of surf lifesaving on the beach' and see local councils replace volunteers with American-style lifeguards.[85]

Phillips' application of White's model to the interrogation and analysis of a specific historical debate is one of the most creative and innovative studies produced by a sport historian.[86] Arguably it lends powerful support to White's contention that historical narratives are as much invented or imagined as discovered.[87] At the very least, Phillips shows that sport historians are no different to other practitioners in imposing themselves on their narratives.[88] This does not mean, however, that White's work is beyond criticism; indeed, the critics are many and their concerns varied.[89] In the first instance, just as the models and paradigms in *The Field* are ideal types, so too are White's categories and few historical works fit into a single category of trope, emplotment, explanation or even ideology. As Keith Windshuttle reminds us, 'the academic historian today who writes within an empirical, realist framework can often be dull and boring, it is true, but it is rare to find one who is so devoid of wit that he or she fails to make one or two ironic observations'.[90] With respect to tropes, White recognises elements of synecdoche, metonymy and irony in the texts of several 'masters of nineteenth-century historical thinking', including Jacob Burckhardt, Karl Marx and Alexis de Tocqueville, which he analyses in *Metahistory*, as well as in E. P. Thompson's twentieth-century classic *The Making of the English Working Class* (1963).[91] A similar case can be made for emplotment and argument. For example, elements of tragedy seep into Jaggard's work (for example, his narrative of the cork plug[92]) and even I can discern elements of romance in my (implicit) support for the individualism associated with surfing.

Several critics have also questioned the precise relationship between ideology and trope.[93] The concept of qualified objectivity and its associated epistemology of practical realism – discussed in Chapter 2 – is a salient reminder that the curious historian with her biases, values, emotions and cultural preferences is the source of all historical knowledge. Thus, in my histories of beach culture in Australia I bring my experiences as a surfboard rider and observations made through the eyes of a surfer;[94] Jaggard likewise brings to his histories of surf lifesaving personal experiences and observations as a 'clubby'.[95] Such foregroundings of what amounts to ideological or political positions in history leads Keith Jenkins to argue that White has mistakenly inverted the relationship between trope and ideology and that rather than tropes prefiguring the modes of ideology, the ideological mode prefigures which trope the historian will use to 'metaphorically "figure things out"'.[96]

Notwithstanding his criticism, Jenkins believes that White provides a serious model for 'constructing histories'. Jenkins wants practitioners to make their dominant trope, ideological position, and type of plot and argument explicit. He urges his colleagues to explicitly acknowledge the 'constituted rather than the found nature of … "the historicised past"'.[97] Paraphrasing White, the sympathetic Jenkins says that 'drawing history nearer to its literary sensibility' and 'recognis[ing] and mak[ing] explicit the fictive element in our histories' can only elevate 'our understanding of historiography … to a higher level of self-consciousness'.[98] Robert Berkhofer agrees. Historians, he says, 'need to investigate not only how literary and rhetorical conventions and forms shape historical discourse but also how those conventions and forms constrain the representation of history and thereby the patterning of the past itself as history'.[99] Even Richard Evans, who is quick to point out that 'most of White's earlier arguments do not stand up', acknowledges that his work has been 'all … to the good' in teaching practitioners to 'examine texts with more care and caution', to 'disclose covert beneath overt messages', and to 'decipher the meaning of subtle shifts of grammar'. White, Evans admits, has helped turn the field into a more creative, self-conscious and critical enterprise that is no longer obsessed with finding unified, unambiguous, meanings.[100]

The first shoots of deconstructionist consciousness are appearing in sport history. In his cultural history of American baseball's Black Sox scandal,[101] Daniel Nathan explicitly responds to White's challenge with a text that 'self-consciously reveals my handiwork, seams and all'. 'I try', Nathan says, 'to replicate the complicated nature of the event and the ways in which representations and memories of it complement and compete with each other'.[102] But it is very early days. Rather than evidence of reflexivity, many of the current references to rhetoric, metaphor, narrative and text in sport history are simply uncritical appropriations of concepts deriving from mainstream cultural history and cultural studies.[103] In this regard contemporary sport historians are mimicking the previous generation who appropriated concepts such as modernisation and hegemony from sociology (see Chapter 3). In Chapter 11, I analyse the active role of language, texts and narrative structures in the creation and description of sport history. The key influences on this shift are Clifford Geertz and Michel Foucault, not Hayden White. Given that Victoria Bonnell and Lynn Hunt have labelled White a patron saint of the cultural turn in history,[104] his absence in sport history seems strange. White's absence manifests itself in two ways. The overwhelming majority of sport historians still present their work, whether narratives or non-narratives, as omniscient narrators, and few enter discussions about the relationships between history and fictional literature.

History and fiction[105]

Historical practitioners, philosophers of history, and writers and literary critics have long discussed the relationship between fiction – novels, short stories, plays, poems, films – and history. Carlo Ginzburg points to the old and wide practice of interweaving fiction and history to overcome a paucity of evidence.[106] Paul Ricoeur describes the relationship between fiction and history as 'more complex than we will ever be able to put into words'. He analyses the relationship through the medium of time which he says is intimately connected to the temporality of life, the very essence of history and fiction.[107] Carolyn Steedman, like White, highlights the figurative relationships that bind conventional readings of history and fiction. In both history and fiction, narratives and metaphors bring together the separate and the distant to create the new and the pertinent. Of course, whether readers accept these connections depends on how well writers order events and entities, and on the plots and metaphors they use to give their compilations coherence.[108] Thus for Steedman, and the deconstructionist school, fiction does not simply mean feigned elements; it also refers to crafting narratives, that is, forming, shaping and moulding all the components.[109]

Sport historians have largely adopted a reconstructionist perspective on the relationship between history and fiction and tend to distinguish the two in ways that in reality are not quite so sharp. Conservative practitioners place fiction in the realms of sentiment, bias, opinion, imagination and memory; fiction debases historical facts and sources, scrupulous obedience to which supposedly defines real history.[110] But clearly 'a large part of literature is properly historical' in the sense of 'recording and interpreting … personal, national, and cosmological events' as Lionel Trilling argued and as Kevin McAleer and Allen Guttmann, among other sport historians, demonstrate.[111] In this section, however, I focus on the thoughts of a small band of deconstructionist-leaning sport historians. While stopping well short of the fully fledged deconstructionist conceptualisation of history as a genre of literature, members of this group have variously delved into the theoretical and structural relationships between history and fiction in fictional histories, historical novels and biographies, explored fiction as a way of knowing the past and as a way of disrupting traditional histories, and commented upon the way fiction produces subjects.

There is a long tradition of historians weaving fact and fiction to produce what is sometimes called 'faction'. The Black Sox scandal has attracted several factional accounts. Eliot Asinof admits to 'reconstruct[ing] dialogues and conjecture about the thoughts and motivations of the many involved' in *Eight Men Out* (1963), while *Say It Ain't So Joe: The True Story of Shoeless Joe Jackson* (1992) and *The Ginger Kid: The Buck Weaver Story* (1992) 'read like novels' in which the respective authors, Donald Gropman and Irving Stein, 'recount conversations and thoughts [they] could only have invented'.[112] Similarly, in *The Book of Fame* (2000), a novel about the 1905 New Zealand national rugby team's tour of Great Britain, Lloyd Jones, interweaves fictitious accounts with authentic sources such as match reports in newspapers, players' mementoes, a diary written by one player (George Dixon) and scrapbooks collated by another (Billy Stead).[113] According to Jones, 'imagination slips easily into the gaps' left by scant sources, especially of events beyond the actual matches. Thus, at a darts sideshow on a visit to the seaside town of Scarborough in 1905, All Black George Tyler won a stuffed rabbit which the team proceeded to throw around 'until Jimmy Duncan scratched his chin and …

mentioned an error he'd seen creep into our play'.[114] Ironcially, this fictitious insertion provides the very coherence that reconstructionists crave in their narratives.

Those who compile historical fiction simply admit that some of the content is true and some fictional, and they 'leave the reader to decide which is which'.[115] Such ambiguity dismays reconstructionists for whom real history must present all the evidence and all the proofs up front.[116] It is beside the point to suggest that only an overly suspicious reader would demand evidence for a well-contextualised, credible and sublimely smooth description of, say, Jones' account of the All Black rugby players relaxing at Scarborough. Reconstructionists refuse to budge from their insistence that real history must demonstrate 'congruence with the surviving record' at every juncture and that historians must reference these records.[117]

Interestingly, conservative reconstructionists also relegate biography into the realm of literature. They can find 'no serious place in historical study' for biographies and autobiographies. The notion of objective autobiographers selecting their own significant events and forging connections between them defies reconstructionist commonsense: 'no matter how carefully we assemble the facts, autobiography involves us, inevitably, in myth', writes Allen Guttmann.[118] Even where biographers present themselves as detached outsiders, suspicions remain that 'anyone who devotes years to the study of one individual can hardly escape some identification with the subject and will inevitably [understand their subject's motives, intentions and actions] through that person's eyes'.[119] Of course, we can only wonder how reconstructionists might distinguish a biographer from a non-biographer who spends a lifetime gathering and interrogating documents on a single small event.

Social historians are more receptive to autobiographies and biographies, seeing them as valuable sources of emotions, ideals, interests, sensations, impressions, private opinions, attitudes, drives and motives of significant individuals.[120] Sport historians David Zang and Douglas Hartmann both cite a raft of autobiographies written by former athletes testifying to the racist, demeaning and dehumanising characteristics of professional and college sport.[121] Historians of sport who have written biographies, notably William Baker (Jesse Owens), Allen Guttmann (Avery Brundage) and John MacAloon (Pierre de Coubertin), largely place their subjects into the broader social and political contexts of their times and try to explain how those individuals either reinforced or resisted a particular *Zeitgeist*. All approached their subjects as detached, objective reconstructionists. While not claiming to fill or close every gap, they compulsively describe their journeys of gathering evidence – travelling widely to interview people with personal knowledge and memories of their subjects including relatives, friends and colleagues, and trawling archives, newspapers and personal correspondence – and stress their care in guarding against retrospective causal interpretations, in contextualising their subjects, and in balancing excessive detail against the bigger picture.[122] The results, not surprisingly, are coherent stories 'with all the details in explanatory order and with everything ... accounted for [and] in its proper ... sequence'.[123]

Deconstructionists have assimilated some of the scepticism surrounding the validity of biography as history. In deconstructionist eyes any history that attempts to recover exactly what happened in the past, or tries to mould what are often coincidental and unrelated events into consistent and continuous logical processes that lead their subjects along a particular course, is tantamount to fiction. Sarah Nuttall finds the same process at work in biography. She says that a biographer 'must break up the surface of life, which would make it a story with a beginning and an ending, and without abolishing these, he or she must decontextualise the fragments in order to recontextualise them. A construction must be made and where there is construction another order also comes into play – that of the imagination'.[124]

Deconstructionists approach biographies quite differently from reconstructionists. Instead of trying to close the gaps (between, for example, inconclusive narrative connections, and the subjects' hesitations, or spontaneous revisions of dates, times and places) that frustrate reconstructionists, deconstructionists leave them wide open for all to see. Deconstructionists acknowledge the unknowable and are sensitive to the fragmentary and partial nature of their historical sources and evidence. Examples in sport history are sparse but William Fotheringham's biography of British Tour de France cyclist Tom Simpson and Nick Tosches' biography of the African American heavyweight boxer Charles 'Sonny' Liston capture much of the deconstructionist sentiment. Fotheringham and Tosches are both hesitant to draw definitive conclusions, especially about their subjects' controversial deaths. Throughout their texts, just when an answer appears forthcoming, Fotheringham and Tosches pose fresh questions that introduce new perspectives and more doubts. This is not just a literary device to build and hold suspense; it is a way of confirming the complicated and complex nature of the truth. Fotheringham finally settles on the causes of Simpson's death – the 'symptoms point to exertional heatstroke' induced by amphetamines and *rage à vaincre* (a 'madness' that drove Simpson to push himself beyond endurance). However, even this verdict does not end the questions: must Simpson take sole responsibility for consuming the performance enhancing drugs that raised his core temperature and hindered the dissipation of body heat, or does the blame lie with the race organisers, team managers, journalists and fans who pushed him 'beyond the point where common sense would dictate withdrawal in the interests of damage limitation?'[125]

Tosches titles the final chapter of Liston's biography 'Astrology'. The title is a clever metaphor for framing the many mysteries of Liston's life and death. So many aspects of his life – date of birth, origins of the Sonny nickname, the two losses to Cassius Clay/Muhammad Ali, his relationship with the mafia, causes of death – will never be known. In the absence of conclusive evidence as to how Liston died (the contenders include natural causes, drug overdose and assassination), Tosches asserts that, 'in the end, it had more to do with that starless astrology of the soul of a man who "died the day he was born"'.[126]

On the other hand, deconstructionist-leaning sport historians interested in the history-fiction nexus, may also be attuned to fiction as a medium for knowing the past, for disrupting traditional histories, and for producing subjects. These deconstructionists may actively promote fiction as a fertile source of knowledge; fiction implants attitudes and beliefs and can help develop strategies to cope with new situations and ideas, and gain knowledge about what it would be like to be placed in circumstances that we would never experience.[127] Peter Mewett shows fiction and history combining among professional runners in Australia as these athletes seek to negotiate the present. Success in professional running requires athletes to conceal their true abilities and thus trick bookmakers into offering the longest odds. Hence the sport abounds with stories of trainers (coaches) protecting their runners from 'snoopers' (spies) belonging to competing 'stables', and of leaks from within stables. These stories, says Mewett, 'relate fragments of the sport's past as it is relevant to the here-and-now and, in turn, this sense of the past provides a guide about "what-to-do", about how to constitute the sport'. In this manner the stories '(re)create a history of the *doing* of the sport that is central to its agenic (re)construction'. But, as Mewett observes, 'remembering is shifting, situational (and perhaps fictional) because it is so inextricably built into and constructed from within the present'. Critically, factual veracity is irrelevant because 'it is the doing of the sport in the here-and-now that selects the relevant narratives'.[128]

Most work examining the power of fiction in sport history focuses on its ability to transfer readers to different worlds. Jeffrey Hill describes Brian Glanville's *The Rise of Gerry Logan* (1963), a novel about the on- and off-field experiences of a fictional Scottish soccer player, as an 'engagement' with British soccer in the late 1950s and early 1960s. The period, says Hill, was one of change that ended

> decades-old restrictions on players' wages and labour mobility, and which in turn gave rise to a new representation of the sport in the press and on television. Soccer was acquiring a new image, emerging from its traditional role as the 'working-man's game', and becoming a subject of interest and debate among a wider audience, including intellectuals.[129]

David McGimpsey goes much further. He locates the cultural reputation of baseball in American society firmly in the literary realm. McGimpsey believes that the 'cultural fascination' with the Black Sox scandal, as evident in contemporary novels such as Harry Stein's *Hoopla* (1983), W. P. Kinsella's *Shoeless Joe* (1984) and Brendan Boyd's *Blue Ruin* (1991), 'is not merely based on a desire to "get the story straight"'. Rather it captures American interest in baseball's 'moral space', a place where different interests collide and 'history is open to interpretation'. For McGimpsey, 'baseball's optimistic tropes are strong because they are contested by an equally present series of cynical tropes'. Thus where baseball is 'America at its best', it is also 'no better than *The Jerry Springer Show*'; where 'baseball shows us a[n] … America where all are judged on merit', it is also 'an exclusive boys' club'; and where 'baseball returns sons to fathers', it also 'keeps fathers and sons enthralled to what William Carlos Williams called "a spirit of uselessness"'.[130] Reflecting on the question of historical interpretation, McGimpsey remarks that on certain questions the truth may reside in statistics and facts but

> most fans and casual observers welcome the subjective and partisan bases for sports arguments. Few have all of baseball's statistics at their fingertips, and even those with a vast historical knowledge harbour basic assumptions about the game that are influenced by affection for certain players or moments. The history of the game is subjective and baseball's cultural products try to appeal to that subjectivity.[131]

More to the point, baseball fiction can say things about America that other genres simply cannot capture.[132]

Finally, deconstructionist-leaning scholars of sport afford fiction the power to produce subjects. 'If the goal is to understand how people thought about [American] football', writes Michael Oriard, then short stories and serialised novels in magazines such as *Post*, *Collier's*, *Tip Top Weekly*, *Boys' Life*, *American Boy* were 'clearly important'. These fictional narratives, Oriard continues, 'insinuated themselves into readers' views of reality in subtle ways. The chief figures in formulaic football films and stories – the hero, the heroine, the coach, the rival, the ethnic teammate, the booster – became absorbed into the public consciousness, to become part of the context when readers contemplated the "real" game'.[133] Hill succinctly sums up Oriard's position, describing him as disposing of notions that the text corresponds with society. Instead he captures the autonomy of the text and its ability to create meaning.[134] Of course, how readers receive and respond to fiction is a notoriously thorny area for historians. I touch on this issue in Chapter 11.

In an analysis of the 2000 Bollywood blockbuster *Lagaan* ('Tax'), Chandrima Chakraborty demonstrates the power of fiction to disrupt dominant meanings and to rewrite the histories of subordinated and marginalised groups who are typically excluded from accounts of the past. The film tells the story of peasants from the village of Champaner who form a cricket team that defeats a British eleven during the colonial era. According to Chakraborty, *Lagaan* shows subaltern groups convincingly co-opting and critiquing the 'master forms and tropes of the West'. For example, in their initial discussions of the meaning of cricket, the peasants describe the game as silly and childish. In so doing they not only offend the East India Company official in charge of Champaner for whom cricket embodies British morality, civilisation, modernity and progress, they invert the terms and tropes of colonial discourses: 'the colonized male, usually denied adult status and described as "childlike", "ignorant", and "boy", now names the "civilized" as child'. The cricketers in *Lagaan* may be fictional but, by introducing the 'experiences of a subaltern group hidden from elite history' and by 'destabilizing the history of colonial cricket', the film poses important questions about historical knowledge and historiography such as who writes history, and who is included and excluded, and from which histories.[135] These questions extend to the very essence of both deconstructionism and constructionism.

Conclusion

Sport historians rarely enter into discussions or debates over the different forms of presenting the past. Mark Dyreson's mild rebuke of Michael Oriard for 'flattening orthodox chronology' in his *King Football* probably captures the extent of concern about presentation within the field.[136] Yet even with his concerns about Oriard's thematic approach, which he says 'confuses certain issues', Dyreson acknowledges that orthodox chronology too poses problems, not least in imposing arbitrary blocks of time – 'the Roaring Twenties, the depressed Thirties, the war-torn Forties, and the tail-fin Fifties' – on twentieth-century American football.[137] Despite their success in contemporary sport history, I consider pure narratives the least satisfying forms of presentation. Usually a record of an event or a single sport, and primarily aimed at non-critical aficionados and devotees, the typical narrative in sport history is a barren treatise, devoid of imagination – whether in the questions asked or the concepts deployed – and all too often guided by a strong faith in some idealised notion of sport.[138] Invariably, the promised insights into life and society are either buried under mountains of minutiae or suffocated by the specificity of sporting cultures that do not readily translate across cultural, regional or national boundaries (such as cricket and baseball, or Australian football and American football).[139]

Defending their forms of presentation and particularly their slavish devotion to sources and evidence, reconstructionists commonly appeal to the 'tenets of history that forbid them from knowingly inventing or excluding things that affect their conclusions'. As David Lowenthal puts it, 'in terming himself an historian and his work a history, [the practitioner] chooses to have it judged for accuracy, internal consistency, and congruence with the surviving record. And he dares not fabricate a character, ascribe unknown traits or incidents to real ones, or ignore incompatible traits so as to make his tale more intelligible, because he could neither hide such inventions from others with access to the public records nor justify them when found out'.[140] Of course, as we have seen, the great irony is that no matter how hard reconstructionists try, even the blandest report extracted verbatim from the sources will involve some degree of imposition on the part of the historian.

The deconstructionist call for self-conscious reflection, and for practitioners to openly acknowledge the limitations of knowing and presenting the past,[141] has attracted few followers in sport history. One might say that Daniel Nathan cuts a pretty solitary figure in this regard. For him, every historical moment contains different versions because, irrespective of our sources and evidence, 'we tend to see what we want to see, believe what we need to believe'.[142] If Nathan is correct, and there are good reasons for accepting that he is, then perhaps Carolyn Steedman's notion of the narrative as a 'transaction' provides the vital clue to understanding how people evaluate historical presentations. 'People may remember the past, and may verbalize their recollections', Steedman explains, 'but to become a story what they say must achieve a coherence and point which are the same for the hearer as the teller'.[143] Hayden White adds to this perspective when he notes that before readers will accept a particular narrative as 'an adequate representation or explanation of a historical phenomenon', it must be congruent with the times, places and cultural conditions.[144] Such congruence returns us to the centrality of ideology and politics that Jeffrey Alexander believes underpins all theory (see Chapter 3) and that Keith Jenkins believes prefigures all historical presentations.

Of course, historians' freedom to impose whatever interpretation they want on the past is not absolute: historians must always work with the remnants of the past. How historians work with the materials from the past is the subject of the next chapter, the last in Part I.

Chapter 5

Remnants of the past

Sources, evidence and traces in sport history

HISTORIANS CANNOT ESCAPE from the remnants of the past that are the basic materials of the discipline. As Arthur Marwick reminds us, 'one cannot travel to the past by ship or plane … the only way we can have knowledge of the past is through studying the relics and traces left by past societies'.[1] Irrespective of the model of inquiry, historical materials are paramount. Whether they subscribe to reconstructionism, constructionism or deconstructionism, all practitioners emphasise their remnants of the past (as manifest in notes and bibliographies) and the methods they use to extract evidence from them.[2] While constructionists and deconstructionists do not agree with reconstructionists who claim that historical knowledge resides solely in the authority of validated sources,[3] they do agree that historians must understand the origins and context of each source, and be able to explain how the source is relevant to the historical question at hand.[4] But as I have shown in preceding chapters, practitioners approach sources in different ways. Reconstructionists treat historical materials as concrete artifacts and interrogate them to ascertain their truthfulness (see Chapter 2); constructionists contexualise historical materials within theoretical frameworks that they hold as the primary means by which historians reveal reality (see Chapter 3); deconstructionists conceptualise historical materials as discourses and texts, and search these linguistic forms for their inherent power relations (see Chapter 4). This final chapter in Part I compares and contrasts the epistemological assumptions underpinning each model by examining four broad categories of historical material found in sport history – official documents, documents of mass communication (newspapers), oral testimony, and visual materials. These categories do not encapsulate the sum total of sources in the field, they simply illustrate the more common types of materials used in sport history.[5] Moreover, historians rarely rely on just one type of material for evidence; rather than answering or clarifying historical questions, a reliance on one type of material typically raises fresh issues.

In other words, historians generally believe that the more vast the array of primary material, the more dependable the historical knowledge.[6]

The epistemological assumptions underpinning reconstructionist, constructionist and deconstructionist treatments of official documents, documents of mass communication (newspapers), oral testimony and visual materials are represented schematically in Table 5.1. Very broadly, reconstructionists and constructionists regard

Table 5.1   Epistemological assumptions of reconstructionism, constructionism and deconstructionism by category of historical material

Historical materials	Epistemological assumptions		
	Reconstructionism	*Constructionism*	*Deconstructionism*
	• Focuses on distortions in historical materials and evidence • Interrogation reveals truths	• Theory drives gathering and interrogation of historical material • Theory reveals reality	• Focuses on how historical knowledge comes into being • Interrogation: another layer of interpretation
Official documents	• Official documents yield knowledge about the past • Archives: sites for the retrieval of knowledge	• Official documents contextualised by theory to reveal reality • Archives: non-theorised	• Official documents serve political interests • Archives: sites for the production of knowledge
Newspapers	• Newspapers: sport's prime historical record • Newspapers represent specific interests (revealed by interrogation)	• Newspapers: contextualised by theory to reveal reality	• Newspapers: mediating texts
Oral testimony	• Oral evidence produced through structured interviews • Detachment from subject essential • Memory variously an obstacle to, or a databank of, the past • Memory and forgetting: distinct conditions • Truth and falsity: absolute values	• Oral testimony contextualised by theory to reveal reality • Memory contextualised by theory to reveal reality	• Oral evidence produced in negotiated dialogue • Involvement with informant a virtue • Memory a creative construction produced in dialogue • Memory and forgetting: one and the same condition • Truth and falsity: obsolete concepts
Visual materials	• Film: a powerful medium for transporting viewers to events • Documentary films and historical practice generally incompatible • Photographs: represent *prima facie* evidence	• Films contextualised by theory to reveal reality • Reception resides in theorised context and circumstances of image • Photographs contextualised by theory to reveal reality	• Documentary films and historical practice both fictional creations • Photographs: ambiguous texts passed through many mediating filters

Principal sources: Robert Berkhofer, *Beyond the Great Story* (1995), Peter Burke, *Eyewitnessing* (2001), Louis Gottschalk, *Understanding History* (1969), Carolyn Hamilton *et al.*, *Refiguring the Archive* (2002), Keith Jenkins and Alun Munslow, *The Nature of History Reader* (2004), Alun Munslow, *Reconstructing History* (1997), Luise White, *Speaking With Vampires* (2000).

the materials of the past as the foundations of historical knowledge which, when tested and interrogated, yield evidence and truths. The difference between reconstructionists and constructionists is that the latter use theory to drive the gathering, or selection, of historical materials, and rely on theory for their contextualisation. Deconstructionists are deeply sceptical of the truth – or reality – bearing properties of the fragments of the past. Whatever evidence historians draw from the remnants of the past, deconstructionists believe that it is always partial and fragmented, and that it involves interpretations replete with gaps, interrupted thoughts and plots. Among deconstructionists the term source is a misleading description of a remnant from the past. Source is a metaphor that implies historians simply 'fill their buckets from the stream of Truth' and that 'their stories become increasingly pure as they move closer to the origins'. But as Peter Burke explains, every account of the past involves intermediaries. These include earlier historians, archivists who arrange documents, scribes who write documents, and witnesses whose words were recorded.[7] Thus, deconstructionists view interrogation as the insertion of another layer of interpretation that brings more contradictions, inversions and secrets.[8] In the following discussion, I address these respective epistemological assumptions across the four categories of historical material. As in Chapter 4, my emphasis is on reconstructionism and deconstructionism which represent the extremes of opinion.

Official documents (and archives)

The term 'official' as adopted here refers to the records of states, governments, corporations and formally constituted organisations. Their records include legislation and by-laws, internal memoranda, correspondence sent to other organisations and individuals, statements of policy, reports, and minutes of meetings. Historians of sport rely heavily on official documents. A royal proclamation issued by James I of England in 1618 – the *Declaration of Lawful Sports* (better known as *The King's Book of Sports*) – testifies to official sanction of popular recreations and pastimes.[9] Details culled from census enumerators' books paint a socio-occupational picture of sportsmen in nineteenth-century central Scotland.[10] Prospectuses issued by soccer clubs adopting company status give insights into the profit motivations of members and directors involved in Scottish football around the turn of the twentieth century.[11] Laden with sporting results, commentaries and photographs, official school magazines have been key sources in numerous historical studies.[12] Official reports of the organising committees help reconstruct accounts of early modern olympic games.[13] Tables of foreign sportspeople travelling to apartheid South Africa, produced in the annual reports of the Department of National Education, effectively monitored the sports boycott.[14] A White Paper (statement of government policy published in advance of legislative proposals), titled *Sport and Recreation* (1975), alerts historians to a crucial shift in official British attitudes towards sport as a legitimate aspect of the welfare state.[15] Although space limitations preclude examining the full range of official documents, in this section I focus on Hansard and the contrasting treatments applied to these verbatim records of parliament by reconstructionists and deconstructionists.

Reconstructionists treat all remnants of past activity, including Hansard, as evidence-bearing material with the truth content emerging through interrogation (see Chapter

2). John O'Hara, for example, found the objectives of the New South Wales Gaming and Betting Act of 1906 in Hansard. (Among other things the Act abolished street betting, betting houses and tote shops, and restricted betting to selected racecourses and sportsgrounds.) Trawling Hansard debates on the Act, which he corroborated with sermons from the pulpit, newspaper editorials and letters to editors, O'Hara concluded that anti-gaming legislators in New South Wales represented white, Protestant, middle-class social and moral reformers, whose primary goal was to discipline the lower orders. In Hansard, O'Hara found evidence that the Act imposed 'greater restrictions' on the 'lower orders than on … their social superiors'. During the parliamentary debates, members admitted that the middle-class Randwick racecourse and 'gentlemen's residential clubs' would 'escape prosecution'; police would only direct their attention to 'less respectable gaming dens and betting shops'. Members also believed that by limiting public racecourses to half-day operations on official holidays, they would reduce absenteeism among working-class men.[16]

By reconstructionist criteria, Hansard is an excellent source for corroborating the motives of members of parliament which, of course, find concrete expression in legislation. Hansard is also an unquestionably reliable account of what members actually said in the chamber with highly trained parliamentary staff transcribing debates, and parliamentary rules and conventions requiring members to sign off their speeches as accurate accounts. Deconstructionists, however, are less concerned about the reliability and accuracy of members' speeches, or even their paralinguistic performances (for example, demeanour) and mode of delivery (for example, eloquence and elegance or rhetorical truth) which, although Hansard does not capture them, are critical to making evidence appear trustworthy. They seek to understand the authority of Hansard to define social problems, such as gambling. To this end deconstructionists ask questions about the way representations of particular problems serve specific political interests; they are especially interested in the way certain voices are silenced and excluded.[17] O'Hara hints at these concerns in references to the debates over gambling in late nineteenth- and early twentieth-century Australia taking place largely within the middle classes and to divisions over gambling within the working classes. However, to the best of my knowledge, no one has examined how debates in official documents such as those produced by parliament and royal commissions might have actually constructed both the working classes and the problem of gambling.[18]

These differences in epistemology and approach between reconstructionists and deconstructionists also appear in their respective approaches to archives, the storage sites of official documents.[19] Whereas the former see archives as neutral sites of knowledge, the latter conceive of them as sites of power. Reconstructionists studying sport in Victorian and Edwardian Britain and in American colleges have made extensive use of public school and university archives. J. A. Magan scoured the archives of Harrow, Lancing, Lorretto, Marlborough, Stoneyhurst and Uppingham schools for his history of the emergence and consolidation of athleticism as an educational ideology.[20] Ronald Smith visited some 50 university archives in researching his history of radio and television in big-time college sport. University archives often contain vast amounts of material on sport, says Smith, including presidential papers, faculty athletic committee minutes, athletic directors' papers, athletic association records, coaches' documents, conference commissioners' correspondence and reports, alumni records, and student diaries and reminiscences. 'Nearly every significant action or problem in intercollegiate athletics is reflected in presidential correspondence', he continues. John Watterson, who draws heavily on university archives in his history of American college football, echoes Smith.[21] Identified by one peer as sport history's most 'diligent excavator of archival material', Watterson singles out the papers of the legendary University of Chicago coach Amos Alonzo Stagg as especially useful. He 'saved almost everything', observes Watterson, while his wife also 'compiled scrapbooks of newspaper articles' that extended for some 50 years. In particular, Stagg's letters build an important profile of his 'relations with William Harper, Walter Camp, and other figures who played a role in big-time football'.[22] Archives are indeed indispensable repositories of primary historical evidence for sport historians, but they are not simple 'stores of transparent sources' from which practitioners freely 'recover total images'.[23]

Sport historians are well aware of gaps and omissions in archives. Few sports clubs or associations archive material, and when they do it is typically uneven and anonymous. Less the result of deliberate political decisions, these haphazard situations largely stem from problems associated with limited space and the perfectly understandable attitudes of (mainly volunteer) officials whose priority is day-to-day survival not preserving the past.[24] The same is not necessarily true of government departments, corporations, and large organisations such as international sporting federations.

All states, governments, corporations and organisations, regardless of their charters and political complexions, operate within a climate of confidentiality and carefully manage the release of information they deem sensitive. Embargoes, commonly lasting between 30 and 50 years, are the principal means of management. Freedom of information legislation allows historians to step around some embargoes and overzealous bureaucrats who both defend and invent official secrets.[25] Freedom of information laws provide for a 'general right' to consult 'documents held by government agencies, subject to exemptions which recognise the need to protect sensitive personal and commercial information and some government records'.[26] The caveat, of course, is unambiguous: freedom of information laws may improve access to historical material but it falls far short of total liberalisation.[27] In 1993 I applied to the Department of Sport under the Australian Commonwealth Freedom of Information Act (1982) to examine a specific document concerning Sydney's bid for the 2000 olympic games. While the Department granted access, for a fee, release of the document still rested on the judgement of a state functionary. Even searchers' rights to appeal – in my case to an Administrative Appeals Tribunal and ultimately the Commonwealth Ombudsman – does not obviate potentially perverse decisions. And, of course, historians rarely have any rights to appeal for access to records held by private individuals, companies, or independent associations.[28]

Sport historians know that governments and associations manipulate, conceal, hide and destroy information.[29] In the former East Germany, the Ministry for State Security classified all documents pertaining to the state's controlled hormonal doping of athletes programme. Only select people could access the documents that included doctoral theses, scientific reports from research institutes and sports associations, and protocol books (giving the times and dosages of androgenic-anabolic steroids administered to athletes). When the East German regime collapsed in 1989, sports officials destroyed many compromising documents and other sensitive materials 'disappeared' from official libraries.[30] Similarly, for 20 years after the deaths of 11 Israeli athletes at the olympic games in Munich, the Bavarian and West German governments concealed information from the athletes' relatives. The families of athletes knew little about the attack on and siege of, the Israeli accommodation in the athletes' village by Black September fedayeen, and even less about the German rescue mission at Fürstenfeldbruck as the captors tried to leave the host nation with their athlete hostages. Officials variously claimed that their investigations were ongoing, that no official reports existed, or that all relevant documents had been destroyed.[31]

Yet, such examples have not dented reconstructionist confidence in the archive which remains a 'beacon of light, a place ... of and for sight', a site where the initiated cry out '"once I was blind, but now I see"'.[32] Reconstructionists privilege stories about the discovery of documents and evidence over those that relate to their disappearance and concealment. Werner Franke and Brigitte Berendonk describe their retrieval of documents pertaining to the German Democratic Republic's secret hormonal doping programme, recounting instances of documents surviving official purges and of Manfred Höppner, the deputy director and chief physician of East Germany's Sports Medical Service and doping system, selling incriminating documents to the weekly magazine *Stern*![33] Simon Reeve devotes almost a chapter in his book on the Munich saga to the release of official documents pertaining to the deaths of the Israeli athletes, which first came to light through the actions of an anonymous worker in the German archives. (The documents, contained in 3,808 files, show that German authorities tried to 'cover up' the inadequate security at the 1972 games and the botched rescue mission of the Israeli athletes.[34]) Such narratives engender a firm belief among reconstructionists that persistence ultimately leads to the truth. But this belief typically comes at the expense of ignoring the circumstances under which archives are assembled and materials excised and excluded.[35]

It is precisely these issues that prompt deconstructionist scepticism in the archive. 'We often forget', writes Achille Mbembe,

> that not all documents are destined to be archives. In any given cultural system, only some documents fulfil the criteria of "archivability". Once they are received, they have to be coded and classified. They are then distributed according to chronological, thematic or geographical criteria. Archives are the product of a process which converts a certain number of documents into items judged to be worthy of preserving and keeping in a public place, where they can be consulted according to well-established procedures and regulations. The archive ... is fundamentally a matter of discrimination and selection, which, in the end, results in the granting of a privileged status to certain written documents, and the refusal of that same status to others ...[36]

Among deconstructionists, then, archives are 'processes of preservation and exclusion', and places where states, corporations and organisations produce knowledge for their own interests as distinct from sites for the retrieval of knowledge.[37] (Interestingly, reconstructionist sport historians have no difficulty conceptualising sport museums and halls of fame, libraries, and the internet in these terms.[38]) Deconstructionists, it must be stressed, do not advocate abandoning archival searches and they agree that questions about the trustworthiness, authenticity and reliability of documents remain pressing. However, they do urge a more cautious engagement with archived materials. As well as alerting historians to the way in which archival documents change over time, the 'turn to the social and political conditions that produced those documents has altered the sense of what trust and reliability might signal and politically entail'.[39] Much deconstructionist analysis of archives is couched in terms of social memory (including forgetting – see below) and imagination. Verne Harris defines the archive as a trilectic of remembering, forgetting and imagining.[40] Just as 'every act of memory is also an act of forgetting',[41] so imagining 'dances between remembering and forgetting ... The dance of imagination, moving effortlessly through both conscious and unconscious spaces, shapes what is remembered and what is forgotten, and how the trace is configured'.[42]

Two brief examples illustrate the deconstructionist approach to archives. My 1993 application to the Department of Sport made under the Australian Commonwealth Freedom of Information Act, was a request for a document prepared by John Coates, chair of the Sydney Olympic Bid Committee (SOBC). Coates presented the document, an outline of his strategy to win the hosting rights for the 2000 games, to the inaugural meeting of SOBC in early 1991.[43] The archived version of the document is, not unexpectedly, bland and unrevealing; it adds nothing to the presumptive and corroborative evidence that Coates overstepped International Olympic Committee (IOC) guidelines on bidding for host city rights (see Chapter 2, note 31). Through the lens of reconstructionism, the document is merely another example of archival silence. Under the lens of deconstructionism, however, it contributes to Australia's forgetfulness of how members and supporters of SOBC actually won the hosting rights for the 2000 olympics.

Similarly, the deconstructionist tenet that 'there is no remembering that cannot become forgetting',[44] calls into question the saliency of the more than 150 documents recovered by Franke and Berendonk pertaining to East Germany's secret hormonal doping programme. Any possibility that these documents might constitute an archival foundation for drug-free sport – a memory reminding future generations of the athletes who died from hormonal doping and a warning to young aspiring sportspeople of the severe side-effects (gynecomastopathy, liver damage, hirsutism, acne, folliculitis, amenorrhea, polycystic ovarian syndrome[45]) – seems improbable. Indeed, Franke and Berendonk believe that only the threat of scandal prevented politicians and sports officials in the West from using the same drugs as their East German counterparts.[46] Signs of forgetting are everywhere. The IOC, for example, studiously avoids advertising former president Juan Antonio Samaranch's close friendship with Manfred Ewald. As the secretary of state for sport in East Germany, Ewald was the ultimate mastermind of the doping programme; at the same time as suspicions raged about East Germany's sporting miracles, Samaranch awarded Ewald an Olympic Order.[47]

Documents of mass communication

Unlike official records, many of which are never published or printed only in small numbers, documents of mass communication are produced in large volumes for wide distribution. Documents of mass communication include newspapers, magazines, comic books, posters and advertisements, each of which offers unique insights into the past and presents different problems. For example, advertisements are useful sources for the study of past attitudes to commodities and are excellent signifiers of cultural values, but in the hands of advertising agencies they tend to sanitise the world.[48] While the young couple appearing with cycles at a homestead in rural Ontario on the cover of the Brantford Red Bird bicycle catalogue for 1898 signify modern notions of social freedom and mobility, it is unlikely that they could present themselves so immaculately after having ridden any distance over the rough dirt roads of the period.[49] This section, however, concentrates on reconstructionist, constructionist and deconstructionist assumptions about, and treatments of, newspapers, which many sport historians regard as the prime record for the field.[50]

Newspapers present information in different forms: lists of events, records of prevailing political and social values, and the results of investigations into events, issues and people. Notices and announcements provide dates, times and venues of sporting fixtures, sporting results and scores, and the names of players, teams, coaches and officials. Editorials and letters convey insights into prevailing social thinking. Thomas Wentworth Wills' letter published in *Bell's Life in Victoria* on 10 July 1858, in which he proposed the formation of a committee to 'draw up a code of laws' for football, reveals something of the mood of the times around the birth of what would become a national game. 'If it is not possible to form a foot-ball club', Wills wrote in his letter, then perhaps they could start a rifle club to help protect the colonists in their 'adopted land against a tyrant's band, that may some day "pop" upon us when we least expect a foe'. In the wake of war in Crimea, many colonists feared a Russian invasion and Wills' proposal painted sport as valuable preparation for military service: 'surely our young cricketers are not afraid of the crack of the rifle, when they face so courageously the leather sphere'.[51] Investigations by journalists can also produce important information. In 'The Black Athlete: A Shameful Story', a five-part series published in *Sports Illustrated* in 1968, Jack Olsen exposed high levels of dissatisfaction, disgruntlement and disillusionment among African American athletes. Describing the report as 'hard-hitting' and 'riveting', Douglas Hartmann says it 'not only called attention to the grievances and discontents of African American athletes, but … point[ed] out the stark contradictions between these problems and the popular image of sport as a leader in race relations'.[52]

Reconstructionists acknowledge that newspaper material varies enormously in reliability. They generally accept sporting notices, announcements, results and scores as reliable although always 'subject to human error' in the processes of 'providing, receiving, or printing the information'.[53] They also regard newspaper stories that capture broad social moods surrounding big events as good evidence, especially when reported by trained journalists who supply eyewitness testimony (compared with those who gather information after an event such as Jack Chalmers' rescue of Milton Coughlan described in Chapter 2).[54] But reconstructionists also identify a plethora of problems and issues concerning newspaper evidence. The 'preferences, bias, knowledge and experiences' of journalists will always influence their observations, descriptions and opinions especially where the subject being written about can be interpreted from different perspectives.[55] The *Bendigo Advertiser* and the *Castlemaine Representative* presented two quite different accounts of an exchange between William Gilbert Grace and Mr Bruce, the chairman of the Bendigo Cricket Club, on the England tour of Australia in 1873–4. The exchange, which occurred at the end of the second day's play of the Bendigo match, was precipitated by Bruce's accusation that Grace displayed discourtesy when he left the lunch interval early. According to the *Bendigo Advertiser*, Grace told

Bruce that his accusation was 'd____ ungentlemanly' and when Bruce retorted by calling Grace a 'd___ blackguard', the latter 'motion[ed] with his clenched fist to strike' his slanderer. The *Castlemaine Representative* reported that despite being 'spoken to in a rude and rough manner', Grace remained 'gentlemanly and quiet'.[56]

'Every story starts with a perspective', observed Leonard Koppett, a former sport journalist with the *New York Times*, and journalists invariably see the world and events through the eyes of the community for which the newspaper purports to speak. Thus, 'when a team representing San Francisco beats one from Dallas, the reporter from the *Dallas Times* writes about Dallas' loss while the reporter from the *San Francisco Herald* describes San Francisco's victory'.[57] Journalists' perspectives narrow further when they travel and live with sporting teams. As they develop close working relationships with players who they present as heroes to the public, journalists tend to shy – consciously or unconsciously – from questioning any behaviour, attitudes and habits that may contradict their perspectives. Cycling journalist William Fotheringham admits that, prior to the drug scandal on the 1998 Tour de France, he had long 'steered away' from the issue of banned drugs.[58]

Koppett advised historians to treat quotes by sportspeople in newspapers with 'suspicion and care'. They capture neither tone nor expression, 'they are nearly always incomplete', and often they do not even come first hand (when 'reporters listen to speeches in huddles they forever ask each other, "what did he say?"'). Moreover, journalists 'do not check the validity of the quote', they are just 'words taken at face value'. Distinguishing between journalistic and historical practice, Koppett admitted that journalists know their quotes are often 'incomplete[and inaccurate but they're writing tomorrow's news not history'. Likewise, when a microphone is thrust in front of a person 'they have an opportunity to play to the crowd and say things that may have little to do with the situation'. Such are the problems with quotations that Koppett recommended that historians avoid writing player A 'said' and to replace it with player A 'was quoted as saying'.[59]

Reconstructionists are well aware that newspapers are actors who strive to build loyal readerships and that they target specific regional affiliations, cultures, social classes and genders through editorials, opinion pieces, cartoons and slants on stories. New York and Chicago tabloids were 'merciless in their opposition' to the 1926 heavyweight boxing title fight between Jack Dempsey and Gene Tunney in Philadelphia, while the Philadelphia press 'supported it under the guise that the fight would help reduce, if not liquidate, the city's debt' that had been swelled by a Sesquicentennial Exhibition.[60] In the 1850s American religious journals such as the *Independent* refused to report the 'loathsome details of prize fights' and other 'low, disgusting sports', as did the publishers of *Turf, Field and Farm* who declared that they sought only the patronage of 'more respectable elements of society'.[61] Similarly, when San Francisco '49er players staged a one-day strike in 1949 for play-off pay, they won support from the *Daily Worker* and the *San Francisco Examiner*'s Prescott Sullivan, while *New York Times* columnist Arthur Daley and the *San Francisco Chronicle*'s Bill Leiser opined in favour of the owners.[62] In the late 1920s, small-town North Carolina newspapers were far more progressive in their reporting of women's high school basketball than their big-city cousins. At the same time as the *Hickory Daily Record* referred to the Hickory High Tornadoes 'walloping' the Lincoln Wolves and was addressing players by their surnames, the *Charlotte Observer* was still using the courtesy title 'Miss'.[63]

Reconstructionists also find vast differences between quality broadsheets and tabloids in the coverage of sports. *The Times* of London snubbed popular sports although it 'reserved a special place for cricket, a game which kept its professionals firmly in their place'. The *Daily Telegraph*, the 'paper of the aspiring middle classes of the Home Counties', was 'unique in maintaining a full reporting of private school sports'.[64] 'Notorious for sensationalism, for pictorial excess, for abandoning news in favor of crass entertainment, for exploiting the ill-educated masses', the tabloids built their success around sex, sport and crime. However, Michael Oriard cautions that 'contrary to the assumption of elitist critics that the tabloids appealed only to the unwashed masses', they were in fact read by all classes.[65]

Last, reconstructionists are acutely aware that journalistic styles and methods of reporting have changed dramatically over time. The early sporting press, says Dennis Brailsford, was part of a 'broader literary culture' that conjoined 'fact and fantasy', each reinforcing the other. By way of illustration Brailsford cites a description of two rounds in a celebrated fight reported by *Sporting Magazine* (April 1808):

> 6. Some obstinate rallying ... Gregson was hit about at pleasure. Gully received a tremendous blow to the right side of his head at the close of this round.
>
> 7. Gully rallied his man ... and hit him about six blows on the head with great ease, and he also stopped those of Gregson, whose left eye was closed, his nose broken, and his face hideously disfigured; Gregson was at length hit off his legs.

'The point is', Brailsford patiently explains, 'that even with men in this apparently hopeless state and with Gregson seeming near death's door, the fight still went on for over twenty more rounds! It was all part of the new world of play, the creating of sporting gods, the reality and the fiction each feeding off and strengthening the other'.[66]

Summing up developments in the British press, Jeffrey Hill describes the style of the mid-Victorian press as 'heavy and detailed', and focused on the 'ebb and flow of the play'. This gave way in the late-Victorian and Edwardian eras to a more readable reporting style complemented by photographs. During the inter-war period the sporting press shifted its attention once again, this time to 'the imaginative, the human drama, and the "behind the scenes" story'.[67] Styles also changed in reports of individual sports. Michael Oriard observes several changes in American football writing from the '"epic" style in the 1890s, to a "heroic" style in the 1920s, then to a "realistic" style in the late 1930s and after'. The 'epic style' embraced 'overblown classic allusion: football players as gladiators, the stadium as a Circus Maximus, contending teams as Greeks and Persian legions'. The heroic style retained embellishments 'but found its metaphors closer to home, in the nicknames of the teams, styles of play, even weather conditions. Writers elaborated imaginatively on USC's "Thundering Herd," Georgia Tech's "Golden Tornado," SMU's "aerial circus," and so on ...'.[68]

Differences in style and content partly reflect different contexts. In keeping with Jim Crow laws and customs, newspaper cartoonists mercilessly caricatured African American heavyweight boxer Joe Louis as a 'crude Sambo', a 'savage ape-like figure with coconut head, long arms, broad shoulders, narrow waist and bulging muscles'. They ridiculed Louis, 'associat[ing] him with the chicken-stealing, razor-toting, crap-shooting, and lazy elements of the Sambo stereotype'. But after Louis knocked out the

German Max Schmeling in a new climate of heightened international tensions on the eve of the Second World War, Americans found in him a new national hero. Newspaper cartoonists responded by removing the 'Sambo mask' and drawing sketches of a handsome young African American.[69]

Notwithstanding newspaper bias towards particular groups or interests, reconstructionists retain their faith in interrogation and corroboration to circumvent bias. Reconstructionists draw particular comfort from the vast range of newspapers which they argue offers them a means to identify and surmount bias by simply reading one paper against another.[70] In contradistinction, constructionists theorise newspapers in such a way that the information contained therein fits very specific interpretations and does not require interrogation to ascertain its truthfulness. For example, left-leaning constructionists interpret the Western mass media as a conduit for the 'special interests that dominate the state and private activity'. The mass media 'fix[es] the premises of discourse', decides what the general population 'sees, hears, and thinks about', and thereby '"manages" public opinion'. According to these constructionists, this model appears in the 'choices, emphases, and omissions' made by industry representatives.[71] The contemporary American mass media's reluctance to address racial controversies surrounding college sport (for example, admission requirements, graduation rates, recruiting practices and compensation for athletes) is one example. In earlier generations, of course, the issues were class, ethnicity, and gender.[72] Why this reluctance?

'Most biased choices in the media', Edward Herman and Noam Chomsky assert,

> arise from the preselection of right-thinking people, internalized preconceptions, and the adaptation of personnel to the constraints of ownership, organization, market, and political power. Censorship is largely self-censorship, by reporters and commentators who adjust to the realities of source and media organizational requirements, and by people at higher levels within media organizations who are chosen to implement, and have usually internalized, the constraints imposed by proprietary and other market and governmental centres of power. ... in most cases media leaders do similar things because they see the world through the same lenses, are subject to similar constraints and incentives, and thus feature stories or maintain silence together in tacit collective action and leader-follower behaviour.[73]

Glen Moore and Pamela Grundy employ this theoretical framework in their respective analyses of the press' involvement in the struggle between professional baseball players and club owners in America during the Gilded Age, and the decline of women's basketball in North Carolina in the mid-twentieth century.

Moore argues that prior to the consolidation of the capitalist political economy, newspapers sided with players against owners. But by the end of the nineteenth century this had changed and newspapers ceased advocating on the players' behalf. The shift was part of a drawn out process that began with club owners trying to form a monopoly league, and curtailing players' rights to organise their labour, and the players retaliating. The latter established their own league with fresh backers. However, once the players became part-owners and managers of baseball, they were no longer merely playing according to the codes of a game; they were participating in an economic system with its own 'logic and instinct for survival'. The new backers and player-owners had to protect their investments and this meant accumulating capital and controlling the wage demands of a new generation of players. By the late nineteenth century, baseball reporters recognised that the game, like the press, had been fully drawn into the capitalist system, and that both were now part of the establishment. Such was the strength of the system, writes Moore in tones reminiscent of Herman and Chomsky, that the baseball establishment no longer had to bribe reporters or threaten editors with shutting down their papers: 'sportswriters already knew what to print'.[74]

According to Grundy, the media replaced its support for women's basketball in the interwar years with open criticism and outright hostility after the Second World War. Not only did newspapers such as the *Winston-Salem Journal-Sentinel* sponsor basketball tournaments for women in the 1930s, they described the athletic feats of young women with epic and heroic rhetoric. The Wilmington girls, said one report in the *Wilmington Morning Star*, exhibited the same 'courage as Leonidas in grim Thermopolae pass', while the *Baltimore Afro-American* described 'the fighting femmes' from Fayetteville State Teachers' College laying a 'path of hardwood destruction reminiscent of Sherman's march through Atlanta' on their tour of South Carolina, Georgia and Alabama. But by the 1950s a general belief prevailed that women's basketball threatened the men's game. Amid a controversy over a high school tournament for girls, one columnist in the *Greensboro Daily News* gave prominence to the sentiments expressed by a leading college coach who ' "blamed girls' basketball for causing a lack of interest around North Carolina in boys' play" '. The same paper also praised the state athletic association's decision to introduce cheerleading contests and Tournament Queen beauty pageants to the boys' state competition. Cheerleaders, wrote a *Greensboro* reporter, are a 'vital part' of athletic programmes and they inject ' "school spirit" into the student body'.[75]

Thus, a theory of the press alerts Moore and Grundy to 'patterns of indignant campaigns and suppressions, of shading and emphasis, and of selection of context, premises, and general agenda'[76] that they observe in reports of baseball and women's basketball. Moreover, that same theory provides the two historians with their interpretations, namely, that the press reports served the interests of club-owners and male sport respectively and without rallying the media neither interest group would have achieved its aims (that is, to limit professional baseballers' demands, or sexualise and trivialise female basketballers' athleticism). According to this theory, then, the media is a source of power rather than a (reconstructionist) mine of facts. It is a view also held by deconstructionists who approach newspapers as mediating texts rather than historical sources.

The notion of sport as a mediated text is especially pertinent given that most people experience sport indirectly via the media, principally newspapers, radio and television. Before satellite communications few people directly witnessed sporting competitions; the majority read or listened to a version 'that screened out much of what a player or spectator at the ground would have seen or heard'. Particularly in the case of international events, 'one nation may have seen the contest directly as spectators at the ground, cheering their side on, barracking their opponents, but the other witnessed it only remotely through newspaper articles'.[77]

Graeme Davidson illustrates these points in his discussion of the 'Bodyline' Test cricket series of 1932–3, 'arguably the most serious crisis in British-Australian relations in more than a century'. While the 'contest excited the passions of millions … only a few thousand Australians and a handful of English players, journalists and officials' personally witnessed the action. However, many more Australians experienced and interpreted the crisis through the press. For example, Melbourne's *Sun News Pictorial* covered its front page of 18 January 1933 with photographs of the Australian wicket-keeper Bert Oldfield slumping to the ground after being hit on the head by a bouncing delivery from Harold Larwood. *The Times* of London, by contrast, carried no photographs and only referred to Oldfield being carried from the field (with a suspected fractured skull) three-quarters of the way down a column on the sports pages. 'If Australians became indignant about "Bodyline" while Englishmen remained largely unmoved', Davidson concludes, 'it was because one was looking, figuratively, through an instant camera with a telephoto lens and the other through a wide-angle camera with a long time-lapse.'[78] Thus, 'unlike romance and popular films, which we all read directly', we overwhelmingly read sport 'as already interpreted'; these media texts 'inscribe many assumptions, preconceptions and "commonsense" attitudes, not only about sport but many other aspects of society including place, gender, ethnicity and class'.[79]

While constructionism and deconstructionism both emphasise the role of reporters in mediating between sporting events and their audiences, and examine sportswriting as the 'text of that mediation', deconstructionists stress the notion of the unique voice. Oriard, for example, discerns neither a 'single voice' speaking for entire classes or groups nor a common meaning of football 'emerging from a clearly articulated debate'. Instead, 'multiple narratives' of the game 'reveal an interplay of interests, both within and between identifiable groups, that [are] as often self-contradictory as they [are] opposed to each other'.[80]

It is not too much of an exaggeration to say that sport history rests on newspapers as historical sources. Certainly the accessibility of newspapers has facilitated the growth of the field. But, as we have seen, the epistemological assumptions about, and approaches to newspapers varies widely within the field although it is probably fair to conclude that few sport historians pay enough attention to interrogating newspaper sources.

Oral testimony (and memory)

Oral history, 'the recording and analysis of oral accounts of the past',[81] is an invaluable and compelling research method. As Jennifer Hargreaves shows in her interviews with marginalised women who struggled against 'particularly harsh forms of discrimination' to partake in sport, oral histories are unique in the questioning of informants and in evoking recollections and understandings of individuals and groups largely hidden from documentary sources.[82] Oral history also adds another analytical dimension – the paralinguistic, or non-verbal. During interviews oral historians can read their subjects' body language, expression and tone, which documents and artifacts cannot convey.[83]

Conservative reconstructionists initially opposed attempts to extract evidence from oral communication which they believed distorted and corrupted accounts of the past. Among the litany of problems they identified were the 'orientations, biases and manipulations' of interviewees and interviewers and the peculiar relationships between them, lack of 'clear chronological organisation', 'accretions over time [and] selective adaptations', and the 'vagaries and deficiencies of memory'.[84] Not only did the respective perceptions, predispositions, experiences and social position (class, cultural affiliation, gender, race, age) of the interviewer and interviewee determine the latter's willingness to talk (in some cases insider status assists the historian, in others it is disadvantageous), they clearly affected the questions asked and accounts heard.[85] The tendency of interviewees to engage in 'impression management' – to emphasise or omit aspects of themselves, or play down events or experiences, as a technique to make favourable impressions and control the perceptions of interviewers – also weighed against oral testimony.[86] Timing of the interview not only influences people's willingness to speak – in the thick of battle, before victory or defeat is certain, key actors tend to vanish – but also what is said.[87] Timing, likewise, will determine the informants' ability to recall detail; most observers and participants have better recall in the immediate aftermath of an event or experience, although 'gains in perspective' may offset the inevitable loss of detail that occurs over time.[88] In the words of experienced interviewer, journalist and historian Gideon Haigh, oral historians work with highly fallible 'sets of synapses' that tend to 'scramble the past, jumble things up, conflate and telescope events, screen out the unpleasant, understate or overstate a personal involvement, [and] indulge in *post hoc* rationalisation'.[89]

Jules Tygiel identifies one piece of testimony in Ken Burns' documentary *Baseball* as an example of overstated personal involvement. In the film Buck O'Neil (a Negro League veteran and former manager of the Kansas City Monarchs) describes the team bus pulling into a Southern gas station to fill the tanks and purchase food. According to O'Neil, when the station owner refused to serve the individual players, Jackie Robinson threatened to purchase the gas elsewhere, whereupon the owner, fearful of losing custom, capitulated. Tygiel labels the gas station incident a 'wonderful tale', one that 'demonstrate[s] Robinson's fiery temperament, his refusal to accept discrimination, and his awareness of the chinks in Jim Crow's armor'. He also notes that 'O'Neil's version appears authoritative' and implies that 'he was an eyewitness to these events'. However, O'Neil was in the army in 1945 and 'never played with or managed Robinson on the Monarchs'.[90]

Despite these problems and the continued privileging of documentary sources, oral testimony gradually gained more acceptance within mainstream reconstructionism, especially among those working with illiterate groups for whom oral communication offers one of their few access points to the past. Reconstructionists thus set out to make oral methodology 'rigorous and equal to any documentary historiography'.[91] Early guidebooks peppered oral practitioners with commonsense advice: prepare, adopt 'a neutral and objective presence', listen carefully, refrain from interrupting, allow for pauses and silences, ask open-ended questions, avoid jargon, probing and leading questions, minimise the presence of the tape recorder. But the formalisation of commonsense advice quickly encountered problems. For example, how precisely, do interviewers balance the need for a neutral presence with the recommendation that they establish good rapport with interviewees? Or, how do interviewers reconcile open-ended questioning with opposing advice to control the 'focus and flow of the interview'?[92]

Nonetheless, reconstructionists convinced themselves that they had worked through these issues and declared their ability to unlock even the dimmest memory and to verify their facts (by reinterviewing informants and interviewing multiple informants).[93] Haigh's account of extracting from Tony Greig, the captain of the England cricket team, the story of his involvement in the formation of World Series Cricket, an alternative international cricket competition put together by Australian media magnate Kerry Packer, is a classic illustration of reconstructionist faith in the oral method. Haigh first interviewed Greig 15 years after the cricketer had undermined the very establishment that embraced him. Greig appeared to have forgotten this 'traumatic period' and unlocking his memory became Haigh's goal, a task he eventually achieved with typical reconstructionist zeal. Just before his second interview with Greig, Haigh chanced upon an item in an English newspaper that referred to a *This Is Your Life* programme featuring Greig. Investigation revealed that the date of the programme coincided with the period of special interest to Haigh, the 'day before he flew to Trinidad to recruit the elite of Pakistan and West Indian cricket on behalf of the Packer organisation'. Thus, after talking to Greig

> long enough to loosen [him] up, I ventured to mention the day he'd been ambushed by ITV and saw his life literally flash before his eyes. Making the general inquiry specific did the trick; he remembered it, all too well, and finally dilated on the topic … '.[94]

It is a serendipitous tale but also a partial one: just as reconstructionist historians working in archives omit from their accounts the files they never track down, so oral historians omit the testimonies never told.[95]

Unlike reconstructionists who seek to extract objective truths from oral sources, deconstructionists locate oral testimonies in 'particular cultural practices' that are 'informed by culturally specific systems and relations of communication'. Among deconstructionists, sensitivity to the 'relational and communicative patterns', practices and contexts of particular subcultures, be they based on gender, race and ethnicity, religion, sexuality, disability or age, are paramount. Thus, where reconstructionists advise detachment, deconstructionists consider some degree of subjective involvement in the lives of informants a virtue.[96] Participants in all conversations, irrespective of how one-sided they seem, bring to them their own 'social, psychological, and cultural biases, perceptions and codes', says Jane De Hart. And whether conscious or unconscious, those elements 'may do as much to shape the information forthcoming as the question asked'.[97]

However, it is in the area of memory that the different tenets of reconstructionist and deconstructionist oral testimony most clearly emerge. As Haigh's exchange with cricketer Tony Greig demonstrates, reconstructionists too often promote the idea that interviewees simply retrieve their memories in response to the right questions posed in the right circumstances. Deconstructionists refer to dialogues between interviewers and interviewees that involve considerably 'more than the retrieval of memory'.[98] Among deconstructionists, memory is not a simple act of retrieving facts and information, it is a process of 'creative construction' in which passion, humanity and trope are no less important than fact.[99]

Deconstructionists do not necessarily assign unreliable memory to the problem basket. Irrespective of whether Buck O'Neil was with Jackie Robinson during the incident at the Southern gas station, his account, cited above, informs us of how African Americans understood their collective situation. O'Neil's story illustrates the refusal of African Americans to accept discrimination and their awareness of the pragmatic limitations of white power. Thus, among deconstructionists the apparent reliability of memory is less important than 'how people make sense of their past, how they connect individual experience and its social context, how the past becomes part of the present, and how people use it to interpret their lives and the world around them'.[100] These questions figure in the works of Phil Vasili, Peter Mewett, and Daniel Nathan.[101]

In his biography of Arthur Wharton, Vasili asks why the British public so easily erased from its memory the achievements of an exceptionally talented black sportsman. In addition to being the first black professional soccer player in England (with a senior career that spanned from 1885–1902), Wharton held the first world record for the 100 yards (10 seconds) from 1886–1923. (Among the texts omitting Wharton's name are the 1900–1 and 1901–2 editions of *Football Who's Who*, *Football and How to Play* [1904], the *Book of Football* [1906] and Maurice Golesworthy's *Encyclopaedia of Association Football* [1973], as well as numerous contemporary works dealing specifically with black footballers and sportsmen.) Vasili answers this question by comparing the social contexts of Wharton's achievements with the African American runner Jesse Owens who won four gold medals at the 1936 olympics in Berlin and who remains fixed in the American memory. (Associated Press named Owens its Athlete of the Half-Century in 1950 and in 1976 he received the Presidential Medal of Freedom.)

According to Vasili, social memory always has a political context and, as a black African sportsman in imperial Britain where racist ideas about white superiority and black inferiority prevailed, Wharton's athletic achievements posed too many contradictions that were easier to forget than trumpet. Owens' olympic successes, in contradistinction, 'flowed with the prevailing current of international politics'. An economic and imperial power, Nazi Germany threatened the leading capitalist nations who sought to capitalise on what they recognised as its vulnerability to 'practical refutations' of its racist ideology. Owens' achievements on the track 'publicly denied the nostrums of Nazism', embarrassed the Germans, and 'provided immense propaganda material to the opponents of fascism'. As Vasili concludes, Owens' medals were 'held up to symbolise not so much a victory for ethnic equality – for this could have dangerous repercussions in house and yard – but rather a defeat for a particular variety of racialism as constructed, implemented and propagandised by the Nazis'.[102]

Mewett's analysis of the stories that circulate among Australia's professional runners (see Chapter 4) also introduces critical questions about memory. Mewett argues that the stories professional runners tell each other serve as 'models of how to win' and as 'strategies to combat threats to winning'. They are, he says, 'of necessity, relevant to the present'. In other words, the specific demands of professional running 'structure remembering, affecting, "the *content* as well as the expression of memory"'. Mewett's comments also bring to the fore Paul Ricoeur's ideas about time and its centrality in understanding history (see Chapter 4). 'The oral narratives pertinent to professional running', says Mewett, 'are selected by the ways of doing the sport *now*'.

> Stories that are not relevant to the present are not told; they are not even remembered. Although professional runners have a sense of continuity with what has gone before them, this is not a strict historical continuity in the sense of a sequence of events and happenings. But a sense of the past as a timeless, undifferentiated set of occurrences is important, because this enables those in the sport to legitimate the ways that they construct it in the present.[103]

And last, Mewett's reference to the irrelevance of factual veracity (see Chapter 4), reminds us of the deconstructionist preference for understanding the broad context from which stories emerge rather than trying to establish the truth of every individual story.[104]

Deconstructionists accept that informants will say 'different things at different times'. In one interview in 1962, Helen Liston described her heavyweight boxer son Charles ('Sonny') as a 'good, obedient boy' who as a child 'never gave me any trouble'; in another interview the following year she referred to Sonny as having been 'a rough boy' who liked the 'rough side of life'.[105] These different accounts are not necessarily due to confusion on Liston's part or a faulty memory, but more likely emanate from her own complex and disrupted life and experiences. 'People do not give testimony that fits neatly into chronological or cosmological accounts', explains Luise White. Rather, 'they talk about different things in personal terms; they talk about what happened to them and about what they did about it, but they also use themselves as a context in which to talk about other things as well'. The reconstructionist idea that a person 'would not change [their] mind or words, serves historians not the speaker's own complicated interests' which may include taking into account different audiences.[106]

Thus, deconstructionists view oral evidence as no different to other forms. It is equally relational and fragmented, bound by assumptions, embedded with intent, in need of interpretation, and revealing of the limitations in representations of historical reality.[107] Rather than framing their thoughts around notions of truth as in 'the most accurate kind of information', when people speak they construct stories 'that carry the values and meanings that most forcibly get their points across'.[108] In this sense, oral evidence is 'produced in contentious dialogue', that is, in a process of negotiation and renegotiation that renders absolute notions of truth and falsity obsolete. Hence, rather than following reconstructionism advice to avoid leading questions, deconstructionists propose '"leading" informants and arguing with them'. Only by conducting interviews in such a manner will the historian learn what the informant believes is important enough to defend.[109] The reconstructionist drive to distinguish between true and false stories is, in many instances, not only irrelevant but 'eclipses all the intricate ways in which people use social truths to talk about the past'. As I have shown in several instances in this section, inaccuracies in certain stories are precisely what make them exceptionally reliable: 'their very falseness is what gives them meaning; they are a way of talking that encourages a reassessment of everyday experience to address the workings of power and knowledge'.[110]

Visual materials: films and photographs

An understanding of sport, which is inextricably tied to corporeality and movement, would be nigh impossible without the testimony of images that appear in numerous mediums such as paintings, lithographs, posters, coins and medals, ceramic arts, stone and metal sculptures, photographs and films.[111] Regular reviews of films in the *Journal of Sport History* imply that sport historians take at least some visual materials seriously; however, these practitioners are very much in the minority.[112] Indeed, some are clearly of the opinion that whatever evidence visual images contain, it is overwhelmingly trivial.[113] I begin by looking at reconstructionist and constructionist perspectives on films and then turn to an examination of photographs as evidence in reconstructionist and deconstructionist sport history.

Reconstructionism finds little of evidential quality in film. Among reconstructionists the process of production relegates film firmly into the realm of fiction: 'pictures are worth a thousand words', says Larry Gerlach, 'but not if you want to explain history'.[114] All films involve some level of control in the production process. In pure fiction films, producers control the scripts (before filming), the sets (during filming) and editing (after filming). In standard documentary films, producers may cede control over events in front of the camera but they retain control over recording and editing; even in compilation documentaries, such as those that assemble archival footage, producers maintain editorial control.[115]

This is not to suggest that reconstructionists totally reject film. On the contrary, they acknowledge its power to connect viewers with events and people.[116] Cycling devotee Ray Pascoe's film, *Something to Aim At*, about British olympic medallist Tom Simpson who died in 1967 during the Tour de France, captures something of the cyclist's colour, voice, accent, manners, facial expressions and style of pedalling.[117] Like good historians, master film-makers transport viewers back in time and connect them emotionally with unfamiliar people, viewpoints and events in the past. Gerlach praises Ken Burns in this regard: his documentary *Baseball* 'accomplished what legions of baseball historians have failed to do – impart to millions an appreciation for and understanding of baseball as the national pastime and the ways in which sport is an integral part of American history'.[118] Archival footage of the agitated crowd attending the funeral procession in Tripoli for the five Black September fedayeen killed during the olympic games in Munich graphically illustrates the claim that many Arabs considered the dead men martyrs.[119] Specialist surf-films – produced by surfers for surfers – in the late 1960s and early 1970s conveyed countercultural messages of 'alternative life styles, the taking of psychedelic drugs and letting tomorrow's problems take care of themselves'.[120]

And, of course, historians study film for the way governments, corporations and private individuals employ visual images to exploit, consciously or unconsciously, particular assumptions about society, or promote propagandist messages. Sport history's classic example is *Olympia* (1938). It remains the subject of ongoing debate: was the producer, Leni Riefenstahl, a propagandist for Nazism or simply an artist?[121] Archival footage in 'Sporting Fever', an episode in the television documentary *The People's Century*, illustrates German and American war propaganda featuring heavyweight boxers Max Schmeling and Joe Louis. Both boxers appeared in recruitment advertisements in official films made for the Second World War efforts of their respective countries.[122]

Reconstructionists generally focus on the motives and interests of producers and directors. Interrogating Burns' *Baseball*, Steve Pope finds a film-maker who is 'liberal on social issues', as is 'evident by his abiding concern for civil rights', but who also respects traditional 'American "values" and institutions'. Pope thus situates Burns' histories within the 'consensus historiography of the 1950s and early 1960s that celebrated the vitality of American culture and posited that while different people may have clashed on certain issues, their disagreements ultimately took place within a broader framework of agreement on underlying principles'.[123] But ultimately reconstructionists find an incompatibility in the crafts of history and film-making.

While admitting that some of the factual errors in Burns' *Baseball* stem from 'technical difficulties' (for example, 'a reversed negative shows right-handed Dennis

Eckersley as a left-hander in set position – his name is spelled backwards on the uniform'), Gerlach nonetheless maintains that the 'vast majority of the visual inaccuracies are deliberate', the manifestations of poetic or artistic license.[124] Jules Tygiel concurs. Individually, none of the flaws seem 'terribly significant', he says, but 'collectively they reveal a disturbing pattern of manipulation and distortion which, if present in a literary history of these events would be clearly unacceptable'.[125] Gerlach insists that

> historians can't make up evidence, combine aspects of different events to form a desired happening, or substitute the deeds of one person for another. But Burns does this repeatedly. What troubles me is that Burns insists on referring to himself as an 'historian', calling his film a documentary and dismissing errors as poetic license. Ken Burns is not an historian. He is a filmmaker. He has not produced a photo-documentary history of baseball, but an illustrated history of baseball geared to the sensory imperatives of television entertainment.[126]

Tygiel and Gerlach condemn numerous historical misrepresentations in *Baseball*. With respect to Burns' treatment of Jackie Robinson breaking the colour bar in major league baseball, and particularly the role of Brooklyn Dodger president Branch Rickey in that event, Tygiel finds 'substantial liberties' in 'sequence, facts, and events'. For example, 'when discussing the announcement of Robinson's signing with the Montreal Royals on 23 October 1945, Burns shows a photograph of Rickey signing Robinson to a contract. Rickey, however, was not at the Montreal signing ceremony. Burns' photo, taken several years later, has the advantage of showing Rickey and Robinson together, but has nothing to do with the historical events presented to the viewing audience'.[127] Herein, lies the problem: the film-maker endeavours to tell what actually happened in an artistic manner that appeals to the maximum number of viewers. Invariably, however, the perfect compilation – a smooth montage crafted from many tiny clips – involves 'sleights of hand' which distort the complexities, contradictions and ambiguities of the past.[128]

Do films have any place in reconstructionism? Yes, says Arthur Marwick, but they should 'concentrate on those topics where visual evidence is genuinely significant' and where 'vast amounts of conceptual analysis' and even 'factual narrative', which are best suited to presentation by the 'traditional printed or spoken word', are not needed. However, Marwick stresses that no film is 'self contained' and every film will require some 'verbal analysis and explanation'.[129]

Theorisation plays a critical role in constructionist approaches to films; theory provides the link between evidence and reality. This can be illustrated in an analysis of a surf video, *Runman 69*. Released in 1989, *Runman 69* primarily shows non-professional surfers riding dangerous conditions at less well-known surf breaks in and around Los Angeles. The video is one in a series that constitutes a genre of underground surf films. The images, signs and messages in this genre differ radically from those conveyed by mainstream surf-industry videos.[130]

Evidence of this difference emerges from comparative viewings with scores of surf videos, and press statements heralding their releases. One press release accompanying *Runmental* (another video in the same series) promised a 'below the radar assault on the unsuspecting … homogenized globally cloned surf species'.[131] We probably cannot 'resurrect the sold-out soul of surfing', this particular press release continues, 'but at the very least we will fucking molten lava roast it'. Further evidence of the *Runman* series as a different genre comes from the reaction of mainstream surf culture. Where magazines did publish reviews, comments were typically brief and condemnatory. *Surfer Magazine* said of *Runman 69*, 'there's enough mean, debauched and evil stuff in [the video] to make [us] a little leery about giving it a good review'.[132] Describing *Runmental* as 'the Anti-surf flick', *The Surfer's Journal* likened it to 'a clown at a rodeo, a bad joke at a wedding, or a loud fart at a funeral'.[133]

But if *Runman 69* is part of a different genre, how precisely, does it differ? Cultural insiders will immediately recognise three key differences. First, *Runman 69* celebrates the counterculture soul-surfing riding style of the 1970s, a style characterised by the appearance of effortlessness on the wave. Second, the video scorns the hyperkinetic style associated with professional surfing in which riders aim to perform the maximum number of manoeuvres on each wave. The third difference emerges in the way the surfers in *Runman 69* distribute prestige, what William Goode calls a prime force in human society and Alain de Botton labels 'one of the finest earthly goods'.[134]

Most explanations of prestige conceptualise it within a rational, utilitarian framework. Within this framework prestige is a reward that is accumulated for the purposes of reproducing and conserving human life.[135] But Georges Bataille argued that utilitarian frameworks conceal and distort a fundamental reality. Prestige, he said, is often conferred not by acts of accumulation but through 'unproductive expenditures: luxury, mourning, war, cults, the construction of sumptuary monuments, games, spectacles, arts, [and] perverse sexual activity (i.e. deflected from genital finality) – activities which … have no end beyond themselves'.[136] Bataille advocated that rather than being part of an economy of accumulation, prestige is actually part of an economy of loss where the yardstick is not how much one accumulates but how much one is prepared to lose. The surfers in *Runman 69* illustrate Bataille's economy of loss in their willingness to incur serious injury in their quest for prestige.

Arguably such forms of 'expenditure' operate in all sports. However, mainstream sports manage this expenditure and co-opt it into schemes of utility. For example, untempered excesses and pleasures – violence, gambling, abuse of women – that are obvious in body-contact sports like football, boxing and ice-hockey are typically concealed behind official rules, referees, elaborate scoring systems and, of course, media and educational institutions that discursively recover social utility in sport. The media and educational institutions simultaneously blast all excesses and insist that sport teaches leadership and discipline that participants carry over into competitive, accumulation-based careers. Far from playing this game, the producers of *Runman 69* encourage followers to 'take a crap in someone's pool' and 'ask your boss if you can take his 13-year-old-daughter away for the weekend'.[137] In this context it is hardly surprising that the video received poor reviews.

Thus constructionists, like reconstructionists, interpret films within the prevailing cultural and political contexts, within the circumstances in which the film was produced or commissioned, and within the context of its physical location. However, constructionists also theorise different elements (for example, the distribution of prestige in *Runman 69*). Such theorising frames constructionists' interpretations and their views of reality; among constructionists alternative interpretations derive from misunderstandings, poor contextualisation or, most probably, inappropriate theorisation (for example, utilitarian concepts of prestige).

Plate 5.1 As these two photographs of Polish sprinter Ewa Klobukowska demonstrate, historians have many opportunities to show people (and events) in an array of negative or positive lights.
© Fotopress and © Keystonepress Agency

Deconstructionists essentially see film, like history, as a genre of fiction (see Chapter 4) and are less concerned with the factual errors therein than with the lessons they teach. In this way films mimic stories discussed in the previous section on oral testimony. Thus, commenting on *The Hurricane* (1999), the story of boxer Rubin 'Hurricane' Carter's nineteen-year wrongful imprisonment for a triple homicide, Daniel Nathan notes that despite its 'cartoonish' and 'manipulative qualities', the film conveys important lessons about racism in America.[138] Of particular interest here in the case of visual materials is the deconstructionist perspective that different interpretations of the same images, or indeed the same event, are normal.[139] This view emerges in the following examination of photographs as historical material. Yet, despite their embrace of different interpretations, deconstructionists also tend to frame these differences within theory.

Reconstructionists deem photographs *prima facie* evidence: 'what is in the picture is ... a direct and true rendering of reality as it existed at the moment when the camera shutter was operated'. They define photographs as 'timeless document[s] that, after a minimum of identification, needed no further context, social background or ideological framework to be understood and creatively redeployed'.[140] Sport historians typically employ photographs in this manner. Photographic portraits of players, athletes and administrators,[141] and photographs of sporting equipment,[142] uniforms,[143] spectators,[144] and settings for events and incidents,[145] regularly appear in monographs as visual facts.[146]

Ironically, however, the ease with which photographs translate visual interpretations of cultural patterns or social behaviours and incidents into concrete facts means that they actually require careful corroboration and contextualisation.[147] Cheryl Cole provides a wonderful illustration with two photographs of olympic 100 meters champion Ewa Klobukowska. The first, from *Time* magazine, shows a masculine-looking Klobukowska crossing a finishing line.

Publication of this photograph coincided with news that Klobukowska had just failed a sex test at a European Cup Track and Field event in 1967 and *Time* 'quite clearly' wanted to cast doubt on Klobukowska's sex. The second photograph appeared twenty years later in *New Scientist*. It accompanied an article by Alison Turnbull who painted Klobukowska as a victim of sex testing and shows the athlete in a victory pose with 'extended arms accentuating her [feminine] slenderness'.

Deconstructionists concur with reconstructionists that historians should interrogate the motives of those who produce and publish visual images. However, the former are more sensitive to the different ways that individuals or groups view or receive the same images.[148] These differences lead deconstructionists to see photographs as 'ambiguous texts rather than accurate records of "the truth"'.[149] They talk about photographs passing through mediating filters including the subjectivity of the photographer, the protocols accompanying occasions at which photographs are taken, the different ways different subjects present themselves to cameras, variations in the technical means of producing prints, the public or private domains in which photographs appear, and the ultimate fates of photographs – framed family portrait, book illustration, file in an archive.[150] Sport historians have been slow to explore these issues, although John Bale offers direction in his detailed examinations of photographs depicting *gusimbuka urukiramende* (literally, high jumping) among Tutsi in the early twentieth century.[151]

Among the photographs that Bale deconstructs is one widely reproduced from *In the Heart of Africa* (London, 1910) which shows the Duke of Mecklenburg and his

Plate 5.2 Tutsi *gusimbuka urukiramende.* The ambiguity of photographic evidence: a Tutsi sporting event or European hegemony in Africa?
Courtesy John Bale

adjunct, von Weise, standing between two high jump uprights with a Tutsi jumper passing over their heads to clear, according to Mecklenburg, a height of 2.50 metres.

The 'preferred meaning' of the photographer, says Bale, is unknown, and the actual image can be read in a number of ways: as 'a means of authenticating the expedition' (that is, to demonstrate to the reader that the writer was actually there), as a record of Tutsi achievement in a western sport, or as a 'personal memento of the African visit'. Bale reads the photograph to connote European power. At first glance this interpretation seems odd: the Tutsi jumper – the apparent subject – sails smoothly over the heads of the 'overdressed Duke ... and his militarily uniformed adjunct', and the low position of the camera outlines the athlete 'against the sky' thus 'heightening the dramatic effects of the jump'. Yet, as Bale observes, the high jumper does not assume an unequivocal 'visual primacy' over the two Germans. On the contrary, 'the Europeans command the center even if they are not the subject of the photograph' and their centrality combined with 'upright posture and military uniform' symbolise 'power and control – the condition of European hegemony over Africa'. Realistically, the Europeans may not have been able to compete with the Tutsi jumpers but their presence, posture and style of dress 'communicate to a European audience their *cultural* superiority over the African', and simultaneously 'preserve the essential *difference* (culture/nature) between European and African'. In these senses the photograph represents a 'power asymmetry'. Further confirmation of this relationship emerges from 'the fact that a European *took* or *shot*' the photograph in which the indigene appears as an '"object of information"', never a subject of communication'.[152]

Bale extends his deconstruction to the captions accompanying different publications of the Mecklenburg photograph which he points out typically frame one reading rather than guiding the reader to multiple or alternative meanings. For example, most captions name and individualise the Germans while generalising the African jumper as a Tutsi, a tribesman, a tall native, a fellow and so forth. In so doing, the jumper – whose identity was 'recorded orally by the indigenous culture' – appears merely as 'an object "to be looked at rather than a self-constituting subject"'.[153]

Bale's deconstruction is a perfect example of an innovative and creative use of evidence. While the Mecklenburg photograph yields scant evidence of *gusimbuka urukiramende* per se, it offers precious testimony into a cultural encounter between colonisers and colonised. Of course, such ingenuity requires that historians learn more advanced techniques for reading images than the commonsensical methods of interrogation and corroboration performed by reconstructionists (see Chapter 2). These advanced techniques immerse historians in psychoanalysis, structuralism and semiotics, areas with which many reconstructionists are unfamiliar and uncomfortable.[154]

Psychoanalytical approaches to photographs search for the unconscious symbols and associations in the image that reveal the self's (that is, the photographer's or the reader's) repressed desires that are projected onto others. Structuralist and semiological approaches conceptualise photographs as systems of signs and they direct attention to the 'internal organization' of a particular work and 'especially the binary oppositions between its parts or the various ways in which its elements may echo or invert one another'.[155] Bale's deconstruction of the Mecklenburg photograph inverts the relationship between the athletic high jumpers and the inactive European officials such that the former are read as the (stereotyped – underdressed, displaying animal prowess) subject of the latter's authority and power.

How much confidence can we place in this type of interpretation which clearly also relies on stereotypes of the European colonial master? Historians cannot, of course, psychoanalyse long dead photographers and 'listen to their free associations'. People do project their unconscious fantasies onto images, but it is impossible to justify this approach to the past according to accepted scholarly criteria because the absence of evidence introduces an irreducible speculative element. Likewise, semiology is removed from its social context.[156] As Peter Burke concludes, silences come in many forms – what is not said in oral discourse, blind spots in visual images (what the author does not see), blanks that the image maker unconsciously leaves for the viewer to fill in. The problem for deconstructionists is to ascertain whether the silence is 'conscious or unconscious' and whether the unconscious is repressed in a Freudian sense or simply a taken-for-granted silence of ordinary language. Either way the historian risks drawing 'intolerably reductionist' conclusions that leave 'no place for ambiguities or for human agency'.[157]

A staple of constructionism, theory is also integral to deconstructionist interpretation. While deconstructionists stress that the producers can neither fix the meanings of their materials that may become historical fragments nor determine their reception among subsequent generations, this does not mean that any interpretation is as good as another. Theory, it seems, still separates strong interpretation from weak interpretation in deconstructionism.

Conclusion

Deconstructionism has undoubtedly raised the bar on assessing what historical materials yield in the way of evidence. Sport historians are slowly realising this potential although two obstacles remain. First, there are the fundamentally different assumptions that reconstructionists, constructionists and deconstructionists make about the nature and roles of evidence, and, subsequently, the different ways they handle historical materials. In their search for the truth, reconstructionists pay particular attention to the distortions to which historical materials and evidence are subject; in their drive to unmask power relations, deconstructionists focus on the conditions under which historical knowledge comes into being. These differences are not beyond reconciliation. It requires reconstructionists to acknowledge that historical materials can produce varied and variable interpretations, and deconstructionists to concede that historical materials impose limitations on interpretations. Sport history already appears to be witnessing positive movements in these directions as Ronald Smith's high praise of Michael Oriard's histories of football and Oriard's careful interpretations testify.[158] Second, however, are deeper disagreements about the objectives of history. For some the past should be studied as the domain of those who resided there, for others the past can belong to anyone who claims it and 'infuse[s] it with meaning for those alive today'.[159] While the latter view remains very much the minority position in sport history, the weight of evidence gathered in Part I of *The Field* confirms that few sport historians actually set out to faithfully reconstruct the past for its own sake. The overwhelming majority of practitioners pose questions about the past that interest them, and they approach their questions from quite specific ideological perspectives.

PART II

Explanatory paradigms

HISTORIANS CARRY WITH THEM, whether consciously or not, any number of assumptions about the objectives of history, the means of handling evidence, the truth quotient of facts, the role of theory, and the form of presentation. In Part I of *The Field*, I grouped these assumptions into three models of historical inquiry: reconstructionism, constructionism and deconstructionism. In Part II, I examine these assumptions in the practice of sport history under the banner of explanatory paradigms. David Hackett Fischer describes history as 'a process of *adductive* reasoning' in which practitioners ask open-ended questions about past events and answer those questions with selected evidence. Arranging questions and evidence, he argues, is a complex iterative process, involving constant adjustments, as the historian strives to achieve the best possible fit. This process also yields a range of explanatory paradigms that, in Fischer's words, take various forms, including 'a statistical generalisation, or a narrative, or a causal model, or maybe an analogy. Most commonly it consists not in any one of these components but in a combination of them'.[1] Each chapter in Part II illustrates one explanatory paradigm – advocacy, comparison, causation, social change, context, and new culture – with examples from sport history. While Fischer explicitly identifies the narrative form of presentation as an explanatory paradigm, it is not discussed here (having been assessed, and found epistemologically wanting, in Chapter 4). More to the point, pure narratives are extremely rare in contemporary sport history; most practitioners consciously incorporate arguments (of varying complexity) into their narratives.

All history, says Fischer, is 'articulated in the form of a reasoned argument'.[2] The basis of what is an adversarial discipline, historical arguments come in a plethora of forms. Among the easiest to recognise arguments in sport history are those that attempt to debunk myths. As William Baker reminds us, 'sport, more than most forms of human activity, lends itself to myth-making',[3] and consistent with their desire to establish the truth, many historians of sport consider it their 'prime duty' to 'set the sports record straight, and thus prevent myths from becoming conventional wisdom'.[4] Setting the record straight usually involves two simple historical methods: forensic interrogation of sources, and a cross-examination of those who propagate mythical versions of the past. In Chapter 6 I investigate the efforts of sport historians to debunk three myths – the amateur status of ancient Olympians, Abner Doubleday's invention of baseball and William Webb Ellis' inauguration of rugby. As they set out to put the record straight, these advocates hold on firmly to the basic (reconstructionist) premise that historians can extract objective truths from the remnants of the past. But in revisiting the question of objectivity (introduced in Chapter 2) in the context of debunking sporting myths, I return to the earlier conclusion that all historical arguments contain some level of partisanship and that 'pure' objectivity is unattainable.

Only a minority of arguments sit comfortably in the advocacy paradigm. Some involve non-adversarial explanations, others non-adversarial interpretations. Most historical explanations and interpretations include theories and concepts, and they incorporate entities such as values, intentions, interests and instincts that are not always directly observable in the remnants of the past, let alone documented. While historians typically blur historical explanations and historical interpretations, in *The Field* I distinguish the two on the basis of causal attributes. An historical explanation proffers a cause of some phenomenon, while an interpretation seeks broader understanding and does not specify causes. In Chapters 7, 8 and 9 I analyse arguments of explanation; in Chapters 10 and 11 I investigate arguments of interpretation.

To strengthen their arguments and explanations, historians often make comparisons across time and space, and between similar and dissimilar events, groups and individuals. The simplest, and most common, comparisons in sport history are allusions where the practitioner refers to other cases to highlight points of similarity or dissimilarity; some practitioners, however, advocate highly complex and systematic comparisons as a means to prove causation. I examine the former under the rubric of the comparison paradigm (see Chapter 7) and investigate systematic comparison as part of the causal paradigm (see Chapter 8). Rigorous systematic comparison is a feature of a strand of constructionism that portrays causation as a science with a methodological and explanatory structure similar to, albeit less precise than, the natural sciences. Sport historians have generally shied away from this approach as, indeed, they have from causal explanations in general.

History may be, in the words of Edward Carr, 'a study of causes',[5] but few sport historians consciously engage with causation as an explanatory paradigm. Rather, causality tends to be implicit in the field, appearing in either the temporal sequencing of events in narrative presentations, or in thematic analyses that touch on relationships between agents and phenomena or structures and phenomena. Thus, as well as looking at an example of systematic comparison as a means of establishing causation, I examine causality in narratives and agents and structures as causal factors (see Chapter 8).

The discussion of agents and structures as causes returns us to the agency-structure debate (see Chapter 3), a debate that dominated social history in the 1970s and 1980s. Few sport historians explicitly articulate their positions with respect to the agency-structure debate. But, when it comes to explaining long-term changes in the nature of sport, the overwhelming majority of practitioners implicitly side with structural causation. The problem confronting these historians, however, is the lack of theoretically rigorous and coherent notions of structure and accounts of how structures themselves change. I examine the problems and issues confronting structural change as an explanatory paradigm in Chapter 9.

Two interpretive paradigms prevail in sport history: context (see Chapter 10) and new culture (see Chapter 11). As well as contextualising the remnants of the past and their evidence, historians also contextualise sporting practices, that is, they make connections between these practices and other phenomena as a means to advance understanding of both sport and broader society at different times. Context also demonstrates the social significance of sport and has helped legitimise sport history in the academy. Contextualist sport historians typically work at the intersection of reconstructionism and constructionism. They are generally interested in big picture history and are comfortable incorporating concepts into their interpretations without necessarily feeling compelled to theorise. On the other hand, orthodox reconstructionists and constructionists tend to shy away from context: the former disconcerted by the broad generalisations and lack of primary sources, the latter perturbed by the absence of rigour when dealing with concepts. (Some sport historians are also recognising the need to contextualise themselves in their work; I discuss this move in the Epilogue.)

Under the influence of cultural history, the context paradigm has lost some of its former gloss in sport history. Contemporary practitioners interested in interpretation are increasingly turning to deconstructionist-aligned tools and concepts such as discourse, textualism and narrativism to advance their arguments. These concepts define new culture as an explanatory paradigm.

Although my focus in Part II is on the operational side of each explanatory paradigm, this aspect cannot be divorced from the epistemological content that gives an explanatory paradigm its form. Indeed, each paradigm aligns with a model – advocacy with reconstructionism, social change with constructionism, new culture with deconstructionism, and comparison, causation and context with either reconstructionism, or constructionism, or at the intersection of reconstructionism / constructionism depending on the level of conceptualisation or theorisation.

Chapter 6

Advocacy

Debunking myths

HISTORIANS ARGUE. Historians of sport studying the early modern olympics argue over Edwin Flack and whether he represented Australia or the London Athletic Club at the 1896 games in Athens. They question claims that British athletes competed in the 1904 olympics in St Louis, and they even debate the correct name of the Italian marathoner who was disqualified from the olympic event in 1908.[1] Good historians take inordinate care when constructing their arguments, blending the gathering, examination and interrogation of sources with rigorous logic. The good historian strives to make her or his argument watertight with no loopholes or openings for the ever-present sceptic who, armed with razor-sharp questions, is only too eager to reveal incomplete and inadequate sources, expose weak comparisons, poor context and errors of logic, and, in particular, prove partisanship. Although they steadfastly shy from the term advocate, and its connotations of bias, subjectivity and partisanship, nearly all historians, irrespective of which model they use, engage in advocacy. Indeed, any scholar who constructs an argument is, by definition, a proponent or advocate. In this chapter I follow David Hackett Fischer's concept of an explanatory paradigm and employ the term advocacy in a specific paradigmatic sense. I apply it to those who construct arguments with the sole objective of debunking sporting myths, and who adhere to the reconstructionist epistemological tenet that the truth resides in the remnants of the past.

Myths abound in sport history. While they assume numerous forms, the most well known involve the origins of individual sports, sporting continuities, and conspiracies.[2] As Wray Vamplew reminds us, many reconstructionist historians believe they have a professional responsibility to lay bare myths which they conceptualise as error-ridden partisan tales.[3] I begin by looking at the efforts of a group of advocates to debunk three grand myths: amateurism in the ancient Olympic games, and the origins of both baseball and rugby.

Yet, even as these advocates appear to have categorically proved their cases, fresh doubts must surely arise when we (re)introduce the issue of objectivity and partisanship. (Few practitioners in the field have explicitly embraced qualified objectivity – see Chapter 2.) Reconstructionists maintain that the remnants of the past are, by definition, objective and that these materials impose real limits on partisan interpretations. But the supposed objectivity of sources has not stopped historical arguments or prevented historians from accusing each other of partisanship when handling and interpreting sources. In fact, partisanship is an unavoidable element of all arguments. Later I apply a framework based on two concepts, involvement and detachment, to identify four distinct levels of partisanship among advocates, from the least partisan 'judge' to the unabashed partiality of the 'leading counsellor'. The framework both reinforces the vital role of interpretation and judgment in history and, in the context of mythmaking, it introduces several critical concepts including function, propagation, circulation and contextualisation. The final section investigates these concepts as the foundations of an alternative, constructionist-based approach to myths and examines their social utility.

Setting the record straight

Followers of sport have been fed a steady diet of myths. Among the more popular and enduring are that olympians in the ancient world were amateur athletes, that Abner Doubleday invented baseball, and that William Webb Ellis initiated the distinctive game of rugby. I analyse the respective arguments of David Young, Robert Henderson, Jenny Macrory and Tony Collins who set out to debunk these myths. In accordance with the advocacy paradigm these historians place greatest weight on forensic interrogations of the sources upon which the myths rest and on the motives and interests of the partisan myth-builders.[4]

Amateurism and the ancient olympic games

'The early qualification to contest an Olympian crown was fourfold: racial, social, moral and technical – in that order. He had to be a pure Hellene; innocent of crime; untainted by blasphemy, sacrilege or any impiety; and trained to a degree of physical perfection: a succession of guarantees unknown to modern society and a firm basis for the unshakeable amateur standing demanded by the international Olympic authority today'. These words, from the souvenir programme for the opening ceremony of the 1956 olympics in Melbourne, convey a view, widely accepted for much of the twentieth century, about an ideological continuity between the ancient and modern olympics. According to the anonymous author, 'the conservative controllers' of the ancient games 'obstinately defended' them against any form of commercialism. Indeed, 'it was as much in accord with the Olympic tradition of amateurism as the Greek scorn of commercialism in art that even artists executing statues of the champions were not entitled to payment – some of them were exempted from taxes; this and free meals at the municipal expense were the sum of their emolument'. Happily, this belief about the ancients survives in the modern games, asserted the writer, thanks to Baron Pierre de Coubertin who revived the event. 'De Coubertin's habit was to rake history like a beachcomber. He clearly saw the part the Games had played in the life of the early Greeks and he never ceased to hold before his eyes the vision of such a festival in global terms and its effect upon the assembled youth of the nations of the world'. Hence the modern version is

> restricted, as were those of the ancients, to amateurs. A competitor from the host country, on behalf of all the competitors, takes the Olympic oath of amateurism. The earliest competitors in the modern Games entered themselves and paid their own expenses; only those, therefore, who could find the time and money could possibly compete. The parade of the athletes and the liberation of the flight of doves, the crowning of the victors with an olive wreath – the only award, today represented by an Olympic medal – all these repeated the pattern of the old Games in the new era.[5]

After scouring the sources, David Young reported he could not find a shred of evidence to support the case that the ancient Greeks had a concept even vaguely similar to amateurism:

> I can find no mention of amateurism in Greek sources, no reference to amateur athletes – no evidence that the concept 'amateurism' was even known in antiquity. The truth is that 'amateur' is one thing for which the ancient Greeks never even had a word.[6]

On the contrary, Greek athletics were 'serious business'. They also embraced a warrior ethos that sanctioned levels of aggression and violence totally unacceptable among nineteenth- and twentieth-century amateur sportspeople.[7]

Having interrogated the sources, Young conforms with the most basic rule of historical practice by investigating the interests of those who propose myths and the benefits that they accrue from propagating their versions of the past. As I discussed (in Chapter 2), reconstructionists and constructionists expect that an advocate's frame of reference and/or their 'religious, political, social, economic, racial, national, regional, local, family, personal, and other ties' will 'dictate a predilection or a prejudice' that reveals their partisanship and weakens the credibility of their argument.[8] Edward Carr placed this rule at the fore of historical practice, advising students to 'study the historian before you study the facts'. The wise reader, he said, will ask who the author is and what bees are in her or his bonnet. While reading, the wise person will keep a sharp ear for the inevitable 'buzzing'.[9]

Searching for the source of the myth about ancient amateur olympians, Young identifies a band of second-rate classical scholars (Paul Shorey, John Mahaffy, Percy Gardner, E. Norman Gardiner, H. A. Harris), and a coterie of olympic officials including Caspar Whitney (a member of the International Olympic Committee [IOC] and a president of the United States Olympic Committee [USOC]), Baron Pierre de Coubertin (founder of the modern olympic games), and Avery Brundage (a president of both USOC and the IOC). With the exception of Gardner, whom Young describes as a 'true Victorian Englishman', these men 'adulated' Victorian aristocracy and indeed '*wished* that they were Victorian aristocrats'. They subscribed to a class-exclusive notion of amateur sport and looked to the olympic games as a bastion for, in Whitney's words, the 'more refined elements'. In this context, ancient Greece became a 'precept for the athletic system which they themselves preferred'.[10] Three of these individuals warrant more attention: Gardiner, de Coubertin and Brundage. Gardiner, who stands as the historical 'source of all our gross misconceptions' about sport in ancient Greece, 'made no pretence of disinterested scholarship', says Young. He openly declared that his objective was to 'mold public opinion on the modern athletic controversy'. Although it was only after he formed the IOC that de Coubertin started to 'promulgate his own nonsense about the ancient Greek "amateurs"', the Baron cunningly exploited amateurism as the burning sporting issue of his generation for his own ends. de Coubertin used amateurism as a ruse to bring international sports officials to Paris in 1894 and then enlisted their help to resurrect the games. Brundage, who represented the United States in the decathlon and pentathlon at Stockholm in 1912, fell under the spell of de Coubertin's ideal of olympism and amateurism very early; throughout his career Brundage never tired of praising 'amateurism, fair play and good sportsmanship. For him, as for Coubertin, Olympism became a secular religion'.[11]

Young's interrogation of the sources pertaining to the ancient Olympic games and his investigation of those propagating the amateur version of ancient athletics would appear to demonstrate the virtues of reconstructionism and the advocacy paradigm as being able to set the record straight. However, before drawing a firm conclusion from a limited sample, it behoves us to look at other myths such as those about the origins of baseball and rugby.

Abner Doubleday and the origins of baseball

In 1905, Albert Spalding, the co-founder of the National League and a sporting goods magnate, established a six-member Commission to investigate the origins of baseball. Over the previous decades two explanations of the game's origins had emerged. One declared baseball 'a descendant of English rounders', the other claimed it as 'an entirely American pastime, with its roots nowhere but in American soil'. Challenged to settle the matter once and for all by Henry Chadwick, his colleague in publishing, friend and supporter of the rounders theory, Spalding, a proponent of the home-grown theory, formed the Commission. Presenting its report in 1907, the Commission deduced that 'Base Ball had its origins in the United States' and that 'the first scheme for playing it, according to the best evidence obtainable to date, was devised by Abner Doubleday at Cooperstown, N. Y., in 1839'. Spalding hailed the finding and publicised it in his *America's National Game* (1911). For the next quarter of a century 'text-book writers, sporting writers, [and] historians seemingly fascinated by the august set-up of the Commission, swallowed uncritically the verdict'.[12]

The key source upon which the Spalding Commission based its findings was a letter from Abner Graves. According to the Commission, Graves claimed to have been a 'playmate and fellow pupil of Abner Doubleday at Green's Select School in Cooperstown' and to have been 'present when Doubleday first outlined with a stick in the dirt the present diamond-shaped Base Ball field, including the location of the players in the field'. The Commission also reported that Graves had seen 'a diagram of the field' and a 'memorandum of the rules', both produced by Doubleday.[13] (Until very recently, historians did not have direct access to Graves' letter. They could only read his words in a press statement released by the Spalding Commission. A fire in 1911 destroyed most of the correspondence gathered by the Commission's secretary and historians assumed that Graves' letter had vanished along with the other remnants. In 2001 the National Baseball Hall of Fame and Museum announced that two letters from Graves had been discovered in scrapbooks kept by or on behalf of Spalding. Graves wrote one letter, dated 3 April 1905, to the editor of the *Akron Beacon-Journal* in response to that newspaper reporting Spalding's appeal for recollections of baseball's origins. He sent the second letter directly to Spalding on 17 November 1905 after the latter's request for more information.[14])

Robert Henderson, from the New York Public Library and the official librarian of the Racquet and Tennis Club of New York, examined the Doubleday story in the 1940s. After interrogating the evidence, Henderson found that Doubleday himself made no claims about inventing baseball: his obituary in the *New York Times* (1893) does not mention the game, nor does the memorial volume published by the New York State Monuments Commission.[15] With respect to Graves, Henderson called into question his ability to tell the truth noting that he was an 'old man' of over eighty years and gave his evidence *'sixty-eight years after the events'*.[16] Henderson also discovered a major discrepancy in dates, namely, that 'Doubleday was not in Cooperstown in 1839 ... . He entered West Point Military Academy on September 1st, 1838, and was not in Cooperstown on leave or otherwise in 1839 ...'. As to Graves being present when 'Doubleday first outlined with a stick in the dirt the present diamond-shaped Base Ball field', Henderson observed that the press release contains 'no such statement'. On the contrary, Graves stated elsewhere that 'I do not know, neither is it possible for anyone to know, on what spot the first game was played according to Doubleday's plan'. Nor does any of Graves' correspondence refer to a diagram of the field or a memorandum of rules. Moreover, the press release includes quotations from several people who testified to 'various forms of baseball long before Doubleday'. Yet the Commission 'utterly disregarded' these references to baseball's forerunners. Thus while Henderson conceded that 'Doubleday may have *played* baseball, ... he did not *invent* it. That idea germinated in the senile brain of the ancient Abner Graves'.[17]

Just as Young would later investigate the motives of those who propagated myths about ancient olympians, Henderson sought to identify the beneficiaries, and key propagators, of the Doubleday myth. Henderson's list comprised only Spalding and the Cooperstown Chamber of Commerce. Spalding wanted acclaim, for himself and his business, for 'unravelling the mystery' of baseball's beginnings, while the Cooperstown Chamber of Commerce was only too happy to 'exploit' the 'historical association', purchasing the local Doubleday Field which it developed to include the National Baseball Museum and Hall of Fame.[18]

Henderson's work thus appears to confirm the earlier finding based on Young's work that historians can reveal at least some truths by simply interrogating the sources.[19] Arguments over the origin of rugby offer another opportunity to test the idea that sources contain truths that learned historians can skilfully tease out.

William Webb Ellis and the origins of rugby

In the Headmaster's wall beside the close at Rugby School is a stone tablet. Erected by the Old Rugbeian Society in 1900, the tablet 'commemorates the exploit of William Webb Ellis who with fine disregard for the rules of football as played in his time first took the ball in his arms and ran with it thus originating the distinctive feature of the rugby game. A. D. 1823'. Among rugby fans and administrators, Ellis' initiative is accepted as gospel. Today, nations participating in the quadrennial Rugby Union World Cup compete for the William Webb Ellis trophy. (Before the 1991 World Cup, the Rugby Football Union even re-enacted the 1823 event as a part of its marketing campaign for the tournament.[20])

Historians of sport dismiss as myth the orthodox version of rugby's origins as proposed by the commemorative stone. But a debate has emerged between historians with Eric Dunning and Kenneth Sheard, William Baker, and Tony Collins advocating one account and Jenny Macrory another. Both sides begin with the three sources that support Ellis as the founder of rugby: a letter written in 1880 by an old boy, Matthew Bloxam, and published in *Meteor*, the Rugby School magazine, and two letters written by Thomas Harris to the four-man Committee formed by the Old Rugbeian Society in 1895 to investigate the origins of the game. Harris entered Rugby in 1819, at age seven and left in 1828.[21]

Macrory finds much truth in the Ellis story. She accepts the letters as evidence that in the early 1820s boys at Rugby occasionally ran carrying the ball, whether legitimately or not, and that such acts prompted attempts to stop them. Although Bloxam left the school in 1821, two years before the alleged event, Macrory deems his testimony reliable. First, he 'had no possible reason to invent the story'; Bloxam's objective was merely to 'set the record straight' and to correct the views of a newspaper correspondent who had claimed that the 'Rugby game was of great and unknown antiquity'. Macrory deems Bloxam an indifferent witness (see Chapter 2): the Bloxam 'family knew Ellis well, and they did not like him at all'. Bloxam was 'certainly not attempting to set Ellis up as some kind of hero'. Second, he 'was a thoroughly honest antiquarian with an impeccable reputation for careful, scholarly investigation. He was a lawyer by profession and the author of a meticulous standard work on Gothic Architecture which ran to eleven editions'. Third, Bloxam's source was, in all probability, his younger brother John who had been a contemporary of Ellis at both Rugby and Oxford. Macrory also finds firm evidence of reliability in Harris' testimony. Harris described Ellis as an 'admirable cricketer' and the records confirm that he went on to play for Oxford University.[22]

Macrory argues that Ellis possessed 'drive' and a 'forceful personality', and she believes it is hardly surprising that 'men who were both senior and junior to him at school' would remember him 60 years later 'as something of a cheat who was prepared to take advantage of his seniority to override the rules'. Elaborating on her position, Macrory explains that a period of social flux descended over Rugby School in the early 1820s as enrolments declined. And although his behaviour was '*not* readily acceptable', Ellis exploited his position as 'a praeposter and fine cricketer' to 'do as he pleased', including running with the ball in violation of the rules of the day.[23] Macrory also praises the Committee of the Old Rugbeian Society for its careful examination of the issue and for its sober conclusions:

THIS STONE
COMMEMORATES THE EXPLOIT OF
WILLIAM WEBB ELLIS
WHO WITH A FINE DISREGARD FOR THE RULES OF FOOTBALL
AS PLAYED IN HIS TIME
FIRST TOOK THE BALL IN HIS ARMS AND RAN WITH IT
THUS ORIGINATING THE DISTINCTIVE FEATURE OF
THE RUGBY GAME.
A.D. 1823.

Plate 6.1   The source of the myth of William Webb Ellis? The tablet commemorating the birth of rugby produced by the Old Rugbeian Society.
Courtesy Tim Chandler

> … at some date between 1820 and 1830 the innovation was introduced of running with the ball, and that this was in all probability done in the latter half of 1823 by Mr W. Webb Ellis … . To this we would add that the innovation was regarded as of doubtful legality for some time, and only gradually became accepted as part of the game, but obtained customary status between 1830 and 1840 and was duly legalized first in 1841–2.[24]

Macrory asserts that these 'unsensational' findings by the Old Rugbeian Committee are congruent with its simple motives: to correct a view propounded by Montague Sherman in his history of football published in 1887 that rugby was the lone example of primitive football surviving in a school. In short, the Committee merely wanted to show that rugby was a modern game.[25]

Macrory contends that the myth of the Ellis story resides in two errors committed by the Old Rugbeian Society. The first was its decision to write the history 'literally in a tablet of stone'. As a result, the media and public 'forgot' the Committee's position that carrying the ball was slow to gain acceptance and embraced the '"big bang" story'. The Society committed a second error when it mentioned Ellis by name. Peers regarded Ellis as more of an 'anti-hero' than a 'hero' and this limited the Society's choice of words for the plaque. Settling on 'a fine disregard for the rules' may have been, in Macrory's words, 'a piece of inspired rhetoric', but it also 'made a virtue of [Ellis'] flagrantly irregular behaviour'. Together these two errors 'captured the collective imagination'.[26]

Dunning and Sheard, Baker, and Collins admit that the official rugby story contains 'a kernel of fact' by virtue of Ellis' attendance at Rugby School (1816–25) and his having been a keen footballer.[27] But these historians maintain that the evidence supporting the official history lacks corroboration. The issue, says Collins, is simple: 'no facts can be adduced to support [the] proclamation' on the commemorative plaque. 'Other than in Bloxam's writings, Ellis's name is not mentioned in connection with the rugby game in any work on the subject published before 1895', Collins observes, adding that even the Old Rugbeian Committee 'could not find a single witness who either saw Ellis's act or could provide hearsay evidence of it'. In questioning Bloxam's motives, Collins challenges Macrory's assertion that Ellis' schoolboy peer was an indifferent witness. Bloxam did have an agenda, says Collins: he wanted to 'prove that the Rugby game was … not a variant of older folk football'. Dunning and Sheard also contest Bloxam's reliability. They note that he 'left the school in 1820, i.e. three years prior to the supposed event. His account, therefore, was based on hearsay recalled at a distance of over fifty years'.[28]

The most substantial disagreement between Macrory and the others concerns the motives of Rugby School and the Rugby Football Union in propagating the Ellis story. Dunning *et al.* are much more sensitive than Macrory to both the context (see Chapter 10) and the motives of different actors. In the case of the School, Collins notes that it stopped interschool fixtures in 1876 after a series of losses against opponents that it charged with 'playing non-school-boys'. Rugby only resumed interschool fixtures two decades later. Thus the 'Ellis myth allowed the school to do something it had been unable to do on the playing field: reassert its leading position in public school football over its more successful imitators'. In the case of the Union, Collins argues that the myth served to separate the Rugby game 'from the older traditions of plebeian folk football'. In so doing it created 'a distinct middle-class lineage for the sport at a time when the middle classes in general were seeking to create exclusive recreational havens for themselves outside the prevailing mass sporting culture'. Moreover, the myth 'helped to delegitimise the 1895 split of the Northern Union by seemingly proving that rugby football was indeed the property of the middle classes'.[29]

Thus, while Young and Henderson demonstrate the ability of reconstructionists to convincingly debunk at least some myths by interrogating sources, the debate between Dunning *et al.* and Macrory reminds us of the complexities that can emerge from what at first glance seems like a straightforward historical analysis involving perhaps only a handful of sources. Notwithstanding reconstructionism's abiding confidence in the remnants of the past to speak for themselves,[30] the three case studies above are further evidence of the centrality of judgement and interpretation in historical practice. And judgements and interpretations return us to the thorny question of objectivity.

Advocacy, partisanship and objectivity

History retains an air of judicial practice. 'The objective historian's role is that of a neutral, or disinterested, judge; it must never degenerate into that of advocate or, even worse, propagandist', warns Peter Novick.[31] But can we really expect historians to ignore their predilections, values and subjectivities when they present their arguments? While many contemporary historians subscribe to the notion of qualified objectivity and insist that their personal beliefs and commitments do not 'diminish the value of our historical understanding',[32] the debate over the origins of rugby reminds us that the field remains highly alert to partisanship, the management of which is as pressing as ever. Partisanship is a particular issue in sport history where so many practitioners are fans – Tony Mason calls sport historians 'fans with typewriters'[33] – who celebrate and eulogise sporting prowess and evince an extraordinary faith in sport's contribution to social wellbeing. Not even the influence of social history with its commitment to studying marginalised groups and the past from below has significantly diluted the fan mindset among sport historians. True, many sport historians focus their attention on the sources of discrimination in sport whether they be race, ethnicity, class, gender, sexuality or geography; a few even adopt what might be called interventionist stances.[34] But the majority ultimately conceptualise the marginalised more as victims of corrupt practices emanating from commercial and political interests than from contradictions and tensions within sport.[35] Thus, most sport historians are predisposed towards, in Hayden White's terminology (see Chapter 4), a conservative or liberal ideology.[36]

So, how do sport historians working within the advocacy paradigm manage the partisanship and objectivity issues? Dennis Smith's model of the relationship between involvement and detachment offers one tool to work through this question. Smith defines involvement as the capacity to empathise with and evoke the situation of participants in specific historical situations, and detachment as the capacity to observe processes and relationships objectively, discounting political/moral commitments and emotion-laden responses. These two positions meld to yield four forms of partisanship that, in keeping with the legal airs of the discipline, I have chosen to refer to as expert witness, judge, partisan eye-witness and leading counsellor.[37] While illustrative, the legal terminology should not be taken literally. Evan Whitton, for example, sees important differences between English common law and history. He maintains that the former is 'not interested in the truth' or 'with getting the facts'. Rather, the system is more preoccupied with '"making and observing rules and procedures than exercising judgement"'. These rules are essentially about determining admissible evidence.[38] Historians, of course, treat every remnant of the past as a potential source and only the most conservative of reconstructionists shy from making judgements. The four forms are as follows:

- *Expert witness*: achieves a high degree of detachment, at the expense of involvement. Referring to legal settings, Whitton believes that the predilections of expert witnesses typically lie with their own position or theory.[39] Indeed, the Crown or the defence call their expert witnesses to bolster a specific position.
- *Leading counsellor*: expresses a high degree of involvement, at the expense of detachment. Leading counsellors often 'identify strongly with the interests of the subordinate groups they have researched'. Interestingly, critics observe that in legal settings, leading counsellors are not averse to lying to opponents and will often 'do things for their clients that they would find immoral if they acted similarly for themselves or non-clients'.[40]
- *Partisan eye-witness*: the historian's involvement with a particular (usually political or moral) viewpoint limits her or his capacity for detachment. However, in some instances, partisan eye-witnesses inhibit overt expressions or cultivations of their viewpoint in order to present themselves as detached. In the legal realm, Whitton notes that witnesses typically display an unconscious partisanship towards 'the party who calls them' and that this disposition 'may lead otherwise honest witnesses to conceal some facts and colour others'. Whitton also cites United States lawyer

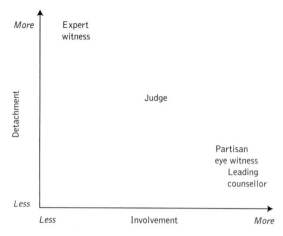

Figure 6.1   Forms of partisanship in historical advocacy

Principal Sources: Dennis Smith, *The Rise of Historical Sociology* (1991), Evan Whitton, *Trial by Voodoo* (1994).

and cross-examination specialist Francis Wellman who argued that the moment witnesses take the stand, 'they instinctively desire to see their side win, although they may be entirely devoid of any other interest in the case whatsoever'.[41]

- *Judge*: by avoiding theory and trying to 'give coherence to as much empirical complexity as possible', judges strive for a creative balance between involvement and detachment, each complementing the other. Of course, it would be naïve to believe that legal practices, including the rules and rituals of the courtroom, could completely restrain and subordinate, let alone eliminate, the personal values and interests of judges.

The four forms are represented schematically in Figure 6.1. Interestingly, Smith does not rank his categories. He associates 'important work' with all four and believes that the healthiest fields and disciplines are those that accommodate all forms of advocacy.[42]

Smith's category of judge is the most conceptually difficult to apply in practice because no judge can claim 'passive observer' status. While many historians have tried to defend objectivity in numerous ways, they invariably fail. Although John Tosh concedes that historians bring to the evidence 'an attitude of mind', he describes this attitude as a fifth sense – which develops over time through a systematic and prudently sceptical engagement with the evidence – and the basis for wise judgements. However, this attitude precludes the operation of definitive principles and rules in historical enquiry,[43] and Tosh logically opens the door for interpretation and partisanship in historical practice and thereby challenges claims to objectivity. A good example of the weaknesses in Tosh's case can be found in the life of C. L. R. James, the native West Indian sportsman, historian, journalist, novelist and political activist. James was raised on a diet of gentlemanly cricket that imbued in him a peculiar ethos and moral code:

> I never cheated, I never appealed for a decision unless I thought the batsman was out, I never argued with the umpire, I never jeered at a defeated opponent,

… . My defeats and disappointments I took as stoically as I could. If I caught myself complaining or making excuses I pulled up. If afterwards I remembered doing it I took an inward decision to try not to do it again. … this code became the moral frame work of my existence. It has never left me.[44]

It was a moral framework that he could never escape and, when confronted by revelations of a scandal in college basketball during his stay in the United States, it became, in the words of *New York Times* sports columnist Robert Lipsyte, a 'blind spot'. James simply 'could not accept … that these athletes were the greedy spawn of an exploitative system' that gave 'teen-aged athletes, often black and poor, sub-minimum wages, ironically called scholarships, that would leave many of them helpless in the job market if they didn't become professional athletes'. James, the 'sophisticated idealist', was simply unable to 'make the complete connection. He could understand why they did what they did, but considered it treachery. He still thought that the school tie was a binding social contract'.[45] It is the classic predicament of all those who hold judicial powers.

It needs noting that Tosh displays an inordinate confidence in the ability of historical practitioners to treat evidence and arguments with scepticism. A hallmark of scholarly inquiry,[46] scepticism demands that advocates prove their cases at every point of the argument, that their logic is impeccable, and that they remove their partisanship. While one finds plenty of scepticism directed at opponents' arguments in the field, advocates rarely apply the same scepticism to their own positions although, as we have seen in the case of James, they typically brim with a heady mixture of faith and partisanship.

Tosh's notion of attitude also alerts us to those historians who insist that the process of securing factual completeness and accuracy is the bedrock of historical practice and more fundamental than conceptually rich and imaginative lines of inquiry, reasoning and argument. These are the very practitioners whose 'concern for detailed accuracy' often 'bur[ies] significance under trivia'.[47] Fischer likens arguments to 'chains of reasoning' and the fact that one link is imperfect does not necessarily mean that all the links are faulty.

> If the argument is a single chain, and one link fails, then the chain itself fails with it. But most historians' arguments are not single chains. They are rather like a kind of chain mail which can fail in some part and still retain its shape and function.

While woe will befall the person who is inside chain mail that fails at a vital point, as Fischer concludes, 'not all points are vital points'.[48] (Theodore Zeldin also issues a pertinent warning here in his reminder that history lost much of its earlier intellectual appeal in the 1920s when it shied from making generalisations and retreated into 'minute scholarship that appealed to only a few specialists'.[49])

In short, the concept of judge is an impossible ideal in history: judges are members of society and carry with them all the values, ideals and beliefs to which they have been exposed and taught. At best, judges can learn their own prejudices and try to limit and restrain them. Smith's notions of detachment and involvement seem to have at least some utility in helping us to position the four advocate historians of sport described earlier. Henderson appears the most detached although he expresses some sympathy for the Cooperstown Chamber of Commerce which acted in 'good faith' when developing the Doubleday Field and the Baseball Museum and Hall of Fame. Debunking Cooperstown as the birthplace of baseball was not, said Henderson, a reason in itself to abandon the site.[50] Indeed, where is the proper place to celebrate the birth of a game that actually evolved over a long period? It may be that the Hall of Fame stands, as Stephen Jay Gould declares, in an 'incongruous and inappropriate locale', but that place still remains, he believes, quite wonderful.[51] An interesting tension emerges here between Henderson's epistemological conservative reconstructionism and the idealism of Gould and Richard Tofel. Cooperstown may hold fast to Abner Doubleday, says Tofel, but it has not inducted him into the Hall of Fame and this fact is sufficient to consign the tale to an 'innocuous conspiracy'.[52] Gould apparently agrees, pointing to the caption on the Doubleday exhibit that he believes 'sets just the right tone: "In the hearts of those who love baseball, he is remembered as the lad in the pasture where the game was invented. Only cynics would need to know more"'.[53] Henderson rejects this position; he demands that these institutions actively teach the truth. Failure to do so, he believes, perpetuates an error that will eventually turn the Museum into an object of 'ridicule'.[54] Of course, Henderson assumes that people only want truths and that the truth must prevail in every circumstance. But if this is so, why do many myths endure long after being debunked by scholars? (I will explore this question in the following section.)

At first glance, Young appears as detached as Henderson, advising readers that he 'sought to minimize any moral judgements ... and to let my subjects speak for themselves'.[55] Yet, following in the footsteps of the fan, Young explicitly links general concerns about truth to his interest in the modern olympics which he describes as 'one of the world's greatest institutions'. According to Young, the olympic movement will not reach its potential as the world's 'greatest hope' unless we understand the truth of its history. Young may stress that this assessment 'scarcely bears' on the content of his work,[56] but his words raise questions about the relationship between idealism and epistemology. As I showed earlier with respect to reconstructionists who conceptualise archives as institutional beacons of truth (see Chapter 5), epistemological assumptions are not necessarily free from idealism and faith.

Of the four advocate historians discussed, Macrory and Collins appear the most overtly involved with their subjects. Both apparently believe that their involvement with rugby, which is prominently advertised on the covers of their texts, adds credibility to their arguments. Macrory is the archivist at Rugby School as indicated on the front cover of *Running With the Ball*; Collins was, as the back-cover of *Rugby's Great Split* describes, 'a barman, bus worker, advertising copywriter and chairperson of the Rugby League Supporters' Association'.[57] If these public pronouncements leave any doubt about their respective sentiments and predilections – historians must be wary of reading individual subjectivities from objective class positions[58] – these surely evaporate in the light of their respective evidence and arguments. Macrory attempts to salvage the involvement of an individual (Ellis) in the origins of rugby, she defends the Old Rugbeian Society and its history Committee, sees no need to place the Society, its Committee or the Rugby Football Union in their broader social contexts, and champions those 'Victorian men who maintained "the fine disregard" for the powerful opposition they faced from the advocates of the dribbling game' (that is, soccer).[59] By contrast, Collins (and Dunning and Sheard, and Baker) contextualise the Old Rugbeian Society and rugby within late-nineteenth-century class relations, and privilege social and economic forces over individuals.

Forensic examinations of historical remnants are a prerequisite of all historical practice. However, reconstructionists working in the advocacy paradigm insist that such examinations define the boundaries of the field and that they are the sole means by which historians discover truths about the past. As noted earlier, in cases dealing with narrowly defined questions or what Fischer calls 'a single chain' (usually involving specific details about an individual or small events or incidents), the forensic examination of historical materials may produce complete and satisfactory answers. However, most historical questions are more complex and incorporate concepts and contexts that exist well outside raw historical materials. Context is a subject rarely discussed by sport historians and is explored more fully later (see Chapter 10). I also introduce it in the next section to help explain why so many sporting myths persist in popular thought despite having been debunked by scholars.

Reconstructionists treat myths as ideologically motivated historical distortions and set out to debunk them by interrogating those sources that they believe sustain them. But even after exposing and publicising fabrications, many historians discover that, much to their chagrin, myths often persist. The typical response in the case of the enduring sporting myth is to blame 'uncritical journalists and gullible fans' for circulating untruths. (Following in the Socratic tradition, in which truth equates to justice, the tendency among reconstructionists is to lament the injustice of the durable myth.) The problem, however, is not so much the credulous journalist or naïve fan, as the narrow definition of myth adopted by reconstructionists. The following section revisits sporting myths through the lens of constructionism which draws on anthropological and sociological concepts and theories to explain why some myths survive 'learned assaults'.[60]

The contexts and functions of sporting myths

David Voigt defines myth as a 'dramatic story' and he identifies a range of functions fulfilled by such stories: justifying a popular institution or custom, explaining a practice or value, expressing a people's wishful thinking and validating present behaviour in terms of what happened in the past.[61] Albert Spalding, for example, appears to have intuitively recognised the power of the Doubleday myth to bolster American nationalism when he submitted Graves' letter to his Committee inquiring into the origins of baseball. 'It certainly appeals to an American's pride', Spalding said, 'to have had the great national game of Base Ball created and named by [Abner Doubleday] a Major General in the United States Army'.[62] Recognising myths as integral to both individual and collective human experiences, James Robertson similarly argues that myths transcend rational analyses that prevent them from simply disappearing: 'just as the analysis of dreams does not make an individual stop dreaming, or indeed deprive him of the effect of a particular dream, so the urge to make myths and the power of particular myths are not destroyed by understanding'.[63]

Voigt links the survival of the Doubleday myth to a general discomfort with uncertainties and random explanations, and to the modern penchant for scientifically precise understandings about the origins of human behaviours.[64] Not surprisingly, given his background as an evolutionary palaeontologist, Stephen Jay Gould offers similar sentiments:

> For some reason ... we are powerfully drawn to the subject of beginnings. We
> yearn to know about origins, and we readily construct myths when we do not
> have data (or we suppress data in favor of legend when a truth strikes us as too
> commonplace). The hankering after an origin myth has always been especially
> strong for the closest subject of all – the human race. But we extend the same
> psychic need to our accomplishments and institutions – and we have origin
> myths and stories for the beginning of hunting, of language, of art, of kindness,
> of war, of boxing, bow ties, and brassieres.[65]

Of course, not all myths reside in the origin category. However, the broader point of
contextualising myths in terms of social needs, interests and priorities is illuminating.
Indeed, Baker describes the Ellis and Doubleday myths as 'period pieces, reflecting
more of the era which gave them birth than of the events to which they referred'.[66]

Here I delve further into the context of myths by examining the works of Brett
Hutchins and Gary Osmond.[67] Hutchins investigates the 'mythical status' of Australian
cricket legend Don Bradman; he is especially interested to know how a cricketer could
survive as the embodiment of Australian nationalism for more than half a century after
retiring from the game. To answer this question, Hutchins looks at the ways that
journalists, politicians, film-makers, writers, biographers, poets, songwriters and cultural
brokers 'figure' Bradman both on and off the field.[68] These agents produce, reproduce,
vigilantly protect and staunchly defend images of Bradman, says Hutchins, and their
efforts provide valuable insights into his cultural significance. Importantly, Hutchins'
concept of the Bradman myth does not refer to false accounts of the cricketer's career
and life, rather it acknowledges that the 'heroic' images of the player are overly simplistic,
unreflective, lacking balance and uncritical.[69]

Under what conditions did the heroic and virtuous images of Bradman come
about and why do they survive? Hutchins proposes three sets of conditions. First, the
positive images and stories of Bradman resonated with prevailing issues and interests;
Bradman the cricketer and man embodied national heroism, signified economic and
social progress, and represented political and masculine landscapes. For example,
Bradman's batting average of 99.94, which far exceeded that of any other cricketer
before or since, 'captured and celebrated the overall mood of social development'.

> Bradman embodied the modernist faith in improvement and progress, which
> is reflected in the mechanistic way that his batting was often understood.
> Descriptions of his batting include: run-machine, automaton, business
> cricketer, adding machine, machinelike, flawless engine, mechanically faultless,
> functional, computer type approach and workmanlike. ... Bradman's choice
> and caution in shot selection conveyed a desire for efficiency by the calculation
> of risk and reward. Bradman symbolised the arrival of a new era, the 'efficient
> age' in which science reigned over the aesthetic and in which the sporting
> body became 'an extension of the technical spirit'. He was a mechanical spirit
> in a mechanical age.[70]

Second, Hutchins argues that Bradman 'exists at the intersection of the material, the
cultural and the symbolic'. This nexus helped 'elevate the Don from mortal cricketer
to mythical hero'. According to Hutchins, the 'continuing production, sale and

consumption of a wide variety of Bradman-related products has become a self-perpetuating cycle that helps to affirm the commercial *and* heroic value of his name and image'. Some might argue that 'the Don's commercial value is a reflection of his heroism: he is famous and historically significant so his heroism is financially lucrative when packaged attractively'. However, Hutchins rejects such reasoning because it ignores the fact that Bradman is 'sold to the public as famous and historically significant'.

> Over the last two decades in particular, a Bradman industry – made up of retailers, memorabilia producers and auctioneers, the Bradman Foundation, and the media, etc. – has emerged that anchors its marketing line on his reputation. In pursuing its own economic objectives, the industry serves to promote, stabilise and perpetuate his heroism and, in the process, ensure the popularity and growing value of Bradmorabilia. In summary, the industry ensures that the Don's symbolic value and his economic value complement and keep pace with one another.[71]

This suggests the operation of a 'two way exchange' whereby 'cultural codes are subject to economic practices, and economic practices are subject to cultural coding'. As Hutchins concludes, 'Bradman's heroism influences the commercial value of his name and image and vice versa'.[72]

Collectively, these two conditions frame a third that further facilitates the survival of the Bradman myth. In short, they act as a barrier to those who might propose a less than celebratory view or 'seek to demythologise' the Don. This 'barrier' comprises institutions (including the media and the memorabilia industry) and people (including the prime minister) who have built a self-perpetuating framework for understanding Bradman's heroism that ensures it 'appears both "natural" and "normal"'. So established, entrenched and sacred is this framework, says Hutchins, that to challenge it is 'considered profane and actually further solidifies the worshipful mindset of the Bradman "true believers"'.[73]

Like Hutchins and other constructionists who look at the social functions of sporting myths, Osmond explores the cultural contexts of myths that reveal 'important themes and tensions in society' and 'disguise vested interests and social struggles'. He investigates the myth in Australian swimming that a young Solomon Islander by the name of Alick Wickham introduced the freestyle 'crawl' stroke in the 1890s. He shows how the Wickham story exposes a racial 'imprint' on white Australia:

> Pacific Islanders were part of a complex web of race relations in Australia. They were often demonised as 'head hunters', 'savages' and 'heathens' and, simultaneously, were positively constructed in terms of physicality, exoticness, and romanticised innocence. The public discourse about Wickham's swimming career and his involvement in the crawl myth reflects the positive social construction of racial identities of Islanders in Australia and reveals the existence of a prominent stereotype about the 'natural' aquatic abilities of Islanders.[74]

Osmond finds a kernel of truth in the Wickham story; the swimmer undoubtedly helped popularise the crawl as a competitive stroke. But the famous Cavill brothers –

Syd, Arthur and Dick – actually developed the crawl before Wickham arrived in Australia.[75] The crawl myth facilitated the accommodation of Wickham within a racial discourse: Sydney's swimming fraternity was more than willing to embrace the non-white 'exoticised Islander' sportsman.[76]

While Pacific Islanders confronted social Darwinian caricatures about their racial inferiority, 'ideas about race were in fact widely disputed rather than rigidly defined; often contradicting, overlapping and converging'. Wickham 'the nimble savage' stands as a classic 'example of racial stereotyping in sport' but, as the champion swimmer, the '"speedy young South Seas Islander", the man who held the world record for fifty yards from 1903–15, challenged the dominant racial discourse' of inferiority.[77]

Unlike reconstructionists who conceptualise myths as historical fallacies ripe for debunking by forensic examination of sources, Voigt, Hutchins and Osmond examine myths as 'tall tales' that perform social 'functions'.[78] Once again, competing ideologies surface here. Whereas Voigt (and Gould) focus on myths as natural tendencies within the human condition, Hutchins and Osmond follow the French social theorist and exponent of semiology Roland Barthes in connecting myths to power structures and vested interests.

Constructionists do, of course, engage in advocacy in the sense of putting forward arguments and defending positions. But, unlike reconstructionists whose arguments tend to revolve around times, places, individuals and incidents (which they seek to validate or affirm by searching the remnants of the past), constructionist arguments generally involve interpretations informed by concepts and theories. Thus, for constructionsts the arguments surrounding a particular myth are less about specific facts and more about trying to understand the very reasons why myths exist.

Conclusion

Through their approach to the past, advocates highlight the indispensability of forensic interrogation of sources in historical practice. Handling the remnants of the past is the one activity that defines all historical practice irrespective of model or paradigm, and advocates make a virtue of this craft. However, history is much more than simply handling the materials of the past or exposing the ideologies of historical practitioners. By emphasising these activities to the exclusion of all others, reconstructionists underestimate the complexity of historical practice. For example, I have shown in this chapter that once a version of the past gains currency it can be exceedingly difficult to dislodge. Indeed, David McGimpsey observes that simply 'revisiting the same legend, even in the hopes of debunking its authority, often ironically reinforces the details of that which was meant to be discredited'.[79]

The following chapters in *The Field* move on to examine more complex forms of historical arguments. These incorporate comparisons, theories and contexts. In each of these chapters we move further away from the remnants of the past and the conservative reconstructionist approach to gathering and interrogating sources as the basis of history. However, as we shall see, none of these approaches guarantee historical truths, nor do they confer a disciplinary unity on the field.

Chapter 7

Comparison

Expanding the evidence

SPORT HISTORIANS ARE FOREVER making comparisons. Whether looking at similar or contrasting cases, they compare the achievements and situations of individuals (Jesse Owens and Jackie Robinson), character, styles and demeanours (Muhammad Ali and Mike Tyson), groups (working classes and middle classes), collective behaviours (tennis crowds and football crowds), cultures (rugby and rugby league), ideologies (socialist and capitalist), institutions (International Olympic Committee and International Rugby Board), nations (Canada and the United States) and eras (feudal and modern). Comparisons help historians understand the nature of sport, its different functions and meanings, the diversity of factors that shape sport and influence participation, and how individuals and groups make sense of sport and use it for their own ends. Showing differences and similarities constitutes evidence in history and, as a method for distilling commonalities and sharpening distinctions between seemingly similar and parallel events and phenomena, comparison has proved invaluable in helping historians to enhance their understanding and improve their classifications and categories.[1] Indeed, the acclaimed scholar of political studies, Samuel Beer, considers comparison one of the more important tools of the historian and ranks it alongside theory as a key mechanism for choosing evidence.[2]

Although scholars use comparison to build evidence across the humanities and the social and natural sciences, the rules of how it can and should be used — for example, in selecting cases and examples to compare, determining the relevance of comparative data and information, verifying the logic of comparative analysis — are not clearly articulated in discussions of historical theory. It seems that the only rules of comparison in history are that cases should be culturally appropriate and they should share a common context.[3] Neither of these rules eliminates the need for judgement, discernment and perspicacity on the part of the historian;[4] the practitioner is the final arbiter of what are appropriate comparisons. But, as I have shown, the decisions historians make are invariably influenced by their own views and cultural dispositions.[5] Nor are these rules sufficient to transform comparison into a method. Indeed, Raymond Grew dismisses the notion of comparison as an historical method. 'There is no comparative method in history', he asserts. Rather, it is 'a kind of attitude' based on questions and searches for answers.[6] Yet, this is how David Hackett Fisher conceptualises his notion of historical paradigms (see above). Here, I identify four distinct types of comparison in sport history: metaphorical allusions, systematic comparisons, post-binary comparisons and scientific comparisons. Collectively they make up the comparative paradigm. Table 7.1 summarises the four types of comparison.

Most comparisons in history take the form of an allusion – to another person, place, event, practice or text. In his history of pistol duelling in late-nineteenth-century Germany, Kevin McAleer alludes to British boxing as a way of illustrating the rigid codes of conduct and peculiar masculinity among the German upper classes.

> Proper German gentlemen harbored a particular distaste for boxing and its two-fisted muscularity, considering it lower class and bestial, a one way ticket to Palookaville. The German duel, on the other hand, was supposedly imbued with a chivalrous patina because it equalized chances between combatants and elevated them above the messy, random, and spontaneous fury of the streets by virtue of its performed rules, which happily also supplied it a unique legal status. But the decisive reason why duelists were so horrified by the sweet science of boxing – though they were unwilling to admit it – was that Gleason's Gym posed a greater threat to dueling's pretentious rigmarole than the most severe penal sanctions. Arrogant Germans could be humbled when leveling challenges across the Channel in Britain. 'In many cases', gloated one critic, 'he immediately receives for his troubles an unpleasantly hard, and unpleasantly sure, fist in the solar plexus'. For the German duelist, aggressive only by rote, swift and real fighting seemed a contingency beyond his spirit's reckoning. Theirs was not a can-do mentality; hidebound duelists were too preoccupied with doing nothing *wrong*. [Renowned proponent of dueling Albert] Von Boguslawski pleaded the case that the Englishman paid special attention to his muscular development, implying that Germans were not physically equipped for the rough work of light sparring. The traditional affiliations signified by the synonymous equation of the word *Boxerei* with the terms *Schlägerei* and *Prügelei* (both meaning a brawl or street fight) died hard. The scrappy English way was wholeheartedly deplored by an old guard of German votaries who had long sworn their allegiance to the Comte de Chatauvillard, not the Marquis of Queensberry. 'Gentleman Jim' Corbett may have been heavyweight champion of the world (1892–97), but for Germans he was certainly no gentleman. The two titles were incompatible in the minds of patrician-nosed duelists.[7]

It is not uncommon in sport history for practitioners to make comparative allusions to the playful, religious, artistic and war-like dimensions of various sports and sporting activities. Many allusions include metaphors to underscore similarities and commonalities in comparative cases, but rarely differences. Indeed, those who use metaphorical language do not usually consider contrary evidence or inconsistencies. Thus, I employ the term 'metaphorical allusion' to single out what amounts to a casual type of comparison that

Table 7.1 Types of comparison in sport history

Type	Objectives and procedures	Limitations
Metaphorical allusion	• Evokes sentiments and conveys impressions • Highlights commonalities	• Metaphorical language leads to one-sided generalisations • Requires judgements • Conflates 'likenesses' with structural similarities / functions / purposes
Systematic	• Enhances arguments, explanations and interpretations • Seeks answers to specific questions / offers limited generalisations • Highlights commonalities and differences • Exposes contradictions / inconsistencies in selected cases	• Requires judgements • Demands access to diverse sources • May require bi- and multi-lingual skills
Post-binary	• Transcends dichotomies and oppositional characteristics of traditional social and cultural relationships / identities • Examines spaces between opposing cultural entities	• Requires judgements • Demands new interpretive theories (semiology, psycho-analysis, poststructuralism)
Scientific	• Seeks universal laws • Provides definitive causal explanations	• Requires judgements • Insensitive to ambiguities and tensions in internal variables

historians use to evoke sentiments and convey impressions rather than systematically build an argument.[8]

The prevalence of allusions in sport history masks a paucity of conscious and systematic comparisons in the field. The difference between a metaphorical allusion and systematic comparison lies in the attention the latter pays to points both of similarity and difference. There are obvious similarities in the splits in Australian and English rugby: both occurred around the same time and both led to breakaway groups forming a new code – rugby league. But looking more closely, Andrew Moore also finds fundamental differences in the two cases. In England the break transpired at the end of a campaign waged by senior members of the Rugby Football Union to rid the organisation of wretched workers from the north who threatened the fabric of their game. While widely portrayed as a strike by working-class players, the famous meeting at the George Hotel in Huddersfield in 1895 was more correctly a response to a lockout. By contrast, the split in antipodean rugby arose from a 'strike by the workers rather than a lockout by the bosses'. The English rugger fraternity may have been keen to see the backs of the proletarians, says Moore, but one finds little evidence of the same levels of antagonism in Australia.[9] Somewhat surprisingly, the number of sport historians who have undertaken this type of systematic comparison with a view to arguing a specific case, or offering an historical explanation or interpretation, is quite small.

More recently, ideas grounded in deconstructionism have added a radical new dimension to comparative work in sport history. Western thought tends to dichotomise natural and social phenomena, describing and defining them in terms of oppositional characteristics and mutually opposed terms.[10] Comparisons of white and black, and male and female, for example, underscore notions of race and gender respectively. Far from being politically neutral, such comparisons fuel 'an insidious way of looking at things' and contribute to the Western penchant for social hierarchies.[11] Comparisons of race and gender in the late nineteenth and early twentieth centuries helped define sport as 'the natural' province of white men, often to the exclusion of black men and all women.[12] The rejection of social hierarchies in deconstructionist thought turned attention towards the intervening spaces or conditions between binary oppositions. In the classic example, the cultural theorist Homi Bhabha looked at instances where English discourses fused with Indian discourses, and vice versa, to generate hybrid discourses that privilege neither one nor the other. Norman Wilson calls these investigations 'symmetrical comparative analyses' which he says 'recognize parallel goals, rather than positing one as first or better'.[13]

Such thinking has seeped into sport studies. Sport sociologists Toni Bruce and Chris Hallinan make the case that popular olympic champion Cathy Freeman, who identifies herself simultaneously as Aboriginal and white, provides an opportunity to combine the distinctive cultures of white and Aboriginal Australia and at least contemplate a new and surprising hybrid amalgamation.[14] Under the term post-binary comparisons, I look at cases where scholars consciously step into the space between seemingly opposing cultural entities to find hybrid and highly complex cultural forms.

The final type of comparison is the scientific. This term refers to an advanced form of systematic comparison that aims to provide definitive causal explanations. Scientific comparisons, a lynchpin of historical sociology,[15] have found little favour with mainstream history and are virtually unheard of in sport history.[16] The only work in the field of which I am aware that comes close to fulfilling the criteria of a scientific comparison is John Hoberman's examination of the Red Cross, the Boy Scout movement, the Esperanto movement, and the Wagnerian and olympic movements. Earlier I looked at Hoberman's 'idealistic internationalisms', a concept he forged from this comparison (Chapter 3).[17] Given the strong causal dimensions of scientific comparisons, I discuss them in Chapter 8.

Metaphorical allusions

C. L. R. James' portrayal of cricket as an art, and George Orwell's description of sport as 'mimic warfare' are prime examples of metaphorical allusions in sport history. While James believed that all sports showed artistic qualities, he felt that these were especially evident in the dramatic qualities of cricket and in the bowling and batting movements of cricketers. The drama in a game of cricket, James claimed, is more intense than in any other sport, and as good as that found in any novel, play or ballet. According to James, cricket's dramatic properties emerge from the structure of a game that pits two individuals against each other in a conflict that is both personal and representative of a social group. By comparison, 'the dramatist, the novelist, the choreographer, must *strive* to make his individual character symbolic of a larger whole'. And, of course, he or she may well fall short. Cricket is also superior to other codes in this respect:

the runner in a relay race must take the plus or minus that his partner or partners give him. The soccer forward and the goalkeeper may at certain rare moments find themselves sole representatives of their sides. Even the baseball batter, who most nearly approaches this particular aspect of cricket, may and often does find himself after a fine hit standing on one of the bases, where he is now dependent upon others.

But in cricket, the batsman who faces the bowler 'does not merely represent his side, [f]or that moment, to all intents and purposes, he is the side'. No other game, James asserted, imposes the relationship between 'the One and the Many, Individual and Social, Individual and Universal, leader and followers, representative and ranks, the part and the whole' on the players in such a deliberate structured manner as in cricket.[18]

James also saw cricket as a visual art, not in the sense of 'the accurate representation of an object', which he set aside as merely a form of reproduction, but as 'a quality that existed in its own right'. Following the art critic Bernhard Berenson, James said that real artistic forms are made up of tactile values and movement. The former refers to the representation of objects in ways that enhance the lives of viewers. In James' words, 'significant form ... sets off physical processes in the spectator which give to him a far greater sense of objective reality ... than would a literal representation, however accurate'. And just as the artist is able to capture tactile values, so too is she or he able to '*extract the significance of movements*'.[19]

James identified batting and bowling actions as the primary sources of tactile values and artistic movement in cricket. He singled out the bowling actions of Maurice Tate and Ray Lindwall as exemplars. The action of the former remains, in the words of John Arlott whom James cites, 'as lovely a piece of movement as ever cricket has produced':

> His run in, eight accelerating and lengthening strides, had a hint of scramble about it at the beginning, but, by the eighth stride and well before his final leap, it seemed as if his limbs were gathered together in one glorious wheeling unity. He hoisted his left arm until it was pointing straight upwards, while his right hand, holding the ball, seemed to counter-poise it at the opposite pole. Meanwhile, his body, edge-wise on to the batsman, had swung its weight back on to the right foot: his back curved so that, from the other end, you might see his head jutting out, as it were, from behind his left arm. Then his bowling arm came over and his body turned; he released the ball at the top of his arm swing, with a full flick of the wrist, and then plunged through, body bending into that earth-tearing, final stride and pulling away to the off side.

Lindwall's action began with 'two walking paces' before 'glid[ing] into the thirteen running strides [that] set the world a model for rhythmic gathering of momentum for speed-giving power'.

> Watching him approach the wicket, Sir Pelham Warner was moved to murmur one word, 'Poetry!' The poetry of motion assumes dramatic overtones in the last couple of strides. A high-lifted left elbow leads Lindwall to the line. The metal plate on his right toe-cap drags through the turf and across the bowling

crease as his prancing left foot thrusts directly ahead of it, to land beyond the popping crease. This side-on stretch brings every ounce of his thirteen stone into play as his muscular body tows his arm over for the final fling that shakes his shirtsleeve out of its fold. In two more strides his wheeling follow-through has taken him well to the side of the pitch.[20]

James' comparison was not only articulate and insightful, it was prophetic given the steadily growing interest in the body shown by sport historians and the field's realisation that bodies 'convey a host of deep-seated cultural beliefs and values'.[21] Yet, ultimately, his comparison is more allusional and metaphorical than systematic and explanatory.[22] The one-sidedness of his comparison becomes immediately apparent when we look at an alternative allusion: war.

'Serious sport', declared George Orwell in 1945 following a tour of Britain by the Moscow Dynamos football team, 'is an unfailing cause of ill-will'; 'it is bound up with hatred, jealousy, boastfulness, disregard of all rules and sadistic pleasure in witnessing violence: in other words it is war minus the shooting'.[23] As evidence for his claim, Orwell cited numerous examples including the 1936 olympic games, a riot at a football match in Spain, incidents of violence between players on the field during the Dynamos tour, and an invasion of a soccer field by spectators at an international football match between India and Burma. In addition, he pointed to the inherent nature of sporting competition. Even if they didn't know from their own observations, it was surely easy enough to deduce that sporting contests 'lead to orgies of hatred', Orwell wrote. By his logic, it could not be otherwise:

> Nearly all the sports practised nowadays are competitive. You play to win, and the game has little meaning unless you do your utmost to win. [W]here you pick up sides and no feeling of local patriotism is involved, it is possible to play simply for the fun and exercise: but as soon as the question of prestige arises, as soon as you feel that you and some larger unity will be disgraced if you lose, the most savage combative instincts are aroused. Anyone who has played even in a school football match knows this.

Orwell may have been in no doubt that sport is 'mimic warfare'[24] but, like James, he did not consider alternative perspectives.

Reflecting on the positions proposed by James and Orwell, an obvious question arises: can sport be simultaneously a form of art and of war? While logically this question supposes at least some form of relationship between the two,[25] for my purpose it highlights the principal deficiency of metaphorical allusions: they can only ever be 'sign[s] of approximation' and are therefore 'indicator[s] of incompleteness and aporias'.[26] Indeed, critics of metaphorical allusions are quick to point to the dissimilarities in the practices or entities being compared. Thus, when analysing the relationship between sport and art, sport and war, or sport and religion, they emphasise the different natures and objectives of the respective practices. Sport and art, wrote Louis Arnaud Reid, are two different categories of human endeavour that merely share certain likenesses – skill, grace, beauty, design, feeling, drama and ritual. But it does not follow that because they share these likenesses that they are one and the same. Skill, for example, 'is not necessarily art, although all art requires skill. The football player is, clearly, not an artist in the same sense as a cellist or the dancer is an artist'.[27] Similarly, it is an overstatement to suggest that all batsman and bowlers are graceful, artistic cricketers.[28] On the contrary, there is no shortage of ungainly bowlers and jerky batsmen, some of who have been immensely successful and achieved great fame. The England and Australian Test cricketer Sammy Woods once described the bowling action of Australian Fred 'Demon' Spofforth as 'all legs, arms and nose'! Derek Birley may have admired the 'highly functional' batting styles of New Zealand great Bert Sutcliffe and Australian legend Don Bradman, but he could not countenance the adjective 'elegant'.[29]

Observing that it is possible to bring an aesthetic attitude to anything – telephone book, slag heap, dirty littered street, battlefield – Reid argues, that 'one has to distinguish carefully between *sporting* intentions and purposes not as such normally aesthetic at all, and the *aesthetic* values which may arise incidentally in the performances of sports'. While aesthetic performance may be the aim in sports such as gymnastics, diving and skating, in most codes it is merely an incidental by-product. And even though it is possible to describe the sporting performance of gymnasts, divers and skaters as artistic, Reid maintained that these sportspeople are still only something of artists. The reason, he said, is because art and sport have different purposes. The objective of the former is aesthetic percipience; the objective of the latter is 'a practical one, to achieve victory in certain ways within a system of strict rules'. Whereas sportspeople play within a defined set of rules, artists do not have to obey rules under the threat of penalty.[30]

Of more historical substance and of greater interest here are the systematic comparisons of the type undertaken by Andrew Moore. As noted above, he uses a comparative approach in his search for an answer to a specific question about the origins of rugby league in Australia. Unlike those practitioners who resort to metaphorical allusions, Moore carefully investigated and weighed up all the evidence, including that which revealed contradictions and inconsistencies in his argument.

Systematic comparisons

Surprisingly few scholars interested in sport have consciously undertaken systematic comparisons. Perhaps this relates to the practical problems (see below) or to perceived associations with historical sociology.[31] One notable exception is Ali Mazrui, the 1979 Reith lecturer and current Chair of the Center for the Study of Islam and Democracy (Washington).

In *The Africans: A Triple Heritage*, Mazrui compares the influences, both positive and negative, of indigenous traditions, Islamic ways and Western tendencies on sport across the continent of Africa. But Mazrui does not treat these three sets of influences as monolithic, uniform forces; he enhances his comparison by looking at contradictions and inconsistencies within each. He analyses traditional African sports in the context of masculinity and initiation into manhood and warrior status. In different parts of the continent, initiation rites involve competitive forms of wrestling and spear-throwing. African culture tends to exclude women from sport. This is somewhat ironic given that women do most of the physical labour in sub-Sahara Africa; they tend crops and often walk long distances to fetch water and firewood that they then carry home. Given their high levels of physicality, why are these women so conspicuously absent from sport?

Mazrui attributes this contradiction to what he calls the 'sexercise gap', the distance between measures of sexual attractiveness and the requirements for fitness. In most African societies 'putting on weight was [traditionally] part of the process of acquiring elegance and poise'. By contrast, 'the demands of athletic prowess require a trimming down ... and a more commensurate balance between weight and height'. As Mazrui concludes, 'the athletics of weight are in conflict with the aesthetics of sex – and the resulting sexercise ratio is wide'.[32]

Several sports flourish in Islamic Africa, including polo in the Islamic Emirates and camel racing in the Horn region. But more generally, Islamic practices militate against sport. First, Islam does not actively encourage 'the arts of relaxation and entertainment'. These survive in the Arab world in spite of, rather than because of, Islam. For example, Islamic education systems devote little place or time to organised leisure. Second, stringent Islamic rules of dress hamper training for, and participation in, sports that sanction and promote exposure of the body. Revealing legs in shorts or wearing swimming costumes in public are forms of nakedness in Islam and violate the moral code of dress. Third, in its opposition to games of chance and making profit through speculation (including rewarding winners of sporting events), Islam effectively reduces the resources available for sports training, the promotion of sport, and the means for attracting new talent and enhancing sport as a social activity. Fourth, by limiting the consumption of food and liquid to non-daylight hours during Ramadhan, Islam reduces energy levels and sporting effectiveness during this month-long period. Fifth, orthodox Islam's code of chivalry protects women from public gaze and deems intermingling with male strangers – which in sport includes players, officials, reporters and spectators – culturally inappropriate. Moreover, by separating women from hard physical labour and confining them to the home, Islam effectively 'encourage[s] a *de facto* fattening of women' that fosters a large sexercise gap among Islamic women. Despite these practices, female athletes and male teams from Tunisia, Morocco and Algeria have achieved international sporting success. Mazrui's explanation is that the Maghreb is 'one of the most secularised and Westernised parts of the Muslim world and therefore among the least affected by traditional Islamic restrictions on sport'.[33] By referring to such exceptions and contradictions, Mazrui captures the essence of systematic comparisons and what distinguishes them from one-sided metaphorical allusions.

The Western influence on sport in Africa varies according to which European power held colonial possession. It is no coincidence, Mazrui argues, that the great African olympians have come disproportionately from former Anglophone rather than Francophone colonies. British colonial administrators placed higher value on sport and physical training in their education systems and the police and armed forces than the French. Class also has a major influence on sporting participation in Africa. Tennis and golf are popular with Westernised middle classes throughout Africa, irrespective of race. In eastern and southern Africa middle-class blacks and whites play rugby, and they are joined in cricket by middle-class Asians. Sporting women in Africa tend to be the Westernised middle classes. With the sexercise gap at its narrowest point in Western culture, middle-class African women do not have to resolve the contradiction between sporting fitness and sexual attractiveness. However, Africa's most popular game is soccer, which is both classless and (with the exception of South Africa) culturally neutral.[34]

Mazrui further pursues his interest in the intersections of class, sex, race and culture with a comparison of 'two significant individuals in the recent history of black people': world heavyweight boxing champion Muhammad Ali, and heavyweight boxing champion of Uganda, soldier and president Idi Amin Dada.[35] In addition to skin colour, gender, physical fearlessness and religious commitment to Islam, Ali and Amin shared a number of other commonalities. Their personalities were, according to Mazrui, similarly 'loud and unpredictable' with both 'constantly playing the buffoon in certain types of public situations'.[36] They also pursued high-risk careers: Amin lived 'a gunshot away from either an assassination or a coup', while every time Muhammad Ali stepped into the ring he risked 'a decisive blow on the chin'.[37]

Early in their careers neither Amin nor Ali held the confidence of their superiors. On his visits to the Royal palace to fight, Amin failed to inspire King Mutesa who thought him 'a comparatively simple, rough character'. Before Cassius Clay/Muhammad Ali won the world title (against Sonny Liston), most observers considered him 'a brash upstart' with moderate skills. Yet, Ali would, in Mazrui's words, 'attain supremacy in boxing with a degree of conclusiveness and skill as unexpected as those which were to be exhibited by soldier Idi Amin in his attainment of supreme political power in Uganda'.[38] Both men were revered abroad by fellow blacks. Many more African Americans hero worshipped Idi Amin than Martin Luther King. The former's 'defiance of Western opinion, his readiness to assert who is boss in Uganda, his mischievous telegrams to mighty leaders of the white world, his rough-and-ready rustic image of the modern African warrior, … fire[d] the imagination of some underprivileged black Americans'. Ali, of course, had 'even more admirers in the African continent' than in the USA.[39]

Just as Mazrui recognises diversity in sporting achievement throughout Africa, with, for example, the Maghreb an enclave of success in North Africa, and Anglophone countries the highest producers of olympic medallists south of the Sahara, so he notes differences between Amin and Ali. While they resented Christian imperialism, Amin was more circumspect in his criticisms compared with Ali, who, 'with fewer political constraints …, was blunter in denouncing Christianity as a white man's religion' and 'more open in declaring his intention to spread the message of Islam to other black people'.[40]

Nor does Mazrui's comparison of the two men stop at their personal traits, attributes and careers. He also compares them in the context of modern technologies of production, destruction and communication. As participants in a brutal labour-intensive sport, boxers Amin and Ali occupied lowly positions in the technology of production, positions commensurate with an international system that allocates sporting opportunities on the basis of socio-economic class.[41] On the other hand, in their primary careers, Ali had a closer relationship with the technology of communication and Amin with the technology of destruction. World championship boxing, such as Ali's title fight against George Foreman in Kinshasa (Zaire/Congo), is 'predicated on instant communication with a large sector of the human race and a capacity to exploit localized drama in a global dimension'.[42] The technology of destruction was as critical to Idi Amin as the technology of communication was to Muhammad Ali. Amin, the career soldier, depended on access to the technology of large-scale destruction, which is more important than control over the means of production in underdeveloped Uganda. It allowed Amin, a member of the relatively small Kakwa ethnic community, to 'establish political pre-eminence over the proud and numerous Baganda' and a further nine million Ugandans.[43]

The rules of Western technology offer Mazrui a final yardstick for comparing Amin and Ali. British training and membership of the King's African Rifles initially constrained Amin's application of destructive technology. But those constraints receded with the withdrawal of the imperial forces from Uganda.

> The phenomenon of men disappearing in the middle of the night, apparently by order of Field Marshall Amin, the phenomenon of decapitation of political opponents, the phenomenon of utilizing a combination of sorcery and technological brutality for the attainment of political ends, have all been a disturbing but real manifestation of the erosion of rules of western technology in a culturally inhospitable environment.

Muhammad Ali, in contradistinction, 'sought to be judged by globally accepted standards' and the rules of boxing.[44]

Summing up the criteria for effective historical comparisons, Grew argues that they are 'most enlightening when the choice of what to compare is made in terms of general and significant problems, the elements compared are clearly distinguished, and attention is paid to the intricate relationships between the elements compared and the particular societies in which they are located'.[45] Mazrui's comparisons meet some of these criteria. He takes care to distinguish between the different elements and to place them in the context of their own societies, which he prefers to the simpler context of universalising grand theories. Indeed, his work produces some unexpected connections between aspects of society usually ignored in broad theories. For example, few theories offer explanations for the diversity of black experiences (especially among women) in Third World sport, or for the different ways that sport intersects with modern technologies. On the other hand, Mazrui's psycho/cultural-profiles of two successful black men, Muhammad Ali and Idi Amin, largely ignores the structural obstacles that limit opportunities and achievements for the overwhelming majority of their race. In the end, we learn little of lasting, let alone predictive value, from this comparison. A more valuable comparison, at least in terms of structural obstacles, would be that between successful female athletes, such as Nawal El Moutawakel (the first woman from an Islamic and an African nation to win an olympic medal and the first ever olympic gold medallist from Morocco) and Wilma Rudolph (the first American woman to capture three gold medals in a single olympics). El Moutawakel and Rudolph both achieved in the face of almost insuperable constraint: Islamic lore and a high sexercise gap in the case of the former, economic poverty, sickness, politics and geography in the case of Rudolph. These women are better illustrations of socio-cultural constraints than the forces that make for a twinning of Muhammad Ali and Idi Amin.[46]

Systematic comparisons have not escaped critical attention. Conservative reconstructionism views comparisons as 'wrong in principle because history is about unique entities and, as a consequence, nothing in the past can be compared with anything else'.[47] Supporters of this model have identified a plethora of practical difficulties associated with comparative approaches. The best historians, they maintain, typically have an expertise in one period, region or theme, all of which shrink as the number of sources increases. Comparative work allegedly violates this 'principle' because it requires historians to gather sources from different regions or across large time spans, and to extend their proficiency in interpretation.[48]

These practical concerns are very much evident in sport history. It is certainly not uncommon to find comparisons based on mismatched categories of primary and secondary sources or, in the case of a comparison of the recreational and sporting pursuits of middle-class women in colonial New Zealand and England, on a single primary source. According to the author of this article, the pioneer culture, with its 'less severe divisions of social class and the relatively spontaneous tenor of community life', afforded women in New Zealand a 'degree of emancipation' in sport and recreation unknown among British women.[49] This may well be true, but what is the evidence for this claim? In the case of New Zealand women, the author makes extensive use of diaries and letters written by women and newspaper accounts. But in the case of English women, the evidence is astonishingly sparse and two key claims are unsupported:

> In the literature that has been written about women during the 'pioneer' period words such as 'strength', 'courage' and 'determination' appear regularly. In Victorian England notions of femininity would not normally have included such characteristics.
>   … the situation in Victorian New Zealand shaped a process of gender socialization where certain women worked with men. The primary sources of information reinforce a picture of an absence of that feeling of antagonism to the environment or to the opposite sex which characterized English society of the day.[50]

In the final analysis, the evidence supporting claims about the restricted lives of English women rests on a single diary entry written by Lady Barker. And she wrote the entry while living on a sheep station in South Canterbury in the late 1860s and early 1870s: 'one's nerves and courage are in very different order out in New Zealand to the low standard which rules for ladies in England, who "live at home in ease!"'[51] Such limited and uncorroborated evidence hardly inspires confidence in the comparative approach.

Proficient interpretations of comparative sources often require advanced levels of cultural and linguistic competence, and too few sport historians are bi- or multi-cultural, let alone bi- or multi-lingual. As well as reducing opportunities for extensive and insightful comparison, this factor can also detract from other types of analysis. Hoberman, for example, attributes the poor understanding of olympic internationalism during the Nazi era to the 'limited number of English-language commentaries'.[52]

Miles Fairburn and John Tosh dismiss outright the grand tenet of reconstructionism that historical instances are unique. 'If taken to its logical conclusion', Fairburn explains, 'the objection would forbid us from using generalising concepts in history such as "social class", "monarchy", "feudalism", "the family", and force us to employ only particular terms, a restriction which would prevent us from talking about almost anything related to the past.'[53] Tosh concurs:

> The very language which historians employ imposes a classification on their material and implies comparisons beyond their immediate field of interest. The only reason why scholars can use the phrase 'feudal tenure' of a particular relationship between lord and tenant, or the word 'revolution' of a major political upheaval, is because they share with their readers a common notion of what those words mean, based on a recognition that the world would be

incomprehensible if we did not all the time subsume particular instances into general categories.[54]

The same is true in sport history. Amateur, professional, working class, middle class and an abundance of other general categories and connotative terms, including sport (Chapter 4), comprise the language that cements the field. Indeed, Norman Wilson reminds us that 'the very concept of "unique" rests on implicit comparison'.[55]

In several cases sport historians have used collaboration to circumvent logistical and resource problems inherent in comparisons. John Nauright and Tim Chandler's edited collection *Making Men: Rugby and Masculine Identity* is a good example. As the initiators and coordinators of the project, they sought explanations for the peculiar forms of manhood and manliness among the upper and middle classes in Victorian societies dominated by liberal political and economic ideals. The contributors provided historical details from different regions, including Northern England, Wales, New Zealand, Natal and New South Wales, and the two editors made the comparisons, and the generalisations, in their introductory and concluding chapters.[56] More about offering interpretations than trying to formally validate universal laws, the real value of this type of comparative work lies in the stimulus that it gives to subsequent research. Indeed, *Making the Rugby World: Race, Gender, Commerce* quickly followed *Making Men*.

Making the Rugby World brought together an even more geographically dispersed set of authors – 'beyond the confines of the predominantly "white old boys" of the British Isles' – in an attempt to understand the adoption, adaptation, incorporation and/or assimilation of rugby among non-European cultures in New Zealand and South Africa, and the expansion of the game into non-British settings such as France, Italy, Japan and the United States. Using this approach, Nauright and Chandler showed that rugby is not a static or monolithic cultural form, nor immune from local or international commercial influences.[57] Conclusions such as these played an important role in alerting historians to the social and cultural complexity of sport and encouraged some in the field to take a closer look at the deficiencies and limitations of traditional binary comparisons.

Post-binary comparisons

The post-binary approach to comparative analysis differs from other comparative approaches in its attempt to transcend the simple dichotomies and oppositional characteristics that mark so many social and cultural forms, relationships and identities in Western thought. Focusing their attention on the complexities and actual lived experiences of different cultures, proponents of post-binary approaches oppose models that promote social hierarchies – superior and inferior, normal and abnormal, worthy and unworthy, chosen and condemned. Rejecting claims that philosophy and science can represent absolute truths, they are especially suspicious of formal definitions – of the sort proposed by James, Orwell and Reid and most prevalent in scientific comparisons – which they say 'obscure the complexities of relationships'. In their recent examination of the relationship between sport and religion, Tara Magdalinski and Tim Chandler advise colleagues against labouring over definitions (of religion) that are often irrelevant to understanding cultural practices and relationships, and are reminiscent of narrowly conceived 'rationalist paradigms that suggest all aspects of culture can be scientifically labelled' and categorised, typically into hierarchical structures.[58] Supporters of post-binary comparative approaches still explore oppositional characteristics, entities, forces and structures. But, whereas earlier generations of practitioners saw only totalising, monolithic and homogenous cultural forms emerging from these relationships, fresh eyes see an array of new cultural forms occupying the fissures, gaps and spaces between oppositional characteristics. The objective of a post-binary comparison, then, is to investigate the openings between oppositional characteristics, entities, forces and structures that both produce new cultural forms and facilitate their reception.[59] I examine works by Grant Farred, James Mills and Paul Dimeo, and John Hughson as examples of this approach.

Farred investigates the identities of soccer players from the Cape Flats Coloured townships during apartheid. Although these players appropriated the names, colours and playing styles of English professional clubs, their actions were not simple mimicry. On the contrary, these players demonstrated a highly complex – and often disguised – form of agency in which they negotiated between idealised notions of Europe and the real conditions of everyday life in the townships.[60] Through this negotiation they create their unique identities. While conceding that some clubs on the Cape Flats were little more than English 'cultural derivatives', with members making only minimal and superficial adjustments to their identities, Farred cites the Everton Amateur Football Club of Heideveld as an example of one club that successfully unshackled township football from the English model to achieve cultural autonomy.[61] Like their brethren at Merseyside, the players at Everton of Heideveld have a loose affiliation with the Anglican Church, wear blue and white, and base their game on a combination of ball skills and defence. Yet, the distinctive offensive bravado and defensive discipline of the Cape Flats amateurs effectively gave a new meaning to Everton, removing all connotations of Merseyside and transforming it into an independent township soccer team:

> On the playing fields of the Cape Flats, 'Everton' evoked only one identity – the local one, because Everton AFC played a brand of football that was not only different from their English namesake, but one that was more highly regarded than the metropolitan model. The Cape Flats amateurs succeeded in wrestling 'Everton' from the county of Lancashire, unmooring it culturally, and then re-inventing it. Everton AFC made Everton FC a Merseyside institution that was not so much unrecognisable as 'undesirable' – Heideveld boys wanted to play like 'their' Everton, not the English model.[62]

Thus, rather than seeing one brand of football as superior or inferior to another, or as a mimic of another, Farred moves beyond traditional forms of comparison and examines the specific conditions on the Cape Flats that produced an entirely new brand with a commensurate and distinct local cultural identity.

In their analysis of the sporting body and corporeal politics in colonial India, Mills and Dimeo also move the comparative approach forward to show that football was neither a simple agent of colonisation nor a site of pure resistance. Unlike earlier generations of scholars who hailed colonial sport as a relatively benign agent of socialisation, or who discovered it as a site of resistance to colonial power and authority, Mills and Dimeo walk between these polar positions. They highlight the simultaneous oppositional and complicit tendencies in football and the complex nature of relationships in and around the game. Their classic example concerns the victory of the Mohun Bagan district football club in the 1911 Indian Football Association Challenge Shield. On their way to victory, Mohun Bagan defeated St Xavier's, Rangers, the Rifle Brigade, the First Middlesex Regiment and, in the final, the British East Yorkshire Regiment. The Indian press celebrated the 2–1 victory in the final as a thorough refutation of British stereotypes that cast Indians as physically inferior. Here Mills and Dimeo cite an editorial from *Nayak*:

> Indians can hold their own against Englishmen in every walk of art and science, in every learned profession, and in the higher grades of the public service . . . . It only remained for Indians to beat Englishmen in that peculiarly English sport, the football. It fills every Indian with joy to learn of the victory of the Mohun Bagan team over English soldiers in the Challenge Shield competition. It fills every Indian with joy and pride to know that rice-eating, malaria-ridden, barefooted Bengalis have got the better of beef-eating, Herculean, booted John Bull in the peculiarly English sport. Never before was there witnessed such universal demonstration of joy, men and women alike sharing it and demonstrating it by showering of flowers, embraces, shouts, whoops, screams and even dances.

Mohun Bagan's success amounted to 'a moment of nationalist triumph' and a 'dramatic and public undoing' of colonial stereotypes about British athletic superiority and Indian effeteness. Yet, as Mills and Dimeo point out, the act of celebration also endorsed British lores that enshrined sporting victories and demonstrations of physical prowess as the truest markers of 'strength and self-reliance', and the body as the proper 'site for judging a people and its destiny'. Hence, Mohun Bagan's victory was simultaneously 'a victory for the bodies of the Bengali team and the people they represented' and 'an acceptance of the legitimation of the discourses of strength and self-discipline that underlay the body politics introduced by the British Raj'.[63] Hence, in their (post-binary) analysis of the sporting body in early-twentieth-century Indian football, Mills and Dimeo show a cultural identity weaving between contradictory positions and opposing tendencies.

In the last example of a post-binary comparison, Hughson examines what he calls the hybrid identity of the Bad Blue Boys (BBB) – a 'neo-tribe' of young Australian men born of Croatian parentage who support Sydney United (formerly Sydney Croatia) soccer club. By blending the old and new and the sacred and the profane, the BBB have forged a highly complex new identity out of their Croatianness. While under constant pressure from the culture of their parents – to marry a Croatian bride, to extend their duty to family relatives and to attend church – members of the BBB do not 'rebel against these potentially coercive aspects of community'. Instead, they 'incorporate them into their neo-tribal culture':

> They do this by amplifying the obligatory aspects of their ethnographic background so that endogamy, family loyalty and religiosity become collective character traits that distinguish the BBB from other Australian age cohorts. Each of these traits is performed via a hypermasculinity – liaisons with non-Croatian

women are regarded as sexual conquests, female family members are to be protected from would-be suitors of non-Croatian background, and religion is used as a means of vilification in public settings such as the soccer stadium.[64]

It is at the soccer stadium, particularly Edensor Park, the home ground of Sydney United, that the BBB 'simultaneously express the sacred and the profane' aspects of their identity. On the one hand, the stadium is a 'sacred place', a 'place [to] worship … the hard toil of Croatian people'. On the other hand, it is a site of profanity. On match days the BBB unashamedly taunt opposition spectators with songs and chants loaded with racism, misogyny and homophobia, and with Nazi-type salutes that symbolically allude to fascism.[65] For Hughson, the hybrid identity of the BBB is a 'loose construction of mixed "cultural elements" put together by individuals in a strategic manner to create new and unexpected meanings'. Most importantly, Hughson sees the BBB as replacing all notions of necessary, essential, absolute and fixed forms of identity with provisional and contingent interpretations.[66] In this way, he too moves beyond traditional forms of comparison.

Irrespective of their success in transcending traditional hierarchical concepts of identity, practitioners engaging in post-binary comparisons do not totally remove Western notions of oppositional characteristics from their analyses of identity. Indeed, the idea of identity seems inescapably shackled to binomialism. As Magdalinski and Chandler note, religious communities use a range of strategies – initiation rites, defined dogmas, prescribed moralities, authoritative teachings, texts and traditions, social structures, organised authority structures – to maintain their differences and to separate themselves from other religions and communities. In their words, 'the production of boundaries between "them" and "us" is crucial to the formation of collective identities' that always depend on locating themselves in relation to others. 'Communities function by establishing who they are *not*, as much as who they *are*'.[67] In short, these forms of differentiation fully retain the threads of comparison, most obviously from the standpoint of the subject. This is particularly evident in the works of Farred, Mills and Dimeo, and Hughson, and raises further thorny questions about relativism and judgement.

Hughson's work on the BBB offers insights into these issues and helps clarify the deconstructionist position. Hughson admits that the traditions to which the BBB subscribe invoke a 'simplistic evocation' and that members appear engaged in a quest to recover a lost peasant community. While conceding that some might view such a collective social persona with scorn or pity, he prefers 'to suspend judgement and to view the BBB as a group of collective social actors who construct a meaningful and relevant identity from the cultural resources they have available to them'.[68] Hughson defends this position on the grounds that it is consistent with contemporary social science which distinguishes between acceptable moral judgements and unacceptable moralising. In this case, to judge members of the BBB by anything other than their own standards is to practise unacceptable moralising. Critics will no doubt charge Hughson with romanticising the BBB and with ethical relativism – of trying to explain away, rather than explain, the less savoury behaviours and attitudes of the BBB. However, such charges would misconstrue his position. In keeping with deconstructionist sentiment, Hughson is not advocating a general position about anti-social behaviour, racism or misogyny among alienated youth. Rather his questions and answers are specific to the BBB and are consciously devoid of abstraction.[69]

Conclusion

Any notion of history as the study of entirely unique events is an illusion. All history involves a comparative dimension – whether implicit or explicit. Sport historians use comparative approaches for a wide variety of reasons. Most simply employ the approach to enhance the evidential quality of an historical interpretation. By comparing German pistol duellists with British boxers, McAleer was able to paint a clearer picture of the former. Similarly, Mazrui used a comparative approach to understand the soul of a continent torn three ways, while Nauright and Chandler sought to develop a greater understanding of the nature of masculinity. Moore compared the origins of rugby league in Australia and England in order to debunk orthodox rugby history. The 'unchallenged mantra' of this history attributes the birth of the antipodean game to 'a heroic response by the battlers, albeit a politically muted one, to the "tyrannies of the Establishment"' and conceives of it as 'a project for promoting "humanitarianism" and "democracy" in sport'.[70] In contradistinction, Hoberman's objective was explicitly political:

> if we are interested in establishing the potential of idealistic internationalisms, then the value of the comparative method lies in establishing realistic parameters of action (and even imagination) over the long term. If we ask, for example, whether the Olympic movement has done what it should have been able to do in fulfilment of its professional aims, what we are really asking is whether it has performed on a par with analogous organizations in comparable historical conditions.[71]

Somewhat surprisingly, few sport historians have used comparisons with the explicit intention of producing causal explanations, although one can discern embryonic elements of causation in *Making Men* and *Making the Rugby World*. The very titles of these two texts imply causation. Moore's piece has a more explicit causal objective. He locates the origin of rugby league in the Eastern states of Australia in, first, 'ties of kinship, allegiance and culture' based on the movement of convicts and assisted migrants between the north of England and New South Wales and Queensland, and, second, local factors. Analysing the latter, Moore notes that 'rugby league emerged from a period when the working class was recovering from the defeats of the 1890s and reasserting itself industrially and politically. The debate about professionalism was part of this broader working-class challenge, a contribution to the project of civilising capitalism, as was the taking of the parliamentary road in the formation of the Australian Labor Party'.[72] Moore makes a major contribution to debunking orthodox rugby history. However, his references to Wales and New Zealand alert us to another type of comparison, one capable of generating universal laws about the class foundations of sport. I will compare the origins of rugby league in different countries in the next chapter as an example of scientific causation and as part of a broader investigation into causation in history.

Chapter 8

Causation

Explaining determinants in sport

ONE OF THE PARADOXES OF HISTORIOGRAPHY is that while historians repeatedly engage with causal reasoning and causal relationships, few consciously offer causal explanations. As Thomas Haskell observes, 'historians are not shy about assigning responsibility or imputing the causal status upon which responsibility rests'. Indeed, they 'routinely bestow praise and assign blame; they talk incessantly about change and presume that acts have consequences; they tell stories showing how one thing leads to another, how things came into being and go out of being'. Yet despite this 'deep preoccupation with relations between particular causes and effects', professional historians 'seldom display any interest in causation per se'.[1] While this disinterest may raise questions about the need for a detailed exploration of causation in history, I believe three factors make such an examination prudent. First, the temporal sequencing of events in narrative presentations implies causation (see Chapter 4), but whether these relationships are truly causal requires further inspection. Second, some strands of constructionism advocate causation as the ultimate paradigm of historical proof, although this remains very much a minority position in the discipline. For its disciples, causation constitutes a science with a methodological and explanatory structure similar to, albeit less precise than, the natural sciences. While I am not aware of any sport historians adopting this position, the fact that it is grounded in systematic comparison opens the door to a potentially rich method, and one that warrants at least some investigation.[2] Third, notions of causation, irrespective of whether they are incorporated into a history implicitly or explicitly, situate practitioners in the debate over whether agents or structures are the prime determinants of social outcomes. Broadly speaking, reconstructionist-leaning historians emphasise individuals, groups and organisations as causal agents who act in pursuit of their goals. Constructionists, in contradistinction, focus on the social and collective worlds of customs and laws which they hold rule, shape, order and structure (in other words, cause) social outcomes. Even though the agency-structure debate, which dominated social history in the 1970s and 1980s, has receded over the last decade, it maintains a presence in the discipline and merits consideration.[3]

Each of these three factors has influenced both the epistemology and thematic content of sport history. However, before discussing these factors, we should look at what makes causation a major issue in history.

A contentious and problematic paradigm

Philosophers and practitioners of history have long seen causation through one of two lenses. E. J. Tapp deemed causation to be the 'great central pillar' of historical thought, while Thomas Haskell placed causal reason at the centre of 'the explanatory schemes on which historians ... rely'; Eric Hobsbawm said that questions of the sort 'why [was] situation A followed by situation B and not C [or] D' are fundamental to history. Edward Carr most famously declared history 'a study of causes'.[4] To others, causation is an unwelcome visitor to history. Michael Oakeshott believed that causation invaded history and brought with it darkness rather than light and chaos rather than order; Theodore Zeldin called causation a 'merciless tyrant', akin to chronology. John Vincent urged practitioners to cast aside cause which he said constricts historical thought, while Geoffrey Barraclough opposed historians' fixation with causes that can only be speculated upon and that are irrelevant when compared with consequences that stay with us.[5]

Amid these general complaints and opposition, some substantive objections to causal analysis emerge. Observing that causality is always determined retrospectively, the French philosopher of history and sociologist, Raymond Aron, said that causal relations are, by definition, historical probabilities rather than past truths, to which he added, 'as for the probability born of the partial character of historical analyses and of causal relations, it exists in our minds, not in things'.[6] In a similar vein, Vincent commented that historians choose their causes from an infinite range of possibilities and that deciding on 'the cause of an event ... is a matter of almost arbitrary choice'.[7] Carr offered what has become perhaps the classic statement of this view in his example of Robinson, a pedestrian killed crossing a road late at night. At first glance the cause of death seems straightforward, even beyond contestation: Robinson died after a car, driven by Jones, knocked him down. But as Carr showed, the cause was not necessarily so obvious; any one of several causal explanations was possible. Although Jones was intoxicated, the brakes of his vehicle were defective despite an overhaul just a week earlier, and Robinson crossed the road at a blind corner that both he and local road authorities knew had notoriously poor visibility. Carr also wanted to know why Robinson crossed the road that night. In reporting that Robinson was on his way to buy cigarettes, Carr opened the door to putting at least some causal responsibility/blame on the pedestrian: Robinson's inability to control his nicotine habit meant that he placed himself at undue risk by crossing the road at an inappropriate time and place.[8]

Most objections to causation arise from historians who believe that the assumptions and methods of causal analysis emanate from the natural sciences and the 'fallacious quest for general social laws'.[9] Haskell attributes to Carl Hempel the widespread view that explaining an event means constructing it as a manifestation of law-like regularities.[10] But, in practice most historians, especially those working in reconstructionism and deconstructionism, inquire into the causes of single events – like the deaths of cyclist Tom Simpson or boxer Sonny Liston (see Chapter 4) – rather than trawling the remnants of the past to propose general causal laws, such as, for example, one which could provide an explanation for all fatalities in all sports which is obviously a flawed endeavour.

Moreover, the majority of historians are 'tentative and diffident' about drawing causal, particularly monocausal, conclusions.[11] With respect to the latter, the preference is for gradations of probable and plausible explanations rather than categorical causal attributions.[12] Rather than saying *a* caused *b*, historians typically invoke synonyms; they tell their readers that *a* led to *b*, or that *a* gave rise to, brought about, made, provided, produced, created or influenced *b*, or that *b* was due to, resulted from, or conditioned by *a*.[13] For example, in his narrative of sport in industrial America, Steven Riess informs us that urbanisation and technical innovation 'dramatically shaped' sport, that rapid urbanisation 'influenced' sport, that concerns over health 'led to' the public health movement, that changing spatial patterns accompanying urbanisation 'impacted upon' athletic participation, that sports journalism helped 'generate' popular interest in sport, that the railroad and trolley cars 'facilitated' sport, that electric lighting had an 'impact on' indoor sport, and that industrialisation 'influenced' the manufacture of cheap sporting goods.[14] While the presumption of causation is evident, the language is diluted and implies that the causal explanation is but a proposal, and perhaps one amongst many.

Many of the problems associated with causal explanations stem from ambiguous and vague causal questions that afford an infinite variety of answers. Consider the question, what caused English and Australian players to abandon rugby and to form a new code, rugby league, in the late nineteenth and early twentieth centuries? Unless they are fully alert to the specific context of the question, historians can offer any number of causal-type answers, all of which may be correct. They might emphasise the purposes, desires, weaknesses and abilities of individual players; they might refer to the political interests and strategies of different groups or alliances such as the working or middle classes, or they might discuss the causes in terms of economic, social or ideological trends and shifts.[15] Interestingly, Patrick Gardiner attributes much of the vagueness associated with causal questions to the very 'looseness' of concepts for which explanations are sought.[16] Robert Paddick illustrated Gardiner's claim in an essay on amateur sport in Australia. The very concept of amateurism, Paddick argued, is extremely difficult to construct because the conservative rhetoric spouted by amateur sports administrators frequently sat at odds with their often quite pragmatic solutions to conflicts involving professional practices. Moreover, in the late nineteenth century the concept of amateurism was treated as commonsensical. (Commonsense, according to Haskell, exists as a tacit ideology that leaves unsaid many of its assumptions about needs, opportunities, conventions and experiences.[17]) In Paddick's words, many of the issues associated with amateurism involved 'complex sets of moral, educational, psychological and social values' that proponents simply left unstated.[18] In short, certain concepts, especially those that carry large doses of commonsense, actually hinder the precise identification of causes.

The upshot of all this is that 'there is no such thing as *the* cause, and no cause for all occasions'. Rather, as Fischer explains, 'there are many different kinds of causal explanation' and each kind has 'different requirements and different uses. The specific kind of causal explanation a historian employs must be selected according to the nature of the object of the explanation'.[19]

Unlike natural scientists, historians cannot isolate one historical factor from all others to test its significance. In the great mix of potential causes for virtually every event, bygone and present, it is very easy for the unwary, and even the experienced, historian to draw causal conclusions from non-causal correlations, or to simply assume that succeeding events are necessarily consequences of earlier events. Causal relationships involve elements of necessity while 'correlations are often mere coincidences that do not indicate any significant connection, or any reason for expecting such correlation to continue'.[20] Of course, observations of correlations between events may suggest, or lead to the discovery of, causal relations.

Ben Rader believes that Allen Guttmann mistakes a correlation for a causal relationship in *From Ritual to Record*, although he admits that 'inconsistent and ambiguous' terminology makes it impossible to make this conclusion with absolute certainty. According to Rader, Guttmann identifies several dependent variables – including Protestant religious affiliation, membership of the upper middle class, adolescence and male sexuality – which all share a positive correlation with participation in contemporary sport. Guttmann then finds the independent variable in the correlation between Protestantism and participation in sports that he says 'disguises the fundamental causal relationship between these two dependent variables and the independent variable which acts upon them'. In Guttmann's words, the 'basic explanatory factor is the scientific world-view ... an empirical, experimental, mathematical *Weltanschauung*'.[21]

Rader lodges three objections to Guttmann's claim that the *Weltanschauung* caused modern sport.[22] First, Guttmann misrepresents the position of sociologist Robert Merton. Guttmann's independent variable derives from Merton who accepted that Protestants were highly receptive to the new science of the seventeenth century and certainly more open than Catholics. But Merton 'emphatically demurred' from any claim that Protestantism caused the new science. Rader believes that Guttmann ignores this latter point.[23] Second, Rader does not find Guttmann's supporting evidence persuasive. Gutmann's 'observation that both important mathematical discoveries and the beginning of the concern for quantification in sports occurred in the eighteenth century' could, Rader suggests, be a 'parallel historical development' or simply amount to a 'cultural transfer of interest in mathematics to sports'. Third, Guttmann's empirical evidence is too scant. It includes the claim that 'French Catholicism in Canada has had a long standing "parochial antagonism" toward the "modern world"', and a couple of survey findings, one that 'theology majors at two Swiss universities have less involvement in sports than natural or social science majors', and another that 'majors in the humanities at Amherst College participate less frequently in sports than either social or natural science majors'. Such evidence, Rader concludes, can at best, only 'suggest correlations not causal relationships'.[24]

Guttmann's predicament is hardly unique. Faced with these issues and problems, advocates of causation have tended to distinguish between what they call necessary and sufficient causes. Richard Evans defines a necessary cause as one where 'if A had not happened, then B could not have happened', and a sufficient cause as one where 'A happening was enough to make B happen'. Evans further divides the necessary category into absolute causes ('if A had not happened, then B *definitely* could not have happened') and relative causes ('if A had not happened then B *probably* could not have happened').[25] Neil Tranter distinguishes between necessary and sufficient causes in his explanation of women's participation in competitive sport. The necessary cause, he says, was a concern about the physical fitness of upper- and middle-class women and their ability to produce healthy offspring in a climate of social anxiety and tension, precipitated by working-class militancy and Social Darwinism. In addition, Tranter identifies four sufficient causes for competitive female sport: a new conceptualisation of femininity that sanctioned displays of overt physicality among women; a belief that participation in sport would produce loyal, rational-thinking, resourceful, determined and good humoured women who would set new standards of morality and behaviour for successful middle-class family life; a recognition that genteel sports (for example, archery, croquet, lawn tennis and golf) facilitated social contact between the sexes; and an incipient feminist movement that endorsed mildly competitive sport.[26]

However, it is not immediately clear what the distinction between necessary and sufficient causes achieves. Referring to his experience of analysing the causes of a major cholera epidemic in Hamburg in 1892, Evans says that he identified a dozen causes in his source material. But in a quite remarkable admission – and one that certainly vindicates Hayden White's views about history as a literary creation (see Chapter 4) – Evans describes experimenting and moving his text around. Here he emphasises not the analysis of evidence to single out *the* cause but a literary construction that 'generate[s] a growing sense of suspense and excitement in the reader as we come closer and closer to the narrative of the epidemic itself'.[27] Leaving to one side the literary dimension of Evans' causal narrative, his account reaffirms that the distinction between necessary and sufficient causes does not eliminate the need for judgement. Indeed, where Tranter, for example, labels the feminist movement a sufficient cause, other sport historians (see below) consider it a necessary cause.

Causal reasoning and causal relationships are ubiquitous in sport history. Nowhere are they more evident than in narrative presentations where the temporal sequencing of events provides a framework of, and indeed reliance on, causal relationships. But whether this temporal sequencing amounts to a true casual relationship is the subject of intense debate.

Narrative and causation

The very structure of narrative, the dominant form of presentation in reconstructionism, implies causal relations: in the Robinson example, the pedestrian died after being hit by a car, an act which appears to be the immediate cause.[28] For some philosophers of history, such relations constitute an example of the fallacy of *post hoc ergo propter hoc*, that succeeding events are necessarily consequences of earlier events.[29] For others, causal relations are integral elements of narrative; I noted earlier that the establishment of causal linkages between events is one of Kenneth Gergen's six criteria for an 'intelligible' or 'well-formed' narrative (see Chapter 4).[30] Indeed, I illustrated this criterion citing Eric Dunning and Kenneth Sheard's narrative of the struggle between middle-class supporters of amateurism and working-class advocates for professionalism within the Rugby Football Union at the end of the nineteenth century. Dunning and Sheard's chronological ordering of events – the working-class Yorkshire Union's proposal to compensate players for *bona fide* loss of time, the rugby establishment's attempts to alert amateurs to the threat posed by the Yorkshire men's proposal, the establishment's counter motion at the general meeting, the vote at the general meeting and the decisive constitutional amendment at a subsequent special general meeting – imply not only interconnection but causality. Historians have long commended narrative presentations for their ability to capture relationships between human actions and outcomes especially in times of crisis and drama when developments often occur in several spheres simultaneously. Narratives are also well suited to the incorporation of contingent causes, '"the recognition that at numerous critical points during [an event] things might have gone altogether differently"'.[31] (The issue of contingent causation is discussed more fully below under the heading 'Agents as causes').

But whether narratives convey true causal relationships is hotly debated. Morris Cohen believed that causal relationships may always involve a temporal sequence but causality is 'more than mere succession in time'.[32] Haskell asserts that narrative is a form of causal thinking, arguing that the logic of narrative 'derives not merely from sequence – one thing after another – but also from productivity':

> Beginnings do not merely precede middles and ends; they prepare them, produce them. At every stage of an effective narrative account the reader must be informed of that, without which, the next stage or scene would not follow. If the reader is to accept narrative's generic claim to constitute a unity that extends through time, connecting events that occurred at different moments, certain needs must be met. Those needs have much to do with causal relevance and they must be met not just section by section (beginning, middle, end) but paragraph by paragraph and sentence by sentence.

Continuing along this line of reasoning, Haskell writes that 'narratives seek to persuade us that at a particular past, present and future are so densely interrelated that they can best be comprehended as a unity'. Elaborating on this point, he insists that

> It won't do to report what happened at T_1, T_2, T_3, T_4. The reader must learn what it was about the event at T_1 that helped *cause* the one at T_2 (or, as the case may be, produce it, bring it about, pave the way for it, conduce to its occurrence, remove obstacles to its happening).[33]

However, Haskell, is also equivocal. In fact it soon becomes clear that his criteria for causation in narrative are not absolute.

Ultimately, 'what is needed', Haskell says, 'is not a rigid chain of cause-and-effect relationships of the necessitarian variety, such that each event mandates the occurrence of the next, like so many falling dominoes lined up in a row'. Rather,

> narrative supplies … a much looser sequence of stage-setting observations, such that the reader who knows what happened at T_1 will respond to what happens at T_2 with a tacit nod of understanding, rather than a scowl of befuddlement. 'Yes,' the reader must think, 'given what went before, and given all the contrariety of human motivation and the cunning of fate, that is one possible/likely outcome'. It is not predictability that is signified by this nod of

understanding, but plausibility – no small thing in a world as short on truth and certainty as ours.[34]

Of course, from the epistemological position of constructionism, any attempt to render the 'infinitely branching tree of causal sequences' as a unified historical entity, looks decidedly odd.[35]

As I noted earlier, Arthur Stinchcombe heartily praises those historians who embed rich detail in their narratives (see Chapter 3). He also believes that the causal structure in most narratives, particularly those that summarise long sweeps of history and that purport to capture the motors of a society's operation, are more literary artefact and illusionary than explanatory. Stinchcombe identifies two verbal conjuring tricks at work here. The first, which he labels 'causal analysis by naming', involves the use of portentous terms to create the illusion that things have particular substance.[36] For example, historians interested in the development of modern sport frequently incorporate notions of bureaucratisation into the process.[37] The insinuation in this term is that whatever sports officials do derives from the historical position of the bureaucrat whose prime interests and focus are the standardisation of rules (and, in the case of sport, the measurement of athletic performance). But sport historians who discuss the bureaucratisation of sport rarely analyse the behaviours of specific sports officials or their work. Where practitioners do investigate, as Paddick did, they invariably confront a host of contradictions and ambiguities that render the generalisation inoperable. The second conjuring trick, says Stinchcombe, seizes advantage of the literary fact that the starting point of a narrative always appears as the prime cause, and that the end always concludes in some kind of culmination or conclusion. More often than not, however, historians do not carefully connect the causally relevant evidence in the body of the text with either the introduction or the conclusion. Thus, 'causes become apparently exogenous by appearing in thin analyses at the beginnings and endings' whose only links to the historical evidence in the course of the narrative appear in portentous terms.[38]

Morris Cohen also recognised these sorts of problems but, like Haskell, he believed that the nature of the discipline warranted a different set of rules for causal explications. History, said Cohen, pressures narrators to tell coherent stories and does not afford them the luxury to stop and indicate every so often that their evidence is in fact inadequate or inconclusive. Thus, most historians compromise by adopting less stringent conceptions of causality.[39] Such positions are, of course, an anathema in constructionism. Stinchcombe's solution is to unshackle narrative from what he calls 'its naïve epistemological moorings', that is from the tones in its language that imply a causal theory. To this end he proposes breaking the unique sequences of historical narratives into 'theoretically understandable bits' and, after subjecting them to theoretical interpretation, reinserting them. Stinchcombe's process of theoretical interpretation, introduced in Chapter 3, involves looking for analogies and comparative examples to construct concepts and general ideas that are relevant at each stage of the narrative (as distinct from grounding the narrative sequence as a whole in general ideas which he says merely leads to 'flaccid … notions with little capacity for illumination').[40] Similarly, Edward Carr proposed distinguishing between major and minor causes of an event where the major cause either bears semblance to a covering law or can be generalised across different cases and examples. Building on this tradition, I investigate a scientific method of causation formulated by Theda Skocpol, and test it on a case study of the emergence and development of professional rugby in England and Australia. While I am not aware of any sport historian applying such a scientific approach to causation, it does, I believe, offer a potentially valuable causal method worthy of closer attention in the field.

The 'science' of causation

In her *magnum opus*, *States and Social Revolutions*, Theda Skocpol proposes a precise method of causation. Her method involves two procedures: analysing cases of agreement and cases of disagreement. In her words:

> First, one can try to establish that several cases having in common the phenomenon one is trying to explain also have a common set of causal factors, although they vary in other ways that might have seemed causally relevant. Second, one can contrast the cases in which the phenomenon to be explained and the hypothesised causes are both absent, but which are otherwise as similar as possible to the positive cases.[41]

One sporting question that appears ripe to test Skocpol's method of agreement and disagreement is why did professional rugby emerge and prosper in England and Australia around the turn of the twentieth century?

As a starting point let me restate Skocpol's approach using information extracted from the history of rugby as propounded by Andrew Moore (see Chapter 7). With respect to the method of agreement, the objective is to test the hypothesis that irreconcilable class-based differences over the meaning of rugby explain the development of professional rugby in Australia and England, notwithstanding the fact that there were key differences in the two schisms that might prove causally relevant (for example, what Moore calls a 'lock-out' in England as opposed to a 'strike' in Australia). With respect to the method of disagreement, the objective is to 'highlight by negation the significance of this cause', that is, class-based differences of meaning.[42] New Zealand, Wales and South Africa offer a potential set of comparative cases that are reasonably similar but sufficiently different to the situation in Australia and England. South Africa did not support professional rugby while professionally based competitions in Wales and New Zealand were weak. If these so-called negative cases do not contain the same outcome (for example, vibrant professional rugby) then the result reinforces the conclusions of the method of agreement. As Miles Fairburn explains, 'the hypothesised causes in the positive cases *must have produced the outcomes, since the negative cases contained neither the same outcomes nor the same postulated causes but were similar in every other respect*'.[43]

Like the orthodox explanations, Moore identifies class tensions as a cause of the schism in rugby in England and Australia. What he adds, however, is greater clarity to the nature of those class tensions. Rather than discussing them in terms of predetermined hostilities based on abstract economic interests, Moore examines class tensions in the context of ideological differences over the meaning of rugby: amateurs played rugby solely for pleasure and physical health, professionals played for material gains. Local conditions meant that those differences were more intense in England than in Australia. Extending the comparison and examining instances of negation (that is, employing the method of difference), sharpens our understanding of why viable professional rugby competitions emerged in England and Australia but not elsewhere. Class tensions were also present in New Zealand, Wales and South Africa[44] but attempts to form alternative professional rugby competitions were either short-lived and essentially ineffective (Wales and New Zealand) or never eventuated (South Africa). Why? Were rugby authorities in those countries able to successfully reconcile the amateur and professional meanings of sport? Certainly not! Rather what they did do was deflect and partially ameliorate class differences in sport by defining rugby as a nationalist project. In so doing they nullified potential working-class defectors.

In a climate of 'growing working-class belligerence' following a series of unfavourable decisions handed down by the Arbitration Court, Albert Baskerville, a Wellington postal worker, organised a team of New Zealand rugby players to tour England and Australia as professionals in 1907–8. The New Zealand Rugby Football Union (NZRFU), an affiliate of the Rugby Football Union in England, immediately expelled the architect of the professional game in New Zealand. Although the tour proceeded and professional rugby gained a 'foothold' in New Zealand, rugby league remained financially impoverished. Even as early as 1907–8 NZRFU, with support from the press, had assigned the mantle of New Zealand's national game to rugby and many New Zealanders viewed it as means of nurturing imperial patriotism. 'Football is the national game of New Zealand', proclaimed the *New Zealand Herald*, 'and the fame that New Zealand has won in it all over the world is worth guarding and should not be risked in any way'.[45]

A similar situation prevailed in Wales. Rugby became an expression of Welsh nationalism although the Welsh, too, tolerated a degree of professionalism 'in order to accommodate working men'. One area of difference between New Zealand and Wales concerned the way national interests conceptualised rugby historically. In the former, rugby was a modern game for an emerging nation while 'the Welsh industrial bourgeoisie promoted an indigenous Welsh culture by connecting the distinctive aspects of contemporary Wales (particularly rugby), to a distant … Celtic past'.[46]

Racial interests largely overrode class interests and shaped nationalist sporting projects in South Africa in the early twentieth century. In Natal, for example, race determined which football code local inhabitants played. In 1907, when Africans formed a soccer association, whites, 'particularly those of the upper classes, … abandon[ed] the round for the oval ball'. White workers in Durban initially continued to play soccer but within a few years rugby had emerged as 'the emblem for the province's white sporting prospects'.[47] Rugby's appeal among Afrikaners was largely limited to the sons of the elite who attended Victoria College, later Stellenbosch University, in the Western Cape. Rugby provided the university with a 'specific Afrikaner identity to counter that of the neighbouring and predominantly English-speaking University of Cape Town'. In the Boer republics the game was virtually unknown at the turn of the century and in Johannesburg 'working Afrikaners had little leisure time for organized sport'. Political union in 1910 united the former British colonies and Boer republics under one flag and a central government. The governing South African Rugby Board might have excluded blacks but it viewed the game as a vehicle for 'promoting understanding' between Afrikaners and English-speakers and nurturing a 'white "South Africanism" [that] could ultimately act in the interest of "the higher scheme of imperial unity"'.[48]

These details add up to support for the causal argument that professional rugby stemmed in the first instance from irreconcilable class-based differences over the meaning of sport. But a strong working class capable of supporting an alternative concept of the game was a prerequisite for the materialisation of those differences. Skocpol's method of difference confirms the significance of these interacting causes. In New Zealand, Wales and South Africa smaller and weaker working class movements found themselves easily distracted and hence co-opted by nationalist sporting ideals propagated by the middle classes. Ultimately, they were unable to effect their class-based sporting aspirations.

Skocpol's method has, of course, been subjected to rigorous cross-examination and attracted a number of criticisms (over and above those directed at the simpler and more common comparative methods – see Chapter 7). Internal diversity within Australia and England raises questions about the validity of generalisations pertaining to the schism in rugby. Why, for example, was professional rugby largely confined to Lancashire, Yorkshire and Cheshire in England, and Sydney and Newcastle in Australia? To what extent did behaviour in those regions represent the whole country? Complete answers probably require further comparisons with soccer and Australian football respectively. Suffice to say, professionalism emerged in soccer and Australian football with minimal opposition from amateur ideologues.[49] And perhaps there are less differences between the positive cases and the cases of negation than first appears. Did the ethos of rugby in New Zealand, Wales and South Africa really conform to English ideals? Did New Zealanders, Welsh and English-speaking South Africans really play the game according to the Christian amateur ethos of English public school boys? Evidence from New Zealand and South Africa suggests not. 'New Zealanders, with their peculiarly pragmatic and unsentimental approach to rugby,' argues Finlay Macdonald, 'often found more in common with the [English] men of the north, whose working lives ... more clearly matched their own'.[50] Although scant, the evidence from South Africa implies that conditions there were similar to New Zealand; certainly in the 1920s and 1930s Afrikaners introduced a particularly aggressive nationalistic ethos to the amateur game in South Africa akin to the professional version in England and Australia.[51]

These questions are a salient reminder of the difficult task historians face when searching for sustainable causal generalisations. For Skocpol,

> even when the cases are roughly approximate, perfect controls for all potentially relevant variables can never be achieved. Thus, strategic guesses have to be made about what causes are actually likely to be operative – that is, which ones could, or could not actually affect the object of study. The upshot is that there always are unexamined contextual features of the historical cases that interact with the causes being explicitly examined in ways the comparative historical analysis either does not reveal, or must simply assume to be irrelevant.[52]

In the same vein, 'comparative historical analysis necessarily assumes (like any multivariate logic) that the units being compared are independent of one another. But actually, this assumption is rarely if ever fully valid for macro-phenomena ... . [T]hese phenomena occur in unique world-historical contexts ..., and they happen within international structures that tie societies to one another'.[53] Indeed, international 'ties of kinship, allegiance and culture' lie at the heart of Andrew Moore's argument: the cultural and political specificities of Yorkshire and Lancashire had a general influence on Australian society (for example, a penchant for fish and chips!) as well as specific regional influences, particularly in 'the epicentres of labour militancy' in New South Wales and Queensland, where Labor Party branches and professional rugby gained early strongholds.[54]

Finally, it bears repeating that narrative and scientific approaches to causation occupy minority positions in sport history. Among those practitioners who employ thematic approaches to present the past and who engage with causality, the antecedents of effects or consequences usually reside in one of two categories: rational thinking and motivated agents, or structures. In very general terms, reconstructionist-leaning practitioners tend to concentrate on agents (individuals, groups and organisations), their goals and the means by which they produce outcomes or bring about ends. Constructionist-leaning practitioners, on the other hand, more commonly focus on the collective worlds of customs and laws that are held to rule, shape, order and structure agents' objectives, interests and goals.[55]

Agents as causes

Historians who offer rational and/or motivated agents as the antecedents of causal explanations make a number of assumptions about those agents; they also typically examine very specific types of events and actions. Before looking at the latter, we need to briefly revisit the assumptions that underpin the concept of agency among mostly reconstructionist-leaning practitioners.

Earlier I noted that reconstructionism views agents as autonomous free-thinking beings who act according to their values and beliefs in pursuit of their objectives, interests and goals (see Chapter 3). Historians who emphasise agents as the antecedents of effects and consequences generally assume that those actors' objectives, interests and goals constitute the mental causes of action.[56] In the words of R. G. Collingwood, 'that which is "caused" is the free and deliberate act of a conscious and responsible agent, and causing him to do it means affording him a motive for doing it'.[57] Thus in trying to identify the cause of a past event, such as the protests by Tommie Smith and John Carlos on the victory podium at the 1968 olympic games in Mexico City, the taking of Israeli athletes as hostages at the olympic games in Munich, or the boycott of the 1976 olympics in Montreal by African nations, sport historians search the remnants of the past for utterances and other evidence that might reveal the motivations, goals and intentions of those directly involved. However, it is no easy task to ascertain and prove motives (see also Chapter 5). Christopher Lloyd is correct when he says that 'actors can be deluded, can deliberately lie, or even can be genuinely unconscious of certain mental antecedents of action', and that they 'always give selective, partial, context-dependent, accounts of their motives'. Thus, historians need to remain aware that reasons cited as motives for action can easily 'mislead as to the real situation'.[58] There is no better demonstration of all these points in sport history than in Douglas Hartmann's insightful analysis of the protests by Smith and Carlos in Mexico City. As he reminds us, there is no evidence that 'Smith and Carlos consciously planned the demonstration symbolic-detail-by-symbolic-detail', nor that they 'would be able to situate it in a comprehensive analytical context'. Rather, their action was based more on a deep tacit *'understanding* of the sociological elements of Olympic ritual and the potential for political expression also made possible by what was simply taken for granted and by what was left out altogether'.[59]

Constructionism generally dismisses rational and/or motivational antecedents of effects and consequences as superficial. But recalling Fischer's advice, cited above, to select causal explanations according to the 'nature of the effect to be explained and the nature of the object of the explanation', quite clearly there are instances where rational and/or motivational antecedents are relevant and legitimate. Explanations involving clearly stated political objectives that seek to cast blame, or entail contingencies, are obvious examples.

Human beings who engage in deliberate and voluntary action to achieve specific outcomes can bring about effects and consequences and these rational and motivational antecedents do have a place in causal explanations, as Herbert Hart and Tony Honoré insist.[60] Sport historians have shown individuals acting to improve human performances by designing new forms of technology (including drugs),[61] and others acting to gain access to competition, facilities and resources by waging political campaigns. Indeed, it is no coincidence that we often refer to human beings pursuing political causes. Women, for example, have long taken action 'to transcend practical and symbolic forms of oppression' in sport.[62] The literature, especially that dealing with the 1920s and 1930s, is rich with examples of such agency. Pamela Grundy recounts several instances of women in North Carolina taking political action to play sport. In 1920, shortly after 'the Nineteenth Amendment wrote women's suffrage into the U.S. Constitution, a group of young women at Charlotte's Central High School banded together and headed toward the principal's office'. They wanted to play basketball and they wanted the school to afford them the same opportunities it gave boys.[63] Susan Cahn cites the case of Madam J. H. Caldwell who placed a 'wanted' notice in the *Chicago Defender* for 'Ladies to Play Ball'. 'Women are voting now, so why not be able to play a real game of baseball?', the advertisement queried.[64] Allen Guttmann refers to the political actions of Amelia Earhart and Alice Milliat. The most famous female pilot of her time (and the first woman to fly across the Atlantic, albeit as a passenger) and an editor for *Cosmopolitan* and *McCall's* magazines, Earhart 'urged women to seize their opportunities for autonomy and adventure'. She also actively 'supported the political efforts of the National Woman's Party, the most aggressively feminist organization of the period'. Milliat served as president of the Fédération des Sociétés Féminines Sportives de France and founded the Fédération Sportive Féminine Internationale, which organised the Jeux Internationaux Féminins (more commonly referred to as the Jeux Olympiques Féminins – Women's Olympic Games) in 1922. She was the 'main force behind three highly successful Women's International Games' and 'presided over no fewer than nine international conferences on women's sports'.[65] These women are cited as people who have effected change in women's sport and in women's status within society, and are invariably cast as bearing individual responsibility for at least some element of transformation.[66]

Blame also affixes responsibility to individuals and occupies an especially prominent place in popular causal explanations. Avery Brundage, the president of the International Olympic Committee, blamed the black-power protests in Mexico City on 'warped mentalities and cracked personalities',[67] while African American sprinter Lee Evans, a colleague of Smith and Carlos, blamed Brundage. According to Lee, Brundage inflamed an already highly charged situation on the eve of the games when he said that supporters of the black-activist Olympic Project for Human Rights were 'lucky to be allowed' to represent the US in Mexico City. According to Evans, 'if he hadn't come out like that, I don't think anything would have happened'.[68]

In academic history the general wariness of practitioners to assign monocausal explanations tends to moderate allocations of blame. In his analysis of the controversy over the selection of Sarah 'Fanny' Durack and Wilhelmina 'Mina' Wylie in the Australian team for the 1912 olympic games, Dennis Phillips clearly blames Rose Scott and A. C. W. Hill, the respective president and secretary of the New South Wales Amateur Swimming Association, for the opposition to selecting women swimmers, an opposition which severely delayed the confirmation of Durack and Wylie. Nonetheless, Phillips goes to considerable length to show the complex 'concerns and motivations on both sides of the debate'. He points out, for example, that despite their differences, Durack, Wylie and Scott agreed that 'women who found themselves a part of public life dominated by men' had to take steps to protect themselves from 'male harassment'.[69] As well as shying from a monocausal explanation, Phillips demonstrates just how easily fresh perspectives can shift blame.

Some historians are reluctant to apportion blame for past wrongs or ills especially those that are seen as the antecedents of contemporary problems or issues. These practitioners are particularly apprehensive about applying current values and standards to the past and ignoring proper historical context.[70] My stance is that the assignment of blame is legitimate and responsible advocacy. Blame is responsible when it identifies the causes of humiliating, harmful or hurtful behaviour such as apartheid sport, the hormonal doping of athletes in East Germany and invasive forms of sex-testing imposed on aspirant female olympians.[71] Disregarding the roles played by agents who are clearly identifiable in the formulation of these policies is tantamount to explaining away, rather than explaining, racism, abuse of power and sexism. Indeed, one must ask where lies the moral and political compass of historians who refuse to apportion blame? Hartmann recognises this as a particular problem among scholars who are uncomfortable with political intrusions into sport but are unable to distinguish between corrupt forms (for example, Hitler's use of the 1936 olympic games in Berlin to glorify Nazism) and socially defensible forms (for example, Smith and Carlos' demonstration on the victory podium at the 1968 games in Mexico City).[72] Presentism (the doctrine that historical practice is centred on questions primarily of concern or interest to the present) is, of course, an unavoidable part of the discipline, as are the values that shape historians' arguments, judgements and the selection of causes.[73]

The fact that some acts achieve the effects and consequences desired by their initiators does not, of course, ring true for every action. No action is ever assured of success and in many cases effects and consequences occur as a result of contingencies.[74] The term contingency carries two quite different meanings in history. When historians say that 'such and such a fact is the accidental cause of a certain event', they may mean that the actual event is a fortuitous structure based on accident. That is, 'the accidental cause is the variable cause which leads to an exceptional draw'. Alternatively, they view the accidental cause as simply an 'opportunity by which an effect implied by the situation is realized'.[75] Most sport historians seem to conceptualise contingency in the latter form. Two examples may help illustrate the difference. Historians of Australian rugby league invariably refer to the role of Alex Burdon's broken collarbone in the formation of the New South Wales Rugby League. Burdon broke his bone playing for a team representing the New South Wales Rugby Union. The Union refused to compensate the incapacitated Burdon for his medical expenses and lost income and, shortly thereafter, players and administrators met to form a new competition for professional players, the New South Wales Rugby League. However, the pressure to form a new code had been building for some time and I am not aware of any historians who seriously conceptualise the League as a fortuitous structure arising from the Union's harsh treatment of a lone player.[76] Mike Cronin treats the appointment of former England representative Jack Charlton to manage the Ireland soccer team in 1986, and that team's subsequent victories in international competition, as contingencies in soccer's rise to the status of national game in the Republic. In Cronin's view, the ephemeral nationalism accompanying the successes of a few Charlton-managed teams were simply small frames in the much bigger picture of the development of Irish nationalism and Irish identity in the late-twentieth century.[77]

In constructionist thought, causal explanations that stop at agents' free will and mental capacities are superficial and ignore the antecedents of structure. As Lloyd explains, the antecedents of agency typically overlook the fact that people often 'act in certain consistently patterned and rule following ways' especially when reacting to environmental influences.[78] Kevin McAleer gives a brilliant illustration of patterned and rule-governed action in his discussion of courage among German pistol duellists. Interestingly, like the example taken from his work that I cited in the previous chapter, this too includes a comparison to strengthen the explanation.

> [T]he German duelist bore an uncanny resemblance to the average soldier in the field. His forlorn courage was not of the rare inborn kind. It was borrowed from a cause, an army, its officers. The cause was his inextricable predicament as defined by the code; the officers were the attending seconds; and the army, which swept him forward into battle, consisted of his tony societal counterparts and their *bien pensant* opinions. If the first great thing to learn about life is to refrain from doing what you really do not want to do, then duelists were to be pitied more than anything else. They lacked the courage not to be brave; like a young woman today lacking the self-confidence to be unapologetically overweight in body-beautiful Southern California – although no one for a moment is pretending that duelists were subject to pressures quite so extreme.[79]

In this case, as in so many others, the antecedents of duelling (and slimming) are clearly structured (see Chapter 3). And notwithstanding the examples of rational and/ or motivational antecedents cited above, structural antecedents retain enormous influence in sport history.

Structures as causes

Among most historians who privilege structured behaviours as the antecedents of effects and consequences, any explanation that focuses solely on the ability of agents to act, and on their interests and motives (and contingencies), generally has no substance. Constructionism rejects all notions of pure agents and holds that 'consciousness, choice and action are all situationally conditioned and constrained'.[80] In constructionist-leaning history, situational conditions and constraints reside in deep-rooted or underlying structures (collections of laws or rules that govern the behaviour of any system such as the economic laws of accumulation and competition that govern the capitalist system). These structures determine everything that happens; indeed, things only happen differently when the structures themselves are different or undergo change. Critics, of course, reject such explanations as predetermined and grossly reductionist; they argue that structures are merely metahistorical doctrines unsupported by historical facts and empirical evidence. Not surprisingly, opponents of structural causality point to the role of agents who make choices and shape their own situations to suit their own ends.

Notions of structural causality have been influential in sport history, especially in situations where practitioners attempt to explain social changes in sport, although, as I point out in the following chapter, the field lacks coherent approaches towards, or theories of, structural change. Most historians of sport still struggle to reconcile the underlying tension between free-thinking individual agents who act and produce causes, and broader social predispositions that cause, or more often constrain, agency. Kathleen McCrone's work on sport in the late Victorian girls' public schools is one example. McCrone identifies a number of agents, including Dorothea Beale (headmistress of Cheltenham Ladies College), Frances Mary Buss (North London Collegiate School) and Jane Francis Dove (St Leonards), who actively championed the social emancipation of women, especially in games and physical exercises at the time when women had virtually no control over their own bodies. But when it comes to effecting substantial change, McCrone paints these agents as virtually impotent. 'The image of the new sportswoman' propounded by Beale and her colleagues, says McCrone, 'accommodated to traditional, Victorian bourgeois mores without radically challenging them'. At best these agents 'revitalized' the prevailing bourgeois mores 'in a way which allowed some adaptation to the broader social changes occurring at the time'. Beale, for example, 'went out of her way to ensure that players projected an image of moderation and respectable femininity'. Over a tenure that spanned nearly half a century, she progressively introduced different systems of gymnastics, games such as tennis, cricket and hockey, and eventually allowed sporting contests between houses. But each new addition was carefully considered in the context of the times. And while proud of her school's sporting facilities, which included twenty-six tennis courts, Beale was 'most anxious that our girls should not overexert themselves or become absorbed in athletic rivalries'. Ultimately, McCrone's formulation places all the weight of change on social structures rather than a reciprocal relationship between agents and structures. The real source of change is that which occurs within the system itself. McCrone even conceptualises the women's movement to which Beale and her colleagues belonged as just one element in those 'powerful economic and social forces that ... produc[ed] unprecedented change, stress and instability'.[81] At the end of the day the reader gains no clear explanation of what caused these changes; the how and why questions of change in the social system are not answered with any precision, and the agents merely hover on the sidelines.

Conclusion

Historians of sport hold different ontological beliefs and epistemological assumptions; they have different interests, aims, objectives and points of view; they work with different explanatory paradigms and employ different methodologies. In short, the field contains an inordinately diverse mix of philosophies and approaches with no single model of enquiry or explanatory paradigm dominating. Yet, for all this diversity, causal reasoning and causal relationships probably underpin more explanations than any other in sport history. Claims that shifts to postmodernism and 'to the form in which historians deploy their stories' have displaced the search for causes and exposed all notions of cause and effect as either 'bad metaphysics' or artificial, appear overstated.[82] It seems highly improbable that the idea of cause, which, as we have seen, embraces everything from 'signifying reason or motive on the part of historical agents' to 'the subsumption of events, actions, or phenomena under causal laws' will simply fade away or vanish.[83] This does not mean that many of the criticisms of causal explanation are without validity. The assumptions practitioners make about the forces and processes that they believe influence people, about agency, intentions and motivations, and about the determining effects of ethics, ideology, geography, gender, race, class, culture and so forth, all guide the type, shape and form of causal questions asked. And

> in asking why did this happen or what if something else had happened so would the effect be the same, the historian is not only predetermining meaning (to a greater or lesser extent) by the form in which he/she casts the problem, but he/she is also working teleologically within his/her own selection and arrangement of the evidence.[84]

I have argued throughout this text, beginning with the observation that facts do not carry predetermined meanings (see Chapter 2), that historians make judgements and decisions at every turn and base these as much on their own values as on objective facts and evidence. This is hardly unique to causal explanations. Thus, in the realist world of reconstructionism and constructionism, Perez Zagorin is undoubtedly correct when he writes that as long as historical thinking 'includes explanation as one of its objectives, causal attribution will remain a necessary ingredient'.[85]

Interest in explaining social changes in sport certainly shows little sign of abating. Indeed, when it comes to explaining social change, sport historians almost invariably assimilate structural antecedents. Such is the prominence of these causal explanations of social change that they can be treated as an explanatory paradigm. However, as we shall encounter in the following chapter, the operationalisation of structure and structural change bedevils the field.

Chapter 9

Social change

Explaining transformations

T HE TITLE OF DAVID LOWENTHAL'S classic historiographical text, *The Past is a Foreign Country* offers historians a useful reminder that studying by-gone eras and elapsed conditions, and what differentiates them from the present, involves questions of social change.[1] Indeed, comparing past and present conditions and circumstances, placing aspects of the past and present in their respective contexts, or examining the causes of change is both implicit and explicit in the very term history. Pamela Grundy illustrates this well in the following short narrative about the emergence of the modern sportswoman:

> During the first part of the nineteenth century, argued Smith College instructor and women's basketball advocate Senda Berenson, 'the so-called ideal woman was a small brained damsel who prided herself on her delicate health, who thought fainting interesting, and hysterics fascinating.' But by 1901 an article appearing in the *Salisbury Daily Sun* ... could announce, 'The old maid has ... disappeared completely, and in her place we have the breezy independent, up to date, athletic and well gowned bachelor girl, who is succeeding in business life or a profession and asks neither pity nor favors from her fellow men.'[2]

Here I treat social change as a paradigmatic case of causation, analysing change from a theoretical perspective.[3]

Why should historians consider theory integral to understanding change? After all reconstructionists reject theory. Their inquiries into change typically proceed by empirical investigation of particular actions, events and ideas rather than by abstract concepts and processes. Reconstructionists who venture into large-scale social change prefer to emphasise the accumulation of modifications, which are often small and gradual, and eventually reach a point that historians agree denotes something fundamentally different. In sport history reconstructionists describe modern sport as the coalescence of sporting and social modifications. These include the introduction of rules, umpires and administrative bodies, the construction of specialised and dedicated facilities (for example, pools, gymnasiums, fields), and the development of transport systems (especially rail which facilitated the movement of sporting teams and spectators), mass production (that lowered costs of sporting equipment and goods), and mass communication (notably penny newspapers that popularised sport).[4] Summarising the accumulation approach, Tom Bottomore wrote that it places social change at the 'intersection of separate and distinct quasi-causal chains and the accumulation of their effects ... which produce a dominant tendency toward a major change'.[5]

The theoretical dimension of social change emerges from two questions ignored or glossed over by reconstructionists. First, what changes? Actors, of course, have relatively short lives and change over time. Yet, although individuals constantly move on, in many instances they are replaced by like-minded types to the extent that neither new actors nor even entire new generations necessarily mean fresh patterns or alternative ways of doing things; the way people play, for example, shows remarkable continuity.[6] Hence change emanates not simply from fresh personnel, but from their beliefs, values, norms, roles, practices, and ways of doing things that differ from past forms and types and which, most importantly, have new structuring effects. Thus, as Grundy observes above, changes in values and assumptions about the ideal woman in the second half of the nineteenth century helped reshape or structure (that is, determine) ideas about sporting females; these ideas in turn translated into new patterns of behaviour. And, as we shall see, Grundy also highlights the importance of competition as a key structuring idea in modern society. The notion of structuring effects derives from the concept of structure as a motor of history, a view that prevails among many constructionists (see Chapters 3, 8 and 9).

A second question logically follows this perspective of social change: how do structures change? There is no single answer. Structural change depends entirely upon the historian's concept of structure and her or his understanding of the relationship between structure and human action. Earlier I described determinist and nondeterminist concepts of structures (see Chapter 3). Determinists (essentialists) view structures as determining action independently of the will of human agents; with respect to structural change, determinists 'locate the fundamental determining sources ... *outside* the conscious agency of human subjects' within the social or physical environment, or within various psychological or behavioural predispositions. Nondeterminists (constructionists) situate structures within the sphere of human action, and they 'locate the fundamental source of change *within* the conscious human agent, albeit an agent who always acts within a structured social, cultural, and geographical environment'.[7]

In this chapter I utilise a determinist-nondeterminist framework to analyse and evaluate different approaches to structural change in sport history.[8] Determinist and nondeterminist concepts of structural change comprise a variety of broad theoretical traditions. Three have established roots in sport history: systematic evolutionism (determinism), structuralism (determinism), and relational structurism (non-determinism). Systematic evolutionism conceptualises social change within 'relatively autonomous "organic" systems'; change 'evolves through several distinct [phases] from lower to higher levels of cultural complexity, technological development, and geographical scope'. Structuralist theories 'concentrate on the continuity of cultures and economic structures beneath superficial changes in society. Certain visible aspects of society change but the structures of the cultural, social, economic, and ecological determinants change very slowly if at all'. Relational structurism recognises change as a dialectical (as opposed to a hierarchical) relationship between agents and objective structures.[9]

At this point the idea of culture as a structure, referred to in the two preceding paragraphs, demands comment. Whether culture constitutes a structure is the subject of considerable theoretical debate. Some interpretive approaches to social history argue that institutionalised cultural forms 'develop', 'legitimise' and 'articulate' the social order; in these senses, they reduce society to culture. The fundamental problem for interpretive approaches is to account for the 'relationship between subjective understandings and the objectivity of society'.[10] In sport history, theoretically driven interpretive concepts of culture have had minimal influence. Occasional studies draw on the works of Erving Goffman (for whom social interaction is a dialectic between individuals as each attempts to manage the impressions that others receive)[11] and Clifford Geertz (who analysed cultural structures as the 'macro contexts of individual and collective action').[12] I discuss Geertz's influence in more detail later (see Chapter 11).

Structuralist approaches to social change hold that structures, particularly those deemed responsible for social exploitation and disadvantage, determine culture, which is synonymous with ideology. Culture functions to reproduce structures by 'redirect[ing] potentially disruptive action towards support for the determining structure'.[13] Theories of hegemony (discussed below) come closest to this approach in sport history.

Arguing from the perspective of relational structurism, Christopher Lloyd maintains that culture 'plays a vital role in motivating, channelling, and even dominating human agency'. He believes that 'social structuring processes … have their origins as much in the beliefs, rituals, and ideologies of people' (that is, culture), 'as in the material, political, and geographical connections between them'.[14] But Lloyd also warns against conflating culture with structure. Culture includes ways of life, systems of belief and customary habits, and how these are transmitted (via language, artefacts, imitation and example); social structures are 'institutionalized rules of behaviour' (as distinct from behaviour) that 'define the relations, status and roles of people'. Structures and cultures obviously overlap but the former defines the social position of people and regulates their behaviour, obligations, rights and privileges; cultures provide us with our ideas about the 'nature of society' and 'social structure'.[15] Sporting structures include the 'ensemble of specific rules, tactics, organizations, facilities, records, and equipment' of sport;[16] when Jeffrey Hill refers to sport as an 'agent of culture', he is describing it as holding 'the power to inscribe and structure habits of thought and behaviour which contribute to our ways of seeing ourselves and others, to making sense of our social relationships and to piecing together some notion of what we call "society"'.[17] According to Hill, sport has helped produce and reproduce ideas about gender, nationalism, hero-worship and bodily exercise.

In analysing and evaluating different approaches to structural change in sport history, I direct particular attention to the ways in which various approaches and theories deal with action and culture. I begin by looking at systematic evolutionism and structuralism as two determinist theoretical traditions of social change; I then examine the nondeterminist theoretical tradition of relational structurism. Using concrete examples,

I show the substantial theoretical problems sport historians face when trying to construct accounts of change that avoid excessive generalisation and abstraction, and that provide satisfactory accounts of structures, human agency and culture. Happily, some sport historians have made progress in overcoming the problems.

Systematic evolutionism: from traditional to modern sport

Systematic evolutionism and structuralism are the two most common forms of deterministic theories of social change in sport history. A branch of functionalism, systematic evolutionism conceives of societies and cultures as 'organic holistic systems' that progressively evolve, becoming increasingly differentiated and complex.[18] Systematic evolutionism is best represented by the highly influential modernisation school, which is underpinned by two key (ideal-type) concepts – the traditional and the modern. Historians commonly employ these two concepts to distinguish premodern rural and agrarian societies from contemporary urban and industrial societies. Stability, localism, unspecialised social roles and paternal social hierarchies characterised traditional societies. Modern societies, by contrast, are dynamic, cosmopolitan, technological, mobile, industrial and constantly modified by rational thought.[19] Traditional and modern societies support different sporting structures. Traditional sport was unorganised, tied to local religious customs and interwoven with agrarian rhythms; 'modern' sport is secular, democratic, bureaucratised, specialised, rationalised, quantified and grounded in an obsession with records.[20] While notions of traditional and modern sport saturate sport history, surprisingly few practitioners theorise the changes from traditional to modern sport. Allen Guttmann and Melvin Adelman are the best known.[21]

The first sport historian to systematically compare traditional and modern sports, and the first to provide a typology – which still endures – of the formal structural properties of each, Guttmann also identified the processes by which sport passed from the traditional to its modern structural form. Prior to Guttmann (and in numerous cases since), sport historians simply attributed the transformation to the 'end products' of urbanisation and industrialisation, notably improved standards of living, communications and transport, reduced working hours and technological innovations.[22] Missing from these explanations are accounts of the processes that drive human thought and make change possible, as well as details of the conditions under which 'social, ideological, and cultural contexts' change.[23] Guttmann located the basic mechanism of structural change in human desire and the quest for achievement, success and status that underpinned the all-crucial scientific revolution.

Guttmann identified modern sport as a cultural expression of the scientific view of, and approach to, the world. 'The emergence of modern sports', he said, 'represents … the slow development of an empirical, experimental, mathematical *Weltanschauung*'. This 'intellectual revolution, … symbolized by the names of Isaac Newton and John Locke and institutionalized in the Royal Society … for the advancement of science', explained, according to Guttmann, the likes of 'athletic achievement' in Eastern Europe after the Second World War. There the 'vestiges of premodern social organization and ideology were suddenly, even ruthlessly, challenged by a relentlessly modern attitude'.[24]

At first glance Guttmann's account of social change rests on an historically grounded notion of culture in the tradition of the German sociologist Max Weber. Indeed,

Guttmann labels his interpretation Weberian.[25] But whereas dialectical interactions between the individual and society, the material and cultural, and the subjective and the objective underpinned Weber's work on structural change (thus classifying his approach to structure as nondeterminist), Guttmann actually embraced what Lloyd calls an objective and a-historical approach that ignores human intentions and their ability to control the environment.[26] Guttmann's foundations of modern sport lie on an obsession with records, which derives from a combination of an 'impulse to quantification' and the 'desire to win, to excel, to be the best'. As I have noted, Guttmann located the origins of this fixation in the scientific culture of seventeenth century England. However, not only was he scant on the detail and silent about the international diffusion of this scientific *Weltanschauung*, he painted the mania for records as the *telos* of Western society and modern sport. This was most evident in his language: 'one *must* count', 'the almost inevitable tendency to transform *every* athletic feat into one that can be quantified and measured', 'the statistics of the game are part and parcel of the statistics of modern society', 'the ingenuity of *Homo mensor* must not be underestimated', 'the record becomes a psychological presence in the mind of everyone involved with the event'.[27] Seen in this light, Guttmann's classification of his theory as nondeterminist seems misplaced.[28]

Guttmann's approach to social change actually combined elements of systematic evolutionism and dispositional-behaviourism. In the first instance, sport moves between two states of equilibrium (the traditional and the modern) with the greater differentiation and complexity of the modern treated as a higher evolutionary state. Guttmann did not analyse the cause of change as a cultural mutation (for example, the rise of a scientific *Weltanschauung*) but as a combination of an internal psychological impulse to quantify and a lust for competition. Ultimately this tallies to a behavioural dispositionalist explanation of human action. Although Guttmann's modern environment technically affords individuals choices, the opportunity to choose remains 'limited' and no actors appear to consciously work to 'alter structural situations'. Nor does modern society depend on agents for its reproduction, 'it just *is* and persists as a reified abstraction'.[29]

Like Guttmann, Adelman analysed the transformation from traditional to modern sport and claimed to ground his account of social change in cultural processes. He also professed a concern with the interactions between individuals and society. 'Actions and attitudes', he wrote, are the 'product of human agencies'. But while they will 'at times run counter to the requirements of the modern system', they also have to be seen 'within the context and boundaries established by modern institutions'.[30] And like Guttmann, Adelman's focus on social complexity and the structural-functional organisation of modern sport fitted the assumptions of systematic evolutionism.[31] On the other hand, Adelman showed more rigour than Guttmann in searching for a causal explanation of modern sport which he located in a rational behaviouralist disposition.

Adelman's key to modern sport is the modern city, a structure emerging from the centralised nation state, industrial production and improved communications, and which requires 'rational order' to function. According to Adelman, rational order lies at the heart of the 'modern identity' and 'way of life'. He analysed the impact of the rational order on sport in three areas: dedicated physical space, organisational structures and collective behaviour. Industrial production, which 'required a new division of urban space based solely on ... economic utility and value', removed traditional recreational lands. In the competition for urban land, sporting groups formed organisations that also 'performed important integrative functions' by bringing together individuals who shared common interests but did not know each other personally. The rational order of the city also aided the 'ideology' of modern sport. Amid fears of a 'physically degenerating' race and a 'decaying' social order, faddists and fanatics upheld sport as a panacea that would 'promote good health', 'encourage morality', and 'instil positive character values'. However, if the modern city was 'both a setting and a stimulant for … athletics, the creation of modern sports structures was not solely a by-product of societal change'. As Adelman noted, 'the institutional needs' of sport were 'equally responsible for the modernization of athletics'.[32]

Finally, Adelman identified competition and commercialisation as factors in the modernisation of sport. While sporting competition stemmed from a 'desire to demonstrate superiority', the organisation of competition helped formalise different behaviours, some of which (for example, specialised managerial, administrative and marketing roles) were integral to professional sport. Commercial sport assisted modernisation by providing a 'method of financing' professional competition. Moreover, the increase in commercial sporting operations (for example, staging events, organising competitions) compelled entrepreneurs to 'coordinate and rationalize their business practices to maximize their profits'.[33] Adelman insisted that competitive and professional sport 'flowed from the search for superiority' and 'always preceded commercialization'. While he followed Guttmann's reference to actors' internal psychological dispositions (that is, their innate desire for competition), Adelman's incorporation of rational behaviour made his approach less deterministic.[34]

Rational behaviour, that which emanates from actors examining the relationship between means and ends, was the lynchpin of Adelman's new urban order and modern sport. It produced, for example, a constant scrutiny and revision of rules, and the employment of science and technology to enhance efficiency. 'A consequence of specific environmental conditions', rational behaviour explanations of social change are stronger than psychological explanations because 'actors can learn new strategies and make genuine choices'.[35] Last, Adelman paid greater attention to structure. His social structures are more than mere epiphenomena at the end of causal chains that begin with the internal states or rational actions of individuals; they play a significant causal feedback role.

Yet, despite his claims to examine social change through nondeterminist cultural processes, Adelman ultimately retreated to the 'innate and supposedly universal disposition to behave in the actor's self interest'. In so doing he locked himself into the ambit of behavioural-determinism.[36] Although he purported to develop a theory of social structure and change, this remained underdeveloped and largely peripheral to concerns with behaviour. Where Adelman established links between structure and action they appear forced and contrived. For example, he concluded his rich discussion of the demise of bear and bull baiting, cockfighting and ratting, and their failure to modernise, with the claim that these blood sports were incompatible with urban society.[37] But this claim does no justice to the complex issues, debates, contradictions and ambiguities surrounding blood sports that Adelman identifies in *A Sporting Time*. Furthermore, it is too categorical, making no allowance for a continuation of these activities underground, or for continued vigilance by opponents against any resurgence of these pastimes. Thus Adelman situates sporting behaviour within a structure that is fixed and does not change – the rationally ordered city.[38]

Marxist structuralism is a second type of determinism in sport history alongside systematic evolutionism. Although not propounded by sport historians, Marxist structuralism commonly appears as a launching pad to introduce theoretical problems associated with structural change, and as a means to criticise sport sociologists for their cavalier treatment of historical details. Marxist structuralism differs sharply from systematic evolutionism in its concept of structure. In systematic evolutionism structures are surface phenomena; in the structuralist tradition they are 'the deep *unobservable* levels of languages, cultures, minds, economies, and societies'. Earlier I noted that the causal powers of deep structures completely override human agents who virtually disappear beneath the abstract social order (Chapter 3).[39] Despite his non-Marxist status, Fernand Braudel is worth citing here to reinforce this notion of the absent historical agent in structuralism. 'When I think of the individual', Braudel wrote, 'I am always inclined to see him imprisoned within a destiny in which he himself has little hand, fixed in a landscape in which the infinite perspectives of the long term stretch into the distance both behind him and before'.[40] Despite their differences, systematic evolutionist and structuralist approaches share common ground in dealing with social change: both focus on the maintenance of social equilibrium. (The difference here is that systematic evolutionism views modern society as essentially nonproblematic, whereas left-leaning structuralisms deem the capitalist structure as problematic and direct their attention to the possibilities of social transformation.) In sport history, the influence of Marxist structuralism lies in the questions practitioners ask about sport's role in the structure of traditional capitalism and, increasingly, late capitalism.

Structuralism: from modern to late capitalist sport

Structuralists view society as a whole made up of a hierarchy of structures. The nature of the hierarchy determines both 'the general form' that society takes at any one time and the possibilities for social transformation.[41] Subscribing to a variety of theoretical tendencies, structuralists disagree about the nature of the social totality (that is, about its hierarchical structure). Structural Marxism assigns primacy to the economy (see Chapter 3). The economy determines the principal characteristic of society, namely, which social class rules, and attributes 'major historical transitions' to the rise and entrenchment of new social classes.[42] Culture plays a critical role in this theory, serving an ideological function by persuading people to accept situations that belie their class (that is, their natural) interests. Hence, culture is reducible to class structures. Such a concept reduces people to cultural dupes who are unable to fathom their situations.[43] So how does structural Marxism explain social change? According to this theory, change emanates from the 'transformation of consciousness' (frequently treated as synonymous with culture), which leads to a 'radical alteration of social arrangements'. In capitalist societies the transformation appears as an inevitable consequence of internal processes, namely declining rates of profit, downward pressure on wages, and the growing immiseration of workers. Ideological statements about the social relations of capitalism seem increasingly contradictory and workers' organisations, trade unions and left-leaning political parties unite the masses who transform society.[44]

Early in the last quarter of the twentieth century, corresponding with a new *Zeitgeist*, several sport historians embraced the Italian Marxist Antonio Gramsci's theory of hegemony. Through hegemony theory they sought to escape the determinism of structural Marxism *and* account for the perseverance of capitalist structures of domination. Hegemony theory infused sport history (see Chapter 3). Others turned to postmodernism, a term signifying radical cultural changes in late-twentieth-century Western society. Observing that Western culture seemed to offer individuals inordinate choices, postmodernists turned their attention to analysing broadening tastes, opinions and lifestyles within a framework of collapsing cultural norms and standards. In postmodern theory, 'culture and society fuse and interpenetrate' with the former ceasing to serve political ideological functions.[45] Among the numerous theories of postmodernism, those put forward by Fredric Jameson and David Harvey found resonance among some sport historians. Jameson and Harvey deem postmodernism to be an ideological handmaiden of late capitalism. In this section, I examine hegemony and postmodern theories in sport history. I argue that neither advances the field's theoretical understanding of social change. On the contrary, too many sport historians conflate hegemony with ideology which they use to explain how structures perpetuate relations of passive domination, while postmodern theories of sport remain shackled to the functionalist assumptions of structural Marxism.

Hegemony and capitalism

A 'mechanism of bourgeois rule over the working class in a *stabilized capitalist society*', Gramsci's concept of hegemony gained currency among left-leaning Western academics in the 1970s.[46] According to Gramsci,

> hegemony works through ideology but it does not consist of false ideas, perceptions, definitions. It works *primarily* by inserting the subordinate class into key institutions and structures which support the power and social authority of the dominant order. It is above all, in these structures and relations that a subordinate class *lives its subordination*.[47]

Just as they appropriate most of their concepts, sport historians seized the prevailing left-leaning Gramscian concept of hegemony which quickly became a standard explanation for the stability of sport in capitalist societies. In so doing, they tended to conflate hegemony with ideology (as a set of false ideas) and viewed it as a force that 'persuades the general public to consider their society and its norms and values to be natural, good, and just [thereby] concealing the inherent system of domination'.[48] The end result has been, according to philosopher of sport William Morgan, 'an explanation of the staying power of capitalism' and its 'forces of containment'.[49] In fact, hegemony theory is the means by which sport studies scholars explain impediments to any form of change and by which they attribute the staying power of any structure of domination.[50]

Most accounts of hegemony are, in Richard Holt's words, too theoretically 'neat'. John Hargreaves' claim that sport in Britain helped 'fragment' the working classes and 'reconstitute them within a unified social formation under bourgeois hegemony' fails to convince Holt who argues that sport did not unite the ruling classes in a 'straightforward way'. 'Despite the manifest importance of amateurism', Holt contends that 'northern businessmen were excluded from "bourgeois" amateur consensus (as, for example, the Northern Union in rugby revealed)'. In addition, Holt suggests that the 'public school ideal of "fair play" was not so much a "bourgeois" doctrine as an adaptation of older aristocratic traditions of honour and style which created the ideal of "effortless superiority" '. Similarly, 'the extent of working-class incorporation into the ideology of amateurism appears to have been fairly restricted. Working-class sportsmen seem to have been more or less indifferent to amateur values ...'.[51]

Holt's criticism contains an irony: Hargreaves (like Stephen Hardy) directs primary attention to the dialectics of hegemonic relationships. Both scholars see hegemonic patterns 'characterized by conflict and consent, [and] coercion and struggle', and find 'outcomes' that are never problem free for either party.[52] Hargreaves and Hardy are, thus, less followers of Gramsci than of Raymond Williams for whom sustaining hegemony is an ongoing and difficult task for dominant groups. Williams did not view hegemony as a form of passive dominance; 'it has continually to be renewed, recreated, defended, and modified. It is also continually resisted, limited, altered, challenged by a host of pressures'.[53] Within this framework, dominant groups can never guarantee their hegemony; they must 'anticipate challenges' and assess the best 'combination of coercion and persuasion'. And this is 'an ongoing process of accommodation and compromise'.[54]

Consistent with Williams, Hargreaves notes that the 'sport-hegemony relation cannot be understood simply as a means of maintaining or reproducing the dominant pattern of social relations'. Hegemony, he continues, does not 'simply reflect', nor is it 'determined by, the mode of production'.[55] Thus his example of a broad coalition of youth workers (including teachers) tackling the problem of non-conforming youth – those who played on the street, gambled, trespassed and slept out – in St Ebbs (Oxford) in the 1890s, paints a picture of success (hegemony) and failure (resistance). On the one hand, the coalition produced some 'respectable', 'conforming' and 'clean-cut' youths who joined organisations, enjoyed sport and subscribed to 'bourgeois norms of respectability'. On the other hand, lower-working-class youths continued to resist 'pressures to conform'. They had their own model, 'the "corner-boy" with a distinctive mode of dress (wide leather belt and bell-bottomed trousers)'.[56]

Even this formulation failed to satisfy some critics. Holt points out that 'it is not enough to show that there were individuals with the *intention* of exercising control over workers'. Rather 'it has to be established that some kind of moral influence was in fact exercised'. Highlighting the tautology in Hargreaves' argument, Holt asserts that it 'cleverly accepts that such control was only partially and incompletely achieved, and in fact interprets this cultural independence as "resistance", thereby providing further proof of the strength of the concept'.[57]

Hardy, and his collaborator Alan Ingham, were more sensitive to Holt's concerns in their case study of the playground movement, a campaign led by middle- and upper-class reformers to provide playgrounds and supervised activities for children and adolescents in American cites in the late nineteenth and early twentieth centuries. Hardy and Ingham demonstrate that the middle classes did not simply impose playgrounds on social subordinates as a form of control. Instead the working classes 'forced middle and upper class reformers to provide ... local recreation space' which they used to 'pursue their own conceptions of leisure'. Hardy and Ingham's analysis has three merits. First, they show that although the agency of subordinate groups remained 'bounded by over-arching structures', these groups were able to 'win space' and to 'warren' into the dominant classes. Second, they explain how the actions of subordinate groups oscillated between 'pragmatic accommodation' and 'conflict'. In the case of the former, there was widespread consensus about the moral value of playgrounds; in the latter, the two classes disagreed as to who would 'regulate' children's activities in the new recreational spaces. Third, Hardy and Ingham shy from assuming that support for values propagated by dominant groups or ruling classes constitutes evidence of hegemony. Nor, conversely, do they assume that acts of what Holt calls 'cultural independence' (for example, young immigrants pulling the trousers of dignitaries visiting urban playgrounds or uprooting shrubbery, or adolescents milling on street corners wearing wide leather belts and bell-bottomed trousers) are tantamount to resistance. Genuine resistance is 'anchored in a recognized opposition of interest', and strives to lay the foundations for a radical transformation of existing social relations or structures.[58]

Hegemony is not the primary theoretical focus of Hardy and Ingham's investigation of the playground movement; it is more concerned with the relationship between agency and structure. Earlier I noted that Hardy and Ingham follow sociologist Anthony Giddens' approach to structures, conceptualising them as 'constituted and transformed over time through social practices' (see Chapter 3). In other words, they are 'constituted by human agency, and yet at the same time are the very medium of this constitution'.[59] Increasingly, social theorists (and social historians) accept this definition as the most feasible way to escape the determining constraints of structures and the shackles of ideology in structural Marxism.[60] It allows Hardy and Ingham to talk about subordinated groups winning space from the dominant, although to what end they do not explain. The point here is that Hardy and Ingham's analysis contains critical elements of a nondeterminist approach to social change that Christopher Lloyd calls relational structurism. I examine this below.

Previously I linked the appeal of hegemony to political pessimism about the potential for social change (see Chapter 3). Among sport historians concerned with structures of domination in apparently fixed societies with homogeneous cultures, hegemony offered explanatory power. But in the last decade of the twentieth century a new *Zeitgeist* attuned some sport historians to what appeared to be massive cultural changes. Operating under the banner of postmodernism, they directed their attention to the changing nature of sport in an emerging structure – late capitalism.

Postmodernism: late capitalism and sport

Sport historians have generally shied from postmodernism.[61] The few who embrace it generally follow Fredric Jameson and David Harvey in conceiving of postmodernism as an ideological handmaiden of late capitalism, and continue to concentrate on the functions of sport in capitalist societies. They have produced some evocative and rich descriptions and help give contemporary sport a fresh context but whether they have advanced the field's theoretical understanding of social change is a moot point.

Jameson ties postmodern culture to late capitalism. He describes the latter as a form of global consumer capitalism that expands markets by facilitating individuals' ability to acquire. Accompanying global capitalism has been an expansion of cultural forms largely disconnected from particular social contexts. There is, says Jameson, 'a prodigious expansion of culture throughout the social realm, to the point at which everything in our social life – from economic value and state power and practices to the very structure of the psyche itself – can be said to have become "cultural" in some original and as yet untheorized sense'.[62] Jameson identified three basic characteristics of postmodern culture: depthlessness, a-historicism and a concept of the world as a technological rather than a natural entity. Depthlessness refers to the absence of emotion and intensity in cultural products that are decentred from the people who produce them and are nothing more than consumable images. No longer signified by external forces, postmodern cultures and traditions are disjointed fragments which individual actors reconstitute for their own interests. This process of reconstitution gives the postmodern world its senses of a-historicism, immediacy and timelessness. Last, information and communication rule technology forms.

The postmodernist interest in information and communication technology draws attention to the media and its relationship to culture. Among postmodernists the media is no longer simply a medium of communication but constitutes a 'network of power' that 'constructs' and 'controls', in part by 'nullifying our senses of history'.[63] Krishan Kumar eloquently summarises one perspective of the modern media which, 'suffused with images and symbols', is said to have 'obliterated' objective reality:

> In the condition of what Jean Baudrillard calls the 'ecstasy of communication', the world, our world, becomes a world purely of 'simulation', 'the generation by models of a real without origin or reality: a hyperreal'. In hyperreality it is no longer possible to distinguish the imaginary from the real, the sign from the referent, the true from the false. The world of simulation is a world of *simulacra*, of images. But unlike conventional images, *simulacra* are copies that have no originals, or of which the originals have been lost. They are images which are 'murderers of the real, murderers of their own model.' In such a condition there can be no concept of ideology, no idea of 'the betrayal of reality' by signs or images. There are only signs and images, only the hyperreal. 'History has stopped meaning …'.[64]

Sport sociologist David Andrews explores the issue of 'superficial historicism' in an analysis of television advertisers who he says 'randomly cannibalise' the sporting past.

One of Andrews' more evocative examples is a television commercial for the sporting goods and clothing company Reebok. The commercial, broadcast in the United Kingdom in the early 1990s, featured Manchester United forward Ryan Giggs.

> The commercial opens with nostalgic images of youthful football supporters *circa* 1950, bedecked in red and white scarves and enthusiastically waving football rattles. Setting the scene, the familiar voice of (Sir) Bobby Charlton (a revered symbol of Manchester United's past triumphs and tragedies) encourages the audience to 'just imagine their greatest side'. Charlton's call to historical reflection is subsequently curtailed by the unfolding televisual narrative, which effectively selects Manchester United's transhistorical XI for the audience. Through computer generated composition – accompanied by the voice of Kenneth Wolstenhome (a renowned commentator on the history of English football) and the strains of an emotive orchestral backdrop (ironically,

an arrangement of the American Civil War song 'Marching through Georgia') – Giggs is seemlessly inserted into a televisual pastiche of noted players drawn from various periods in the team's post-war history. Dismantling historical boundaries, Giggs is depicted as the orchestrator and finisher of a flowing move designed to trigger the embodied memories residing within English football's collective consciousness (George Best's hip swerve, Steve Coppel's scuttling runs, Bobby Charlton's passing etc.). Having curled the ball with the outside of his left foot into the top right hand corner of the net (a move thus thrust into collective consciousness as a sign of Giggs*ness*), he is then flanked in celebration by the talismanic Best and Charlton, as Charlton himself proclaims 'their greatest ever side. Giggs would be in it, and he'd be wearing Reebok boots'.[65]

What Andrews doesn't tell us, of course, is how viewers interpret such advertisements. Ian Harriss also addresses the issue of postmodern superficiality in his analysis of one-day cricket, although this too raises issues.

According to Harriss, one-day cricket exhibits several unique characteristics. Among them are the negation of individual strategies, particularly those pertaining to batting (the one-day version confines batters' 'portfolio of strokes' as the game draws to its maximum fifty overs), and a technological infrastructure (including flood lights and electronic scoreboards) that displaces the pitch as the focal point of attention. A 'decentred spectacle that emphasises a glossy surface without depth', postmodern cricket is 'consumed as a commodity package'. Harriss likens the one-day spectacle to 'a one-hour television melodrama'.

> The paradox of one-day cricket is that, like the television melodrama, while it emphasises action it does so only within the framework of a formula. Also like the television melodrama, the plot of each game is circumscribed by the structure of the series as a whole. This eliminates complexity and allows the viewer to be immersed quickly and easily in the immediate plot … the story is essentially limited, repetitive and predictable.[66]

But how does he explain postmodern cricket as a new sporting form?

Harriss contends that traditional and postmodern cricket both serve ideological functions. While traditional cricket 'masked the contradiction and oppression inherent in the labour/capital relationship' (by virtue of serving as an analogy to the 'fair contest between capital and labour, which is adjudicated by an impartial legal system signified by umpires in ceremonial robes'), postmodern cricket 'presents the act of consumption as though it were totally unrelated to the social relations of production'.[67] The problem with this explanation is that it rests on discredited functionalist assumptions (see Chapter 3). It simply assumes, for example, that cricket performs functions vital to the orderly operation of contemporary capitalism. As such, postmodern cricket offers no fresh insights into our theoretical understanding of social change.[68]

Like Jameson, Harvey locates the emergence of postmodern culture in the logic of capitalist development. But, whereas Jameson privileges the media and the way it accelerates the process of commodification, Harvey examines the methods of capitalist production under the rubric of Fordism and post-Fordism.

In the early twentieth century the principles of scientific management propounded by Frederick Taylor (known as Taylorism),[69] and the automated factory introduced by Henry Ford at his motor-vehicle assembly lines (known as Fordism), underpinned the methods of capitalist production. But in its objective to produce cheap, standardised products for mass markets, Fordism moved beyond the factory gates into the private home as it sought to regulate every aspect of workers' lives. As Antonio Gramsci wrote in 'Americanism and Fordism' (1931), 'the new methods of work are inseparable from a specific mode of living and of thinking and feeling'.[70] In the spirit of Gramsci, disciples of post-Fordism maintain that its hallmarks – diversity, differentiation and fragmentation – are not purely economic phenomenon. Rather, the productive flexibility of capitalism also spills over into politics and industrial relations, and culture and ideology. The characteristics of post-Fordist politics include 'the fragmentation of social classes', 'social movements and "networks" based on religion, race, or gender or on single-issue politics', 'core and periphery' labour forces, and 'private provision in welfare'. Among the features of post-Fordist culture are 'individualist modes of thought and behaviour', 'fragmentation and pluralism in values and life-styles', and 'privatization in domestic life and leisure pursuits'. On the question of social change, post-Fordists disagree about the causes of the shift from Fordism to post-Fordism. One of the more persuasive explanations, put forward by the French 'regulation school', maintains that the Taylorist-Fordist mode of development, which produced the great postwar economic boom, simply 'exhausted its potential for growth'.[71] Following in the vein of Marxist structuralism, the theoretical logic of this explanation attributes wider changes to the consequences of stresses or contradictions within the capitalist structure.[72]

Several scholars have applied post-Fordist analysis to alternative sports. Duncan Humphreys ascribes the social acceptance of snowboarding to a post-Fordist 'celebration of difference and diversification' combined with capitalism's appropriation of snowboarding's unique 'styles, meanings and values' to enhance profits. Banned by ski-field operators, snowboarding initially survived as an 'underground' culture supported by a post-Fordist economy in which small businesses produced boards, boots and clothes for a niche market.[73] The situation changed in the 1980s and Humphreys offers some evidence to support the regulationists' notion of Fordist economic 'exhaustion':

> Skiing reached a growth plateau … and snowboarding offered ski fields a new market and ongoing economic prosperity. *Ski Magazine* summed up the importance of snowboarding when it described it as one of the greatest things that ever happened to the sport: 'It attracted a whole new generation of young riders to the ski resorts, giving the ski world a much needed shot in the arm'. Ski field managers simply could not continue to oppose snowboarders.[74]

Snowboarding may have given skiing 'a shot in the arm' but, in Humphreys' colourful language, 'opening the ski fields gave snowboarding a dose of steroids'. Over the course of the 1980s the number of board manufacturers, for example, escalated from around eight to more than 35. The commodification of snowboarding, which proceeded in tandem with the commercialisation of skateboarding, relied heavily on exploiting the two cultures' '"irresponsible" and "uncontrolled" images and attitudes to sell their products to youth'. Advertising images intended to 'shock and stun' – such as the poster for Black Flys sunglasses showing a male with hooks attached to taut strings piercing his nostril, tongue and ear – illustrate this point.[75]

As I have already noted, post-Fordism is not a purely economic phenomenon. Post-Fordists associate changes in the nature of industrial organisation and work (for example, 'flatter' organisations, flexible and casual labour, demand for constant upskilling) with a 'general move away from large-scale organization, centralization, bureaucracy and hierarchy' and the emergence of individualisation and privatisation as the 'master themes of contemporary western life'.[76] What are the implications of these specific 'master themes' for sport? Post-Fordist theory points towards some greater measures of individual freedom and different levels of opposition to sporting structures. But Humphreys does not theoretically explore these structures; moreover, he is wary of equating cultural opposition to a fully fledged social transformation.

Theories of postmodernism find little favour among theorists and historians interested in social change. Steven Best and Douglas Kellner accuse postmodern theorists of excessive abstraction and reductionism. Although they praise postmodern theories for analysing 'micro and marginal phenomena ignored by much classical social theory' and 'valoriz[ing] differences, pluralities, and heterogeneities that were often suppressed by the grand theories of the past', Best and Kellner criticise them for ignoring the patterns and relations of social structures. Similarly, they note that postmodern claims of an historical rupture or a 'radically new sociohistorical situation' have been neither substantiated nor theorised.[77] Indeed, postmodern notions of discontinuity rest on inadequate historical research.[78] At least two sport historians echo this latter claim.

While he agrees with Andrews' notion that media conglomerates produce 'disembodied history', Hardy remains unconvinced that media distortions of history are a new phenomenon.[79] In a case study of the New South Wales Rugby League (NSWRL), Murray Phillips contends that the most significant changes in the competition occurred in the interwar years, long before postmodernism. He maintains that 'the termination of clubs and expansion of competitions' are not, as claimed by Harriss and other postmodernists, the 'exclusive features of contemporary sport'. Phillips informs readers that in the 1920s NSWRL simultaneously invited new clubs into its competition and excluded others. This does not mean that the social structures and relations of rugby league have remained static. On the contrary, Phillips identifies 'essential differences' in motives and effects: the economic potential of sponsors and television have replaced working-class demographics, and non-working-class regional and parochial identities have supplanted working-class tribalism. Like Hardy and Ingham, and Holt, Phillips steps back from theoretical generalisations: 'neither simple continuities nor abrupt discontinuities' satisfactorily explain the changes associated with the 'widespread commercialisation and globalisation of sport.' And, like Hardy *et al.*, Phillips finds no substitute for careful empirical research. In the case of NSWRL, he accuses commentators who focus exclusively on corporate management of ignoring the substantial economic contributions made by passionate volunteers.[80]

Unable to reconcile generalising theories with the demands of their guild that practitioners present full and complete accounts of their topic, historians overwhelmingly reject determinist theories of social change. They deem inadequate any theory that advocates a single motor of change, whether a human disposition or a contradiction in a deep structure. So what do constructionist sport historians look for in a theory of change? The critiques above suggest three criteria. First, the theory must avoid assigning primacy to single factors or conditions in explaining change and should take cognisance of the prevailing economic, social and cultural situation. Second, it must be attuned to general human motivations, acknowledging their complexities and their cultural and psychological orientations. And third, the theory must 'retain a central place for the structuring and transforming power of individual and collective conscious action' and acknowledge that this 'often leads to unintended consequences'.[81] These three criteria fulfil the definition of a nondeterminist framework of social change that Christopher Lloyd calls relational structurism.

Relational structurism: making modern sporting culture

Relational structurism examines 'human agency, rationality, and praxis' as essential forces for social change. Agents have 'real capacities' and act in accordance with their perceived interests whether they be individual or collective. But even though structures within this tradition are the products of human agents, the capacity of actors to transform structures remains constrained by various biological, social, cultural and environmental parameters. Thus, 'agency is never completely free but always constrained and enabled by its structural and ideological situation and the experience of the actor'. In short, people 'make history but always in particular enabling and disabling conditions'. Relational structurists also acknowledge the 'significance of unintended consequences of action and unrealised results of intentions for social structure and social change'. Both intended and unintended consequences of action turn into objective and seemingly unalterable conditions of action and thought.[82]

Relational structurism is less a theory of social change than a 'methodological position' or a process whereby the historian looks for 'forces' of change in the 'relations between action, consciousness, institutions, and structures'.[83] Relational structurists empirically investigate the specific; they retain general concepts but ally them with particular descriptions instead of marrying them to sociological theories or general social historical descriptions. In these ways relational structurism bears similarities to contextualisation. But relational structurism differs from contextualisation in its consideration of causation and structure, and in its analytical approach. In relational structurism the term structure denotes causation while in the context paradigm it merely implies a relationship or a correspondence between two sets of conditions or circumstances. The context paradigm typically leaves structure untheorised and synonymous with broader general conditions (for example, demography, geography, human disposition); relational structurism conceptualises structures around the rules and resources of social relationships and their unintended consequences. Finally, in keeping with their theoretical stance, relational structurists systematically explore relationships between abstract concepts – action, consciousness, institutions and structures – which they present as a non-narrative. By contrast, those working in the context paradigm choose the forces, events, agents, and convergences and contingencies on the basis of personal judgement and present their histories as narratives.[84]

Pamela Grundy's *Learning to Win* is an examplar of relational structurism in sport history.[85] Seeking to understand how sport became 'a model for a conservative view of the American social and economic order', Grundy finds the answer in a new ideology that emerged in the nineteenth century to portray competition as an inevitable and generally admirable fact of life. Such was the power of this ideology that it effectively obscured the dark side of sport (for example, violence, bribery, corruption), shrouding it in a 'celebratory rhetoric' that accompanies most sporting discourse.[86] The historian's analytical process, rather than obedience to predetermined conclusions, is the key to good relational structurism, and Grundy explores six theoretical relationships as she constructs her history: action and consciousness, action and institutions, action and structures, consciousness and institutions, consciousness and structures, and institutions and structures.[87]

Action and consciousness

Relational structurism conceives of actors as reflective rational beings, and acknowledges that what they know or believe about their social situation will shape their actions. *Learning to Win* contains rich examples of sportsmen and women, usually from minority groups, consciously appraising their social world and strategising accordingly. For example, as young women stepped into the abounding opportunities of a late nineteenth-century North Carolina society in transition, they 'cautiously negotiated their changing roles, seeking to expand their realm of action while avoiding overt threats to the status quo'. Early advocates of physical culture for middle-class women couched their programmes in terms of non-threatening 'genteel respectability, evoking the images of dignified self-control associated with conventional ideals of well-bred ladies'.[88]

Action and institutions

North Carolina society comprised a myriad of institutions that served as social bulwarks and appeared timeless. But Grundy reminds readers that the 'shape and purpose' of all institutions, and the rituals associated with them, are the product of endless political battles. Far from fixed, eternal and changeless, institutions are 'contingent' and 'freighted with the circumstances and assumptions that influence their making'. The decline of women's competitive basketball after the Second World War is an apt illustration. By the 1930s women's school and college basketball in North Carolina boasted high quality play, large crowds of spectators and enthusiastic media coverage. Proponents of this style of basketball, however, confronted opposition from the national women's physical education movement that 'championed "moderate" exercise over high-level competition' and by the 1950s competitive women's college basketball had virtually collapsed.[89]

Action and structure

Grundy acknowledges both the determining effects of structure and the power of agents to transform structures. She refers, for example, to 'residents from every walk of life ... refashion[ing their] lives and identities' under the 'demands of industrial labor, urban life, and the ideas and images of national mass culture', and to 'athletic fields' as sites where minority groups could, on occasion, 'effectively challenge the assumptions that cast them as unworthy of full participation in US society'. Through sport, women and African Americans demonstrated that they 'possessed the discipline, intelligence, and poise to contend for position or influence in every arena of national life'.[90]

Consciousness and institutions

Political struggles within existing institutions, and those leading to new institutions, invariably occur where actors are conscious of their social situations and are willing to defend their interests and beliefs. In this regard Grundy refers to 'female activists' in the 1970s who 'saw sports as a way for women to throw off physical and emotional restrictions, developing skills, pride, and confidence' and ultimately to winning their 'place in the public spotlight'.[91] In this instance, however, Bruce Kidd offers a better example than Grundy who is sparse on detail. Kidd analyses the competing values and political activities of the National Hockey League, the Amateur Athletic Union, the Workers' Sports Association, and the Women's Amateur Athletic Federation in Canada during the interwar years. Whereas the primary objectives of the Union and the Federation were to make ideal men and to promote the health and well-being of sportswomen respectively, the Association acted as a vehicle for socialism, while the League sought to promote financially lucrative spectacles.[92]

Consciousness and structures

Conscious actors interrelate with the broader structures of society in complex ways. Grundy describes a cross-section of citizens using sport for their own ends amid widespread social changes in North Carolina in the first few decades of the twentieth century. Sport, she says, enabled 'North Carolinians to engage this new society'; it became 'an arena where residents could school themselves in the discipline and coordinated effort that were becoming hallmarks of American achievement, experiment with the pleasures of self-expression and public performance, and negotiate the boundaries between local cultures and national ideals'. African American intellectuals who subscribed to institutionalised sport negotiated a 'troubling dilemma' between 'artistic creativity rooted in vernacular culture' and 'disciplined organization'. These 'negotiations' enabled them to 'claim allegiance both to [white] middle-class ideals ... and to a specifically black heritage'.[93]

Institutions and structures

Institutions can reinforce or challenge social structures. Prestigious North Carolina universities sponsored sports programmes in the late nineteenth century to reinforce a view that society reflected the competitive order of the natural world. College sport, especially football, became the domain of 'educated', 'ambitious', young white men who 'represented an emerging elite, the pinnacle of the state's new social hierarchy', in the new capitalist society.[94]

Other theories of social change incorporate some of these relationships, but only relational structurism captures them in their entirety. As Grundy demonstrates, it is the totality of these relationships that provide an ideal nondeterminst template for the social change explanatory paradigm in sport history. In *Learning to Win* Grundy deals with the three essential criteria of social change theory: structure, human action and culture. Historians seeking to understand social change cannot avoid dealing with structure and one structure is inescapable in the contemporary world: capitalism.[95] Grundy allocates a prime seat to capitalism. It is the structure that determined nineteenth-century North Carolina society, economy and culture (including sport). As Grundy puts it, competitive sport 'meshed neatly' with the goals of capitalism; sporting and capitalist endeavour were one and the same. In both capitalism and sport each citizen must not only 'win' their own places, they must 'win it anew each day'.[96]

Grundy provides a convincing account of human action. While she links the ideology of sport to the logic of capitalist accumulation to provide a materialist account of human action, her explanation is nonreductionist because she also shows sport fostering nonmaterial notions such as status and pride. Grundy's comparison of the different meanings of sport among industrialists and workers illustrates these differing accounts of human action. Sport offered industrialists a 'mirror' on the material world. Here Grundy cites the football pioneer and clock manufacturing executive Walter Camp who described the game as the '"best school for instilling into the young man those attributes which business desires and demands"'. Wage labourers, in contradistincton, joined industrial sporting teams to earn status and prestige and thereby 'blunt the disdain' often accorded manual labourers.[97]

In addition to showing different motives for human action, analysis of industrialist and worker sporting teams highlights the distinction between social structures and symbolic cultures. It demonstrates that the relationship between structure and culture is not necessarily one of correspondence or simple resemblance. Indeed, relational structurism deems the relationship 'fundamentally problematic'.[98] Not surprisingly, this is the weakest aspect of *Learning to Win*. Notwithstanding her emphasis on agency and cultural autonomy, and the ability of minority groups such as African Americans to negotiate their own cultural space within institutionalised sport, ultimately Grundy privileges structure. As she concludes, the very institution of sport – which is built upon a 'model of competition and individual effort' – offers participants little space in which to question the 'larger meaning of competition' that structures contemporary American society.[99]

Conclusion

Constructionist sport historians have embraced numerous theories in their efforts to explain social change. As we have seen, success has been limited.[100] At one level this is understandable given that theories of social change are, by definition, vulnerable to abstractionism, reductionism and historical inaccuracy. Of course, no theory could escape such charges from those reconstructionists who insist that history's sole objective is to find the causes of unique events. Neither general concepts and categories, nor consideration of long sweeps of time have any place in reconstructionism. Perhaps only a minority of historians subscribe to this view – they are the ones who do not explain how they deal with their own mental categories or cultural biases when selecting their facts. Nonetheless, most historians maintain that a single exception is suffice to debunk a theory, or that incorrect claims deriving from a particular theory are grounds for rejecting the corpus of a theory.[101] But as this chapter shows, historians interested in social change cannot realistically avoid theory, irrespective of how much detail is available to them.

The critical question for sport historians is, which theory? Many of the logical dead ends that sport historians run into stem from their failure to seriously explore this question. Just as they appropriate their concepts from outside the discipline, so too they appropriate their theories and often apply them in a shallow and uncritical manner. Frequently the choice of theory is more a reflection of the social mood than it is a concern with scientific or intellectual issues. The evidence presented here suggests that theories of social change cannot avoid the concept of structures and how they change. Logically, this means delving into relationships between structures and agents, and structures and cultures. While avoiding structural determinism is no easy matter, adopting a concept of structure as sets of rules and behaviours both constituted by, and constituting of, human agency, gives historians a manageable theory of change. However, even those theories that see the motor of historical transformation as deriving from internal contradictions within structures, recognise that these contradictions 'establish only the preconditions, or potentiality, for large-scale social change'. 'Nonstructural processes' such as 'new social groups', 'new interests and values', and 'new culture and consciousness' must occur before change is realised.[102]

Culture, rather than structure, currently holds the attention of sport historians. Like their colleagues in social history, historians of sport are increasingly investigating the 'production of meaning', especially 'by relations of power rather than for "external" or "objective" class structures, or other "social" referents'.[103] Sport is a key producer of meaning, especially identity. 'To race or shoot a puck is', in Bruce Kidd's words, 'not only to exercise a skill, but to embody, express, and elaborate a complex code about self and culture – in short, to acquire an identity'.[104] And sport historians are slowly beginning to approach culture in more diffuse ways, most notably through language or discourse. Grundy, for example, observes the fusion of sporting and business language solidifying sport's place in modern society. While coaches refer to teams as 'well-oiled machines' and describe winning combinations as 'clicking on all cylinders', business leaders (and politicians) broadcast their successes 'in terms of home runs, of fast breaks, and of hitting the line hard'. Such language, Grundy says, 'blurs distinctions between athletics and society'.[105] Of course, this shift raises new questions. What is language? How do actors receive and formulate language? Are actors passive recipients of language? These questions involve interpretations of culture.

I begin the process of historical interpretation in the next chapter with an examination of context, a term that has appeared throughout this text. What, precisely, does it involve, and does it distort our interpretations of historical materials? These questions frame Chapter 10. In Chapter 11 I examine language as a deconstructionist explanatory paradigm.

Context

Interpreting the big picture

NOTHING, IT WOULD SEEM, is more fundamental in the lexicon and practice of history than context. E. P. Thompson defines history as the 'discipline of context',[1] while Robert Berkhofer observes that 'historians do not question the basic desirability of finding [a context] as the appropriate background for understanding past ideas, behaviors and institutions'.[2] While sport historians eagerly contextualise their sources and evidence, and even their concepts and theories,[3] when it comes to contextualising the practice of sport, enthusiasm wanes. This is especially true among the fan element who, after all, are the great majority in the phenomenon we call sport. Perhaps fans fear that broad inquiry will reveal the dark side of sport,[4] or perhaps they sincerely believe that the natural essence of sport transcends context. Steven Jay Gould, for example, subscribes to the latter view. Although not a sport historian, Gould's intellectual reputation undoubtedly lends credibility to his views. In keeping with his belief that baseball is intrinsically 'profound', Gould dismisses those scholars who connect the game to supposedly 'deeper issues' of morality and history. To him they are ridiculous and merely pursuing ulterior motives and agendas.[5]

Despite the misgivings and apprehensions of the fan element, context emerged as a paradigm in sport history, largely to counter the marginalisation of the field. Charged by detractors of playing games and engaging in frivolity, many practitioners sought to highlight the social significance and implications of sport. Some described sport as 'the mirror of all things ... shed[ding] light on political, social, legal and economic systems and processes',[6] a position which Joseph Strutt articulated in the early nineteenth century in *Sports and Pastimes of the People of England* (1801). As he put it, 'in order to form a just estimation of the character of any particular people, it is absolutely necessary to investigate the Sports and Pastimes most generally prevalent among them'.[7]

Other practitioners linked sport to the project of total history, one which gained currency among social historians in the 1970s. The French philosopher Michel Foucault described total history as an attempt to link all the events, structures, institutions, customs, mental attitudes, technical practices and political behaviours of a 'well-defined spatio-temporal area' and 'to establish a system of homogeneous relations'. The system collates all these phenomena in such a manner that they both 'symbolize one another' and express a 'central core – a principle, a meaning, a spirit, a world view, an overall shape'.[8]

Irrespective of their language, and whether they referred to the mirror of sport or to total history, key sport historians agreed that placing sport in its broader economic, political and social contexts would demonstrate the intellectual and scholarly credentials of their field.[9] Early examples include works by Robert Malcolmson and Tony Mason. The former looked at recreation among English commoners in the eighteenth century in the context of ties with family, neighbours and working colleagues;[10] Mason examined the development of Association Football (soccer) in England in the context of working-class solidarity, sociability and consciousness.[11]

Notwithstanding the sceptical fans, seeking context has an important presence in the field. James Olson trumpets context as the premier paradigm. He believes that the finest sport histories 'successfully analyze a particular topic and then shed light on much broader issues'. Olson praised John Watterson's *College Football* in this regard. According to Olson, Watterson 'transcends the narrow confines of sport history' by placing 'college football in the larger context of American social, economic, cultural and political life'.[12] Similarly, Colin Howell applauds Nancy Bouchier for locating the sporting history of Woodstock and Ingersoll, two small nineteenth-century Ontario towns, in a broad historical context.[13]

Yet, despite the prominence of context, historians hardly discuss the concept or its implications for practitioners and their readers.[14] Here I analyse the nature of context in sport history and the problems it raises for the field, then I propose a contextual model that systematically links sport to the geography, demography, economy, technology, ideology, institutions, agents, politics and other phenomena in defined areas at specific times. Such a model allows sport historians to satisfy two fundamental goals of the field: to highlight the social significance of sport and to offer insights into particular societies at different conjunctures.

The nature of context

Despite the prominence of context in history, few practitioners discuss it as an historical form or method. Context establishes relationships between historical events, beliefs, objects and individuals that share more than a temporal juxtaposition or contiguity. Describing contextualisation as a process of colligation, William Walsh said that historians 'initially confront what looks like a largely unconnected mass of material' and they set out to make sense of the jumble 'by revealing certain pervasive themes or developments'. The art is to identify significant events, circumstances and people, and to explain why they are significant, 'significant here being what points beyond itself and connects with other happenings as phases in a continuous process'.[15] Establishing the significance of individual parts in the mass is also a priority for Hayden White. However, for White, establishing a context is no simple task. In the process, historians do not integrate every event and trend in a holistic manner. Rather, they select particular 'threads' that link the event under study to different areas of the context. They join these in 'a chain of provisional and restricted characterizations of finite provinces' that they hold constitutes a 'manifestly "significant" occurrence'.[16] The contextualist also traces these threads outward into the surrounding social environment in which the event occurred, and both backward and forward in time. Tracing the threads backwards enables the historian to determine the origins of the event; tracing them forwards allows the practitioner to determine the impact or influence of the event on subsequent events. The process of contextualism ends, White says, when the 'threads either disappear into the context of some other event or converge to cause the occurrence of some new event'.[17]

While White evidently allows space for causation in context, most historians approach it as one of understanding wholes rather than establishing causes between the phenomena that make up the mass. In this sense, finding the context is an approach whereby the historian seeks to understand phenomena by placing them in the circumstances in which they occurred. Most contextual arguments are interpretations of a phenomenon within a unitary, intelligible whole. Whereas historical explanations typically include relationships of the form *a* caused *b* (for example, *the appointment of Jack Charlton as manager of the Ireland national soccer team* caused *a new sporting nationalism in the Republic*), historical interpretations, although not precluding causal explanations (which often appear as contingencies), more typically take the form *a*, *b* and *c* amount to *d*. The *d* may constitute a holistic summation, a generalisation, or a concept (for example, *the new 'civic and banal' Irish nationalism of the 1990s* represented the coalescence of *successes at the 1990 and 1994 World Cups*, *policies of social liberalisation of Ireland introduced by Mary Robinson [the nation's first woman president]*, *economic transformation and the emergence of the 'Celtic Tiger'*, and *the peace process in Northern Ireland*).[18] Of course, it must be stressed that a narrative structure of an historical presentation may leave the impression of a causal explanation (see Chapters 4 and 8) irrespective of the author's intent or paradigm.[19]

Sport historians working in the context paradigm typically sit at the intersection of reconstructionism and constructionism. The influence of reconstructionism on the paradigm is most apparent in the assumption that the subject or unit of study (irrespective of whether it consists of 'a set of events, an era or all of history') is 'unique'.[20] Analogies and comparisons, the foundations of constructionist concepts and theories (see Chapter 3), are sparse in the context paradigm; Berkhofer goes so far as to describe comparison in contextualisation as an oxymoron.[21] Certainly few sport historians working in the area of context undertake comparisons. Colin Tatz, a strong advocate of context, explicitly rejects the need for comparisons in his history of Aboriginal sport. The experiences of African Americans, Māori and Pacific Islanders in New Zealand, or West Indians in England, he argues, tell us little about the nature and extent of racism in Australia.[22] Support for Tatz's position comes from E. P. Thompson. Well-constructed contexts are successful, he said, because they show a coherent and internally consistent set of relationships between all the parts in a cultural or social system; in contradistinction, many historical comparisons are insignificant, 'muddled' and 'pretentious'.[23] Where sport historians working in the context paradigm do make comparisons, they typically highlight dissimilarities that emphasise the particular or unique rather than the common.[24] However, orthodox reconstructionists are conspicuously less enamoured with big-picture contexts which they deem sullied and tainted by broad generalisations and limited archival work.

On the other hand, the contextualist penchant for incorporating vaguely defined concepts into their interpretations offends orthodox constructionists who prefer rigorously defined, tested and theorised concepts. Constructionists interested in social wholes or holistic arrangements of social phenomena also prefer to theorise the connections between components. They insinuate that context without theory is arbitrary and bankrupt.[25] Theories of structure are the most widely used to connect relationships within a unitary whole.[26] Interestingly, the key assumptions implicit in the concept of structure also underscore the context paradigm. According to Malcolm Waters, the term structure implies,

> first, that the phenomenon under inspection can be analysed as a series of component units of a specified type (e.g. roles, classes, value-commitments, genders, societies); second, that these units are related to each other in quite definite ways; third, that the relationships between units connect together to give the phenomenon under observation a characteristic pattern which needs to be understood as a totality; and fourth, that the pattern of relationships is relatively stable and enduring over time.[27]

The similarities with Walsh's process of colligation should be immediately apparent.

Orthodox constructionists roundly condemn reconstructionists for their descriptive and generally vague approaches to structural concepts, such as modern society or modern sport. Yet, constructionists can overstate the need for theory-making which does not necessarily enhance historical interpretation. Indeed, in their efforts to espouse generalising theories, constructionists often ignore details that may be crucial to the explanation but do not qualify as necessary conditions (see Chapter 8).[28] And, of course, there are many examples of colligatory interpretations exposing broad social aspirations and values unseen by highly theorised explanations. Contextualists are no less adroit at conjuring profound insights into social, cultural and political pursuits than fully fledged theorists.[29] William Baker's contextualisation of modern sport in *Sports in the Western World* is a good example. Baker draws connections between sport and urbanisation, technological advancements, and the vagaries of economics and politics.

Baker's initial context for sport was of population shifts from the countryside to the city and from Europe to North America and various colonies in the southern hemisphere. Mass congregations of people in modern cities contextualise issues such as sociability, identity and entertainment, all of which connect to sport. The modern city also provided the context for understanding the technological developments that Baker eloquently links to the growing popularity of playing and watching sport:

> City tram systems, first drawn by horses and later by electricity, provided transportation. Cheap train service[s] carried both players and spectators to games in other cities. Newspapers exploited innovative print technology to publicize forthcoming events, and then they gave instant reportage by means of new telegraph and telephone systems. Editors soon discovered that more sports coverage meant higher circulation figures, particularly with the arrival of yet another nineteenth-century invention, photography. By 1900 some sportswriters were pecking away at a new contraption called a typewriter.

Technological advances also played a major role in sports equipment. Tougher iron and steel went into the making of goals for soccer, rugby and American football, ice hockey, and basketball, and for golf clubs, ice skates, bicycle frames, gymnastic equipment, spiked shoes, and face masks, not to mention the construction of sturdy stadiums. Vulcanized rubber provided resilient, air filled balls of all shapes and sizes and pneumatic tires for bicycles and harness-racing rigs. Mechanical sewing machines turned out uniforms at a pace and a low cost never before possible; new synthetic dyes added touches of color to the fabrics. Most important of all, perhaps, was the invention of the incandescent light bulb. By the mid-1880s indoor gymnasiums and sports arenas began scheduling evening prizefights, gymnastic classes, wrestling matches, and pedestrian contests under electric lights rather than by the earlier inadequate, foul-smelling gas lamps and torches.[30]

Baker complemented the social and technological context of sport with political and economic events referring to the 'dark clouds of war and economic depression [that] hung heavy over fields of play' in the early twentieth century:

A male born in 1895 enjoyed youthful athletic options unknown to his grandfather, but by 1914 he was a ripe candidate for canon fodder. If he survived World War I (and ten million men did not), he returned home to pick up the pieces of his life, only to see his society plunge into the devastating Great Depression in the early 1930s. Scarcely did he recover from that pit of despair before he had to pack his sons off to World War II.[31]

By simply painting a general scene, and by pointing to general goals and general cultural and political trends, Baker made modern sport highly intelligible. His interpretations were as insightful as many highly theorised (and empirically richer) but narrower explanations of modern sport.

Context also allows historians to examine a phenomenon in two different eras without having to theorise social change. Brett Hutchins interprets Australian champion Don Bradman's batting average of 99.94 runs per innings in official international cricket matches in two distinct periods, the 1930s and the 1990s. The first interpretation falls within the context of productivity and performance.

During the interwar years, modern Western industrial economies were characterised by a push towards 'positivistic, technocratic and rationalistic' social orders. The Australian economy, for instance, experienced a manu-facturing production increase of 70 per cent from the start of World War I to the Great Depression; in the 1930s it doubled despite the Depression, and technological and industrial innovations unfurled in the transport and construction sectors. Communications technology was also developing, and radio broadcasts, particularly of cricket, led to large increases in the sales of radio sets. By 1934, over one million wireless receivers were licensed ... . Given the emphasis on production and technology, Bradman's relentless run accumulation captured and celebrated the overall mood of social development. Bradman ... possessed the potential to fulfil the modernist project of linear progress towards an ideal goal, in cricket symbolised by the 'perfect' average of 100 runs per innings.[32]

Hutchins' second interpretation places Australia's continuing celebration of Bradman's batting achievements, long after the cricketer's retirement, in the context of contemporary political ideology. As he tells it, in an age where 'social and political activity is measured and managed according to the logic of the market and "economically rational" outputs and returns', it is hardly surprising that Bradman's 99.94 average remains 'to the fore' and in 'the spotlight'.[33]

The distinction between context and theory, however, is not always clear-cut. Frank Ankersmit referred to 'colligatory concepts', such as modernisation or the counterculture, which 'permit the historian to bring a large range of different phenomena under a common denominator'.[34] Notwithstanding his use of modernisation as a theoretical framework, Mel Adelman noted that some proponents advocated its application as 'a heuristic device to organize material on cultural developments during a specific time period, particularly within the context of Western society, and then to relate these developments to broader societal change'.[35]

The context paradigm adds further weight to a now familiar position: historians cannot avoid judgements. Just as historians must make judgements when they select their facts and evidence, so too they must make judgements when deciding contextual relationships. And judgement is no simple matter when the object is to capture the full complexity and diversity of the past where each event and phenomenon comprises a thousand possible ties to others. Frederick Cozens and Florence Stumpf reminded sport historians of this complexity in their observation that the list of factors which affect the sporting lives of any given group includes 'virtually all major manifestations of the culture, with only a *degree* of influence as the differentiating characteristic. No knowledge of how people dressed, ate, thought, worshipped, governed themselves, educated their children, built their homes and cities – nothing would be irrelevant to a complex understanding of the how, when, what, and why' of sporting lives.[36] Of course, historical judgements inevitably comprise a teleological dimension, as Harry Ritter explained. 'To have a notion of "context"', he said, 'one needs to have a notion of "how things turned out," and this is where the element of "hindsight" or "perspective" comes in. The historian is able to develop a clear conception of "wholes" into which the individual event can fit because he knows the outcome of past events'.[37] These preliminary thoughts provide the basis for examining a range of problems associated with contextualisation in sport history.

Problems of context

Given that historians can 'always get another context' and that 'no "context" is ever exhaustive',[38] readers might anticipate some rigorous debates over the subject in sport history. Yet, debates are rare in the field and discussion is muted. Mark Dyreson recently queried John Watterson's context for American college football and suggested that the nature and structure of higher education in the United States, and the changes therein, would have been a more appropriate context for understanding the history of the game.[39] Implicit in Catriona Parratt's overview of women's sport is an argument that modernisation is an overly narrow, male-specific context and that many connections exclude women. Parratt notes, for example, that modernisation has contributed to 'the neglect and trivialization of those activities that do not conform to the dominant pattern', and to 'the marginalization of women and female sport forms'.[40] As a concrete example of a uniquely female sporting practice that does not conform to the orthodox context of modernisation, Parratt refers to Nancy Struna's work on spinning contests among American women in the late eighteenth century. Struna provides a fascinating discussion of these contests as part of a larger investigation into women in early American sporting culture that includes a well developed contextual interpretation of women's sport in the middle third of the eighteenth century. At one point Struna notes that women lagged up to a century behind men with respect to transforming domestic activities into modern-type sporting contests. But Struna presents this as a statement of fact rather than a point to launch debate over how scholars might better contextualise the place of women in modern society.[41]

Breadth of context has generated some discussion in sport history. The orthodox view, articulated by Geoff Lawrence and David Rowe in their analysis of the commercialisation of sport, advocated broad social, political and economic contexts such as capitalism for comprehending the significance and implications of sporting practices and cultures.[42] One of the first practitioners to contest orthodox wisdom that broad contexts are the most relevant for interpreting sport was Stephen Hardy. He advised colleagues to conceptualise sport as an industry that, 'like agriculture, steel, or medicine', can be understood independently of the wider society.[43] Understanding how individual sports 'developed along the lines they have, and why the industry's system and structure took on its particular shape and logic', says Hardy, means 'consider[ing] developments from the inside out'. According to Hardy, inside history begins with the practitioner identifying the central issues that concern sport organisations themselves. It is reasonable to assume, he argues, that the basic concerns of sports organisations

> center upon the acquisition and maintenance of facilities, supplies, and players; the staging of events, the minimizing of costs, the garnering of publicity; in short the concerns of business. In turn, these will probably revolve around the key functions of management – planning, coordinating, and controlling human, material and financial resources in order to reach some objectives, either clear or hazy.

Thus Hardy proposes that historians should focus less on the broad context and target questions at 'ongoing issues within the sport industry'.[44]

Hardy is not alone in these views. Leaving to one side the inimitable Stephen Jay Gould, sociologist Maurice Roche and philosopher William Morgan also share Hardy's perspective. Roche laments the current tendency in sport studies to 'lose touch with the dramatological', that is, the various 'ritualistic and theatrical features which contribute to the charisma, aura and popular attraction' of sport.[45] Morgan concurs with those scholars who warn that broad social contexts do not exhaust the interpretation of practices. Morgan, like Hardy, does not deny that social and historical forces 'fashion' sport. But he argues that connecting sporting practices to large-scale processes and forces such as feudalism or capitalism merely strips the real meaning and significance from these 'fragments of social life'. 'It may be appropriate', Morgan continues, to claim that

> football intimates a certain violent posture toward life. It may be further appropriate to track [this] disposition back to the social conditions [from where it] sprang. But it won't do to claim that ... football is essentially a capitalist practice, or alternatively that football is 'indissolubly' connected to capitalism. To assert such ... is to ignore ... the important wedge driven between sport and its social context by its constitutive rules.

Thus, for Morgan, the broad social, economic and political context ignores 'the constitutive rules of sporting practices' that 'partition' and 'separate' them from 'the whole round of social life'.[46]

Hardy believes that sport historians should shy away from general contexts on strategic grounds. While he attributes the legitimation of sport history to the field's willingness to contextualise sport and its embrace of gender, race and class frameworks emanating from social and cultural history, Hardy worries that these approaches may erode the field's autonomy. He observes that social, cultural and economic historians ask different questions about sport than those asked by sport historians. Among the former, sport is a vehicle to test theories, especially those relating to popular culture or social development in cities. A cultural or social historian, for example, might enquire into how baseball or basketball complemented movie theatres and vaudeville in the construction of a new, cross-ethnic, white male bourgeois ethos that excluded women and blacks. Historians of sport, in contradistinction, place the sport experience at the centre. For example, women concerned with alienation in sport might ask, why are people

> now celebrating the Women's World Cup as a moment of liberation and triumph? How can this be a moment of triumph? Women still hold few positions of authority in the sport industry. Things are really no different from when I played. Has this always been the case? Have there ever been alternative models available to women, ones that they controlled?

Although Hardy agrees that the questions asked by sport historians are not better than those posed by social or cultural historians, he wants sport history to be 'its own field, with ... its own set of questions'. Bowing down to the 'weightier' questions of the parent discipline will only leave sport historians to pick up the pieces when scholars in the former 'move onto greener pastures – popular fiction, clothing, cosmetics, and food'.[47]

Hardy, Roche and Morgan raise important issues. But ultimately their concerns remind the field that historians do not work in one framework and that practitioners choose the paradigm best suited to answering a specific question. Tatz illustrates this point with respect to Aboriginal history, a topic which he too says has inside and outside perspectives. 'The first is personal and internal, the ingredients that are the essence of Aboriginality. These include the nature of and attitudes to life and death, the agonies, joys, inheritance of traditions, folkways, outlooks and idioms'. Delving into these matters requires the practitioner to understand culture and the tools and methods of the cultural paradigm (see Chapter 11). By contrast, 'the second is the record and aggregate of past events, the narrative in time, the chronicle of what has befallen them, with good and (mostly) bad faith, these past two centuries'. For Tatz no interpretation of the outside history of Aboriginal life could possibly be complete without the context of geography and law. Critically, Tatz does not privilege inside history over outside history. Rather, both are 'central to Aboriginal life'.[48]

More recently deconstructionists have raised new philosophical concerns about context under the rubric of textualism (see Chapter 11). Textualists challenge contextualisation on three grounds. First, they argue that contextualisation constitutes a form of *intratextualisation* because it always

> occurs within the text itself by comparing one part to another or a part to the whole. In normal reading and reviewing such (con)textualism shows as the consistency of the argument or story, especially through a comparison of annotation and the generalizations it supports.

Second, from an *intertextuality* perspective, the context of a text emanates from other texts that provide the pretext. Historians inevitably begin their explorations into the past with the interpretations proffered by other practitioners; in this sense they address the past in terms of how it is defined by the discipline. Professional intertextual conversations extend to the nature of sources, and how to read sources for facts and evidence. Third, any claim that the context of a text exists outside the text in society, culture and polity – the so-called *extratextual* perspective – flounders on the fact that such notions are themselves categories, interpretations and abstractions. And 'since the latter are obvious textual constructions, so contextualizations employing them are also textual constructions'. In short, an extratextual social construction is nothing more than a form of textual sociality. Social reality is both constituted and understood through textualisation broadly conceived.[49]

At first glance, the deconstructionist critique of context is tautological. In deconstructionism, context always appears as 'a self-contained, endless, internal self-referential system of signifiers, whose meanings are generated by their own network'.[50] Yet, it is true that much academic history comprises narrowly focused intertextual conversations that restrict what is seen. Brian Stoddart alludes to this problem in his observation that sport history has assumed a 'patina of "sameness"' with respect to limited 'examinations of issues pertaining to colour, caste, class and stratification'.[51] Certainly the literature – the intertextual conversations – on the modern olympic games almost universally contextualise the phenomenon within twentieth-century nationalism and international political relations.[52] The threads of nationalism and international politics link to fascism, the Cold War and decolonisation, all of which allegedly sharpened the olympic games as surrogate war. International political crises invariably spilled over into the games. The Soviet invasion of Hungary in 1956 precipitated a bloody, torrid encounter when the two countries met in a water polo match in Melbourne. Apartheid and the Soviet invasion of Afghanistan precipitated boycotts. Different presidents of the International Olympic Committee (IOC), notably Pierre de Coubertin (1896–1925), Avery Brundage (1952–72) and Juan Antonio Samaranch (1980–2001), fit neatly into the political context. John Hoberman, for example, notes that de Coubertin occupied a central position in the idealistic internationalisms of the *fin de siècle* and the pre-World War I era, that Brundage was a 'pronounced germanophile and anti-Semite' whose 'ideological ambivalence' created space for the Nazis and their sympathisers within the olympic movement, and that Samaranch's political activities and tastes also extended to fascism.[53]

But these intertextual conversations do not compel historians of the modern olympic games to work within the context of twentieth-century nationalism and international political relations. Maurice Roche recently severed the ties of orthodox intertextuality by examining the modern olympic games in the context of modernity. (Although Roche sets out to theorise the olympic games as a function of modernity, the connections he makes between the world's largest sporting pageant and modernity can also serve as a framework of contextualisation. This point is elaborated further in the introduction to the following section.) According to Roche, the olympic games offered early moderns an opportunity to review their lives and relationships in a world that promised to satisfy their needs for identity but which, under the impetus of industrial development, scientific approaches to progress, heightened military activity and totalitarian states, threatened their very social and individual existence per se. Similarly, contemporary mega-events offer late-moderns 'cultural resources' to help them adapt to 'incessant technological and organisational change' in the labour force, '"information overload" … and the chaos of "choice" in consumer markets', and an increasingly plural and complex cultural and political life. The olympics have contributed to the 'development and promulgation' of ideas about national collective identity, the inclusion of diverse groups in the traditions and destinies of specific nations, and an understanding of the 'obligations and rights of participation' associated with national life. Olympic games provide us with 'enduring motivations and special opportunities to participate in collective projects' that, *inter alia*, 'structure social space and time, display the dramatic and symbolic possibilities of organised and effective social action, and reaffirm the embodied agency of people as individual actors'. Lastly, the allure of positive international images and status consolidated mega-events as permanent features of modernity, with producers largely oblivious to fears about high costs and public debt. Competition to host olympic games existed from before the First World War and continued into the 1920s (two cities bid for 1904, three for 1908, four for the cancelled games of 1916, and six for 1924). Interest declined in the 1930s and 1940s, during which the IOC aligned itself with fascism, but new mega-sporting events, such as workers' games, women's olympics and Empire games (Commonwealth games from 1952) filled the void. Interest in hosting the olympics games returned after the Second World War with seven and nine cities bidding for the 1952 and 1956 games respectively. Similarly, while threats of boycotts and exorbitant costs appear to have put a brake on hosting the olympics in the late 1970s and early 1980s, that pressure did not extend to other mega-sporting events, such as the goodwill games, gay games and fresh interest in FIFA's world cup.[54]

Contextualisation is a form of synthesis based on interpretations of historical sources and evidence. It is highly adaptive to new questions and eras, and is a powerful tool in the historian's armoury. Arguing the case for 'putting text in context', Douglas Hartmann demonstrates how contexts change through time. Analysing the photograph (text) of Tommie Smith and John Carlos protesting on the victory podium at the 1968 olympic games in Mexico City, Hartmann notes that the image of the two athletes – gloved-fists raised and heads bowed – has carried two very different meanings in mainstream American

Plate 10.1   In the 1970s Tommie Smith and John Carlos were enemies of the state;
by the 1990s they were heroes of the civil rights movement. The photograph that
defined them had not changed but the context had. © Fotopress

society. In the 1970s Smith and Carlos were traitors; by the 1990s they had been rehabilitated as heroes of the civil rights movement. As Hartmann comments, 'the image itself did not change at all during this period', nor did Smith or Carlos say or do anything 'that could have affected how it was interpreted'. Hence, 'the only recourse for explaining this dramatic transformation', Hartmann says, is 'to look to the broader sociohistorical context within which its meaning was produced and imputed'.[55]

Nonetheless, neither the proponents nor opponents of contextualisation are forthcoming with what they believe context should include or exclude. Nor do they offer advice as to how practitioners might organise their material in a manner that might develop and or enhance their generalisations or conclusions.[56] The following section moves to rectify these oversights by proposing a model to guide the process of contextualisation. Of course, no model can eliminate the need for judgement when colligating events into an interpretive context. However, the proposed model arguably removes at least some of the arbitrariness from the process and promotes a more systematic approach. This model follows that employed by Arthur Marwick in his history of the Cultural Revolution in the 1960s.

A model for contextualisation

In *The Sixties*, Marwick sets out to explain the causes of the Cultural Revolution that occurred in the West between the late 1950s and the mid-1970s.[57] But the promised explanation does not eventuate.[58] In Chapter 8 I referred to the implicit idea in the notion of historical causation that a phenomenon can be abstracted from the past, unshackled from its relations and connections, and signalled as the cause of other selected events and phenomena. But Marwick does not proceed in this manner. Rather he explores the Cultural Revolution as the coalescence of 16 characteristics – including new subcultures and movements generally critical of, or in opposition to, one or more aspects of established society, an unprecedented influence of young people, far-reaching international cultural exchanges, and upheavals in race, class, and family relationships – all of which are linked and interconnected. He then superimposes what he calls a causal model. While this model does not reveal the causes of the Cultural Revolution, it does provide a master context and a good template for the context paradigm.[59] The essence of its success as a contextual model lies in opening a vast range of phenomena to broader perspectives that expose more general values and relationships in any period.

Marwick's model comprises four principal components: major forces and constraints, events, human agencies, and convergences and contingencies. Major forces and constraints (that is, structures – see Chapters 3, 8 and 9) consist of three main forms: structural (geographical, demographic, economic and technological), ideological (what is believed and can be believed, and existing political and social philosophies), and institutional (systems of government, justice, policing and voting, educational, religious and working-class organisations and the family). Events include those that have effects and consequences such as the Great Depression and the Second World War. Similarly, human agencies also have effects and consequences. Politicians, presidents, prime ministers and protest movements comprise the more obvious human agents. Finally, convergences and contingencies refer to the interrelationships between events and human agencies that generate unforeseen events and circumstances.[60]

It is not difficult to see these components collectively operating as a macro-context for any number of sporting phenomena and, indeed, a number of sport histories focus on capturing these dimensions. Elliot Gorn's account of gouging in the southern backwoods of North America from the late eighteenth century through the antebellum era is a case in point.[61] Arguably what makes Gorn's history an exemplary contextualisation is his incorporation of each of Marwick's components.

Gouging in the backwoods

A brutal form of fighting that involved maximum disfigurement of one's opponents — including cutting out tongues, biting off lips, noses and ears, gouging out eyes, and tearing at and kicking genitals — flourished in American frontier societies from the late eighteenth century through the antebellum era. Through his use of context, Gorn increases our understanding of this violent pastime and offers powerful insights into the nature of a pre-modern American society.

Gouging took place within a peculiar combination of structural, ideological and institutional 'forces'. Geographically and socially isolated, the male-dominated backwoods supported a pre-capitalist semi-subsistence economy of hunting, herding and agriculture, and weak legal and political institutions. It was a harsh, impoverished world that nurtured a strong sense of fatalism among populations who assumed pain and suffering to be their lot. In a world where 'aggressive self-assertion and manly pride were the real marks of status … brutal recreations toughened men for a violent social life in which the exploitation of labor, the specter of poverty, and a fierce struggle for status were daily realities'. Gorn identifies two types of events: unsuccessful attempts by different legislatures to stem 'the carnage', and tales of heroic encounters that passed into folklore and legend and thus contributed to the reproduction of gouging culture. The key agents in the backwoods were not political leaders but legendary gougers. In Tennessee they included the likes of Ab 'Bully of the Hill' Gaines (from Big Hatchie Country), Neil Brown (Totty's Bend), William Holt (Vernon) and Jim Willis (Smithfield). These 'legendary champions were real individuals … who attained their status by being the meanest, toughest, and most ruthless fighters, who faced disfigurement and never backed down'. As Gorn emphasises, 'violent sports, heavy drinking, and impulsive pleasure seeking were appropriate for men whose lives were hard, whose futures were unpredictable, and whose opportunities were limited'.

Gouging eventually declined as new forces emerged and introduced new agents: market-orientated staple crop production replaced hunting, and improved transport systems, towns, schools, churches and families gradually smothered the backwoods. 'In a slow and uneven process, keelboats gave way to steamers, then railroads; squatters to cash crop farmers; hunters and trappers to preachers'. 'Emergent social institutions engendered a moral ethos that warred against the old ways. For many individuals, the justifications for personal violence grew stricter, and mayhem became unacceptable'. These new conditions did not end violence; rather they facilitated a new context. 'Modern' men, Gorn observes, turned to alternative means to display their status and defend their honour. In this they were assisted by a contingent technology: the revolver. Gunplay, rather than fighting tooth and nail, offered a cleaner, more dignified, method by which to settle disputes and confirm one's social position.

Through a process of contextualisation, Gorn demonstrates that gouging was a rational activity within the prevailing values of the American backwoods from the late eighteenth century through the antebellum era. But, more importantly, he is able to offer an interpretation of the pastime:

> [M]en labored so that they might indulge the joys of the flesh. Neither a compulsive need to save time and money nor an obsession with progress haunted people's imaginations. The backcountry folk who lacked a bourgeois or Protestant sense of duty were little disturbed by exhibitions of human passions and were resigned to violence as part of daily life. Thus the relative dearth of capitalistic values (such as delayed gratification and accumulation), the absence of a strict work ethic, and a cultural tradition that winked at lapses in moral rigor limited society's demand for sober self control.

While the orthodox constructionist historian might prefer to decipher these connections in causal terms and perhaps to theorise gouging, contextualists like Gorn simply set out to identify the circumstances of its occurrence in the American backwoods, and to highlight the values and behaviours it incorporated. Gorn links many of these values and behaviours to the concept of honour, which he discusses at length. But Gorn neither theorises honour (although he makes some comparisons to codes of honour in other places and times) nor reduces gouging to a theory of honour.[62]

Early cricket in the Antipodes

A similar example of contextualisation is apparent in Greg Ryan's study of New Zealand cricket. Although New Zealanders are better known for their rugby prowess, cricket was considered the national game until early in the twentieth century. Like Gorn's history, Ryan's study not only increases our understanding of this particular (gentlemanly) pursuit (including its development and decline), he also offers powerful insights into the nature of colonial New Zealand through his use of context. Ryan describes the effects of structural, ideological and institutional forces and constraints on cricket. Immigration, economic boom and urban growth, associated with the discovery of gold, facilitated cricket's expansion. Urbanisation congregated people and assisted new sporting competitions among city dwellers who craved entertainment and sought different ways to demonstrate physical prowess and status. However, as Ryan notes, there were limits as to who played with whom, with the working classes significantly underrepresented in cricket as players and officials. Yet, he maintains that the constraints on working-class participation stemmed more from restricted opportunities bound up with a paucity of educational opportunities, long working hours and the transient nature of their lives, than from deliberate strategies of exclusion pursued by the middle class. He also underlines climate as a second major structural constraint on cricket in New Zealand: rain inevitably interrupts play and shortens seasons and, combined with cold temperatures, produces damp and inferior pitches.

Ryan identifies cricket as a moral ideology that he says was especially strong in secondary schools. Middle-class Victorian colonists conceptualised cricket as a metaphor for 'the relationship between physical and mental health, the maintenance of appropriate standards of morality, [and] the cultivation of "manly" character'. Indeed, so strong was this ideology among cricket's patrons that they relegated economic costs, notably those associated with organising international matches against England, to a secondary consideration; after all, international cricket relations with England would preserve New Zealand's 'niche within the Empire'. But ideology also imposed constraints, most notably in the area of women's participation: the Victorians believed cricket was too vigorous for women and that it posed grave threats to their reproductive capacities.

Institutional support for cricket came from the military, elite middle-class secondary schools (including girls' schools where the game survived in a cloistered environment), provincial associations, and the New Zealand Cricket Council (NZCC). On the other hand, provincial antagonism and self-interest worked against the NZCC which struggled to produce a viable product to sell to the public. Perhaps the greatest institutional constraint on New Zealand cricket was the Public Reserves Acts of 1877 and 1881. These pieces of legislation prevented cricket authorities from enclosing public grounds and charging admission. By the time an amendment in 1885 allowed cricket authorities to establish permanent facilities and generate income, Canterbury, Otago and Wellington had already committed themselves to private ventures that remained financial millstones for 20 years.

It was not just broader social forces that shaped cricket in New Zealand; events precipitated different trajectories for the game as well. James Lillywhite's All England XI tour in February 1877 hastened the formation of the Otago and Canterbury Cricket Associations. By contrast, defeats at the hands of Australian and English touring teams in the early twentieth century dented 'public enthusiasm for international cricket'.

Ryan names scores of agents, mostly individuals, who were integral to cricket's development. They include patrons 'with the right mix of English public school and Oxbridge grooming, wealth and influential connections', entrepreneurs who brought touring teams to the country, and secondary school headmasters and teachers. In many instances the latter 'injected athletic life into school cricket'. Among their number were Charles Corfe (Christ's College), Joseph Firth (Wellington College), Walter Empson (Wanganui), C. F. Bourne (Auckland Grammar School) and William Justice Ford (Nelson College).

Last, Ryan examines the impact of convergences and contingencies. In Dunedin, two associations competed for political control of cricket. The middle-class Otago Cricket Association eventually gained power and the working-class Dunedin and Suburban Cricket Association disintegrated. But the former paid a heavy price for its increasing alienation of the working class: declining bank balances limited its ability to stage interprovincial matches. Similarly, New Zealand's refusal to join the Commonwealth of Australia, and its determination to pursue a more conventional imperial role that prized cultural and political links with Britain, had detrimental consequences for cricket in this country.[63]

Ryan identifies a wide-ranging set of circumstances, relationships, forces, values and behaviours pertinent to understanding the rise and decline of cricket as New Zealand's national game in the nineteenth century. In so doing he demonstrates the virtues of context as a paradigm in the field.

Conclusion

Sport historians contextualise the remnants of the past and their evidence; they also contextualise sport, seeking to understand it in the circumstances of different places and times. Through this latter process, contextualisation operates as an explanatory paradigm in the field. Some practitioners still appear hesitant and reluctant to contextualise sport; certainly sport historians appear more at ease with comparison and theoretical interpretation. As this chapter shows, context can simultaneously inform, arouse awareness and extend perspectives. For example, in his contextualisation of American football, Gerald Gems connects the cultural meanings of the game to the emergence of the United States as a modern society after the Civil War. According to him, 'the symbols, rituals and meanings' found in football 'resulted in a clear definition of the United States as an aggressive, commercial, patriarchal culture ready to promote its ideals on the world stage'.[64] Interestingly, Maurice Mandelbaum considers the 'relationship of part to whole' even more 'fundamental in historiography' than the 'relationship of antecedent to consequent'.[65]

   Context achieved prominence in sport history under the rubrics of total history and social history, although surprisingly few practitioners either articulated the process or publicly sang its praises. Like James Olson, Brian Stoddart identifies the enormous insights into human behaviour, attitudes and ideals offered by context. For Stoddart contextualisation is a powerful way of seeing.[66] Stoddart's applause for this paradigm should not come as a surprise given that he discusses it in an overview of C. L. R. James' contribution to sport studies. James' *Beyond the Boundary* stands as the exemplar of contextualisation. But Stoddart also observes that the emergence of new concepts, such as postcolonialism, is introducing new ways of interpreting sport.[67] Similarly, Norman Wilson talks of the 'broad framework of meaning' generated by contextualisation fading under the weight of the cultural turn with its emphasis on smaller units of analysis and micro-interpretations.[68] However, as I shall argue in the Epilogue, calls for historians to show greater reflexivity has encouraged more practitioners to reflect on the context of their own work and to locate their views and experiences (that is, their personal context) in the broader context.

Chapter 11

New culture

Interpreting language and discourse

IN PART I OF *THE FIELD* I discussed the different approaches to language in reconstructionism and deconstructionism. Among reconstructionists, cross-examination of evidence requires interrogation of language to ascertain the tone and accuracy of sources, and involves questions about word usage, figures of speech and stylistic cadence, and how they articulate bias and partisanship. Reconstructionists maintain a strong vigilance over style and rhetoric in their sources and especially in colleagues' texts. While granting style 'enormous evidential value, both in getting and in giving evidence', reconstructionists dismiss rhetoric as a 'mechanical trick' associated with propaganda, poetics and oratory.[1] Deconstructionists also direct attention to language. They focus on the form and structure of narratives and search for what they claim are the power relations inherent in narratives. They pose questions such as, who is speaking? And who is speaking for whom?[2] But underpinning the deconstructionist approach to language lies a quite different epistemological position. Whereas reconstructionists regard language as a generally transparent medium and recognise a close correspondence between the language found in sources/texts and past reality, deconstructionists question the degree to which language corresponds to the social world in the past and the present.[3] They are sensitive to the persuasive, deceptive, manipulative and controlling nature of language. Whereas reconstructionists typically present their histories as omniscient narrators of coherent, unified stories, deconstructionists prefer fragmenting and differentiating what they charge are the spurious unities in reconstructionist narratives.[4] Thus, deconstructionists devote more attention to the form and narrative structure of their sources and texts, that is, to the *meaning of the message*, compared with reconstructionists for whom the language issue is principally one of clear writing, or the *mode of the medium*.[5]

In this chapter I analyse the way a group of sport historians – including John Bloom, Douglas Brown, Susan Cahn, John Hargreaves, Peter Mewett, Michael Oriard, Catriona Parratt, Synthia Sydnor and Patricia Vertinsky – approach language. I link their works to the cultural turn in the field and the beginnings of a shift away from social history; in so doing I direct particular attention to the language-culture nexus. Whereas earlier I located the origins of the language-culture nexus in the thoughts of Hayden White (see Chapter 4), here I examine the contributions of Michel Foucault and Clifford Geertz. I begin by describing some early and subsequent applications of discourse theory in sport history. In general, sport historians have accommodated epistemologically non-threatening forms of discourse analysis that emerged in the late 1980s. Indeed, the approach has become orthodox among scholars examining the policing of female physicality. I then focus on what could be called the newer language strands of culture, textualism and narrativism, that are beginning to diffuse into sport history. Textualism and narrativism raise a number of epistemological issues and questions about the objectives of contemporary historical practice. In delving into these issues and questions I point to an emerging accommodation of selected elements of deconstructionist ideas about language and discourse. I also address the question of whether this small, but perceptible, shift might spark a new emphasis on presentism in the field.

Language and discourse: avenues of knowledge, truth and power

Deconstructionist theories of language start from the premise that language has a material reality. According to this proposition, language determines consciousness, and ultimately being, by virtue of facilitating, or excluding from consideration, certain ways of thinking about experiences and by framing behaviour. In this sense, linguistic structures are said to shape social structures and cultural practices, such as sport, and therefore to *constitute* history. Such a concept stands in marked contrast to earlier theories which held that language essentially corresponded to, or unproblematically represented, reality.[6] Following the influential French philosopher and intellectual historian Michel Foucault, this more specific sense of language is now termed discourse.[7] At the heart of Foucauldian discourse analysis are variable and contested meanings and notions of truth and knowledge embroiled in struggles for power.

Foucault's later historical projects connected the deployment of power to the body.[8] Here he focused on 'the body as produced by and existing in discourse' and the body as '*the* link between daily practices on the one hand and the large scale organisation of power on the other'.[9] With respect to discourse, Foucault argued that scientific, rational and implicitly modern discourses of the human body, especially medicine, psychiatry and psychology, provided both the philosophical and organisational bases to repress bodies. Foucault's interest in the body as the link between practice and power derived from his study of different technologies of discipline and in particular the emergence of public surveillance as a prominent technology. Initially encouraging and stimulating convicted criminals to monitor and exert self-control over their behaviour,[10] the gaze of surveillance quickly diffused from prisons, first into other state institutions such as army barracks, hospitals and schools, and then into everyday public life; for example, in the street, at the shopping mall, in the open-plan office. At these sites individuals constitute themselves as 'normal' by making themselves highly visible.[11] Critical to the successful operation of surveillance as a technology of discipline in everyday life is the stimulation of desire by a consumer culture that compels individuals to address the presentation of their bodies in public. Foucault found in consumer culture a new mode of control that proceeds not through institutional repression but by individual investment in, and stimulation of, the body. In his words, 'Get undressed – but be slim, good looking, tanned!'[12]

Foucauldian theories of, and insights into, the knowledge-body-power trilogy attracted the attention of sport historians interested in the corporeal dimensions of sport and physical activity, and issues related to power.[13] Patricia Vertinsky brought discourse to the fore in *The Eternally Wounded Woman*. Referring to the controlling power of discourse and its ability to subordinate women, Vertinsky observed that by 'speaking as experts through written sources such as medical manuals, pedagogical treatises and case histories', medical practitioners on both sides of the Atlantic in the late nineteenth and early twentieth centuries 'constituted women in particular ways'.

> Medicine took on the authority to label female complaints, or to declare women potentially sick even if they did not complain. The labelling of normal female functions such as menstruation and menopause as signs of illness requiring rest and medical observation did not, in itself, *make* women sick or incapable of vigorous activity. It did, however, provide a powerful rationale to persuade them from acting in any other way.[14]

Vertinsky uses the experience of feminist Charlotte Perkins Gilman to illustrate how medical discourse controlled middle-class girls. Embittered by marriage and motherhood, the once physically active Gilman sank into depression, a condition exacerbated by guilt and shame. A prominent establishment neurologist, Silas Weir Mitchell, diagnosed neurasthenia and mapped out a cure based on 'complete rest, seclusion and excessive feeding' followed by 'moral and physical re-education' that 'gradually taught [Gilman and other patients] not to yield to hysterical behaviour but to display order, control and self restraint'. The so-called rest cure, Vertinsky concludes, was nothing more than a

> behaviour modification treatment designed to make nervous, overactive and dissatisfied women more passive, feminine and healthy, and to help them to learn that domesticity was the cure, not the cause, of their problems. The female neurasthenic was thus 'returned to her menfolk's management, recycled and taught to make the will of the male her own'.

Complete rest, seclusion and cessation of physical, intellectual and social activities may have allowed some women to relax, and perhaps helped others to at least gain weight and colour. But in Gilman's case they 'deprived her of all that she held most important'. More broadly, suspension of physical activity, intellectual work and social contacts amounted to a 'potent form of punishment in the process of social control. Deprived of reading or writing, freedom of vigorous activity in the open air and ready access to understanding friends, the mental and physical incarceration imposed by the rest cure became a devastating medical experience from which some women never recovered'.[15] Thus, from a Foucauldian perspective, discourse became the material reality of female subordination by defining their problems (of the body) and the solutions.

References to discourse as a method of constituting and controlling women's bodies proliferated in sport studies during the 1990s, although more so among sport sociologists[16] than sport historians, and the concept became something of an orthodoxy. Nowhere is this more evident than in works that examine the production and policing of women's bodies and female physicality and sexuality. Susan Cahn, for example, analyses women's sport in *Coming on Strong: Gender and Sexuality in Twentieth-Century Women's Sport* as a cultural product in which popular discourses about the meaning of gender and sexuality compete against each other. In the struggle over women's participation, she notes that 'matters went far beyond the issue of decorum' and the 'kinds of behaviour … deemed appropriate for the female sex'. They in fact 'broached fundamental questions about the content and definition of American woman- and man-hood'. These included, 'would women engaging in traditionally male activity become more manlike? What exactly were "manly" and "womanly" qualities?'[17] The discourse of lesbianism emerged as a powerful weapon to police female coaches, athletes and administrators in the twentieth century. 'Discomfit with lesbianism', Cahn writes, affects decisions at every possible level including hiring, recruiting and publicity.

> Women coaches suspect that one reason for the increasing proportion of male coaches is the bias, especially among male administrators, against lesbians … . They admit to choosing dress and hair styles with the intention of deflecting lesbian suspicions; in some cases lesbian coaches have even married men in order to protect their careers. The issue comes up repeatedly at recruitment as well, with some coaches reassuring parents that they accept only 'feminine' players and do not permit lesbians on the team. The impulse to deny lesbianism governs publicity … . Pressed to fill the often empty stands at women's events, administrators have attempted to package college athletes as feminine and 'sexy'. … women leaders are not immune from pressure to suppress the issue. At the 1983 New Agenda Conference, organizers agreed to table a resolution that dealt openly with lesbianism when corporate sponsors of the conference threatened to withdraw funding if the word *lesbian* entered into the printed record. Conference members pushed through a resolution about homophobia but consented to withdraw another resolution and delete the word *lesbian* from official conference documents.[18]

In short, Cahn maintains that the discourse of female heterosexuality and homosexuality has a material reality in the distribution and allocation of opportunities and rewards in the sporting world.

Sport historians have been less receptive to Foucauldian insights into the interrelationships between sport, consumer culture, the stimulation of desire and the subordination of bodies. Most sport historians merely touch on the debates, emanating largely from sport sociology, as to whether commercial sport liberates or represses women. Discussions typically conclude on the claim that media images of activities like aerobics seduce women to strive for unattainable ideal body types and thus 'reproduce inequalities and inadequacies among participants'.[19] The lack of attention given to these interrelationships is surprising in light of the directions provided by John Hargreaves in *Sport, Power and Culture*.

Hargreaves rejects the view that the 'economic power' of cultural producers and brokers can fully explain the 'power-generating capacity of consumer culture'. Rather, consumer culture derives its 'coherence and power' from the articulation of key discourses and practices.[20] The 'dominant discourses/practices' of contemporary social life, according to Hargreaves, are 'organised around consumer culture'. They include 'youth, beauty, romance, sexual attraction, energy, fitness and health, movement, excitement, adventure, freedom, exotica, luxury, enjoyment, entertainment, fun'. Hargreaves explores the relationship between sporting practices and the organisation of power by examining how consumer culture controls the public representation of bodies.

> The dominant icon of consumer culture is the youthful, sexually attractive, healthy, physically fit person; and the cultural imperative to all alike, irrespective of age, appearance and sex, is to look, act and feel as if we are so. The objective of [the new disciplinary technology], which is installed through consumer culture, is to produce the 'normal person' by making each as visible as possible to the other, and by meticulous work on persons' bodies – at the instigation of subjects themselves. Our increased visibility to each other in public space, in the street, work, office, school, college, the media, the swimming pool, the beach, the health club, etc., constitutes a comprehensive system of mutual discipline and surveillance, which can be far more relentless than repressive discipline. Witness the disciplined enjoyment of freely chosen activities like jogging, dieting, dressing fashionably, keeping clean, applying unguents and cosmetics, playing sports, displaying at discos, etc.; and consider the volume of freely chosen goods and services that is consumed in the process of producing oneself as the youthful, authentic man or woman.[21]

It was a powerful analysis offering rich insights which few sport historians have followed.

Hargreaves' analysis influenced my work on the history of the beach and my examination of different methods used to discipline Australian beachgoers in the early twentieth century. For example, although briefer bathing costumes introduced onto Australian beaches after the First World War 'gave women new freedoms, … they also enticed them to reveal more of their bodies which were then subjected to new disciplinary methods – exercise, dieting, toiletries, cosmetics, accessories – to ensure that they conformed to the correct shape, colour, smell and demeanour'.[22] In his general history of Canadian sport, Colin Howell premises his discussion of sporting bodies on Foucauldian notions of mass consumer culture disciplining the modern body. Although 'liberated from Victorian prudery', Howell writes, the body is now 'subjected to the cultural technologies of consumer capitalism, which through advertising presents the body as a commodity for consumption'.[23]

Under the sway of postmodernism, poststructuralism and literary criticism, the cultural turn's emphasis on the meaning of the message continued to expand, with style, rhetoric and other linguistic approaches to the form and structure of texts undergoing radical reconceptualisation. Rhetoric now includes the study of the 'psycho-logic of the argument' and 'its persuasive effects on the audience', poetics delves into the 'rhetorical strategies' of texts, and discourse analysis has moved into a more 'inclusive consideration of texts as a whole both in themselves and in their larger social context'.[24] Within cultural history, the notion of texts has expanded to include non-literary forms such as paintings, films, television programmes, clothing styles, sport spectacles, political rallies and even societies and cultures. And, instead of 'a concrete phenomenological object with a fixed meaning', texts are now viewed by cultural historians as 'systems or structures of meaning flowing from semiotic, social and cultural processes' which are subjected to 'diverse readings and various interpretations'.[25] In the following section, I examine the emergence of textualism and its counterpart, narrativism, in sport history.

Sport, cultural texts, narratives

Elaborating on the idea of life as a text, Robert Berkhofer explains that

> not only do human behaviour and social interaction produce texts, but humans and their societies understand themselves through and as interpretive textualizations. It is only through such textualizations that humans can reproduce their cultures and social institutions. All behaviour can be interpreted like texts because it was produced in the first place through a process of textualization broadly conceived.[26]

The idea of sport as an interpretive text first emerged in Clifford Geertz's seminal essay on Balinese cockfighting.[27]

'To treat the cockfight as a text', Geertz said, 'is to bring out a feature of it (in my opinion the central feature of it) that treating it as a rite or a pastime, the two most obvious alternatives, would tend to obscure – its use of emotion for cognitive ends':

> What the cockfight says it says in a vocabulary of sentiment – the thrill of risk, the despair of loss, the pleasure of triumph. Yet what is says is not merely that risk is exciting, loss depressing, or triumph gratifying, banal tautologies of effect, but that it is of these emotions, thus exampled, that society is built and individuals put together. Attending cockfights and participating in them is, for the Balinese, a kind of sentimental education. What he learns there is what his culture's ethos and his private sensibility (or, anyway, certain aspects of them) look like when spelled out externally in a collective text.[28]

Thus, the cockfight 'provides a metasocial commentary' upon Balinese social life, especially its hierarchical structure. And 'its function … is interpretive: it is a Balinese reading of Balinese experience; 'a story they tell themselves about themselves'.[29] Yet, if Geertz teaches historians to interpret what participants in cultural events already know, he also issues a caution: 'the cockfight is not the master key to Balinese life, any more than bullfighting is to Spanish. What it says about life is not unqualified nor even unchallenged by what other equally eloquent cultural statements say about it'. 'The culture of a people', he continues, 'is an ensemble of texts, themselves ensembles'. Hence the scholar's task is to 'read over the shoulders of those to whom [the texts] properly belong'.[30]

Surprisingly, constructionist sport historians have not appropriated or applied Geertz's model to other Western sports, even though he referred in his essay to America revealing itself in the ball park, on the golf links, at the race track and around the poker table, just as 'Bali surfaces in a cock ring'.[31] In fact textual approaches did not emerge in sport history until the early 1990s by which time Geertzian-type approaches had benefited enormously from some two decades of theoretical advances in cultural interpretation. One crucial development was the shift from ideological readings of texts to reader-oriented readings. Whereas the former tended to present popular or mass culture as monolithic, the latter recognise that no single reading can represent the diversity of responses that readers assign texts; the breadth of readers' personal and social experiences is just too great.[32] Early examples in sport history include works by H. F. Moorehouse, Jeffrey Hill and Richard Holt.[33] However, Michael Oriard's interpretation of American football's inaugural years and its development as a mass spectacle is more theoretically explicit and widely cited in the field.

Oriard captures well the limitless possibilities for spectators interpreting a sporting text when he describes a range of responses (readings) to a particular 'exemplary moment' in football, in this case a violent collision between a receiver and defender.

> While fans probably choose teams most often for reasons of personal connection or regional rootedness, several other factors come easily to mind. Imagine our receiver as black, the defender white. Or one of them from Notre Dame, the other from Brigham Young; one from the Big Ten, the other from the Southeast Conference; one a candidate for a Rhodes Scholarship, the other a known drug-user or sex-offender; one a street kid from the inner city, the other the son of a wealthy cardiologist; one a well-known volunteer for the Special Olympics, the other a arrogant publicist of his own athletic brilliance. Certain teams have their own distinctive images: think of the Cowboys, the Bears, the Raiders, the 49ers in the National Football League; or, of Penn State, Miami, Oklahoma, Southern California among the colleges. And imagine the fans watching these players and teams not as a 'mass' audience but as actual people: European-, African-, Hispanic-, and Asian-American; Catholic, Protestant, Jew, and nonbeliever; WASP and redneck; college graduate and high-school dropout; conservative and liberal; racist and humanitarian; male and female, rich and poor, urban and rural, sick and well; ones just fired from jobs and ones just promoted; ones just fallen in love and ones just separated from a spouse; some pissed off at the world and some blissfully content.[34]

Acknowledging that any reading of American football will confront a plurality of meanings, Oriard sets out to highlight the diversity of audiences and to explain textual power as a force, whether oppressive or empowering, in people's lives. For Oriard, textual analysis restores what people actually experience and, in this sense, he wants to break away from master narratives and abandon allegorical approaches that impose ideological formalism and predetermined meanings.[35]

In his foreword to *Reading Football*, Alan Trachtenberg describes Oriard's work as one that 'tells the story of how stories are told'. According to Trachtenberg, the text conjoins 'fields and methods', connecting sport history with narrative theory and popular cultural studies. 'Presiding over the encounter', he continues, 'is the powerful idea of mediation, the idea that culture consists not of pure acts and events but of texts; ... . The story told in *Reading Football* is that the game emerged as narrative through a process of reading, of mediated interpretation on the part of several cohorts of historical actors'.[36] While *Reading Football* has not launched a plethora of imitations, at least two sport historians approach their subjects in a manner closely resembling Oriard. Where Geertz and Oriard conceptualised Balinese cockfighting and early American football as texts, Catriona Parratt and Peter Mewett approach the Haxey Hood (a folk-football-type game played at Haxey village in north-west Lincolnshire) and the dying Australian sport of professional running, respectively, as sets of narratives.

Seeking to understand the different 'meanings that can be read in the Hood, and specifically with what it has to say about the people and the place of Haxey and about their connections with the game and with each other', Parratt approaches the practice as 'a set of narratives'. Many narratives constitute the Hood; there are narratives relating to the actual game, narratives of the rituals and practices that precede the game, and narratives about its origins.[37] Of particular interest to Parratt are those narratives that assign women crucial roles:

> it is a woman (Lady de Mowbray) who inspires the 'original' playing for the Hood. And they are crucial in a symbolic sense because, in accordance with longstanding cultural conventions, 'woman' is the metonymy for home, hearth, refuge, even the pub to which male participants in the Hood return, to which the victors bring the actual Hood once their odyssey is over.[38]

Mewett approaches professional running as a network of narratives that the runners and their coaches employ as 'models of how to win and strategies to combat threats to winning' (see Chapters 4 and 5).[39] Illustrating the latter, Mewett offers a story told by one runner, 'Tony Holborn', who described the tactics used by his coach, 'Charlie Davis', during trials (full-speed runs over race distances), and 'the consequences that could befall snoopers' – spies working for competing stables or for bookmakers.

> *Holborn:* We couldn't talk out of the stable, at all ... . Before running the trials he [Davis] would get some binoculars and look around the tree tops, you know, to make sure that there was no one out there watching. We used to laugh at this until one day he found someone up there with a stopwatch – we had to chase him off. Years ago Charlie said that he found a guy and they tarred and feathered him, in the Depression years. They tarred and feathered this bloke. Because, fair comment, they had to win to eat. That was a very serious offence.[40]

Narratives such as these, Mewett suggests, make professional running in the sense that they offer runners and coaches courses of action in a whole range of circumstances.

Parratt and Oriard concur. Narratives, says Parratt, 'help to define Haxey as a distinctive place and Haxonians as a distinctive people, to produce a sense of community and attachment within and across generations, even across centuries, and to evoke feelings of belonging to the land and locale'.[41] Similarly, Oriard argues that 'the very experience of playing [football] is determined to a considerable degree by the narratives through which boys and young men consciously and unconsciously learn to read its meanings'.[42]

Critics, however, are less convinced. Edward Said sums up their position. While Said agrees that under certain conditions some texts may have a material reality, he maintains that 'the realities of power and authority – as well as the resistances offered by men, women and social movements to institutions, authorities and orthodoxies – are the realities that make texts possible, that deliver them to their readers'.[43] Bryan Palmer applies Said's logic to the entire deconstruction project and questions whether it can 'transcend its limitation' of forever turning inward towards interpretation and denying that understanding of the past can exist outside of texts, discourses, languages and signification.[44] I do not know whether all the sport historians cited above are aware of Palmer's criticism but his words appear to resonate with Vertinsky and Hargreaves, both of whom treat language as a supplementary analytical tool; language assists in shaping and understanding lived experiences rather than constituting them.[45] Vertinsky, for example, sees 'networks of discursive practices' as being 'clearly moulded and influenced by social institutions' while Hargreaves links discourse to the 'production system'.[46] Indeed, its broad acceptance can probably be explained by the fact that discourse analysis in sport history typically runs in tandem with the traditional focus on institutions and practices associated with social history, and that concerns about its epistemology have not yet been raised.

But what about textualism and narrativism, the newer strands of the cultural turn? In the following section I examine some of the epistemological issues associated with these new strands. In their focus on heterogeneous interpretations, have textualists and narrativists in sport history abandoned the search for single truths and realities about the past? What role does context play in the new cultural histories? Do new narratives give others their voices? The answers to these questions have implications for future directions in sport history.

Epistemological issues

Classifying textualism as a form of idealism, Richard Rorty alerts historians to the limitations of discourse and textual analysis as independent avenues to discovering the past. Rorty describes scholars who search for 'secret codes', in the belief that they will reveal the 'right meaning', as decoders and weak textualists. He considers them 'victim[s] of realism'. The decoder, says Rorty,

> thinks that if he stays within the boundaries of a text, takes it apart, and shows how it works, then he will have 'escaped the sovereignty of the signifier', broken with the myth of language as mirror of reality, and so on. But in fact he is just doing his best to imitate science – he wants a *method*, and he wants everybody to agree that he has cracked the code.

Thus, decoders are no less concerned with achieving consensus among their peers than any other scholar.[47]

Whatever their deconstructionist proclivities, all of the sport historians cited above employ linguistic analysis as a scientific method to extract truths. Vertinsky interrogates the vocabulary of her sources for the secret code that she believes will deliver her social reality. 'The study of the particular discursive formations or networks of experts', Vertinsky writes, 'may bring us closer to an understanding of the social reality of the time' as it determined the 'health and exercise needs of women and children'. Questions about discourses and the body can aid our knowledge of 'how social practices are linked up with the large-scale organization of power'.[48] Hargreaves deconstructs the discourses of the consumer and body cultures to enhance his interpretation of reality. 'A good deal of the strength of consumer culture', he says, 'resides in its ability to harness and channel bodily needs and desires'.[49] Although Oriard finds a plurality of meanings emerging from readings of nineteenth-century American football, he also 'discovers' in the press and the 'texts of popular journalism' a single reality that exists 'somewhere between totalizing allegory and the specific interpretations of a million readers':

> The sportswriter mediates between the athletic contest and its audience; sportswriting is the text of that mediation. … overwhelmingly we read football as already interpreted. We attend a few games but read about dozens the next day in the newspaper. Even with television, we read the games themselves through and against the nearly instantaneous interpretations of non-stop talking commentators.[50]

Thus, in creating football as a public spectacle, the press provides a concrete illustration or reality of this sporting culture: 'the popular press was primary, the game itself secondary, in football's extraordinary rapid emergence as a popular spectacle and cultural force'.[51]

Perhaps the best example of a secret code in sport history can be found in the 'hidden transcripts' that John Bloom claims to discover in an interview conducted in 1967 between Arthur Harris, a Native American, and two anthropologists – Elizabeth Euler and Patricia McGee. Bloom reads Harris' stories of specific sporting events and leisure activities as a 'counternarrative … that critically reflects upon race, national identity, and assimilation' in the United States.[52]

Upon first reading Harris' narrative, Bloom found a 'rather straightforward celebration of ideologies that have been a core aspect of dominant culture in the United States: ideologies such as those elevating individual success and upward mobility, nonwhite subservience, and white privilege and paternal responsibility'. Subsequent readings, however, revealed a series of 'hidden transcripts' or conversations. These provide important 'clues' into the 'complex nature of boarding schools, Native American history, and the role of sports within these'. 'Harris's story', Bloom continues, 'might seem to accommodate those in power, but it is also about using dominant society to survive and about drawing upon hidden stories to fashion critique'.[53]

Harris' decision to leave the San Carlos reservation in Arizona and attend the Hampton Normal and Agricultural Institute in Virginia, an institution originally established to educate freed slaves, is one example of a 'hidden transcript'. Harris, says Bloom,

> recalls that he learned of Hampton while a student at the Phoenix Indian School when a teacher had him read Booker T. Washington's memoir *Up from*

Slavery. However, he made the decision to attend the school over the Fourth of July weekend in 1910 while participating in a baseball tournament playing for Phoenix Indian School against both Indian and white teams. Even more significantly, he takes special care to remind his interviewers that July 4, 1910 was an eventful day in sports history. On that date, Jack Johnson, the first African American heavyweight boxing champion, successfully defended his title against a white fighter named Jim Jeffries in Reno, Nevada.

Although Harris makes only fleeting reference to the fight, Bloom insists that 'it shapes his narrative in very important ways'. (At this point Bloom provides the racial context of the Johnson-Jeffries bout, referring in particular to the negative sentiments expressed by the American press. On the eve of the fight, the *Chicago Daily Tribune* praised Jeffries, referring to him as a minister's son, while vilifying Johnson as a 'coward' and a shirker who gravitated to boxing with the desire to make easy money. Bloom also notes that white-led race riots erupted in several cities and towns in the United States following Johnson's victory.) Harris, Bloom believes, uses an ironic trope to frame his decision to leave for Hampton. In Bloom's words,

> Harris constructs an ... ironic narrative in which he is able to resist identification with whiteness during a time of intense hatred toward blacks by embracing African American institutions like Hampton and heroes like Washington. Harris's narrative, particularly in the way that he evokes sports, suggests that beneath the surface, Native Americans and African Americans shared common interests at a particular moment of danger in relation to racial politics.

Bloom finds further support for his argument in Harris' decision to stay at Hampton after the federal government, fearful of, in Harris' words, 'Indians ... intermarry[ing] ... Negroes', refused to financially support Native Americans studying at the Virginian institute. Leaving Hampton and attending an Indian school would have financially benefited Harris. Further, 'he could have followed the lead of someone like Charles Carter, attempting to gain social advancement by embracing the potential privileges of whiteness and, in turn, accepting a racial polarity in which its opposite, blackness, is associated with degradation'. However, by remaining at Hampton, Harris 'chooses to defy terms of success based on identification with "whiteness," siding his own more ambiguous racial identity with "blackness"'.

While sport, leisure and play occupy only a small portion of Harris' narrative they are crucial in Bloom's deconstruction 'for they connect his story to "hidden transcripts"',

> that can be read as building a powerful critique of race and racism in the United States from the multiple social locations that Harris has occupied: as a Yavapia who was brutally displaced and as a Native American who played sports, identified with blacks, and became educated into white society.[54]

But how much of Bloom's argument actually rests on evidence pertaining to race issues that is external to Harris' narrative? How persuasive would Bloom be if he did not, for example, put the Johnson–Jeffries bout into context? In fact, despite his claim to have discovered hidden transcripts, Bloom still relies heavily on the historical guild's practice of contextualisation (see Chapter 10).

Just as historians who claim to find new truths in language cannot escape more traditional explanatory paradigms, so too do their attempts to break from master narratives, to restore people's actual experiences and to give others their own voices, confront innumerable problems. Historians can, of course, achieve 'epistemic humility' and 'methodological caution' by simply putting others' experiences in full quotations.[55] But the real problem for historians, as Bloom discovered, is that their job is not just to reclaim voices but to contextualise them.[56] And contextualisation means that historians must draw overall conclusions about the relationships between multiple viewpoints. Ultimately, this means that historians' narratives will consider one perspective 'best or right no matter how diverse the subjects' voices in the represented world of the text'.[57] In other words, historians remain system makers, authorities, those who organise and bring together contested identities within one structure or system of truth according to the principles of an underlying model.

Sport historians are no exception. Parratt is explicit on this point in her article on the Haxey Hood. 'My main purpose', she writes, is to trace a number of 'themes through the Hood narratives and to indicate how they seem *to me* to construct a certain sense of the place and people of Haxey'.[58] With respect to gender relationships, despite the crucial roles played by women in the Hood – 'they are always in men's "field of vision"' and act as 'potential catalysts of male action' – women remain 'marginal in the sense that they do not participate physically in any of the core action'. Moreover, they are marginal in many of the popular songs – narratives – sung during the 12 days of festivities that accompany the event. Songs such as 'Drink Old England Dry', 'John Barleycorn' and 'Farmer's Boy' 'feature male characters or metaphorical men possessing, penetrating, fighting over, defending, or winning the land (the metaphorical woman) and real women'.[59] In the end, historians who attempt to combine actors' viewpoints with their own in a single text confront an insurmountable task; historians cannot avoid privileging their viewpoints over those of the actors. Berkhofer is surely correct when he concludes that plural voices do not lead to plural pasts.[60]

Oriard's claim that the popular press created football by producing standard narratives is a further illustration of historians privileging their own viewpoints. He claims that 'no single voice' defined football and that sports journalists, like spectators, brought their own interests and agendas to games. He finds 'power' constrained by a 'lack of consensus' among journalists and by the 'freedom' of readers to 'choose among the available interpretations, or even to impose their own'.[61] Yet, ultimately Oriard ascribes a set of standard narratives to historical readers who, as Stephen Hardy reminds us, were not interrogated. For Hardy, Oriard 'may be too quick to assume that yesterday's readers would agree with *his* interpretation'. Hardy's conclusion that 'there is no easy read of a text', especially old newspapers and magazines, that cannot be corroborated by 'extensive observation and interviews with living subjects', exposes a key shortcoming of textualism.[62]

Does this mean that historians are shackled to reconstructionism? Rorty discusses the possibility of historians freeing themselves from reconstructionism under the heading of strong textualism. Strong textualists, like Fredrich Nietzsche and William James, says Rorty, recognise that the *idea* of method presupposes that of a *privileged vocabulary*, the vocabulary which gets to the essence of the object, the one which expresses the properties which it has itself as opposed to those which we read into it. Nietzsche and James said that the notion of such a vocabulary was a myth – that even in science, not to mention philosophy, we simply cast around for a vocabulary which lets us get what we want.[63]

Thus 'strong textualists' are practitioners who 'ask neither the author nor the text about their intentions but simply beat the text into a shape which will serve [their] own purpose[s]'.[64] For many sport historians, Synthia Sydnor's defiance of standard historical protocols in her 'A History of Synchronized Swimming' amounted to a form of strong textualism.

Sydnor classifies her text as Benjaminian, after the German Marxist and cultural critic Walter Benjamin. 'Listen to Benjamin's words in his "Theses on the Philosophy of History"', says Sydnor: '"to articulate the past historically does not mean to recognise it 'the way it really was' (Ranke). It means to seize hold of a memory as it flashes up at a moment of danger"'.[65] Benjamin conceptualised history as a series of snapshots, a model that derived from his interest in the montage production techniques used in photography and film, and which he translated into 'showing' history.[66] Sydnor follows Benjamin, describing her essay on the history of synchronised swimming as 'a hybrid text that "seizes hold of memory as it flashes up at a moment of danger"'.[67] To this end she assembles a series of evocatively titled tableaux ('Proem', 'Also Known As', 'Fin de Millennium Synchronized Swimming'). Most tableaux are lists of words, each of which amounts to a 'show' of images and ideas about synchronised swimming. 'The History of the Science of Synchronized Swimming' includes

'Archimedes' Principle of Buoyancy'; 'Newton's Law of Inertia'; 'Newton's Law of Acceleration'; 'Newton's Law of Action and Reaction'; 'Center of Gravity'; 'Centre of Buoyancy'; 'Static Equilibrium in the Water'; Bernoulli's Principle; 'Hydrostatics'; "'Fat and Air'; 'Water Pressure', 'Ear Trouble', 'Anatomical Differences'; 'Theoretical Square Law'; Labanotation; Sports Medicine.

Another tableau, 'Type of Meet', is a much smaller and simpler 'show':

Intermediate, Senior, Midwestern, Invitational, Association Meet, North Zone Championships, Junior Nationals, Jantzen U.S. Nationals.[68]

Sydnor's style is deliberately poetic and literary; her text shies away from description and explanation, and avoids all analysis and (arguably) context. She wants readers to 'swim in circles, above and below, without having to gulp linear argument'.[69]

The *Journal of Sport History* published Sydnor's history but few colleagues shared her enthusiasm for the Benjaminian approach. On the contrary, open hostility greeted her presentation of the work to the North American Society for Sport History conference in 1997.[70] Yet, if Sydnor's history abandons context and lacks either an argument or narrative (the traditionally essential tools for the facilitation of historical comprehension), it is more substantial than a pastiche of images 'without any apparent interjection of the historian's viewpoint'.[71] Not only does she affirm her role as a narrator and organiser of text by inviting readers to 'dive into *my* narrative',[72] Sydnor declares herself 'loyal to the canon of historical methodology and theory', 'faithful to observing continuity and change', and 'conscious of the complex problems concerning truth, relativism, and representation that are entangled in the practices of being an historian'.[73] With respect to her use of sources, the meticulously referenced 105 notes – an average of 12.35 per page – confirm Sydnor's claim that she is 'true [to her] grounding in classical source use'.[74] In short, in the words of Phillipe Carrard, Sydnor is clearly 'playing the game by the rules'.[75] Thus while Sydnor's history offers a new 'way of handling ... subject matter',[76] her approach affirms Penelope Corfield's views that in practice historians do not have much leeway and that interpretation is not infinitely malleable.[77]

The message should be clear to those sport historians who fear that discourse analysis, textualism and narrativism pose a threat to traditional historical practice. As the above examples illustrate, in many respects these elements of the cultural turn have not transcended traditional historical practices grounded in reconstructionism.

Conclusion: returning to the present

Since the mid-1980s, sport historians have shown a growing interest in the cultural aspects of sport and have recognised the importance of language as integral to cultural analysis. This is most evident in the incorporation of discourse analysis into sport history. In certain areas, notably the policing of female physicality, discourse analysis has become something of an orthodoxy although it has also diffused into other areas such as the analysis of the olympics. Douglas Brown's deconstruction of early editions of *Revue Olympique*, the official organ of the International Olympic Committee (IOC), is one example. While most sport historians dismiss the journal as 'little more than a clearinghouse' for the founder of the IOC, Pierre de Coubertin, 'to disseminate his esoteric writing projects',[78] Brown argues that *Revue Olympique* located 'the Olympic Movement and its specific type of sport festival firmly within the dominant [modernist] discourse of aesthetics, art and culture'. It

> bound sport to aesthetic concepts such as the autonomy or disinterestedness of beauty, the intellectual enlightenment and the universality of beauty and truth. In de Coubertin's theory, sport and physical activity belonged to the realm of high culture. These were forms of culture that could lead to higher insights about the human condition; they could illuminate universal truths. In effect, the *Revue Olympique* aligned sport with the central tenets of aesthetic modernism.[79]

However, the language foundations of the cultural turn have not totally transformed the longstanding themes that have dominated sport history. Many sport historians now examining culture are social historians simply incorporating into their works the cultural traits associated with identity.[80] Among these practitioners, discourse analysis merely supplements the examination of social and economic relationships that are held to constitute social reality. They continue to deny culture absolute autonomy and they are reluctant to use literary theory in any direct way.

Catriona Parratt calls the new culture paradigm an 'accommodation' between constructionism and deconstructionism. Parratt is undoubtedly correct when she says that 'most sport and leisure historians are probably quite comfortable' with this form of deconstruction.[81] Bryan Palmer's celebration of C. L. R. James' *Beyond a Boundary* is a classic example of the marriage between language and signification on the one hand and historical materialism on the other. Although James wrote 'well before the implosion of theory and outside of any awareness of the stress on language that would figure forcefully in structuralism and poststructualism', *Beyond a Boundary* ostensibly treats cricket as a text in which the language of the game 'illuminates class and race relations in a colonial setting'.[82]

Perhaps only a handful of sport historians are seriously engaging with the 'heterogeneous, interrelated worlds of meaning we call culture' and attempting to analyse the ways that historical subjects use language to constitute, transmit, transform and represent their worlds.[83] Nonetheless, they are leading sport history's move away from its earlier concerns with events, economic causation, and class conflict and stratification. Logically, one would expect the study of sport as ensembles of texts, narratives and voices to accelerate this shift in emphasis.[84] While it is not clear where this trend will lead the field, I believe that Peter Mewett's narratives of professional runners is suggestive of one possible direction towards a greater curiosity about the everyday lives of ordinary sportspeople and, with it, perhaps a new focus on presentism (a perspective that places interests in, and concerns about, the present at the heart of the historian's questions) in sport history.

Although he makes no reference to Harry Harootunian, Mewett's approach offers a brilliant example of one of the American historian's central theses. In *History's Disquiet*, Harootunian begins with a fact familiar to all historians: history is present centred. Historians study the past to answer questions and concerns about the present.[85] However, historians assume that they are examining a fixed past, a platform, for understanding the present as a continuous movement from a past to a present, irrespective of whether the present shares continuities or discontinuities with the past. Following Walter Benjamin, Harootunian inverts this model to 'privilege the present and experience as a condition of constructing the past'.[86] Recognising the primacy of the present, Harootunian wants to abandon 'the fixity' of the past that dominates historical practice in favour of a new 'relationship to a past' based on the '"exceptional" structured from the present's desire'. 'What has been absent in the practice of history devoted to reconstructing the past of a present', Harootunian argues, 'is the present, what is given as the historical present and how it shows itself'.[87]

Mewett illustrates Harootunian's thoughts in representing the stories told by professional runners. He finds that among professional runners, 'the past is slave to the here-and-now'. While they 'use examples of past exploits, as related in oral narratives, to reproduce the *ways* of the sport, … these ways, of necessity, are relevant to the present'.[88] Mewett does not claim to exhaust all conceptions of history and admits that his primary concern is popular notions of history. But his emphasis on everyday life resonates with Harootunian. The ordinary events of everyday life perpetuated by ordinary people, Harootunian argues, is where the present is reproduced long after any curiosity in the historical past has faded.[89]

Interestingly, talking to young black and white Americans, John Hoberman found a 'thoroughly racialised social universe' in which sport is a critical medium for promoting 'racial folklore'. According to Hoberman 'the realities of race' find their most vocal expression in this racialised universe of 'everyday encounters' where large 'numbers of people engage in race relations, absorb ideas about racially specific traits and abilities, and grapple with their own racial dramas'.[90] Yet, as Hoberman observes, scholars pay little attention to this aspect. Perhaps the cultural turn will guide sport historians to a better understanding of those everyday encounters through the discourses, texts, narratives, stories and voices that emerge from them. As Harry Harootunian and Peter Mewett ably demonstrate, the potential for new and exciting revelations about the past, and the present, is very real.

Epilogue

SPORT HISTORIANS PRESENT THEIR EVIDENCE of, and arguments about, the past in different ways. These involve, *inter alia*, telling stories, comparing practices, establishing causes, contextualising events and theorising change. For many historians, the diversity of paradigms – combined with mixed techniques for gathering and interrogating sources and an array of themes that include race, class, gender, and national relations, cultural practices and identity[1] – is proof of the discipline's richness and creativity, its ability to adapt and accommodate fresh approaches and trends, and its development.[2] Certainly new themes generate excitement, and even controversy, when they first appear with their novel questions about the past and the present. Yet fresh approaches have not fundamentally revised the epistemological foundations of sport history.

Dwight Zakus and Synthia Slowikowski might find the field alive with 'richly multifarious' ways of knowing and telling about the past,[3] but accepted and acceptable epistemology in mainstream academic sport history generally remains firmly anchored to a bedrock of empiricism and to an unshakeable belief that historians can recover the past, its realities and truths.[4] Furthermore, most sport historians do not welcome or even tolerate alternatives.[5] On the other hand, individual practitioners cited in *The Field* are evidence of a small but rising number of scholars who, influenced by the cultural turn and deconstructionism, are beginning to critically examine traditional ways of knowing and telling, and to grapple with alternative models.

I begin these concluding thoughts with a discussion of the main tenet of an alternative model namely, reflexivity – a heightened state of self-awareness in which practitioners make continual references to their own involvement in their histories. The call for reflexivity allows historians to explain their conscious engagement with historical representations – that is, how they represent the past as history and the different ways they unavoidably distort its representation – and to enter into fuller dialogues with other viewpoints. I do not advocate reflexivity as either a prescription for 'proper' history or as a 'new rule' for historical practice;[6] Michael Oriard is surely correct when he reminds us that 'our discipline is most richly productive when least constrained by orthodoxies of any sort'.[7] I am also well aware that sport historians are more reflexive under certain conditions, such as when they write historiography,[8] reviews and rejoinders,[9] and in specific parts of their texts such as prefaces and footnotes. Nonetheless, I believe that reflexivity can help historians deal with the key question that bedevils the discipline: what is the purpose of history?[10]

Reflexivity

Historians are forever making judgements and choices about which sources to include or exclude, the best interpretation, context or theory, the most appropriate trope or emplotment. Rarely do they describe these judgements and choices to their readers, much less explain how they might affect or shape a narrative or argument. Such descriptions are the essence of reflexive historical practice. Reflexive historians are not only highly conscious and self-critical of their assumptions, theoretical outlooks and practices, but they also make explicit references to them in their work. At the heart of reflexivity is a self-awareness within the historian that she or he plays a creative role in the production and presentation of history and that this role even extends to gathering and interrogating the remnants of the past.[11] Reflexive historians do not reject historical reality. Rather, they question our access to and apprehension of that reality and challenge its meaning. The reflexive historian is always alert to the possibility of multiple truths in any interpretation.[12] The multiplicity of truth leaves room for reflexive historians to grow comfortable with, and even express, doubt: doubt about the coherence of events they narrate, about the relationships between causes and consequences, about the relationships between the remnants of the past and evidence, about the ease with which the remnants of the past translate into representations of the past, and about the ascription of meaning by both historians and those who participated in actual historical events.[13]

Disciples of the mainstream reconstructionist-constructionist alliance in sport history often define themselves as reflexive. They might admit their arguments derive from positions, that their objectivity is qualified (see Chapter 2), and that their conclusions are always tentative. At first glance their histories might even appear to lend support to their claims. In his analysis of the revolt by African American athletes, Douglas Hartmann issues repeated warnings against the superficial treatment of sources. He identifies sources that cannot be corroborated and notes his lack of access to some sources. He even comments on a shortfall in the record of what many would consider the defining moment of the revolt – Tommie Smith and John Carlos raising their black-gloved clenched fists on the victory podium at the 1968 olympic games. As he says, the photograph is silent about who conceived and planned the protest.[14] By the epistemological standards of the reconstructionist-constructionist alliance, Hartmann is highly reflexive. Yet, from a deconstructionist perspective his reflexivity falls short in that his text seemingly allows for a recovery of the past. Deconstructionist reflexivity requires authors to admit that history is an interpretation, rather than a recovery, of the past.

Similarly, growing numbers of sport historians are locating themselves in their work, at least in their prefaces. In *Mortal Engines* John Hoberman recounts an offer 'to buy a can of chemical powder' that came with a promise to make him a 'stronger and faster' athlete. For the avid runner this was no time to ask whether such a purchase might be 'licit or illicit behaviour for an athlete'; he seized the opportunity for 'a chemical advantage', even paying more money than he could afford. The can in fact contained only powdered amino acids (the building blocks of protein), but such was the 'intoxicating feeling' associated with the potential for superior performances that it would temper Hoberman's 'judgements of athletes who take drugs in secret to outperform their competitors'. Indeed, Hoberman uses this narrative to position himself in the debate over performance enhancing drugs. While stating his opposition to athletes who take illicit drugs, he can nonetheless 'understand something about why they do'.[15] It is an evocative story and one that critically transports Hoberman across the boundary of qualified objectivity and partisanship; unlike so many sport historians he uses this story to provide a viewpoint from which to criticise the subculture with which he closely identifies. Yet, it cannot be said that Hoberman explicitly integrates his viewpoint into the text in a dialectical manner that informs all his judgements and decisions with respect to his evidence and arguments.[16]

A fully reflexive historian will engage with her or his ontology, epistemology, sources, theory, ethics, morality, politics, viewpoints, concept of time and space, context, narrative, rhetoric, genre and field,[17] preferably in the text but at least in the footnotes. In the remainder of this section I will survey the concept of reflexivity in sport history and its relationship with selected elements from this list under three headings: remnants of the past, historical arguments, and presentism.

Reflexivity and remnants of the past

All historians agree that the remnants of the past lie at the heart of historical evidence and are the technical foundations upon which the discipline rests. But in acknowledging the potential to handle every single piece of historical material in a myriad of ways – historians also examine the remnants of the past for their silences and omissions (see Chapter 2) – those who embrace reflexivity are more cautious about drawing conclusions. They are also more willing to bring to the fore ambiguities in the evidence. Although I looked at a few examples in Chapter 4 including Nick Tosches' *The Devil and Sonny Liston* (2000) and William Fotheringham's *Put Me Back on My Bike: In Search of Tom Simpson* (2003), it appears that film-makers have been more attracted to this issue than historians. Akira Kurosawa's *Rashomon* (1950) – a film that David Hackett Fischer includes in a package of mid-twentieth century intellectual and political thoughts and cultural products that he believes fuelled relativism and contributed to historians rethinking their relationship with the past[18] – provides a useful heuristic device for understanding the role of interpretation in the presentation of historical fact.

In *Rashomon*, four narrators in medieval Japan describe the rape of a woman and the murder of her samurai warrior husband in a forest. Each describes the same characters and many of the same details, although their accounts are at odds on significant points. The bandit (the alleged rapist and murderer) admits to the murder but denies the charge of rape which he insists was an act of mutual consent; the woman says that the bandit attacked her but suggests that she may have murdered her husband; the dead husband (who tells his version through a medium) claims rape and suicide; the tale told by the woodcutter (an 'independent' witness) is so convoluted that viewers can only wonder whether he actually saw anything. Kurosawa does not set out to determine what really happened in the forest; nor does he seek to apportion blame or establish innocence. Rather, he wants to show how difficult it is to establish absolute truth. As historians or jurors, all that we can say is *something* happened in the forest which left a man dead, his body offering incontrovertible proof of this fact. But the how, who, why and when all require interpretation and will always be open to distortion by different perspectives. In short, the belief that the remnants of an event – including in this case oral testimony – can reveal the ultimate truth is highly unlikely.

Reconstructionists reject such claims as an affront to, and a violation of, the *raison d'être* of history, namely, to establish certainties and find the truth. Historian of baseball David Block captures what amounts to the missionary zeal of reconstructionist certainty when he describes his 'yearn[ing] for … a consensus vision of the game's evolution that is faithful to the details of history' and sidesteps 'the enduring folk tales and misguided notions of baseball's beginnings'.[19] But Block's own history of the 'roots of our beloved National Pastime' paradoxically reaffirms the impossibility of ascertaining the origins of baseball, a game that has footprints in medieval Europe, children's games, and a host of spontaneous and whimsical behaviours. Harold Seymour was surely correct when he wrote many years ago that 'to ascertain who invented baseball would be equivalent to trying to locate the discoverer of fire'.[20] It is also worth noting that the consolidation of baseball as America's national pastime took well over half a century – a salient reminder that 'meaning is only made manifest retrospectively' and requires much more than simply knowing what happened.[21] Perhaps the greatest irony here is Block's willingness to smooth over conflicting evidence to preserve his 'reconstruction of baseball's odyssey'. Block reassures readers that his history is 'based almost exclusively upon documented evidence … verif[ied] with my own eyes' and 'written in the applicable historical periods', and that his evidence refers 'unambiguously to baseball and related games' as distinct from broader references to 'base or playing at ball'. Despite these reassurances he has to admit that his evidence is still 'somewhat selective' and his history only 'plausible'.[22]

In the final analysis, Block's history of baseball is no more reliable than the bandit's, the bride's, the husband's or the woodcutter's version of events in *Rashomon*. All are points of view. Block's assumption that memory is necessarily less reliable than documentary evidence is unfounded,[23] as discussed earlier (see Chapter 5). The real difference between the respective approaches of Block and Kurosawa lies in epistemology and a derogatory label. Because Kurosawa refuses to interrogate the testimony further, look for other sources, or privilege one version over the others, reconstructionists accuse him of relativism and of undermining all sense of objective knowledge.[24] While the abandonment of certainty and truth may be a logical conclusion of relativism, deconstructionism does not regard this as a problem. As I showed in 'Oral Testimony (and Memory)' (see Chapter 5), in the hands of deconstructionists, the absence of certainties can be as fascinating as knowing the truth about the past, and equally powerful.[25]

Cultural relativism may have facilitated the decline of history as 'an empirical and analytically founded problem-solving epistemology'[26] but it also enabled historians to approach raw materials with much greater creativity and imagination. Such ingenuity and inventiveness appears in sport history most notably in the way some scholars approach memory – which historian Alon Confino calls 'perhaps *the* leading term in cultural history'[27] – and monuments. 'Such is the nature of memory, private and collective', writes Daniel Nathan, that any reading should be 'eclectic, wide-ranging, fragmentary, and necessarily conditional'.[28] Some reconstructionists might see this as a short step from concluding that any interpretation is as good as another. This is not Nathan's intent. Referring to narratives of baseball's Black Sox scandal in America's collective memory, Nathan agrees that they 'can be twisted into many shapes, used in various ways, made to serve a range of purposes. But in practice, there are limits. The Black Sox narrative could not be reshaped to support any purpose or historical interpretation'.[29] Indeed, historians are generally highly alert to weak, poor and ridiculous interpretations. As Munslow reminds us, the potential to draw multiple conclusions does not mean that any one interpretation is as good as another, 'it simply means that there are no definitive interpretations'.[30] Nor does relativism remove hierarchies of values or mean that there are not absolute ethics such as freedom, equality and diversity.[31] In short, cast-iron historical arguments involve much more than simply the remnants of the past. They also include logic, theory, ethics, context and the like.

Reflexivity and historical arguments

Whatever the subject, be it a precise name or date, the exact cause of a sportsperson's death, the function of sport, the meaning of a sporting monument, the objectives of a sporting movement, or a debate over an historical memory, historians build arguments to support one position – using fact, explanation, theory, interpretation – over another. What is apparent to me, and evident in the likes of Hartmann's *Race, Culture, and the Revolt of the Black Athlete* (2003) and Nathan's *Saying It's So* (2003), and other recent works such as John Bale and Mike Cronin's *Sport and Postcolonialism* (2003), Jeffrey Hill's *Sport, Leisure and Culture in Twentieth Century Britain* (2002), Tara Magdalinski and Timothy Chandler's *With God on their Side* (2002), and Patricia Vertinsky and Sherry McKay's *Disciplining Bodies in the Gymnasium* (2004), is the increasingly sophisticated and creative nature of arguments in sport history. In the last mentioned volume, Patricia Vertinsky, Sherry McKay and Stephen Petrina follow Walter Benjamin's vision of history as 'a porous surface whose holes provide windows into discarded memories'. They fix their gaze 'upon the porous surface of the history of the War Memorial Gymnasium' at the University of British Columbia which includes the Memorial Window, the entrances to the monument, the bleachers on the basketball court, the bowling alley and so forth. Their objective is not simply to document the history of the War Memorial Gymnasium; their understanding of history extends far beyond extracting evidence from the remnants of the past. Rather, they want to 'illuminate meanings and memories of the past and to elicit new understandings about the ideal modern body of architectural discourse and the education of the athletic body in higher education in the years following World War II'. As they candidly admit, 'places of memory inspire creative thinking and story-telling about the historical past', and historians' own perspectives and experiences will influence the histories they write.[32]

There is, of course, no magic formula or method for such histories.[33] However, a closer look at what these scholars accept as given and requiring no further evidence or proof, and what they reject as ill-founded, reveals a new emphasis on context (and theories that accept multiple truths and subjective epistemologies[34]). I am not referring here to the contextualisation of the past as described in Chapter 10, a form conscious of its evidence. I am highlighting the historian's personal context that shapes her or his history and is less bound by evidence. Berkhofer calls this form of context reflexive contextualisation, and it requires historians to explain their choices about different levels of context, including the relationship between the personal context and more traditional contextualised versions of the past.[35]

The editors of and contributors to *Disciplining Bodies in the Gymnasium* offer a good illustration of reflexive contextualisation. As faculty at the University of British Columbia they have an intimate knowledge of the War Memorial Gymnasium and acknowledge that the memories they 'have *chosen* to record ... resonate with some of *our own experiences* and have thus been imprinted upon our writing bodies too'.[36] For example, in their essay 'No Body/ies in the Gym', Vertinsky, McKay and Petrina record that women occupying offices in the War Memorial Gymnasium as faculty in the School of Human Kinetics regard the building as 'the bastion of "the basement boys", the male scientists who [take] up most of the working space there'. They cite a female faculty member who registers her 'disappointment' at men who refuse 'to play ball with us' and who exclude women from the team. This example is clearly one with which the authors personally identify and, in this sense, it is part of their own context. But they also put this personal context into a broader context of civil rights for women and the movement towards affirmative action and gender sensitive policies in the 1990s. These trends encouraged university administrators at the University of British Columbia to hire female faculty in the School of Human Kinetics. Importantly, they also extend the broader context into a commentary on change and continuity in gender attitudes and policies. On the one hand, women and men now 'share playing space and practice times' in the War Memorial Gymnasium and 'it is widely accepted that games such as basketball are good for developing physical mastery and group coordination for women, just as they are for men'. On the other hand, women's intercollegiate basketball games are still scheduled as preludes to the men's games, the Department of Athletics and Sports Services employs only one female coach compared to 21 male coaches, and 'the lion's share of the athletic budget still flows to the men's sports'.[37]

Reflexive contextualisation resonates closely with the cultural turn in sport history (see Chapter 11). Nowhere is this more apparent than in the overlapping concerns with presentism.

Reflexivity and presentism

In general historical parlance, presentism connotes the distortion of the past by the insertion of the present into either, or both, questions and conclusions. I take a less negative view of presentism and see it simply as a perspective that places interests in, and concerns about, the present at the heart of the historian's questions. Conservative reconstructionists condemn presentism as an anathema to the discipline; they argue that the experiences, thoughts and actions of the people of the past, not those of the present, must be to the fore.[38] By contrast, a present-minded perspective situates 'the study of the past and its "living existence" in the present'.[39] In the words of Canadian novelist Margaret Atwood, the past no longer belongs to those who once lived in it; the past belongs to those who claim it, and are willing to explore it, and to infuse it with meaning for those alive today. The past belongs to us, because we are the ones who need it.[40]

Indeed, the need for a past undoubtedly explains why new generations of historians continually proffer new interpretations when raking over bygone events, and why different groups often read the past so differently. The fact that so many historians pose their questions against backdrops of contemporary events, issues and observations, and that so many questions involve, either directly or indirectly, issues that relate to contemporary identity, social position and social change, are good evidence of presentism in the discipline and the field.

While presentism always makes historical truths the subject of prevailing consciousness and tentative, it does not mean upholding the present as 'true, given, natural, foundational, and so on'.[41] Nor does it mean forsaking the relationship between knowledge of the past and predictions of the future. On the contrary, it is not uncommon for practitioners to employ historical knowledge to warn their readers of 'the dangers inherent within certain modes of thought and institutional practice'.[42] In *Darwin's Athletes*, John Hoberman uses historical examples to show that sport perpetuates rather than alleviates racial stereotypes. He argues that the rise of the black athlete gave new life to biological racism that continues to block the social progress of African Americans.[43] Similarly, in *Sport and Nationalism in Ireland*, Mike Cronin uses historical examples to show that sport does not unite disparate groups as a single national identity in anything other than the most fleeting and superficial manner – what he calls evanescent nationalism – and that sport will continue to reflect competing identities among broader population groups.[44]

Implicit in these texts is a view that the presentation of historical knowledge can influence the future.[45] This view is infused with notions of ethical responsibility which, in turn, logically requires reflexivity. In Berkhofer's words, 'ethics stresses as it envisages the "ought" of … power and social relations', and, in addressing issues about how people ought to live and conduct their lives, the historian has to decide whether to promote a status quo or oppositional efforts. Additionally, the historian might have to make decisions about whether ethics are relative (contextualised) or absolute.[46]

In conclusion, irrespective of which model and paradigm they work with, all historians are concerned with the question, what makes good history? Reflexive historians, however, subscribe to an additional set of criteria in judging good history. These criteria do not necessarily resolve the debates about what makes history 'good'. As I have shown, deconstructionism has alerted sport historians to the rhetorical, poetic and metaphorical elements in narrative and to the power of language to shape meaning and create understanding.[47] But only a handful of practitioners have ventured into this area (see Chapters 4 and 11) and embraced the call to adopt reflexivity in the presentation of their histories. The mainstream of the field continues to hold tightly to the view that language corresponds to reality and is the medium through which one gains access to the past. Nonetheless, a greater reflexivity just might help the field negotiate the ongoing tension about the purposes and objectives of sport history, that is, the history of a practice that connotes human freedom but is simultaneously shackled to the structures of social constraint and discrimination. This tension returns me to where I began, the politics of history.[48]

Politics and the purpose of history

What is the purpose of history? Few practitioners welcome this question.[49] It is one that historians of sport, who continue to face professional marginalisation, probably fend off more than their colleagues working in other branches of the discipline.[50] Yet, if key themes in sport history – class, race, gender, identity – afford practitioners ideal opportunities to highlight the social and political relevance of their field,[51] disciplinary customs impose impediments. The number of historians subscribing to Geoffrey Elton's principle that 'the past must be studied for its own sake', as 'an intellectual pursuit, an activity of the reasoning mind', may be small and declining, but his stance that the desire to demonstrate social purpose leads to the selection of evidence that meets only preconceived ends (that is, determinism), continues to exert a powerful hold.[52] My position is that reflexivity will help sport historians gain more confidence and feel more comfortable when dealing with explicitly political issues.

Notions of sport as a mirror of society and total history have helped sport historians to explain the relevance of their field. Out of these notions emerged a solid tradition of challenging mainstream views about sport and, in particular, analysing the history of institutions and structures held responsible for marginalising minority groups and limiting their sporting participation. To give but one example, at the height of international condemnation of apartheid, an oppressive political system based on race that not only discriminated against black sportspeople but also demeaned and denigrated them, Robert Archer and Antoine Bouillon reported rich and vibrant rugby, soccer and cricket competitions and cultures in different black communities.[53] Their aim was to record the history of black sport in South Africa, to correct white South African ignorance of black sporting culture, and to challenge official history as relayed by the organs of the apartheid state. Citing an incident involving police interrogation of the South African Black Consciousness leader Steve Biko, who later died of brutality in police detention, Archer and Bouillon showed black people using their knowledge of sport to unsettle white stereotypes.

> His interrogators had been astonished by his interest in what they regarded as exclusively 'white' matters. For example, a rugby tour by the New Zealanders was in progress at the time, and the Security Police asked if he was following the tour. He told them he was. What did he think of the Springbok team? Steve replied: 'I wouldn't have Bosch at fly-half, I'd pick Gavin Cowley'. This he said appeared to flabbergast them. Such black knowledge of white sport . . . [54]

Over the last two decades, such approaches towards challenging mainstream views have proliferated. In so doing they have exposed sport history as a 'political battleground' with different versions in 'constant dialogue and competition' as those committed to upholding authority and those intent on its subversion both seek the sanction of the past.[55]

Nathan offers a particularly good illustration of the 'combative and political nature of representing the past' in his analysis of over 80 years of narratives about the Black Sox scandal. Some versions of the scandal, he remarks, like the one advanced by Baseball Commissioner Judge Kenesaw Mountain Landis, 'contributed to the status quo' while others, such as those put forward by Harry Stein in *Hoopla* (1983), John Sayle's *Eight Men Out* (1988) and Brendan Boyd's *Blue Ruin* (1991), 'complicate historical simplification and resist traditional power relations'.[56]

On this battlefield, radical historians strive to demystify conceptual and cultural categories, denaturalise past and present discourses, and destabilise social and political institutions. Among these dissenting scholars, the task of the historian is to critique, revamp and transform the dominant culture rather than facilitate its reproduction and transmission. The more radical the transformation sought, the more comprehensive historians should be in expressing their oppositional point of view. In particular they need to show that inequalities of power are inherent in every interaction.[57] This is not necessarily an onerous task. According to Alan Trachtenberg, it can be as simple as demonstrating that 'ordering facts into meaning, data into history ... is not an idle exercise but a political act, a matter of judgement and choice about the emerging shape of the present and the future'.[58] As I have shown throughout *The Field*, political viewpoints pervade even the most seemingly innocuous historical texts and practices. The reason is simple. In Berkhofer's words, all historians 'presume models of human behavior, human agency, or the nature of human nature, and they offer them implicitly if not explicitly as the lessons of history for today's understanding of the world'. Furthermore,

> whether humans prefer peace or war, whether human nature is a constant or culturally emergent, what the human will can achieve in the face of adverse circumstances and social structures, what are the nature and roles of the sexes, and even what constitutes causation and proof, are among a multitude of questions whose answers necessitate taking positions basic to political stances. In the end even the long, long ago must be textualized according to present-day historical practice with all the political implications embodied in that form of discourse; otherwise the reader will not understand the story or argument.[59]

In sport history, however, most critiques are still liberal rather than radical in their ideological orientation (see Chapter 4). While consistent with the fan mentality, this state of affairs suggests to me an inherent unease with the politicisation of history. I believe that a more reflexive stance could reconcile this unease by conveying more honest and ultimately stronger arguments. I will illustrate this by building on a critique that Douglas Hartmann makes of a particular conclusion drawn by David Wiggins.

A well-respected scholar of the African American sporting experience, Wiggins offers what appears to be a balanced overview of the revolt by black athletes at three American campuses in the late 1960s and early 1970s.

> White athletes did not take kindly to the fact that black students hid behind a façade of racial discrimination for breaking rules for which they themselves would have been seriously reprimanded. The majority of white athletes, moreover, were disturbed by the seeming attempt of their black counterparts to disrupt the institution of sport, an institution that relied heavily on humbleness, submissiveness, and respect for authority. White athletes believed that their black counterparts mistakenly confused racial discrimination with the discipline that was necessary for the success of any athletic team.

Black athletes did not confuse discrimination with discipline as much as they probably used their coaches as scapegoats. They conveniently alleged discrimination as a justification for their actions, according to Harry Edwards' interpretation, in an attempt 'to ameliorate and help resolve the dilemma of conflicting demands in which they found themselves.' The black athletes at Berkeley, Syracuse, and Oregon State were enrolled at institutions with a relatively small number of blacks in the total school population. Their informal social contacts at these institutions were limited to a small minority of black students on campus. While this situation provided black athletes at the three schools with an important support system, it also placed enormous pressure on them because they were unable to seek out new social contacts when their role as athletes conflicted with the political views of the majority of blacks on campus. By alleging discrimination, black athletes could at once express empathy with or become actively involved in the black protest movement and convince themselves that they had not violated their proper role as athletes.[60]

Hartmann agrees with Wiggins that 'these protests were an important and even calculated part of a much broader and larger symbolic attack on antiblack racism in a post-civil rights United States'. And he concurs that 'African American athletes often had to be convinced against their initial inclinations, by more politically progressive members of the black community to take part in race-based protests'. But Wiggins' apparent downplaying of the real claims of racial discrimination and injustice that underscored these protests troubles Hartmann. The logical conclusion of ignoring these claims is to 'see these revolts merely as symbolic appropriations of sport; that is, the allegations of discrimination in sport were simply used for political purpose with no real basis in fact'.[61]

An examination of Wiggins' body of work demonstrates that this logical conclusion is not the only possible one.[62] And I agree that there is something amiss with Wiggins' conclusion in this specific piece. Looking more closely, it seems to me that he wants to reconcile three competing positions: his commitment to reconstructionism which defines real history as fair, balanced and objective, his knowledge that black athletes suffered discrimination, and his own role as what he calls a 'tangential' actor in the protests. In the introduction to *Glory Bound*, Wiggins describes the nature of historical research in terms of locating primary source material, organising historical materials and careful writing, and he appears committed to objective, neutral, a-political history. His apparent definition of objectivity would help explain a preparedness to give equal weight to both sides of any argument.[63] As an experienced researcher of the African American sporting experience, Wiggins is familiar with the institutional neglect, social isolation, racial insensitivity and prejudice that African American athletes suffered on white campuses.[64] Last, Wiggins witnessed at close quarters at least three episodes of racial politics between African American athletes and University officials at Oregon State.[65]

These competing positions place Wiggins in a predicament. First, by giving equal weight in the conclusion to both the black and white views, he ends up favouring the latter because the two sides were so unequal in the first place. Second, his a-political stance does not preserve the neutrality that he apparently seeks to convey. As the historian of social policy and gender issues Linda Gordon reminds us, 'the pose of objectivity is worse than explicit partisanship, because those who claim neutrality are misleading people about their actual positions, and worse, ... they lack a viewpoint from which to be critical of their own culture'.[66] In a much earlier article, Wiggins admitted that sport in the United States 'has not always been the democratic savior as some people have portrayed it, but rather a white built, white-owned, and white-serving institution characterized by subjugation of the black athlete'.[67] However, those unfamiliar with this other work could be forgiven for thinking that he does not want to critique sport. Adding weight to this view is an admission that he found the decision to ask for the resignation of a baseball coach (one of the three episodes of racial politics at Oregon State University in which he had an involvement) 'terribly difficult', given that he was 'a nineteen-year-old college student who had always been taught to respect those in authority'.[68] In short, he avoids discussion of an institution that in the late 1960s and early 1970s was riven with a set of tensions and contradictions that David Zang would later label SportsWars.[69]

How might Wiggins resolve this predicament? I believe that greater reflexivity on his part would have helped; furthermore, it could have strengthened his history. Bringing himself into the narrative and openly reflecting on his (partial) viewpoint as a young white college athlete at a time of political turmoil, and then comparing this viewpoint to the one he held as an experienced researcher nearly two decades later, would have given Wiggins the opportunity to say something insightful about the meaning of sport and, in particular, why so many participants readily accept its qualities such as submissiveness and respect for authority. Undoubtedly such a comparison would have altered his history, possibly in a quite radical way. By posing questions such as 'Do I still subscribe to the view that coaches are worthy of respect by virtue of their position?' and 'Would I make the same decisions now as then?', and engaging with the answers in his text, Wiggins could have avoided the pretence of offering a purely objective and neutral viewpoint. He may also have been able to show how the discourse of sport works to obscure, erase and mystify racial issues. Hartmann links this discourse to a liberal democratic ideology that makes it 'impossible for outsiders to the racial injustice and discontent ... to even begin to understand the protesters' ... grievances and concerns'.[70] However, Wiggins was there and has studied the issues for decades. He is perfectly – perhaps uniquely – positioned to demystify and debunk many of the popular notions and ideas about sport and race. But he can only do that if he is prepared to make his own position utterly explicit, which is, of course, the essence of decon-structionism.[71]

Some sport historians will argue that the degree of reflexivity recommended here is 'not real history' and that it exceeds the historian's brief. They may describe it as too messy and excessive for their readers – especially general readers for whom most history texts are targeted. They might argue that general readers demand only that the author cites her or his evidence, and they will possibly suggest that the majority of readers are satisfied knowing they are reading work by a trained 'expert'. Such statements misconstrue the issue. History is the study of the past in the present and not the reconstruction of the past in its totality. Without reflexivity historians contribute to the illusion that they have a firm grip on the past.

Finale

A real problem for those practitioners grappling with a new model for sport history is the lack of exemplars. However, recent texts suggest some sport historians are inching forward under their own steam. As Lynn Hunt identified long before the cultural turn had taken hold in sport history, rigorous cultural analysis will inevitably sharpen the methods and goals of history. In her words, 'as historians learn to analyze their subjects' representations of their worlds, they inevitably begin to reflect on the nature of their own efforts to represent history; the practice of history is, after all, a process of text creating and of "seeing", that is, giving form to subjects'.[72] A recent plethora of books on historiography, historical knowledge and history methods vindicate Hunt and suggest that mainstream history is finally beginning to seriously reflect on historical practice. This might well be seen as a good example of the margins of a discipline refiguring the center.[73] Unfortunately, many sport historians still misinterpret this reflection as, first, an unsubstantiated attack on the reliability of historical evidence, and, second, a metaphysical epistemological issue best left to philosophers. The result has been a tendency towards conformity and a stifling of experimentation. Even those sport historians who are pursuing the study of culture and language are only just beginning to reflect on their own representations of history.

Notes

Prologue

1   The olympics do not warrant the veneration of a capital letter. The ancient games were held at Olympia, hence the use of the upper case as a recognised geographical name. Any resemblance that the modern sports pageant may have to the ancient version or to the place called Olympia is remote and allusional – hence the lower case 'o'. Nor does the philosophy of olympism have a greater claim to a capital letter than liberalism, humanitarianism, authoritarianism, utopianism or fascism.

2   The key texts were only published at the end of the decade: Malcolm Templeton, *Human Rights and Sporting Contacts: New Zealand Attitudes to Race Relations in South Africa 1921–94* (Auckland: Auckland University Press, 1998), David Black and John Nauright, *Rugby and the South African Nation* (Manchester: Manchester University Press, 1998), Trevor Richards, *Dancing on Our Bones: New Zealand, South Africa, Rugby and Racism* (Wellington: Bridget Williams Books, 1999), and Shona Thompson, 'The Tour', in Brad Patterson (ed.), *Sport, Society and Culture in New Zealand* (Wellington: Stout Research Centre, 1999), pp. 79–91.

3   E. P. Thompson, *The Poverty of Theory: Or an Orrery of Errors*, second edition (London: Merlin, 1995), p. 51. Similarly Keith Jenkins writes that, 'while most historians would agree that a rigorous method is important [to history], there is a problem as to which rigorous method they are talking about ... Thus, would you like to follow Hegel or Marx or Dilthey or Weber or Popper or Hempel or Aron or Collingwood or Dray or Oakeshott or Danto or Gallie or Walsh or Atkinson or Leff or Hexter? Would you care to go along with modern empiricists, feminists, the Annales School, neo-Marxists, new-stylists, econometricians, structuralists or post-structuralists, or ... Marwick ..., to name but twenty-five possibilities? And this is a short list! The point is that even if you could make a choice, what would be the criteria? How would you know which method would lead to a 'truer' past? ... Talk of method as the road to truth is misleading. There is a range of methods without any agreed criteria for choosing' (*Re-Thinking History* [London: Routledge, 1991], p. 15).

4   Allen Guttmann, *From Ritual to Record* (New York: Columbia University Press, 1978), J. A. Mangan, *Athleticism in the Victorian and Edwardian Public School* (Cambridge: Cambridge University Press, 1981), Richard Holt's *Sport and the British* (Oxford: Oxford University

Press, 1989), and Patricia Vertinsky's *The Eternally Wounded Woman* (Urbana, IL: University of Illinois Press, 1994). Manchester University Press first published the latter in 1989.

5   Thompson, *The Poverty of Theory*, p. 68.

6   Although as Keith Jenkins points out, sport historians are not unique in this respect (*Refiguring History: New Thoughts on an Old Discipline* [London: Routledge, 2003], pp. 36–9).

7   Alex Callinicos, *Theories and Narratives: Reflections on the Philosophy of History* (Cambridge: Polity Press 1995), p. 3. See also, Mark Cousins, 'The Practice of Historical Investigation', in Derek Attridge, Geoff Bennington and Robert Young (eds), *Structuralism and the Question of History* (Cambridge: Cambridge University Press, 1989), pp. 126–36.

8   Hayden White, *Metahistory: The Historical Imagination in Nineteenth-century Europe* (Baltimore, MD: The Johns Hopkins University Press, 1973), p. xi.

9   Miles Fairburn, *Social History: Problems, Strategies and Methods* (New York: St Martin's Press, 1999), p. 7, and Nancy Struna, 'Social History and Sport', in Jay Coakley and Eric Dunning (eds), *Handbook of Sports Studies* (London: Sage, 2000), p. 187 and p. 189. Anglo-American historians attribute the *wie es eigentlich gewesen* – as it really was, or as it actually happened – approach to the nineteenth century German historian Leopold von Ranke, who is widely regarded as the father of modern historical scholarship. Peter Novick argues that successive generations of historians have misinterpreted Ranke for whom the term *eigentlich* meant 'essentially' rather than 'really'. In the context of 'essential', Ranke 'reflected a widespread romantic desire to open oneself to the flow of intuitive perception'. As Peter Novick puts it, 'the young historian who in the 1970s proposed a "psychedelic" approach to history – altered states of consciousness as a means for historians to project themselves back into the past – was thus in some respects truer to the essence of Ranke's approach than empiricists who never lifted their eyes from the documents.' Ironically, German historians attacked Ranke for his idealism while 'American historians venerated him for being precisely what he was not' (*That Noble Dream: The 'Objectivity Question' and the American Historical Profession* [Cambridge: Cambridge University Press, 1988], pp. 26–31, quotes p. 28).

10   Mike Huggins, *Flat Racing and British Society 1790–1914* (London: Frank Cass, 2000), Pamela Grundy, *Learning to Win: Sports, Education, and Social Change in Twentieth-Century North Carolina* (Chapel Hill, NC: The University of North Carolina Press, 2001), Robert Barney, Stephen Wenn and Scott Martyn, *Selling the Five Rings: The International Olympic Committee and the Rise of Olympic Commercialism* (Salt Lake City, UT: University of Utah Press, 2002), Daniel Nathan, *Saying It's So: A Cultural History of the Black Sox Scandal* (Urbana, IL: University of Illinois Press, 2003). *Saying It's So* also won the North American Society for the Sociology of Sport Book Award.

11   Robert Berkhofer, *Beyond the Great Story: History as Text and Discourse* (Cambridge, MA: Harvard University Press, 1995), p. 12.

12   Hans Kellner attributes the 'marginality of historical theory [in] the historical profession' to a paucity of jobs, lack of direct influence on other historical endeavours, and 'a set of conceptual concerns unique to itself' ('A Bedrock of Order: Hayden White's Linguistic Humanism', *History and Theory*, 19, 4 [1980], p. 10).

13   Michael Postan, *Fact and Relevance: Essays on Historical Method* (Cambridge: Cambridge University Press, 1971), p. 64.

1 An introduction to sport historiography

1   Several sport historians have described the origins and rise of the field. See, for example, Richard Cashman, 'The Making of Sporting Traditions', *Bulletin* [of the Australian Society for Sports History] (December 1989), pp. 15–28, Alan Metcalfe, 'North American Sport History: A Review of North American Sport Historians and Their Works', *Exercise and Sport Sciences Reviews*, 2 (1974), pp. 225–38, and Nancy Struna, 'Sport History', in John Massengale and Richard Swanson (eds), *The History of Exercise and Sport Science* (Champaign, IL: Human Kinetics, 1997), pp. 143–79. Struna offers a good overview of the different themes in the

field in, 'Social History and Sport', in Jay Coakley and Eric Dunning (eds), *Handbook of Sports Studies* (London: Sage, 2000), pp. 191–6.

2   Nancy Struna, 'Historical Research in Physical Activity', in Jerry Thomas and Jack Nelson (eds), *Research Methods in Physical Activity* (Champaign, IL: Human Kinetics, 1996), pp. 251–75. Mel Adelman presented a very early version of Struna's approach in, 'The Role of the Sport Historian', *Quest*, 12 (1969), pp. 61–5. Citing Louis Gottschalk, Adelman described two groups of sport historians. 'One may be called "descriptive historians"; they attempt to give an account of the event or situation under consideration in its own unique setting. The other may be called "theoretical historians"; they try to find in their subject matter a basis for comparison, classification, interpretation or generalization. Every historian is likely to be in both groups at the same time or different times even though he may emphasize his adherence to one rather than the other' (p. 62). Roberta Park proposed a useful introductory broad schema of sport history by linking the field to the contents of social history, cultural history, and intellectual history ('Sport History in the 1990s: Prospects and Problems', *American Academy of Physical Education Papers*, 20 [1987], pp. 98–9, and 'Research and Scholarship in the History of Physical Education and Sport: The Current State of Affairs', *Research Quarterly for Exercise and Sport*, 54, 2 [1983], pp. 98–100). Park's categories do, I believe, offer a good introduction to the content of sport history to 100 and 200 level classes.

3   Struna, 'Historical Research', p. 257.

4   Struna, 'Historical Research', p. 258. See also, Thomas Haskell, *Objectivity Is Not Neutrality: Explanatory Schemes in History* (Baltimore, MD: The Johns Hopkins University Press, 1998), p. 7, and John Tosh, *The Pursuit of History: Aims, Methods and New Directions in the Study of Modern History*, second edition (London: Longman, 1991), p. 112.

5   E. P. Thompson, *The Poverty of Theory: Or an Orrery of Errors* (London: Merlin, 1995), p. 64. In his objection to the still approach, Thompson raised questions about the relationship between history and time. I touch on this throughout *The Field*. It is discussed in great detail by Paul Ricoeur, *Time and Narrative*, volume 1, translated by Kathleen McLaughlin and David Pellauer (Chicago, IL: University of Chicago Press, 1983), volume 2 translated by Kathleen McLaughlin and David Pellauer (Chicago, IL: University of Chicago Press, 1984), volume 3, translated by Kathleen Blamey and David Pellauer (Chicago, IL: University of Chicago Press, 1985).

6   Keith Jenkins and Alun Munslow (eds), *The Nature of History Reader* (London: Routledge, 2004), p. 4. The clearest outline of the three models is found in, Alun Munslow, *Deconstructing History* (London: Routledge, 1997).

7   Geoffrey Elton, *Return to Essentials: Some Reflections on the Present State of Historical Study* (Cambridge: Cambridge University Press, 1991), p. 27.

8   Munslow, *Deconstructing History*, p. 14 and p. 15.

9   David Hackett Fischer, *Historians' Fallacies: Toward a Logic of Historical Thought* (New York: Harper & Row, 1970), p. xv note 1.

10 Robert Eaglestone offers an excellent clarification of the deconstructionist position on evidence in his, *Postmodernism and Holocaust Denial* (Cambridge: Icon, 2001).

11 Michael Stanford, *A Companion to the Study of History* (Oxford: Basil Blackwell, 1994), p. 91.

12 Yves-Pierre Boulongne, 'Pierre de Coubertin and Women's Sport', *Olympic Review* (February/March 2000), pp. 23–6.

13 Louis Gottschalk, *Understanding History: A Primer of Historical Method*, second edition (New York: Alfred A. Knopf, 1969), pp. 149–50.

14 Peter Gay, *Style in History* (New York: Basic Books, 1974), pp. 3; See also Gottschalk, *Understanding History*, pp. 17–19.

15 Tosh, *The Pursuit of History*, p. 113, and J. A. Mangan, 'The End of History Perhaps – But the End of the Beginning for the History of Sport! An Anglo-Saxon Autobiographical Perspective', *Sporting Traditions*, 16, 1 (1999), pp. 62–3. See also, Toni Bruce, 'Postmodernism and the Possibilities for Writing "Vital" Sports Texts', in Geneviève Rail (ed.), *Sport and Postmodern Times* (Albany, NY: State University of New York Press, 1998), pp. 8–9. For a critical comment

on these views see, Phillipe Carrard, *Poetics of the New History: French Historical Discourse from Braudel to Chartier* (Baltimore, MD: The Johns Hopkins University Press, 1992), pp. 141–6.

16 Michael Postan, *Fact and Relevance: Essays on Historical Method* (Cambridge: Cambridge University Press, 1971), p. 62.

17 May Brodbeck, 'Methodological Individualisms: Definition and Reduction', in William Dray (ed.), *Philosophical Analysis and History* (New York: Harper & Row, 1966), pp. 297–329, and Steven Lukes, *Individualism* (Oxford: Blackwell, 1973).

18 Elton, *Return to Essentials*, p. 15 and p. 19.

19 Munslow, *Deconstructing History*, pp. 22–3, and Tosh, *The Pursuit of History*, pp. 154–5.

20 Tosh, *The Pursuit of History*, pp. 160–1. See also, Peter Burke, *History and Social Theory* (Cambridge: Polity Press, 1992), p. 29.

21 Werner Sombart, 'Economic Theory and Economic History', *The Economic History Review*, 2, 1 (1929), p. 3.

22 Munslow, *Deconstructing History*, p. 23 and p. 40.

23 Munslow, *Deconstructing History*, p. 48.

24 Haskell, *Objectivity Is Not Neutrality*, pp. 6–7.

25 Stephen Hardy, 'Entrepreneurs, Structures, and the Sportgeist: Old Tensions in a Modern Industry', in Donald Kyle and Gary Stark (eds), *Essays on Sport History and Sport Mythology* (College Station, TX: Texas A & M Press, 1990), pp. 47–51.

26 Norman Denzin, *The Research Act*, third edition (Englewood Cliffs, NJ: Prentice Hall, 1989), p. 49.

27 Hardy, 'Entrepreneurs, Structures, and the Sportgeist', p. 47.

28 Munslow, *Deconstructing History*, p. 46.

29 Denzin, *The Research Act*, p. 13.

30 According to Wayne Wilson, concepts typically enter sport history a decade after they first appear in mainstream fields ('A Bibliometric Analysis of NASSH Literature, 1973–2001: Assessing Innovation, Continuity and Impact', paper presented to the North American Society for Sport History convention, 28 May 2004).

31 John Hoberman, 'Toward a Theory of Olympic Internationalism', *Journal of Sport History*, 22, 1 (1995), pp. 1–37.

32 Arthur Stinchcombe, *Theoretical Methods in Social History* (New York: Academic Press, 1978), p. 17.

33 Stinchcombe, *Theoretical Methods*, p. 22.

34 Stinchcombe, *Theoretical Methods*, pp. 17–19, and Denzin, *The Research Act*, p. 53 and pp. 59–60.

35 Munslow, *Deconstructing History*, p. 71.

36 Munslow, *Deconstructing History*, p. 188.

37 Munslow, *Deconstructing History*, p. 118.

38 Munslow, *Deconstructing History*, p. 74.

39 Munslow, *Deconstructing History*, pp. 100–1.

40 Hayden White, *Metahistory: The Historical Imagination in Nineteenth-century Europe* (Baltimore, MD: The Johns Hopkins University Press, 1973), p. 283.

41 Joyce Appleby, Lynn Hunt and Margaret Jacob, *Telling the Truth About History* (New York: W. W. Norton, 1994).

42 Fischer, *Historians' Fallacies*, p. xv.

43 Robert Berkhofer, *Beyond the Great Story: History as Text and Discourse* (Cambridge, MA: Harvard University Press, 1995), p. 37.

44 Munslow, *Deconstructing History*, p. 10.

45 Peter Novick, *That Noble Dream: The "Objectivity Quest" and the American Historical Profession* (Cambridge: Cambridge University Press, 1988), p. 2.

46 Berkhofer, *Beyond the Great Story*, p. 165 and pp. 213–14.

47 Tony Collins, *Rugby's Great Split: Class, Culture and the Origins of Rugby League Football* (London: Frank Cass, 1998), Robert Henderson, *Ball, Bat and Bishop: The Origin of Ball Games* (Urbana,

IL: University of Illinois Press (1947/2001), and David Young, *The Olympic Myth of Greek Amateur Athletics* (Chicago, IL: Ares Publishers, 1984).

48 Dennis Smith, *The Rise of Historical Sociology* (Cambridge: Polity Press, 1991), p. 163.

49 Gary Osmond, '"Look at that Kid Crawling": Race, Myth and the "Crawl" Stroke', *Australian Historical Studies*, forthcoming, and Brett Hutchins, *Don Bradman: Challenging the Myth* (Melbourne: Cambridge University Press, 2002).

50 Miles Fairburn, *Social History: Problems, Strategies and Methods* (New York: St Martin's Press, 1999), p. 92.

51 Kevin McAleer, *Dueling: The Cult of Honor in Fin-de-Siècle Germany* (Princeton, NJ: Princeton University Press, 1994), pp. 77–8.

52 Ali Mazrui, 'Boxer Muhammad Ali and Soldier Idi Amin as International Political Symbols: The Bioeconomics of Sport and War', *Comparative Studies in Society and History*, 19, 2 (1977), pp. 189–215, and Ali Mazrui, *The Africans: A Triple Heritage* (London: BBC Publications, 1986).

53 James Mills and Paul Dimeo, '"When Gold is Fired It Shines": Sport, the Imagination and the Body in Colonial and Postcolonial India', in John Bale and Mike Cronin (eds), *Sport and Postcolonialism* (Oxford: Berg, 2003), pp. 107–22, Grant Farred, '"Theatre of Dreams": Mimicry and Difference in Cape Flats Township Football', in Bale and Cronin, *Sport and Postcolonialism*, pp. 123–45, and John Hughson, '"We Are Red, White and Blue, We Are Catholic, Why Aren't You?": Religion and Soccer Subculture and Symbolism', in Tara Magdalinski and Timothy Chandler (eds), *With God on their Side: Sport in the Service of Religion* (London: Routledge, 2002), pp. 56–70.

54 Jennifer Hargreaves, *Sporting Females: Critical Issues in the History and Sociology of Women's Sports* (London: Routledge, 1994), p. 36. See, for example, Pamela Grundy, *Learning to Win: Sports, Education, and Social Change in Twentieth-Century North Carolina* (Chapel Hill, NC: The University of North Carolina Press, 2001), pp. 130–1, and Susan Cahn, *Coming on Strong: Gender and Sexuality in Twentieth-Century Women's Sport* (Cambridge, MA: Harvard University Press, 1995), p. 38.

55 Peter Stearns, 'Goals in History Teaching', *International Review of History Education*, 2 (1998), p. 281, and Tosh, *The Pursuit of History*, pp. 154–5.

56 See, for example, Steven Riess, *Sport in Industrial America 1850–1920* (Wheeling, IL: Harlan Davidson, 1995), pp. 11–42.

57 Berkhofer, *Beyond the Great Story*, p. 32.

58 E. P. Thompson, 'Anthropology and the Discipline of Historical Context', *Midland History*, 3 (1972), p. 43.

59 Marwick, Arthur, *The Sixties: Cultural Revolution in Britain, France, Italy, and the United States, c.1958 – c.1974* (Oxford: Oxford University Press, 1998), pp. 23–5.

60 Elliot Gorn, '"Gouge and Bite, Pull Hair and Scratch": The Social Significance of Fighting in the Southern Backcountry', *American Historical Review*, 90, 1 (1985), pp. 18–43, and Greg Ryan, *The Making of New Zealand Cricket 1832–1914* (London: Frank Cass, 2004).

61 Jeffrey Hill, 'British Sports History: A Post-modern Future?', *Journal of Sport History*, 23, 1 (1996), p. 18.

62 Hill, 'British Sports History', p. 17.

63 See for example, Cahn, *Coming on Strong*, Patricia Vertinsky, *The Eternally Wounded Woman: Women, Doctors, and Exercise in the Late Nineteenth Century* (Urbana, IL: University of Illinois Press, 1994), and Douglas Brown, 'Modern Sport, Modernism and the Cultural Manifesto: De Coubetin's Revue Olympique', *The International Journal of the History of Sport*, 18, 2 (2001), pp. 78–109.

64 John Bloom, *To Show What an Indian Can Do: Sports at Native American Boarding Schools* (Minneapolis, MN: University of Minnesota Press, 2000), Cahn, *Coming on Strong*, John Hargreaves, *Sport, Power and Culture: A Social and Historical Analysis of Popular Sports in Britain* (Cambridge: Polity Press, 1986), Peter Mewett, 'History in the Making and the Making of History: Stories and the Social Construction of Sport', *Sporting Traditions*, 17, 1 (2000), pp.

1–17, Michael Oriard, *Reading Football: How the Popular Press Created an American Spectacle* (Chapel Hill, NC: University of North Carolina Press, 1993), Michael Oriard, *King Football: Sport and Spectacle in the Golden Age of Radio and Newsreels, Movies and Magazines, the Weekly and the Daily Press* (Chapel Hill, NC: University of North Carolina Press, 2001), Catriona Parratt, 'Of Place and Men and Women: Gender and Topophilia in the "Haxey Hood"', *Journal of Sport History*, 27, 2 (2000), pp. 229–45, Synthia Sydnor, 'A History of Synchronized Swimming', *Journal of Sport History*, 25, 2 (1998), pp. 252–67, and Vertinsky, *The Eternally Wounded Woman*.

65 Pat Hudson, *History by Numbers: An Introduction to Quantitative Approaches* (London: Arnold, 2000), p. 53. See for example, Nancy Struna, 'Gender and Sporting Practice in Early America, 1750–1810, *Journal of Sport History*, 18, 1 (1991), pp. 10–30.

66 Catriona Parratt, 'From the History of Women in Sport to Women's Sport History: A Research Agenda', in Margaret Costa and Sharon Guthrie, *Women and Sport: Interdisciplinary Perspectives* (Champaign, IL: Human Kinetics, 1994), p. 6, and Susan Birrell, 'Discourses on the Gender/Sport Relationship. From Women in Sports to Gender Relations', *Exercise and Sport Sciences Review*, 16 (1988), pp. 467–9.

67 Parratt, 'A Research Agenda', p. 9.

68 Patricia Vertinsky, 'Gender Relations, Women's History and Sport History: A Decade of Changing Enquiry, 1983–1993', *Journal of Sport History*, 21, 1 (1994), pp. 13–24. For a more general discussion of this shift see, Joan Scott, 'Women's History', in Peter Burke (ed.), *New Perspectives on Historical Writing*, second edition (Cambridge: Polity Press, 2001), pp. 43–70.

69 Antoinette Burton, *Dwelling in the Archive: Women Writing House, Home and History in Late Colonial India* (Oxford: Oxford University Press, 2003), p. 23. See, for example, Struna, 'Gender and Sporting Practice', pp. 10–30.

70 Parratt, 'A Research Agenda', pp. 11–12, and Struna, 'Social History and Sport', p. 189.

71 Vertinsky, 'Gender Relations', pp. 16–18 and pp. 22–3, and Jennifer Hargreaves, 'Querying Sport Feminism: Personal or Political', in Richard Giulianotti (ed.), *Sport and Modern Social Theorists* (Basingstoke: Palgrave Macmillan, 2004), pp. 201–3. For a good example see, Patricia Vertinsky and Sherry McKay (eds), *Disciplining Bodies in the Gymnasium: Memory, Monument, Modernism* (London: Routledge, 2004). I discuss this text in the Epilogue.

72 See, in particular, Joan Scott, *Gender and the Politics of History* (New York: Columbia University Press, 1988).

73 Alun Munslow, *The Routledge Companion to Historical Studies* (London: Routledge, 2000), pp. 228–32, Berkhofer, *Beyond the Great Story*, p. 258, and M. Ann Hall, *Feminism and Sporting Bodies: Essays on Theory and Practice* (Champaign, IL: Human Kinetics, 1996), p. 71 and p. 86.

74 Richard Mandell, 'Modern Criticism of Sport', in Kyle and Stark, *Essays on Sport History*, pp. 118–38.

75 Cited in, Berkhofer, *Beyond the Great Story*, pp. 271–2.

76 Hall, *Feminism and Sporting Bodies*, pp. 70–6.

77 Penelope Corfield, 'History and the Challenge of Gender History', *Rethinking History*, 1, 3 (1997), p. 241 and p. 245.

78 Burton, *Dwelling in the Archive*, pp. 143–4.

79 Jenkins and Munslow, *History Reader*, p. 6.

80 For a good example, see Robert Barney, 'Setting the Record Straight – Again: Dorando Pietri It Is', *Olympika*, 10 (2001), pp. 129–30.

81 Here I am thinking about broad questions pertaining to social change.

2 Facts, objectivity and interpretation: truth in sport history

1 Geoffrey Elton, *Return to Essentials: Some Reflections on the Present State of Historical Study* (Cambridge: Cambridge University Press, 1991), p. 48. Today, Elton represents the conservative reconstructionist position as evident in the following quote: 'uncertainty around

historical truth and a true view of the past arises from the deficiencies of the evidence and the problems it poses, rather than from the alleged transformation of events in the organizing mind of the historian. That doctrine, however dressed up, leads straight to a frivolous nihilism which allows any historian to say whatever he likes. We historians are firmly bound by the authority of our sources ... And though gaps and ambiguities close the road to total reconstruction, the challenges they pose lead to those fruitful exchanges, even controversies, among historians which do as much as anything does to advance our outworks ever nearer to the fortress of truth' (*Return to Essentials*, pp. 48–9).

2   David Hackett Fischer, *Historians' Fallacies: Toward a Logic of Historical Thought* (New York: Harper & Row, 1970), p. 40.

3   Robert Berkhofer, *Beyond the Great Story: History as Text and Discourse* (Cambridge: Harvard University Press, 1995), p. 56.

4   Joyce Appleby, Lynn Hunt and Margaret Jacob, *Telling The Truth About History* (New York: W. W. Norton, 1994), p. 259.

5   The origins of this model lie in the scientific revolution. See, Peter Novick, *That Noble Dream: The 'Objectivity Question' and the American Historical Profession* (Cambridge: Cambridge University Press, 1988), Part I, and Appleby, Hunt and Jacob, *Telling The Truth*, Chapters 1 and 2. See also, Gareth Stedman Jones, 'History: The Poverty of Empiricism', in Robin Blackburn (ed.), *Ideology in Social Science: Readings in Critical Social Theory* (London: Fontana, 1972), pp. 96–115.

6   Michael Postan, *Fact and Relevance: Essays on Historical Method* (Cambridge: Cambridge University Press, 1971), p. 48 and p. 49, and John Murphy, 'The Voice of Memory: History, Autobiography and Oral Memory', *Historical Studies*, 22, 87 (1986), p. 158.

7   Bernard Whimpress, 'The Value of Facts in Sports History', *Sporting Traditions*, 9, 1 (1992), p. 2. While he goes on to argue that historians must put their facts into context, his underlying assumption appears to be that it is as easy to determine a context as it is to gather the facts. On the contrary, determining a context is as difficult as deciding the facts (Chapter 10). Indeed, the latter formulation highlights the deficiencies of the map analogy: maps only provide a sense of place if the reader knows how to translate cartographic symbols and scales into real terrain.

8   Historians use notes – as footnotes or endnotes – to record where they found their facts/ evidence/testimony. In this sense these are the sites where historians prove that they have consulted relevant historical materials. They are also frequently the sites where historians engage with and challenge each other (Louis Gottschalk, *Understanding History: A Primer of Historical Method*, second edition [New York: Alfred A. Knopf, 1969], p. 19) and describe their own reflexivity. I discuss the issue of reflexivity more fully in the epilogue. Sloppy noting, excessive and pedantic noting, and especially the absence of notes, expose historians to intense peer criticism (Daniel Nathan, *Saying It's So: A Cultural History of the Black Sox Scandal* [Urbana, IL: University of Illinois Press, 2003], p. 112 and pp. 131–2). Reviewers criticised the lack of notes in Brian Stoddart's *Saturday Afternoon Fever* (1986) (see, Bob Stewart, 'Stoddart on Sport', *Sporting Traditions*, 3, 1 [1986], p. 93 and David Rowe, 'Saturday Afternoon Theory', *Sporting Traditions*, 4, 1 [1987], pp. 56–7 and pp. 64–5) and Colin Howell's *Blood, Sweat, and Cheers* (2001) (see, Greg Gillespie, 'Canadian Sport Studies', *International Sports Studies*, 24, 2 [2002], p. 66). Of course, notes 'guarantee nothing in themselves'. Practitioners use them in a myriad of ways: to deny or assert the same facts, 'to amass citations and quotations of no interest to any reader', or 'to attack anything that resembles a new thesis' (Anthony Grafton, *The Footnote: A Curious History* [London: Faber and Faber, 1997], pp. 4–5 and p. 235. See also, p. 7).

9   Keith Windschuttle, *The Killing of History* (Sydney: Macleay Press, 1994), p. 22 and p. 212. Induction takes its name from the English philosopher and statesman Francis Bacon who advanced a method that 'derives its axioms from the senses and the particulars, rising by a gradual and unbroken ascent, so that it arrives at the most general axioms last of all' (cited in, Fischer, *Historians' Fallacies*, p. 4 note 2). But as Fischer comments, Bacon's major work

'did not defend an induction as simple-minded as this, but rather a more complex method of interdependent inquiry and research' (p. 5).

10   Gerald Redmond, *The Sporting Scots of Nineteenth-Century Canada* (Toronto: Associated University Presses, 1982), pp. 232–3. While 'probably', the opening word in this quote, underscores the conservative reconstructionist's penchant for caution, it hardly diminishes the certainty of the conclusion.

11   Primary and secondary are not 'cast-iron categories', the distinction depends on the questions that the historian asks (Luise White, *Speaking With Vampires: Rumor and History in Colonial Africa* [Berkeley, CA: University of California Press, 2000], p. 311). Evidence spatially and temporally removed from an event may qualify as a primary source. Often historians are as interested in what contemporary commentators *thought* was happening, or thought had happened, as in what actually did happen (John Tosh, *The Pursuit of History: Aims, Methods and New Directions in the Study of Modern History*, third edition [London: Longman, 2000], p. 38). In their respective analyses of the conquest of Mount Everest, for example, Gordon Stewart and Peter Hansen pay as much attention to the account given by John Hunt, the ascent team's captain who stayed at the base camp, as to Edmund Hillary and Tenzing Norgay who climbed to the summit. Hunt's views constitute a primary source for Stewart and Hansen who seek to understand the conquest of Everest in the context of British imperialism (Gordon Stewart, 'Tenzing's Two Wrist-Watches: The Conquest of Everest and Late Imperial Culture in Britain 1921–1953', *Past and Present*, 149 [1995], pp. 170–97, and Peter Hansen, 'Comment' [on Gordon Stewart's 'Tenzing's Two Wrist-Watches'], *Past and Present*, 157 [1997], pp. 159–77). Historians mostly use secondary sources to contextualise their subject (Chapter 10). When historians use secondary sources as evidence, as they often must, they access evidence through an intermediary who mediates, or filters, the information (Tosh, *The Pursuit of History*, p. 38). In the search for evidence about the physical ascent of Mount Everest, John Hunt is a secondary source: he neither accompanied nor observed Hillary and Tenzing on the summit.

12   Ronald Smith, 'Intercollegiate Athletics/Football History at the Dawn of a New Century', *Journal of Sport History*, 29, 2 (2002), p. 231. See also, p. 234.

13   Fischer, *Historians' Fallacies*, p. 4.

14   R. G. Collingwood, *The Principles of History* (Oxford: Oxford University Press, 1999), pp. 12–13.

15   Murphy, 'The Voice of Memory', p. 158 and p. 162.

16   Appleby, Hunt and Jacob, *Telling The Truth*, pp. 260–1.

17   Appleby, Hunt and Jacob, *Telling The Truth*, p. 242.

18   Simon Milton, Review of John Sugden and Alan Tomlinson, *FIFA and the Contest for World Football, Who Rules the Peoples' Game?* (Cambridge: Polity Press, 1998), *International Sports Studies*, 21, 2 (1999), pp. 77–8. The classic example of fact pouncing in sport history is Ronald Smith's review of Steve Pope's *Patriotic Games*. Smith's paper begins with a list of 34 alleged factual errors (Roundtable Discussion: Sport, Nationalism and *Patriotic Games*, paper presented at the North American Society for Sport History Conference, 24 May 1998, University of Windsor).

19   Andrew Moore, 'Testosterone Overdose: Popular Culture and Historical Memory', *Sporting Traditions*, 10, 1 (1993), p. 17. As author of *The Mighty Bears! A Social History of North Sydney Rugby League* (1995), Moore is well qualified to judge the facts in question: that Gary – not Greg – Larson was Norths' forward lock who played State of Origin for Queensland, and that Don McKinnon – not Norm Strong – holds the club record for most games. See also, Smith, Sport, Nationalism and *Patriotic Games*, and Richard Holt, Review of Derek Birley's trilogy, *Sport and the Making of Britain*, *Land of Sport and Glory*, and *Playing the Game* (Manchester: Manchester University Press, 1993, 1995 and 1996), *The Sports Historian*, 18, 2 (1998), p. 170.

20   Some historians at least have the grace to apologise for their own errors. After castigating Bill Mallon and Ian Buchanan 'for perpetuating … a long held error in the expression of the

name of the celebrated [1908 olympic games] Italian marathoner Dorando Pietri', Robert Barney revisited the issue and on the basis of fresh evidence magnanimously conceded that his appellation Pietri Dorando was incorrect (Robert Barney, 'Setting the Record Straight – Again: Dorando Pietri It Is', *Olympika*, 10 [2001], pp. 129–30).

21 Arthur Marwick draws the useful distinction here between human 'inaccuracy' and 'wilful dishonesty' (Arthur Marwick, *The Nature of History*, second edition [London: Macmillan, 1981], p. 162).

22 Berkhofer, *Beyond the Great Story*, p. 56.

23 Milton, Review, p. 78. Edward Carr likened bestowing praise on historians for factual accuracy to congratulating 'an architect for using … properly mixed concrete'. 'It is a necessary condition of [their] work', he says, 'but not [their] essential function'. Carr maintains that historians do not require the expertise 'to determine the origin and period of a fragment of pottery or marble, to decipher an obscure inscription, or to make the elaborate astronomical calculations to establish a precise date'. These are the 'so-called basic facts', they are the 'same for all historians', and 'belong to the category of the raw materials of the historian rather than of history itself' (Edward Carr, *What Is History?*, second edition [Harmondsworth: Penguin, 1990], pp. 10–11. See also, Appleby, Hunt and Jacob, *Telling The Truth*, p. 248). But not everyone agrees. Fischer called this a 'haughty attitude' and 'unfortunate habit'. 'The apparent fact that historians often assume that particular statements will be accurate, or that somebody else is responsible for their accuracy', Fischer argued, 'explain[s] why so many historical statements are in fact inaccurate'. In a telling point against Carr, Fischer correctly reminded historians that 'there are *no* auxillary sciences' to which they can send their 'verification problems'; responsibility rests solely with the individual historian (Fischer, *Historians' Fallacies*, p. 41). Of course, the sheer volume of raw material in most cases makes checking every fact unrealistic and unfeasible. Like Carr, Postan pointed to history as an act of interpretation rather than the discovery and regurgitation of facts when he ranked practitioners who show an 'aptitude for theoretical synthesis' ahead of those who 'cautiously and painstakingly' check the facts (Postan, *Fact and Relevance*, p. 16). On the other hand, every historian will, at some time or another, regret their failure to systematically check their own references (Marwick, *Nature of History*, pp. 162–3).

24 Postan, *Fact and Relevance*, p. 51.

25 Carr, *What Is History?*, p. 11, p. 12 and p. 23. Carr likened facts to free swimming fish. He said that they reside in a 'vast and inaccessible ocean and what the historian catches will depend, partly on chance, but mainly on what part of the ocean he chooses to fish in and what tackle he chooses to use – these two factors being, of course, determined by the kind of fish he wants to catch. By and large the historian will get the kind of facts he wants. History means interpretation' (p. 23). See also, Postan, *Fact and Relevance*, pp. 51–2.

26 'It is easy to forget, in the heat of the argument, how transient evidence, fact, and truth have historically been, and how regularly they have been replaced by new and equally replaceable facts', writes Luise White (*Speaking With Vampires*, p. 311. See also Fischer, *Historians' Fallacies*, p. 5).

27 Carr, *What Is History?*, p. 12 and p. 13. Here Carr added that in most cases a particular interpretation 'has been preselected and predetermined for us by people who were consciously or unconsciously imbued with a particular view and thought the facts which supported that view worth preserving'.

28 Berkhofer, *Beyond the Great Story*, p. 53. See also, Alun Munslow, *Deconstructing History* (London: Routledge, 1997), p. 6, Arthur Marwick, 'Two Approaches to Historical Study: The Metaphysical (Including Postmodernism) and the Historical', *Journal of Contemporary History*, 30 (1995), p. 21, and Appleby, Hunt and Jacob, *Telling The Truth*, p. 261.

29 Format adapted from Berkhofer, *Beyond the Great Story*, pp. 53–4. See also Jacques Barzun and Henry Graff, *The Modern Researcher*, third edition (New York: Harcourt Brace Jovanovich, 1977), pp. 111–12. Information on Grace from Simon Rae, *W. G. Grace: A Life* (London: Faber, 1998), Ric Sissons, *The Players: A Social History of the Professional Cricketer* (Sydney: Pluto

Press, 1988), C. L. R. James, *Beyond a Boundary* (Durham, NC: Duke University Press, 1993), and Philip Bailey, 'W. G. Grace Revisited', *The Cricket Statistician*, 58 (Summer 1987). Details of the dates pertaining to the Athens olympics comes from 'Athens 1896', a discussion on the Sport History Scholars List, SPORTHIST@ PDOMAIN.UWINDSOR.CA, 18 October 2001. Description of John Bull from 'John Bull', Micropaedia, *Encyclopaedia Britannica*, fifteenth edition, 6 (1987), p. 588. For a critical comment on the list of British sporting performances see, Frank Keating, 'A preposterous slander on no end of performances', *Guardian*, 8 October 2001. For an explicit statement on the need to contextualise raw sporting statistics see, Brett Hutchins, *Don Bradman: Challenging the Myth* (Melbourne: Cambridge University Press, 2002), pp. 21–2.

30   Berkhofer, *Beyond the Great Story*, p. 55.

31   Raphael Samuel, 'History and Theory', in Samuel (ed.), *People's History and Socialist Theory* (London: Routledge and Kegan Paul, 1981), p. xlvii. Martha Howell and Walter Prevenier warn that an argument from silence constitutes presumptive evidence only against those who withhold or suppress information and 'purport to give a full account' of the event or story 'from which [they] omitted the crucial information'. Historians who claim that silence constitutes concealment must first prove that the silenced information was 'integral' to the account and 'so central' that it should have been automatically included (*From Reliable Sources: An Introduction to Historical Methods* [Ithaca, NY: Cornell University Press, 2001], p. 74). There is presumptive evidence that John Coates, the chair of the Sydney Olympic Bid Committee (SOBC), withheld information from the written version of the paper he gave to SOBC outlining the lobbying needed to secure olympic hosting rights (John Coates, The Process of Bidding for an Olympic Games, paper presented to the inaugural meeting of the Sydney Olympic Games Bid Committee, 6 March 1991). Although Coates makes no claim that his paper gives a full account of how to lobby members of the International Olympic Committee (IOC), the seasoned campaigner for hosting rights knew that cities had to step beyond the IOC's own guidelines. Moreover, an official investigation into Sydney's bid, initiated by the New South Wales minister responsible for the olympics, confirmed that Sydney lobbyists, including Coates, breached IOC guidelines (Tom Sheridan, *Report on the Independent Examination for SOCOG* [Sydney Organising Committee for the Olympic Games], 12 March 1999).

32   Keith Jenkins and Alun Munslow (eds), *The Nature of History Reader* (London: Routledge, 2004), p. 14. See also, Paul Ricoeur, *Time and Narrative*, volume 1, translated by Kathleen McLaughlin and David Pellauer (Chicago, IL: University of Chicago Press, 1983).

33   Murphy, 'The Voice of Memory', p. 97.

34   Windschuttle, *The Killing of History*, p. 219 and p. 220.

35   Windschuttle, *The Killing of History*, p. 220. See also Elton, *Return to Essentials*, p. 52.

36   Gottschalk, *Understanding History*, p. 42, Appleby, Hunt and Jacob, *Telling The Truth*, p. 257, Arthur Marwick, *The New Nature of History: Knowledge, Evidence, Language* (Basingstoke: Palgrave, 2001), p. 164, Elton, *Return to Essentials*, p. 55, John Tosh, *The Pursuit of History: Aims, Methods and New Directions in the Study of Modern History*, second edition (London: Longman, 1991), p. 133, and E. P. Thompson, 'On History, Sociology and Historical Relevance', *British Journal of Sociology*, 27, 3 (1976), p. 391.

37   Gottschalk, *Understanding History*, p. 140 and p. 150. See also Marwick, *The New Nature of History*, pp. 179–82.

38   Book forums are a good starting point to examine the complexities of evaluating historical arguments. See, for example, Jeffrey Sammons, 'A Proportionate and Measured Response to the Provocation That is *Darwin's Athletes*', *Journal of Sport History*, 24, 3 (1997), pp. 378–88 and John Hoberman, 'How Not to Read *Darwin's Athletes*: A Response to Jeffrey T. Sammons', *Journal of Sport History*, 24, 3 (1997), pp. 389–96.

39   Joan Patrick, Bathing and Drowning in Late Victorian Manly (BA Honours dissertation, University of Sydney, 1997), p. 4 and p. 79. For Lowe's account of events see, Arthur Lowe, *Surfing, Surf-shooting and Surf-lifesaving Pioneering* (Manly: Arthur Lowe, 1958), p. 76.

40   Berkhofer, *Beyond the Great Story*, p. 55. This shares common ground with Karl Popper's principle of falsifiability which states that scientists use evidence to falsify scientific conjectures,

as distinct from verifying them (Karl Popper, *Conjectures and Refutations: The Growth of Scientific Knowledge* [London: Routledge and Kegan Paul, 1963]).

41   Susan Philips, 'Evidentary Standards for American Trials: Just the Facts', in Judith Irvine and Jane Hill (eds), *Responsibility and Evidence in Oral Discourse* (Cambridge: Cambridge University Press, 1992), p. 250, and Michael Poliakoff, *Combat Sports in the Ancient World: Competition, Violence and Culture* (New Haven, CT: Yale University Press, 1987), p. 6.

42   Gottschalk, *Understanding History*, p. 157.

43   Lowe, *Surf-lifesaving Pioneering*, pp. 76–8 and p. 104.

44   Olympic Games Melbourne 1956, Opening Ceremony, Official Souvenir Programme (author's copy).

45   'Fists fly in pool fracas', and 'Russia, Hungary in wild clash', *Argus*, 7 December 1956.

46   Robert Menzies, 'A Green and Pleasant Memory', *The Official Report of the Organizing Committee for the Games of the XVI Olympiad, Melbourne 1956* (Melbourne: Organizing Committee of the XVI Olympiad, 1958), pp. 13–14.

47   Berkhofer, *Beyond the Great Story*, pp. 55–6.

48   'Struggle with shark: Surfer's terrible death at Coogee', *Sun*, 5 February 1922, 'Into the jaws of death', *Sunday Times*, 5 February 1922, 'Chalmer's story of shark tragedy', *Daily Telegraph*, 6 February 1922, 'Surf tragedy: Fight with shark', *Sydney Morning Herald*, 6 February 1922, and 'Surf tragedy: Mangled swimmer torn from shark's jaws', *Referee*, 8 February 1922.

49   In its account, the Royal Shipwreck and Relief Humane Society of New South Wales, which issued a bravery award to Chalmers, said witnesses to the event alerted the beach crowd, that Chalmers 'momentarily stunned' himself when he fell on rocks, and that Coughlan's body was 'floating helplessly' when Chalmers arrived (Report quoted in Graham Lomas, *The Will to Win: The Story of Frank Beaurepaire* [London, Heinemann, 1960], pp. 71–2). Beaurepaire also received a bravery award for swimming to Coughlan's aid behind Chalmers.

50   Berkhofer, *Beyond the Great Story*, p. 56.

51   Gottschalk, *Understanding History*, p. 167.

52   Joachim Rühl, 'Sports Quantification in Tudor and Elizabethan Tournaments', in John Marshall Carter and Arnd Krüger (eds), *Ritual and Record: Sports Records and Quantification in Pre-modern Societies* (New York: Greenwood Press, 1990), pp. 70–1. The standard apparently improved over subsequent days.

53   Rühl, 'Sports Quantification', p. 77.

54   Gottschalk, *Understanding History*, p. 167.

55   Ali Crombie, 'Mr Olympics chases his own gold', *Business Review Weekly*, 16 April 1999, pp. 85–91, and 'Five rings, four stars, no conflict', *Business Review Weekly*, 23 April 1999, pp. 149–57.

56   Sheridan, *Report on the Independent Examination*, pp. 41–2, and Gerard Ryle and Gary Hughes, 'Breaking China: How Sydney stole the games', *Sydney Morning Herald*, 6 March 1999.

57   Catriona Parratt, 'Of Place and Men and Women: Gender and Topophilia in the "Haxey Hood"', *Journal of Sport History*, 27, 2 (2000), p. 242 note 2.

58   Appleby, Hunt and Jacob, *Telling The Truth*, p. 248. Fischer offers a long list of fallacies associated with factual verification (*Historian's Fallacies*, pp. 40–63).

59   Mark Golden, *Sport and Society in Ancient Greece* (Cambridge: Cambridge University Press, 1998), p. 178.

60   Golden, *Sport in Ancient Greece*, p. 4, p. 77, p. 84 and p. 85. See also Frank Nisetich, *Pindar's Victory Songs* (Baltimore, MD: The Johns Hopkins University Press, 1980), p. 2. In interrogating Pindar's works, reconstructionists emphasise that he was 'a paid artist who also used embellishment and myth' (Donald Kyle, *Athletics in Ancient Athens* [Leiden: E. J. Brill, 1987], p. 7).

61   Choice of framework, of course, often rests on personal preferences. The notion of sport as a set of integrative relationships has its origins in ideas that link it to religion. A religious framework dominates the study of ancient Greek sport. See, for example, Kyle, *Ancient Athens*,

pp. 10–11 and p. 13, and David Sansone, *Greek Athletics and the Genesis of Sport* (Berkeley, CA: University of California Press, 1988). Golden does not dismiss this framework. On the contrary, he observes that 'there is surely something in the connection of sport and religion in ancient Greece'; more specifically, he describes Kyle's contention of a 'harmonious and lasting' relationship between sport and religion as 'a careful and, I think, uncontroversial formulation' (Golden, *Sport in Ancient Greece*, p. 15 and p. 23).

62 Golden, *Sport in Ancient Greece*, p. 176.

63 Golden, *Sport in Ancient Greece*, p. 84.

64 Briefly, Golden argues that victorious Olympians differentiated themselves from mere mortals by their athletic achievements, and that epinicians and statues confirmed social distinction and added to them by helping to elevate champion athletes to god-like status. Such elevation, of course, risked promoting envy and jealousy among ordinary people, especially if the victors assumed an air of arrogance and became dismissive of the rights and status of others. The wealthy classes, who extended patronage to Olympians, were well aware that they needed to assuage social tensions. This need, Golden suggests, might explain the switch in commemorative strategies away from odes, which the elites used to communicate with the masses, to statues which were messages to the victors' own class, wealthy Greeks able to regularity visit the precincts in which the statues stood' (Golden, *Sport in Ancient Greece*, p. 82, pp. 85–6 and p. 103). Social distinction and community are the subject of intense theorising and debate. Kevin Crotty, for example, argues that the preservation of distinction is a vital function of all communities. Crotty cites René Girard who wrote that 'it is not these distinctions but the loss of them that gives birth to fierce rivalries and sets members of the same family or social group at one another's throats' (*Song and Action: The Victory Odes of Pindar* [Baltimore, MD: The Johns Hopkins University Press, 1982], pp. 60–2).

65 'No sensible historian', wrote Geoffrey Elton, 'would now wish to treat history as a science in the sense that its study produces proven, verifiable and unvarying truths …' (*Return to Essentials*, p. 51).

66 Phil Vasili, *The First Black Footballer, Arthur Wharton 1865–1930: An Absence of Memory* (London: Frank Cass, 1998), p. 201. This point is well made by Richard Crepeau in his commentary on the death of the German boxer Max Schmeling ('Courage, contradictions: Schmeling vs Louis vs '30s world', *Orlando Sentinel*, 8 February 2005).

67 Berkhofer, *Beyond the Great Story*, p. 56.

68 Jim Sharpe, 'History from Below', in Peter Burke (ed.), *New Perspectives on Historical Writing*, second edition (Cambridge: Polity Press, 2001), pp. 30–1.

69 Gottschalk, *Understanding History*, p. 161.

70 Michael Laws, *Gladiator: The Norm Hewitt Story* (Wellington: Darius Press, 2001), p. 195.

71 Gottschalk, *Understanding History*, p. 161.

72 Laws, *Gladiator*, p. 23.

73 Gottschalk, *Understanding History*, p. 161.

74 Dawn Fraser with Harry Gordon, *Gold Medal Girl: The Confessions of an Olympic Champion* (Melbourne: Lansdowne Press, 1965), p. 21. The official report into the conduct of Australian women swimmers at the Tokyo olympics is housed in the Australian olympic archives. All references to Fraser's behaviour have been removed! (Harry Gordon, *Australia and the Olympic Games* [Brisbane: University of Queensland Press, 1994], pp. 262–3, and Dennis Phillips, *Australian Women at the Olympic Games, 1912–1992* [Sydney: Kangaroo Press, 1992], p. 84). In Chapter 5 I discuss the archives as a site where knowledge is produced rather than found.

75 W. F. Mandle, 'Sports History', in Graeme Osborne and Mandle (eds), *New History: Studying Australia Today* (Sydney: Allen & Unwin, 1982), p. 88. Of course, people also romanticise and fanaticise their pasts as bullies, or as outsiders, for their own psyches and for their hearers. In either of these senses, 'prejudicial truth' may be false or at least exaggerated.

76 Gottschalk, *Understanding History*, pp. 161–3.

77 Alan Bairner, *Sport, Nationalism, and Globalization: European and North American Perspectives* (Albany, NY: State University of New York Press, 2001), p. 164.

78   Gottschalk, *Understanding History*, pp. 163–4.

79   Gottschalk, *Understanding History*, p. 163.

80   Gottschalk, *Understanding History*, p. 164.

81   Interview, in 'Sport and Apartheid', *Current Affairs Bulletin* [Australia], November 1970, pp. 188–90. African American sprinter Tommie Smith's endorsement of the olympic boycott in 1967 is another classic example of a statement contrary to expectations (Douglas Hartmann, *Race, Culture, and the Revolt of the Black Athlete: The 1968 Olympic Protests and Their Aftermath* [Chicago, IL: Chicago University Press, 2003], pp. 38–9).

82   Howell and Prevenier, *From Reliable Sources*, p. 75.

83   Carolyn Hamilton, Verne Harris and Graeme Reid, 'Introduction', in Carolyn Hamilton, Verne Harris, Jane Taylor, Michele Pickover, Graeme Reid and Razia Saleh (eds), *Refiguring the Archive* (Cape Town: David Philip, 2002), p. 12, and Carlo Ginzburg, 'Checking the Evidence: The Judge and the Historian', in James Chandler, Arnold Davidson and Harry Harootunian, *Questions of Evidence: Proof, Practice, and Persuasion across the Disciplines* (Chicago, IL: University of Chicago Press, 1991), p. 294.

84   Joseph Maguire, 'Common Ground? Links Between Sports History, Sports Geography and the Sociology of Sport', *Sporting Traditions*, 12, 1 (1995), p. 21.

85   Marwick, 'Two Approaches to Historical Study', p. 23.

86   Appleby, Hunt and Jacob, *Telling The Truth*, pp. 259–60.

87   Marvin Eyler, 'Some Reflections on Objectivity and Selectivity in Historical Inquiry', *Journal of Sport History*, 1, 1 (1974), p. 63.

88   Munslow, *Deconstructing History*, p. 42, and Elton, *Return to Essentials*, p. 55.

89   Thomas Haskell, *Objectivity Is Not Neutrality: Explanatory Schemes in History* (Baltimore, MD: The Johns Hopkins University Press, 1998), p. 2.

90   Carr, *What Is History?*, p. 29.

91   Appleby, Hunt and Jacob, *Telling The Truth*, p. 259 and p. 260. Carr described an embryonic form of practical realism when he referred to historians continuously moulding their facts to their interpretations and their interpretations to their facts without ever assigning primacy to one or the other. 'The historian starts with a provisional selection of facts, and a provisional interpretation in the light of which that selection has been made – by others as well as by himself. As he works, both the interpretation and the selection and ordering of facts undergo subtle and perhaps partly unconscious changes, through the reciprocal action of one or the other. And this reciprocal action also involves reciprocity between present and past, since the historian is part of the present and the facts belong to the past. The historian and the facts of history are necessary to one another. The historian without his facts is rootless and futile; the facts without their historian are dead and meaningless' (*What Is History?*, pp. 29–30).

92   Appleby, Hunt and Jacob, *Telling The Truth*, p. 246 and p. 254. See also, Tosh, *Pursuit of History*, second edition, p. 137.

93   Miles Fairburn, *Social History: Problems, Strategies and Methods* (New York: St Martins Press, 1999), p. 6.

94   Berkhofer, *Beyond the Great Story*, p. 165 and p. 168.

95   Bill Murray, ' "Amateurs at Play": Sport and the Making of the British Ruling Class', *Sporting Traditions*, 16, 2 (2000), pp. 117–18. Originally commissioned by the book reviews editor of *Culture, Sport, Society*, the journal's general editor blocked publication. *Sporting Traditions* subsequently printed the review. It is impossible to know whether the general editor opposed the inflammatory comments Murray levelled at him – see especially note 19 – or genuinely believed that the piece lacked scholarship. However, the fact that Richard Holt and Catriona Parratt make precisely the same criticisms, albeit in more moderate tones, suggest that the opposition to the review stemmed from personal angst. For example, Holt described the text as 'full of splendid stories of hard riding squires and hard fought matches …' and said that Birley prefers to 'plough his own furrow, telling us rather more than we want to know about yachting or hunting – the upper classes are over-represented here …' (Holt, Review,

p. 169). Parratt commented that '"vulgarians studied racing forms ... the better sort preferred the cricket scores"' (Catriona Parratt, Review of Derek Birley's, *Land of Sport and Glory* and *Playing the Game* [Manchester: Manchester University Press, 1995 and 1996], *Journal of Sport History*, 24, 2 [1997], p. 210).

96 Appleby, Hunt and Jacob, *Telling The Truth*, pp. 255–7 and pp. 260–1.

97 Appleby, Hunt and Jacob, *Telling The Truth*, pp. 256–7.

98 S. W. Pope, *Patriotic Games: Sporting Traditions in the American Imagination, 1876–1926* (New York: Oxford University Press, 1997), especially pp. 27–9, Ronald Smith, *Sports and Freedom: The Rise of Big-Time College Athletics* (New York: Oxford University Press, 1988), especially p. 172, and Smith, Sport, Nationalism and *Patriotic Games*, pp. 7–8.

99 Like many historians critical of interpretations that disagree with their own, Smith erroneously believes that a more careful use of the sources would have led Pope to 'a different interpretation' (Sport, Nationalism and *Patriotic Games*, p. 9). Andrew Ritchie makes the same error in his critique of Nancy Struna ('Seeing the Past as the Present that it once was: A Response to Nancy Struna's "Reframing the Direction of Change in the History of Sport" [*IJHS*, December 2001]', *The International Journal of the History of Sport*, 20, 3 [2003], p. 149).

100 Elton, *Return to Essentials*, p. 51 and p. 62.

101 Andrew Ritchie, Discussion of methodology in history, ISPHES – Sport History Scholars List, SPORTHIST@PDOMAIN.UWINDSOR.CA, 10 November 2001.

102 Fischer, *Historians' Fallacies*, p. xv. Fischer combines Charles Sanders Peirce's concepts of abduction and induction to produce adduction. Peirce's abduction refers to 'the process of forming an explanatory hypothesis' while his induction is 'the experimental testing of a theory' (*Historians' Fallacies*, p. xvi note 1).

103 This list comes from, Christopher Lloyd, 'For Realism and Against the Inadequacies of Common Sense: A Response to Arthur Marwick', *Journal of Contemporary History*, 31 (1996), p. 194. See also, Geoffrey Nowell Smith, 'Common Sense', *Radical Philosophy*, 7 (1974), pp. 15–16.

104 Lloyd, 'Response to Arthur Marwick', p. 194.

105 Hayden White, 'Response to Arthur Marwick', *Journal of Contemporary History*, 30 (1995), pp. 239–40.

106 Munslow, *Deconstructing History*, p. 168.

107 See, for example, Roy Hay, 'The Last Night of the Poms: Australia as a Postcolonial Sporting Society?', in John Bale and Mike Cronin (eds), *Sport and Postcolonialism* (Oxford: Berg, 2003), pp. 15–28.

108 Nancy Struna, 'Reframing the Direction of Change in the History of Sport', *The International Journal of the History of Sport*, 18, 4 (2001), p. 3.

109 Munslow, *Deconstructing History*, pp. 168–9.

110 Munslow, *Deconstructing History*, p. 169. See also, Verne Harris, 'A Shaft of Darkness: Derrida in the Archive', in Hamilton *et al.*, *Refiguring the Archive*, p. 81.

111 Munslow, *Deconstructing History*, p. 169.

112 Michael Oriard, 'Football, Cultural History and Democracy', *Journal of Sport History*, 29, 2 (2002), pp. 246–8. See also Mark Dyreson, 'Reading Football History: New Vistas in the Landscape of Sport', *Journal of Sport History*, 29, 2 (2002), p. 212.

113 White, *Speaking With Vampires*, p. 311. See also, Robert Eaglestone, *Postmodernism and Holocaust Denial* (Cambridge: Icon, 2001), p. 56.

114 Berkhofer, *Beyond the Great Story*, p. 55.

115 White, 'Response to Arthur Marwick', p. 239.

116 Appleby, Hunt and Jacob, *Telling The Truth*, p. 230.

3 Facts, concepts and structures: theory in sport history

1   Geoffrey Elton, *Return to Essentials* (Cambridge: Cambridge University Press, 1991), p. 15 and p. 19. 'Historians captured by theory', he continues, 'may tell you that they test their constructs by empirical research, but they do nothing of the sort; they use empirical research to prove the truth of the framework, never to disprove it. ... adherents of theory do not allow facts to disturb them but instead try to deride the whole notion that there are facts independent of the observer'.

2   Werner Sombart, 'Economic Theory and Economic History', *Economic History Review*, 2, 1 (1929), p. 3.

3   George Kneller defines theory as 'a set of statements describing the nature and operation of an unobserved entity or process postulated as the cause of certain observed facts' (*Science as a Human Endeavour* [New York: Columbia University Press, 1978], p. 10). In the social sciences and humanities the level of formality varies. At one extreme, formal theories consist of two sets of concepts – descriptive (describe what the theory is about) and operational (specify relationships between elements) – placed in a deductive scheme. Emile Durkheim's theory of suicide is an appropriate example given its application in sport sociology although, it bears noting, that despite their claims to working in a highly theoretical discipline, few sport sociologists have constructed, or tested, formal theories. While Durkheim did not explicitly formalise his theory, Robert Merton provides a useful summary: 1) social cohesion provides psychic support to group members subjected to acute stresses and anxieties, 2) suicide rates are functions of *unrelieved* anxieties and stresses to which persons are subjected, 3) Catholics have greater social cohesion than Protestants, 4) therefore, lower suicide rates should be anticipated among Catholics than among Protestants (*Social Theory and Social Structure*, second edition [Glencoe, IL: Free Press, 1957], p. 97). Following Durkheim, Wally Karnilowicz hypothesised that the frequency of suicide should be lower on, and around, national religious and civil holidays and major sporting events than on, and around, non-ceremonial days. Karnilowicz tested his hypothesis in an analysis of daily suicide rates in America between 1972 and 1978. More specifically, he sought to ascertain whether the suicide rate declined on and around the last day of the World Series in American professional baseball and Super Bowl Sunday (the national championship game of American professional football), 4 July and Thanksgiving Day (American national civil holidays), and Easter Sunday and Christmas Day (national religious holidays). Empirical evidence supported Karnilowicz's Durkheimian theory that public ceremonial occasions increase social integration and lessen the incidence of suicides (James Curtis, John Loy, and Wally Karnilowicz, 'A Comparison of Suicide-dip Effects of Major Sports Events and Civil Holidays', *Sociology of Sport Journal*, 3, 1 [1986], pp. 1–14).

4   John Tosh, *The Pursuit of History: Aims, Methods and New Directions in the Study of Modern History*, third edition (London: Longman, 2000), p. 134, and Alun Munslow, *Deconstructing History* (London: Routledge, 1997), p. 46. Thomas Haskell captures the historian's vagueness towards theory when he refers to it as 'nothing more than a freewheeling recognition that events are interrelated in more ways than are immediately apparent' (*Objectivity Is Not Neutrality: Explanatory Schemes in History* [Baltimore, MD: The Johns Hopkins University Press, 1998], p. 6).

5   Heated discussions about theory and sport history surfaced at the Australian Society for Sports History conference at the University of Queensland in 1995, and at the North American Society for Sport History conference at Springfield College in 1997. The *Victorian Bulletin of Sport and Culture*, a newsletter published by the Department of Physical Education and Recreation at the Victoria University of Technology (Melbourne), kept the Queensland debate running for a few issues (see, numbers 4 [September 1995], 5 [December 1995], 6 [March 1996], and 7 [June 1996]).

6   Jeffrey Alexander, 'Modern, Anti, Post and Neo', *New Left Review*, 210 (1995), pp. 75–6, and see also, pp. 79–80.

7   In sport history, see the comments by Ronald Smith, 'Intercollegiate Athletics/Football History at the Dawn of a New Century', *Journal of Sport History*, 29, 2 (2002), pp. 231–2.

8   Michael Postan, *Fact and Relevance: Essays on Historical Method* (Cambridge: Cambridge University Press, 1971), p. 62.

9   For an introduction to the vast topic of agency see, Christopher Lloyd, *Explanations in Social History* (Oxford: Basil Blackwell, 1988), pp. 17–19, and p. 186.

10   Arthur Marwick, *The New Nature of History: Knowledge, Evidence, Language* (Basingstoke: Palgrave, 2001), pp. 246–7. See also, Murray Phillips, 'Tunnel Vision: The Production of Sport History', in Jan Wright (ed.), *Researching in Sport, Physical and Health Education* (Wollongong: University of Wollongong, 2004), p. 28. Pointing to the polymorphous nature of most historical subjects, deconstructionists also argue for a version of this perspective (see, for example, Jeffrey Hill, *Sport, Leisure and Culture in Twentieth Century Britain* [Basingstoke: Palgrave, 2002], pp. 182–3).

11   Elton, *Return to Essentials*, p. 9, p. 10 and p. 20. Experience shows, Elton continued, that few scholars will abandon their theories even when they find contradictory evidence: 'it takes a mental revolution equal to a spiritual conversion to separate a devotee from his theory, and the chances are that that will happen only if another theory stands by to catch the convert' (*Return to Essentials*, p. 23). See also, John Tosh, *The Pursuit of History: Aims, Methods and New Directions in the Study of Modern History*, second edition (London: Longman, 1991), pp. 157–8. All subsequent references to Tosh cite the second edition.

12   E. P. Thompson, *The Poverty of Theory: Or an Orrery of Errors* (London: Merlin, 1995), p. 63. Anthony Giddens attributes Thompson's renown in both history and the social sciences to his emphasis on, and incorporation of, agency into his work (*Social Theory and Modern Sociology* [Cambridge: Polity Press, 1987], pp. 203–4). See also, Matt Perry, *Marxism and History* (Basingstoke: Palgrave, 2002), p. 19, pp. 99–102 and p. 128.

13   Perry Anderson, *Arguments Within English Marxism* (London: Verso, 1980), pp. 32–3.

14   Haskell, *Objectivity*, p. 17.

15   Anderson, *Arguments*, p. 19. Explaining her preference for focusing 'more on times of conflict than on periods of calm', Pamela Grundy argues that 'conflict forces participants to articulate ideas with especial clarity and force' (Pamela Grundy, *Learning to Win: Sports, Education, and Social Change in Twentieth-Century North Carolina* [Chapel Hill, NC: The University of North Carolina Press, 2001], p. 8).

16   Haskell, *Objectivity*, pp. 19–20.

17   For details see: Bob Stewart, 'Boom-time Football, 1946–1975', in Rob Hess and Bob Stewart (eds), *More Than a Game: An Unauthorised History of Australian Rules Football* (Melbourne: Melbourne University Press, 1998), pp. 195–7, Braham Dabscheck, 'The Professional Cricketers Association of Australia', *Sporting Traditions*, 8, 1 (1991), pp. 2–27, Richard Holt and Tony Mason, *Sport in Britain, 1945–2000* (Oxford: Blackwell, 2000), pp. 63–92, and Charles Korr, *The End of Baseball As We Knew It* (Urbana, IL: University of Illinois Press, 2002). Andrew Sayer distinguishes generalisations from abstractions. 'A generalisation is an approximate quantitative measure of the number of objects belonging to some class or a statement about certain common properties of objects' (for example, most professional sportspeople are men) and, unlike abstractions, 'seek out formal relationships' (*Method in Social Science: A Realist Approach*, second edition [London: Routledge, 1992], pp. 100–2).

18   Fernand Braudel, *Capitalism and Material Life, 1400–1800* (New York: Harper & Row, 1973), p. 444, and Haskell, *Objectivity*, p. 2.

19   Tosh, *Pursuit of History*, pp. 160–1.

20   Including concepts within what he variously calls 'ordering devices' and 'mediating mental structures', Haskell describes them as 'utterly indispensable' to the way people 'make sense' of experience (*Objectivity*, p. 2 and p. 3).

21   Norman Denzin, *The Research Act*, third edition (Englewood Cliffs, NJ: Prentice Hall, 1989), p. 13. See also, Peter Burke, *History and Social Theory* (Cambridge: Polity Press, 1992), p. 29,

and Kevin Wamsley, 'Power and Privilege in Historiography: Constructing Percy Page', *Sport History Review*, 28, 2 (1997), pp. 146–55.

22 Munslow, *Deconstructing History*, pp. 22–3, Tosh, *Pursuit of History*, pp. 154–5, Arthur Stinchcombe, *Theoretical Methods in Social History* (New York: Academic Press, 1978), pp. 17–19, and Denzin, *The Research Act*, p. 53 and pp. 59–60. For a brief but useful discussion of sport as an abstract concept see, Hugh Cunningham, *Leisure in the Industrial Revolution c.1780–c.1880* (London: Croom Helm, 1980), pp. 12–13.

23 Gareth Stedman Jones, 'Class Expression Versus Social Control: A Critique of Recent Trends in the Social History of "Leisure"', *History Workshop*, 4 (1977), p. 164.

24 Stinchcombe, *Theoretical Methods*, pp. 2, 4, 5 and 16. James Walvin makes the same point ('Sport, Social History and the Historian', *British Journal of Sports History*, 1, 1 [1984], p. 10).

25 Stinchcombe, *Theoretical Methods*, pp. 23–4.

26 Stinchcombe, *Theoretical Methods*, p. 16. See also, Peter Knapp, 'Can Social Theory Escape From History: Views of History in Social Science', *History and Theory*, 24 (1984), pp. 34–52. In contradistinction to Stinchcombe, Karl Marx argued in the *Grundisse* that the concrete only reveals itself through the analysis of abstract concepts. For summaries of this position see, Raphael Samuel, 'History and Theory', in Samuel (ed.), *People's History and Socialist Theory* (London: Routledge & Kegan Paul, 1981), pp. xlviii–xlix, and Alex Callinicos, *Theories and Narratives: Reflections on the Philosophy of History* (Cambridge: Polity Press, 1995), pp. 129–30. Needless to say this position finds little if any support in sport history.

27 Stinchcombe, *Theoretical Methods*, p. 17, p. 21 and pp. 28–9.

28 Thompson, *The Poverty of Theory*, pp. 61–2. See also, pp. 51–3.

29 John Hoberman, 'Toward a Theory of Olympic Internationalism', *Journal of Sport History*, 22, 1 (1995), p. 3, p. 6, p. 7, pp. 9–10 and pp. 11–12. As a point of clarification and interest, despite their language, many of the 'internationalist projects of this period were not negations of nationalism'. Instead they were 'cultural projections of nationalist impulses employing cosmopolitan vocabularies rooted in ethnocentric ideas of national grandeur' (p. 8).

30 Hoberman, 'Toward a Theory', p. 19, p. 27 and p. 28.

31 Stinchcombe, *Theoretical Methods*, p. 22. Agency is integral to Hoberman's 'theory' although he does not explicitly expound on the subject.

32 Hoberman, 'Toward a Theory', p. 35.

33 Thompson, *The Poverty of Theory*, p. 62.

34 Hoberman, 'Toward a Theory', pp. 33–4.

35 Haskell, *Objectivity*, p. 3.

36 Jones, 'Class Expression Versus Social Control', p. 164.

37 Cited by Lewis Coser in, Lewis Coser and Robert Nisbet, 'Merton and the Contemporary Mind: An Affectionate Dialogue', in Coser (ed.), *The Idea of Social Structure: Papers in Honor of Robert K. Merton* (New York: Harcourt Brace Jovanovich, 1975), p. 9.

38 Jones, 'Class Expression Versus Social Control', p. 164.

39 Joseph Maguire, Grant Jarvie, Louise Mansfield and Joe Bradley, *Sport Worlds: A Sociological Perspective* (Champaign, IL: Human Kinetics, 2002), p. 160, and Tosh, *Pursuit of History*, pp. 154–5. See also, Munslow, *Deconstructing History*, pp. 22–3.

40 Braudel, *Capitalism and Material Life*, p. 442.

41 Joseph Maguire, 'Common Ground? Links Between Sports History, Sports Geography and the Sociology of Sport', *Sporting Traditions*, 12, 1 (1995), pp. 20–21.

42 Wray Vamplew, 'Sports Crowd Disorder in Britain, 1870–1914: Causes and Controls', *Journal of Sport History*, 7, 1 (1980), pp. 5–20, and Maguire, 'Common Ground?', p. 21.

43 Munslow, *Deconstructing History*, p. 23.

44 Maguire, 'Common Ground?', p. 18.

45 Munslow, *Deconstructing History*, p. 40. It is a fallacy, David Hackett Fischer argues, to believe that historians can 'operate without the aid of preconceived questions, hypotheses, ideas, assumptions, theories, postulates, prejudices, presumptions or general presuppositions of

any kind' (*Historians' Fallacies: Toward a Logic of Historical Thought* [New York: Harper & Row, 1970], p. 4).

46   Richard Holt, *Sport and the British: A Modern History* (Oxford: Oxford University Press, 1989), p. 367.

47   Tosh, *Pursuit of History*, pp. 153–4.

48   For a list of examples see, Nancy Struna, 'Social History and Sport', in Jay Coakley and Eric Dunning (eds), *Handbook of Sports Studies* (London: Sage, 2000), p. 189.

49   For reviews of the discipline in the 1970s see: Melvin Adelman, 'Academicians and American Athletics: A Decade of Progress', *Journal of Sport History*, 10, 1 (1983), pp. 80–106, William Baker, 'The State of British Sport History, *Journal of Sport History*, 10, 1 (1983), pp. 53–66, Allen Guttmann, 'Recent Works on European Sport History', *Journal of Sport History*, 10, 1 (1983), pp. 35–52, Robert Malcolmson, 'Sports in Society: A Historical Perspective', *British Journal of Sports History*, 1, 1 (1984), pp. 60–72, Richard Mandell, 'Modern Criticism of Sport', in Donald Kyle and Gary Stark (eds), *Essays on Sport History and Sport Mythology* (College Station, TX: Texas A & M Press, 1990), pp. 118–38, W. F. Mandle, 'Sports History', in G. Osborne and Mandle (eds), *New History: Studying Australia Today* (Sydney: George Allen & Unwin, 1982), pp. 82–93, Don Morrow, 'Canadian Sport History: A Critical Essay', *Journal of Sport History*, 10, 1 (1983), pp. 67–79, Gerald Redmond, 'Sport History in Academe: Reflections on a Half Century of Peculiar Progress', *British Journal of Sports History*, 1, 1 (1984), pp. 24–40, and Walvin, 'Sport, Social History and the Historian', pp. 5–13.

50   Morrow, 'Canadian Sport History', p. 73, and Richard Holt, 'Sport and History: The State of the Subject in Britain', *Twentieth Century British History*, 7, 2 (1996), p. 251.

51   Tosh, *Pursuit of History*, pp. 154–5, and Jones, 'Class Expression Versus Social Control', p. 167.

52   Walvin, 'Sport, Social History and the Historian', p. 8, and Bruce Kidd, *The Struggle for Canadian Sport* (Toronto: University of Toronto Press, 1996), p. 8.

53   The uses and meanings of functionalism and structuralism differ widely. See, for example, Mark Abrahamson, *Functionalism* (Englewood Cliffs, NJ: Prentice-Hall, 1978), and Peter Blau (ed.), *Approaches to the Study of Social Structure* (New York: The Free Press, 1975). While the intellectual sources of functionalism derive primarily from the works of the classical sociologist Emile Durkheim, the sources of structuralism are more diverse and include Ferdinand Saussure, Durkheim, Karl Marx and Sigmund Freud (Lloyd, *Explanations*, p. 237).

54   Malcolm Waters, *Modern Sociological Theory* (London: Sage, 1994), p. 173.

55   Keith Sandiford, 'The Victorians at Play: Problems in Historiographical Methodology', *Journal of Social History*, 15, 2 (1981), p. 272. Commonly cited examples include: Frederick Paxson, 'The Rise of Sport', *Mississippi Valley Historical Review*, 4 (1917), pp. 143–68, reprinted in George Sage (ed.), *Sport and American Society: Selected Readings* (Reading, MA: Addison-Wesley, 1974), pp. 80–103, Arthur Schlesinger, *The Rise of the City, 1878–1898* (New York: Macmillan, 1933), and Foster Rhea Dulles, *A History of Recreation: America Learns to Play* (New York: Appleton-Century-Crofts, 1965).

56   Stephen Hardy, 'The City and the Rise of American Sport: 1820–1920', *Exercise and Sport Sciences Reviews*, 9 (1981), pp. 193–4.

57   Peter McIntosh, 'An Historical View of Sport and Social Control', *International Review of Sport Sociology*, 6 (1971), p. 6 and pp. 10–11. See, for example, Adelman, 'Academicians and American Athletics', pp. 84–5.

58   Lloyd, *Explanations*, p. 149 and p. 154. George Lakoff and Mark Johnson argue that 'most of our ordinary conceptual system is metaphorical in nature' (*Metaphors We Live By* [Chicago, IL: University of Chicago Press, 1980], p. 4 and p. 239). See also, Chapter 4.

59   For a discussion of the complex interrelationships between functions and structures in structural-functionalism see Abrahamson, *Functionalism*, pp. 13–14 and p. 16. For a good example of this type of structure see the description of Stephen Hardy's Sportgeist in note 100 below.

60 James Frey, 'College Athletics: Problems of a Functional Analysis', in C. Roger Rees and Andrew Miracle (eds), *Sport and Social Theory* (Champaign, IL: Human Kinetics, 1986), p. 203.

61 McIntosh, 'Sport and Social Control', pp. 5–13, Robert Malcolmson, *Popular Recreations in English Society, 1700–1850* (Cambridge: Cambridge University Press, 1973), pp. 75–88, and John Daly, *Elysian Fields: Sport, Class and Community in Colonial South Australia 1836–1890* (Adelaide: John Daly, 1982).

62 Malcolmson, *Popular Recreations*, p. 76, p. 77, p. 79, p. 84, p. 85 and p. 86.

63 Quote Allen Guttmann, '*From Ritual to Record*: A Retrospective Critique', *Sport History Review*, 32, 1 (2001), p. 5. See also, Jones, 'Class Expression Versus Social Control', pp. 163–4, Adelman, 'Academicians and American Athletics', pp. 86–7, Richard Gruneau, 'Modernization or Hegemony: Two Views of Sport and Social Development', in Jean Harvey and Hart Cantelon (eds), *Not Just a Game: Essays in Canadian Sport Sociology* (Ottawa: University of Ottawa Press, 1988), pp. 15–16, Holt, *Sport and the British*, pp. 359–60, Tony Mason, 'Afterword', in Mason (ed.), *Sport in Britain: A Social History* (Cambridge: Cambridge University Press, 1989), p. 345, Kidd, *Canadian Sport*, p. 9. For examples of general critiques see: Anthony Giddens, *Sociology, A Brief But Critical Introduction* (Basingstoke: Macmillan, 1986), p. 144, and Tony Judt, 'A Clown in Regal Purple: Social History and the Historians', *History Workshop*, 7 (1979), pp. 69–71.

64 For a retrospective review of Malcolmson's contribution to the field see, Catriona Parratt, 'Robert W. Malcolmson's *Popular Recreations in English Society, 1700–1850*: An Appreciation', *Journal of Sport History*, 29, 2 (2002), pp. 313–23.

65 Lloyd, *Explanations*, pp. 155–6. See also, Nicos Mouzelis, *Sociological Theory: What Went Wrong?* (London: Routledge, 1995), pp. 128–9.

66 Malcolmson, *Popular Recreations*, p. 75 and p. 76.

67 Daly, *Elysian Fields*, p. 5. See also, note 3 for an example of functionalism as expounded by Robert Merton. One of the arch-theorists of functionalism (along with Talcott Parsons and Marion Levy), Merton is a key source for Malcolmson and McIntosh. Daly's principal functionalist theorist is Lewis Coser, a student of Merton at Columbia University in the late 1940s. Interestingly, Malcolmson was a student of E. P. Thompson.

68 Lloyd, *Explanations*, p. 155.

69 McIntosh, 'Sport and Social Control', p. 10.

70 Benjamin Rader, *American Sports: From the Age of Folk Games to the Age of Television* (Englewood Cliffs, NJ: Prentice Hall, 1983), p. 360. A few years earlier Rader had been more explicit about his attachment to functionalism when he implored his colleagues to pay more attention to 'analyz[ing] the social functions of sports' ('Modern Sports: In Search of Interpretations', *Journal of Social History*, 13, 2 [1979], p. 319).

71 Daly, *Elysian Fields*, p. 173.

72 Tosh, *Pursuit of History*, p. 161.

73 Lloyd, *Explanations*, p. 16.

74 Thompson, *The Poverty of Theory*, p. 198.

75 Mouzelis, *Sociological Theory*, p. 87.

76 Emile Durkheim, *The Rules of Sociological Method*, eighth edition (Glencoe, IL: Free Press, 1964), pp. 4–5.

77 Lloyd, *Explanations*, p. 6 and p. 16, and Tosh, *Pursuit of History*, p. 154.

78 Sayer, *Method in Social Science*, pp. 92–4.

79 Vamplew, 'Sports Crowd Disorder', p. 9.

80 Waters, *Modern Sociological Theory*, p. 93.

81 Waters, *Modern Sociological Theory*, p. 92.

82 Jean-Marie Brohm, *Sport: A Prison of Measured Time* (London: Ink Links, 1978), Bero Rigauer, *Sport and Work* (New York: Columbia University Press, 1981), and Gerhard Vinnai, *Football Mania* (London: Ocean Books, 1973). See also, Paul Hoch, *Rip Off the Big Game* (New York: Anchor Books, 1972).

83   Waters, *Modern Sociological Theory*, pp. 118–19. Marx did not use the economic base, or mode of production, in 'any single, consistent sense' and hence it has been subjected to great debate and theorising in which Althusser's formulation appears as one of many. At the heart of the debate is whether the forces of production can be described independently of the relations of production given that the former includes labour processes that are integral aspects of the latter. For overviews see, Laurence Harris, 'Forces and Relations of Production', and Susan Himmelweit, 'Mode of Production', in Tom Bottomore (ed.), *A Dictionary of Marxist Thought* (Oxford: Blackwell, 1983), pp. 178–80 and pp. 335–7. For useful introductions to Marx see, Giddens, *Critical Introduction*, pp. 33–7, and Perry, *Marxism and History*.

84   Waters, *Modern Sociological Theory*, pp. 119–20.

85   Waters, *Modern Sociological Theory*, p. 120. See also, Grant Jarvie and Joseph Maguire, *Sport and Leisure in Social Thought* (London: Routledge, 1994), pp. 95–8.

86   Cited in Waters, *Modern Sociological Theory*, pp. 121–2.

87   Brohm, *Sport*, pp. 55–6.

88   Mason, 'Afterword', p. 346 and p. 347. See also, Richard Gruneau, 'Sport and the Debate on the State', in Hart Cantelon and Richard Gruneau (eds), *Sport, Culture and the Modern State* (Toronto: University of Toronto Press, 1982), p. 23.

89   Pierre Laguillaumie cited in, Allen Guttmann, *From Ritual to Record: The Nature of Modern Sports* (New York: Columbia University Press, 1978), p. 66. See also, Brohm, *Sport*, pp. 55–6, pp. 105–6 and p. 176.

90   Gruneau, 'Sport and the State', p. 23, and Mason, 'Afterword', p. 347.

91   John Hargreaves, *Sport, Power and Culture* (Cambridge: Polity Press, 1987), pp. 114–15. See also, Mason, 'Afterword', p. 346.

92   Richard Gruneau, *Class, Sports, and Social Development* (Amherst, MA: University of Massachusetts Press, 1983), p. 48. See also, Tony Mason, *Sport in Britain* (London: Faber and Faber, 1988), p. 75, Adelman, 'Academicians and American Athletics', p. 94, and Rader, 'Modern Sports', pp. 312–13.

93   Gruneau, *Class, Sports, and Social Development*, p. 37. See also, Gruneau, 'Sport and the State', p. 25, and Holt, 'Sport and History', p. 248. For other broader critiques see, Bero Rigauer, 'Marxist Theories', in Coakley and Dunning, *Handbook*, p. 41, and Jarvie and Maguire, *Sport and Leisure*, p. 104. Feminist historians find such analyses problematic because they reduce gender to 'a by-product of ... economic structures. Consequently it is difficult to see historically how economic systems determine gender relationships' (Patricia Vertinsky, 'Gender Relations, Women's History and Sport History: A Decade of Changing Enquiry, 1983–1993', *Journal of Sport History*, 21, 1 [1994], p. 3. See also, Hill, *Sport*, p. 10, and Jennifer Hargreaves, *Sporting Females: Critical Issues in the History and Sociology of Women's Sport* [London: Routledge, 1994], p. 18 and p. 21). On these topics see: Arnd Krüger and James Riordan, *The Story of Worker Sport* (Champaign, IL: Human Kinetics, 1996) and Harry Edwards, *The Revolt of the Black Athlete* (New York: Free Press, 1969). The reference to Muhammed Ali comes from, David Zang, *SportsWars: Sport in the Age of Aquarius* (Fayetteville, AR: The University of Arkansas Press, 2001), p. 112.

94   Alan Tomlinson, 'Good Times, Bad Times and the Politics of Leisure: Working-Class Culture in the 1930s in a Small Northern English Working-Class Community', in Hart Cantelon and Robert Hollands (eds), *Leisure, Sport and Working-Class Cultures: Theory and History* (Toronto: Garamond Press, 1988), p. 48.

95   Hargreaves, *Sport, Power and Culture*, pp. 114–15. Vamplew agrees that 'most studies' of modern North-American sport have accepted that clubs are 'profit maximizers', but he argues that profit motives in late-nineteenth century British sport varied between sports and entrepreneurs. While cycling, horse-racing, and ice-rinks aimed to 'deliver dividends' to shareholders, Scottish soccer clubs strove to 'win matches and championships rather than make money'. Among many members of the working-class, 'shareholding [was] merely an extension of their role as supporters', a form of 'consumption rather than investment' ('The

Economics of a Sports Industry: Scottish Gate-Money Football, 1890–1914', *Economic History Review*, 35, 4 [1982], p. 550, pp. 557–8, and p. 567).

96   Eric Hobsbawm, 'Mass-producing Traditions: Europe, 1870–1914', in Eric Hobsbawm and Terence Ranger (eds), *The Invention of Tradition* (Cambridge: Cambridge University Press, 1983), p. 307.

97   Sayer, *Method in Social Science*, p. 95. A good example of the failure to separate the latter is Shona Thompson, 'Challenging the Hegemony: New Zealand Women's Opposition to Rugby and the Reproduction of a Capitalist Patriarchy', *International Review for the Sociology of Sport*, 23, 3 (1988), pp. 205–10.

98   Stephen Hardy and Alan Ingham, 'Games, Structure, and Agency: Historians on the American Play Movement', *Journal of Social History*, 17 (1983), p. 286.

99   Patrick Joyce, 'The End of Social History?', *Social History*, 20, 1 (1995), pp. 89–90.

100   Stephen Hardy, 'Entrepreneurs, Structures, and the Sportgeist: Old Tensions in a Modern Industry', in Donald Kyle and Gary Stark (eds), *Essays on Sport History and Sport Mythology* (College Station, TX: Texas A & M Press, 1990), pp. 49–82. The Sportgeist comprises four sets of values – physicality, competition, creativity, and achievement – each of which begets social tensions. Within the physicality of sport, 'the enthusiasm for aggressive play … alternates with outcries against violence'. Competition produces tensions between 'passion for victory' and 'indignation over cheating'. Creativity engenders tensions between the 'freedom to engage in the contest with few restrictions' and regimens of rules and systematic training. Achievement fuels tensions between the success of the individual athlete or team, and the community that basks in the reflected glory of sporting victory and that claims success as its own. These values form relationships that constitute structural patterns within any 'loose membrane of a game form that demands some physical skill'. On the one hand, the Sportgeist allows individuals to 'invigorate' sport with their own meanings: 'players, fans, and coaches constantly make their own decisions on physicality, achievement, competition and creativity'. On the other, while 'every participant has … a measure of agency in making sport history', individuals can only make history within external constraints that they cannot change, such as the sport structure (rules, tactics, organisations, facilities, records, equipment) and the general structure (climate, topography, economic systems, class, gender and race relations). Hardy appropriates the word 'Geist' from the German philosopher Georg Hegel (1770–1831). Hegel regarded spirit (Geist) as a 'certain kind of self-conscious activity'. It is a 'dialectical interplay between self-knowledge, self-actualization, and practical striving, in which the striving for a given set of goals, founded on a given knowledge of oneself, leads in time to new self-knowledge, new goals, and so to an altered striving' (Allen Wood, 'Hegel and Marxism', in Frederick Beiser (ed.), *The Cambridge Companion to Hegel* [Cambridge: Cambridge University Press, 1993], p. 427 and p. 428).

101   Hardy, 'The Sportgeist', pp. 54–5 and p. 63.

102   Alexander, 'Modern, Anti, Post and Neo', p. 69, p. 71, p. 73, pp. 75–6, p. 77 and p. 78. See also, Samuel, 'History and Theory', p. li, and Postan, *Fact and Relevance*, pp. 154–82. Alexander places the death of functionalism 'between the assassination of President Kennedy and the San Francisco "summer of love" of 1967'. Alexander specifically talks about the death of modernisation theory rather than functionalism. However, modernisation theory was a form of functionalism with most of the critiques attacking its functionalist assumptions. For a summary of the origins and nature of modernisation see Lloyd, *Explanations*, pp. 205–6. Writing in 1975, one of the arch-theorists of functionalism, Talcott Parsons, dismissed the death of functionalism as 'slightly exaggerated'. He insisted that 'there was less talk about functional analysis because essentially all serious theory in the field had become functional and took this for granted' ('The Present Status of "Structural-Functional" Theory in Sociology', in Coser, *Social Structure*, p. 79). Indeed, neo-functionalists such as Alexander are not the only ones to point to the indispensability of functionalist logic in macro-social analyses. See, for example, Mouzelis, *Sociological Theory*.

103   Alexander, 'Modern, Anti, Post and Neo', p. 71. See also, Alex Callinicos, *Against Postmodernism: A Marxist Critique* (Cambridge: Polity Press, 1989), David Harvey, *The Condition of Postmodernity: An Enquiry into the Origins of Cultural Change* (Oxford: Basil Blackwell, 1989), and Krishan Kumar, *From Post-Industrial to Post-Modern Society: New Theories of the Contemporary World* (Oxford: Basil Blackwell, 1995).

104   David Zang uses the term 'SportsWars' to capture the times. The term expresses the tensions and issues in the 1960s around the claims that sport built character and that participation involved 'sacrificial effort, submission to authority, controlled physical dominance, victory with honour, and manliness'. Zang borrows sportswriter Robert Lipsyte's phrase SportsWorld to encapsulate these claims. Lipsyte describes SportsWorld as 'a sweaty Oz you'll never find in a geography book, ... an ultimate sanctuary, a university for the body, a community for the spirit, a place to hide that glows with the time of innocence when we believed that rules and boundaries were honored, that good triumphed over evil' (Zang, *SportsWars*, p. xii).

105   'Disenchanted with the values of mainstream sport', especially win-at-all-costs competition, disciples of the new leisure movement experimented with activities such as snowboarding, skateboarding, frisbee throwing, hot dog skiing, surfing and high risk activities like rock climbing and parachuting. The essences of these practices were 'fun and personal growth' (Peter Donnelly, 'Subcultures in Sport: Resilience and Transformation', in Alan Ingham and John Loy, *Sport in Social Development: Traditions, Transitions, and Transformations* [Champaign, IL: Human Kinetics, 1993], pp. 133–4 and p. 137). For an anti-modern perspective of sport pertaining to coaches in this period see, Bob Stewart and Aaron Smith, 'Australian Sport in a Postmodern Age', in J. A. Mangan and John Nauright (eds), *Sport in Australasian Society* (London: Frank Cass, 2000), pp. 285–6.

106   Adelman, 'Academicians and American Athletics', p. 84 and p. 85. See also, Alan Ingham and Peter Donnelly, 'A Sociology of North American Sociology of Sport: Disunity in Unity, 1965 to 1996', *Sociology of Sport Journal*, 14, 4 (1997), p. 363.

107   Jones, 'Class Expression Versus Social Control', p. 168.

108   Eric Hobsbawm, *On History* (London: Abacus, 1998), pp. 193–4.

109   Gruneau, *Class, Sports, and Social Development*, p. 36.

110   Adelman, 'Academicians and American Athletics', pp. 86–7. Good examples of the critiques levelled at social order and social control theories in the late 1970s can be found in Richard Cashman and Michael McKernan (eds), *Sport: Money, Morality and the Media* (Sydney: University of New South Wales Press, 1981), pp. 223–303. However, the authors of these critiques were not so much looking to abandon the social control paradigm as trying to better understand 'the ways social control operates in concrete historical situations' and to refine the concept for its application to sport (Bill Murray, 'Sport and Social Control: Introduction', in Cashman and McKernan, *Sport: Money, Morality and the Media*, p. 222).

111   For an overview of Williams' thinking and his impact on sport studies see, Ingham and Donnelly, 'North American Sociology of Sport', p. 385, and Alan Ingham and Stephen Hardy, 'Introduction: Sport Studies Through the Lens of Raymond Williams', in Ingham and Loy, *Sport in Social Development*, pp. 1–19.

112   Jones, 'Class Expression Versus Social Control', p. 168. Hargreaves is vulnerable here. See, for example, *Sport, Power and Culture*, pp. 82–3.

113   William Morgan, *Leftist Theories of Sport: A Critique and Reconstruction* (Urbana, IL: University of Illinois Press, 1994), p. 60.

114   Colin Howell, 'On Metcalfe, Marx, and Materialism: Reflections on the Writing of Sport History in the Postmodern Age', *Sport History Review*, 29, 1 (1998), p. 101. The three principal texts that introduced sport historians to hegemony were Hardy and Ingham's 'Games, Structure, and Agency', Hargreaves' *Sport, Power and Culture*, and Gruneau's *Class, Sports, and Social Development*. Gruneau, Hardy and Ingham studied together at the University of Massachusetts. Hargreaves first presented his ideas on hegemony to a conference at Queens University in late 1979. Gruneau was one of the conference organisers and Hargreaves' paper was subsequently published under the title 'Sport and Hegemony: Some Theoretical Problems', in Cantelon and Gruneau, *Sport, Culture and the State*, pp. 103–40. For an essential

overview of the influences on the field at this juncture see, Ingham and Donnelly, 'North American Sociology of Sport', pp. 362–418 but especially pp. 377–9.

115 Alexander, 'Modern, Anti, Post, Neo', p. 80.

116 Interestingly, Jeffrey Hill also identifies a link between hegemony and postmodernism, describing the architect of the former, Antonio Gramsci, as a 'postmodernist *avant la lettre*' for his view that subordinate groups need to engage with the status quo 'culturally as well as politically' (Hill, *Sport*, p. 4).

117 Alexander, 'Modern, Anti, Post and Neo', p. 81 and p. 82, and Callinicos, *Against Postmodernism*, pp. 162–71.

118 Hargreaves, *Sport, Power and Culture*, pp. 82–3.

119 Jan Cameron, 'The Issue of Gender in Sport: "No Bloody Room for Sheilas ..."', in Chris Collins (ed.), *Sport in New Zealand Society* (Palmerston North: Dunmore Press, 2000), pp. 178–9.

120 For an overview of one recent debate between reconstructionists and constructionists in sport history (written from a constructionist perspective) see, David Rowe and Jim McKay, 'Out of the Shadows: The Critical Sociology of Sport in Australia, 1986 to 1996', *Sociology of Sport Journal*, 14, 4 (1997), pp. 354–7.

121 Bernard Whimpress, Review of Mike Coleman and Ken Edwards, *Eddie Gilbert: The True Story of an Aboriginal Cricketing Legend* (Sydney: ABC Books, 2002), *Sporting Traditions*, 19, 1 (2002), pp. 91–4.

122 E. P. Thompson, 'On History, Sociology and Historical Relevance', *British Journal of Sociology*, 27, 3 (1976), p. 387.

4 Narratives, non-narratives and fiction: presenting the sport past

1 Robert Berkhofer, *Beyond the Great Story: History as Text and Discourse* (Cambridge, MA: Harvard University Press, 1995), p. 37, W. B. Gallie, *Philosophy and Historical Understanding* (London: Chatto & Windus, 1964), pp. 12–13, David Lowenthal, *The Past is a Foreign Country* (Cambridge: Cambridge University Press, 1985), p. 219, Lawrence Stone, 'The Revival of Narrative: Reflections on a New Old History', *Past and Present*, 85 (1979), p. 5, Harry Ritter, *Dictionary of Concepts in History* (Westport, CT: Greenwood Press, 1986), pp. 279–80, and Michael Stanford, *A Companion to the Study of History* (Oxford: Blackwell, 1994), pp. 87–8 and 95–6. See Ann Rigney for a good overview of different definitions of narrative ('Narrativity and Historical Representation', *Poetics Today*, 12, 3 [1991], pp. 591–605).

2 Alun Munslow, *Deconstructing History* (London: Routledge, 1997), p. 58, and Keith Jenkins and Alun Munslow (eds), *The Nature of History Reader* (London: Routledge, 2004), p. 7.

3 Munslow, *Deconstructing History*, p. 57.

4 John Warren describes a more extreme version of this form of deconstructionism:

> [W]e are all prisoners of language. We can know most things only indirectly, and only through words. This is particularly true for history ... because we can have no direct experience of the past. Being dependent upon words would not matter if we were in control of the words used by others or even by ourselves. But we are not. If we settle down to write ... an accurate, calm, factual and objective account of some event in history ... we ... use documents – texts – from the past. But each text, including our own, is anything but an objective and factual account. Texts ... are full of metaphors, symbols, signs, gaps, deliberate and accidental omissions and distortions. They reflect power-relationships, the conscious and unconscious attitudes of the author towards those relationships ... and a host of distortions ... which cannot be allowed for in any typical and superficial analysis of 'bias'. [As long as we] use words ... in writing up our conclusions [so we] are going to be the prisoners of language. [H]istorians

who claim to be writing about the past as it actually happened are almost laughably naïve. The history we write is really fiction

> (*History and the Historians* [London: Hodder & Stoughton, 1999], p. 112 and
> p. 114).

5   John Watterson, *College Football: History, Spectacle, Controversy* (Baltimore, MD: The Johns Hopkins University Press, 2000), Ronald Smith, *Play-by-Play: Radio, Television and Big-Time College Sport* (Baltimore, MD: The Johns Hopkins University Press, 2001), Charles Alexander, *Breaking the Slump: Baseball in the Depression Era* (New York: Columbia University Press, 2002) (winner of the 2003 Seymour Medal, awarded by the Society for American Baseball Research for the best book on baseball history or biography), Robert Barney, Stephen Wenn and Scott Martyn, *Selling the Five Rings: The International Olympic Committee and the Rise of Olympic Commercialism* (Salt Lake City, UT: University of Utah Press, 2002), Charles Korr, *The End of Baseball As We Knew It* (Urbana, IL: University of Illinois Press, 2002). *The End of Baseball As We Knew It* was runner up in the 2003 Seymour Medal and received an honourable mention in the North American Society for Sport History award.

6   Kenneth Gergen, 'Narrative, Moral Identity and Historical Consciousness: A Social Constructionist Account' (2004), http://www.Swarthmore.edu/SocSci/kgergen1/text3.html, pp. 2–3. For a more expansive set of criteria see, Stanford, *The Study of History*, pp. 89–92.

7   Eric Dunning and Kenneth Sheard, *Barbarians, Gentlemen and Players: A Sociological Study of the Development of Rugby Football* (Oxford: Martin Robertson, 1979), pp. 167–9.

8   Gergen, 'Narrative, Moral Identity and Historical Consciousness', p. 2. Gergen stresses that the value may be desirable or undesirable. See also note 15.

9   Gergen, 'Narrative, Moral Identity and Historical Consciousness', p. 2.

10   Gergen, 'Narrative, Moral Identity and Historical Consciousness', p. 2. See also, Alex Callinicos, *Theories and Narratives: Reflections on the Philosophy of History* (Cambridge: Polity Press, 1995), p. 46.

11   Gergen, 'Narrative, Moral Identity and Historical Consciousness', p. 3. See also, Callinicos, *Theories and Narratives*, p. 46, and Tony Collins, *Rugby's Great Split: Class, Culture and the Origins of Rugby League Football* (London: Frank Cass, 1998), p. xiii.

12   Gergen, 'Narrative, Moral Identity and Historical Consciousness', pp. 2–3.

13   Gergen, 'Narrative, Moral Identity and Historical Consciousness', p. 3.

14   As David Carr puts it,

> narrative is not merely a … way of describing events; its structure inheres in the events themselves. Far from being a formal distortion of the events it relates, a narrative account is an extension of one of their primary features. [Stories] are told in being lived and lived in being told. The actions and sufferings of life can be viewed as a process of telling ourselves stories, listening to those stories, acting them out, or living them through
>
> ('Narrative and the Real World: An Argument for Continuity', *History and Theory*, 25, 2 [1986], p. 117 and p. 126)

See also, Wilhelm Dilthey, 'The Understanding of Other Persons and Their Life-Expressions', in Patrick Gardiner (ed.), *Theories of History* (Glencoe, IL: The Free Press, 1959), pp. 213–25, Stanford, *The Study of History*, pp. 99–102, and Joyce Appleby, Lynn Hunt and Margaret Jacob, *Telling The Truth About History* (New York: W. W. Norton, 1994), pp. 262–3.

15   Appleby, Hunt and Jacob, *Telling The Truth*, p. 263, and Munslow, *Deconstructing History*, p. 114. Indeed, historians should not overlook the arbitrary nature of endings or beginnings (Jenkins and Munlsow, *The Nature of History Reader*, p. 252).

16   Lowenthal, *The Past is a Foreign Country*, p. 225.

17   R. G. Collingwood, *The Principles of History* (Oxford: Oxford University Press, 1999), pp. 12–13.

18   Munslow, *Deconstructing History*, p. 10.

19   Nancy Struna, 'Social History and Sport', in Jay Coakley and Eric Dunning (eds), *Handbook of Sports Studies* (London: Sage, 2000), pp. 188–9. As a reviewer for several journals I can attest that scissors-and-paste forms of presentation still cross my desk with surprising regularity. For a recently published example see, John Lucas, 'Setting the Foundation and Governance of the American Olympic Association: The Efforts of Robert Means Thompson, 1911–1919 and 1922–1926', *Journal of Sport History*, 29, 3 (2002), pp. 457–68.

20   Munslow, *Deconstructing History*, p. 70.

21   David Thelen (ed.), 'The Movie Maker as Historian: Conversations with Ken Burns', *Journal of American History*, 81, 3 (1994), p. 1039. See also, Arthur Marwick, 'Two Approaches to Historical Study: The Metaphysical (Including Postmodernism) and the Historical', *Journal of Contemporary History*, 30, 1 (1995), pp. 21–2.

22   Hayden White, *Tropics of Discourse: Essays in Cultural Criticism* (Baltimore, MD: The Johns Hopkins University Press, 1978), p. 134.

23   Berkhofer, *Beyond the Great Story*, p. 160.

24   Geoffrey Elton, *Return to Essentials: Some Reflections on the Present State of Historical Study* (Cambridge: Cambridge University Press, 1991), pp. 70–1.

25   J. A. Mangan, 'The End of History Perhaps – But the End of the Beginning for the History of Sport! An Anglo-Saxon Autobiographical Perspective', *Sporting Traditions*, 16, 1 (1999), pp. 64–5. See also, Richard Holt, *Sport and the British: A Modern History* (Oxford: Oxford University Press, 1989), p. 357.

26   Thelen, 'Conversations with Ken Burns', p. 1047.

27   Richard Evans, *In Defence of History* (London: Granta Books, 1997), p. 70.

28   Elton, *Return to Essentials*, pp. 70–1.

29   Mangan, 'The End of History Perhaps', pp. 64–5. Mangan recently drew the ire of Bill Murray who accused him of developing 'severe clichéitis' and for 'demonstrat[ing] in his own writing style the faults he is claiming to expose in others' (Bill Murray, '"Amateurs at Play": Sport and the Making of the British Ruling Class', *Sporting Traditions*, 16, 2 [2000], p. 126 note 19).

30   Munslow, *Deconstructing History*, p. 10.

31   John Tosh, *The Pursuit of History: Aims, Methods and New Directions in the Study of Modern History*, second edition (London: Longman, 1991), pp. 59–60.

32   Michael Oriard, *Sporting with the Gods: The Rhetoric of Play and Game in American Culture* (Cambridge: Cambridge University Press, 1991), p. xii, and Michael Oriard, *Reading Football: How the Popular Press Created an American Spectacle* (Chapel Hill, NC: The University of North Carolina Press, 1993), pp. 274–5. John Hoberman similarly alerts us to the different ideological meanings of sport in the twentieth century (*Sport and Political Ideology* [Austin, TX: University of Texas Press, 1984]). For changes in the meaning of the related concept of manliness see, J. A. Mangan, *The Games Ethic and Imperialism: Aspects of Diffusion of an Ideal* (Harmondsworth: Viking, 1986), p. 18.

33   Louis Gottschalk, *Understanding History: A Primer of Historical Method*, second edition (New York: Alfred A. Knopf, 1969), p. 134.

34   David Zang, *SportsWars: Athletes in the Age of Aquarius* (Fayetteville, AR: The University of Arkansas Press, 2001), p. 103.

35   Zang, *SportsWars*, p. 103.

36   Stone, 'The Revival of Narrative', p. 4. Stone's views on narrative in contemporary social history have been largely dismissed. See, for example, Callinicos, *Theories and Narratives*, p. 45 and p. 77, Eric Hobsbawm, 'The Revival of Narrative: Some Comments', *Past and Present*, 86 [1980], pp. 3–8, and Munslow, *Deconstructing History*, p. 89 and p. 110.

37   Lowenthal, *The Past is a Foreign Country*, p. 227, Lynn Hunt, '"No Longer an Evenly Flowing River": Time, History, and the Novel', *American Historical Review*, 103, 5 (1998), pp. 1517–18, and Birgitte Possing, 'The Historical Biography: Genre, History and Methodology', in John Bale, Mette Christensen and Gertrude Pfister (eds), *Writing Lives in Sport: Biographies, Life-histories and Methods* (Aarhus: Aarhus University Press, 2004), p. 21.

38   Stone, 'The Revival of Narrative', p. 5.

39   Lowenthal, *The Past is a Foreign Country*, p. 223. Non-narrative forms of presentation had their 'antecedents in nineteenth-century positivism' and did not simply emerge in response to the 'problems with reconstructionist approaches' (Jenkins and Munslow, *The Nature of History Reader*, p. 9). For different views on the ability of narrative to causally relate and contextualise evidence see Munslow, *Deconstructing History*, p. 52, and Philippe Carrard, *Poetics of the New History: French Historical Discourse from Braudel to Chartier* (Baltimore, MD: The Johns Hopkins University Press, 1992), p. 74 and p. 75.

40   Stanford, *The Study of History*, p. 106. See also, E. P. Thompson, *The Poverty of Theory: Or an Orrery of Errors* (London: Merlin, 1995), p. 64.

41   Munslow, *Deconstructing History*, p. 44.

42   R. G. Collingwood, *The Idea of History* (London: Oxford University Press, 1961), pp. 269–82, and R. G. Collingwood, *An Autobiography* (London: Oxford University Press, 1939), pp. 37–9. Notwithstanding his use of the term scientific historian, Collingwood rejected nineteenth-century positivism and the notion that 'historical persons and actions could be approached "externally" like the phenomena of nature' (Gardiner, *Theories of History*, p. 250).

43   In the words of Alex Callinicos, 'conceiving the historian's practice ... as the interplay of question and answer, in which the autonomy of the process is established when the historian poses her own questions, rather than taking them ready made from the sources, displaces the attempt to reduce historiography to narrative. [R. G.] Collingwood acknowledges that viewing historical enquiry as a process of question and answer is a development of Lord Acton's famous injunction ... "study problems in preference to periods"'. Precisely the same conception of historiography is to be found in the *Annales* school [where] 'the science of history' is 'a history of problems which does not start from facts encountered, but which must on each occasion construct its research object' (*Theories and Narratives*, p. 77).

44   Struna, 'Social History and Sport', p. 189, S. W. Pope, 'Introduction', in Pope (ed.), *The New American Sport History: Recent Approaches and Perspectives* (Urbana, IL: University of Illinois Press, 1997), p. 3, and Steven Riess, 'What Is Sport History', in Riess (ed.), *Major Problems in American Sport History: Documents and Essays* (Boston, MA: Houghton Mifflin, 1997), p. 1.

45   Mangan, *The Games Ethic and Imperialism*, p. 91.

46   Jeffrey Sammons, for example, charges John Hoberman with sweeping too widely in *Darwin's Athletes* ('A Proportionate and Measured Respone to the Provocation That is *Darwin's Athletes*', *Journal of Sport History*, 24, 3 [1997], pp. 378–9).

47   See, for example, Susan Cahn, *Coming on Strong: Gender and Sexuality in Twentieth-Century Women's Sport* (Cambridge, MA: Harvard University Press, 1995), Richard Cashman, *Paradise of Sport: The Rise of Organised Sport in Australia* (Melbourne: Oxford University Press, 1995), Holt, *Sport and the British*, Colin Howell, *Blood, Sweat, and Cheers: Sport and the Making of Modern Canada* (Toronto: University of Toronto Press, 2001), and Steven Riess, *City Games: The Evolution of American Urban Society and the Rise of Sports* (Urbana, IL: University of Illinois Press, 1991).

48   Berkhofer, *Beyond the Great Story*, p. 81. John Tosh, *The Pursuit of History: Aims, Methods and New Directions in the Study of Modern History*, third edition (London: Longman, 2000), pp. 96–9. Sport historians Roberta Park and Nancy Struna both stress this point (Roberta Park, 'Research and Scholarship in the History of Physical Education and Sport: The Current State of Affairs', *Research Quarterly for Exercise and Sport*, 54, 2 [1983], pp. 97–8, and Nancy Struna, 'Historical Research in Physical Activity', in Jerry Thomas and Jack Nelson [eds], *Research Methods in Physical Activity* [Champaign, IL: Human Kinetics, 1996], pp. 267).

49   Watterson, *College Football*, pp. 4–5, pp. 379–82 and pp. 392–8. Even in his scissors-and-paste narrative of the sporting Scots in nineteenth-century Canada (Chapter 2), Gerald Redmond still argues that female participation in the Scottish games of curling and golf played an important role in the overall emancipation of women in sport (*The Sporting Scots of Nineteenth-Century Canada* [Toronto: Associated University Presses, 1982], p. 232).

50   Mangan, *The Games Ethic and Imperialism*, pp. 71–2.

51   Dunning and Sheard, *Barbarians, Gentlemen and Players*, p. 1.

52   Berkhofer, *Beyond the Great Story*, p. 81 and p. 313 note 16.

53   Holt, *Sport and the British*, p. 9, p. 357, and p. 367.

54   Hayden White, *The Content of the Form: Narrative Discourse and Historical Representation* (Baltimore, MD: The Johns Hopkins University Press, 1987), p. 2.

55   Louis Mink, 'History and Fiction as Modes of Comprehension', *New Literary History*, 1, 3 (1970), p. 557.

56   Munslow, *Deconstructing History*, p. 70, Jenkins and Munslow, *The Nature of History Reader*, pp. 12–13, and Hans Kellner, *Language and Historical Representation: Getting the Story Crooked* (Madison, WI: The University of Wisconsin Press, 1989), p. 10.

57   Tosh, *The Pursuit of History*, second edition, p. 112.

58   Kevin McAleer, *Dueling: The Cult of Honor in Fin-de-Siècle Germany* (Princeton, NJ: Princeton University Press, 1994), p. 47.

59   Hayden White, 'The Value of Narrativity in the Representation of Reality', in W. J. T. Mitchell (ed.), *On Narrative* (Chicago, IL: University of Chicago Press, 1981), p. 23.

60   Munslow, *Deconstructing History*, p. 52, and Warren, *History and the Historians*, p. 117.

61   Redmond, *Sporting Scots*, pp. 233–4.

62   Hayden White, 'Response to Arthur Marwick', *Journal of Contemporary History*, 30, 2 (1995), p. 243.

63   Hayden White, *Metahistory: The Historical Imagination in Nineteenth-century Europe* (Baltimore, MD: The Johns Hopkins University Press, 1973). White's project is part of the textualist movement's rejection of the science of history.

64   Keith Jenkins, *On "What is History?" From Carr and Elton to Rorty and White* (London: Routledge, 1995), p. 167. See also, White, *Tropics of Discourse*, pp. 94–5, White, *Metahistory*, p. xi, and Munslow, *Deconstructing History*, p. 156. Roland Barthes notes 'it is very rare that [language] imposes at the outset a full meaning which it is impossible to distort. ... there always remains, around the final meaning, a halo of virtualities where other possible meanings are floating: the meaning can almost always be *interpreted*' (*Mythologies*, translated by Annette Lavers [Frogmore: Paladin, 1973], p. 132). Clearly, the intrusion of rhetoric, such as metaphors, into the language of physics and chemistry (for example, 'the big bang theory') suggests that problems of description and understanding are not peculiar to the humanities. Moreover, while history does not possess its own specialised technical language, this does not mean that many historical works 'require a good deal of technical language in order to be understood'. As far as Richard Evans is concerned, the distinction between scientific and non-scientific language 'seems entirely artificial' (*In Defence of History*, p. 67). For a good example see, Vasilia Christidou, Kostas Dimopoulos and Vasilis Koulaidis, 'Constructing Social Representations of Science and Technology: The Role of Metaphors in the Press and the Popular Scientific Magazines', *Public Understanding of Science*, 13, 4 (2004), pp. 347–62.

65   Lloyd Kramer, 'Literature, Criticism, and Historical Imagination: The Literary Challenge of Hayden White and Dominick LaCapra', in Lynn Hunt (ed.), *The New Cultural History* (Berkeley, CA: University of California Press, 1989), p. 109. See also, Munslow, *Deconstructing History*, p. 177. Interestingly, George Lakoff and Mark Johnson argue that 'metaphor is as much a part of our functioning as our sense of touch, and as precious' (*Metaphors We Live By* [Chicago, IL: University of Chicago Press, 1980], p. 4 and p. 239).

66   Adrian Beard, *The Language of Sport* (London: Routledge, 1998). See also, Frederick Cozens and Florence Stumpf, *Sports in American Life* (New York: Arno Press, 1976), pp. 232–48, and Douglas Hartmann, *Race, Culture, and the Revolt of the Black Athlete: The 1968 Olympic Protests and Their Aftermath* (Chicago, IL: Chicago University Press, 2003), pp. 259–61.

67   Pamela Grundy, *Learning to Win: Sports, Education, and Social Change in Twentieth-Century North Carolina* (Chapel Hill, NC: The University of North Carolina Press, 2001), p. 297 and p. 298. See also, Hartmann, *The 1968 Olympic Protests*, p. 79. A prominent metaphor in sport studies has been that of the mirror, with sport said to reflect practically every dimension of

social, economic and political life. For a brief example of the latter see, William Baker, *Sports in the Western World* (Urbana, IL: University of Illinois Press, 1988), p. 189. For the fullest explication of sport as a reflection of twentieth century political ideologies and doctrines see, Hoberman, *Sport and Political Ideology*. Mangan even uses a metaphor to describe the growth of sport history that he says 'has developed from a seed into a sapling in some 25 years' (Mangan, 'The End of History Perhaps', p. 61).

68   White, *Metahistory*, p. 34. White best explicates these relationships in *Tropics of Discourse* (a collection of his previously published articles) while Jenkins' *On "What is History?"* offers an excellent summary.

69   W. F. Mandle, 'Cricket and Australian Nationalism in the Nineteenth Century', *Journal of the Royal Australian Historical Society*, 59, 4 (1973), p. 225.

70   Grant Jarvie, 'Sport, Nationalism and Cultural Identity', in Lincoln Allison (ed.), *The Changing Politics of Sport* (Manchester: Manchester University Press, 1993), p. 74 and p. 76. See also, Epilogue note 51.

71   David Andrews and Jeremy Howell, 'Transforming Into a Tradition: Rugby and the Making of Imperial Wales, 1890–1914', in Alan Ingham and John Loy (eds), *Sport in Social Development: Traditions, Transitions and Transformations* (Champaign, IL: Human Kinetics, 1993), pp. 77–8.

72   Trevor Richards, *Dancing On Our Bones: New Zealand, South Africa, Rugby and Racism* (Wellington: Bridget Williams Books, 1999), p. 237 and p. 243.

73   White, *Metahistory*, p. 7.

74   Munslow, *Deconstructing History*, p. 158. See also White, *Metahistory*, pp. 7–11.

75   White, *Metahistory*, pp. 13–19.

76   Munslow, *Deconstructing History*, pp. 158–9.

77   White, *Metahistory*, pp. 19–20.

78   White, *Metahistory*, pp. 24–5.

79   Murray Phillips, 'A Critical Appraisal of Narrative in Sport History: Reading the Surf Lifesaving Debate', *Journal of Sport History*, 29, 1 (2002), pp. 25–40. In an earlier example Peter Carino employs White's model to analyse the way novels explain the Black Sox scandal – see note 101 – in American baseball ('Novels on the Black Sox Scandal: History / Fiction / Myth', *Nine: A Journal of Baseball History and Social Policy Perspectives*, 3, 2 [1995], pp. 276–92).

80   For a complete listing see Phillips, 'A Critical Appraisal of Narrative', p. 37 note 2.

81   Phillips, 'A Critical Appraisal of Narrative', p. 26.

82   Phillips, 'A Critical Appraisal of Narrative', pp. 29–30.

83   Phillips, 'A Critical Appraisal of Narrative', pp. 31–2. Using this same approach, Daniel Nathan cites David Voigt's coverage of the Black Sox scandal in the second volume of his trilogy *American Baseball* (1970) as an example of a tragic emplotment (*Saying It's So: A Cultural History of the Black Sox Scandal* [Urbana, IL: University of Illinois Press, 2003], p. 125).

84   Phillips, 'A Critical Appraisal of Narrative', pp. 32–3.

85   Phillips, 'A Critical Appraisal of Narrative', pp. 34–5.

86   Following Phillips' lead I have twice applied White's model to individual texts. See Douglas Booth, 'Post-Olympism? Questioning Olympic Historiography', in John Bale and Mette Christensen (eds), *Post-Olympism? Questioning Sport in the Twenty-First Century* (Oxford: Berg, 2004), pp. 13–32, and Douglas Booth, 'Searching for the Past: Sport Historiography in New Zealand', *Sporting Traditions*, 21, 2 (2005), pp. 7–9. In a more recent work, Phillips discusses the review process associated with the publication of the surf lifesaving debate and reveals the unease that such work engenders among sport historians ('Tunnel Vision: The Production of Sport History', in Jan Wright [ed.], *Researching in Sport, Physical and Health Education* [Wollongong: University of Wollongong, 2004], pp. 19–35).

87   White, *Metahistory*, p. ix.

88   Phillips, 'A Critical Appraisal of Narrative', p. 35.

89   The editors of *History and Theory* produced an entire edition of the journal devoted to a critical assessment of *Metahistory*. The edition included articles by Hans Kellner, Philip Pomper,

Maurice Mandelbaum, Eugene Golob, Nancy Struever, and John Nelson ('*Metahistory*: Six Critiques', *History and Theory*, 19, 4 [1980]).

90   Keith Windschuttle, *The Killing Of History* (Sydney: Macleay Press, 1994), p. 241.

91   White, *Metahistory*, p. xi, p. 203, p. 250, p. 262, p. 281, p. 282, pp. 285–6, p. 296, pp. 315–16, pp. 324–5, pp. 377–8 and pp. 429–30, and White, *Tropics of Discourse*, pp. 15–19.

92   Facing suspension from a forthcoming state championships for breaching patrol regulations, viz, using a plug made of cork rather than foam in a rescue ski, the North Cottesloe Club issued a writ against Western Australian officials in the Supreme Court (Ed Jaggard, 'Writing Australian Surf Lifesaving's History', *Journal of Sport History*, 29, 1 [2002], pp. 18–19).

93   As well as trope and plot. See, for example, Hans Kellner, 'A Bedrock of Order: Hayden White's Linguistic Humanism', *History and Theory*, 19, 4 (1980), p. 21.

94   Douglas Booth, *Australian Beach Cultures: The History of Sun, Sand and Surf* (London: Frank Cass, 2001), p. xx and p. xxi.

95   Jaggard, 'Writing Australian Surf Lifesaving', p. 15.

96   Jenkins, *On "What is History?"*, p. 171. See also, Appleby, Hunt and Jacob, *Telling The Truth About History*, pp. 228–9.

97   Jenkins, *On "What is History?"*, p. 176 and p. 10.

98   Jenkins, *On "What is History?"*, p. 177. Hans Kellner concurs although 'he believes that historians resolved the issue of ideology and objectivity long ago. 'Objectivity', Kellner says, 'is not a fashionable term among historians today because of their sensitivity to the ideological implications of any position within an historical context. Once "value neutral" social science itself came under examination as a tool of domination, the universality of ideology came to be taken for granted'. Paradoxically, he continues, rather than 'a disabling blow to historical writing', recognition of the 'universality of ideology' actually 'added to the feeling of security' within the discipline: 'Since ideological demystification of any given text or artifact is basic to both the Marxist and non-Marxist practice today, and since the position of the scholar within society is also continuously scrutinized ideologically, the "ideological scepticism" really becomes a confrontation between two or more reasonably knowable positions. In fact, the loss of willed objectivity which followed the ideologizing of all thought and action offers the sense of a firmer grasp on a "reality", however complex and elusive that reality may be' (Kellner, 'A Bedrock of Order', p. 12).

99   Berkhofer, *Beyond the Great Story*, p. 135.

100   Evans, *In Defence of History*, p. 126. Evans here is citing Lawrence Stone, 'History and Post-Modernism', *Past and Present*, 135 (1992), p. 190.

101   The scandal erupted in 1920 when a Chicago Grand Jury investigating an alleged fix of a regular-season game between two lowly clubs found evidence that members of the Chicago White Sox had accepted money to give less than their best against the rival Cincinnati Reds in the previous season's World Series.

102   Nathan, *Saying It's So*, p. 9.

103   See, for example, John Bale, 'The Rhetoric of Running', in Jørn Hansen and Niels Kayser Nielsen (eds), *Sports, Body and Health* (Odense: Odense University Press, 2000), pp. 123–31, Bernard Whimpress (ed.), *The Imaginary Grandstand: Identity and Narrative in Australian Sport* (Kent Town: Australian Society for Sports History, 2001), Hugh Dauncey and Geoff Hare, *The Tour de France 1903–2003: A Century of Sporting Structures, Meanings and Values* (London: Frank Cass, 2003), and John Bale, 'Scientific and Romantic: The Rhetorics of the First Four-Minute Mile', *The International Journal of the History of Sport*, 21, 1 (2004), pp. 118–26. Bale does display deconstructionist consciousness in a more recent work (John Bale, 'The Mysterious Professor Jokl', in Bale *et al.*, *Writing Lives*, pp. 25–39). Sport historians are not the only culprits in this respect. David Carroll's words, penned in 1993, remain almost as true a decade later: 'historians have for the most part ignored or simply rejected the … critical strategies associated with poststructuralist and deconstructionist theories of discourse and textuality' ('Poetics, Theory, and the Defence of History', *Clio*, 22, 3 [1993], p. 273).

104   Victoria Bonnell and Lynn Hunt, 'Introduction', in Bonnell and Hunt (eds), *Beyond the Cultural Turn: New Directions in the Study of Society and Culture* (Berkeley, CA: University of California Press, 1999), p. 2.

105   While this discussion refers to both history used in fiction (for example, historical novels and films) and fiction used in history (for example, fiction as source material), the primary focus is on the former.

106   Carlo Ginzburg, 'Checking the Evidence: The Judge and the Historian', in James Chandler, Arnold Davidson and Harry Harootunian, *Questions of Evidence: Proof, Practice, and Persuasion across the Disciplines* (Chicago, IL: University of Chicago Press, 1991), p. 297.

107   Paul Ricoeur, *Time and Narrative*, volume 3, translated by Kathleen Blamey and David Pellauer (Chicago, IL: University of Chicago Press, 1985), p. 154. See also, Hunt, 'Time, History, and the Novel', pp. 1518–21.

108   Carolyn Steedman, *Landscape For A Good Woman* (London: Virago, 1989), p. 132.

109   Jenkins and Munslow, *The Nature of History Reader*, p. 3.

110   Antoinette Burton, *Dwelling in the Archive: Women Writing House, Home and History in Late Colonial India* (Oxford: Oxford University Press, 2003), p. 20. Many reconstructionists still presume that 'memory is closer to fiction than history is to "truth"' (p. 22). I discuss memory in more detail in Chapter 5.

111   Trilling cited in McAleer, *Dueling*, p. 6. McAleer praises Alexander Pushkin, Heinrich and Thomas Mann, Theodor Fontane, Arthur Schnitzler, Guy de Maupassant, and Mark Twain for their 'expert renditions on the dueling theme' and concludes that 'these writers were first-rate social historians'. See also John Demos, 'In Search of Reasons for Historians to Read Novels', *American Historical Review*, 103, 5 (1998), pp. 1526–29, and E. P. Thompson, 'Anthropology and the Discipline of Historical Context', *Midland History*, 3 (1972), p. 49. These sources all point to Jack Berryman's misdirected criticism of Allen Guttman's use of 'fictitious' novels in *From Ritual to Record*. According to Berryman, novels lack explanatory power (Review of Allen Guttmann, *From Ritual to Record*, *American Historical Review*, 84, 2 [1979], p. 429). But Guttmann consulted novels for their evocative descriptions and distillations of, and corroborative insights into, the social and moral milieux of American football and its peculiar codes, not to extract facts or causal explanations (Allen Guttmann, *From Ritual to Record: The Nature of Modern Sports* [New York: Columbia University Press, 1978], pp. 122–5). Concerns about the historical fidelity of different literary genres persists among some practitioners. Greg Gillespie and David Wiggins both raise the issue in their analyses of travel narratives which are widely included in the literary genre (Greg Gillespie, '*Wickets in the West*: Cricket, Culture, and Constructed Images of Nineteenth-Century Canada', *Journal of Sport History*, 27, 1 [2000], p. 53, and David Wiggins, 'Work, Leisure and Sport in America: The British Travelers Image, 1830–1860', *Canadian Journal of History of Sport*, 18, 1 [1982], pp. 28–9).

112   Carino, 'Novels on the Black Sox Scandal', p. 278, and Nathan, *Saying It's So*, pp. 106–16 and pp. 164–9.

113   Lloyd Jones, *The Book of Fame* (Auckland: Penguin, 2000), pp. 177–8.

114   Jones, *The Book of Fame*, p. 177.

115   Lowenthal, *The Past is a Foreign Country*, p. 227.

116   Gordon Wood, 'Novel History', *New York Review of Books*, 27 June 1991, p. 15. Here Wood is reviewing Simon Schama's *Dead Certainties (Unwarranted Speculations)* (1991), which he describes as a mingling of 'fact with fiction' and an 'experiment in narration' (p. 12). He disapproves: 'historians may never see and represent the truth wholly and finally, but some of them will come closer than others, be more nearly complete, more objective, more honest in their written history, and we will know it, have known it, when we see it. That knowledge is the best antidote to the destructive skepticism that is troubling us today' (p. 15).

117   Lowenthal, *The Past is a Foreign Country*, p. 229, Wood, 'Novel History', p. 15, and Carino, 'Novels on the Black Sox Scandal', p. 284.

118   Allen Guttmann, *The Games Must Go On: Avery Brundage and the Olympic Movement* (New York: Columbia University Press, 1984), p. 1.

119   Tosh, *The Pursuit of History*, third edition, pp. 75–6, Gertrude Pfister, 'We Love Them and We Hate Them: On the Emotional Involvement and Other Challenges during Biographical Research', in John Bale *et al.*, *Writing Lives*, pp. 131–2, Possing, 'The Historical Biography', p. 18, and Brett Hutchins, *Don Bradman: Challenging the Myth* (Melbourne: Cambridge University Press, 2002), pp. 156–7.

120   See, for example, John Lucas, 'Sport History Through Biography', *Quest*, 31, 2 (1979), pp. 216–21.

121   Zang, *SportsWars*, p. xv, and Hartmann, *The 1968 Olympic Protests*, p. 192. Common to both lists are Jim Bouton's *Ball Four* (1970) and Dave Meggyesy's *Out of Their League* (1971).

122   William Baker, *Jesse Owens: An American Life* (New York: The Free Press, 1986), pp. xi–xii, Guttmann, *The Games Must Go On*, and John MacAloon, *This Great Symbol: Pierre de Coubertin and the Origins of the Modern Olympic Games* (Chicago: University of Chicago Press, 1981), p. xiii. While MacAloon informs his readers that he has borrowed a number of concepts from cultural theory, sociology and psychology, he stresses that these are purely 'strategic recourses' in the 'absence' of primary sources (p. xiii). MacAloon's suspicion of concepts appears later in the text where he dismisses different classifications of de Coubertin as 'enlightened reactionary' and 'bourgeois liberal'. 'There is little to recommend one shorthand over the other', he writes: 'like most men', de Coubertin 'possessed ... views which do not easily amalgamate under simple labels' (p. 312 note 142). But it is Victor Turner's testimony to *This Great Symbol* that is most revealing of MacAloon's epistemology: his 'art consists in allowing Coubertin's story to tell itself in an apparently natural flow of facts. The conceptual apparatus is skilfully concealed though unobtrusively present at all developmental nodes of the narrative ... . He never abandons the historian's and biographer's alertness to the refractory details of individual life and the particular history in which it is embedded' (*This Great Symbol,* back cover). Birgitte Possing provides a very useful schema of different historical biographical forms (Possing, 'The Historical Biography', pp. 22–3), Gary Whannel identifies various types of sport biographies most of which he places in the celebratory category (*Media Sport Stars: Masculinities and Moralities* [London: Routledge, 2002]), and Bale and his colleagues discuss whether sport biographies constitute a distinct genre (John Bale, Mette Christensen and Gertrude Pfister, 'Introduction', in Bale *et al.*, *Writing Lives in Sport*, pp. 9–11).

123   Steedman, *Landscape For A Good Woman*, pp. 5–7 and p. 21.

124   Sarah Nuttall, 'Literature and the Archive: The Biography of Texts', in Carolyn Hamilton, Verne Harris, Jane Taylor, Michele Pickover, Graeme Reid and Razia Saleh (eds), *Refiguring the Archive* (Cape Town: David Philip, 2002), pp. 297–8. See also, Pfister, 'We Love Them and We Hate Them', p. 141.

125   William Fotheringham, *Put Me Back on My Bike: In Search of Tom Simpson* (London: Yellow Jersey Press, 2003), pp. 6–8 and pp. 189–90. See also Bale, 'Jokl', p. 33.

126   Nick Tosches, *The Devil and Sonny Liston* (Boston, MA: Little, Brown, 2000), p. 252, p. 253, and p. 254. See also, pp. 127–8.

127   Tosh, *Pursuit of History*, second edition, p. 38, Mary Louise Pratt, *Imperial Eyes: Travel Writing and Transculturation* (London: Routledge, 1992), p. 220, Louis Ferleger and Richard Steckel, 'Faulkner's South: Is There Truth in Fiction?', in Elizabeth Fox-Genovese and Elisabeth Lasch-Quinn (eds), *Reconstructing History: The Emergence of a New Historical Society* (New York: Routledge, 1999), p. 362, Natalie Zemon Davis, *Fiction in the Archives: Pardon Tales and Their Tellers in Sixteenth-Century France* (Stanford, CA: Stanford University Press, 1987), p. 3, and Jeffrey Hill, New Historicism for Historians: Sport, Literature and Society, keynote address presented to the North American Society for Sport History conference, Pacific Grove, CA, May 2004, p. 12.

128   Peter Mewett, 'History in the Making and the Making of History: Stories and the Social Construction of Sport', *Sporting Traditions*, 17, 1 (2000), p. 2 and pp. 14–15. Compare this with the oft-cited view of Karl Marx for whom 'the tradition of all dead generations weighs

like a nightmare on the brain of the living' (Karl Marx, 'The Eighteenth Brumaire of Louis Bonaparte', in David McLellan (ed.), *Karl Marx Selected Writings* [Oxford: Oxford University Press, 1977], p. 300). Maurice Roche makes an important point with respect to connecting experience and events: 'people reflect on and periodise their biographies in relation to the readily identifiable and memorable great public events which affect them during their lives'. In other words, mega-events act as temporal and cultural markers in the formation of identity (*Mega-events and Modernity: Olympics and Expos in the Growth of Global Culture* [London: Routledge, 2000], p. 5).

129   Hill, 'New Historicism for Historians', pp. 12–13. See also the comments of Kevin McAleer in note 111 above.
130   David McGimpsey, *Imagining Baseball: America's Pastime and Popular Culture* (Bloomington, IN: Indiana University Press, 2000), p. 2.
131   McGimpsey, *Imagining Baseball*, pp. 51–2.
132   McGimpsey, *Imagining Baseball*, p. 161.
133   Oriard, *King Football*, p. 17 and pp. 55–6. See also, p. 85, p. 89, and pp. 101–12.
134   Hill, 'New Historicism for Historians', p. 8.
135   Chandrima Chakraborty, 'Bollywood Motifs: Cricket Fiction and Fictional Cricket', *The International Journal of the History of Sport*, 21, 3/4 (2004), pp. 549–72. See also Carino, 'Novels on the Black Sox Scandal', p. 290.
136   On the other hand, concerns certainly followed Synthia Sydnor's presentation of 'A History of Synchronized Swimming' at the North American Society for Sport History conference in 1997. Describing her text as a Benjaminian (after the German Marxist and cultural critic Walter Benjamin) montage and a hybrid text, Sydnor visibly riled her audience by presenting the history as a series of tableau. The *Journal of Sport History* (25, 2 [1998], pp. 252–67) subsequently published the text. But Sydnor does not advocate the tableau form of presentation as a model for others to emulate. In contradistinction, her objectives appear to resonate with the broad deconstructionist project and are discussed as such in Chapter 11.
137   Mark Dyreson, 'Reading Football History: New Vistas in the Landscape of Sport', *Journal of Sport History*, 29, 2 (2002), p. 206. See also, Collins, *Rugby's Great Split*, pp. xiii–xiv.
138   See also, Holt, *Sport and the British*, p. 358.
139   McGimpsey, *Imagining Baseball*, p. 61, and Brian Stoddart, 'Sport, Colonialism and Struggle: C. L. R. James and Cricket', in Richard Giulianotti (ed.), *Sport and Modern Social Theorists* (Basingstoke: Palgrave Macmillan, 2004), p. 125.
140   Lowenthal, *The Past is a Foreign Country*, p. 229.
141   Munslow, *Deconstructing History*, p. 70.
142   Nathan, *Saying It's So*, p. 220.
143   Steedman, *Landscape For A Good Woman*, p. 132.
144   White, 'Response to Arthur Marwick', p. 244. See also Margaret Atwood, 'In Search of *Alias Grace*: On Writing Canadian Historical Fiction', *American Historical Review*, 103, 5 (1998), p. 1504.

5 Remnants of the past: sources, evidence and traces in sport history

1   Arthur Marwick, *The New Nature of History: Knowledge, Evidence, Language* (Basingstoke: Palgrave, 2001), p. 26.
2   Gordon Stewart is a good example of a deconstructionist-leaning historian who appeals to the validity of empirical evidence. This is clear in his reply to Peter Hansen with whom he debated the soundness of using imperial culture as a theoretical framework to analyse the conquest of Mount Everest. Highlighting the 'weight and variety' of his evidence, Stewart appears affronted by Hansen's charge that he 'rel[ied] on second-hand accounts' to describe

the views of Tenzing Norgay (who with Edmund Hillary was the first to reach the summit). Countering the latter, Stewart concludes that 'my case was much strengthened by the long quotation from Tenzing' ('Reply' [to Peter Hansen], *Past and Present*, 157 [1997], p. 180 and p. 183 note 20. See also, p. 184 and p. 190). See Chapter 2 note 8 for a discussion of the place and role of notes in academic histories.

3   Geoffrey Elton, *Return to Essentials: Some Reflections on the Present State of Historical Study* (Cambridge: Cambridge University Press, 1991), p. 51.

4   Marwick, *The New Nature of History*, p. 164.

5   The categories derive from Arthur Marwick, *The Nature of History*, second edition (London: Macmillan, 1981), pp. 139–41, and Marwick, *The New Nature of History*, pp. 166–72.

6   Luise White, *Speaking With Vampires: Rumor and History in Colonial Africa* (Berkeley, CA: University of California Press, 2000), p. 310, and Robert Malcolmson, *Popular Recreations in English Society, 1700–1850* (Cambridge: Cambridge University Press, 1973), p. 3. Of course, historians often examine what one category of material says about a particular issue. Roberta Park recently analysed British and American medical journals between 1870 and 1910 to ascertain the medical profession's opinion on football injuries. Among the medical journals she consulted were *Medical Record*, *British Medical Journal*, *Lancet*, *Medical Record*, *Journal of the American Medical Association*, *Boston Medical Surgery Journal*, *American Journal of the Medical Sciences*, *Medical and Surgical Reporter*, and *American Medico-Surgical Bulletin* ('"Mended or Ended?" Football Injuries and the British and American Medical Press, 1870–1910', *The International Journal of the History of Sport*, 18, 2 [2001], pp. 110–33).

7   Peter Burke, *Eyewitnessing: The Uses of Images as Historical Evidence* (London: Reaktion Books, 2001), p. 13.

8   Joyce Appleby, Lynn Hunt and Margaret Jacob, *Telling The Truth About History* (New York: W. W. Norton, 1994), p. 267, and Verne Harris, 'A Shaft of Darkness: Derrida in the Archive', in Carolyn Hamilton, Verne Harris, Jane Taylor, Michele Pickover, Graeme Reid and Razia Saleh (eds), *Refiguring the Archive* (Cape Town: David Philip, 2002), p. 81.

9   William Baker, *Sports in the Western World* (Urbana, IL: University of Illinois Press, 1988), p. 79. For the text of the proclamation see Steven Riess (ed.), *Major Problems in American Sport History: Documents and Essays* (Boston, MA: Houghton-Mifflin, 1997), pp. 22–4.

10   Neil Tranter, 'The Social and Occupational Structure of Organized Sport in Central Scotland During the Nineteenth Century', *The International Journal of the History of Sport*, 4, 3 (1987), pp. 301–14.

11   Wray Vamplew, 'The Economics of a Sports Industry: Scottish Gate-Money Football, 1890–1914', *Economic History Review*, 35, 4 (1982), p. 551.

12   For example, Ray Crawford, 'Moral and Manly: Girls and Games in Prestigious Church Secondary Schools of Melbourne 1901–1914', in J. A. Mangan and Roberta Park (eds), *From Fair Sex to Feminism: Sport and the Socialization of Women in the Industrial and Post-industrial Eras* (London: Frank Cass, 1987), pp. 182–207, Pamela Grundy, *Learning to Win: Sports, Education, and Social Change in Twentieth-Century North Carolina* (Chapel Hill, NC: The University of North Carolina Press, 2001), and J. A. Mangan, *Athleticism in the Victorian and Edwardian Public School* (Cambridge: Cambridge University Press, 1981).

13   For example, Bill Mallon and Ian Buchanan, *The 1908 Olympic Games: Results of All Events, with Commentary* (London: McFarland, 2000), and Bill Mallon and Ture Widlund, *The 1912 Olympic Games: Results of All Events, with Commentary* (London: McFarland, 2002).

14   Douglas Booth, *The Race Game: Sport and Politics in South Africa* (London: Frank Cass, 1998), p. 144.

15   Jeffrey Hill, *Sport, Leisure and Culture in Twentieth Century Britain* (Basingstoke: Palgrave, 2002), p. 157.

16   John O'Hara, *A Mug's Game: A History of Gaming and Betting in Australia* (Sydney: University of New South Wales Press, 1988), pp. 142–3. For further examples of legislation as historical sources see Richard Holt, *Sport and the British: A Modern History* (Oxford: Oxford University Press, 1989), pp. 33–6 and p. 38, Mike Huggins, *Flat Racing and British Society 1790–1914:*

A Social and Economic History (London: Frank Cass, 2000), pp. 195–9, Ross McKibbin, 'Working-Class Gambling in Britain 1880–1939', *Past and Present*, 82 (1979), pp. 147–78, and Nancy Struna, *People of Prowess: Sport, Leisure, and Labor in Early Anglo-America* (Urbana, IL: University of Illinois Press, 1996), pp. 155–61.

17   White, *Speaking With Vampires*, p. 31 and pp. 37–8, and Adam Ashforth, *The Politics of Official Discourse in Twentieth-Century South Africa* (Oxford: Clarendon Press, 1990), p. 5 and p. 253. See also, Susan Philips, 'Evidentary Standards for American Trials: Just the Facts', in Judith Irvine and Jane Hill (eds), *Responsibility and Evidence in Oral Discourse* (Cambridge: Cambridge University Press, 1992), p. 254, and Evan Whitton, *Trial by Voodoo: Why the Law Defeats Justice and Democracy* (Sydney: Random House, 1994), p. 342 and p. 343.

18   O'Hara, *A Mug's Game*, p. 94 and p. 122.

19   A portmanteau term, archive, broadly defined, is a repository of primary historical material; more narrowly conceived it is an unpublished primary source existing as a single copy (Marwick, *The New Nature of History*, p. 158).

20   Mangan, *Athleticism*, pp. 309–18.

21   Ronald Smith, *Play-by-Play: Radio, Television and Big-Time College Sport* (Baltimore, MD: The Johns Hopkins University Press, 2001), p. 283, and John Watterson, *College Football: History, Spectacle, Controversy* (Baltimore, MD: The Johns Hopkins University Press, 2000), p. xiii and p. 438. Smith also trawled over thirty archives in researching his history of big-time college athletes (Ronald Smith, *Sports and Freedom: The Rise of Big-Time College Athletics* [New York: Oxford University Press, 1988], p. xi).

22   Watterson, *College Football*, pp. 439–40. See also, Robin Lester, *Stagg's University: The Rise and Fall of Big-Time Football at Chicago* (Champaign, IL: University of Illinois Press, 1995). Watterson's expertise in the archives is praised by Mark Dyreson ('Reading Football History: New Vistas in the Landscape of Sport', *Journal of Sport History*, 29, 2 [2002], p. 208).

23   Tony Ballantyne, 'Reading the Archive and Opening up the Nation-State: Colonial Knowledge in South Asia (and Beyond)', in Antoinette Burton (ed.), *After the Imperial Turn: Thinking With and Through the Nation* (Durham, NC: Duke University Press, 2003), p. 102. The status of the archive in contemporary history is the subject of intense debate as critics argue that in their original constructions they excluded the voices of subordinate groups and classes. Even today primary sources housed within recognised repositories will draw less critical attention than those outside (Antoinette Burton, *Dwelling in the Archive: Women Writing House, Home and History in Late Colonial India* (Oxford: Oxford University Press, 2003), p. 24 and p. 140. See also, Murray Phillips, 'Tunnel Vision: The Production of Sport History', in Jan Wright (ed.), *Researching in Sport, Physical and Health Education* (Wollongong: University of Wollongong, 2004), p. 27.

24   Patricia Hayes, Jeremy Silvester and Wolfram Hartmann, ' "Picturing the Past" in Namibia: The Visual Archive and its Energies', in Hamilton *et al.*, *Refiguring the Archive*, p. 115, Colin Tatz, *A Course of History: Monash Country Club 1931–2001* (Sydney: Allen & Unwin, 2002), pp. 8–9, and Douglas Hartmann, *Race, Culture, and the Revolt of the Black Athlete: The 1968 Olympic Protests and Their Aftermath* (Chicago, IL: Chicago University Press, 2003), p. 305 note 10.

25   John Tosh, *The Pursuit of History: Aims, Methods and New Directions in the Study of Modern History*, third edition (London: Longman, 2000), pp. 52–3.

26   Wording from the website of the Australian government ombudsman: http://www.comb. gov.au/publications_information/freedom_information

27   Tosh, *The Pursuit of History*, pp. 52–3. Using freedom of information requests, Douglas Hartmann found numerous documents filed with the CIA on, or relating to, olympic protesters Tommie Smith and John Carlos. But as he notes, full searches require extensive personal details about the individuals and their consent before information is released to third parties (*The 1968 Olympic Protests*, p. 305 note 9).

28   When writing his history of English soccer, Tony Mason asked 33 clubs for access to their records; seven refused and two did not reply (Tony Mason, *Association Football and English*

Society, 1863–1915 [Brighton: Harvester Press, 1980], p. 6). An obsessive official at the Royal Automobile Club in London recently denied colleague Steve Pope access to the association's archives because he was not wearing attire appropriate for a gentleman, viz, a proper jacket and tie (Steve Pope, personal correspondence, 14 August 2003).

29 See, for example, John Watterson, 'Out of Baseball's Shadow: The Paradox of College Football Scholarship', *Journal of Sport History*, 29, 2 (2002), p. 225, and Hartmann, *The 1968 Olympic Protests*, p. 139.

30 Werner Franke and Brigitte Berendonk, 'Hormonal Doping and Androgenization of Athletes: A Secret Program of the German Democratic Republic Government', *Clinical Chemistry*, 43, 7 (1997), p. 1263, p. 1267 and p. 1268.

31 Simon Reeve, *One Day in September* (New York: Arcade, 2000), pp. 219–24.

32 Harris, 'A Shaft of Darkness', p. 75. Ronald Smith is one sport historian who is clearly of the view that properly archived historical materials constitute 'the standard against which all other evidence must be measured' (Burton, *Dwelling in the Archive*, p. 21–2) ('Intercollegiate Athletics/Football History at the Dawn of a New Century', *Journal of Sport History*, 29, 2 [2002], p. 235. See also, Robert Barney, 'Studying Stuff: Research in National and International Archives', in Kevin Wamsley [ed.], *Method and Methodology in Sport and Cultural History* [Dubuque, IA: Brown and Benchmark Publishers, 1995], pp. 104–10, and, Stephen Wenn, 'Archival Wanderings: Rubbing Shoulders with History', in Wamsley, *Method and Methodology*, pp. 121–6).

33 Franke and Berendonk, 'Hormonal Doping', p. 1263, p. 1267 and p. 1268.

34 Reeve, *One Day in September*, pp. 224–7. Relatives of the dead athletes have launched legal proceedings against the German government.

35 Carolyn Hamilton, Verne Harris and Graeme Reid, 'Introduction', in Hamilton *et al.*, *Refiguring the Archive*, p. 9 and p. 16.

36 Achille Mbembe, 'The Power of the Archive and its Limits', in Hamilton *et al.*, *Refiguring the Archive*, pp. 19–20. See also, Burton, *Dwelling in the Archive*, p. 26 and p. 138, and Robert Berkhofer, *Beyond the Great Story: History as Text and Discourse* (Cambridge, MA: Harvard University Press, 1995), p. 222.

37 Hamilton, Harris and Reid, 'Introduction', p. 9, p. 11 and p. 13, Ballantyne, 'Reading the Archive', p. 102, Ann Stoler, 'Colonial Archives and the Arts of Governance: On the Content in the Form', in Hamilton *et al.*, *Refiguring the Archive*, p. 85, and Verne Harris, 'The Archival Sliver: A Perspective on the Construction of Social Memory in Archives and the Transition from Apartheid to Democracy', in Hamilton *et al.*, *Refiguring the Archive*, p. 143. As well as being sites of excision, archives are also sites of excess in the sense that they can allow for unlimited and imaginative readings (Sarah Nuttall, 'Literature and the Archive: The Biography of Texts', in Hamilton *et al.*, *Refiguring the Archive*, p. 295).

38 In 1996, at the initiative of Steve Pope and under his leadership and direction, the *Journal of Sport History* introduced a section devoted to reviewing sport museums and halls of fame ('Sport Films and Hall of Fame Museums: An Editorial Introduction', *Journal of Sport History*, 23, 3 [1996], pp. 309–12). Referring to the growing use of the internet as an on-line archive, Stephen Hardy asks 'who will decide what "real" sources should be scanned into a virtual archive …?' This process, he adds, 'is not quite the same as creating bound, hard-copy compilations of primary sources. Most of those are transcribed; many are annotated. Even the lay reader recognises they are processed by intermediaries. Virtual archives are different. The question is: *which* experts will decide *what* the public researchers surf? Sports historians, as collectives, have been slow to jump into this issue. The future history of sport depends on the interrogation of diverse source material. To that end, sports historians must become more aggressive in their involvement with the growth of on-line archives' ('Where did You Go, Jackie Robinson? Or, the End of History and the Age of Sport Infrastructure', *Sporting Traditions*, 16, 1 [1999], pp. 92–3). 'Museum' is a much abused term for what is often nothing more than a glass case housing a few ad hoc sporting memorabilia. For a good

overview of sport museums see, Wray Vamplew, 'Facts and Artefacts: Sports Historians and Sports Museums', *Journal of Sport History*, 25, 2 (1998), pp. 268–82.

39   Stoler, 'Colonial Archives', p. 85, and Hamilton, Harris and Reid, 'Introduction', p. 9. An influential critic of the archive is Jacques Derrida, see particularly his *Archive Fever: A Freudian Impression* (Chicago, IL: University of Chicago Press, 1996). Verne Harris provides a useful summary of Derrida's principal assertions: '1) the event, the origin, the *arkhé*, in its uniqueness, is irrecoverable, unfindable. "The possibility of the archiving trace, this simple *possibility*, can only divide the uniqueness"; 2) The archiving trace, the archive, is not simply a recording, a reflection, an image of the event. It shapes the event. "The archivization produces as much as it records the event"; 3) The object does not speak for itself. In interrogating and interpreting the object, the archive, scholars inscribe their own interpretation into it. The interpretation has no meta-textual authority. There is no meta-archive. There is no closing of the archive. "It opens out of the future"; 4) Scholars are not, can never be, exterior to their objects. They are marked before they interrogate the markings, and this pre-impression shapes their interrogation' ('A Shaft of Darkness', p. 65). Derrida's *Archive Fever* provides little actual analysis of the archive as a repository of information. It is more about psychoanalysis and the political and social misuses of power (Carolyn Steedman, 'Something She Called a Fever: Michelet, Derrida, and Dust', *American Historical Review*, 106, 4 [2001], pp. 111–13).

40   Harris, 'A Shaft of Darkness', p. 75.

41   Jane Taylor, 'Holdings: Refiguring the Archive', in Hamilton *et al.*, *Refiguring the Archive*, p. 243, and David Bearman, 'Electronic Record-keeping, Social Memory and Democracy', in Hamilton *et al.*, *Refiguring the Archive*, pp. 324–5. In a discussion of remembering and forgetting, Jacques Derrida calls the archive 'a destruction of the memory'; societies deposit materials in archives in order to keep them safe which is tantamount to forgetting about them ('Archive Fever in South Africa', in Hamilton *et al.*, *Refiguring the Archive*, p. 54 and p. 68).

42   Harris, 'A Shaft of Darkness', p. 75.

43   John Coates, The Process of Bidding for an Olympic Games, paper presented to the inaugural meeting of the Sydney Olympic Games Bid Committee, 6 March 1991. A snippet in a newspaper article ('Coates tales', *Australian*, 9 October 1993) alerted me to Coates' address. Rod McGeoch, CEO of the Sydney Olympic Bid Committee, also referred to the address in his book, *The Bid: How Australia Won the 2000 Games* (Melbourne: William Heineman, 1994), p. 35.

44   Harris, 'A Shaft of Darkness', p. 75.

45   Franke and Berendonk, 'Hormonal Doping and Androgenization of Athletes', p. 1273.

46   Franke and Berendonk, 'Hormonal Doping and Androgenization of Athletes', pp. 1276–7.

47   Steven Ungerleider, *Faust's Gold: Inside the East German Doping Machine* (New York: St Martin's Press, 2001).

48   Burke, *Eyewitnessing*, pp. 94–102. In 1964, Marshall McLuhan wrote that historians will 'one day discover that the ads of our times are the richest and most faithful daily reflections that any society ever made of its entire range of activities' (*Understanding Media: The Extensions of Man* [New York: McGraw-Hill, 1964], p. 232).

49   Glen Norcliffe, *The Ride to Modernity: The Bicycle in Canada, 1869–1900* (Toronto: University of Toronto Press, 2001), pp. 146–7. The advertisement also appears in full colour on the cover of Norcliffe's book; for the state of rural roads in Canada at the time see the photograph on page 162.

50   Dennis Brailsford, *A Taste for Diversions: Sport in Georgian England* (Cambridge: The Lutterworth Press, 1999), p. 11. See also, David Block, *Baseball Before We Knew It: A Search for the Roots of the Game* (Lincoln, NB: University of Nebraska Press, 2005), pp. 225–8.

51   Leonie Sandercock and Ian Turner, *Up Where, Cazaly?: The Great Australian Game* (London: Granada, 1982), p. 19. Sandercock and Turner describe the letter as 'the Declaration of Independence of a new national game' (see also, Ken Inglis, *Australian Colonists* [Melbourne: Melbourne University Press, 1993], p. 153) but there is no evidence of Wills (or his rules)

being involved in the first game of football played between two grammar schools less than a month after the letter's publication (Geoffrey Blainey, *A Game of Our Own: The Origins of Australian Football* [Melbourne: Information Australia, 1990], pp. 14–18). For another similar newspaper example see also, Greg Ryan, *The Making of New Zealand Cricket 1832–1914* (London: Frank Cass, 2004), p. 86. While reconstructionists agree that letters are often 'patchy' and 'unrepresentative', they nonetheless praise them for the information they yield 'about individuals and their perceptions not readily obtained elsewhere' (Marwick, *The Nature of History*, p. 140).

52   Hartmann, *The 1968 Olympic Protests*, p. 219. The feature was subsequently published as a book, Jack Olsen, *The Black Athlete: A Shameful Story* (New York: Time-Life Books, 1968).

53   Thomas Jable, The Reliability of Newspaper Sources, paper presented at the North American Society for Sport History conference, Ohio State University, 26 May 2003.

54   John Betts, 'Sporting Journalism in Nineteenth-century America', *American Quarterly*, 5 (1953), p. 45.

55   Jable, Newspaper Sources.

56   Simon Rae, *W. G. Grace: A Life* (London: Faber, 1998), pp. 172–3. Rae sees the two accounts as part of a consistent pattern in which 'papers in places Grace had yet to visit dismissed the accusations against him as baseless smears, but the tune tended to change after they had had first-hand experience of him'.

57   Leonard Koppett, The Reliability of Newspaper Sources, paper presented at the North American Society for Sport History conference, Ohio State University, 26 May 2003.

58   Koppett, Newspaper Sources, and William Fotheringham, *Put Me Back on My Bike: In Search of Tom Simpson* (London: Yellow Jersey Press, 2003), p. 8.

59   Koppett, Newspaper Sources, and personal correspondence 26 May 2002. See also, Brailsford, *A Taste for Diversions*, p. 11.

60   Jable, Newspaper Sources, p. 6. See also, Betts, 'Sporting Journalism', p. 54.

61   Betts, 'Sporting Journalism', p. 45 and p. 46. See also, p. 47.

62   Michael Oriard, *King Football: Sport & Spectacle in the Golden Age of Radio and Newsreels, Movies and Magazines, the Weekly and the Daily Press* (Chapel Hill, NC: The University of North Carolina Press, 2001), p. 250.

63   Grundy, *Learning to Win*, pp. 233–4. Irwin Silber argues that sports journalist Lester Rodney helped break the colour bar in American sport with his writings in the *Communist Daily Worker* (*Press Box Red* [Philadelphia, PA: Temple University Press, 2003]).

64   Hill, *Sport, Leisure and Culture*, pp. 46–7.

65   Oriard, *King Football*, p. 26. See also, Frank Luther Mott, *American Journalism*, third edition (New York: Macmillan, 1962), pp. 666–73.

66   Brailsford, *A Taste for Diversions*, pp. 11–12. See also, the wonderful description of a ninth inning reported in an 1888 edition of the Chicago *Times* cited in Betts, 'Sporting Journalism', pp. 54–5.

67   Hill, *Sport, Leisure and Culture*, p. 11 and pp. 44–5.

68   Oriard, *King Football*, p. 29. See also, Grundy, *Learning to Win*, p. 142.

69   William Wiggins, 'Boxing's Sambo Twins: Racial Stereotypes in Jack Johnson and Joe Louis Newspaper Cartoons, 1908 to 1938', *Journal of Sport History*, 15, 3 (1988), p. 249, p. 251 and p. 253, and Mott, *American Journalism*, p. 588. LeRoy Carl believes that cartoons actually reach fewer readers than scholars might suspect. He describes cartoons as 'complicated puzzles mixing current events with analogies'. As a form of language, he says, they conjure 'many barriers and … evoke different meanings in different persons everywhere'. Newspaper readers will not always see the axiom, the double meaning, the parable ('Political Cartoons: "Ink Blots" of the Editorial Page', *Journal of Popular Culture*, 4 [1970], pp. 39–40, and 'Editorial Cartoons Fail to Reach Many Readers', *Journalism Quarterly*, 45, 3 [1968], pp. 533–5).

70   Roy Rosenzweig, *Eight Hours For What We Will: Workers and Leisure in an Industrial City, 1870–1920* (Cambridge: Cambridge University Press, 1983), pp. 290–1.

71 Edward Herman and Noam Chomsky, *Manufacturing Consent: The Political Economy of the Mass Media* (New York: Pantheon Books, 1988), p. xi.

72 Oriard, *King Football*, p. 226, and Grundy, *Learning to Win*.

73 Herman and Chomsky, *Manufacturing Consent*, p. xii.

74 Glenn Moore, 'Ideology on the Sportspage: Newspapers, Baseball, and Ideological Conflict in the Gilded Age', *Journal of Sport History*, 23, 3 (1996), quotes p. 249 and p. 250.

75 Grundy, *Learning to Win*, pp. 140–4, p. 243 and p. 246. See also, pp. 227–9.

76 Herman and Chomsky, *Manufacturing Consent*, p. xv.

77 Graeme Davidson, 'The Imaginary Grandstand: International Sport and the Recognition of Australian Identity', in Bernard Whimpress (ed.), *The Imaginary Grandstand: Identity and Narrative in Australian Sport* (Kent Town: Australian Society for Sports History, 2001), p. 17. See also, Michel Oriard, *Reading Football: How the Popular Press Created an American Spectacle* (Chapel Hill, NC: University of North Carolina Press, 1993), p. 17.

78 Davidson, 'The Imaginary Grandstand', pp. 17–18.

79 Oriard, *Reading Football*, p. 17. See also, Hill, *Sport, Leisure and Culture*, p. 43.

80 Oriard, *Reading Football*, p. 17 and p. 141.

81 Carolyn Hamilton, ' "Living by Fluidity": Oral Histories, Material Custodies and the Politics of Archiving', in Hamilton *et al.*, *Refiguring the Archive*, p. 212. See also, pp. 214–15, and Tosh, *The Pursuit of History*, p. 193.

82 Jennifer Hargreaves, *Heroines of Sport: The Politics of Difference and Identity* (London: Routledge, 2000), p. 1. See also, Alistair Thomson, 'Fifty Years On: An International Perspective on Oral History', *Journal of American History*, 85, 2 (1998), p. 584, and John Murphy, 'The Voice of Memory: History, Autobiography and Oral Memory', *Historical Studies*, 22, 87 (1986), p. 159.

83 Jane De Hart, 'Oral Sources and Contemporary History: Dispelling Old Assumptions', *Journal of American History*, 80, 2 (1993), p. 589.

84 Hamilton, 'Oral Histories', p. 212. See also, Jan Vansina, *Oral Tradition as History* (London: James Currey, 1985), pp. 175–85, Burton, *Dwelling in the Archive*, p. 21, and White, *Speaking With Vampires*, p. 42.

85 De Hart, 'Oral Sources', p. 591.

86 Mark Leary and Robin Kowalski, 'Impression Management: A Literature Review and Two-Component Model', *Psychology Bulletin*, 107, 1 (1990), pp. 34–47.

87 De Hart, 'Oral Sources', p. 591. As well as timing, a number of historians also recognise the importance of place as a mediating variable in obtaining oral testimony (Hamilton, 'Oral Histories', p. 219).

88 De Hart, 'Oral Sources', p. 591.

89 Gideon Haigh, 'Confessions of a Primitive Ethnographer', in Whimpress, *The Imaginary Grandstand*, p. 87.

90 S. W. Pope (ed.), 'Roundtable: Ken Burns's *Baseball*', *Journal of Sport History*, 23, 1 (1996), pp. 69–70. For the transcript of O'Neil's testimony see Geoffrey Ward and Ken Burns, *Baseball: An Illustrated History* (New York: Alfred A. Knopf, 1994), pp. 285–6.

91 White, *Speaking With Vampires*, p. 39, p. 48 and p. 52.

92 Thomson, 'Fifty Years On', pp. 581–2, De Hart, 'Oral Sources', p. 588, Vansina, *Oral Tradition*, p. 61, and Paul Thompson, *The Voice of the Past: Oral History*, third edition (Oxford: Oxford University Press, 2000).

93 White, *Speaking With Vampires*, p. 48 and p. 53. Critics observed that people often revise their answers when they are interviewed for a second time (White, *Speaking With Vampires*, p. 38).

94 Haigh, 'Confessions', pp. 88–9. Interestingly, Haigh finds himself repeatedly struck by what he calls 'naff interviewing' in sport history. The approaches, he says, are typically 'formulaic, inhibiting and stale'; they appear to follow the approach, ' "hello nice old sportsman. Tell me your stories" '. Such approaches are 'pointless' and 'patronising'; they assume that the subject is incapable of discussion and reflection' ('Confessions', pp. 86–7).

95 Burton, *Dwelling in the Archive*, p. 23 and p. 144.

96 Thomson, 'Fifty Years On', p. 582 and p. 583, and De Hart, 'Oral Sources', p. 588.

97 De Hart, 'Oral Sources', p. 590.

98 De Hart, 'Oral Sources', p. 590 and p. 592.

99 Murphy, 'The Voice of Memory', p. 165, Thomson, 'Fifty Years On', p. 585, and De Hart, 'Oral Sources', p. 595.

100 Thomson, 'Fifty Years On', p. 586.

101 In addition to his work on fiction and history (Chapter 4), Nathan offers a useful introduction to the notion of collective memory (*Saying It's So: A Cultural History of the Black Sox Scandal* [Urbana, IL: University of Illinois Press, 2003], pp. 60–2). The French sociologist Maurice Halbwachs is a principal source for Nathan (and Mewett – see note 103 below). Many scholars credit him with being the first to propose that remembering and forgetting are socially constructed and present-orientated processes: 'a remembrance is in a very large measure a reconstruction of the past achieved with data borrowed from the present, a reconstruction prepared, furthermore, by reconstructions of earlier periods wherein past images had already been altered' (Maurice Halbwachs, *The Collective Memory* [New York: Harper Colophon, 1980], p. 69).

102 Phil Vasili, *The First Black Footballer, Arthur Wharton 1865–1930: An Absence of Memory* (London: Frank Cass, 1998), p. 148, pp. 180–1, pp. 186–7, pp. 190–1, p. 192 and pp. 194–5. But are the sporting abilities of Wharton and Owens really comparable? Matthew Taylor charges Vasili with 'overemphasizing' Wharton's significance and argues that he was little more than a footballer 'journeyman' (Review of P. Vasili, *Colouring Over the White Line* [Edinburgh: Mainstream Press, 2000], *Soccer and Society*, 2, 1 [2001], p. 120). Taylor, however, does not address Wharton's running prowess which was significant and, when combined with his football career, should have been sufficient to keep Wharton in the national sporting memory, had, as Vasili maintains, the social climate been different.

103 Peter Mewett, 'History in the Making and the Making of History: Stories and the Social Construction of Sport', *Sporting Traditions*, 17, 1 (2000), p. 2 and pp. 14–15.

104 White, *Speaking With Vampires*, p. 4, p. 5, pp. 9–10, p. 12, p. 19 and p. 41.

105 Nick Tosches, *The Devil and Sonny Liston* (Boston, MA: Little, Brown, 2000), pp. 27–8.

106 White, *Speaking With Vampires*, p. 39 and p. 40.

107 De Hart, 'Oral Sources', p. 591, Hamilton, 'Oral Histories', p. 217, and White, *Speaking With Vampires*, p. 51.

108 White, *Speaking With Vampires*, p. 30.

109 White, *Speaking With Vampires*, pp. 32–4.

110 White, *Speaking With Vampires*, p. 42 and p. 43, and Burton, *Dwelling in the Archive*, p. 25.

111 Burke, *Eyewitnessing*, p. 9. For examples in sport history see, Carol Clark and Allen Guttmann, 'Artists and Athletes', *Journal of Sport History*, 22, 2 (1995), pp. 85–110, Anthony Milavic, 'Pankration and Greek Coins', *The International Journal of the History of Sport*, 18, 2 (2001), pp. 179–92, and Mari Womack, *Sport as Symbol: Images of the Athlete in Art, Literature and Song* (Jefferson, NC: McFarland, 2003).

112 Richard Cashman, *Paradise of Sport: The Rise of Organised Sport in Australia* (Melbourne: Oxford University Press, 1995), p. 171.

113 Stephen Bann cited in Burke, *Eyewitnessing*, p. 184.

114 Pope, 'Roundtable', p. 77.

115 Robert Allen and Douglas Gomery, *Film History: Theory and Practice* (New York: Alfred A. Knopf, 1985), pp. 215–16. Harvey Zucker and Lawrence Babich chronicle and describe some 2,000 sport films released prior to the end of 1984 (*Sports Films: A Complete Reference* [Jefferson, NC: McFarland, 1987]).

116 Burke, *Eyewitnessing*, p. 159.

117 Fotheringham, *Put Me Back on My Bike*, p. 3 and p. 18.

118 Pope, 'Roundtable', p. 77.

119 *One Day in September*, producers John Battsek and Arthur Cohn (Passion Pictures and Dan Valley Film, 1999), videocassette. See also, Reeve, *One Day in September*, p. 147.

120 *History of Australian Surfing*, producer Nat Young (CBS/Fox, 1986), videocassette.

121 *Olympia*, produced by Leni Riefenstahl (International Historic Films, 1938), videocassette. See also, Allen Guttmann, *The Olympics: A History of the Modern Games* (Urbana, IL: University of Illinois Press, 1992), pp. 70–1.

122 *People's Century*, writer, producer, director and editor Mark Davis (BBC/WGBH, 1995), videocassette. For a good analysis of the social assumptions and messages in mainstream fictional film see, Aaron Baker, *Contesting Identities: Sports in American Film* (Urbana, IL: University of Illinois Press, 2003).

123 Pope, 'Roundtable', p. 61. See also, Nathan, *Saying It's So*, pp. 200–1 and p. 206.

124 Pope, 'Roundtable', p. 73.

125 Pope, 'Roundtable', p. 71.

126 Pope, 'Roundtable', p. 71 and pp. 73–4.

127 Pope, 'Roundtable', p. 69 and p. 70. See also the comments by Larry Gerlach on p. 73 of 'Roundtable'.

128 Marwick, *The Nature of History*, p. 237, and Burke, *Eyewitnessing*, p. 159.

129 Marwick, *The Nature of History*, pp. 234–5 and p. 237.

130 This section draws on two conference presentations: Douglas Booth and Kevin Fisher, Film as an historical trace: A case study of *Runman 69*, paper presented to the North American Society for Sport History conference, Pacific Grove, California, May 2004, and Kevin Fisher, Economies of loss, Aesthetics of abjection in *Dogtown and Z-Boys* and *Runman 69*, paper presented to the On the Beach: Interdisciplinary Encounters conference, Fremantle, February 2004. The latter appears as Kevin Fisher, 'Economies of Loss and Questions of Style in Cotemporary Surf Cultures', *Junctures: The Journal of Thematic Dialogue*, 4 (2005), pp.13–21.

131 Runman resurrection, press release. At www.runmanfilms.com/images/pressRelease.jpg, accessed 22 July 2003.

132 Reviews of *Runman 69*. At www.runmanfilms.com/pages/review69.html, accessed 14 November 2002.

133 Reviews of *Runman 69*. At www.runmanfilms.com/pages/reviewsJournal.html, accessed 14 November 2002.

134 William Goode, *The Celebration of Heroes* (Berkeley, CA: University of California Press, 1978), p. vii, and Alain de Botton, *Status Anxiety* (London: Hamish Hamilton, 2004), p. 3.

135 Georges Bataille, 'The Notion of Expenditure', in A. Stoekl (ed.), *Visions of Excess: Selected Writings, 1927–39* (Minneapolis, MN: University of Minnesota Press, 1932), pp. 116–17.

136 Bataille, 'The Notion of Expenditure', p. 118.

137 Runman resurrection.

138 Daniel Nathan, 'The Story of the Hurricane', *Journal of Sport History*, 27, 2 (2000), pp. 299–303, and Robert Rosenstone, (ed.), *Revisioning History: Film and The Construction of a New Past* (Princeton, NJ: Princeton University Press, 1995).

139 Burke, *Eyewitnessing*, p. 177.

140 Hayes, Silvester and Hartmann, 'The Visual Archive', p. 118, Burke, *Eyewitnessing*, p. 10 and p. 184, and Hartmann, *The 1968 Olympic Protests*, pp. 8–10.

141 For example, J. A. Mangan, *The Games Ethic and Imperialism* (Harmondsworth: Viking, 1986), opposite p. 112.

142 For example, Norcliffe, *The Ride to Modernity*, pp. 102–3.

143 For example, Mangan, *Athleticism*, pp. 166–7.

144 For example, Holt, *Sport and the British*, plate 12, and Smith, *Sports and Freedom*, plates 17 and 22.

145 For example, the cover of Jim Riordan and Arnd Krüger (eds), *The International Politics of Sport in the 20th Century* (London: E & F N Spon, 1999).

146 Echoing Keith Windschuttle's notion of fixed evidence (Chapter 2), Andrew Ritchie insists that photographs are not 'methodologically manipulable – photographs do not face in any direction, or move in any direction, or express any opinion – as evidence they are simply themselves' ('Seeing the Past as the Present that it once was: A Response to Nancy Struna's

"Reframing the Direction of Change in the History of Sport" [*IJHS*, December 2001]', *The International Journal of the History of Sport*, 20, 3 [2003], p. 149).

147 Hayes, Silvester and Hartmann, 'The Visual Archive', p. 111, and Cheryl Cole, 'One Chromosome Too Many', in Kay Schaffer and Sidonie Smith (eds), *The Olympics at the Millennium: Power, Politics and the Games* (New Brunswick, NJ: Rutgers University Press, 2000), p. 130.

148 Burke, *Eyewitnessing*, p. 167. Deconstructionists substitute the term gaze for point of view. Borrowed from the French psychoanalyst Jacques Lacan, gaze expresses collective attitudes – as in the western gaze, scientific gaze, colonial gaze, tourist gaze, male gaze – which may be subconscious (Burke, *Eyewitnessing*, p. 125).

149 John Bale, 'Capturing "The African" Body? Visual Images and "Imaginative Sports"', *Journal of Sport History*, 25, 2 (1998), pp. 235–6.

150 Hayes, Silvester and Hartmann, 'The Visual Archive', pp. 103–33.

151 Bale, 'Capturing "The African" Body?', p. 235. See also, John Bale, 'The Rhetoric of Running', in Jørn Hansen and Niels Kayser Nielsen (eds), *Sports, Body and Health* (Odense: Odense University Press, 2000), pp. 123–31.

152 Bale, 'Capturing "The African" Body?', p. 237, p. 238, pp. 240–1, p. 242, p. 243 and p. 244.

153 Bale, 'Capturing "The African" Body?', p. 244 and p. 245, and Hayes, Silvester and Hartmann, 'The Visual Archive', pp. 114–15.

154 Burke, *Eyewitnessing*, p. 169. Joan Chandler, for example, bemoans historians who 'bury themselves in Foucault, Derrida, and other literary theorists' ('"The End of Sports History?" Or the Beginning of Oral History Archives?', *Sporting Traditions*, 16, 1 [1999], p. 46).

155 Burke, *Eyewitnessing*, pp. 172–3.

156 Burke, *Eyewitnessing*, p. 171 and p. 172, and Nuttall, 'Literature and the Archive', p. 291, pp. 293–4 and p. 296.

157 Burke, *Eyewitnessing*, pp. 174–5.

158 Smith, 'Football History', p. 231 and p. 232.

159 Margaret Atwood, 'In Search of *Alias Grace*: On Writing Canadian Historical Fiction', *American Historical Review*, 103 (1998), p. 1516.

Part II Explanatory paradigms

1 Fischer formally defines an explanatory paradigm as 'an interactive structure of workable questions and the factual statements which are adduced to answer them' (*Historians' Fallacies: Toward a Logic of Historical Thought* [New York: Harper & Row, 1970], p. xv note 1).

2 Fischer, *Historians' Fallacies*, p. xv and p. 263.

3 William Baker, 'William Webb Ellis and the Origins of Rugby Football: The Life and Death of a Victorian Myth', *Albion*, 13, 2 (1981), p. 117.

4 Wray Vamplew, *Pay Up and Play the Game* (Cambridge: Cambridge University Press, 1988), p. 13.

5 Edward Carr, *What Is History?*, second edition (Harmondsworth: Penguin, 1990), p. 87.

6 Advocacy: debunking myths

1 Douglas Booth and Colin Tatz, *One-Eyed: A View of Australian Sport* (Sydney: Allen & Unwin, 2000), pp. 81–2, David Young, *The Modern Olympics: A Struggle for Revival* (Baltimore, MD: The Johns Hopkins University Press, 1996), p. 141, Harry Gordon, *Australia and the Olympic Games* (Brisbane: University of Queensland Press, 1994), pp. xxiii–xxvi, and Robert Barney,

'Setting the Record Straight – Again: Dorando Pietri It Is', *Olympika*, 10 (2001), pp. 129–30.

2   Gary Osmond, '"Look at that Kid Crawling": Race, Myth and the "Crawl" Stroke', *Australian Historical Studies*, forthcoming, p. 8. One important myth that stands outside this typology concerns sport as a vehicle of social mobility. See, for example, Steven Riess, 'Professional Sports as an Avenue of Social Mobility in America: Some Myths and Realities', in Donald Kyle and Gary Stark (eds), *Essays on Sport History and Sport Mythology* (College Station, TX: Texas A & M Press, 1990), pp. 83–117.

3   Wray Vamplew, *Pay Up and Play the Game* (Cambridge: Cambridge University Press, 1988), p. 13. Jack Berryman defines mythologising as 'a tendency to misinterpret, oversimplify, misrepresent or even falsify the actual record' ('Introduction', in Kyle and Stark, *Essays on Sport History*, p. 3. See also, Donald Kyle, 'E. Norman Gardiner and the Decline of Greek Sport', in Kyle and Stark, *Essays on Sport History*, p. 8).

4   Tony Collins, *Rugby's Great Split: Class, Culture and the Origins of Rugby League Football* (London: Frank Cass, 1998), Robert Henderson, *Ball, Bat and Bishop: The Origin of Ball Games* (Urbana, IL: University of Illinois Press, 2001), Jennifer Macrory, *Running With the Ball: The Birth of Rugby Football* (London: Collins Willow, 1991), and David Young, *The Olympic Myth of Greek Amateur Athletics* (Chicago, IL: Ares Publishers, 1984).

5   'The Olympic Story', Official Souvenir Programme of the Opening Ceremony, Melbourne Olympic Games, 1956, pp. 7–8 and p. 20. Author's copy. See also Young, *The Olympic Myth*, pp. 85–8.

6   Young, *The Olympic Myth*, p. 7.

7   Young, *The Olympic Myth*, p. 172, and Eric Dunning, 'Sport in the Civilising Process: Aspects of the Development of Modern Sport', in Dunning, Joseph Maguire and Robert Pearton (eds), *The Sports Process: A Comparative and Developmental Approach* (Champaign, IL: Human Kinetics, 1993), pp. 49–51.

8   Louis Gottschalk, *Understanding History: A Primer of Historical Method*, second edition (New York: Alfred A. Knopf, 1969), pp. 156–7. See also, Jeremy Black and Donald MacRaild, *Studying History* (Basingstoke: Macmillan, 1997), pp. 12–14.

9   Edward Carr, *What Is History?*, second edition (Harmondsworth: Penguin, 1964), p. 23.

10 Young, *The Olympic Myth*, p. x, p. 8, pp. 26–7 and p. 35.

11 Young, *The Olympic Myth*, pp. 51–2, pp. 63–7, p. 73, p. 76 and pp. 85–8. For more on Gardiner's influence on the history of sport see Kyle, 'Gardiner and the Decline of Greek Sport', and for details of Brundage's fanaticism on the subject of amateurism see Young, *The Olympic Myth*, pp. 82–3 note 78, and Allen Guttmann, *The Games Must Go On: Avery Brundage and the Olympic Movement* (New York: Columbia University Press, 1984), especially pp. 115–19, pp. 122–31, pp. 168 and pp. 197–9.

12 Henderson, *Ball, Bat and Bishop*, pp. 170–5 and p. 180. Henderson offers a timely reminder here: 'no historian [should be] bold enough, all inclusive enough, to settle any matter without any possibility that the disclosure of further evidence in the future, may modify or upset his findings' (p. 173).

13 Henderson, *Ball, Bat and Bishop*, pp. 176–7.

14 Henderson, *Ball, Bat and Bishop*, pp. 176–7. Henderson reproduces Graves' words in the press release on pp. 184–6. For details of the discovery of the original letters see *Richard Tofel,* 'The "innocuous conspiracy" of baseball's birth: Two long-lost letters show how Doubleday was credited with the game's invention', *Wall Street Journal*, 19 July 2001. The letters are reproduced in David Block, *Baseball Before We Knew It: A Search for the Roots of the Game* (Lincoln, NB: University of Nebraska Press, 2005), pp. 252–6.

15 Henderson, *Ball, Bat and Bishop*, p. 182 and pp. 188–9. Another obituary written by a West Point classmate and lifelong friend described Doubleday as 'a man who did not care for or go into any outdoor sports' (*Tofel,* 'The "innocuous conspiracy"').

16 Henderson, *Ball, Bat and Bishop*, pp. 188–9. Paul Thompson argues that an informant's interests will determine the reliability of her memory. He draws attention to the case of an

elderly man who, when asked to name the occupiers of 108 farms in his district in 1900, correctly named 106 against the parish electoral list (*The Voice of the Past: Oral History*, third edition [Oxford: Oxford University Press, 2000], p. 132).

17 Henderson, *Ball, Bat and Bishop*, pp. 183–6 and p. 188.

18 Henderson, *Ball, Bat and Bishop*, p. 173, p. 190 and pp. 192–3. When asked by a reporter some years later whether there was 'conclusive evidence' for Cooperstown as the birthplace of baseball, the chair of the Commission, Abraham Mills, admitted that there was none. Nonetheless, he insisted that the Commissioners were 'honorable men and their decision was unanimous' (*Tofel*, 'The "innocuous conspiracy"').

19 David Block recently claimed that 'Henderson proved beyond reasonable doubt that the Doubleday story was pure fiction' (*Baseball Before We Knew It*, p. 18).

20 Eric Dunning, Joseph Maguire and Robert Pearton, 'Introduction: Sports in Comparative and Development Perspective', in Dunning, Maguire and Pearton (eds), *The Sports Process: A Comparative and Developmental Approach* (Champaign, IL: Human Kinetics, 1993), p. 1. For copious examples of where the Ellis myth has been propagated see, Baker, 'William Webb Ellis', p. 128–9. Football had been played in England for hundreds of years. The games were usually annual matches played between competing towns with the objective being to kick or carry a ball to a defined goal. Rules were local (Eric Dunning and Kenneth Sheard, *Barbarians, Gentlemen and Players: A Sociological Study of the Development of Rugby Football* [Oxford: Martin Robertson, 1979], pp. 21–45).

21 Macrory, *Running With the Ball*, p. 25, pp. 26–7 and pp. 41–2. See also Baker, 'William Webb Ellis', p. 119 and p. 121.

22 Macrory, *Running With the Ball*, p. 24, p. 27 and pp. 29–32. Macrory's reference to Bloxam's honest character and scholarship is, of course, irrelevant to the actual truth of his claims about Ellis and is an example of what Fischer calls a fallacy of argument *ad verecundiam* (*Historians' Fallacies*, pp. 282–4).

23 Macrory, *Running With the Ball*, p. 32 and p. 34. Macrory also refers to Ellis cheating at schoolwork. This reference concerned an allegation that Ellis' mother assisted him in the competition for the school's Latin prize (pp. 30–1).

24 Macrory, *Running With the Ball*, pp. 34–5. The Committee's findings were published in a booklet entitled *The Origin of Rugby Football* (1897).

25 Macrory, *Running With the Ball*, p. 23 and pp. 34–5.

26 Macrory, *Running With the Ball*, p. 23 and pp. 35–6.

27 Baker, 'William Webb Ellis', p.118.

28 Collins, *Rugby's Great Split*, p. 6, and Dunning and Sheard, *Barbarians, Gentlemen and Players*, p. 60. Dunning and Sheard also raise the issue of theoretical credibility: 'It is just not sociologically plausible that a deeply entrenched traditional game could have been changed fundamentally by a single act, particularly that of a low-status individual such as Webb Ellis is reputed to have been'. And they point to the incompleteness of the account that 'fails to consider how, in the social circumstances which prevailed at Rugby in the early nineteenth century, the practice of "running in" became institutionalised; i.e. it fails to show what it was that led the boys to accept [Ellis'] innovation, not as a punishable misdemeanour, but as a desirable modification, worthy of incorporation into their football as a permanent and legitimate feature' (Dunning and Sheard, *Barbarians, Gentlemen and Players*, p. 61).

29 Collins, *Rugby's Great Split*, pp. 6–7. See also, Dunning and Sheard, *Barbarians, Gentlemen and Players*, pp. 60–1, and Baker, 'William Webb Ellis', p. 124. Macrory accuses Dunning and Sheard of 'allow[ing] their twentieth century preconceptions to intrude upon their evaluation of the historical facts' (Macrory, *Running With the Ball*, p. 47). Interestingly, historians examining the development of baseball viewed it as a middle-class sport played initially by middle-class gentlemen before it was dominated by skilled urban craftsmen and small shopkeepers (Melvin Adelman, *A Sporting Time: New York City and the Rise of Modern Athletics, 1820–1870* [Urbana, IL: University of Illinois Press, 1986], pp. 121–83).

30 See, for example, Collins, *Rugby's Great Split*, p. xviii.

31   Peter Novick, *That Noble Dream: The 'Objectivity Question' and the American Historical Profession* (Cambridge: Cambridge University Press, 1988), p. 2. Continuing on in this conservative reconstructionist vein, Novick says that 'the historian's conclusions are expected to display the standard judicial qualities of balance and even-handedness. As with the judiciary, these qualities are guarded by the insulation of the historical profession from social pressure or political influence, and by the individual historian avoiding partisanship or bias – not having any investment in arriving at one conclusion rather than another. Objectivity is held to be at grave risk when history is written for utilitarian purposes. One corollary of all this is that historians, as historians, must purge themselves of external loyalties: the historian's primary allegiance is to "the objective historical truth," and to professional colleagues who share a commitment to cooperative, cumulative efforts to advance toward that goal.' Harry Ritter's understanding of objectivity and interpretation offers an interesting comparison with the views of Novick (*Dictionary of Concepts in History* [Westport, CT: Greenwood Press, 1986], pp. 243–8 and pp. 302–8). A number of scholars have compared judicial and historical practices including Raymond Aron, Eric Hobsbawm and Max Weber (Raymond Aron, *Introduction to the Philosophy of History: An Essay on the Limits of Historical Objectivity*, translated by George Irwin [Boston, MA: Beacon Press, 1961], p. 157, Eric Hobsbawm, 'The Contribution of History to Social Science', *International Social Science Journal*, 33, 4 [1981], p. 626, and Max Weber, *The Methodology of the Social Sciences*, translated and edited by Edward Shils and Henry Finch [New York: Free Press, 1949], pp. 168–70). In his judgement on the libel case in which military historian David Irving sued professor of modern Jewish studies Deborah Lipstadt, Mr Justice Gray made a clear distinction between a court of law and a court of history. 'It is important that I stress at the outset of this judgement that I do not regard it as being any part of my function as the trial judge to make findings of fact as to what did and what did not occur during the Nazi regime in Germany. It will be necessary for me to rehearse, at some length, certain historical data. The need for this arises because I must evaluate the criticisms of … [Irving's] conduct as an historian in the light of the available historical evidence. But it is not for me to form, still less to express, a judgement about what happened. That is a task for historians. It is important that those reading this judgement should bear well in mind the distinction between my judicial role in resolving the issues arising between these parties and the role of the historian seeking to provide an accurate narrative of past events' (*The Irving Judgement*, http://www.nizkor.org/hweb/people/i/irving-david/judgment-01.html, 1.3, see also 13.3). In their analysis of the law, Herbert Hart and Tony Honoré observe that lawyers and historians both make judgements about causes and 'frequently assert that one particular event was the "effect" or "the consequence" or "the result" of another or of some human action' (*Causation in the Law* [Oxford: Clarendon Press, 1959], p. 8).

32   Alun Munslow, *Deconstructing History* (London: Routledge, 1997), p. 7 and p. 24.

33   Tony Mason cited in Jeff Hill, 'British Sports History: A Post-modern Future?', *Journal of Sport History*, 23, 1 (1996), p. 2.

34   Among the best recent examples are two works by Helen Lenskyj, *The Best Olympics Ever?: Social Impacts of Sydney 2000* (Albany, NY: State University of New York Press, 2002), and *Inside the Olympic Industry: Power, Politics, and Activism* (Albany, NY: State University of New York Press, 2000).

35   The classic statement of sporting faith and the corruption of sport is Michael Novak, *The Joy of Sports*, revised edition (Lanham, MD: Madison Books, 1994).

36   'There can be little doubt', writes John Tosh, 'that conservatives are disproportionately represented in the ranks of the historical profession' (*The Pursuit of History: Aims, Methods and New Directions in the Study of Modern History*, second edition [London: Longman, 1991], p. 25).

37   Dennis Smith, *The Rise of Historical Sociology* (Cambridge: Polity Press, 1991), p. 163 and p. 165. Smith uses the terms examining magistrate, partisan expert witness, scientist, and advocate. For an extended discussion on the nature of detachment in history see Thomas

Haskell, *Objectivity Is Not Neutrality: Explanatory Schemes in History* (Baltimore, MD: The Johns Hopkins University Press, 1998), pp. 145–73.

38 Evan Whitton, *Trial by Voodoo: Why the Law Defeats Justice and Democracy* (Sydney: Random House, 1994), p. ix and p. 23.

39 Whitton, *Trial by Voodoo*, p. 345.

40 Whitton, *Trial by Voodoo*, p. x.

41 Whitton, *Trial by Voodoo*, p. 348.

42 Smith, *Historical Sociology*, p. 164. Mitchell Dean argues that Michel Foucault's notions of genealogy and archaeology and the relationships between them 'provide a way of resolving the problems of involvement and detachment' (*Critical and Effective Histories: Foucault's Methods and Historical Sociology* [London: Routledge, 1994], p. 28). Neither genealogy nor archaeology have touched sport history in any significant way and Dean's discussion places them in the context of presentism (see Epilogue).

43 Tosh, *The Pursuit of History*, pp. 70–1.

44 C. L. R. James, *Beyond a Boundary* (Durham, NC: Duke University Press, 1993), p. 26. Although James works primarily within the context paradigm (Chapter 10), he also figures in the comparison paradigm (Chapter 7).

45 Robert Lipsyte, 'Introduction', in James, *Beyond a Boundary*, p. xiv. See also Douglas Hartmann, 'What Can We Learn from Sport If We Take Sport Seriously as a Racial Force? Lessons from C. L. R. James's *Beyond a Boundary*', *Ethnic and Racial Studies*, 26, 3 (2003), pp. 473–4.

46 In the words of Geoffrey Elton, 'the historian … [who] values his integrity, must be a professional sceptic' (Geoffrey Elton, *Return to Essentials* [Cambridge: Cambridge University Press, 1991], pp. 23–4).

47 Raymond Grew, 'The Case for Comparing Histories', *American Historical Review*, 85, 4 (1980), p. 771.

48 Fischer, *Historians' Fallacies*, p. 305.

49 Theodore Zeldin, 'Social History and Total History', *Journal of Social History*, 10, 2 (1976), p. 239. Similarly, Geoffrey Barraclough appeals to historians to cast off their specialised interests in favour of 'wide, systematic interpretations', and appears to rebuke those practitioners who 'dogmatic[ally] concentrate on the particular and individualistic aspects of history rather than on trying to discover such common features (such patterns, if you like), as can be discerned in past events (History and the Common Man, Presidential address to the Historical Association, London, 12 April 1966. The Historical Association, pamphlet, p. 7 and p. 10).

50 Henderson, *Ball, Bat and Bishop*, p. 193.

51 Stephen Jay Gould, *Bully for Brontosaurus: Reflections in Natural History* (New York: W. W. Norton, 1991), p. 52.

52 Tofel, 'The "innocuous conspiracy"'.

53 Gould, *Bully for Brontosaurus*, p. 52.

54 Henderson, *Ball, Bat and Bishop*, pp. 193–4.

55 Young, *The Olympic Myth*, p. ix.

56 Young, *The Olympic Myth*, p. ix.

57 Collins is also archivist of the British Rugby Football League. See also, Tony Collins, 'Ahr Waggy': Harold Wagstaff and the Making of Anglo-Australian Rugby League Culture, Fifth Annual Tom Brock Lecture, 4 July 2003, Australian Society for Sport History, p. 3.

58 See, for example, C. Behan McCullagh, *The Logic of History: Putting Postmodernism in Perspective* (London: Routledge, 2004), pp. 78–85.

59 See especially, Macrory, *Running With the Ball*, p. 212 and p. 145, p. 169 and pp. 194–6, and Baker, 'William Webb Ellis', p. 126.

60 David Voigt, 'Myths After Baseball: Notes on Myths in Sports', *Quest*, 30 (1978), p. 49. In the early 1970s, the emphasis on history as advocacy shifted to history as text which had important consequences for historical practice. Whereas the debunker of myth focused on sources, the analyst of text turned to reading and interpretation and an acknowledgment that 'readers bring to texts a host of responses, arising from the breadth of their personal

and social experiences, to produce a range of interpretations …'. Hence, 'meaning resides not simply in texts but in the negotiations between texts and readers' (Michael Oriard, *Reading Football: How the Popular Press Created an American Spectacle* [Chapel Hill, NC: University of North Carolina Press, 1993], p. 11 and p. 13). I discuss these approaches further in Chapter 11.

61   Voigt, 'Myths After Baseball', p. 46. See also Baker, 'William Webb Ellis', p. 121.

62   Henderson, *Ball, Bat and Bishop*, p. 178.

63   James Oliver Robertson, *American Myth, American Reality* (New York: Hill & Wang, 1980), p. 346. See also, Gary Osmond and Murray Phillips, '"The Bloke with the Stroke": Alick Wickham, the "Crawl" and Social Memory', *The Journal of Pacific History*, 39, 3 (2004), p. 309.

64   Voigt, 'Myths After Baseball', pp. 47–9. In contradistinction, Baker talks about the 'attractiveness of a facile explanation for a complex historical process' ('William Webb Ellis', p. 119).

65   Gould, *Bully for Brontosaurus*, p. 45. 'The very principle of myth', said Roland Barthes, is to 'transform history into nature, … it is not read as a motive but as a reason' (*Mythologies* [Frogmore: Paladin, 1973], pp. 129–30).

66   Baker, 'William Webb Ellis', p. 117 and p.118. See also, p. 130.

67   Brett Hutchins, *Don Bradman: Challenging the Myth* (Melbourne: Cambridge University Press, 2002), and Osmond, '"Look at that Kid Crawling"'. Hutchins and Osmond both worked on their doctorates at the University of Queensland under Murray Phillips.

68   Hutchins, *Don Bradman*, p. 2. For a discussion of the role of biographies and autobiographies in manufacturing myths see, John Bale, Mette Christensen and Gertrude Pfister, 'Introduction', in Bale, Christensen and Pfister (eds), *Writing Lives in Sport: Biographies, Life-histories and Methods* (Aarhus: Aarhus University Press, 2004), p. 15, and Birgitte Possing, 'The Historical Biography: Genre, History and Methodology', in Bale *et al.*, *Writing Lives in Sport*, p. 18.

69   Hutchins, *Don Bradman*, p. 9, p. 10 and pp. 24–5.

70   Hutchins, *Don Bradman*, pp. 22–3. Commenting on the initial prosperousness of the William Webb Ellis myth, Baker similarly notes that it 'flourished because it rode the crest of several literary and intellectual currents of the period. In fact it built upon an image already firmly established: a proto-muscular Christian, full of pluck but charmingly oblivious to the restrictive traditions of his society, Ellis in his "fine disregard for the rules of football, as played in his time" was a romantic hero in the Tom Brown vein' ('William Webb Ellis', p. 125).

71   Hutchins, *Don Bradman*, p. 79.

72   Hutchins, *Don Bradman*, p. 80.

73   Hutchins, *Don Bradman*, p. 10 and p. 25. Barthes similarly discusses myths as functioning to purify things, make them innocent, give them a 'natural' and 'eternal' justification (*Mythologies*, p. 155).

74   Osmond, '"Look at that Kid Crawling"', p. 3. The myth of the 'crawl' stroke in Australian swimming emanates largely from the recollections of Dudley Hellmrich, the chief honorary coach of the New South Wales Amateur Swimming Association (pp. 1–2). The case of Aboriginal runner Bobby McDonald, who invented the crouch start in running, provides an interesting comparison with Wickham. See, Colin Tatz, *Obstacle Race: Aborigines in Sport* (Sydney: University of New South Wales Press, 1995), pp. 92–3.

75   Osmond, '"Look at that Kid Crawling"', p. 4.

76   Osmond, '"Look at that Kid Crawling"', p. 12. See also, Osmond and Phillips, '"The Bloke with the Stroke"', p. 323.

77   Osmond, '"Look at that Kid Crawling"', p. 13, p. 14 and pp. 15–16.

78   Voigt, 'Myths After Baseball', p. 46. The pejorative notion of function (see Chapter 3) has seen historians with deconstructionist tendencies conceptualise myths as cultural discourses. Of course, some reconstructionists claim that they too investigate the functions of myths by virtue of examining the motives of myth-makers. Constructionist approaches are both

quantitatively and qualitatively different with constructionists acknowledging that consequences exist behind the realm of individuals.

79   David McGimpsey, *Imagining Baseball: America's Pastime and Popular Culture* (Bloomington, IN: Indiana University Press, 2000), p. 3 and p. 52.

7 Comparison: expanding the evidence

1   Raymond Grew, 'The Case for Comparing Histories', *American Historical Review*, 85, 4 (1980), p. 776 and p. 777. Arthur Marwick believes that 'highlighting both similarities and differences' can serve as 'a source of new syntheses, new questions and, sometimes, convincing answers' (*The Nature of History*, second edition [London: Macmillan, 1981], p. 75). Arthur Stinchcombe noted that careful comparison can often 'yield rich concepts that fruitfully enter into many causal statements' (*Theoretical Methods in Social History* [New York: Academic Press, 1978], p. 22). Grew also emphasises that comparisons are central in every stage of historical work, whether asking questions, identifying historical problems, designing research, or reaching and testing conclusions ('Comparing Histories', pp. 768–70).

2   Samuel Beer, 'Causal Explanation and Imaginative Re-enactment', *History and Theory*, 3, 1 (1963), pp. 15–16.

3   William Irwin, '*What Is An Allusion?*', *Journal of Aesthetics and Art Criticism*, 59, 3 (2001), pp. 287–9.

4   Grew, 'Comparing Histories', p. 771.

5   See also, Alun Munslow, *Deconstructing History* (London: Routledge, 1997), p. 7.

6   Grew, 'Comparing Histories', p. 776.

7   Kevin McAleer, *Dueling: The Cult of Honor in Fin-de-Siècle Germany* (Princeton, NJ: Princeton University Press, 1994), pp. 77–8.

8   This is not to diminish the important role of metaphor in developing understanding (see Chapter 4). Indeed, Samuel Beer recently claimed that 'thought advances through metaphor rather than through precept. I really believe that metaphors – those corny expressions, almost a kind of street poetry – tell you more about the future than the think tanks' (Ken Gewertz, 'CES professor honored on 90th birthday', *Harvard University Gazette*, 1 November 2001).

9   Andrew Moore, Jimmy Devereux's Yorkshire Pudding: Reflections on the Origins of Rugby League in New South Wales and Queensland, Tom Brock Lecture, 1999 (Sydney: Australian Society for Sports History), p. 7, p. 9 and p. 11. Moore rests this latter claim on the interesting comments by H. M. Moran, a rugby union player at Sydney University and an 'astute observer' of rugby affairs: 'For the students of Sydney University the establishment of professionalism in sport meant serious loss. In my time, the undergraduates were in danger of all being stamped into a single mould. They were being given one uniform pattern in their prejudices and preferences. Sport provided an extramural course in a totally different discipline. We tussled with factory hands and fireman, with miners, wharf-labourers and carters. These players might have rough manners, but in many of the elementary virtues of life they were our superiors. Above all they had a hard edge to their characters, and a robust humour. By contact with them we gained immeasurably more than they. When professionalism came, University players were shut out from friendships with men in ranks called lower and their education suffered by it. Whatever polite scholarship they might possess they now were sentenced to be weaker in humanity'.

10   Roberta Park, 'Sport, Gender and Society in a Transatlantic Perspective', in J. A. Mangan and Park (eds), *From Fair Sex to Feminism: Sport and the Socialization of Women in the Industrial and Post-industrial Eras* (London: Frank Cass, 1987), p. 59. See also, Tara Magdalinski and Timothy Chandler, 'With God on their Side: An Introduction', in Magdalinski and Chandler (eds), *With God on their Side: Sport in the Service of Religion* (London: Routledge, 2002), p. 3.

11   Keith Jenkins and Alun Munslow (eds), *The Nature of History Reader* (London: Routledge, 2004), p. 191, Robert Berkhofer, *Beyond the Great Story: History as Text and Discourse* (Cambridge, MA: Harvard University Press, 1995), p. 10, and Alun Munslow, *The Routledge Companion to Historical Studies* (London: Routledge, 2000), p. 229.

12   See, for example, Douglas Booth, *The Race Game: Sport and Politics in South Africa* (London: Frank Cass, 1998), p. 55, and Park, 'Sport, Gender and Society', p. 58.

13   Norman Wilson, *History in Crisis: Recent Directions in Historiography* (Upper Saddle River, NJ: Prentice Hall, 1999), p. 136.

14   Toni Bruce and Christopher Hallinan, 'Cathy Freeman: The Quest for Australian Identity', in David Andrews and Steven Jackson (eds), *Sports Stars: The Cultural Politics of Sporting Celebrity* (London: Routledge, 2001), p. 267.

15   Miles Fairburn, *Social History: Problems, Strategies and Methods* (New York: St. Martin's Press, 1999), p. 86. For example, Emile Durkheim and Max Weber, two of the founding fathers of sociology, stressed the importance of comparison. According to Durkheim, 'comparative sociology is not a special branch of sociology. It is sociology itself'. Similarly, Weber wrote, 'we are absolutely in accord that history should establish what is specific, say, to the medieval city; but this is only possible if we first find what is missing in other cities' (Jeremy Black and Donald MacRaild, *Studying History* [Basingstoke: Macmillan, 1997], p. 104).

16   Certainly reconstructionist sport historians have shied from historical sociology in the misguided belief that it is a guaranteed route to a theoretical quagmire and predetermined structural explanations. At first glance the renowned historical sociologist and practitioner of comparison Theda Skocpol appears to lend support to this view when she argues that theoretical concepts and hypotheses are integral to comparative historical analysis: 'the comparative method alone cannot define the phenomenon to be studied. It cannot select the appropriate units of analysis or say which historical cases should be studied. Nor can it provide the causal hypotheses to be explored. All of these must come from the macro-sociological imagination, informed by the theoretical debates of the day, and sensitive to the patterns of evidence for sets of historical cases'. However, Skocpol also advocates comparison in history on the grounds that it can prompt 'new ways of looking at concrete historical cases' (*States and Social Revolutions: A Comparative Analysis of France, Russia and China* [Cambridge: Cambridge University Press, 1979], p. 39 and p. 40). (I discuss Skocpol's scientific method of comparison in Chapter 8.) See also, Victoria Bonnell, 'Theory, Concepts and Comparison in Historical Sociology', *Comparative Studies in Society and History*, 22, 2 (1980), pp. 156–73, Gareth Stedman Jones, 'From Historical Sociology to Theoretical History', *British Journal of Sociology*, 27 (1976), pp. 295–305, and C. Wright Mills, *The Sociological Imagination* [New York: Oxford University Press, 1959], especially pp. 143–63). Joseph Maguire has been prominent in calling for the breakdown of arbitrary boundaries between sport history and sport sociology ('Common Ground? Links Between Sports History, Sports Geography and the Sociology of Sport', *Sporting Traditions*, 12, 1 [1995], pp. 3–25). See also, Jean Harvey, 'Historical Sociology and Social History: Même Combat', in Kevin Wamsley (ed.), *Method and Methodology in Sport and Cultural History* (Dubuque, IA: Brown and Benchmark Publishers, 1995), pp. 2–15.

17   John Hoberman, 'Toward a Theory of Olympic Internationalism', *Journal of Sport History*, 22, 1 (1995), pp. 1–37.

18   C. L. R. James, *Beyond a Boundary* (Durham, NC: Duke University Press, 1993), pp. 196–7.

19   James, *Beyond a Boundary*, pp. 199–201.

20   James, *Beyond a Boundary*, pp. 202–4.

21   Roberta Park, 'Physiology and Anatomy are Destiny!?: Brains, Bodies and Exercise in Nineteenth Century American Thought', *Journal of Sport History*, 18, 1 (1991), p. 63. Park and Patricia Vertinsky have led the field in this area. For a review of the early literature, see Roberta Park, 'A Decade of the Body: Researching and Writing About The History of Health, Fitness, Exercise and Sport, 1983–1993', *Journal of Sport History*, 21, 1 (1994), pp. 59–82. I discuss Vertinsky's work more fully in Chapter 11.

22 James himself declared that he was not talking figuratively. Rather than 'a bastard or a poor relation', cricket, he said, stands alongside 'theatre, ballet, opera and the dance' as 'a full member of the community' (*Beyond a Boundary*, p. 196).

23 George Orwell, 'The Sporting Spirit', in Sonia Orwell and Ian Angus (eds), *The Collected Essays, Journalism and Letters of George Orwell, Volume IV 1945–1950* (London: Secker & Warburg, 1968), p. 41 and p. 42. See also, J. M. Coetzee, 'The 1995 Rugby World Cup', *Stranger Shores: Essays 1986–1999* (London: Vintage, 2002), p. 351.

24 Orwell, 'The Sporting Spirit', p. 41.

25 'Bloody violence cannot be caught to any great extent in truly noble form; hence [war] can only be experienced and enjoyed as a social and aesthetic fiction', wrote Johan Huizinga. Writer and art critic John Ruskin may have declared that 'no great art ever yet rose on earth, but among a nation of soldiers' and 'there is no great art possible to a nation but that which is based on battle', but according to Huizinga he quickly 'arrested the flight of his thought so as to bring in a denunciation of [the first] "modern" war' – the American Civil War (Johan Huizinga, *Homo Ludens: A Study of the Play Element in Culture* [Boston, MA: The Beacon Press, 1955], pp. 101–4.

26 Grant Farred, '"Theatre of Dreams": Mimicry and Difference in Cape Flats Township Football', in John Bale and Mike Cronin (eds), *Sport and Postcolonialism* (Oxford: Berg, 2003), p. 135. As Muhammad Ali bluntly told Congressman Robert Michel, 'there's one hell of a lot of difference in fighting in the ring and going to the War in Vietnam' (cited in, David Zang, *SportsWars: Athletes in the Age of Aquarius* [Fayetteville, AR: The University of Arkansas Press, 2001], p. 103).

27 Louis Arnaud Reid, 'Aesthetics and Education', in H. T. A. Whiting and D. W. Masterson (eds), *Readings in the Aesthetics of Sport* (London: Lepus Books, 1974), p. 17. For a contemporary example see, Søren Damkjær, 'Post-Olympism and the Aestheticization of Sport', in John Bale and Mette Christensen (eds), *Post-Olympism? Questioning Sport in the Twenty-First Century* (Oxford: Berg, 2004), pp. 223–7.

28 Reid, 'Aesthetics and Education', p. 14.

29 Derek Birley, *The Willow Wand: Some Cricket Myths Explored* (London: Queen Anne Press, 1979), p. 168. Birley was particularly contemptuous of the sport-is-art metaphorical allusion as proposed by the doyen of cricket writing Neville Cardus. The 'spirit' of Reggie Spooner's cricket, Cardus once wrote, was 'kin with sweet music, and the wind that makes long grasses wave, and the singing of Elizabeth Schumann in Johan Strauss, and the poetry of Herrick' (cited in, Birley, *The Willow Wand*, p. 165). Cardus employed C. L. R. James at the *Manchester Guardian*. Although well aware of James' arguments about cricket and art, Birley ignores them. The reasons are especially interesting in light of the allegations of a bias towards elitism made by Bill Murray, Richard Holt and Catriona Parratt (see Chapter 2, note 95) in their reviews of Birley's three-volume history of British sport. In his essay 'Cardus and the Aesthetic Fallacy', Birley said Cardus 'deserves special attention' because of the 'distinct social overtones' in his writings. First, 'he was apt to confuse style with pedigree' and, second, 'he gives the distinct impression that he is merely using cricket for his own loftier purposes. His autobiographies suggest that he may even have felt that he was slumming, culturally speaking, when he was at Old Trafford rather than at Hallé concerts or the theatre. So he needed to elevate cricket by high-brow comparisons with the world of art' (Birley, *The Willow Wand*, p. 164).

30 Reid, 'Aesthetics and Education', p. 7, p. 15, p. 17, p. 18 and p. 19. See also, Birley, *The Willow Wand*, p. 168 and p. 173, and Damkjær, 'Aestheticization of Sport', pp. 224–5.

31 In addition to Moore, 'The Origins of Rugby League', examples in sport history include, Mike Cronin, 'Catholics in Sport in Northern Ireland: Exclusiveness or Inclusiveness', in Magdalinski and Chandler, *With God on their Side*, pp. 20–36, Malcolm MacLean, 'Football as Social Critique: Protest Movements, Rugby and History in Aotearoa, New Zealand', in J. A. Mangan and John Nauright (eds), *Sport in Australasian Society* (London: Frank Cass, 2000), pp. 255–77, Robert Morford and Martha McIntosh, 'Sport and the Victorian Gentleman',

in Alan Ingham and John Loy (eds), *Sport in Social Development: Traditions, Transitions, and Transformations* (Champaign, IL: Human Kinetics, 1993), pp. 51–76, Paul Silverstein, 'Stadium Politics: Sport, Islam and Amazigh Consciousness in France and North Africa', in Magdalinski and Chandler, *With God on their Side*, pp. 37–55, Brian Stoddart, 'Sport, Cultural Imperialism, and Colonial Response to the British Empire', *Comparative Studies in Society and History*, 30, 4 (1988), pp. 649–73, and David Wiggins, 'The Future of College Athletics Is at Stake', in *Glory Bound: Black Athletes in a White America* (Syracuse, NY: Syracuse University Press, 1997), pp. 123–51. Jean Harvey, Rob Beamish and Jacques Defrance refer to Skocpol's work in their proposal for a systematic approach towards a comparison of physical exercise policies in welfare states ('Physical Exercise Policy and the Welfare State: A Framework for Comparative Analysis', *International Review for the Sociology of Sport*, 28, 1 [1993], pp. 53–63). However, they are more interested in Skocpol's understanding of the relationship between the state and civil society than her comparative method (see Chapter 8).

32 Ali Mazrui, *The Africans: A Triple Heritage* (London: BBC Publications, 1986), pp. 115–16 and pp. 125–8. For an insightful review see, Coetzee, 'Ali Mazrui' in *Stranger Shores*, pp. 240–9.

33 Mazrui, *The Africans*, p. 117, p. 119, p. 124, p. 125 and p. 128.

34 Mazrui, *The Africans*, pp. 120–4 and p. 128.

35 Ali Mazrui, 'Boxer Muhammad Ali and Soldier Idi Amin as International Political Symbols: The Bioeconomics of Sport and War', *Comparative Studies in Society and History*, 19, 2 (1977), p. 190.

36 Mazrui, 'International Political Symbols', p. 195.

37 Mazrui, 'International Political Symbols', p. 196.

38 Mazrui, 'International Political Symbols', p. 194 and p. 195.

39 Mazrui, 'International Political Symbols', p. 209.

40 Mazrui, 'International Political Symbols', p. 196.

41 Mazrui, 'International Political Symbols', pp. 205–6.

42 Mazrui, 'International Political Symbols', p. 199.

43 Mazrui, 'International Political Symbols', p. 200.

44 Mazrui, 'International Political Symbols', pp. 202–3.

45 Grew, 'Comparing Histories', p. 773.

46 Although El Moutawakel did not win her gold medal in the 400 metre hurdles until 1984, seven years after Mazrui published his article on Muhammad Ali and Idi Amin, her career began much earlier, nurtured and encouraged by her parents. Mazrui writes about El Moutawakel in *The Africans* (pp. 123–4 and p. 157). See also, Wayne Wilson, 'Nawal El Moutawakel', in Karen Christensen, Allen Guttmann and Gertrud Pfister (eds), *International Encyclopedia of Women and Sports*, volume 1 (New York: Macmillan, 2001), pp. 362–3. On Rudolph see, Urla Hill, 'Wilma Rudolph', in Christensen, Guttmann and Pfister, *International Encyclopedia of Women and Sports*, volume 2, pp. 956–8. Australian Aboriginal sportswomen, such as Mabel Campbell, Edna Crouch and Sharon Firebrace, who achieved success while subject to state and federal laws as draconian as any Islamic lore offer potentially even more valuable comparisons with African sportswomen. For details of these women see, Colin Tatz, *Obstacle Race: Aborigines in Sport* (Sydney: University of New South Wales Press, 1995). For a more theoretically framed overview of El Moutawakel, Rudolph, Campbell, Crouch and Firebrace see, Jennifer Hargreaves, *Heroines of Sport: The Politics of Difference and Identity* (London: Routledge, 2000).

47 Fairburn, *Social History*, p. 92, and John Tosh, *The Pursuit of History: Aims, Methods and New Directions in the Study of Modern History*, second edition (London: Longman, 1991), pp. 157–8.

48 Black and MacRaild, *Studying History*, p. 102, and Tosh, *Pursuit of History*, pp. 159–60. Of course, many historians would not consider these obstacles but simply part of what they do, part of the craft.

49 Scott Crawford, '"One's Nerves and Courage are in Very Different Order Out in New Zealand": Recreational and Sporting Opportunities for Women in a Remote Colonial Setting', in Mangan and Park, *From Fair Sex to Feminism*, pp. 161–81.

50 Crawford, 'Recreational and Sporting Opportunities', p. 162 and p. 171.

51 Crawford, 'Recreational and Sporting Opportunities', pp. 164–5.

52 Hoberman, 'Olympic Internationalism', p. 17.

53 Fairburn, *Social History*, p. 93.

54 Tosh, *Pursuit of History*, pp. 159–60.

55 Wilson, *History in Crisis*, p. 86.

56 John Nauright and Tim Chandler (eds), *Making Men: Rugby and Masculine Identity* (London: Frank Cass, 1996).

57 Tim Chandler and John Nauright (eds), *Making the Rugby World: Race, Gender, Commerce* (London: Frank Cass, 1999), pp. 201–2.

58 Magdalinski and Chandler, 'With God on their Side', pp. 1–2.

59 Wilson, *History in Crisis*, p. 134.

60 Farred, 'Cape Flats Township Football', p. 127.

61 Farred, 'Cape Flats Township Football', pp. 128–9.

62 Farred, 'Cape Flats Township Football', pp. 142–3.

63 James Mills and Paul Dimeo, '"When Gold is Fired It Shines": Sport, the Imagination and the Body in Colonial and Postcolonial India', in John Bale and Mike Cronin (eds), *Sport and Postcolonialism* (Oxford: Berg, 2003), pp. 119–21.

64 John Hughson, '"We Are Red, White and Blue, We Are Catholic, Why Aren't You?": Religion and Soccer Subculture and Symbolism', in Tara Magdalinski and Timothy Chandler (eds), *With God on their Side: Sport in the Service of Religion* (London: Routledge, 2002), p. 66 and pp. 67–8.

65 Hughson, 'Religion and Soccer Subculture', p. 64 and pp. 67–8.

66 John Hughson, David Inglis and Marcus Free, *The Uses of Sport: A Critical Study* (London: Routledge, 2005), p. 111.

67 Magdalinski and Chandler, 'With God on their Side', p. 3.

68 Hughson, 'Religion and Soccer Subculture', p. 65.

69 On this point see, Ludmilla Jordanova, *History in Practice* (London: Arnold, 2000), pp. 169–71.

70 Moore, 'The Origins of Rugby League', p. 7 and p. 9.

71 Hoberman, 'Olympic Internationalism', p. 14.

72 Moore, 'The Origins of Rugby League', p. 4, pp. 12–14, p. 16 and pp. 17–18.

8 Causation: explaining determinants in sport

1 Thomas Haskell, *Objectivity Is Not Neutrality: Explanatory Schemes in History* (Baltimore, MD: The Johns Hopkins University Press, 1998), p. 12. Similarly, David Hackett Fischer, notes that 'most of the trouble historians get themselves into in causal explanation consists in asking one kind of causal question and seeking another kind of causal answer. Or it consists of a stubborn determination to locate *the* cause. And both of these problems are aggravated by the unfortunate tendency of historians to hide their causal models from everybody – including themselves' (*Historians' Fallacies: Toward a Logic of Historical Thought* [New York: Harper & Row, 1970], p. 186).

2 Paul Ricoeur praises Raymond Aron for distinguishing these two different forms of causal analysis. According to Ricoeur: 'there is no better way of emphasizing the traditional role ascribed to historical causality, set in this way between understanding which possesses all the features of narrative understanding, and sociological causality, which has all the features of nomological explanation' (*Time and Narrative*, volume 1, translated by Kathleen McLaughlin

and David Pellauer [Chicago, IL: University of Chicago Press, 1983], p. 183 note 6. See also, Raymond Aron, *Introduction to the Philosophy of History: An Essay on the Limits of Historical Objectivity*, translated by George Irwin [Boston, MA: Beacon Press, 1961], pp. 156–264).

3   Indeed, the debates about human agency and structure underpinned constructionism in history (Keith Jenkins and Alun Munslow, 'Introduction', in Jenkins and Munslow [eds], *The Nature of History Reader* [London: Routledge, 2004], p. 10).

4   E. J. Tapp, 'Some Aspects of Causation in History', *Journal of Philosophy*, 49, 3 (1952), p. 67, Haskell, *Objectivity Is Not Neutrality*, p. 4, Eric Hobsbawm, 'The Contribution of History to Social Science', *International Social Science Journal*, 33, 4 (1981), p. 633, and Edward Carr, *What Is History?*, second edition (Harmondsworth: Penguin, 1990), p. 87.

5   Michael Oakeshott, 'Historical Continuity and Causal Analysis', in William Dray (ed.), *Philosophical Analysis and History* (New York: Harper & Row, 1966), pp. 196–9, Theodore Zeldin, 'Social History and Total History', Journal of Social History, 10, 2 (1976), p. 243, John Vincent, *An Intelligent Person's Guide to History* (London: Gerald Duckworth, 1995), p. 49, and Geoffrey Barraclough, History and the Common Man, Presidential address to the Historical Association, London, 12 April 1966. The Historical Association, pamphlet, pp. 10–12.

6   Aron, *Philosophy of History*, p. 165.

7   Vincent, *Guide to History*, p. 45. See also, Morris Cohen, 'Causation and Its Application to History', *Journal of the History of Ideas*, 3, 1 (1942), p. 15, and Max Weber, *The Methodology of the Social Sciences*, translated and edited by Edward Shils and Henry Finch (New York: Free Press, 1949), p. 169.

8   Carr, *What is History?*, pp. 104–5.

9   Charles Beard, president of the American Historical Association, cited in Harry Ritter, *Dictionary of Concepts in History* (Westport, CT: Greenwood Press, 1986), p. 33. See also, Vincent, *Guide to History*, p. 46.

10 Haskell, *Objectivity Is Not Neutrality*, pp. 12–13. See, Carl Hempel, 'The Function of General Laws in History', in Patrick Gardiner (ed.), *Theories of History* (Glencoe, IL: The Free Press, 1959), pp. 344–56.

11 William Dray, *Philosophy of History* (Englewood Cliffs, NJ: Prentice-Hall, 1964), p. 41, and Maurice Mandelbaum, 'Causal Analysis in History', *Journal of the History of Ideas*, 3, 1 (1942), p. 30.

12 Richard Evans, *In Defence of History* (London: Granta Books, 1997), p. 157.

13 Cohen, 'Causation and History', p. 13, Fischer, *Historians' Fallacies*, p. 165, Haskell, *Objectivity Is Not Neutrality*, p. 22, Christopher Lloyd, *Explanations in Social History* (Oxford: Basil Blackwell, 1988), p. 293, and Ricoeur, *Time and Narrative*, volume 1, p. 125.

14 Steven Riess, *Sport in Industrial America, 1850–1920* (Wheeling, IL: Harlan Davidson, 1995), p. 11, p. 13, p. 16, p. 20, p. 29, p. 33, p. 36 and p. 37.

15 Patrick Gardiner, *The Nature of Historical Explanation* (London: Oxford University Press, 1968), pp. 105–7.

16 Gardiner, *Historical Explanation*, pp. 105–7. On the other hand, Frank Ankersmit insists that concepts 'cannot properly be said to have a causal influence upon one another'. Whereas Ankersmit favours dispensing with causality as a means to gain historical understanding, Gardiner simply issues a warning that cause is an extremely slippery notion (Frank Ankersmit, *Narrative Logic: A Semantic Analysis of the Historian's Language* [The Hague: Martinus Nijhoff, 1983], pp. 154–5).

17 Haskell, *Objectivity Is Not Neutrality*, p. 16 and p. 17. See also, Geoffrey Nowell Smith's discussion of common sense ('Common Sense', *Radical Philosophy*, 7 [1974], pp. 15–16).

18 Robert Paddick, 'Amateurism', in Wray Vamplew, Katharine Moore, John O'Hara and Richard Cashman (eds), *The Oxford Companion to Australian Sport*, second edition (Melbourne: Oxford University Press, 1994), p. 12.

19 Fischer, *Historians' Fallacies*, p. 186.

20 Cohen, 'Causation and History', p. 16. See also, Fischer, *Historians' Fallacies*, pp. 167–9.

21   Benjamin Rader, 'Modern Sports: In Search of Interpretations', *Journal of Social History*, 13, 2 (1979), p. 315. See also, Allen Guttmann, *From Ritual to Record: The Nature of Modern Sports* (New York: Columbia University Press, 1978), pp. 84–5.

22   For Rader the key word in Guttmann's account is 'represents'. In the latter's words, 'the emergence of modern sports *represents* neither a triumph of capitalism nor the rise of Protestantism but rather the slow development of an empirical, experimental, mathematical *Weltanschauung*' (emphasis added). As Rader explains, 'if Guttmann intends the *Weltanschauung* to be merely a symbol, then his case may be plausible. But at other places in the book the scientific *Weltanschauung* becomes a 'correlation', a 'relationship', 'roots of', a 'causal relationship', 'the basic explanatory factor', and simply an 'interpretation' (Rader, 'Modern Sports', p. 315).

23   Rader, 'Modern Sports', p. 315.

24   Rader, 'Modern Sports', pp. 315–16.

25   Evans, *In Defence of History*, p. 157. See also, Michael Stanford, *A Companion to the Study of History* (Oxford: Blackwell, 1994), pp. 199–200.

26   Neil Tranter, *Sport, Economy and Society in Britain 1750–1914* (Cambridge: Cambridge University Press, 1998), pp. 85–6. Another reasonably common distinction is that between essential and particular causes. Essential causes have at least a kernel of explanatory power across religious, cultural, national and historical boundaries; particular causes are confined to specific circumstances, events or developments in one of the places or periods under investigation (Jeremy Black and Donald MacRaild, *Studying History* [Basingstoke: Macmillan, 1997], p. 103). Referring to the essential causes that made sporting men in the late nineteenth and early twentieth centuries, Tim Chandler and John Nauright conclude that manhood is not an immutable construct but an adaptation to social environments. They describe rugby helping to reinforce masculine hegemony at different times and different places when white men felt their identities and power threatened by female political and social emancipation or, in some settler societies, by large indigenous populations. Referring to the particular, Chandler and Nauright observe that while rugby is an international game it is also 'a nuanced activity' with distinct regional histories. Although it remained a largely middle- and upper-class game in England and Scotland, rugby developed into a mass sport in Wales, New Zealand and white South Africa (Tim Chandler and John Nauright, 'Introduction: Rugby, Manhood and Identity', in Nauright and Chandler [eds], *Making Men: Rugby and Masculine Identity* [London: Cass, 1996], pp. 1–12).

27   Evans, *In Defence of History*, pp. 144–5. On the following page he writes that 'my reason for devising twelve parallel causal narratives was mainly aesthetic: it simply seemed the neatest, most economical and above all the most exciting and most interesting way of organizing and presenting the evidence'. For Evans' views on White see, p. 126.

28   Haskell, *Objectivity Is Not Neutrality*, p. 22, Philippe Carrard, *Poetics of the New History: French Historical Discourse from Braudel to Chartier* (Baltimore, MD: The Johns Hopkins University Press, 1992), p. 74 and p. 75, David Lowenthal, *The Past is a Foreign Country* (Cambridge: Cambridge University Press, 1985), p. 224, and Ann Rigney, 'Narrativity and Historical Representation', *Poetics Today*, 12, 3 (1991), p. 592.

29   Cohen, 'Causation and History', p. 14, and Fischer, *Historians' Fallacies*, pp. 166–7.

30   Kenneth Gergen, 'Narrative, Moral Identity and Historical Consciousness: A Social Constructionist Account' (2004), http://www.Swarthmore.edu/SocSci/kgergen1/text3.html, pp. 2–3.

31   Alex Callinicos, *Theories and Narratives: Reflections on the Philosophy of History* (Cambridge: Polity Press, 1995), p. 46.

32   Cohen, 'Causation and History', p. 14.

33   Haskell, *Objectivity Is Not Neutrality*, p. 22.

34   Haskell, *Objectivity Is Not Neutrality*, pp. 22–3.

35   Arthur Stinchcombe, *Theoretical Methods in Social History* (New York: Academic Press, 1978), p. 13.

36   Stinchcombe, *Theoretical Methods*, p. 10 and p. 11.

37   Guttmann, *From Ritual to Record*, pp. 45–7.

38   Stinchcombe, *Theoretical Methods*, p. 11 and p. 12.

39   Cohen, 'Causation and History', p. 20.

40   Stinchcombe, *Theoretical Methods*, pp. 13–14.

41   Theda Skocpol, *States and Social Revolutions: A Comparative Analysis of France, Russia and China* (Cambridge: Cambridge University Press, 1979), p. 35.

42   Miles Fairburn, *Social History: Problems, Strategies and Methods* (New York: St Martin's Press, 1999), p. 101.

43   Emphasis in original. Fairburn, *Social History*, p. 97. Fairburn has modified Skocpol's method in an attempt to add even greater precision and sophistication. He employs a fourfold typology: sufficient condition, necessary condition, sufficient and necessary condition, and neither a sufficient nor a necessary condition. A sufficient condition is one where x and y are present and are always succeeded by z. However, although x and y will always produce the outcome, and have completely predictable consequences, other factors can also bring about z: groups that subscribe to different meanings of sport (x and y) predispose social tensions in sport (z) but different meanings of sport do not explain all the tensions in sport that can arise from financial disputes, personality conflicts, competing media interests, hostile fans, and so forth. A necessary condition for an outcome, though essential to that outcome, will not by itself produce the outcome. Wherever there is z (conflict in sport), there is x and y (competing groups with different interests) but x and y are not enough to produce z, rather there needs to be a precipitating factor. For example, the mere presence of amateur ideologues and supporters of professionalism does not necessarily mean a conflict situation in sport. The most important cause and perfect predictor of an event is a sufficient and necessary condition. Thus in the preceding example, an event, issue or personality spurs either the amateur ideologues or supporters of professionalism into taking action against their opponents, whether perceived or real. Lastly, conditions that are neither necessary nor sufficient have no causal role in relation to the outcome (Fairburn, *Social History*, p. 89).

44   At first glance this violates Skocpol's method because the negative cases contain the same postulated causes as the positive cases, that is, class-based antagonisms were present in rugby playing New Zealand, Wales and South Africa in the late nineteenth and early twentieth centuries just as they were in Australia and England. I discuss this apparent violation below.

45   Geoffrey Vincent and Toby Harfield, 'Repression and Reform: Responses within New Zealand Rugby to the Arrival of the "Northern Game", 1907–8', *New Zealand Journal of History*, 31, 2 (1997), pp. 237–8 and p. 239. Finlay Macdonald argues that the Great War settled 'the battle for rugby's amateur soul' in New Zealand: 'The wasteful carnage of the First World War meant that rugby, like most male sports, emerged in tatters; so many young men dead, injured or psychologically damaged; no fees paid for so long that clubs struggled for years to regain their pre-war strength. There would have been little fight left for the right to play rugby the New Zealand way. For most of the century the New Zealand Rugby Football Union would obey the laws set down in England by the inheritors of an elite tradition' (*The Game of Our Lives: The Story of Rugby and New Zealand – And How They've Shaped Each Other* (Auckland: Viking, 1996), p. 33 and p. 37). For further details of the early history of rugby in New Zealand see, Jock Phillips, 'The Hard Man: Rugby and the Formation of Male Identity in New Zealand', and John Nauright, 'Colonial Manhood and Imperial Race Virility: British Responses to the Post-Boer War Colonial Rugby Tours', in Nauright and Chandler, *Making Men*, pp. 70–90 and pp. 130–1.

46   David Andrews, 'Sport and the Masculine Hegemony of the Modern Nation: Welsh Rugby, Culture and Society, 1890–1914', in Nauright and Chandler, *Making Men*, p. 53 and p. 58. See also, David Andrews and Jeremy Howell, 'Transforming Into a Tradition: Rugby and the Making of Imperial Wales, 1890–1914', in Alan Ingham and John Loy (eds), *Sport in Social Development: Traditions, Transitions and Transformations* (Champaign, IL: Human Kinetics, 1993), pp. 77–96, Gareth Williams, 'From Popular Culture to Public Cliché: Image and Identity in

Wales, 1890–1914', in J. A. Mangan (ed.), *Pleasure, Profit, Proselytism: British Culture and Sport at Home and Abroad 1700–1915* (London: Frank Cass, 1988), pp. 128–43.

47   Robert Morrell, 'Forging a Ruling Race: Rugby and White Masculinity in Colonial Natal, *c.*1870–1910', in Nauright and Chandler, *Making Men*, p. 114.

48   Morrell, 'Masculinity in Colonial Natal', p. 114, and Albert Grundlingh, 'Playing for Power? Rugby, Afrikaner Nationalism and Masculinity in South Africa, *c.*1900–*c.*1970', in Nauright and Chandler, *Making Men*, p. 181, p. 182, p. 184 and p. 185.

49   Tony Collins, *Rugby's Great Split: Class, Culture and the Origins of Rugby League Football* (London: Frank Cass, 1998), pp. 180–9, Leonie Sandercock and Ian Turner, *Up Where Cazaly? The Great Australian Game* (London: Granada, 1982), pp. 46–53, and Rob Hess and Bob Stewart (eds), *More Than a Game: An Unauthorised History of Australian Rules Football* (Melbourne: Melbourne University Press, 1998), pp. 75–90.

50   Macdonald, *Game of Our Lives*, p. 31.

51   Robert Archer and Antoine Bouillon, *The South African Game: Sport and Racism* (London: Zed Press, 1982), pp. 64–75.

52   Skocpol, *States and Social Revolutions*, pp. 38–9. I discuss the relationship between causation and contextualisation further in Chapter 10.

53   Skocpol, *States and Social Revolutions*, p. 39.

54   Andrew Moore, 'Jimmy Devereux's Yorkshire Pudding: Reflections on the Origins of Rugby League in New South Wales and Queensland', Tom Brock Lecture, 1999 (Sydney: Australian Society for Sports History), p. 4, p. 12 and pp. 14–15.

55   Fischer identifies eight relatively common categories of antecedents used to address causal explanations in history (*Historians' Fallacies*, p. 186). The category 'abnormal antecedents' warrants a brief note here in recognition of the fact that most events which attract causal explanations, especially those involving considerations of agency, do indeed depart from what is 'normal, ordinary or reasonably expected' (Herbert Hart and Tony Honoré, *Causation in the Law* [Oxford: Clarendon Press, 1959], p. 31, Fischer, *Historians' Fallacies*, p. 185, Haskell, *Objectivity Is Not Neutrality*, p. 16, and Morton White, *Foundations of Historical Knowledge* [New York: Harper & Row, 1965], pp. 115–19). Robinson would have died one day but it was the nature of his premature death – at the hands of the intoxicated Jones – that invites a causal explanation. Most nations want to participate at olympic games which means that boycotts – such as those by African nations in 1976, the USA and its allies in 1980, and the Soviet Union and its allies in 1984 – have become ripe for causal explanations (for example, Christopher Hill, *Olympic Politics: Athens to Atlanta 1896–1996*, second edition [Manchester: Manchester University Press, 1996], and Alfred Senn, *Power, Politics, and the Olympic Games* [Champaign, IL: Human Kinetics, 1999]). Olympic villages are ordinarily sites of international harmony, so the taking of Israeli athletes as hostages during the games in Munich warranted a causal explanation (for example, Simon Reeve, *One Day in September* [New York: Arcade, 2000]). Olympic victory podiums are normally sites of celebration, thus the protests by Tommie Smith and John Carlos at the 1968 olympic games in Mexico City attract causal explanations (for example, Douglas Hartmann, *Race, Culture, and the Revolt of the Black Athlete: The 1968 Olympic Protests and Their Aftermath* [Chicago, IL: Chicago University Press, 2003]). While notions of ordinary and extraordinary are always context dependent, the key point here is that historians rarely proffer causal explanations of ordinary, mundane, everyday happenings. At the philosophical level, the focus on the extraordinary is consistent with popular notions of commonsense (see above) where most people simply leave unsaid the assumptions that they make about their needs, opportunities, conventions and experiences in the belief that these are widely shared. Hence in the world of commonsense, what is said, ruminated upon or pontificated about tends to be that which deviates from the normal, average, expected and anticipated; and the extraordinary and the unusual become 'prime candidates' for causal analysis (Haskell, *Objectivity Is Not Neutrality*, p. 16 and p. 17).

56   Human beings act with both tacit and overt awareness that their actions will produce certain outcomes and results, and they generally understand that alternative actions will lead to different outcomes. 'All practical activity', wrote Cohen, 'involves weighing the consequences

of alternatives only one of which is realized' ('Causation and History', p. 20. See also, Fischer, *Historians' Fallacies*, p. 185, Haskell, *Objectivity Is Not Neutrality*, p. 11, Weber, *The Social Sciences*, p. 165, and White, *Foundations of Historical Knowledge*, p. 147).

57   Cited in, Fischer, *Historians' Fallacies*, p. 186.

58   Lloyd, *Explanations*, p. 183.

59   Hartmann, *The 1968 Olympic Protests*. See especially pp. 22–3, p. 55, p. 67 and p. 279 note 27. Establishing motives has proved exceptionally difficult for scholars trying to understand instances where 'righteous Gentiles' saved Jews at great personal risk and for no monetary reward. According to Colin Tatz, at least a dozen major research projects have tried to produce a taxonomy of motives: because they were true Christians, because they were raised in liberal households, because they were associated with Communism, because they had a prior connection with matters or people Jewish. However, none of these explanations has proved satisfactory. In order to resolve this problem, Tatz distinguishes between motive and intent with the latter providing a more solid foundation for explanation. Thus, 'the *genocidaire*'s intent to destroy can even be arrived at via a moral alibi of acting in "good faith" and "in the best interests" of the victims or of the nation as a whole' (Colin Tatz, *With Intent to Destroy: Reflecting on Genocide* [London: Verso, 2003], p. 175).

60   Hart and Honoré, *Causation in the Law*, pp. 38–9.

61   See, for example, Caroline Daley, *Leisure and Pleasure: Reshaping and Revealing the New Zealand Body 1900–1960* (Auckland: Auckland University Press, 2003), John Hoberman, *Mortal Engines: The Science of Performance and the Dehumanization of Sport* (New York: Free Press, 1992), Carolyn Thomas de la Peña, 'Dudley Allen Sargent and Gustav Zander: Health Machines and the Energized Male Body', *Research in Philosophy and Technology*, 21 (2002), pp. 9–47.

62   Jennifer Hargreaves, *Sporting Females: Critical Issues in the History and Sociology of Women's Sports* (London: Routledge, 1994), p. 36.

63   Pamela Grundy, *Learning to Win: Sports, Education, and Social Change in Twentieth-Century North Carolina* (Chapel Hill, NC: The University of North Carolina Press, 2001), pp. 130–1.

64   Susan Cahn, *Coming on Strong: Gender and Sexuality in Twentieth-Century Women's Sport* (Cambridge, MA: Harvard University Press, 1995), p. 38.

65   Allen Guttmann, *Women's Sports: A History* (New York: Columbia University Press, 1991), pp. 149–50 and pp. 167–8, and Allen Guttmann, 'Alice Milliat', in Karen Christensen, Guttmann and Gertrud Pfister (eds), *International Encyclopedia of Women and Sports*, volume 2 (New York: Macmillan, 2001), pp. 743–4.

66   In another example, David Wiggins argues that the recommendations made by commissions set up in the 1970s by Chancellor Heyns (University of California, Berkeley), Chancellor Corbally (Syracuse University) and President Jensen (Oregon State University) to investigate the grievances of African American athletes, led to substantial reforms in university policies (David Wiggins, *Glory Bound: Black Athletes in a White America* [Syracuse, NY: Syracuse University Press, 1997], pp. 123–51).

67   Allen Guttmann, *The Games Must Go On: Avery Brundage and the Olympic Movement* (New York: Columbia University Press, 1984), p. 243.

68   Kenny Moore, 'A Courageous Stand: In '68, Olympians Tommie Smith and John Carlos Raised Their Fists For Racial Justice', *Sports Illustrated*, 5 August 1991, p. 70.

69   Dennis Phillips, *Australian Women at the Olympic Games, 1912–1992* (Sydney: Kangaroo Press, 1992), pp. 22–5.

70   John Tosh, *The Pursuit of History: Aims, Methods and New Directions in the Study of Modern History*, third edition (London: Longman, 2000), pp. 120–1.

71   See, for example, Douglas Booth, *The Race Game: Sport and Politics in South Africa* (London: Frank Cass, 1998), pp. 60–2 and pp. 90–1, Steven Ungerleider, *Faust's Gold: Inside the East German Doping Machine* (New York: St Martin's Press, 2001), p. 49, and Ian Ritchie, 'Sex Tested, Gender Verified: Controlling Female Sexuality in the Age of Containment', *Sport History Review*, 34, 1 (2003), pp. 88–9.

72   Hartmann, *The 1968 Olympic Protests*, p. 205 and p. 304 note 68.

73   Aron, *Philosophy of History*, pp. 166–73, Carr, *What is History?*, p. 107, Dray, *Philosophy of History*, p. 47 and p. 55, and White, *Foundations of Historical Knowledge*, pp. 167–74. White insists that 'no one should judge an action as right or wrong unless he thinks it is voluntary' (p. 289).

74   Aron, *Philosophy of History*, pp. 173–9.

75   Aron, *Philosophy of History*, p. 166 note 24. See also, Beverley Southgate, *History: What and Why? Ancient, Modern, and Postmodern Perspectives*, second edition (London: Routledge, 2001), pp. 57–61.

76   Murray Phillips, 'Football, Class and War', in Nauright and Chandler, *Making Men*, pp. 161–2.

77   Mike Cronin, *Sport and Nationalism in Ireland: Gaelic Games, Soccer and Irish Identity Since 1884* (Dublin: Four Courts Press, 1999), pp. 131–3.

78   Lloyd, *Explanations*, p. 184.

79   Kevin McAleer, *Dueling: The Cult of Honor in Fin-de-Siècle Germany* (Princeton, NJ: Princeton University Press, 1994), p. 37.

80   Lloyd, *Explanations*, p. 186.

81   Kathleen McCrone, 'Play up! Play up! And Play the Game! Sport at the Late Victorian Girls' Public Schools', in J. A. Mangan and Roberta Park (eds), *From Fair Sex to Feminism: Sport and the Socialization of Women in the Industrial and Post-industrial Eras* (London: Frank Cass, 1987), pp. 107–9, p. 116 and p. 118. Philip Abrams offers the classic statement of this relationship: 'When we refer to the two-sidedness of society we are referring to the ways in which, in time, actions become institutions and institutions are in turn changed by action. Taking and selling prisoners becomes the institution of slavery. Offering one's services to a soldier in return for his protection becomes feudalism. Organising the control of an enlarged labour force on the basis of standardised rules becomes bureaucracy. And slavery, feudalism and bureaucracy become the fixed, external settings in which struggles for prosperity or survival or freedom are then pursued. By substituting cash payments for labour services the lord and peasant jointly embark on the dismantling of the feudal order their great-grandparents had constructed' (*Historical Sociology* [Ithaca, NY: Cornell University Press, 1982], pp. 2–3).

82   Alun Munslow, *The Routledge Companion to Historical Studies* (London: Routledge, 2000), p. 42, and Perez Zagorin, 'Historiography and Postmodernism: Reconsiderations', *History and Theory*, 29, 3 (1990), pp. 268–9.

83   Zagorin, 'Historiography', pp. 269–70.

84   Munslow, *Historical Studies*, p. 40.

85   Zagorin, 'Historiography', pp. 269–70.

9 Social change: explaining transformations

1   David Lowenthal, *The Past is a Foreign Country* (Cambridge: Cambridge University Press, 1985). Lowenthal extracted his title from an aphorism – 'the past is a foreign country, they do things differently there' in L. P. Hartley's novel, *The Go Between* (London: Hamish Hamilton, 1966), p. 9.

2   Pamela Grundy, *Learning to Win: Sports, Education, and Social Change in Twentieth-Century North Carolina* (Chapel Hill, NC: The University of North Carolina Press, 2001), p. 41.

3   Not unexpectedly, historians disagree about the concept of social change. Some conceive of society as 'a fixed, stable and persisting structure'; others view it as a 'process in which there is continual breakdown and renewal, development and decline, the disappearance of old forms and the creation of new ones' (Tom Bottomore, 'Structure and History', in Peter Blau (ed.), *Approaches to the Study of Social Structure* [New York: The Free Press, 1975], p. 159). Nancy Struna recently proposed that historians should focus on social change as a nondeterministic process of 'moving away from the past' rather than 'moving toward' the

creation of new social forms ('Reframing the Direction of Change in the History of Sport', *The International Journal of the History of Sport*, 18, 4 [2001], pp. 1–15).

4   See, for example, Steven Riess, *Sport in Industrial America, 1850–1920* (Wheeling, IL: Harlan Davidson, 1995), pp. 11–42.

5   Bottomore, 'Structure and History', p. 164.

6   Stephen Hardy, 'Entrepreneurs, Structures, and the Sportgeist: Old Tensions in a Modern Industry', in Donald Kyle and Gary Stark (eds), *Essays on Sport History and Sport Mythology* (College Station, TX: Texas A & M Press, 1990), pp. 45–82. While sport historians must guard against over emphasising change at the expense of continuity (Jeffrey Hill, *Sport, Leisure and Culture in Twentieth Century Britain* [Basingstoke: Palgrave, 2002], p. 3), few practitioners focus on continuities over long periods. Stephen Hardy and Allen Guttmann are two exceptions. See, Stephen Hardy, 'The Long Residuals of Sport', paper presented at the Tenth Yale-Smithsonian Seminar on Material Culture, Washington, DC, May 1997, and Allen Guttmann, *The Erotic in Sports* (New York: Columbia University Press, 1996), and *Sports: The First Five Millennia* (Amherst, MA: University of Massachusetts Press, 2004).

7   Christopher Lloyd, *Explanations in Social History* (Oxford: Basil Blackwell, 1988), p. 192 and p. 193.

8   Most sport historians, it should be stressed, are reconstructionists who examine change through empirical enquiry into particular actions, events, classes and social movements. While they may direct some attention to general structures and structural processes, the majority oppose theory.

9   Lloyd, *Explanations*, p. 192.

10   Lloyd, *Explanations*, pp. 18–19, p. 263 and p. 267.

11   Lloyd, *Explanations*, pp. 266–7. See for example, Clare Simpson, 'Respectable Identities: New Zealand Nineteenth-Century "New Women" – On Bicycles!', *The International Journal of the History of Sport*, 18, 2 (2001), pp. 54–77, and Douglas Booth, *Australian Beach Cultures: The History of Sun, Sand, and Surf* (London: Frank Cass, 2001), pp. 9–10.

12   Lloyd, *Explanations*, p. 265. See, for example, Michael Oriard, *Reading Football: How the Popular Press Created an American Spectacle* (Chapel Hill, NJ: The University of North Carolina Press, 1993).

13   Malcolm Waters, *Modern Sociological Theory* (London: Sage, 1994), pp. 213–15.

14   Christopher Lloyd, *The Structures of History* (Oxford: Basil Blackwell, 1993), p. 98.

15   Lloyd, *Structures*, p. 152, and Ian Heywood, 'Culture Made, Found and Lost', in Chris Jenks (ed.), *Cultural Reproduction* (London: Routledge, 1993), p. 105. See also, Chris Jenks, *Culture* (London: Routledge, 1993), p. 26.

16   Hardy, 'Entrepreneurs, Structures, and the Sportgeist', p. 53.

17   Hill, *Sport*, p. 2, p. 4 and pp. 12–13. Similarly, Maguire *et al.* argue that 'sport and culture cannot be separated' and that 'sport is structured by culture' (Joseph Maguire, Grant Jarvie, Louise Mansfield and Joe Bradley, *Sport Worlds: A Sociological Perspective* [Champaign, IL: Human Kinetics, 2002], p. 128).

18   Lloyd, *Explanations*, pp. 200–1. See also, p. 176.

19   Modern is, of course, a relative term. Fifth-century Roman Christians called themselves modern to distinguish their religiosity from heathens and Jews while medieval scholars reinvented the term modern to differentiate cultivated learning from custom and ritual. Since the Enlightenment, modern has meant notions of rationality, science and progress which are also often arbitrary signifiers (Jeffrey Alexander, 'Modern, Anti, Post and Neo', *New Left Review*, 210 [1995], p. 65).

20   Allen Guttmann, *From Ritual to Record: The Nature of Modern Sports* (New York: Columbia University Press, 1978), pp. 15–55. For good descriptions of traditional folk sports see, Dennis Brailsford, *Sport and Society: Elizabeth to Anne* (London: Routledge and Kegan Paul, 1969), pp. 52–3, and Eric Dunning and Kenneth Sheard, *Barbarians, Gentlemen and Players: A Sociological Study of the Development of Rugby Football* (Oxford: Martin Robertson, 1979), pp. 29–30.

21 Sport sociologist Eric Dunning is another leading theorist of the change from traditional to modern sport. His figurational approach has been the subject of much debate with critics pointing to its functionalist tendencies, a charge vigorously denied by Dunning. See, for example, Eric Dunning and Kenneth Sheard, *Barbarians, Gentlemen and Players: A Sociological Study of the Development of Rugby Football*, second edition (London: Routledge, 2005), pp. 275–9.

22 Melvin Adelman, *A Sporting Time: New York City and the Rise of Modern Athletics, 1820–1870* (Urbana, IL: University of Illinois Press, 1986), p. 3, and Hill, *Sport,* p. 2. See, for example, John Lucas and Ronald Smith, *Saga of American Sport* (Philadelphia, PA: Lea and Febiger, 1978), pp. 125–33, Ian Jobling, 'Urbanization and Sport in Canada, 1867–1900', in Richard Gruneau and John Albinson (eds), *Canadian Sport: Sociological Perspectives* (Don Mills, Ontario: Addison-Wesley, 1976), pp. 64–77, Wray Vamplew, *Pay Up and Play the Game: Professional Sport in Britain, 1875–1914* (Cambridge: Cambridge University Press, 1988), and Wray Vamplew, 'Sport and Industrialization: An Economic Interpretation of the Changes in Popular Sport in Nineteenth-Century England', in J. A. Mangan (ed.), *Pleasure, Profit, Proselytism: British Culture and Sport at Home and Abroad 1700–1914* (London: Frank Cass, 1988), pp. 7–20. Of course, most sport historians simply refer to traditional and modern sport as static structures and pay little attention to processes of change (Hugh Cunningham, *Leisure in the Industrial Revolution c. 1780–c. 1880* [London: Croom Helm, 1980], p. 193).

23 Lloyd, *Explanations*, p. 208.

24 Guttmann, *From Ritual to Record*, pp. 80–2 and pp. 85–6.

25 Guttmann, *From Ritual to Record*, p. 80.

26 Lloyd, *Explanations*, p. 300. See also, Jenks, *Culture*, p. 55.

27 Guttmann, *From Ritual to Record*, p. 47, p. 48, pp. 50–1, p. 51, p. 52, p. 54 and p. 55.

28 For a quite different perspective of the nature of modernity, and one more fitting of the nondeterminist label, see Glen Norcliffe, *The Ride to Modernity: The Bicycle in Canada, 1869–1900* (Toronto: University of Toronto Press, 2001). Norcliffe follows Marshall Berman in highlighting the dialectical and janus-faced nature of modernity (*All that is Solid Melts Into Air* [Harmondsworth: Penguin, 1982]). Berman also provided the foundation of my critique of *From Ritual to Record* (Douglas Booth, '*From Ritual to Record*: Allen Guttmann's Insights into Modernization and Modernity', *Sport History Review*, 32, 1 [2001], pp. 183–91).

29 Lloyd, *Explanations*, p. 215, p. 217 and p. 219.

30 Melvin Adelman, 'Academicians and American Athletics: A Decade of Progress', *Journal of Sport History*, 10, 1 (1983), p. 89. See also p. 90, and Adelman, *A Sporting Time*, p. 294 note 15.

31 For example, 'modern society is … marked by a functional social structure', and modernisation facilitates examinations of 'the relationship between sport and the modernizaton of society and/or its component parts' and 'the evolution of modern sports structures and ideology' (Adelman, *A Sporting Time*, p. 5).

32 Adelman, *A Sporting Time*, pp. 7–9.

33 Adelman, *A Sporting Time*, pp. 9–10; see also, p. 102, pp. 146–51 and p. 244. Guttmann is all but silent on the issue of commercialised sport in *From Ritual to Record*.

34 At the conclusion of his text Adelman appears to modify his earlier insinuation of innate pre-rational competition by incorporating notions of 'ideological reasons for the surge of competitive sport after the middle of the nineteenth century' (Adelman, *A Sporting Time*, pp. 284–6).

35 Lloyd, *Explanations*, p. 220 and p. 221.

36 Lloyd, *Explanations*, p. 220.

37 Adelman, *A Sporting Time*, p. 243.

38 See also, Cunningham, *Leisure*, pp. 9–10.

39 Lloyd, *Explanations*, p. 237, p. 238 and pp. 239–40. See also p. 242 and p. 246.

40   Cited in Lloyd, *Explanations*, p. 251. For accessible summaries of Braudel's views on structures and Marxism see, Fernand Braudel, *On History* (Chicago, IL: University of Chicago Press, 1980).

41   Lloyd, *Explanations*, p. 256, and Bottomore, 'Structure and History', p. 165.

42   Bottomore, 'Structure and History', p. 165.

43   Waters, *Modern Sociological Theory*, p. 174. See also p. 182.

44   Waters, *Modern Sociological Theory*, pp. 177–8.

45   Waters, *Modern Sociological Theory*, p. 206. Postmodernism is an elusive and thorny subject. Even after three decades of discussion little general consensus has emerged as to its meaning. Krishan Kumar offers a useful starting point for discussion by likening the prefix to the 'post of *post-mortem*: obsequies performed over the dead body of modernity, a dissection of the corpse'. In this sense postmodernity is a 'condition of reflectiveness', 'the occasion for reflecting on the experience of modernity' (*From Post-Industrial to Post-Modern Society: New Theories of the Contemporary World* [Oxford: Basil Blackwell, 1995], pp. 66–7).

46   Perry Anderson, 'The Antinomies of Antonio Gramsci', *New Left Review*, 100 (1976/77), p. 20, emphasis added. A 'persistent *slippage*' in Gramsci's use of the terms state, civil society, political society, hegemony, domination and direction poses fundamental problems for an analysis of the bourgeoisie state (Anderson, 'Gramsci', p. 25). For details of the arrival of hegemony in sport history see, Chapter 3 note 114.

47   Quintin Hoare and Geoffrey Nowell Smith (eds), *Selections from the Prison Notebooks of Antonio Gramsci* (London: Lawrence and Wishart, 1971), p. 164.

48   George Sage, *Power and Ideology in American Sport: A Critical Perspective* (Champaign, IL: Human Kinetics, 1990), p. 19. One exception to the tendency to conflate hegemony with ideology is Kevin Wamsley's history of rifle shooting in nineteenth-century Canada. Proceeding from a belief that hegemonic analyses of sport must examine the interrelationships between economy, politics and culture at specific historical conjunctures, Wamsley illustrates the potential of hegemonic analysis. A popular cultural practice in Canada during the nineteenth century, rifle shooting was 'predicated on the pleasures of competition, fraternization, social prestige and monetary rewards'. But the cultural and the political fused as fears of military intervention from the United States rose with preparations by regular British troops to withdraw from North America. The Canadian government administration identified citizen shooters as a readily available coercive force and not surprisingly promoted their activities. However, the fusion of the cultural and the political rested on far more than public officials patronising clubs, the administration's construction and maintenance of ranges, or annual grants, peppercorn rents, and free and discounted ammunition to the Dominion of Canada Rifle Association. Canadian 'state' hegemony derived from the freedom of individual rifle shooters to internalise their own experiences and apply their own interpretations to the activity from within a range of potentially contradictory political positions – patriotic–nonpatriotic, loyal–unloyal, Canadian–unCanadian, active–apathetic. Two conditions swayed most participants towards a dominant interpretation: the cultural significations of rifle shooting as manly, comradely, and challenging, and a political threat that 'valorized' shooting as a 'cultural signifier of patriotism, duty, contribution to collective purpose, and protection of territory and society' ('Cultural Signification and National Ideologies: Rifle-shooting in Late Nineteenth-century Canada', *Social History*, 20, 1 [1995], p. 65 and pp. 66–7. See also, Douglas Hartmann, *Race, Culture, and the Revolt of the Black Athlete: The 1968 Olympic Protests and Their Aftermath* [Chicago, IL: Chicago University Press, 2003], p. 310 note 1). Yet, although it is rich in detail and introduces an agency driven account of culture into a nonhierarchical holistic structure that avoids the simple economic determinism of Marxist structuralism, Wamsley's history primarily focuses on the initiation of social consensus at a specific moment in Canadian history rather than social change or the lack thereof.

49   William Morgan, *Leftist Theories of Sport: A Critique and Reconstruction* (Urbana, IL: University of Illinois Press, 1994), p. 95. Allen Guttmann makes the same point with respect to 'ludic diffusion', observing that 'most discussions ... refer not to *cultural hegemony* but rather to

cultural imperialism' which is tantamount to simple cultural domination (*Games and Empires: Modern Sports and Cultural Imperialism* [New York: Columbia University Press, 1994], p. 5). Morgan's concept of, and views on, hegemony sparked intense debate within sport sociology. See, Alan Ingham and Rob Beamish, 'Didn't Cyclops Lose His Vision? An Exercise in Sociological Optometry', *Sociology of Sport Journal*, 14, 2 (1997), pp. 164–75, and William Morgan, 'Yet Another Critical Look at Hegemony Theory: A Response to Ingham and Beamish', *Sociology of Sport Journal*, 14, 2 (1997), pp. 187–95.

50   This is particularly pronounced in historical investigations dealing with gender relations and masculine hegemony. For a brilliant critique of the limitations of incorporating masculine hegemony into studies of sport see, Mike Donaldson, 'What is Hegemonic Masculinity?', *Theory and Society*, 22, 5 (1993), pp. 643–57.

51   Richard Holt, *Sport and the British: A Modern History* (Oxford: Oxford University Press, 1989), p. 364, and John Hargreaves, *Sport, Power and Culture: A Social and Historical Analysis of Popular Sports in Britain* (Cambridge: Polity Press, 1986), p. 209. For further criticisms of Hargreaves' arguments see Tony Collins, *Rugby's Great Split: Class, Culture and the Origins of Rugby League Football* (London: Frank Cass, 1998), p. 232. See also Guttmann, *Games and Empires*, p. 179.

52   John Hargreaves, 'Sport and Hegemony: Some Theoretical Problems', in Hart Cantelon and Richard Gruneau (eds), *Sport, Culture, and the Modern State* (Toronto: University of Toronto Press, 1982), pp. 134–5. Hugh Cunningham was another early critic of determinist approaches to hegemony and an advocate for more careful analysis of its real historical conditions (*Leisure*, p. 11 and pp. 195–9).

53   Raymond Williams, *Marxism and Literature* (Oxford: Oxford University Press, 1977), p. 112.

54   Sage, *Power and Ideology*, p. 20. See also, Alan Ingham and Stephen Hardy, 'Introduction: Sport Studies Through the Lens of Raymond Williams', in Alan Ingham and John Loy (eds), *Sport in Social Development: Traditions, Transitions and Transformations* (Champaign, IL: Human Kinetics, 1993), pp. 1–19, and Hargreaves, *Sport, Power and Culture*, p. 7.

55   Hargreaves, 'Sport and Hegemony', p. 134. See also, Richard Gruneau, *Class, Sports, and Social Development* (Amherst, MA: University of Massachusetts Press, 1983), p. 89.

56   Hargreaves, *Sport, Power and Culture*, pp. 62–3.

57   Holt, *Sport and the British*, pp. 363–4. See also, Norman Baker, 'Whose Hegemony? The Origins of the Amateur Ethos in Nineteenth Century English Society', *Sport in History*, 24, 1 (2004), pp. 1–20. Interestingly, Holt's critique appears in a theoretical appendix which is consistent with the widespread view that historians should not make explicit either their methodology or theories (Richard Holt, 'Sport and History: The State of the Subject in Britain', *Twentieth Century British History*, 7, 2 [1996], p. 251, and Don Morrow, 'Canadian Sport History: A Critical Essay', *Journal of Sport History*, 10, 1 [1983], p. 73).

58   Stephen Hardy and Alan Ingham, 'Games, Structure, and Agency: Historians on the American Play Movement', *Journal of Social History*, 17 (1983), p. 290, pp. 295–6 and p. 297, and Alan Ingham and Stephen Hardy, 'Sport: Structuration, Subjugation and Hegemony', *Theory, Culture and Society*, 2, 2 (1984), p. 94; Morgan, *Theories*, p. 100. Jeffrey Hill provides an alternative approach to hegemony, regarding it 'less conspiratorially as "knowledge formation"', that is, as a process of "knowing" and "understanding" in which sport is intimately implicated' (*Sport*, p. 4).

59   Hardy and Ingham, 'Games, Structure, and Agency', p. 286. See also, Ingham and Hardy, 'Sport: Structuration, Subjugation and Hegemony', p. 100 notes 1 and 2.

60   Patrick Joyce, 'The End of Social History?', *Social History*, 20, 1 (1995), pp. 89–90.

61   Arguably because of the jargon rather than the content and the context. For reviews by sport historians see, Jeffrey Hill, 'British Sports History: A Post-modern Future?', *Journal of Sport History*, 23, 1 (1996), pp. 1–19, and Murray Phillips, 'Deconstructing Sport History: The Postmodern Challenge', *Journal of Sport History*, 28, 3 (2001), pp. 327–43.

62   Fredric Jameson, 'Postmodernism, or The Cultural Logic of Late Capitalism', *New Left Review*, 146 (1984), p. 87.

63   Fredric Jameson, *Postmodernism, or The Cultural Logic of Late Capitalism* (London: Verso, 1991), p. 38.

64   Kumar, *From Post-Industrial to Post-Modern Society*, pp. 123–4.

65   David Andrews, 'Dead and Alive?: Sports History in the Late Capitalist Moment', *Sporting Traditions*, 16, 1 (1999), pp. 79–80. Another interesting Andrews' example is the 'renaissance' of Muhammad Ali. In the 1990s, Ali appeared in 'carefully and consistently choreographed advertising campaigns for Apple, Wheaties, Morton's steakhouses, Rockport shoes' and in so doing 'corroborated his status as a cultural icon of historical proportions, while simultaneously erasing' his past as 'an outwardly Muslim, Pan-Africanist, anti-colonial, and anti-American imperialist' (pp. 80–1). Hardy also offers an example with ESPN's presentation of the fiftieth anniversary of Jackie Robinson's integration into major league baseball ('Where did You Go, Jackie Robinson? Or, the End of History and the Age of Sport Infrastructure', *Sporting Traditions*, 16, 1 [1999], p. 97).

66   Ian Harriss, 'Packer, Cricket and Postmodernism', in David Rowe and Geoff Lawrence (eds), *Sport and Leisure: Trends in Australian Popular Culture* (Sydney: Harcourt Brace Jovanovich, 1990), pp. 117–19. Interestingly, while Guttmann argues that 'the *production* of sports spectacles continues to be relentlessly modern', he concedes that 'the *consumption* of sports spectacles has … become sufficiently discordant to warrant references to "the postmodern condition"' (*Sports*, p. 325).

67   Harriss, 'Cricket and Postmodernism', p. 116 and p. 120.

68   Indeed, this argument shares many similarities with hegemony. Supporters of hegemony direct particular attention to the mass media's portrayal of sport that they deem critical to the stabilisation and persistence of the twentieth-century capitalist order. Media sport, writes Hargreaves, 'often reads like a handbook of conventional wisdom on social order and control. There are homilies on good firm management, justice, the nature of law, duty and obligation, correct attitudes to authority, the handling of disputes, what constitutes reasonable and civilized behaviour, on law and order and on the state of society in general. Media sport encodes an ideology of order and control, in the way the conduct of participants in sports events and that of spectators is depicted' (*Sport, Power and Culture*, p. 145). This view became particularly popular among historians looking at the relationship between the media and gender in sport. Referring to the development of organised netball in New Zealand, for example, John Nauright and Jane Broomhall conclude that 'the media … hailed it as a great game for women especially as it fits into the dominant conceptions of proper female behaviour and physical activity. As a sport, netball does not challenge notions about ways in which women should express themselves physically and therefore does not pose a threat to the gender order' (John Nauright and Jane Broomhall, 'A Woman's Game: The Development of Netball and a Female Sporting Culture in New Zealand, 1906–70', *The International Journal of the History of Sport*, 10, 3 [1994], p. 404).

69   After working as the chief engineer at a Philadelphia steelworks, Taylor (1856–1915) consulted in 'scientific management', a field that advised on efficient and economical ways of performing physical tasks.

70   Hoare and Nowell Smith, *Prison Notebooks*, p. 302. The fact that American workers tolerated regimented Fordist working conditions perplexed Gramsci; their position embodied hegemony. But from their perspective, they were well paid and able to enjoy the fruits of American consumerism.

71   Kumar, *From Post-Industrial to Post-Modern Society*, pp. 50–6.

72   Bottomore, 'Structure and History', pp. 165–6.

73   Duncan Humphreys, 'Snowboarders: Bodies Out of Control and in Conflict', *Sporting Traditions*, 13, 1 (1996), p. 13, p. 14 and p. 15.

74   Duncan Humphreys, '"Shredheads Go Mainstream": Snowboarding and Alternative Youth', *International Review for the Sociology of Sport*, 32, 2 (1997), p. 152.

75   Humphreys, 'Snowboarders', p. 13, p. 14 and pp. 15–16.

76   Kumar, *From Post-Industrial to Post-Modern Society*, pp. 168–70.

77   Steven Best and Douglas Kellner, *Postmodern Theory: Critical Interrogations* (London: Macmillan, 1991), p. 256, p. 257, p. 261 and p. 263. See also Kumar, *From Post-Industrial to Post-Modern*

Society, p. 109, p. 126, p. 131, p. 154 and p. 192. As Kumar puts it, the historical distinction between Fordist and post-Fordist forms of production is largely arbitrary. Both have existed side-by-side throughout the twentieth century and small batch production is in fact a 'general tendency of capitalism'. Kumar refers to a 'comprehensive rejection' of all notions of a 'new order' of capitalism: 'in so far as new features can be distinguished, they are simply the expressions of capitalism's well-known disposition to change and modify its practices in accordance with the requirements of survival and growth' (pp. 167–8).

78 Alex Callinicos, *Against Postmodernism: A Marxist Critique* (Cambridge: Polity Press, 1989), p. 5.

79 Hardy, 'Jackie Robinson', p. 96.

80 Murray Phillips, 'From Suburban Football to International Spectacle: The Commodification of Rugby League in Australia 1907–1995', *Australian Historical Studies*, 110 (1998), p. 39 and p. 48. As well as Harriss' work, Phillips also questions some of the claims made by Bob Stewart. For an example of the latter's work see, Bob Stewart and Aaron Smith, 'Australian Sport in a Postmodern Age', in J. A. Mangan and John Nauright (eds), *Sport in Australasian Society* (London: Frank Cass, 2000), pp. 278–304.

81 Lloyd, *Structures*, p. 186 and p. 285.

82 Lloyd, *Explanations*, p. 193, p. 281, p. 282 and p. 283. See also John Tosh, *The Pursuit of History: Aims, Methods and New Directions in the Study of Modern History*, second edition (London: Longman, 1991), p. 161.

83 Lloyd, *Explanations*, p. 287, p. 288, p. 289 and p. 310.

84 For a good comparison of a contextual and social change approach to one subject see, respectively, Malcolm MacLean, 'Football as Social Critique: Protest Movements, Rugby and History in Aotearoa, New Zealand', in J. A. Mangan and John Nauright (eds), *Sport in Australasian Society* (London: Frank Cass, 2000), pp. 255–77, and Shona Thompson, 'The Tour', in Brad Patterson (ed.), *Sport, Society and Culture in New Zealand* (Wellington: Stout Research Centre, 1999), pp. 79–91.

85 See also, Bruce Kidd, *The Struggle for Canadian Sport* (Toronto: University of Toronto Press, 1996), and, notwithstanding his descent into functionalism (see Chapter 3), Robert Malcolmson's chapter on social change in *Popular Recreations in English Society, 1700–1850* (Cambridge: Cambridge University Press, 1973), pp. 158–71.

86 Grundy, *Learning to Win*, p. 299.

87 While Lloyd identifies the relationships, readers will have no difficulty finding copious examples throughout Grundy's text.

88 Grundy, *Learning to Win*, pp. 42–3.

89 Grundy, *Learning to Win*, p. 229 and p. 301.

90 Grundy, *Learning to Win*, p. 296 and p. 297.

91 Grundy, *Learning to Win*, p. 295. Examples from the North American and international fronts would include the professional leagues in softball and basketball, and a professional circuit in tennis (Susan Cahn, *Coming on Strong: Gender and Sexuality in Twentieth-Century Women's Sport* [Cambridge, MA: Harvard University Press, 1995], p. 254).

92 Kidd, *Canadian Sport*. See also, Mike Cronin's analysis of the competing nationalist versions of Irish sport propagated by the Gaelic Athletic Association and the Irish Football Association (*Sport and Nationalism in Ireland: Gaelic Games, Soccer and Irish Identity Since 1884* [Dublin: Four Courts Press, 1999]).

93 Grundy, *Learning to Win*, p. 180 and pp. 296–7.

94 Grundy, *Learning to Win*, p. 296 and p. 300.

95 David Harvey, *The Condition of Post-Modernity: An Enquiry into the Origins of Cultural Change* (Oxford: Basil Blackwell, 1990), p. 344, and Best and Kellner, *Postmodern Theory*, p. 262. See also, Hargreaves, 'Sport and Hegemony', p. 109, and Hargreaves, *Sport, Power and Culture*, p. 121.

96 Grundy, *Learning to Win*, p. 5, p. 100, p. 217 and p. 220.

97 Grundy, *Learning to Win*, p. 19 and p. 120. See also, Kidd, *Canadian Sport*, pp. 262–70.

98   Lloyd, *Explanations*, p. 282.
99   Grundy, *Learning to Win*, p. 301.
100   See also, Lawrence Stone, 'The Revival of Narrative: Reflections on a New Old History', *Past and Present*, 85 (1979), pp. 6–7 and p. 19.
101   Arthur Stinchcombe, *Theoretical Methods in Social History* (New York: Academic Press, 1978).
102   Bottomore, 'Structure and History', p. 167.
103   Joyce, 'The End of Social History?', p. 82.
104   Kidd, *Canadian Sport*, p. 5.
105   Grundy, *Learning to Win*, p. 298.

10 Context: interpreting the big picture

1   E. P. Thompson, 'Anthropology and the Discipline of Historical Context', *Midland History*, 3 (1972), p. 45.
2   Robert Berkhofer, *Beyond the Great Story: History as Text and Discourse* (Cambridge, MA: Harvard University Press, 1995), p. 31. As Berkhofer notes, 'historians constantly urge themselves and others to "put things into their context(s)"'. Words and sentences must be read in the context of the document, and the document as part of its community of discourse or of the ideological and belief system that gave it meaning at the time. Discourses and worldviews in turn demand the context of their cultures and times. Likewise, human activities and institutions are to be understood in relation to the larger network of behavior or social organization and structure of which they are said to be part. Social, political, religious, economic, family, philanthropic, and other institutional practices make sense only when placed in their proper social and cultural contexts. Thus eras and nations, wars and social movements, individuals and events, and speeches and diaries must all be situated in their contexts'. See also, Thompson, 'The Discipline of Historical Context', p. 43, Richard Evans, *In Defence of History* (London: Granta Books, 1997), p. 158, and Nancy Struna, 'Social History and Sport', in Jay Coakley and Eric Dunning (eds), *Handbook of Sports Studies* (London: Sage, 2000), p. 187.
3   I referred to the importance of contextualising theory in Chapter 3 under the heading 'The Politics of Theory'. Antonio Gramsci's theory of hegemony is a good example given its wide application in sport studies. As Perry Anderson notes, Gramsci placed hegemony in several historical contexts in notebooks that he wrote while languishing in a fascist prison and unravelling a single concept from these different contexts is no easy matter. Gramsci, like all original theorists, 'worked towards radically new concepts in an old vocabulary designed for other purposes and times, which overlaid and deflected their meaning'. This is a common enough problem, but the fact that a fascist censor also scrutinised the thoughts and ideas of a Marxist meant double censorship. In Anderson's words, 'the involuntary disguise that inherited language so often imposes on a pioneer was superimposed by a voluntary disguise which Gramsci assumed to evade his jailers' ('The Antinomies of Antonio Gramsci', *New Left Review*, 100 [1976/7], p. 6). See also, Chapter 11 note 27.
4   Brian Stoddart, 'Sport, Colonialism and Struggle: C. L. R. James and Cricket', in Richard Giulianotti (ed.), *Sport and Modern Social Theorists* (Basingstoke: Palgrave Macmillan, 2004), p. 123. Douglas Hartmann sums up the issue particularly well: 'those who know the most about sport tend not to have the inclination or ability to realize its broader social connections and significance, while, … those who have the requisite skills to understand the broader social dimensions tend to ignore or dismiss sport as a phenomenon worthy of social scientific investigation or serious political consideration' ('What Can We Learn from Sport If We Take Sport Seriously as a Racial Force? Lessons from C. L. R. James's *Beyond a Boundary*', *Ethnic and Racial Studies*, 26, 3 [2003], pp. 454–5).

5   Stephen Jay Gould, *Bully for Brontosaurus: Reflections in Natural History* (New York: W. W. Norton, 1991), p. 46. Gould reveals his hand when he writes, 'people who don't know [that baseball is profound] are not fans and are therefore unreachable anyway'.

6   Colin Tatz, *Obstacle Race: Aborigines in Sport* (Sydney: University of New South Wales Press, 1995), p. 14.

7   Cited in William Baker, *Sports in the Western World* (Urbana, IL: University of Illinois Press, 1988), p. 354. Douglas Hartmann argues that sports activism in the late 1960s and early 1970s (see, for example, Harry Edwards, *The Revolt of the Black Athlete* [New York: Free Press, 1969]) had a 'profound impact' on the emergence of the mirror thesis in sport studies. He also argues that the first text to formerly develop this thesis was Harry Edwards' *Sociology of Sport* (1973) (*Race, Culture, and the Revolt of the Black Athlete: The 1968 Olympic Protests and Their Aftermath* [Chicago, IL: Chicago University Press, 2003], p. 204). Addison-Wesley publishers launched a series titled The Social Significance of Sport around this time with the first book in the series being Donald Ball and John Loy (eds), *Sport and Social Order* (Reading, MA: Addison-Wesley, 1975). The University of Illinois Press began its series Sport and Society in 1986. Edwards still firmly holds to the mirror thesis (see, Harry Edwards, 'The Decline of the Black Athlete', in David Wiggins and Patrick Miller, *The Unlevel Playing Field: A Documentary History of the African American Experience in Sport* [Urbana, IL: University of Illinois Press, 2003], pp. 435–41).

8   Michel Foucault, *The Archaelogy of Knowledge*, translated by A. M. Sheridan-Smith (London: Routledge, 2002), p. 10. Well into the twentieth century, historians approached their topics from the perspective of a limited number of thematic specialisations, notably politics, economics or ideas. In the interwar years a group of French historians led by Marc Bloch (a medievalist) and Lucien Febvre (who specialised in the sixteenth century) founded a historical journal called *Annales d'histoire social et economique*, more widely known as *Annales*. They demanded contributors broaden their approaches and embrace other social sciences, especially economics, sociology, social psychology and geography. Only by drawing upon the insights offered by these disciplines, Bloch and Febvre argued, could historians become aware of the full range of questions that they could put to their sources. According to Bloch and Febvre, historians should strive to recapture human life in all its variety. In short, they proposed that historians write total history. After the Second World War and concomitant with the rise of total history under Bloch and Febvre's successor, Fernand Braudel, social historians – long the poor cousins of political and economic historians – redefined the subject matter of their field that hitherto focused on social problems (poverty, ignorance, insanity, disease), everyday life in the home, workplace and community, and common people or working classes. Increasingly they examined the history of social relationships between different groups of people. Not surprisingly, analyses and accounts of class dominated the field but social historians increasingly turned their attention to race, gender, age, occupation, minority groups and social groups of all types. The result was that social history began to approximate the history of society in its broadest sense and in this sense shared important similarities with total history. See, Ludmilla Jordanova, *History in Practice* (London: Arnold, 2000), pp. 39–42, S. W. Pope, 'Introduction', in Pope (ed.), *The New American Sport History: Recent Approaches and Perspectives* (Urbana, IL: University of Illinois Press, 1997), p. 3, John Warren, *History and the Historians* (London: Hodder & Stoughton, 1999), pp. 95–104, and Theodore Zeldin, 'Social History and Total History', *Journal of Social History*, 10, 2 (1976), pp. 240–2.

9   Stephen Hardy, 'Entrepreneurs, Organizations, and the Sport Marketplace: Subjects in Search of Historians', *Journal of Sport History*, 13, 1 (1986), p. 15, Robert Malcolmson, 'Sports in Society: A Historical Perspective', *British Journal of Sports History*, 1, 1 (1984), p. 60, Tony Scherman, 'Sports history: How games tell us who we are', *New York Times*, 28 November 1983, James Walvin, 'Sport, Social History and the Historian', *British Journal of Sports History*, 1, 1 (1984), p. 8, Karen Winkler, 'A lot more than trading baseball cards: Sport history gains a new respectability', *Chronicle of Higher Education*, 5 June 1985, and Stephen Hardy, 'Where

did You Go, Jackie Robinson? Or, the End of History and the Age of Sport Infrastructure',
Sporting Traditions, 16, 1 (1999), p. 93. Jack Berryman put forward a voice of dissention
arguing against an alignment with social history on the grounds that it 'occupies a similarly
tenuous position with reference to more established areas of history' ('Sport History as
Social History?', *Quest*, 20 [1973], p. 69). One point worth noting here is that notwithstanding
their abiding fascination with sport, historians (and sport sociologists) in the 1970s and
1980s showed no real interest in essentialising (identifying the absolute truths or essences
of) the practice. This task largely remained with philosophers of sport (see, for example,
Bernard Suits, *The Grasshopper: Games, Life and Utopia* [Toronto: University of Toronto Press,
1978]). Essentialism, of course, carries pejorative connotations. But given the rush in the
1990s to emphasise sport as an essential property of the modern nation (another social
construction), it seems unlikely that pejorative connotations alone were sufficient to dissuade
historians from essentialising sport.

10 Robert Malcolmson, *Popular Recreations in English Society, 1700–1850* (Cambridge: Cambridge
University Press, 1973), pp. 52–74.

11 Tony Mason, *Association Football and English Society, 1863–1915* (Brighton: Harvester Press,
1980). An early and enduring exemplar of the context paradigm in sport history was C. L R.
James' *Beyond a Boundary* (1963). See also Chapters 6 and 7 and for useful commentaries see,
Stoddart, 'C. L. R. James and Cricket', Grant Farred, 'The Maple Man: How Cricket Made
a Postcolonial Intellectual', in Farred (ed.), *Rethinking C. L. R. James* (Oxford: Basil Blackwell,
1996), pp. 165–87, and Hartmann, 'Lessons from C. L. R. James'. In the words of the
latter, 'every page of James's seminal text is … predicated on … the proposition that one
cannot understand cricket … unless one situates it in the context of British culture and
colonialism'. 'The broader implications of this formulation should be clear enough', Hartmann
adds: 'if, for example, we are to understand the racial form and function of American sport,
we have to approach it with an informed sense of the meaning and structure of race in the
United States in general' (p. 454).

12 Cited in, John Watterson, *College Football: History, Spectacle, Controversy* (Baltimore, MD: The
Johns Hopkins University Press, 2000), back cover. For example, Watterson links attempts
by college presidents and politicians to eliminate brutal violence from football in the early
twentieth century with broader concerns about unethical practices, high levels of risk in
everyday life, and general calls for social reforms (p. xi, p. 98 and pp. 109–10. See also pp.
64–5 and p. 140).

13 Cited in, Nancy Bouchier, *For the Love of the Game: Amateur Sport in Small-town Ontario, 1838–
1895* (Montreal: McGill-Queen's University Press, 2003), backcover. Even the *New York
Times* compliments Jules Tygiel for 'examining the social and historical context of [Jackie]
Robinson's entrance into white organized baseball' in his book *Baseball's Great Experiment*
(cited in Jules Tygiel, *Baseball's Great Experiment* [New York: Oxford University Press, 1993],
backcover). What makes the *New York Times'* tribute noteworthy is the lack of context in
most media reporting on sport. Absence of context explains why so many academic sport
historians dismiss sports reporting as shallow and superficial. Colin Tatz advocates this view
and has spoken on the subject at several seminars including, 'Can We Take Sports Writing
Seriously?', University of Waikato, 8 September 2004. On the other side of the coin, Elizabeth
Roberts criticises Catriona Parratt for engaging a theoretical framework that obscures the
historical context of leisure among English working-class women in the late eighteenth and
nineteenth centuries (Elizabeth Roberts, Review, *English Historical Review*, 119, 483 [2004],
p. 1079).

14 Berkhofer, *Beyond the Great Story*, p. 32.

15 William Walsh, 'Colligatory Concepts in History', in Patrick Gardiner (ed.), *The Philosophy
of History* (Oxford: Oxford University Press, 1974), p. 136. Elsewhere Walsh writes that
'different historical events can be regarded as going together to constitute a single process, a
whole of which they are all parts and in which they belong together in a specially intimate
way. And the first aim of the historian, when … asked to explain some event or other, is to

see it as part of such a process, to locate it in its context by mentioning other events with which it is bound up' (*An Introduction to the Philosophy of History*, third edition [London: Hutchinson, 1967], pp. 24–5.). See also Frank Ankersmit, *Narrative Logic: A Semantic Analysis of the Historian's Language* (The Hague: Martinus Nijhoff, 1983), p. 99, Louis Mink, 'The Autonomy of Historical Understanding', *History and Theory*, 5, 1 (1965), pp. 32–3, and Nancy Struna, 'E. P. Thompson's Notion of "Context" and the Writing of Physical Education and Sport History', *Quest*, 38 (1986), p. 23.

16   Hayden White, *Metahistory: The Historical Imagination in Nineteenth-century Europe* (Baltimore, MD: The Johns Hopkins University Press, 1973), p. 19.

17   White, *Metahistory*, pp. 18–19. See also, Evans, *In Defence of History*, p. 159.

18   Walsh, 'Colligatory Concepts', pp. 134–6, Mink, 'The Autonomy of Historical Understanding', p. 42, William Dray, '"Explaining What" in History', in Patrick Gardiner (ed.), *Theories of History* (Glencoe, IL: The Free Press, 1959), p. 406, and C. Behan McCullagh, 'Colligation and Classification in History', *History and Theory*, 17, 3 (1978), p. 270. The examples are from Mike Cronin, *Sport and Nationalism in Ireland: Gaelic Games, Soccer and Irish Identity Since 1884* (Dublin: Four Courts Press, 1999), pp. 44–6 and pp. 129–42. As I commented in Chapter 8, Cronin clearly regards the successes of the Charlton-managed national soccer teams as contingencies in the context of Irish national identity (see especially, p. 133). By contrast, in his analysis of the development of rugby league, Tony Collins is concerned with both causal relationships and context. Indeed, he appears to hold the social context of late Victorian and Edwardian England as the antecedent of rugby league (*Rugby's Great Split: Class, Culture and the Origins of Rugby League Football* [London: Frank Cass, 1998], p. xi).

19   Berkhofer, *Beyond the Great Story*, p. 34.

20   Berkhofer, *Beyond the Great Story*, p. 34. The same assumption also appeals to some deconstructionists. This is apparent in Foucault's archaeological approach for example (*Archaeology*, pp. 179–82).

21   Berkhofer, *Beyond the Great Story*, p. 34. Of course, as I discussed in Chapter 7, the study of supposedly unique events logically involves implicit comparison (Norman Wilson, *History in Crisis: Recent Directions in Historiography* [Upper Saddle River, NJ: Prentice Hall, 1999], p. 86).

22   Tatz, *Obstacle Race*, p. 14. Even the staunch advocate of comparison, Raymond Grew concedes that history need not involve comparison, 'except in the broad sense that judgement always has some comparative elements' ('The Case for Comparing Histories', *American Historical Review*, 85, 4 [1980], p. 771).

23   Thompson, 'The Discipline of Historical Context', p. 43. Miles Fairburn sums up the argument when he says that there are obviously many instances where historians simply want to explain a particular case without parallel in any general case. And when this occurs 'no amount of systematic comparison of the general case' will identify 'the important components' of the particular case (*Social History: Problems, Strategies and Methods* [New York: St Martins Press, 1999], p. 92). Liberal-orientated social scientists in apartheid South Africa frequently chastised critics of the regime and state who failed to compare the Republic with the rest of Africa, or the Soviet Union, or Communist China. Comparisons, they argued, would reveal that South Africa was not unique or an exception. In the hands of apologists for, and sympathisers of, the apartheid regime, these arguments helped deflect attention from racial discrimination in South Africa. See, for example, the editor's introduction to Douglas Booth, 'Sport and Society: The Real Boycott Issues', *Indicator South Africa (Urban Monitor)*, 3, 4 (1986), p. 1.

24   Greg Ryan offers an apt example in his history of New Zealand cricket (see below) in which he makes occasional comparisons to highlight dissimilarities with Australian cricket (*The Making of New Zealand Cricket 1832–1914* [London: Frank Cass, 2004], p. 206).

25   See for example, Herbert Hart and Tony Honoré, *Causation in the Law* (Oxford: Clarendon Press, 1959), pp. 33–4, Bryan Palmer, Review, *Social History*, 10, 3 (1985), pp. 400–4, and

Richard Mandell, 'Modern Criticism of Sport', in Donald Kyle and Gary Stark (eds), *Essays on Sport History and Sport Mythology* (College Station, TX: Texas A & M Press, 1990), p. 135.

26   John Tosh, *The Pursuit of History: Aims, Methods and New Directions in the Study of Modern History*, second edition (London: Longman, 1991), p. 154.

27   Malcolm Waters, *Modern Sociological Theory* (London: Sage, 1994). p. 92.

28   Thomas Haskell, *Objectivity Is Not Neutrality: Explanatory Schemes in History* (Baltimore, MD: The Johns Hopkins University Press, 1998), p. 17.

29   C. Behan McCullagh, *The Logic of History: Putting Postmodernism in Perspective* (London: Routledge, 2004), p. 151.

30   Baker, *Sports in the Western World*, pp. 116–17.

31   Baker, *Sports in the Western World*, p. 190.

32   Brett Hutchins, *Don Bradman: Challenging the Myth* (Melbourne: Cambridge University Press, 2002), p. 22.

33   Hutchins, *Don Bradman*, p. 23.

34   Ankersmit, *Narrative Logic*, p. 99.

35   Melvin Adelman, *A Sporting Time: New York City and the Rise of Modern Athletics, 1820–1870* (Urbana, IL: University of Illinois Press, 1986), pp. 3–4. See also Wray Vamplew, *Pay Up and Play the Game: Professional Sport in Britain, 1875–1914* (Cambridge: Cambridge University Press, 1988).

36   Frederick Cozens and Florence Stumpf, *Sports in American Life* (New York: Arno Press, 1976), p 10.

37   Harry Ritter, *Dictionary of Concepts in History* (Westport, CT: Greenwood Press, 1986), p. 52. Similarly, Ankersmit notes that historians use colligatory concepts to illuminate, rather than fit, the facts. The function of colligatory concepts, he says, is to guide historians in constructing their narratives, and to embody the content or cognitive core of historical narratives (Ankersmit *Narrative Logic*, pp. 99–100).

38   Keith Jenkins and Alun Munslow (eds), *The Nature of History Reader* (London: Routledge, 2004), p. 3. See also, Evans, *In Defence of History*, p. 158. The implication is, of course, that contextualisation does not ensure historical certainty which remains epistemologically impossible.

39   Mark Dyreson, 'Reading Football History: New Vistas in the Landscape of Sport', *Journal of Sport History*, 29, 2 (2002), p. 206.

40   Catriona Parratt, 'From the History of Women in Sport to Women's Sport History: A Research Agenda', in Margaret Costa and Sharon Guthrie, *Women and Sport: Interdisciplinary Perspectives* (Champaign, IL: Human Kinetics, 1994), p. 9.

41   Nancy Struna, '"Good Wives" and "Gardeners", Spinners and "Fearless Riders": Middle- and Upper-rank Women in the Early American Sporting Culture', in J. A. Mangan and Roberta Park (eds), *From Fair Sex to Feminism: Sport and the Socialization of Women in the Industrial and Post-industrial Eras* (London: Frank Cass, 1987), pp. 240–1 and pp. 244–5.

42   Geoffrey Lawrence and David Rowe, 'Introduction: Towards a Sociology of Sport in Australia', in Lawrence and Rowe (eds), *Power Play: The Commercialisation of Australian Sport* (Sydney: Hale & Iremonger, 1986), p. 14.

43   Hardy, 'Entrepreneurs, Organizations, and the Sport Marketplace', p. 15. While Berryman's thoughts on the matter ('Sport History as Social History?') preceded Hardy by more than a decade, his views were much more idiosyncratic.

44   Hardy, 'Entrepreneurs, Organizations, and the Sport Marketplace', p. 16. See also Berryman, 'Sport History as Social History?', pp. 71–2.

45   Maurice Roche, *Mega-Events and Modernity: Olympics and Expos in the Growth of Global Culture* (London: Routledge, 2000), p. 12 and p. 20.

46   William Morgan, *Leftist Theories of Sport: A Critique and Reconstruction* (Urbana, IL: University of Illinois Press, 1994), p. 86 and p. 87.

47   Hardy, 'Where did You Go, Jackie Robinson?', pp. 93–5. See also Berryman, 'Sport History as Social History?', p. 70.

48   Tatz, *Obstacle Race*, pp. 29–30.
49   Berkhofer, *Beyond the Great Story*, pp. 22–3. See also, John Toews, 'Intellectual History After the Linguistic Turn: The Autonomy of Meaning and the Irreducibility of Experience', *American Historical Review*, 92 (1987), p. 886.
50   Art Berman cited in, Berkhofer, *Beyond the Great Story*, p. 23. See also, William Irwin, 'Against Intertextuality', *Philosophy and Literature*, 28, 2 (2004), pp. 227–42.
51   Stoddart, 'C. L. R. James and Cricket', p. 123.
52   See, for example, Richard Espy, *The Politics of the Olympic Games* (Berkeley, CA: University of California Press, 1979), Allen Guttmann, *The Olympics: A History of the Modern Games* (Urbana, IL: University of Illinois Press, 1992), Christopher Hill, *Olympic Politics: Athens to Atlanta 1896–1996*, second edition (Manchester: Manchester University Press, 1996), Alfred Senn, *Power, Politics, and the Olympic Games* (Champaign, IL: Human Kinetics, 1999).
53   John Hoberman, 'Toward a Theory of Olympic Internationalism', *Journal of Sport History*, 22, 1 (1995), p. 4, pp. 10–11, p. 29 and p. 34.
54   Roche, *Mega-events and Modernity*. Quotes p. 152, p. 198 and pp. 218–22. Similarly, Douglas Hartmann offers an excellent example of a sport historian severing the ties of orthodox intertextuality pertaining to explanations for the protests by African American athletes at the 1968 olympic games (*The 1968 Olympic Protests*), pp. 20–4.
55   Hartmann, *The 1968 Olympic Protests*, pp. 10–12. Hartmann also stresses the importance of proper historical context in his discussion of Martin Luther King's backing of a proposed boycott of the 1968 olympic games by African American athletes. 'From our perspective early in the twenty-first century – when the civil rights leader's life and work have been deified and in effect depoliticised – it would be easy', Hartmann writes, to misinterpret King's endorsement as evidence of wide support among athletes and the public. However, by the late 1960s King had alienated many of his earlier followers including liberal whites, the federal government, moderate blacks and conservative blacks (pp. 96–7).
56   Berkhofer, *Beyond the Great Story*, p. 24.
57   Arthur Marwick, *The Sixties: Cultural Revolution in Britain, France, Italy, and the United States, c.1958–c.1974* (Oxford: Oxford University Press, 1998).
58   Reviewers were generally critical. See, for example, Van Gosse, Review, *Journal of American History*, 86, 3 (1999), pp. 1311–12, Christopher Hitchens, Review, *Times Literary Supplement*, 13 November 1998 (on-line subscriber archive), Luisa Passerini, Review, *American Historical Review*, 104, 5 (1999), pp. 1642–3, and Clive Webb, Review, *History Today*, 49, 1 (1999), p. 54.
59   As Behan McCullagh comments, poor explanations do not necessarily translate into deficient colligations (*The Logic of History*, p. 183). Interestingly, Marwick makes no references to either colligation or contextualisation in *The New Nature of History: Knowledge, Evidence, Language* (Basingstoke: Palgrave, 2001).
60   Marwick, *The Sixties*, pp. 23–5.
61   Elliot Gorn, '"Gouge and Bite, Pull Hair and Scratch": The Social Significance of Fighting in the Southern Backcountry', *American Historical Review*, 90, 1 (1985), pp. 18–43.
62   Gorn, '"Gouge and Bite, Pull Hair and Scratch"'. Quotes, p. 22, p. 36, p. 37 and p. 43.
63   Ryan, *New Zealand Cricket*. Quotes, p. 81, p. 85, p. 107, p. 176, p. 214 and p. 233.
64   Gerald Gems, *For Profit Pride and Patriarchy: Football and The Incorporation of American Cultural Values* (Lanham, MD: The Scarecrow Press, 2000), p. 1 and p. 7.
65   Maurice Mandelbaum, 'A Note on History as Narrative', *History and Theory*, 6, 3 (1967), p. 418.
66   Stoddart, 'C. L. R. James and Cricket', p. 126.
67   Stoddart, 'C. L. R. James and Cricket', pp. 123–4. I discussed postcolonial analyses of sport under the rubric of post-binary comparisons in Chapter 7.
68   Wilson, *History in Crisis*, p. 76.

11 New culture: interpreting language and discourse

1   Peter Gay, *Style in History* (New York: Basic Books, 1974), p. 3.

2   Of course, this is not a uniquely deconstructionist position as the following example from Catriona Parratt reveals. As she notes, 'working class "voices" … are few and far between in the documentary history of women's rational recreation' and that most 'pass through several middle- and upper-class filters. The circumstances and motivations – social and personal, altruistic and self-interested – that impelled privileged women to [reform recreation for working class women and girls] have left a far more accessible record' ('Making Leisure Work: Women's Rational Recreation in Late Victorian and Edwardian England', *Journal of Sport History*, 26, 3 [1999], p. 476).

3   Decontructionists do not regard language 'as simply a medium, relatively or potentially transparent, for the representation or expression of a reality outside of itself'; they 'entertain … form[s] of semiological theory in which language is conceived of as a self-contained system of "signs" whose meanings are determined by their relations to each other, rather than by their relation to some "transcendental" or extralinguistic object or subject' (John Toews, 'Intellectual History After the Linguistic Turn: The Autonomy of Meaning and the Irreducibility of Experience', *American Historical Review*, 92 [1987], pp. 881–2; see also, p. 885).

4   Robert Berkhofer, *Beyond the Great Story: History as Text and Discourse* (Cambridge, MA: Harvard University Press, 1995), p. 220.

5   For a fuller explanation see, Philippe Carrard, *Poetics of the New History: French Historical Discourse from Braudel to Chartier* (Baltimore, MD: The Johns Hopkins University Press, 1992). For an example of the two approaches in sport history see, Richard Peterson, *Extra Innings: Writing on Baseball* (Urbana, IL: University of Illinois Press, 2001), especially Chapters 4, 5, 9 and 11. Peterson, like several others whose sport history focuses on the 'meaning of the message' – notably Michael Oriard (see below) and David McGimpsey (*Imagining Baseball: America's Pastime and Popular Culture* [Bloomington, IL: Indiana University Press, 2000]) have backgrounds in English.

6   John Tosh, *The Pursuit of History: Aims, Methods and New Directions in the Study of Modern History*, second edition (London: Longman, 1991), p. 87 and p. 89, and Alun Munslow, *Deconstructing History* (London: Routledge, 1997), p. 122.

7   Toews, 'Intellectual History', pp. 889–93.

8   For example, Michel Foucault, *The History of Sexuality: An Introduction*, translated by Robert Hurley (Harmondsworth: Penguin, 1981), p. 151 and p. 152.

9   Chris Shilling, *The Body and Social Theory* (London: Sage, 1993), p. 75.

10 Michel Foucault, *Discipline and Punish: The Birth of the Prison*, translated by Alan Sheridan (Harmondsworth: Penguin, 1977), pp. 202–3.

11 Foucault, *Discipline and Punish*, especially pp. 3–6, p. 211 and p. 223.

12 Colin Gordon (ed.), *Michel Foucault: Power/Knowledge, Selected Interviews and Other Writings 1972–1977* (Brighton: Harvester Press, 1980), p. 78.

13 Catriona Parratt, 'Reflecting on Sport History in the 1990s', *Sport History Review*, 29, 1 (1998), pp. 8–9. Foucault did not consider himself an historian and many in the discipline regard him as a problem. Allan Megill offers a nice summary of the relationship. Although Foucault is 'not *of* the discipline, he is important *to* it, partly because he fosters a self-reflection that is needed to counteract the sclerosis, the self-satisfaction, the smugness that constantly threaten' ('The Reception of Foucault by Historians', *Journal of the History of Ideas*, 48, 1 [1987], p. 134). At the same time a number of feminists criticised Foucault for ignoring women's experiences. See, for example, Nancy Hartsock, 'Foucault on Power: A Theory For Women?', in Charles Lemert (ed.), *Social Theory: The Multicultural and Classic Readings* (Boulder, CO: Westview Press, 1993), pp. 545–54, Caroline Ramazanoglu, *Up Against Foucault: Explorations of Some Tensions Between Foucault and Feminism* (London: Routledge, 1989), and Jana Sawicki, *Disciplining Foucault: Feminism, Power, and the Body* (London: Routledge, 1991).

14   Patricia Vertinsky, *The Eternally Wounded Woman: Women, Doctors, and Exercise in the Late Nineteenth Century* (Urbana, IL: University of Illinois Press, 1994), p. 10 and pp. 11–12.

15   Vertinsky, *The Eternally Wounded Woman*, pp. 208–15.

16   David Andrews, 'Posting-up: French Post-structuralism and the Critical Analysis of Contemporary Sporting Culture', in Jay Coakley and Eric Dunning (eds), *Handbook of Sports Studies* (London: Sage, 2000), pp. 123–6.

17   Susan Cahn, *Coming on Strong: Gender and Sexuality in Twentieth-Century Women's Sport* (Cambridge, MA: Harvard University Press, 1995), p. 3.

18   Cahn, *Coming on Strong*, pp. 266–8.

19   Martin Polley, *Moving the Goalposts: A History of Sport and Society Since 1945* (London: Routledge, 1998), p. 94. See also, Douglas Booth and Colin Tatz, *One-Eyed: A View of Australian Sport* (Sydney: Allen & Unwin, 2000), pp. 204–6, Richard Cashman, *Paradise of Sport: The Rise of Organised Sport in Australia* (Melbourne: Oxford University Press, 1995), pp. 79–82, and Allen Guttmann, *Women's Sports: A History* (New York: Columbia University Press, 1991), pp. 261–3.

20   For an excellent discussion of the concept of practice that addresses both history and sport see, Bruce Kuklick, 'Writing the History of Practice: The Humanities and Baseball, With a Nod to Wrestling', in Elizabeth Fox-Genovese and Elisabeth Lasch-Quinn (eds), *Reconstructing History: The Emergence of a New Historical Society* (New York: Routledge, 1999), pp. 176–88.

21   John Hargreaves, *Sport, Power and Culture: A Social and Historical Analysis of Popular Sports in Britain* (Cambridge: Polity Press, 1986), pp. 132–5. Although he makes numerous references to Foucault's work Hargreaves' Foucaldian perspective derives more directly from Bryan Turner, *The Body and Society* (Cambridge: Basil Blackwell, 1984) and Mike Featherstone, 'The Body in Consumer Culture', *Theory, Culture and Society*, 1, 2 (1982), pp. 18–33. Hargreaves also discusses the discourse of physical education. 'Even when the discourse [of physical education] is ostensibly otherwise, the sub-text is concerned to a very large extent with the theme of socialisation and social control', he comments. 'The subject is conceived overwhelmingly as providing opportunities for monitoring and influencing pupils' social behaviour, for them to experience role play and for learning to adjust to the "demands of society". Such terms and phrases as "preparation for society", "knowledge of right and wrong", "socially acceptable behaviour", "emotional and social adjustment" and "integrating the odd man out", pepper the discourse. Discourse on the function of the subject at the secondary school stage focuses ... on the problem of integrating the less academic pupils. PE's contribution is seen as compensating those who, for want of academic achievement, are destined to spend their lives in unrewarding work, by preparing them to use their leisure. The predominant value underpinning this discourse is clearly individualism, but it is hardly the competitive, achievement-orientated variety applauded in media sport; rather it is a more socially responsible variety considered appropriate for "educational" aims' (*Sport, Power and Culture*, p. 164).

22   Douglas Booth, *Australian Beach Cultures: The History of Sun, Sand and Surf* (London: Frank Cass, 2001), p. 46. See also, p. 33, p. 54 and pp. 169–70. For an explicitly Foucauldian-inspired discussion of swimming pools as sites for disciplining bodies see, Robert Rinehart, 'Born-Again Sport: Ethics in Biographical Research', in Geneviève Rail (ed.), *Sport and Postmodern Times* (Albany, NY: State University of New York Press, 1998), pp. 36–43.

23   Colin Howell, *Blood, Sweat, and Cheers: Sport and the Making of Modern Canada* (Toronto: University of Toronto Press, 2001), p. 108. Howell cites one of my earlier works on the beach but Hargreaves' name does not appear in his select bibliography.

24   Berkhofer, *Beyond the Great Story*, p. 93.

25   Berkhofer, *Beyond the Great Story*, p. 21.

26   Berkhofer, *Beyond the Great Story*, p. 11 and p. 21.

27   In keeping with earlier discussions about the politics of theory (Chapters 3 and 9), Geertz's essay needs to be put into the context of the theoretical period in which it was written. In 1970, Geertz, an anthropologist, and Paul de Man, a literary critic, proposed to the American

Academy of Arts and Science that it host a small gathering of scholars from many disciplines, but principally anthropology and literature, to discuss the theme 'The Systematic Study of Meaningful Forms'. Elaborating on the theme in their subsequent letter of invitation, Geertz and de Man argued that 'meaningful forms, whether they be African passage rites, nineteenth century novels, revolutionary ideologies, grammatical paradigms, scientific theories, English landscape paintings, or the ways in which moral judgments are phrased, have as good a claim to public existence as horses, stones, and trees, and are therefore as susceptible to objective investigation and systematic analysis as these apparently harder realities'. Yet, they added, 'everything from modern logic, computer technology, and cybernetics at one extreme to phenomenological criticism, psychohistory, and ordinary language philosophy at the other has conspired to undermine the notion that meaning is ... so deeply subjective, that it is incapable of being firmly grasped, much less analysed'. Thus, the invitees met to 'construct concepts and methods' to deal with 'meaningful forms'; eight of the papers, including Geertz's, were subsequently published in the Academy's journal, *Dædalus* (Stephen Graubard, 'Preface', *Dædalus*, 101 [1972], pp. v–viii). De Man subsequently found himself at the centre of allegations that he had collaborated with fascism between 1940 and 1942 by writing for Belgium newspapers that supported Nazism. See for example, Bryan Palmer, *Descent into Discourse: The Reification of Language and the Writing of Social History* (Philadelphia, PA: Temple University Press, 1990), pp. 189–98.

28   Clifford Geertz, 'Deep Play: Notes on the Balinese Cockfight', *Dædalus*, 101 (1972), p. 27.

29   Geertz, 'Deep Play', p. 26. Douglas Hartmann draws useful links here between Geertz and the master contextualist C. L. R. James (Chapter 10) noting that both offer, in the words of the latter, 'windows onto a world'. Hartmann also comments on the appearance of functionalist language in the works of Geertz and James. But whereas the former, a highly 'sophisticated interpreter and practitioner of functionalist theory', assumed that 'cultural practices play an essentially conservative, reproductive role in the maintenance and perpetuation of social order', the latter conceptualised the modern world as beset by 'tension, contradiction and struggle' and 'fraught with deep inequalities' ('What Can We Learn from Sport If We Take Sport Seriously as a Racial Force? Lessons from C. L. R. James's *Beyond a Boundary*', *Ethnic and Racial Studies*, 26, 3 [2003], pp. 456–7 and pp. 460–2).

30   Geertz, 'Deep Play', p. 29.

31   Geertz, 'Deep Play', p. 5.

32   Michael Oriard, *Reading Football: How the Popular Press Created an American Spectacle* (Chapel Hill, NC: University of North Carolina Press, 1993), p. 11. With respect to Geertz's reading of Balinese cockfighting, Oriard comments that 'whether a single interpretation of the cockfight can suffice, Geertz and his colleagues must determine' (p. 11. See also, p. 14 and p. 16).

33   H. F. Moorehouse, 'Shooting Stars: Footballers and Working-Class Culture in Twentieth Century Scotland', in Richard Holt (ed.), *Sport and the Working Class in Britain* (Manchester: Manchester University Press, 1990), pp. 179–97, Jeffrey Hill, 'Reading the Stars: A Post-Modernist Approach to Sports History', *The Sports Historian*, 14 (1994), pp. 45–55, and Richard Holt, 'King Across the Border: Denis Law and Scottish Football', in Grant Jarvie and Graham Walker (eds), *Scottish Sport in the Making* (Leicester: Leicester University Press, 1994), pp. 58–74.

34   Oriard, *Reading Football*, pp. 2–3. Hartmann makes the same point with respect to different readings of the protests made by Tommie Smith and John Carlos at the 1968 olympic games in Mexico City (*Race, Culture, and the Revolt of the Black Athlete: The 1968 Olympic Protests and Their Aftermath* [Chicago, IL: Chicago University Press, 2003], p. 157 and p. 173).

35   Oriard, *Reading Football*, p. 15.

36   Alan Trachtenberg, 'Foreword', in Oriard, *Reading Football*, pp. xiv–xv. See also, Jeffrey Hill, 'Cocks, Cats, Caps and Cups: A Semiotic Approach to Sport and National Identity', *Culture, Sport, Society*, 2, 2 (1999), pp. 1–21.

37   Catriona Parratt, 'Of Place and Men and Women: Gender and Topophilia in the "Haxey Hood"', *Journal of Sport History*, 27, 2 (2000), pp. 229–30.

38   Parratt, 'Of Place and Men and Women', p. 239.

39   Peter Mewett, 'History in the Making and the Making of History: Stories and the Social Construction of Sport', *Sporting Traditions*, 17, 1 (2000), p. 2 and pp. 14–15.

40   Mewett, 'History in the Making and the Making of History', p. 5.

41   Parratt, 'Of Place and Men and Women', p. 229.

42   Oriard, *Reading Football*, p. xxii.

43   Cited in Palmer, *Descent Into Discourse*, p. 42. See also, John Murphy, 'The Voice of Memory: History, Autobiography and Oral Memory', *Historical Studies*, 22, 87 (1986), p. 170.

44   Palmer, *Descent Into Discourse*, p. 197. This comment comes at the end of Palmer's powerful critique of Jacques Derrida's defence of Paul de Man (see note 27 above).

45   Toews, 'Intellectual History', p. 882.

46   Hargreaves is also alert to the dangers of Foucauldian analyses which assume 'that control programmes actually achieve their desired effects'. He warns that programmes associated with commodified sport typically falter and fail, especially among subordinate groups. Attempts to transform British soccer from a working-class to a middle-class game offers a 'salutary' example: 'the more up-market it has moved and the more it has been packaged as "family entertainment", the greater the propensity for unruly crowd behaviour. The remoteness of the stars and those who control the game has reduced the effectiveness of traditional informal processes of maintaining order, so that other agencies, notably the police, have had to assume responsibility for it' (*Sport, Power and Culture*, p. 135 and p. 136. See also, pp. 217–18).

47   Richard Rorty, *Consequences of Pragmatism (Essays: 1972–1980)* (Brighton: The Harvester Press, 1982), p. 152. Rorty objects to textualism primarily on moral grounds: without a common vocabulary there can be no sacred wisdom (p. 158).

48   Vertinsky, *The Eternally Wounded Woman*, p. 10.

49   Hargreaves, *Sport, Power and Culture*, p. 134.

50   Oriard, *Reading Football*, p. 17 and pp. 19–20. Oriard's plurality of meanings bears the hallmarks of methodological individualism while his discovery of a single reality in the texts of popular journalism implies a level of structuralism. For a discussion of the debates between methodological individualism and structuralism see, Alex Callinicos, *Making History* (Cambridge: Polity Press, 1988), pp. 64–91.

51   Oriard, *Reading Football*, p. xxi.

52   John Bloom, *To Show What an Indian Can Do: Sports at Native American Boarding Schools* (Minneapolis, MN: University of Minnesota Press, 2000), p. 105. Bloom reproduces an edited version of the interview, pp. 105–10.

53   Bloom, *To Show What an Indian Can Do*, p. 111.

54   Bloom, *To Show What an Indian Can Do*, pp. 114–21. Like Geertz and Oriard, Bloom sees sport as a 'polysemic cultural form', a form that 'gives voice to a variety of historical perspectives, social contexts, and cultural interpretations' (*To Show What an Indian Can Do*, p. xiii. See also p. 102). I think Harris raises interesting questions for those scholars pursuing post-binary comparisons (see Chapter 7). How, for example, do individuals see the 'space' between clearly identified races and ethnicities?

55   For a discussion of quotations see Carrard, *Poetics of the New History*, pp. 182–9; for a discussion of the political problems of representing others' voices and experiences see, Ruth Roach Pierson, 'Experience, Difference, Dominance and Voice in the Writing of Canadian Women's History', in Karen Offen, Ruth Roach Pierson and Jane Rendall (eds), *Writing Women's History: International Perspectives* (London: Macmillan, 1991), pp. 85–90.

56   Pierson, 'Experience, Difference, Dominance and Voice', p. 94. In the words of Luise White, 'establishing the authenticity of the voice – or cacophony of voices' all too often leaves it 'disembodied and decontextualized' (*Speaking With Vampires: Rumor and History in Colonial Africa* [Berkeley, CA: University of California Press, 2000], p. 50. See also, p. 309).

57   Berkhofer, *Beyond the Great Story*, p. 169. Carrard believes that 'historians tell their stories, organise their descriptions, and conduct their analyses from a perspective which is neither that of the people they are considering, nor that of an external observer who would have little understanding of events he or she is reporting' (*Poetics of the New History*, p. 105).

58   Parratt, 'Of Place and Men and Women', p. 230. Emphasis added.

59   Parratt, 'Of Place and Men and Women', p. 239 and p. 240.

60   Berkhofer, *Beyond the Great Story*, p. 190.

61   Oriard, *Reading Football*, p. xxi, pp. 17–18 and p. 141.

62   Stephen Hardy, 'Sport in Urbanizing America: A Historical Review', *Journal of Urban History*, 23, 6 (1997), p. 692.

63   Rorty, *Consequences of Pragmatism*, p. 152.

64   Rorty, *Consequences of Pragmatism*, pp. 151–2.

65   Synthia Sydnor, 'A History of Synchronized Swimming', *Journal of Sport History*, 25, 2 (1998), p. 259.

66   For Benjamin, the production of history was an 'act of reading/writing, more aesthetic and ethical than the scientific claims of historians in the practices of Marxists and non-Marxists alike' (Harry Harootunian, *History's Disquiet: Modernity, Cultural Practice, and the Questions of Everyday Life* [New York: Columbia University Press, 2000], p. 13). As we shall see, Benjamin also influenced Harry Harootunian who shares important theoretical similarities with Peter Mewett.

67   Sydnor, 'Synchronized Swimming', p. 259.

68   Sydnor, 'Synchronized Swimming', p. 256–7.

69   Sydnor, 'Synchronized Swimming', p. 254.

70   Sydnor called the piece her 'finest' work of sport history ('Synchronized Swimming', p. 260). At the time this seemed hyperbole, but from the perspective of 2005, and particularly in the light of Alun Munslow and Robert Rosenstone's *Experiments in Rethinking History* (London, Routledge, 2004), it can only be concluded that Sydnor was at least a generation ahead of the field and ahead of the great majority in the discipline.

71   Berkhofer, *Beyond the Great Story*, p. 199.

72   Sydnor, 'Synchronized Swimming', p. 254.

73   Sydnor, 'Synchronized Swimming', p. 260.

74   That is, the reconstructionist rule that every historical fact should be accompanied by a reference (Carrard, *Poetics of the New History*, p. 159).

75   Carrard, *Poetics of the New History*, p. 160.

76   Berkhofer, *Beyond the Great Story*, p. 25 and p. 199.

77   Penelope Corfield, 'Review Article: The State of History', *Journal of Contemporary History*, 36, 1 (2001), p. 159. Corfield also notes that singular events cannot be plotted outside their wider contexts.

78   Douglas Brown, 'Modern Sport, Modernism and the Cultural Manifesto: De Coubetin's *Revue Olympique*', *The International Journal of the History of Sport*, 18, 2 (2001), p. 81. For an example of de Coubertin's use of the *Revue* see, Per Jørgensen, 'From Balck to Nurmi: The Olympic Movement and the Nordic Nations', *The International Journal of the History of Sport*, 14, 3 (1997), p. 74.

79   Brown, 'Modern Sport, Modernism and the Cultural Manifesto', p. 79 and p. 101. Some readers may interpret my summary as Brown simply putting *Revue Olympique* into a new, and better, context. However, Brown's discourse analysis is much more sophisticated than this and assigns a primary role to language in shaping modern culture (Douglas Brown, 'Discourse and Discontinuity: Interpreting the Cultural History of Sport', in Kevin Wamsley [ed.], *Method and Methodology in Sport and Cultural History* [Dubuque, IA: Brown and Benchmark Publishers, 1995], pp. 37–48).

80   The literature on sport and identity is huge but two texts strike me as pivotal. The first is Lincoln Allison (ed.), *The Changing Politics of Sport* (Manchester: Manchester University Press, 1993). Especially important are the chapters by Allison, 'The Changing Context of Sporting

Life', pp. 1–14, and Grant Jarvie, 'Sport, Nationalism and Cultural Identity', pp. 58–83. See also Epilogue note 51. The second text is, John Nauright and Timothy Chandler (eds), *Making Men: Rugby and Masculine Identity* (London: Frank Cass, 1996).

81 Parratt, 'Reflecting on Sport History', p. 13. See also, Lawrence Stone, 'History and Post-Modernism', *Past and Present*, 135 (1992), p. 191.

82 Palmer, *Descent into Discourse*, pp. 57–61. Grant Farred concurs ('The Maple Man: How Cricket Made a Postcolonial Intellectual', in Farred [ed.], *Rethinking C. L. R. James* [Oxford: Basil Blackwell, 1996], pp. 172–4). Farred argues that 'the outstanding feature of *Beyond a Boundary*' is its integration of Marxist analysis, the politics of cricket and James' interest in literature 'to produce a rare socio-political critique that takes sport as its starting point, its metaphorical axis, and as a site of radical cultural opposition' (p. 174).

83 Toews, 'Intellectual History', p. 906.

84 For example, John Nauright's discussion of community identity among Coloured people in South Africa's Western Cape largely hinges on giving voice to Coloured rugby players (*Sport Cultures and Identities in South Africa* [Leicester: Leicester University Press, 1997], pp. 47–56). Lawrence Stone makes the identical point in, 'The Revival of Narrative: Reflections on a New Old History', *Past and Present*, 85 (1979), p. 13. However, see Carrard's critique of Stone in, *Poetics of History*, p. 68. As Luise White notes, 'letting [people] speak for themselves' has become a major publishing enterprise' (*Speaking With Vampires*, p. 49).

85 It is worth reminding ourselves that literally anything in the present can trigger an interest in the past. As Fernand Braudel puts it, 'a bend in a path or a street can take anyone back to the past' (Fernand Braudel, *Capitalism and Material Life, 1400–1800* [New York: Harper & Row, 1973], p. 441).

86 Harootunian, *History's Disquiet*, p. 13.

87 Harootunian, *History's Disquiet*, p. 18.

88 Mewett, 'History in the Making and the Making of History', p. 2.

89 'In this sense', Harootunian continues, 'history is not mere memory, the remembrance of the way things were, the detached view promising to show what "actually happened", conservation, or even the archive. The tendency still to identify history with memory is nothing more than the sign of a conservative epoch dreaming only of the status quo, desiring no more than what has already arrived. If the term has any sense, history thus envisioned must always be a history of the present which means a politically driven history' (*History's Disquiet*, pp. 21–2). See also, Joe Moran, 'History, Memory and the Everyday', *Rethinking History*, 8, 1 (2004), pp. 51–68.

90 As Hoberman puts it, 'here we find the schoolchild who cannot believe that the black college student who is his mentor is not a football player, since television has persuaded him that every black male student is an athlete; here too is the academically precocious child whose athletic skills save him from harassment by his black peers, whose hostility to intellectual development (and even "whitey's" habit of using seatbelts) only intensifies as they enter adolescence. Some black children still face overt hostility in interracial games. In east Texas in the 1990s, black junior high school boys sometimes play football against whites whose parents shout "Niggers!" from the stands as they watch their sons lose' (*Darwin's Athletes: How Sport Has Damaged Black America and Preserved the Myth of Race* [Boston, MA: Mariner Books, 1997], pp. xxiv–xxv).

Epilogue: Towards an alternative model?

1 Stanley Fish believes that religion is poised to 'succeed high theory and the triumvirate of race, gender, and class as the center of intellectual energy in the academy' ('One University Under God?', *Chronicle of Higher Education*, 7 January 2005). For an excellent pioneering

investigation of religion in sport see, Tara Magdalinski and Timothy Chandler (eds), *With God on their Side: Sport in the Service of Religion* (London: Routledge, 2002).

2   See, for example, Penelope Corfield, 'History and the Challenge of Gender History', *Rethinking History*, 1, 3 (1997), pp. 241–58, and Dwight Zakus and Synthia Slowikowski, 'Alternative Research Theories and Methodologies for Sport History: From Mills and Carr, Through Hesse, to Non-equilibrium Theory', in Kevin Wamsley (ed.), *Method and Methodology in Sport and Cultural History* (Dubuque, IA: Brown and Benchmark Publishers, 1995), pp. 16–36.

3   Zakus and Slowikowski, 'Alternative Research', p. 32. See also, Nancy Struna, 'E. P. Thompson's Notion of "Context" and the Writing of Physical Education and Sport History', *Quest*, 38 (1986), p. 23.

4   This is not peculiar to sport history as Eric Hobsbawm's support for 'old-fashioned positivist evidence' testifies (*On History* [London: Abacus, 1998], p. ix).

5   In the words of Patrick Joyce, 'the elders of social history remain in station still, supported by a younger generation of scholars largely immune to the intellectual history of our own times' ('The End of Social History?', *Social History*, 20, 1 [1995], pp. 80–1). Murray Phillips observes an indifference and lack of self reflection among sport historians on the issue of the production of historical knowledge ('Tunnel Vision: The Production of Sport History', in Jan Wright [ed.], *Researching in Sport, Physical and Health Education* [Wollongong: University of Wollongong, 2004], p. 20).

6   Robert Berkhofer, *Beyond the Great Story: History as Text and Discourse* (Cambridge, MA: Harvard University Press, 1995), pp. 282–3.

7   Michael Oriard, 'Football, Cultural History and Democracy', *Journal of Sport History*, 29, 2 (2002), p. 245.

8   See for example, Murray Phillips (ed.), *Deconstructing Sport History: A Postmodern Analysis* (Albany, NY: State University of New York Press, 2005), and Allen Guttmann, '*From Ritual to Record*: A Retrospective Critique', *Sport History Review*, 32, 1 (2001), pp. 2–11.

9   See for example, Jeffrey Sammons, 'A Proportionate and Measured Response to the Provocation That is *Darwin's Athletes*', *Journal of Sport History*, 24, 3 (1997), pp. 378–88, and John Hoberman, 'How Not to Read *Darwin's Athletes*: A Response to Jeffrey T. Sammons', *Journal of Sport History*, 24, 3 (1997), pp. 389–96.

10 David Hackett Fischer, *Historians' Fallacies: Toward a Logic of Historical Thought* (New York: Harper & Row, 1970), p. 307, and Berkhofer, *Beyond the Great Story*, p. 202.

11 Alun Munslow and Robert Rosenstone (eds), *Experiments in Rethinking History* (London, Routledge, 2004), p. 13 and p. 14.

12 Alun Munslow, *Deconstructing History* (London: Routledge, 1997), p. 102.

13 Berkhofer, *Beyond the Great Story*, and Munslow, *Deconstructing History*.

14 Douglas Hartmann, *Race, Culture, and the Revolt of the Black Athlete: The 1968 Olympic Protests and Their Aftermath* (Chicago, IL: Chicago University Press, 2003), pp. 23–4.

15 John Hoberman, *Mortal Engines: The Science of Performance and the Dehumanization of Sport* (New York: Free Press, 1992), p. x.

16 Berkhofer, *Beyond the Great Story*, p. 247.

17 Berkhofer systematically works through each of these dimensions (*Beyond the Great Story*, pp. 243–83).

18 A fully fledged history of relativism, says Fischer, 'would embrace a major school of German historical and philosophical thought, the epistemology of fascism, Stalin's hostility to "archive rats" and "bourgeois objectivism", the great Japanese movie *Rashomon*, several popular anthologies of Hindu folk legends, the novels of Aldos Huxley, Thomas Mann and André Gide, the essays of Renan and Croce, the poetry of Edward Arlington Robinson and E. E. Cummings, the theology of Reinhold Niebuhr, and the aesthetics of abstract art' (*Historians' Fallacies*, p. 42).

19 David Block, *Baseball Before We Knew It: A Search for the Roots of the Game* (Lincoln, NB: University of Nebraska Press, 2004), p. 162.

20   Cited in, Thomas Altherr, 'A Place Leavel Enough to Play Ball', *Nine: A Journal of Baseball History and Social Policy Perspectives*, 8, 2 (2000), pp. 15–49. Block reproduces this essay as an appendix (*Baseball Before We Knew It*, pp. 229–51. Seymour's quote appears on p. 250).

21   Raphael Samuel, 'History and Theory', in Samuel (ed.), *People's History and Socialist Theory* (London: Routledge & Kegan Paul, 1981), p. xlv.

22   Block, *Baseball Before We Knew It*, pp. 152–4. The holocaust is the classic example. The evidence of the holocaust is overwhelming and irrefutable, but this does not stop historians debating the subject and deriving 'different interpretations from the same sources'. For example, in *Hitler's Willing Executioners* (1997), Daniel Goldhagen argues that 'Germans in general and the killers specifically were willing accomplices, motivated by a thoroughgoing and deep-seated hatred of the Jews', while Christopher Browning puts the case in *Ordinary Men* (1998) that 'average men were transformed into killers' by 'indoctrination, peer pressure, wartime Nazi propaganda and the very nature of the Second World War' (Robert Eaglestone, *Postmodernism and Holocaust Denial* [Cambridge: Icon, 2001], p. 14 and pp. 30–3).

23   Block, *Baseball Before We Knew It*, pp. 152–4.

24   Fischer, *Historians' Fallacies*, pp. 42–3.

25   The holocaust, for example, raises questions for 'the believers in a God who interacted with the world, rewarding the righteous, punishing the evil. Where was the rescuer, the God of Exodus, when the innocents were murdered?' Auschwitz similarly 'challenged the believers in Man, the proponents of Enlightenment ideals of human progress, rationality and the rule of reason'. It 'revealed the blood lust that had defied civilisation, the seeming limitless power to corrupt, the capacity to normalise evil' (Andrew Markus, 'Factory of Death', *The Age* [Melbourne], 29 January 2005).

26   Munslow, *Deconstructing History*, pp. 112–13.

27   Alon Confino, 'Collective Memory and Cultural History: Problems of Method', *American Historical Review*, 102, 5 (1997), p. 1386.

28   Daniel Nathan, *Saying It's So: A Cultural History of the Black Sox Scandal* (Urbana, IL: University of Illinois Press, 2003), p. 59. See also, Jaime Schultz, '"A Wager Concerning a Diplomatic Pig": Remembering and Forgetting in the Iowa-Minnesota Football Contests, 1934–1935', *Journal of Sport History*, forthcoming. On sporting monuments see, Mark O'Neill, Artefacts of the Present: Monuments to Indigenous Athletic Heroes in Australian Social Memory, BA (Hons) Dissertation, School of Human Movement Studies, University of Queensland, 2004, Gary Osmond and Murray Phillips, '"The Bloke with the Stroke": Alick Wickham, the "Crawl" and Social Memory', *The Journal of Pacific History*, 39, 3 (2004), pp. 309–24, and Patricia Vertinsky and Sherry McKay (eds), *Disciplining Bodies in the Gymnasium* (London: Routledge, 2004). Nathan, Schultz and O'Neill all acknowledge the French sociologist Maurice Halbwachs, see Chapter 5 note 101.

29   Nathan, *Saying It's So*, p. 219. See also, Samuel, 'History and Theory', p. xlix, and Eaglestone, *Postmodernism and Holocaust Denial*, p. 56.

30   Munslow, *Deconstructing History*, p. 29.

31   Berkhofer, *Beyond the Great Story*, p. 248, and Munslow, *Deconstructing History*, p. 102.

32   Patricia Vertinsky, Sherry McKay and Stephen Petrina, 'No Body/ies in the Gym', in Vertinsky and McKay, *Disciplining Bodies*, p. 157 and p. 171, and Vertinsky and McKay, *Disciplining Bodies*, p. xii.

33   Berkhofer, *Beyond the Great Story*, p. 257.

34   For a general overview of the trend away from grand theories see, Steven Best and Douglas Kellner, *Postmodern Theory: Critical Interrogations* (London: Macmillan, 1991), especially Chapter 8, and Yvonna Lincoln and Egon Guba, 'Paradigmatic Controversies, Contradictions, and Emerging Confluences', in Norman Denzin and Lincoln (eds), *Handbook of Qualitative Research*, second edition (London: Sage, 2000), pp. 163–88.

35   Berkhofer, *Beyond the Great Story*, p. 244 and p. 249. In one sense reflexivity and reflexive contextualisation restores some status to intuition or *verstehen*. Although maligned by conservative reconstructionists as subjective, *verstehen* based on experience can offer insights and facilitate different connections. To exclude these insights and connections because they

cannot be demonstrated in the documents is to constrict the boundaries of history. See also, Prologue note 9.

36   Emphasis added. Vertinsky and McKay, *Disciplining Bodies*, p. xii. See also, Jennifer Hargreaves, 'Querying Sport Feminism: Personal or Political?', in Richard Giulianotti (ed.), *Sport and Modern Social Theorists* (Basingstoke: Palgrave, 2004), pp. 198–203, and Grant Farred's very useful discussion of the context in which C. L. R. James wrote *Beyond a Boundary* ('The Maple Man: How Cricket Made a Postcolonial Intellectual', in Farred [ed.], *Rethinking C. L. R. James* [Oxford: Basil Blackwell, 1996], pp. 175–80).

37   Vertinsky, McKay and Petrina, 'No Body/ies in the Gym', pp. 163–4.

38   Geoffrey Elton, *The Practice of History*, second edition (Oxford: Basil Blackwell, 2002), p. 43. See also the views of Joyce Appleby in, 'The Power of History', *American Historical Review*, 103, 1 (1998), p. 12.

39   Antoinette Burton, *Dwelling in the Archive: Women Writing House, Home and History in Late Colonial India* (Oxford: Oxford University Press, 2003), p. 138. See also, Mitchell Dean, *Critical and Effective Histories: Foucault's Methods and Historical Sociology* (London: Routledge, 1994), p. 14, and Harry Harootunian, *History's Disquiet: Modernity, Cultural Practice, and the Questions of Everyday Life* (New York: Columbia University Press, 2000).

40   Margaret Atwood, 'In Search of *Alias Grace*: On Writing Canadian Historical Fiction', *American Historical Review*, 103, 5 (1998), p. 1516.

41   Dean, *Critical and Effective Histories*, p. 32.

42   Dean, *Critical and Effective Histories*, p. 29.

43   John Hoberman, *Darwin's Athletes: How Sport Has Damaged Black America and Preserved the Myth of Race* (Boston, MA: Mariner Books, 1997).

44   Mike Cronin, *Sport and Nationalism in Ireland: Gaelic Games, Soccer and Irish Identity Since 1884* (Dublin: Four Courts Press, 1999).

45   Dean, *Critical and Effective Histories*, p. 29.

46   Berkhofer, *Beyond the Great Story*, p. 248. These issues are touched upon by Vicky Paraschak, Michael Heine and James McAra in, 'Native and Academic Knowledge Interests: A Dilemma', in Kevin Wamsley (ed.), *Method and Methodology in Sport and Cultural History* (Dubuque, IA: Brown and Benchmark Publishers, 1995), pp. 62–8.

47   Deconstructionism emphasises 'the orchestration of narrative in the creation of historical knowledge. When historians say that they are confronting the past, they are actually confronting language. Language, like memory, can recollect, but it can never be reality' (Munslow, *Deconstructing History*, p. 103).

48   For a good recent statement of this tension see, Hartmann, *The 1968 Olympic Protests*, pp. 271–4.

49   Fischer, *Historians' Fallacies*, p. 307.

50   Elliot Gorn and Michael Oriard, 'Taking Sports Seriously', *Chronicle of Higher Education*, 24 March 1995.

51   Lincoln Allison's comments on the relationship between sport and identity offer a particularly clear statement of the relevance of sport history. In his words, sport is 'one of the most potent of human activities in its capacity to give meaning to life, to create and interconnect senses of achievement and identity. Above all, and increasingly, sport has a complex and important interaction with nationality and the phenomenon of nationalism' ('The Changing Context of Sporting Life', in Allison [ed.], *The Changing Politics of Sport* [Manchester: Manchester University Press, 1993], pp. 4–5). See also, Mark Dyreson, *Making the American Team: Sport, Culture, and the Olympic Experience* (Urbana, IL: University of Illinois Press, 1998), and Eric Hobsbawm, 'Mass Producing Traditions: Europe, 1870–1914', in Hobsbawm and Terence Ranger (eds), *The Invention of Tradition* (Cambridge: Cambridge University Press, 1983), pp. 298–303. Grant Jarvie provides a particularly good explanation of the (synecdochic) relationship between sport and nationalism (Chapter 4). In his account, sport provides 'a form of symbolic action which states the case for the nation itself'. First, victories incarnate positive images of national virtues, strengths and way of life. Similarly, hosts of international sporting pageants, such as the olympic games, display national wealth, technical expertise

and organisational competence. Second, the symbols, icons, anthems and songs of representative teams are signifiers that separate and distinguish nations from each other. And third, sporting events provide 'shared memories of specific events and personages' which occasionally act as 'turning points for national history' and help forge ideas about 'common destiny' ('Sport, Nationalism and Cultural Identity', in Allison, *The Changing Politics of Sport*, p. 74 and p. 76).

52 Elton, *The Practice of History*, p. 42 and p. 44.

53 Robert Archer and Antoine Bouillon, *The South African Game: Sport and Racism* (London: Zed Press, 1982), pp. 58–60 and pp. 88–94.

54 Archer and Bouillon, *The South African Game*, p. 60.

55 John Tosh, *The Pursuit of History: Aims, Methods and New Directions in the Study of Modern History*, second edition (London: Longman, 1991). Moreover, this battleground operates independently of the truth: 'when we have something invested in a historical moment and a particular version of it, we tend to see what we want to see, believe what we need to believe. We can give reasons in support of an interpretation or a position and can cite evidence and authorities, but at the end of the day different – sometimes competing, sometimes complementary, sometimes equally plausible and legitimate – versions of the moment in question persist' (Nathan, *Saying It's So*, p. 220).

56 Nathan, *Saying It's So*, p. 219.

57 Berkhofer, *Beyond the Great Story*, p. 215.

58 Cited in, Berkhofer, *Beyond the Great Story*, p. 217. See also, pp. 214–15.

59 Berkhofer, *Beyond the Great Story*, pp. 213–14.

60 David Wiggins, *Glory Bound: Black Athletes in a White America* (Syracuse, NY: Syracuse University Press, 1997), pp. 148–9. This work first appeared in the *Journal of Sport History*, 15, 3 (1988), pp. 304–33 under the same title ' "The Future of College Athletics is at Stake": Black Athletes and Racial Turmoil on Three Predominantly White University Campuses, 1968–1972'.

61 Hartmann, *The 1968 Olympic Protests*, p. 115.

62 See in particular, David Wiggins, 'Clio and the Black Athlete in America: Myths, Heroes, and Realities', *Quest*, 32, 2 (1980), pp. 217–25, and David Wiggins, 'Prized Performers, but Frequently Overlooked Students: The Involvement of Black Athletes in Intercollegiate Sports on Predominantly White University Campuses, 1890–1972', *Research Quarterly for Exercise and Sport*, 62, 2 (1991), pp. 164–77.

63 Wiggins, *Glory Bound*, p. xiv. See also, Wiggins, 'Clio and the Black Athlete', p. 217, p. 221 and p. 222. In the latter, Wiggins comments that 'historians ... should not become preoccupied as moral critics, which could obviously be very dangerous. But they should make the effort to be as objective as possible and at the same time be willing to confront ethical issues' (p. 221).

64 In addition to this chapter see, Wiggins, 'Prized Performers', pp. 164–5, p. 174 and p. 175.

65 Wiggins, *Glory Bound*, p. xiv, p. xviii, p. 125 and pp. 145–6.

66 Berkhofer, *Beyond the Great Story*, p. 215. The words are Berkhofer's.

67 Wiggins, 'Clio and the Black Athlete', p. 221.

68 Wiggins, *Glory Bound*, p. xviii.

69 David Zang, *SportsWars: Athletes in the Age of Aquarius* (Fayetteville, AR: The University of Arkansas Press, 2001).

70 Hartmann, *The 1968 Olympic Protests*, p. 76 and p. 80.

71 Eaglestone, *Postmodernism and Holocaust Denial*, pp. 50–2.

72 Lynn Hunt, 'Introduction: History, Culture, and Text', in Hunt (ed.), *The New Cultural History* (Berkeley, CA: University of California Press, 1989), p. 20.

73 It is also worth noting one of the ironies in literary criticism and the social sciences, namely, their call for a renewed historicism to mediate conflicts of politics and theory. See for example, Terrence McDonald (ed.), *The Historic Turn in the Human Sciences* (Ann Arbor, MI: The University of Michigan Press, 1996), and Mitchell Dean, *Critical and Effective Histories*, pp. 10–12.

Glossary

Advocacy, the 'brick by brick' building of an argument, blending the gathering, examination and interrogation of sources with rigorous logic. An **advocate**, or proponent, strives to make her or his argument, or case, unassailable against **scepticism**. All arguments contain some level of **partisanship**. Practitioners working in the advocacy explanatory paradigm focus their arguments on historical sources that they insist can reveal the truth under forensic examination and interrogation.

Advocate, a proponent who constructs an argument. See also **advocacy**. Employing legal terminology, *The Field* categorises advocates on the basis of their **partisanship**. The least partisan advocate is the judge; partisanship rises in the expert-witness and the partisan-eyewitness, and appears unabashed in the leading counsellor.

Approach, see **historical approaches**.

Causal reasoning, a form of **explanation** that accounts for why situation *c* rather than *b* followed *a*. In many cases, the **narrative** structure of an historical interpretation creates the impression of a causal **explanation**. While many historians believe that causal explanations are at the heart of historical practice, the tendency in the discipline is to replace cause with synonyms such as 'led to', 'gave rise to', 'brought about', 'made', 'provided', 'produced', 'created', 'conditioned', 'influenced'.

Chronicle, a sequence of events or actions. See also **story**.

Concept, a class of object (for example, alternative sports), a general notion (for example, hegemony), a theme (for example, urbanisation), a period (for example, Victorian era, the 1960s), or a constellation of interrelated traits (for example, sportsperson) that alerts historians to recurrent features and patterns. Concepts open new realms of observation and analysis to historians by enabling them to move past the single case and transcend immediate perceptions. While abstract and sociologically orientated concepts are the building blocks of theories, defining their shape and content, historians rarely circumscribe their concepts. They typically prefer concepts that employ the language of everyday life. The problem with everyday concepts is that they lack precision and mostly refer to something that is sensed rather than carefully analysed.

Constructionism, a **model** of historical enquiry that looks for patterns, processes, and relationships as a way of explaining the past (compared with **reconstructionism** that attempts to reconstruct the past as it actually was, and **deconstructionism** that focuses on the role of language in making history).

Contextualisation, an approach in which the historian attempts to understand phenomena by placing them in the circumstances in which they occurred. Most contextual arguments are forms of **interpretation** in which the practitioner conceptualises phenomena as a part connected to, or sharing a relationship with, other parts to form a unitary, intelligible whole. Most contextualists are reconstructionists and distinguishable from constructionists who typically attempt to theorise social wholes or holistic arrangements of social phenomena.

Deconstructionism, a **model** of historical enquiry that questions the assumptions of truth and objectivity that underpin **reconstructionism** (a model that emphasises reconstructing the past as it actually was) and **constructionism** (a model that examines patterns, processes, and relationships to explain the past) and focuses on the role of language, especially **discourse** in shaping the content of history.

Discourse, (1) The arrangement, or conveying and shaping, of the content in narrative and non-narrative histories; the vehicle of the argument or story. (2) The result of placing text into its context (**textualisation**) and so providing a coherent meaning to authors and readers. Such discourses, or shared terrains of language, typically contain extra-linguistic dimensions of institutional and economic power.

Discursive practice, multifarious practices and rituals, verbal and non-verbal, through which a certain sense of reality and understanding of something (for example, the nature of sport) is constituted and maintained. Discursive analyses of the lexicon and practices that shape and inform the construction of sport – such as promoting health, social stability, national unity, and so forth – do not seek to penetrate below the surface of sport to uncover dimensions glossed over by ordinary language and practices. Rather, they begin from the assumption that the sporting world is present and open to view in its ordinary, everyday language and material practices. See also **textualisation** (2).

Empiricism, a method of knowledge in which the latter is gained by observation and experience. Empiricism is usually accompanied by the corollary that objective observations provide access to reality. A key problem faced by empiricism is that thought does not emerge solely from experience; rather thoughts provide concepts and mental categories that people use to organise and make sense of their experiences. One question that logically flows from this situation is, to what extent is reality known by our experiences or mind?

Emplotment, the story line – in Aristotle's words, 'the ordered arrangement of the incidents' – or plot structure of a narrative (for example, romance, tragedy, comedy, satire or some combination of these) that historians give to their work and which imposes coherence and meaning on the very evidence and events that reconstructionists and constructionists purport to discover.

Epistemology, a branch of philosophy concerned with questions about the possibilities for reliable knowledge. Largely ignored by reconstructionist and constructionist historians, who are more interested in **methodology**, epistemological issues have been taken up by deconstructionist historians.

Evidence, that which historians bring to bear on a particular question. While conservative reconstructionists tend to confine evidence to **sources**, there is a growing recognition across the discipline that gathering evidence is as much a process of interpretation which includes comparison, **contextualisation**, **theory** and logic.

Explanation, proffers a clear cause of some action or event in the form, 'whenever x then y', in contradistinction to an historical **interpretation** that conveys a broader understanding – such as a, b and c amount to d where d constitutes a holistic summation, a generalisation, or a **concept** – and does not set out to specify a cause. See also **teleology**.

Explanatory paradigm, a mode of practice. David Hackett Fischer formally defines an explanatory paradigm as 'an interactive structure of workable questions and the factual statements which are adduced to answer them'. Sport historians generally work within one of six explanatory paradigms: **advocacy**, comparison, causation, social change, context and new culture.

Fact, a **reconstructionist** concept assuming truth values. When defined by early reconstructionists as an accepted truth, the **concept** of fact usually sinks into a trivial statement – Stella Walsh won the women's 100-metre event at the 1932 olympic games. Rather than viewing facts as absolute truths, contemporary reconstructionists see facts as contingent truth-bearing statements – Stella Walsh was one of the most controversial female athletes in the twentieth century. In this sense, contemporary reconstructionists tend to conceptualise facts as relevances.

Faith, a belief based on minimal or weak evidence and intense **partisanship**.

Heuristic device, a general concept constructed to aid historical analysis rather than to provide a full explanation

Historical anti-realism, a perspective that historians cannot accurately represent the past.

Historical approaches, ways of addressing a task that are distinguished from each other by the questions historians ask, the kinds of evidence they use, and assumptions about **epistemology**, **theory**, **narrative** and **evidence**.

Historical materials, remnants of the past irrespective of form including official documents (reports, memoranda, letters, legislation), newspapers, advertisements, films, paintings, photographs, recordings of oral interviews. See also **sources** and **evidence**.

Historicism, an approach that regards truth as relative to historical conditions, to particular **methods**, and to the interests of the inquirer.

Historiography, a **discourse** about the past, including all the methods and concepts used in its creation.

History, (1) the object of historical research. Once referring to the sum total of all the events, including the interconnections between them, that happened in the past, history is increasingly treated by professional historians as a synonym for **historiography**. According to this framework, historians distinguish between history and '**the past**' – all that has gone before. Implicit in this distinction is an acknowledgement that there will always be a gap between history/**historiography** and **'the past'**. (2) In most European languages the word for history is the same as that used for story: French, *histoire*; Italian, *storia*; German, *Geschichte*.

Interpretation, conveys a broader understanding of some action or event of the form '*x*, *y*, and *z* amount to a *q*', without proffering a clear cause as in the case of an historical **explanation**.

Intertextuality, a deconstructionist notion that there is nothing outside texts and that all texts are based on other texts.

Irony, see **trope**.

Language, an important ingredient in deconstructonist history involved in the construction and interpretation of social reality. Deconstructionists conceptualise language as a highly structured yet radically arbitrary system that constructs meaning out of the relations or differences between signifiers, rather than out of any functional or natural relation between signifier and thing signified. Within this framework, rhetoric, **tropes**, and other figures of speech (found in both **historical materials** and historians' own texts) assume particular importance for the way they alter or modify literal meaning.

Metaphor, a highly conspicuous **trope** (found in both **historical materials** and historians' own texts) that transfers meaning from the familiar to the unfamiliar. Metaphorical relations are not 'natural' entities, but linguistic relations constructed for the social purpose of conveying meaning. In this process of construction, or transferring of meaning, metaphors create resemblances rather than finding and expressing them. Thus deconstructionists define metaphors as expressions of creativity. The most powerful metaphorical clichés are those that assume a patina of naturalness and obviousness as, for example, the view that sport is a metaphor for democracy and opportunity.

Method, a mode of procedure to obtain an object. The historical method includes the techniques and strategies employed to gather and interrogate data and to acquire knowledge about the past. The methods of **reconstructionism** focus primarily on gathering and interrogating materials from the past, those of **constructionism** include the development of concepts and theories, and those of **deconstructionism** involve deep interpretation.

Methodology, the branch of knowledge dealing with method and its application in a particular discipline or field.

Metonymy, see **trope**.

Model, a descriptive term for a strand of inquiry. Alun Munslow identifies three basic models in history: **reconstructionism**, **constructionism** and **deconstructionism**. Each model systematically frames the analysis of a core set of empirical and theoretical problems and contains its own **metaphors** and values.

Narrative, the organisation of historical material into a chronological order and a coherent story.

Objectivity, a condition stressing the presentation of neutral, value-free facts, uncoloured by personal feelings, opinions and biases, as the basis of detached history. See also **qualified objectivity**.

Ontology, the branch of philosophy dealing with the nature of being and existence. Ontology is thus concerned with such things as how we apprehend, comprehend, judge, categorise, make assumptions about, and construct reality. While **recon-**

structionism and **constructionism** rarely directly engage with ontological problems and certainly do not consider ontology as the final arbiter of truth, ontological assumptions implicitly underscore beliefs about how the discipline of history creates '**the past**'. Among deconstructionists this is a major issue and one that they explicitly put at the fore of their work.

Partisanship, the predilections, biases, values and subjectivities, whether implicit or explicit, that constitute partialities in the arguments proposed by an **advocate** or proponent.

Practical realism, the epistemological foundation of Joyce Appleby, Lynn Hunt and Margaret Jacob's theory of **qualified objectivity**. Practical realism: (1) assumes a correspondence between perceptions of the world and the world, (2) views all knowledge as provisional but accepts some as prevailing for centuries, and (3) rejects the categorical doubt of relativism.

Presentism, the doctrine that views history as a practice centred on those interests and concerns which are irrevocably linked to the present or contemporary world. The underlying object of most present-minded history is to demonstrate the historical foundations of a particular problem or issue. The recent discovery of an obesity epidemic in the Western world, for example, has precipitated a rush to investigate the origins of obesity and the perspectives of past societies.

Qualified objectivity, a theory of **objectivity**, put forward by Joyce Appleby, Lynn Hunt and Margaret Jacob, with its own epistemology known as **practical realism**. Qualified objectivity acknowledges the subjective position of the practitioner who initiates historical questions; it also insists that the realities of historical materials force historians to deal with proofs that ultimately distinguish the discipline from fiction and good history from bad history.

Reconstructionism, a **model** of historical enquiry that emphasises the use of empiricism to reconstruct the past (compared with **constructionism** that looks at patterns, processes and relationships to explain the past, and **deconstructionism** that focuses on the role of language in making history).

Reductionism, an over emphasis of one particular aspect of an **explanation** while neglecting others that do not fit the preferred explanation.

Reflexivity, a heightened state of self-awareness in which one is self-conscious and self-critical in theoretical outlook and practice. Reflexive authors make continual reference to the process by which they construct their work and are thus self-referring and self-reflecting.

Relativism, an idea that emphasises divergent bodies of knowledge, conceptual schemes, theories, values and cultures. The logical conclusion of extreme versions of relativism is that there are no fixed certainties, only differences and uncertaintities.

Rhetoric, an argument that uses techniques such as imagery and metaphors to persuade and influence others. Reconstructionists often use the term pejoratively and associate it with distorting the truth.

Scepticism, sharp questions asked of arguments and intended to expose logical errors and, in particular, **partisanship**. A hallmark of scholarly inquiry, scepticism leaves room for doubt and demands the **advocate** or proponent prove their case at every point of the argument.

Social history, a branch of history investigating social relationships and social life especially among the masses and marginalised and minority groups.

Sources, fragments of the past – such as official documents, newspapers, photographs, films and recordings of oral testimony – which, after verification, reconstructionists assume correspond with the past.

Story, a sequence of interconnected events or actions. See also **chronicle**, and **history** (2).

Synedoche, see **trope**.

Teleology, the theory that certain phenomena should be explained by their ends, aims, intentions or purposes rather than their prior causes. In history, teleological explanations usually take one of two forms. The first implies that large forces and processes are the motors of human society, driving it towards unavoidable conclusions. Reconstructionists in particular reject these (usually functional and evolutionary) forms of teleological explanation that they say are purely speculative, devoid of evidence, and a-historical. A second form of teleological explanation emanates from the assumption that human beings act with intent and purposefulness in pursuit of their goals and objectives. Hence any investigation of agents' beliefs, values and interests as explanations of actions is logically teleological.

Textualisation, (1) The placement of text into context. (2) The process whereby semiotic, social and cultural processes constitute texts (systems or structures of meaning). The process of textualisation also constitutes social subjects and cultural objects. Foucault traced this process as a form of discursive practice.

Theory, (1) A body of formal propositions that describe the nature and operation of an unobserved entity or process postulated as the cause of certain observed facts. (2) Sets of vaguely interrelated conceptual schemes better defined as models. Most constructionist sport historians use theory to guide their hypotheses and propositions, and to guide the gathering and interrogation of their **sources** and **evidence**. Constructionist sport historians rarely set out to construct theories.

The past, see **history** (1).

Traces, see **historical materials**.

Trope, a figure of speech used to create specific effects in the process of modifying the literal meaning of **language**.

Select bibliography

This bibliography comprises two sections:

1 Works relating to the practice and theory of general history, and
2 Works relating to the practice and theory of sport history.

1 Works relating to the practice and theory of general history

Abrahamson, Mark, *Functionalism* (Englewood Cliffs, NJ: Prentice-Hall, 1978).

Abrams, Philip, *Historical Sociology* (Ithaca, NY: Cornell University Press, 1982).

Alexander, Jeffrey, 'Modern, Anti, Post and Neo', *New Left Review*, 210 (1995), pp. 63–101.

Allen, Robert and Douglas Gomery, *Film History: Theory and Practice* (New York: Alfred A. Knopf, 1985).

Anderson, Perry, 'The Antinomies of Antonio Gramsci', *New Left Review*, 100 (1976/7), pp. 5–78.

Anderson, Perry, *Arguments Within English Marxism* (London: Verso Books, 1980).

Ankersmit, Frank, *Narrative Logic: A Semantic Analysis of the Historian's Language* (The Hague: Martinus Nijhoff, 1983).

Appleby, Joyce, 'The Power of History', *American Historical Review*, 103, 1 (1998), pp. 1–14.

Appleby, Joyce, Lynn Hunt and Margaret Jacob, *Telling The Truth About History* (New York: W. W. Norton, 1994).

Aron, Raymond, *Introduction to the Philosophy of History: An Essay on the Limits of Historical Objectivity*, translated by George Irwin (Boston, MA: Beacon Press, 1961).

Ashforth, Adam, *The Politics of Official Discourse in Twentieth-Century South Africa* (Oxford: Clarendon Press, 1990).

Atwood, Margaret, 'In Search of *Alias Grace*: On Writing Canadian Historical Fiction', *American Historical Review*, 103, 5 (1998), pp. 1503–16.

Ballantyne, Tony, 'Reading the Archive and Opening up the Nation-State: Colonial Knowledge in South Asia (and Beyond)', in Antoinette Burton (ed.), *After the Imperial Turn: Thinking with and through the Nation* (Durham, NC: Duke University Press, 2003), pp. 102–21.

Barraclough, Geoffrey, History and the Common Man, Presidential address to the Historical Association, London, 12 April 1966. The Historical Association, pamphlet, pp. 15.

Barthes, Roland, *Mythologies*, translated by Annette Lavers (Frogmore: Paladin, 1973).

Barzun, Jacques and Henry Graff, *The Modern Researcher*, third edition (New York: Harcourt Brace Jovanovich, 1977).

Bataille, Georges, 'The Notion of Expenditure', in A. Stoekl (ed.), *Visions of Excess: Selected Writings, 1927–39* (Minneapolis, MN: University of Minnesota Press, 1932), pp. 116–29.

Bearman, David, 'Electronic Record-keeping, Social Memory and Democracy', in Carolyn Hamilton, Verne Harris, Jane Taylor, Michele Pickover, Graeme Reid and Razia Saleh (eds), *Refiguring the Archive* (Cape Town: David Philip, 2002), pp. 323–31.

Beer, Samuel, 'Causal Explanation and Imaginative Re-enactment', History and Theory, 3, 1 (1963), pp. 6–29.

Berkhofer, Robert, *Beyond the Great Story: History as Text and Discourse* (Cambridge, MA: Harvard University Press, 1995).

Berman, Marshall, *All that is Solid Melts Into Air* (Harmondsworth: Penguin, 1982).

Best, Steven and Douglas Kellner, *Postmodern Theory: Critical Interrogations* (Basingstoke: Macmillan, 1991).

Black, Jeremy and Donald MacRaild, *Studying History* (Basingstoke: Macmillan, 1997).

Blau, Peter (ed.), *Approaches to the Study of Social Structure* (New York: The Free Press, 1975).

Bonnell, Victoria, 'Theory, Concepts and Comparison in Historical Sociology', Comparative Studies in Society and History, 22, 2 (1980), pp. 156–73.

Bonnell, Victoria and Lynn Hunt, 'Introduction', in Bonnell and Hunt (eds), *Beyond the Cultural Turn: New Directions in the Study of Society and Culture* (Berkeley, CA: University of California Press, 1999), pp. 1–32.

Bottomore, Tom, 'Structure and History', in Peter Blau (ed.), *Approaches to the Study of Social Structure* (New York: The Free Press, 1975), pp. 159–71.

Braudel, Fernand, *Capitalism and Material Life, 1400–1800* (New York: Harper & Row, 1973).

Braudel, Fernand, *On History* (Chicago, IL: University of Chicago Press, 1980).

Brodbeck, May, 'Methodological Individualisms: Definition and Reduction', in William Dray (ed.), *Philosophical Analysis and History* (New York: Harper & Row, 1966), pp. 297–329.

Burke, Peter, *History and Social Theory* (Cambridge: Polity Press, 1992).

Burke, Peter, *Eyewitnessing: The Uses of Images as Historical Evidence* (London: Reaktion Books, 2001).

Burton, Antoinette, *Dwelling in the Archive: Women Writing House, Home and History in Late Colonial India* (Oxford: Oxford University Press, 2003).

Callinicos, Alex, *Making History* (Cambridge: Polity Press, 1988).

Callinicos, Alex, *Against Postmodernism: A Marxist Critique* (Cambridge: Polity Press, 1989).

Callinicos, Alex, *Theories and Narratives: Reflections on the Philosophy of History* (Cambridge: Polity Press, 1995).

Carl, LeRoy, 'Editorial Cartoons Fail to Reach Many Readers', Journalism Quarterly, 45, 3 (1968), pp. 533–5.

Carl, LeRoy, 'Political Cartoons: "Ink Blots" of the Editorial Page', Journal of Popular Culture, 4 (1970), pp. 39–45.

Carr, Edward, *What Is History?*, second edition (Harmondsworth: Penguin, 1990).

Carr, David, 'Narrative and the Real World: An Argument for Continuity', History and Theory, 25, 2 (1986), pp. 117–31.

Carrard, Philippe, *Poetics of the New History: French Historical Discourse from Braudel to Chartier* (Baltimore, MD: The Johns Hopkins University Press, 1992).

Carroll, David, 'Poetics, Theory, and the Defence of History', Clio, 22, 3 (1993), pp. 273–89.

Christidou, Vasilia, Kostas Dimopoulos and Vasilis Koulaidis, 'Constructing Social Representations of Science and Technology: The Role of Metaphors in the Press and the Popular Scientific Magazines', Public Understanding of Science, 13, 4 (2004), pp. 347–62.

Cohen, Morris, 'Causation and Its Application to History', *Journal of the History of Ideas*, 3, 1 (1942), pp. 12–29.

Collingwood, R. G., *An Autobiography* (London: Oxford University Press, 1939).

Collingwood, R. G., *The Idea of History* (London: Oxford University Press, 1961).

Collingwood, R. G., *The Principles of History* (Oxford: Oxford University Press, 1999).

Confino, Alon, 'Collective Memory and Cultural History: Problems of Method', *American Historical Review*, 102, 5 (1997), pp. 1386–403.

Corfield, Penelope, 'History and the Challenge of Gender History', *Rethinking History*, 1, 3 (1997), pp. 241–58.

Corfield, Penelope, 'Review Article: The State of History', *Journal of Contemporary History*, 36, 1 (2001), pp. 153–61.

Coser, Lewis and Robert Nisbet, 'Merton and the Contemporary Mind: An Affectionate Dialogue', in Coser (ed.), *The Idea of Social Structure: Papers in Honor of Robert K. Merton* (New York: Harcourt Brace Jovanovich, 1975), pp. 3–10.

Cousins, Mark, 'The Practice of Historical Investigation', in Derek Attridge, Geoff Bennington and Robert Young (eds), *Structuralism and the Question of History* (Cambridge: Cambridge University Press, 1989), pp. 126–36.

Davis, Natalie Zemon, *Fiction in the Archives: Pardon Tales and Their Tellers in Sixteenth-Century France* (Stanford, CA: Stanford University Press, 1987).

Dean, Mitchell, *Critical and Effective Histories: Foucault's Methods and Historical Sociology* (London: Routledge, 1994).

De Botton, Alain, *Status Anxiety* (London: Hamish Hamilton, 2004).

De Hart, Jane, 'Oral Sources and Contemporary History: Dispelling Old Assumptions', *Journal of American History* 80, 2 (1993), pp. 582–95.

Demos, John, 'In Search of Reasons for Historians to Read Novels', *American Historical Review*, 103, 5 (1998), pp. 1526–9.

Denzin, Norman, *The Research Act*, third edition (Englewood Cliffs, NJ: Prentice Hall, 1989).

Derrida, Jacques, 'Archive Fever in South Africa', in Carolyn Hamilton, Verne Harris, Jane Taylor, Michele Pickover, Graeme Reid and Razia Saleh (eds), *Refiguring the Archive* (Cape Town: David Philip, 2002), pp. 38–80.

Dilthey, Wilhelm, 'The Understanding of Other Persons and Their Life-Expressions', in Patrick Gardiner (ed.), *Theories of History* (Glencoe, IL: The Free Press, 1959), pp. 213–25.

Donaldson, Mike, 'What is Hegemonic Masculinity?', *Theory and Society*, 22, 5 (1993), pp. 643–57.

Dray, William, *Philosophy of History* (Englewood Cliffs, NJ: Prentice-Hall, 1964).

Dray, William, '"Explaining What" in History', in Patrick Gardiner (ed.), *Theories of History* (Glencoe, IL: The Free Press, 1959), pp. 403–8.

Durkheim, Emile, *The Rules of Sociological Method*, eighth edition (Glencoe, IL: Free Press, 1964).

Eaglestone, Robert, *Postmodernism and Holocaust Denial* (Cambridge: Icon, 2001).

Elton, Geoffrey, *Return to Essentials: Some Reflections on the Present State of Historical Study* (Cambridge: Cambridge University Press, 1991).

Elton, Geoffrey, *The Practice of History*, second edition (Oxford: Basil Blackwell, 2002).

Evans, Richard, *In Defence of History* (London: Granta Books, 1997).

Fairburn, Miles, *Social History: Problems, Strategies and Methods* (New York: St Martins Press, 1999).

Featherstone, Mike, 'The Body in Consumer Culture', *Theory, Culture and Society*, 1, 2 (1982), pp. 18–33.

Ferleger, Louis and Richard Steckel, 'Faulkner's South: Is There Truth in Fiction?', in Elizabeth Fox-Genovese and Elisabeth Lasch-Quinn (eds), *Reconstructing History: The Emergence of a New Historical Society* (New York: Routledge, 1999), pp. 361–9.

Fischer, David Hackett, *Historians' Fallacies: Toward a Logic of Historical Thought* (New York: Harper & Row, 1970).

Fish, Stanley, 'One University Under God?', *Chronicle of Higher Education*, 7 January 2005.

Foucault, Michel, *Discipline and Punish: The Birth of the Prison*, translated by Alan Sheridan (Harmondsworth: Penguin, 1977).

Foucault, Michel, *The History of Sexuality: An Introduction*, translated by Robert Hurley (Harmondsworth: Penguin, 1981).

Foucault, Michel, *The Archaelogy of Knowledge*, translated by A. M. Sheridan-Smith (London: Routledge, 2002).

Gallie, W. B., *Philosophy and Historical Understanding* (London: Chatto & Windus, 1964).

Gardiner, Patrick (ed.), *Theories of History* (Glencoe, IL: The Free Press, 1959).

Gardiner, Patrick, *The Nature of Historical Explanation* (London: Oxford University Press, 1968).

Gay, Peter, *Style in History* (New York: Basic Books, 1974).

Geertz, Clifford, 'Deep Play: Notes on the Balinese Cockfight', *Dædalus*, 101 (1972), pp. 1–37.

Gergen, Kenneth, 'Narrative, Moral Identity and Historical Consciousness: A Social Constructionist Account' (2004), http://www.Swarthmore.edu/SocSci/kgergen1/text3.html.

Giddens, Anthony, *Sociology: A Brief But Critical Introduction*, second edition (Basingstoke: Macmillan, 1986).

Giddens, Anthony, *Social Theory and Modern Sociology* (Cambridge: Polity Press, 1987).

Ginzburg, Carlo, 'Checking the Evidence: The Judge and the Historian', in James Chandler, Arnold Davidson and Harry Harootunian, *Questions of Evidence: Proof, Practice, and Persuasion across the Disciplines* (Chicago, IL: University of Chicago Press, 1991), pp. 290–303.

Goode, William, *The Celebration of Heroes* (Berkeley, CA: University of California Press, 1978).

Gordon, Colin (ed.), *Michel Foucault: Power/Knowledge, Selected Interviews and Other Writings 1972–1977* (Brighton: Harvester Press, 1980).

Gosse, Van, Review of Arthur Marwick *The Sixties* (Oxford: Oxford University Press, 1998), *Journal of American History*, 86, 3 (1999), pp. 1311–12.

Gottschalk, Louis, *Understanding History: A Primer of Historical Method*, second edition (New York: Alfred A. Knopf, 1969).

Grafton, Anthony, *The Footnote: A Curious History* (London: Faber and Faber, 1997).

Graubard, Stephen, 'Preface', *Dædalus*, 101 (1972), pp. v-viii.

Grew, Raymond, 'The Case for Comparing Histories', *American Historical Review*, 85, 4 (1980), pp. 763–78.

Halbwachs, Maurice, *The Collective Memory*, translated by Francis Ditter and Vida Yazdi Ditter (New York: Harper Colophon, 1980).

Hamilton, Carolyn, '"Living by Fluidity": Oral Histories, Material Custodies and the Politics of Archiving', in Carolyn Hamilton, Verne Harris, Jane Taylor, Michele Pickover, Graeme Reid and Razia Saleh (eds), *Refiguring the Archive* (Cape Town: David Philip, 2002), pp. 209–27.

Hamilton, Carolyn, Verne Harris, Jane Taylor, Michele Pickover, Graeme Reid and Razia Saleh (eds), *Refiguring the Archive* (Cape Town: David Philip, 2002).

Harootunian, Harry, *History's Disquiet: Modernity, Cultural Practice, and the Questions of Everyday Life* (New York: Columbia University Press, 2000).

Harris, Verne, 'A Shaft of Darkness: Derrida in the Archive', in Carolyn Hamilton, Verne Harris, Jane Taylor, Michele Pickover, Graeme Reid and Razia Saleh (eds), *Refiguring the Archive* (Cape Town: David Philip, 2002), pp. 61–81.

Harris, Verne, 'The Archival Sliver: A Perspective on the Construction of Social Memory in Archives and the Transition from Apartheid to Democracy', in Carolyn Hamilton, Verne Harris, Jane Taylor, Michele Pickover, Graeme Reid and Razia Saleh (eds), *Refiguring the Archive* (Cape Town: David Philip, 2002), pp. 135–51.

Hart, Herbert and Tony Honoré, *Causation in the Law* (Oxford: Clarendon Press, 1959).

Hartsock, Nancy, 'Foucault on Power: A Theory For Women?', in Charles Lemert (ed.), *Social Theory: The Multicultural and Classic Readings* (Boulder, CO: Westview Press, 1993), pp. 545–54.

Harvey, David, *The Condition of Postmodernity: An Enquiry into the Origins of Cultural Change* (Oxford: Basil Blackwell, 1989).

Haskell, Thomas, *Objectivity Is Not Neutrality: Explanatory Schemes in History* (Baltimore, MD: The Johns Hopkins University Press, 1998).

Hayes, Patricia, Jeremy Silvester and Wolfram Hartmann, ' "Picturing the Past" in Namibia: The Visual Archive and its Energies', in Carolyn Hamilton, Verne Harris, Jane Taylor, Michele Pickover, Graeme Reid and Razia Saleh (eds), *Refiguring the Archive* (Cape Town: David Philip, 2002), pp. 103–33.

Hempel, Carl, 'The Function of General Laws in History', in Patrick Gardiner (ed.), *Theories of History* (Glencoe, IL: The Free Press, 1959), pp. 344–56.

Herman, Edward and Noam Chomsky, *Manufacturing Consent: The Political Economy of the Mass Media* (New York: Pantheon Books, 1988).

Heywood, Ian, 'Culture Made, Found and Lost', in Chris Jenks (ed.), *Cultural Reproduction* (London: Routlege, 1993), pp. 104–19.

Hitchens, Christopher, Review of Arthur Marwick *The Sixties* (Oxford: Oxford University Press, 1998), *Times Literary Supplement*, 13 November 1998 (on-line subscriber archive).

Hoare, Quintin and Geoffrey Nowell Smith (eds), *Selections from the Prison Notebooks of Antonio Gramsci* (London: Lawrence and Wishart, 1971).

Hobsbawm, Eric, 'The Revival of Narrative: Some Comments', *Past and Present*, 86 (1980), pp. 3–8.

Hobsbawm, Eric, 'The Contribution of History to Social Science', *International Social Science Journal*, 33, 4 (1981), pp. 624–40.

Hobsbawm, Eric, 'Mass-producing Traditions: Europe, 1870–1914', in Hobsbawm and Terence Ranger (eds), *The Invention of Tradition* (Cambridge: Cambridge University Press, 1983), pp. 263–307.

Hobsbawm, Eric, *On History* (London: Abacus, 1998).

Howell, Martha and Walter Prevenier, *From Reliable Sources: An Introduction to Historical Methods* (Ithaca, NY: Cornell University Press, 2001).

Hudson, Pat, *History by Numbers: An Introduction to Quantitative Approaches* (London: Arnold, 2000).

Hunt, Lynn, 'Introduction: History, Culture, and Text', in Hunt (ed.), *The New Cultural History* (Berkeley, CA: University of California Press, 1989), pp. 1–22.

Hunt, Lynn, ' "No Longer an Evenly Flowing River": Time, History, and the Novel', *American Historical Review*, 103, 5 (1998), pp. 1517–21.

Irwin, William, *'What Is An Allusion?'*, *Journal of Aesthetics and Art Criticism*, 59, 3 (2001), pp. 287–97.

Irwin, William, 'Against Intertextuality', *Philosophy and Literature*, 28, 2 (2004), pp. 227–42.

Jameson, Fredric, 'Postmdernism, or The Cultural Logic of Late Capitalism', *New Left Review*, 146 (1984), pp. 53–91.

Jameson, Fredric, *Postmodernism, or The Cultural Logic of Late Capitalism* (London: Verso, 1991).

Jenkins, Keith, *Re-Thinking History* (London: Routledge, 1991).

Jenkins, Keith, *On "What is History?" From Carr and Elton to Rorty and White* (London: Routledge, 1995).

Jenkins, Keith, *Refiguring History: New Thoughts on an Old Discipline* (London: Routledge, 2003).

Jenkins, Keith and Alun Munslow (eds), *The Nature of History Reader* (London: Routledge, 2004).

Jenks, Chris, *Culture* (London: Routledge, 1993).

Jones, Gareth Stedman, 'History: The Poverty of Empiricism', in Robin Blackburn (ed.), *Ideology in Social Science: Readings in Critical Social Theory* (London: Fontana, 1972), pp. 96–115.

Jones, Gareth Stedman, 'From Historical Sociology to Theoretical History', *British Journal of Sociology*, 27 (1976), pp. 295–305.

Jordanova, Ludmilla, *History in Practice* (London: Arnold, 2000).

Joyce, Patrick, 'The End of Social History?', *Social History*, 20, 1 (1995), pp. 73–91.

Judt, Tony, 'A Clown in Regal Purple: Social History and the Historians', *History Workshop*, 7 (1979), pp. 66–94.

Kellner, Hans, 'A Bedrock of Order: Hayden White's Linguistic Humanism', *History and Theory*, 19, 4 (1980), pp. 1–29.

Kellner, Hans, *Language and Historical Representation: Getting the Story Crooked* (Madison, WI: The University of Wisconsin Press, 1989).

Knapp, Peter, 'Can Social Theory Escape From History: Views of History in Social Science', *History and Theory*, 24 (1984), pp. 34–52.

Kneller, George, *Science as a Human Endeavour* (New York: Columbia University Press, 1978).

Kramer, Lloyd, 'Literature, Criticism, and Historical Imagination: The Literary Challenge of Hayden White and Dominick LaCapra', in Lynn Hunt (ed.), *The New Cultural History* (Berkeley, CA: University of California Press, 1989), pp. 97–128.

Kumar, Krishan, *From Post-Industrial to Post-Modern Society: New Theories of the Contemporary World* (Oxford: Basil Blackwell, 1995).

Lakoff, George and Mark Johnson, *Metaphors We Live By* (Chicago, IL: University of Chicago Press, 1980).

Leary, Mark, and Robin Kowalski, 'Impression Management: A Literature Review and Two-Component Model', *Psychology Bulletin*, 107, 1 (1990), pp. 34–47.

Lincoln, Yvonna and Egon Guba, 'Paradigmatic Controversies, Contradictions, and Emerging Confluences', in Norman Denzin and Yvonna Lincoln (eds), *Handbook of Qualitative Research*, second edition (London: Sage, 2000), pp. 163–88.

Lloyd, Christopher, *Explanations in Social History* (Oxford: Basil Blackwell, 1988).

Lloyd, Christopher, *The Structures of History* (Oxford: Basil Blackwell, 1993).

Lloyd, Christopher, 'For Realism and Against the Inadequacies of Common Sense: A Response to Arthur Marwick', *Journal of Contemporary History*, 31, 1 (1996), pp. 191–207.

Lowenthal, David, *The Past is a Foreign Country* (Cambridge: Cambridge University Press, 1985).

Lukes, Steven, *Individualism* (Oxford: Blackwell, 1973).

Mandelbaum, Maurice, 'Causal Analysis in History', *Journal of the History of Ideas*, 3, 1 (1942), pp. 30–50.

Mandelbaum, Maurice, 'A Note on History as Narrative', *History and Theory*, 6, 3 (1967), pp. 413–19.

Markus, Andrew, 'Factory of Death', *The Age* (Melbourne), 29 January 2005.

Marwick, Arthur, *The Nature of History*, second edition (London: Macmillan, 1981).

Marwick, Arthur, 'Two Approaches to Historical Study: The Metaphysical (Including Postmodernism) and the Historical', *Journal of Contemporary History*, 30, 1 (1995), pp. 5–35.

Marwick, Arthur, *The Sixties: Cultural Revolution in Britain, France, Italy, and the United States, c.1958–c.1974* (Oxford: Oxford University Press, 1998).

Marwick, Arthur, *The New Nature of History: Knowledge, Evidence, Language* (Basingstoke: Palgrave, 2001).

Marx, Karl, 'The Eighteenth Brumaire of Louis Bonaparte', in David McLellan (ed.), *Karl Marx Selected Writings* (Oxford: Oxford University Press, 1977), pp. 300–25.

Mbembe, Achille, 'The Power of the Archive and its Limits', in Carolyn Hamilton, Verne Harris, Jane Taylor, Michele Pickover, Graeme Reid and Razia Saleh (eds), *Refiguring the Archive* (Cape Town: David Philip, 2002), pp. 19–26.

McCullagh, C. Behan, 'Colligation and Classification in History', *History and Theory*, 17, 3 (1978), pp. 267–84.

McCullagh, C. Behan, *The Logic of History: Putting Postmodernism in Perspective* (London: Routledge, 2004).

McDonald, Terrence (ed.), *The Historic Turn in the Human Sciences* (Ann Arbor MI: University of Michigan Press, 1996).

McLuhan, Marshall, *Understanding Media: The Extensions of Man* (New York: McGraw-Hill, 1964).

Megill, Allan, 'The Reception of Foucault by Historians', *Journal of the History of Ideas*, 48, 1 (1987), pp. 117–41.

Merton, Robert, *Social Theory and Social Structure*, second edition (Glencoe, IL: Free Press, 1957).

Mills, C. Wright, *The Sociological Imagination* (New York: Oxford University Press, 1959).

Mink, Louis, 'The Autonomy of Historical Understanding', *History and Theory*, 5, 1 (1965), pp. 24–47.

Mink, Louis, 'History and Fiction as Modes of Comprehension', *New Literary History*, 1, 3 (1970), pp. 541–58.

Moran, Joe, 'History, Memory and the Everyday', *Rethinking History*, 8, 1 (2004), pp. 51–68.

Mott, Frank Luther, *American Journalism*, third edition (New York: Macmillan, 1962).

Mouzelis, Nicos, *Sociological Theory: What Went Wrong?* (London: Routledge, 1995).

Munslow, Alun, *Deconstructing History* (London: Routledge, 1997).

Munslow, Alun, *The Routledge Companion to Historical Studies* (London: Routledge, 2000).

Munslow, Alun and Robert Rosenstone (eds), *Experiments in Rethinking History* (London, Routledge, 2004).

Murphy, John, 'The Voice of Memory: History, Autobiography and Oral Memory', *Historical Studies*, 22, 87 (1986), pp. 157–75.

Novick, Peter, *That Noble Dream: The 'Objectivity Question' and the American Historical Profession* (Cambridge: Cambridge University Press, 1988).

Nuttall, Sarah, 'Literature and the Archive: The Biography of Texts', in Carolyn Hamilton, Verne Harris, Jane Taylor, Michele Pickover, Graeme Reid and Razia Saleh (eds), *Refiguring the Archive* (Cape Town: David Philip, 2002), pp. 282–99.

Oakeshott, Michael, 'Historical Continuity and Causal Analysis', in William Dray (ed.), *Philosophical Analysis and History* (New York: Harper & Row, 1966), pp. 193–212.

Palmer, Bryan, Review of Roy Rosenzweig, *Eight Hours For What We Will* (Cambridge: Cambridge University Press, 1983) and Francis Couvares, *The Remaking of Pittsburgh* (Albany, NY: State University of New York Press, 1984), *Social History*, 10, 3 (1985), pp. 400–4.

Palmer, Bryan, *Descent into Discourse: The Reification of Language and the Writing of Social History* (Philadelphia, PA: Temple University Press, 1990).

Parsons, Talcott, 'The Present Status of "Structural-Functional" Theory in Sociology', in Lewis Coser (ed.), *The Idea of Social Structure: Papers in Honor of Robert K. Merton* (New York: Harcourt Brace Jovanovich, 1975), pp. 67–83.

Passerini, Luisa, Review of Arthur Marwick, *The Sixties* (Oxford: Oxford University Press, 1998), *American Historical Review*, 104, 5 (1999), pp. 1642–3.

Perry, Matt, *Marxism and History* (Basingstoke: Palgrave, 2002).

Philips, Susan, 'Evidentary Standards for American Trials: Just the Facts', in Judith Irvine and Jane Hill (eds), *Responsibility and Evidence in Oral Discourse* (Cambridge: Cambridge University Press, 1992), pp. 248–59.

Pierson, Ruth Roach, 'Experience, Difference, Dominance and Voice in the Writing of Canadian Women's History', in Karen Offen, Ruth Roach Pierson and Jane Rendall (eds), *Writing Women's History: International Perspectives* (London: Macmillan, 1991), pp. 79–106.

Popper, Karl, *Conjectures and Refutations: The Growth of Scientific Knowledge* (London: Routledge and Kegan Paul, 1963).

Postan, Michael, *Fact and Relevance: Essays on Historical Method* (Cambridge: Cambridge University Press, 1971).

Pratt, Mary Louise, *Imperial Eyes: Travel Writing and Transculturation* (London: Routledge, 1992).

Ramazanoglu, Caroline, *Up Against Foucault: Explorations of Some Tensions Between Foucault and Feminism* (London: Routledge, 1989).

Ricoeur, Paul, *Time and Narrative*, volume 1, translated by Kathleen McLaughlin and David Pellauer (Chicago, IL: University of Chicago Press, 1983).

Ricoeur, Paul, *Time and Narrative*, volume 2, translated by Kathleen McLaughlin and David Pellauer (Chicago, IL: University of Chicago Press, 1984).

Ricoeur, Paul, *Time and Narrative*, volume 3, translated by Kathleen Blamey and David Pellauer (Chicago, IL: University of Chicago Press, 1985).

Rigney, Ann, 'Narrativity and Historical Representation', *Poetics Today*, 12, 3 (1991), pp. 591–605.

Ritter, Harry, *Dictionary of Concepts in History* (Westport, CT: Greenwood Press, 1986).

Robertson, James Oliver, *American Myth, American Reality* (New York: Hill & Wang, 1980).

Rorty, Richard, *Consequences of Pragmatism (Essays: 1972–1980)* (Brighton: Harvester Press, 1982).

Rosenstone, Robert (ed.), *Revisioning History: Film and The Construction of a New Past* (Princeton, NJ: Princeton University Press, 1995).

Rosenzweig, Roy, *Eight Hours For What We Will: Workers and Leisure in an Industrial City, 1870–1920* (Cambridge: Cambridge University Press, 1983).

Samuel, Raphael, 'History and Theory', in Samuel (ed.), *People's History and Socialist Theory* (London: Routledge & Kegan Paul, 1981), pp. xl–lvi.

Sawicki, Jana, *Disciplining Foucault: Feminism, Power, and the Body* (London: Routledge, 1991).

Sayer, Andrew, *Method in Social Science: A Realist Approach*, second edition (London: Routlege, 1992).

Scott, Joan, *Gender and the Politics of History* (New York: Columbia University Press, 1988).

Scott, Joan, 'Women's History', in Peter Burke (ed.), *New Perspectives on Historical Writing*, second edition (Cambridge: Polity Press, 2001), pp. 43–70.

Sharpe, Jim, 'History from Below', in Peter Burke (ed.), *New Perspectives on Historical Writing*, second edition (Cambridge: Polity Press, 2001), pp. 25–42.

Shilling, Chris, *The Body and Social Theory* (London: Sage, 1993).

Skocpol, Theda, *States and Social Revolutions: A Comparative Analysis of France, Russia and China* (Cambridge: Cambridge University Press, 1979).

Smith, Dennis, *The Rise of Historical Sociology* (Cambridge: Polity Press, 1991).

Smith, Geoffrey Nowell, 'Common Sense', *Radical Philosophy*, 7 (1974), pp. 15–16.

Sombart, Werner, 'Economic Theory and Economic History', *The Economic History Review*, 2, 1 (1929), pp. 1–19.

Southgate, Beverley, *History: What and Why? Ancient, Modern, and Postmodern Perspectives*, second edition (London: Routledge, 2001).

Stanford, Michael, *A Companion to the Study of History* (Oxford: Blackwell, 1994).

Stearns, Peter, 'Goals in History Teaching', *International Review of History Education*, 2 (1998), pp. 281–93.

Steedman, Carolyn, *Landscape For A Good Woman* (London: Virago, 1989).

Steedman, Carolyn, 'Something She Called a Fever: Michelet, Derrida, and Dust', *American Historical Review*, 106, 4 (2001), pp. 1159–80.

Stinchcombe, Arthur, *Theoretical Methods in Social History* (New York: Academic Press, 1978).

Stoler, Ann, 'Colonial Archives and the Arts of Governance: On the Content in the Form', in Carolyn Hamilton, Verne Harris, Jane Taylor, Michele Pickover, Graeme Reid and Razia Saleh (eds), *Refiguring the Archive* (Cape Town: David Philip, 2002), pp. 83–101.

Stone, Lawrence, 'The Revival of Narrative: Reflections on a New Old History', *Past and Present*, 85 (1979), pp. 3–24.

Stone, Lawrence, 'History and Post-Modernism', *Past and Present*, 135 (1992), pp. 187–94.

Tapp, E. J., 'Some Aspects of Causation in History', *Journal of Philosophy*, 49, 3 (1952), pp. 67–79.

Tatz, Colin, *With Intent to Destroy: Reflecting on Genocide* (London: Verso, 2003).

Taylor, Jane, 'Holdings: Refiguring the Archive', in Carolyn Hamilton, Verne Harris, Jane Taylor, Michele Pickover, Graeme Reid and Razia Saleh (eds), *Refiguring the Archive* (Cape Town: David Philip, 2002), pp. 243–81.

The Irving Judgement, http://www.nizkor.org/hweb/people/i/irving-david/judgment-01.html.

Thelen, David (ed.), 'The Movie Maker as Historian: Conversations with Ken Burns', *Journal of American History*, 81, 3 (1994), pp. 1031–50.

Thompson, Paul, *The Voice of the Past: Oral History*, third edition (Oxford: Oxford University Press, 2000).

Thompson, E. P., 'On History, Sociology and Historical Relevance', *British Journal of Sociology*, 27, 3 (1976), pp. 387–402.

Thompson, E. P., 'Anthropology and the Discipline of Historical Context', *Midland History*, 3 (1972), pp. 41–55.

Thompson, E. P., *The Poverty of Theory: Or an Orrery of Errors* (London: Merlin, 1995).

Thomson, Alistair, 'Fifty Years On: An International Perspective on Oral History', *Journal of American History*, 85, 2 (1998), pp. 581–95.

Toews, John, 'Intellectual History After the Linguistic Turn: The Autonomy of Meaning and the Irreducibility of Experience', *American Historical Review*, 92 (1987), pp. 879–907.

Tosh, John, *The Pursuit of History: Aims, Methods and New Directions in the Study of Modern History*, second edition (London: Longman, 1991).

Tosh, John, *The Pursuit of History: Aims, Methods and New Directions in the Study of Modern History*, third edition (London: Longman, 2000).

Turner, Bryan, *The Body and Society* (Cambridge: Basil Blackwell, 1984).

Vansina, Jan, *Oral Tradition as History* (London: James Currey, 1985).

Vincent, John, *An Intelligent Person's Guide to History* (London: Gerald Duckworth, 1995).

Walsh, William, *An Introduction to the Philosophy of History*, third edition (London: Hutchinson, 1967).

Walsh, William, 'Colligatory Concepts in History', in Patrick Gardiner (ed.), *The Philosophy of History* (Oxford: Oxford University Press, 1974), pp. 127–44.

Warren, John, *History and the Historians* (London: Hodder & Stoughton, 1999).

Waters, Malcolm, *Modern Sociological Theory* (London: Sage, 1994).

Weber, Max, *The Methodology of the Social Sciences*, translated and edited by Edward Shils and Henry Finch (New York: Free Press, 1949).

Webb, Clive, Review of Arthur Marwick *The Sixties* (Oxford: Oxford University Press, 1998), *History Today*, 49, 1 (1999), p. 54.

White, Hayden, *Metahistory: The Historical Imagination in Nineteenth-century Europe* (Baltimore, MD: The Johns Hopkins University Press, 1973).

White, Hayden, *Tropics of Discourse: Essays in Cultural Criticism* (Baltimore, MD: The Johns Hopkins University Press, 1978).

White, Hayden, 'The Value of Narrativity in the Representation of Reality', in W. J. T. Mitchell (ed.), *On Narrative* (Chicago, IL: University of Chicago Press, 1981), pp. 3–25.

White, Hayden, *The Content of the Form: Narrative Discourse and Historical Representation* (Baltimore, MD: The Johns Hopkins University Press, 1987).

White, Hayden, 'Response to Arthur Marwick', *Journal of Contemporary History*, 30, 2 (1995), pp. 233–46.

White, Luise, *Speaking With Vampires: Rumor and History in Colonial Africa* (Berkeley, CA: University of California Press, 2000).

White, Morton, *Foundations of Historical Knowledge* (New York: Harper & Row, 1965).

Whitton, Evan, *Trial by Voodoo: Why the Law Defeats Justice and Democracy* (Sydney: Random House, 1994).

Williams, Raymond, *Marxism and Literature* (Oxford: Oxford University Press, 1977).

Wilson, Norman, *History in Crisis: Recent Directions in Historiography* (Upper Saddle River, NJ: Prentice Hall, 1999).

Windschuttle, Keith, *The Killing Of History* (Sydney: Macleay Press, 1994).

Wood, Allen, 'Hegel and Marxism', in Frederick Beiser (ed.), *The Cambridge Companion to Hegel* (Cambridge: Cambridge University Press, 1993), pp. 414–44.

Wood, Gordon, 'Novel History', *New York Review of Books*, 27 June 1991, pp. 12–16.

Zagorin, Perez, 'Historiography and Postmodernism: Reconsiderations', *History and Theory*, 29, 3 (1990), pp. 263–74.

Zeldin, Theodore, 'Social History and Total History', *Journal of Social History*, 10, 2 (1976), pp. 237–45.

2 Works relating to the practice and theory of sport history

Adelman, Melvin, 'The Role of the Sport Historian', *Quest*, 12 (1969), pp. 61–5.
Adelman, Melvin, 'Academicians and American Athletics: A Decade of Progress', *Journal of Sport History*, 10, 1 (1983), pp. 80–106.
Adelman, Melvin, *A Sporting Time: New York City and the Rise of Modern Athletics, 1820–1870* (Urbana, IL: University of Illinois Press, 1986).
Alexander, Charles, *Breaking the Slump: Baseball in the Depression Era* (New York: Columbia University Press, 2002).
Allison, Lincoln, 'The Changing Context of Sporting Life', in Allison (ed.), *The Changing Politics of Sport* (Manchester: Manchester University Press, 1993), pp. 1–14.
Andrews, David, 'Sport and the Masculine Hegemony of the Modern Nation: Welsh Rugby, Culture and Society, 1890–1914', in John Nauright and Tim Chandler (eds), *Making Men: Rugby and Masculine Identity* (London: Frank Cass,1996), pp. 50–69.
Andrews, David, 'Dead and Alive?: Sports History in the Late Capitalist Moment', *Sporting Traditions*, 16, 1 (1999), pp. 73–83.
Andrews, David, 'Posting-up: French Post-structuralism and the Critical Analysis of Contemporary Sporting Culture', in Jay Coakley and Eric Dunning (eds), *Handbook of Sports Studies* (London: Sage, 2000), pp. 106–37.
Andrews, David and Jeremy Howell, 'Transforming Into a Tradition: Rugby and the Making of Imperial Wales, 1890–1914', in Alan Ingham and John Loy (eds), *Sport in Social Development: Traditions, Transitions and Transformations* (Champaign, IL: Human Kinetics, 1993), pp. 77–96.
Archer Robert and Antoine Bouillon, *The South African Game: Sport and Racism* (London: Zed Press, 1982).
Bailey, Philip, 'W. G. Grace Revisited', *The Cricket Statistician*, 58 (Summer 1987).
Bairner, Alan, *Sport, Nationalism, and Globalization: European and North American Perspectives* (Albany, NY: State University of New York Press, 2001).
Baker, Aaron, *Contesting Identities: Sports in American Film* (Urbana, IL: University of Illinois Press, 2003).
Baker, Norman, 'Whose Hegemony? The Origins of the Amateur Ethos in Nineteenth Century English Society', *Sport in History*, 24, 1 (2004), pp. 1–20.
Baker, William, 'William Webb Ellis and the Origins of Rugby Football: The Life and Death of a Victorian Myth', *Albion*, 13, 2 (1981), pp. 117–30.
Baker, William, 'The State of British Sport History, *Journal of Sport History*, 10, 1 (1983), pp. 53–66.
Baker, William, *Sports in the Western World* (Urbana, IL: University of Illinois Press, 1988).
Baker, William, *Jesse Owens: An American Life* (New York: The Free Press, 1986).
Bale, John, 'Capturing "The African" Body? Visual Images and "Imaginative Sports"', *Journal of Sport History*, 25, 2 (1998), pp. 234–51.
Bale, John, 'The Rhetoric of Running', in Jørn Hansen and Niels Kayser Nielsen (eds), *Sports, Body and Health* (Odense: Odense University Press, 2000), pp. 123–31.
Bale, John, 'Scientific and Romantic: The Rhetorics of the First Four-Minute Mile', *The International Journal of the History of Sport*, 21, 1 (2004), pp. 118–26.
Bale, John, 'The Mysterious Professor Jokl', in John Bale, Mette Christensen and Gertrude Pfister (eds), *Writing Lives in Sport: Biographies, Life-histories and Methods* (Aarhus: Aarhus University Press, 2004), pp. 25–39.
Bale, John and Mike Cronin (eds), *Sport and Postcolonialism* (Oxford: Berg, 2003).

Bale, John, Mette Christensen and Gertrude Pfister, 'Introduction', in Bale, Christensen and Pfister (eds), *Writing Lives in Sport: Biographies, Life-histories and Methods* (Aarhus: Aarhus University Press, 2004), pp. 9–16.

Ball, Donald and John Loy (eds), *Sport and Social Order* (Reading, MA: Addison-Wesley, 1975).

Barney, Robert, 'Studying Stuff: Research in National and International Archives', in Kevin Wamsley (ed.), *Method and Methodology in Sport and Cultural History* (Dubuque, IA: Brown and Benchmark Publishers, 1995), pp. 104–10.

Barney, Robert, 'Setting the Record Straight – Again: Dorando Pietri It Is', *Olympika*, 10 (2001), pp. 129–30.

Barney, Robert, Stephen Wenn and Scott Martyn, *Selling the Five Rings: The International Olympic Committee and the Rise of Olympic Commercialism* (Salt Lake City, UT: University of Utah Press, 2002).

Beard, Adrian, *The Language of Sport* (London: Routledge, 1998).

Berryman, Jack, 'Sport History as Social History?', *Quest*, 20 (1973), pp. 65–72.

Berryman, Jack, Review of Allen Guttmann, *From Ritual to Record*, *American Historical Review*, 84, 2 (1979), p. 429.

Berryman, Jack, 'Introduction', in Donald Kyle and Gary Stark (eds), *Essays on Sport History and Sport Mythology* (College Station, TX: Texas A & M Press, 1990), pp. 3–6.

Betts, John, 'Sporting Journalism in Nineteenth-century America', *American Quarterly*, 5 (1953), pp. 39–56.

Birley, Derek, *The Willow Wand: Some Cricket Myths Explored* (London: Queen Anne Press, 1979).

Birrell, Susan, 'Discourses on the Gender/Sport Relationship. From Women in Sports to Gender Relations', *Exercise and Sport Sciences Review*, 16 (1988), pp. 459–502.

Black, David and John Nauright, *Rugby and the South African Nation* (Manchester: Manchester University Press, 1998).

Blainey, Geoffrey, *A Game of Our Own: The Origins of Australian Football* (Melbourne: Information Australia, 1990).

Block, David, *Baseball Before We Knew It: A Search for the Roots of the Game* (Lincoln, NB: University of Nebraska Press, 2005).

Bloom, John, *To Show What an Indian Can Do: Sports at Native American Boarding Schools* (Minneapolis, MN: University of Minnesota Press, 2000).

Booth, Douglas, 'Sport and Society: The Real Boycott Issues', *Indicator South Africa (Urban Monitor)*, 3, 4 (1986), pp. 1–6.

Booth, Douglas, *The Race Game: Sport and Politics in South Africa* (London: Frank Cass, 1998).

Booth, Douglas, *Australian Beach Cultures: The History of Sun, Sand and Surf* (London: Frank Cass, 2001).

Booth, Douglas, '*From Ritual to Record*: Allen Guttmann's Insights into Modernization and Modernity', *Sport History Review*, 32, 1 (2001), pp. 183–91.

Booth, Douglas, 'Post-olympism? Questioning Olympic Historiography', in John Bale and Mette Christensen (eds), *Post-Olympism? Questioning Sport in the Twenty-First Century* (Oxford: Berg, 2004), pp. 13–32.

Booth, Douglas, 'Searching for the Past: Sport Historiography in New Zealand', *Sporting Traditions*, 21, 2 (2005), pp. 1–28.

Booth, Douglas and Colin Tatz, *One-Eyed: A View of Australian Sport* (Sydney: Allen & Unwin, 2000).

Bouchier, Nancy, *For the Love of the Game: Amateur Sport in Small-town Ontario, 1838–1895* (Montreal: McGill-Queen's University Press, 2003).

Boulongne, Yves-Pierre, 'Pierre de Coubertin and Women's Sport', *Olympic Review* (February/ March 2000), pp. 23–6.

Brailsford, Dennis, *Sport and Society: Elizabeth to Anne* (London: Routledge and Kegan Paul, 1969).

Brailsford, Dennis, *A Taste for Diversions: Sport in Georgian England* (Cambridge: The Lutterworth Press, 1999).

Brohm, Jean-Marie, *Sport: A Prison of Measured Time* (London: Ink Links, 1978).

Brown, Douglas, 'Discourse and Discontinuity: Interpreting the Cultural History of Sport', in Kevin Wamsley (ed.), *Method and Methodology in Sport and Cultural History* (Dubuque, IA: Brown and Benchmark Publishers, 1995), pp. 37–48.

Brown, Douglas, 'Modern Sport, Modernism and the Cultural Manifesto: De Courbetin's *Revue Olympique*', *The International Journal of the History of Sport*, 18, 2 (2001), pp. 78–109.

Bruce, Toni, 'Postmodernism and the Possibilities for Writing "Vital" Sports Texts', in Geneviève Rail (ed.), *Sport and Postmodern Times* (Albany, NY: State University of New York Press, 1998), pp. 3–19.

Bruce, Toni and Christopher Hallinan, 'Cathy Freeman: The Quest for Australian Identity', in David Andrews and Steven Jackson (eds), *Sports Stars: The Cultural Politics of Sporting Celebrity* (London: Routledge, 2001), pp. 257–70.

Cahn, Susan, *Coming on Strong: Gender and Sexuality in Twentieth-Century Women's Sport* (Cambridge, MA: Harvard University Press, 1995).

Cameron, Jan, 'The Issue of Gender in Sport: "No Bloody Room for Sheilas …"', in Chris Collins (ed.), *Sport in New Zealand Society* (Palmerston North: Dunmore Press, 2000), pp. 171–85.

Carino, Peter, 'Novels on the Black Sox Scandal: History/Fiction/Myth', *Nine: A Journal of Baseball History and Social Policy Perspectives*, 3, 2 (1995), pp. 276–92.

Cashman, Richard, 'The Making of Sporting Traditions', *Bulletin* [of the Australian Society for Sports History] (December 1989), pp. 15–28.

Cashman, Richard, *Paradise of Sport: The Rise of Organised Sport in Australia* (Melbourne: Oxford University Press, 1995).

Cashman, Richard and Michael McKernan (eds), *Sport: Money, Morality and the Media* (Sydney: New South Wales University Press, 1981).

Chakraborty, Chandrima, 'Bollywood Motifs: Cricket Fiction and Fictional Cricket', *The International Journal of the History of Sport*, 21, 3/4 (2004), pp. 549–72.

Chandler, Joan, '"The End of Sports History?" Or the Beginning of Oral History Archives?', *Sporting Traditions*, 16, 1 (1999), pp. 41–9.

Chandler, Tim and John Nauright (eds), *Making the Rugby World: Race, Gender, Commerce* (London: Frank Cass, 1999).

Clark, Carol and Allen Guttmann, 'Artists and Athletes', *Journal of Sport History*, 22, 2 (1995), pp. 85–110.

Coates, John, The Process of Bidding for an Olympic Games, paper presented to the inaugural meeting of the Sydney Olympic Games Bid Committee, 6 March 1991.

Coetzee, J. M., 'The 1995 Rugby World Cup', in Coetzee, *Stranger Shores: Essays 1986–1999* (London: Vintage, 2002), pp. 351–6.

Cole, Cheryl, 'One Chromosome Too Many', in Kay Schaffer and Sidonie Smith (eds), *The Olympics at the Millennium: Power, Politics and the Games* (New Brunswick, NJ: Rutgers University Press, 2000), pp. 128–46.

Collins, Tony, *Rugby's Great Split: Class, Culture and the Origins of Rugby League Football* (London: Frank Cass, 1998).

Collins, Tony, 'Ahr Waggy': Harold Wagstaff and the Making of Anglo-Australian Rugby League Culture, Fifth Annual Tom Brock Lecture, 4 July 2003, Australian Society for Sports History, p. 20.

Cozens, Frederick and Florence Stumpf, *Sports in American Life* (New York: Arno Press, 1976).

Crawford, Ray, 'Moral and Manly: Girls and Games in Prestigious Church Secondary Schools of Melbourne 1901–1914', in J. A. Mangan and Roberta Park (eds), *From Fair Sex to Feminism: Sport and the Socialization of Women in the Industrial and Post-industrial Eras* (London: Frank Cass, 1987), pp. 182–207.

Crawford, Scott, '"One's Nerves and Courage are in Very Different Order Out in New Zealand": Recreational and Sporting Opportunities for Women in a Remote Colonial Setting', in J. A. Mangan and Roberta Park (eds), *From Fair Sex to Feminism: Sport and the Socialization of Women in the Industrial and Post-industrial Eras* (London: Frank Cass, 1987), pp. 161–81.

Crepeau, Richard, 'Courage, contradictions: Schmeling vs Louis vs '30s world', *Orlando Sentinel*, 8 February 2005.

Crombie, Ali, 'Mr Olympics chases his own gold', *Business Review Weekly* [Australia], 16 April 1999, pp. 85–91.

Crombie, Ali, 'Five rings, four stars, no conflict', *Business Review Weekly* [Australia], 23 April 1999, pp. 149–57.

Cronin, Mike, *Sport and Nationalism in Ireland: Gaelic Games, Soccer and Irish Identity Since 1884* (Dublin: Four Courts Press, 1999).

Cronin, Mike, 'Catholics in Sport in Northern Ireland: Exclusiveness or Inclusiveness', in Tara Magdalinski and Timothy Chandler (eds), *With God on their Side: Sport in the Service of Religion* (London: Routledge, 2002), pp. 20–36.

Crotty, Kevin, *Song and Action: The Victory Odes of Pindar* (Baltimore, MD: The Johns Hopkins University Press, 1982).

Cunningham, Hugh, *Leisure in the Industrial Revolution c.1780–c.1880* (London: Croom Helm, 1980).

Curtis, James, John Loy, and Wally Karnilowicz, 'A Comparison of Suicide-dip Effects of Major Sports Events and Civil Holidays', *Sociology of Sport Journal*, 3, 1 (1986), pp. 1–14.

Dabscheck, Braham, 'The Professional Cricketers Association of Australia', *Sporting Traditions*, 8, 1 (1991), pp. 2–27.

Daley, Caroline, *Leisure and Pleasure: Reshaping and Revealing the New Zealand Body 1900–1960* (Auckland: Auckland University Press, 2003).

Daly, John, *Elysian Fields: Sport, Class and Community in Colonial South Australia 1836–1890* (Adelaide: John Daly, 1982).

Damkjær, Søren, 'Post-Olympism and the Aestheticization of Sport', in John Bale and Mette Christensen (eds), *Post-Olympism? Questioning Sport in the Twenty-First Century* (Oxford: Berg, 2004), pp. 211–30.

Dauncey, Hugh and Geoff Hare, *The Tour de France 1903–2003: A Century of Sporting Structures, Meanings and Values* (London: Frank Cass, 2003).

Davidson, Graeme, 'The Imaginary Grandstand: International Sport and the Recognition of Australian Identity', in Bernard Whimpress (ed.), *The Imaginary Grandstand: Identity and Narrative in Australian Sport* (Kent Town: Australian Society for Sports History, 2001), pp. 12–26.

Donnelly, Peter, 'Subcultures in Sport: Resilience and Transformation', in Alan Ingham and John Loy, *Sport in Social Development: Traditions, Transitions, and Transformations* (Champaign, IL: Human Kinetics, 1993), pp. 119–45.

Dulles, Foster Rhea, *A History of Recreation: America Learns to Play* (New York: Appleton-Century-Crofts, 1965).

Dunning, Eric, 'Sport in the Civilising Process: Aspects of the Development of Modern Sport', in Dunning, Joseph Maguire and Robert Pearton (eds), *The Sports Process: A Comparative and Developmental Approach* (Champaign, IL: Human Kinetics, 1993), pp. 39–70.

Dunning, Eric, Joseph Maguire and Robert Pearton, 'Introduction: Sports in Comparative and Development Perspective', in Dunning, Maguire and Pearton (eds), *The Sports Process: A Comparative and Developmental Approach* (Champaign, IL: Human Kinetics, 1993), pp. 1–9.

Dunning, Eric and Kenneth Sheard, *Barbarians, Gentlemen and Players: A Sociological Study of the Development of Rugby Football* (Oxford: Martin Robertson, 1979).

Dunning, Eric and Kenneth Sheard, *Barbarians, Gentlemen and Players: A Sociological Study of the Development of Rugby Football*, second edition (London: Routledge, 2005).

Dyreson, Mark, *Making the American Team: Sport, Culture, and the Olympic Experience* (Urbana, IL: University of Illinois Press, 1998).

Dyreson, Mark, 'Reading Football History: New Vistas in the Landscape of Sport', *Journal of Sport History*, 29, 2 (2002), pp. 203–20.

Edwards, Harry, *The Revolt of the Black Athlete* (New York: Free Press, 1969).

Edwards, Harry, 'The Decline of the Black Athlete', in David Wiggins and Patrick Miller (eds), *The Unlevel Playing Field: A Documentary History of the African American Experience in Sport* (Urbana, IL: University of Illinois Press, 2003), pp. 435–41.

Espy, Richard, *The Politics of the Olympic Games* (Berkeley, CA: University of California Press, 1979).

Eyler, Marvin, 'Some Reflections on Objectivity and Selectivity in Historical Inquiry', *Journal of Sport History*, 1, 1 (1974), pp. 63–76.

Farred, Grant, 'The Maple Man: How Cricket Made a Postcolonial Intellectual', in Farred (ed.), *Rethinking C. L. R. James* (Oxford: Basil Blackwell, 1996), pp. 165–87.

Farred, Grant, ' "Theatre of Dreams": Mimicry and Difference in Cape Flats Township Football', in John Bale and Mike Cronin (eds), *Sport and Postcolonialism* (Oxford: Berg, 2003), pp. 123–45.

Fisher, Kevin, 'Economies of Loss and Questions of Style in Cotemporary Surf Cultures', *Junctures: The Journal of Thematic Dialogue*, 4 (2005), pp. 13–21.

Fotheringham, William, *Put Me Back on My Bike: In Search of Tom Simpson* (London: Yellow Jersey Press, 2003).

Franke, Werner and Brigitte Berendonk, 'Hormonal Doping and Androgenization of Athletes: A Secret Program of the German Democratic Republic Government', *Clinical Chemistry*, 43, 7 (1997), pp. 1262–79.

Fraser, Dawn with Harry Gordon, *Gold Medal Girl: The Confessions of an Olympic Champion* (Melbourne: Lansdowne Press, 1965).

Frey, James, 'College Athletics: Problems of a Functional Analysis', in C. Roger Rees and Andrew Miracle (eds), *Sport and Social Theory* (Champaign, IL: Human Kinetics, 1986), pp. 199–210.

Gems, Gerald, *For Profit Pride and Patriarchy: Football and The Incorporation of American Cultural Values* (Lanham, MD: The Scarecrow Press, 2000).

Gillespie, Greg, '*Wickets in the West*: Cricket, Culture, and Constructed Images of Nineteenth-Century Canada', *Journal of Sport History*, 27, 1 (2000), pp. 51–66.

Gillespie, Greg, 'Canadian Sport Studies', *International Sports Studies*, 24, 2 (2002), pp. 65–7.

Golden, Mark, *Sport and Society in Ancient Greece* (Cambridge: Cambridge University Press, 1998).

Gordon, Harry, *Australia and the Olympic Games* (Brisbane: University of Queensland Press, 1994).

Gorn, Elliot, ' "Gouge and Bite, Pull Hair and Scratch": The Social Significance of Fighting in the Southern Backcountry', *American Historical Review*, 90, 1 (1985), pp. 18–43.

Gorn, Elliot and Michael Oriard, 'Taking Sports Seriously', *Chronicle of Higher Education*, 24 March 1995.

Gould, Stephen Jay, *Bully for Brontosaurus: Reflections in Natural History* (New York: W. W. Norton, 1991).

Grundlingh, Albert, 'Playing for Power? Rugby, Afrikaner Nationalism and Masculinity in South Africa, c.1900–c.1970', in John Nauright and Tim Chandler (eds), *Making Men: Rugby and Masculine Identity* (London: Frank Cass, 1996), pp. 181–204.

Grundy, Pamela, *Learning to Win: Sports, Education, and Social Change in Twentieth-Century North Carolina* (Chapel Hill, NC: The University of North Carolina Press, 2001).

Gruneau, Richard, 'Sport and the Debate on the State', in Hart Cantelon and Richard Gruneau (eds), *Sport, Culture, and the Modern State* (Toronto: University of Toronto Press, 1982), pp. 1–38.

Gruneau, Richard, *Class, Sports, and Social Development* (Amherst, MA: University of Massachusetts Press, 1983).

Gruneau, Richard, 'Modernization or Hegemony: Two Views of Sport and Social Development', in Jean Harvey and Hart Cantelon (eds), *Not Just a Game: Essays in Canadian Sport Sociology* (Ottawa: University of Ottawa Press, 1998), pp. 9–32.

Guttmann, Allen, *From Ritual to Record: The Nature of Modern Sports* (New York: Columbia University Press, 1978).

Guttmann, Allen, 'Recent Works on European Sport History', *Journal of Sport History*, 10, 1 (1983), pp. 35–52.

Guttmann, Allen, *The Games Must Go On: Avery Brundage and the Olympic Movement* (New York: Columbia University Press, 1984).

Guttmann, Allen, *Women's Sports: A History* (New York: Columbia University Press, 1991).

Guttmann, Allen, *The Olympics: A History of the Modern Games* (Urbana, IL: University of Illinois Press, 1992).

Guttmann, Allen, *Games and Empires: Modern Sports and Cultural Imperialism* (New York: Columbia University Press, 1994).

Guttmann, Allen, *The Erotic in Sports* (New York: Columbia University Press, 1996).

Guttmann, Allen, '*From Ritual to Record*: A Retrospective Critique', *Sport History Review*, 32, 1 (2001), pp. 2–11.

Guttmann, Allen, 'Alice Milliat', in Karen Christensen, Allen Guttmann and Gertrud Pfister (eds), *International Encyclopedia of Women and Sports*, volume 2 (New York: Macmillan, 2001), pp. 743–4.

Guttmann, Allen, *Sports: The First Five Millennia* (Amherst, MA: University of Massachusetts Press, 2004).

Haigh, Gideon, 'Confessions of a Primitive Ethnographer', in Bernard Whimpress (ed.), *The Imaginary Grandstand: Identity and Narrative in Australian Sport* (Kent Town: Australian Society for Sports History, 2001), pp. 82–96.

Hall, M. Ann, *Feminism and Sporting Bodies: Essays on Theory and Practice* (Champaign, IL: Human Kinetics, 1996).

Hansen, Peter, 'Comment' (on Gordon Stewart's 'Tenzing's Two Wrist-Watches'), *Past and Present*, 157 (1997), pp. 159–77.

Hardy, Stephen, 'The City and the Rise of American Sport: 1820–1920', *Exercise and Sport Sciences Reviews*, 9 (1981), pp. 183–219.

Hardy, Stephen, 'Entrepreneurs, Organizations, and the Sport Marketplace: Subjects in Search of Historians', *Journal of Sport History*, 13, 1 (1986), pp. 14–33.

Hardy, Stephen, 'Entrepreneurs, Structures, and the Sportgeist: Old Tensions in a Modern Industry', in Donald Kyle and Gary Stark (eds), *Essays on Sport History and Sport Mythology* (College Station, TX: Texas A & M Press, 1990), pp. 45–82.

Hardy, Stephen, 'Sport in Urbanizing America: A Historical Review', *Journal of Urban History*, 23, 6 (1997), pp. 675–708.

Hardy, Stephen, 'The Long Residuals of Sport', paper presented at the Tenth Yale-Smithsonian Seminar on Material Culture, Washington, D. C., May 1997.

Hardy, Stephen, 'Where did You Go, Jackie Robinson? Or, the End of History and the Age of Sport Infrastructure', *Sporting Traditions*, 16, 1 (1999), pp. 85–100.

Hardy, Stephen and Alan Ingham, 'Games, Structure, and Agency: Historians on the American Play Movement', *Journal of Social History*, 17 (1983), pp. 285–301.

Hargreaves, Jennifer, *Sporting Females: Critical Issues in the History and Sociology of Women's Sports* (London: Routledge, 1994).

Hargreaves, Jennifer, *Heroines of Sport: The Politics of Difference and Identity* (London: Routledge, 2000).

Hargreaves, Jennifer, 'Querying Sport Feminism: Personal or Political', in Richard Giulianotti (ed.), *Sport and Modern Social Theorists* (Basingstoke: Palgrave, 2004), pp. 187–205.

Hargreaves, John, 'Sport and Hegemony: Some Theoretical Problems', in Hart Cantelon and Richard Gruneau (eds), *Sport, Culture, and the Modern State* (Toronto: University of Toronto Press, 1982), pp. 103–40.

Hargreaves, John, *Sport, Power and Culture: A Social and Historical Analysis of Popular Sports in Britain* (Cambridge: Polity Press, 1986).

Harriss, Ian, 'Packer, Cricket and Postmodernism', in David Rowe and Geoff Lawrence (eds), *Sport and Leisure: Trends in Australian Popular Culture* (Sydney: Harcourt Brace Jovanovich, 1990), pp. 109–21.

Hartmann, Douglas, 'What Can We Learn from Sport If We Take Sport Seriously as a Racial Force? Lessons from C. L. R. James's *Beyond a Boundary*', *Ethnic and Racial Studies*, 26, 3 (2003), pp. 451–83.

Hartmann, Douglas, *Race, Culture, and the Revolt of the Black Athlete: The 1968 Olympic Protests and Their Aftermath* (Chicago, IL: Chicago University Press, 2003).

Harvey, Jean, 'Historical Sociology and Social History: Même Combat', in Kevin Wamsley (ed.), *Method and Methodology in Sport and Cultural History* (Dubuque, IA: Brown and Benchmark Publishers, 1995), pp. 2–15.

Harvey, Jean, Rob Beamish and Jacques Defrance, 'Physical Exercise Policy and the Welfare State: A Framework for Comparative Analysis', *International Review for the Sociology of Sport*, 28, 1 (1993), pp. 53–63.

Hay, Roy, 'The Last Night of the Poms: Australia as a Postcolonial Sporting Society?', in John Bale and Mike Cronin (eds), *Sport and Postcolonialism* (Oxford: Berg, 2003), pp. 15–28.

Henderson, Robert, *Ball, Bat and Bishop: The Origin of Ball Games* (Urbana, IL: University of Illinois Press, 1947/2001).

Hess, Rob and Bob Stewart (eds), *More Than A Game: An Unauthorised History of Australian Rules Football* (Melbourne: Melbourne University Press, 1998).

Hill, Christopher, *Olympic Politics: Athens to Atlanta 1896–1996*, second edition (Manchester: Manchester University Press, 1996).

Hill, Jeffrey, 'Reading the Stars: A Post-Modernist Approach to Sports History', *The Sports Historian*, 14 (1994), pp. 45–55.

Hill, Jeffrey, 'British Sports History: A Post-modern Future?', *Journal of Sport History*, 23, 1 (1996), pp. 1–19.

Hill, Jeffrey, 'Cocks, Cats, Caps and Cups: A Semiotic Approach to Sport and National Identity', *Culture, Sport, Society*, 2, 2 (1999), pp. 1–21.

Hill, Jeffrey, *Sport, Leisure and Culture in Twentieth Century Britain* (Basingstoke: Palgrave, 2002).

Hill, Jeffrey, New Historicism for Historians: Sport, Literature and Society, keynote address presented to the North American Society for Sport History conference, Pacific Grove, May 2004.

Hill, Urla, 'Wilma Rudolph', in Karen Christensen, Allen Guttmann and Gertrud Pfister (eds), *International Encyclopedia of Women and Sports*, volume 2 (New York: Macmillan, 2001), pp. 956–8.

Hoch, Paul, *Rip Off the Big Game* (New York: Anchor Books, 1972).

Hoberman, John, *Sport and Political Ideology* (Austin, TX: University of Texas Press, 1984).

Hoberman, John, *Mortal Engines: The Science of Performance and the Dehumanization of Sport* (New York: Free Press, 1992).

Hoberman, John, 'Toward a Theory of Olympic Internationalism', *Journal of Sport History*, 22, 1 (1995), pp. 1–37.

Hoberman, John, *Darwin's Athletes: How Sport Has Damaged Black America and Preserved the Myth of Race* (Boston, MA: Mariner Books, 1997).

Hoberman, John, 'How Not to Read *Darwin's Athletes*: A Response to Jeffrey T. Sammons', *Journal of Sport History*, 24, 3 (1997), pp. 389–96.

Holt, Richard, *Sport and the British: A Modern History* (Oxford: Oxford University Press, 1989).

Holt, Richard, 'King Across the Border: Denis Law and Scottish Football', in Grant Jarvie and Graham Walker (eds), *Scottish Sport in the Making* (Leicester: Leicester University Press, 1994), pp. 58–74.

Holt, Richard, 'Sport and History: The State of the Subject in Britain', *Twentieth Century British History*, 7, 2 (1996), pp. 231–52.

Holt, Richard, Review of Derek Birley's trilogy, *Sport and the Making of Britain*, *Land of Sport and Glory*, and *Playing the Game* (Manchester: Manchester University Press, 1993, 1995 and 1996), *The Sports Historian*, 18, 2 (1998), pp. 169–75.

Holt, Richard and Tony Mason, *Sport in Britain 1945–2000* (Oxford: Blackwell, 2000).

Howell, Colin, 'On Metcalfe, Marx, and Materialism: Reflections on the Writing of Sport History in the Postmodern Age', *Sport History Review*, 29, 1 (1998), pp. 96–102.

Howell, Colin, *Blood, Sweat, and Cheers: Sport and the Making of Modern Canada* (Toronto: University of Toronto Press, 2001).

Huggins, Mike, *Flat Racing and British Society 1790–1914: A Social and Economic History* (London: Frank Cass, 2000).

Hughson, John, ' "We Are Red, White and Blue, We Are Catholic, Why Aren't You?": Religion and Soccer Subculture and Symbolism', in Tara Magdalinski and Timothy Chandler (eds), *With God on their Side: Sport in the Service of Religion* (London: Routledge, 2002), pp. 56–70.

Hughson, John, David Inglis and Marcus Free, *The Uses of Sport: A Critical Study* (London: Routledge, 2005).

Huizinga, Johan, *Homo Ludens: A Study of the Play Element in Culture* (Boston, MA: The Beacon Press, 1955).

Humphreys, Duncan, 'Snowboarders: Bodies Out of Control and in Conflict', *Sporting Traditions*, 13, 1 (1996), pp. 3–23.

Humphreys, Duncan, ' "Shredheads Go Mainstream": Snowboarding and Alternative Youth', *International Review for the Sociology of Sport*, 32, 2 (1997), pp. 147–60.

Hutchins, Brett, *Don Bradman: Challenging the Myth* (Melbourne: Cambridge University Press, 2002).

Ingham, Alan and Rob Beamish, 'Didn't Cyclops Lose His Vision? An Exercise in Sociological Optometry', *Sociology of Sport Journal*, 14, 2 (1997), pp. 160–86.

Ingham, Alan and Peter Donnelly, 'A Sociology of North American Sociology of Sport: Disunity in Unity, 1965 to 1996', *Sociology of Sport Journal*, 14, 4 (1997), pp. 362–418.

Ingham, Alan and Stephen Hardy, 'Sport: Structuration, Subjugation and Hegemony', *Theory, Culture and Society*, 2, 2 (1984), pp. 85–103.

Ingham, Alan and Stephen Hardy, 'Introduction: Sport Studies Through the Lens of Raymond Williams', in Alan Ingham and John Loy (eds), *Sport in Social Development: Traditions, Transitions and Transformations* (Champaign, IL: Human Kinetics, 1993), pp. 1–19.

Inglis, Ken, *Australian Colonists* (Melbourne: Melbourne University Press, 1993).

Jable, Thomas, The Reliability of Newspaper Sources, paper presented at the North American Society for Sport History conference, Ohio State University, 26 May 2003.

Jaggard, Ed, 'Writing Australian Surf Lifesaving's History', *Journal of Sport History*, 29, 1 (2002), pp. 15–23.

James, C. L. R., *Beyond a Boundary* (Durham, NC: Duke University Press, 1993).

Jarvie, Grant, 'Sport, Nationalism and Cultural Identity', in Lincoln Allison (ed.), *The Changing Politics of Sport* (Manchester: Manchester University Press, 1993), pp. 58–83.

Jarvie, Grant and Joseph Maguire, *Sport and Leisure in Social Thought* (London: Routledge, 1994).

Jobling, Ian, 'Urbanization and Sport in Canada, 1867–1900', in Richard Gruneau and John Albinson (eds), *Canadian Sport: Sociological Perspectives* (Don Mills, Ontario: Addison-Wesley, 1976), pp. 64–77.

Jones, Gareth Stedman, 'Class Expression Versus Social Control: A Critique of Recent Trends in the Social History of "Leisure" ', *History Workshop*, 4 (1977), pp. 162–70.

Jones, Lloyd, *The Book of Fame* (Auckland: Penguin, 2000).

Jørgensen, Per, 'From Balck to Nurmi: The Olympic Movement and the Nordic Nations', *The International Journal of the History of Sport*, 14, 3 (1997), pp. 69–99.

Keating, Frank, 'A preposterous slander on no end of performances', *Guardian*, 8 October 2001.

Kidd, Bruce, *The Struggle for Canadian Sport* (Toronto: University of Toronto Press, 1996).

Koppett, Leonard, The Reliability of Newspaper Sources, paper presented at the North American Society for Sport History conference, Ohio State University, 26 May 2003.

Korr, Charles, *The End of Baseball As We Knew It* (Urbana, IL: University of Illinois Press, 2002).

Krüger, Arnd and James Riordan, *The Story of Worker Sport* (Champaign, IL: Human Kinetics, 1996).

Kuklick, Bruce, 'Writing the History of Practice: The Humanities and Baseball, With a Nod to Wrestling', in Elizabeth Fox-Genovese and Elisabeth Lasch-Quinn (eds), *Reconstructing History: The Emergence of a New Historical Society* (New York: Routledge, 1999), pp. 176–88.

Kyle, Donald, *Athletics in Ancient Athens* (Leiden: E. J. Brill, 1987).

Kyle, Donald, 'E. Norman Gardiner and the Decline of Greek Sport', in Kyle and Gary Stark (eds), *Essays on Sport History and Sport Mythology* (College Station, TX: Texas A & M Press, 1990), pp. 7–44.

Lawrence, Geoffrey and David Rowe, 'Introduction: Towards a Sociology of Sport in Australia', in Lawrence and Rowe (eds), *Power Play: The Commercialisation of Australian Sport* (Sydney: Hale & Iremonger, 1986), pp. 13–45.

Laws, Michael, *Gladiator: The Norm Hewitt Story* (Wellington: Darius Press, 2001).

Lenskyj, Helen, *Inside the Olympic Industry: Power, Politics, and Activism* (Albany, NY: State University of New York Press, 2000).

Lenskyj, Helen, *The Best Olympics Ever?: Social Impacts of Sydney 2000* (Albany, NY: State University of New York Press, 2002).

Lester, Robin, *Stagg's University: The Rise and Fall of Big-Time Football at Chicago* (Champaign, IL: University of Illinois Press, 1995).

Lomas, Graham, *The Will to Win: The Story of Frank Beaurepaire* (London, Heinemann, 1960).

Lowe, Arthur, *Surfing, Surf-shooting and Surf-lifesaving Pioneering* (Manly: Arthur Lowe, 1958).

Lucas, John, 'Sport History Through Biography', *Quest*, 31, 2 (1979), pp. 216–21.

Lucas, John, 'Setting the Foundation and Governance of the American Olympic Association: The Efforts of Robert Means Thompson, 1911–1919 and 1922–1926', *Journal of Sport History*, 29, 3 (2002), pp. 457–68.

Lucas, John and Ronald Smith, *Saga of American Sport* (Philadelphia, PA: Lea and Febiger, 1978).

MacAloon, John, *This Great Symbol: Pierre de Coubertin and the Origins of the Modern Olympic Games* (Chicago, IL: University of Chicago Press, 1981).

Macdonald, Finlay, *The Game of Our Lives: The Story of Rugby and New Zealand—And How They've Shaped Each Other* (Auckland: Viking, 1996).

MacLean, Malcolm, 'Football as Social Critique: Protest Movements, Rugby and History in Aotearoa, New Zealand', in J. A. Mangan and John Nauright (eds), *Sport in Australasian Society* (London: Frank Cass, 2000), pp. 255–77.

Macrory, Jennifer, *Running With The Ball: The Birth of Rugby Football* (London: Collins Willow, 1991).

Magdalinski, Tara and Timothy Chandler, 'With God on their Side: An Introduction', in Magdalinski and Chandler (eds), *With God on their Side: Sport in the Service of Religion* (London: Routledge, 2002), pp. 1–19.

Maguire, Joseph, 'Common Ground? Links Between Sports History, Sports Geography and the Sociology of Sport', *Sporting Traditions*, 12, 1 (1995), pp. 3–25.

Maguire, Joseph, Grant Jarvie, Louise Mansfield and Joe Bradley, *Sport Worlds: A Sociological Perspective* (Champaign, IL: Human Kinetics, 2002).

Malcolmson, Robert, *Popular Recreations in English Society, 1700–1850* (Cambridge: Cambridge University Press, 1973).

Malcolmson, Robert, 'Sports in Society: A Historical Perspective', *British Journal of Sports History*, 1, 1 (1984), pp. 60–72.

Mallon, Bill and Ian Buchanan, *The 1908 Olympic Games: Results of All Events, with Commentary* (London: McFarland, 2000).

Mallon, Bill and Ture Widlund, *The 1912 Olympic Games: Results of All Events, with Commentary* (London: McFarland, 2002).

Mandell, Richard, 'Modern Criticism of Sport', in Donald Kyle and Gary Stark (eds), *Essays on Sport History and Sport Mythology* (College Station, TX: Texas A & M Press, 1990), pp. 118–38.

Mandle, W. F., 'Cricket and Australian Nationalism in the Nineteenth Century', *Journal of the Royal Australian Historical Society*, 59, 4 (1973), pp. 225–46.

Mandle, W. F., 'Sports History', in Graeme Osborne and Mandle (eds), *New History: Studying Australia Today* (Sydney: Allen & Unwin, 1982), pp. 82–93.

Mangan, J. A., *Athleticism in the Victorian and Edwardian Public School* (Cambridge: Cambridge University Press, 1981).

Mangan, J. A., *The Games Ethic and Imperialism: Aspects of Diffusion of an Ideal* (Harmondsworth: Viking, 1986).

Mangan, J. A., 'The End of History Perhaps – But the End of the Beginning for the History of Sport! An Anglo-Saxon Autobiographical Perspective', *Sporting Traditions*, 16, 1 (1999), pp. 61–72.

Mason, Tony, *Association Football and English Society, 1863–1915* (Brighton: Harvester Press, 1980).

Mason, Tony, *Sport in Britain* (London: Faber and Faber, 1988).

Mason, Tony (ed.), *Sport in Britain: A Social History* (Cambridge: Cambridge University Press, 1989).

Mazrui, Ali, 'Boxer Muhammad Ali and Soldier Idi Amin as International Political Symbols: The Bioeconomics of Sport and War', *Comparative Studies in Society and History*, 19, 2 (1977), pp. 189–215.

Mazrui, Ali, *The Africans: A Triple Heritage* (London: BBC Publications, 1986).

McAleer, Kevin, *Dueling: The Cult of Honor in Fin-de-Siècle Germany* (Princeton, NJ: Princeton University Press, 1994).

McCrone, Kathleen, 'Play up! Play up! And Play the Game! Sport at the Late Victorian Girls' Public Schools', in J. A. Mangan and Roberta Park (eds), *From Fair Sex to Feminism: Sport and the Socialization of Women in the Industrial and Post-industrial Eras* (London: Frank Cass, 1987), pp. 97–129.

McGeoch, Rod with Glenda Korporaal, *The Bid: How Australia Won the 2000 Games* (Melbourne: William Heineman, 1994).

McGimpsey, David, *Imagining Baseball: America's Pastime and Popular Culture* (Bloomington, IN: Indiana University Press, 2000).

McIntosh, Peter, 'An Historical View of Sport and Social Control', *International Review of Sport Sociology*, 6 (1971), pp. 5–13.

McKibbin, Ross, 'Working-Class Gambling in Britain 1880–1939', *Past and Present*, 82 (1979), pp. 147–78.

Menzies, Robert, 'A Green and Pleasant Memory', *The Official Report of the Organizing Committee for the Games of the XVI Olympiad, Melbourne 1956* (Melbourne: Organizing Committee of the XVI Olympiad, 1958), pp. 13–14.

Metcalfe, Alan, 'North American Sport History: A Review of North American Sport Historians and Their Works', *Exercise and Sport Sciences Reviews*, 2 (1974), pp. 225–38.

Mewett, Peter, 'History in the Making and the Making of History: Stories and the Social Construction of Sport', *Sporting Traditions*, 17, 1 (2000), pp. 1–17.

Milavic, Anthony, 'Pankration and Greek Coins', *The International Journal of the History of Sport*, 18, 2 (2001), pp. 179–92.

Mills, James, and Paul Dimeo, ' "When Gold is Fired It Shines": Sport, the Imagination and the Body in Colonial and Postcolonial India', in John Bale and Mike Cronin (eds), *Sport and Postcolonialism* (Oxford: Berg, 2003), pp. 107–22.

Milton, Simon, Review of John Sugden and Alan Tomlinson, *FIFA and the Contest for World Football, Who Rules the Peoples' Game?* (Cambridge: Polity Press, 1998), *International Sports Studies*, 21, 2 (1999), pp. 76–8.

Moore, Andrew, 'Testosterone Overdose: Popular Culture and Historical Memory', *Sporting Traditions*, 10, 1 (1993), pp. 2–22.

Moore, Andrew, Jimmy Devereux's Yorkshire Pudding: Reflections on the Origins of Rugby League in New South Wales and Queensland, Tom Brock Lecture, 1999 (Sydney: Australian Society for Sports History).

Moore, Glenn, 'Ideology on the Sportspage: Newspapers, Baseball, and Ideological Conflict in the Gilded Age', *Journal of Sport History*, 23, 3 (1996), pp. 228–55.

Moore, Kenny, 'A Courageous Stand: In '68, Olympians Tommie Smith and John Carlos Raised Their Fists For Racial Justice', *Sports Illustrated*, 5 August 1991, pp. 60–73.

Moorehouse, H. F., 'Shooting Stars: Footballers and Working-Class Culture in Twentieth Century Scotland', in Richard Holt (ed.), *Sport and the Working Class in Britain* (Manchester: Manchester University Press, 1990), pp. 179–97.

Morford, Robert and Martha McIntosh, 'Sport and the Victorian Gentleman', in Alan Ingham and John Loy (eds), *Sport in Social Development: Traditions, Transitions, and Transformations* (Champaign, IL: Human Kinetics, 1993), pp. 51–76.

Morgan, William, *Leftist Theories of Sport: A Critique and Reconstruction* (Urbana, IL: University of Illinois Press, 1994).

Morgan, William, 'Yet Another Critical Look at Hegemony Theory: A Response to Ingham and Beamish, *Sociology of Sport Journal*, 14, 2 (1997), pp. 187–95.

Morrell, Robert, 'Forging a Ruling Race: Rugby and White Masculinity in Colonial Natal, *c.*1870–1910', in John Nauright and Tim Chandler (eds), *Making Men: Rugby and Masculine Identity* (London: Frank Cass, 1996), pp. 91–120.

Morrow, Don, 'Canadian Sport History: A Critical Essay', *Journal of Sport History*, 10, 1 (1983), pp. 67–79.

Murray, Bill, 'Sport and Social Control: Introduction', in Richard Cashman and Michael McKernan (eds), *Sport: Money, Morality and the Media* (Sydney: New South Wales University Press, 1981), pp. 219–22.

Murray, Bill, '"Amateurs at Play": Sport and the Making of the British Ruling Class', *Sporting Traditions*, 16, 2 (2000), pp. 117–26.

Nathan, Daniel, 'The Story of the Hurricane', *Journal of Sport History*, 27, 2 (2000), pp. 299–303.

Nathan, Daniel, *Saying It's So: A Cultural History of the Black Sox Scandal* (Urbana, IL: University of Illinois Press, 2003).

Nauright, John, 'Colonial Manhood and Imperial Race Virility: British Responses to the Post-Boer War Colonial Rugby Tours', in Nauright and Tim Chandler (eds), *Making Men: Rugby and Masculine Identity* (London: Frank Cass,1996), pp. 121–39.

Nauright, John, *Sport, Cultures and Identities in South Africa* (London: Leicester University Press, 1997).

Nauright, John and Jane Broomhall, 'A Woman's Game: The Development of Netball and a Female Sporting Culture in New Zealand, 1906–70', *The International Journal of the History of Sport*, 10, 3 (1994), pp. 387–407.

Nauright, John and Tim Chandler (eds), *Making Men: Rugby and Masculine Identity* (London: Frank Cass, 1996).

Nisetich, Frank, *Pindar's Victory Songs* (Baltimore, MD: The Johns Hopkins University Press, 1980).

Norcliffe, Glen, *The Ride to Modernity: The Bicycle in Canada, 1869–1900* (Toronto: University of Toronto Press, 2001).

Novak, Michael, *The Joy of Sports*, revised edition (Lanham, MD: Madison Books, 1994).

O'Hara, John, *A Mug's Game: A History of Gaming and Betting in Australia* (Sydney: University of New South Wales Press, 1988).

Olsen, Jack, *The Black Athlete: A Shameful Story* (New York: Time-Life Books, 1968).

Olympic Games Melbourne 1956, Opening Ceremony, Official Souvenir Programme (author's copy).

O'Neill, Mark, Artefacts of the Present: Monuments to Indigenous Athletic Heroes in Australian Social Memory, BA (Hons) Dissertation, School of Human Movement Studies, University of Queensland, 2004.

Oriard, Michael, *Sporting with the Gods: The Rhetoric of Play and Game in American Culture* (Cambridge: Cambridge University Press, 1991).

Oriard, Michael, *Reading Football: How the Popular Press Created an American Spectacle* (Chapel Hill, NC: The University of North Carolina Press, 1993).

Oriard, Michael, *King Football: Sport & Spectacle in the Golden Age of Radio and Newsreels, Movies and Magazines, the Weekly and the Daily Press* (Chapel Hill, NC: The University of North Carolina Press, 2001).

Oriard, Michael, 'Football, Cultural History and Democracy', *Journal of Sport History*, 29, 2 (2002), pp. 241–9.

Orwell, George, 'The Sporting Spirit', in Sonia Orwell and Ian Angus (eds), *The Collected Essays, Journalism and Letters of George Orwell, 1945–1950*, volume iv (London: Secker & Warburg, 1968), pp. 40–4.

Osmond, Gary, '"Look at that Kid Crawling": Race, Myth and the "Crawl" Stroke', *Australian Historical Studies*, forthcoming.

Osmond, Gary, and Murray Phillips, '"The Bloke with the Stroke": Alick Wickham, the "Crawl" and Social Memory', *The Journal of Pacific History*, 39, 3 (2004), pp. 309–24.

Paddick, Robert, 'Amateurism', in Wray Vamplew, Katharine Moore, John O'Hara and Richard Cashman (eds), *The Oxford Companion to Australian Sport*, second edition (Melbourne: Oxford University Press, 1994), pp. 11–15.

Paraschak, Vicky, Michael Heine and James McAra, 'Native and Academic Knowledge Interests: A Dilemma', in Kevin Wamsley (ed.), *Method and Methodology in Sport and Cultural History* (Dubuque, IA: Brown and Benchmark Publishers, 1995), pp. 62–8.

Park, Roberta, 'Research and Scholarship in the History of Physical Education and Sport: The Current State of Affairs', *Research Quarterly for Exercise and Sport*, 54, 2 (1983), pp. 93–103.

Park, Roberta, 'Sport, Gender and Society in a Transatlantic Perspective', in J. A. Mangan and Roberta Park (eds), *From Fair Sex to Feminism: Sport and the Socialization of Women in the Industrial and Post-industrial Eras* (London: Frank Cass, 1987), pp. 58–93.

Park, Roberta, 'Sport History in the 1990s: Prospects and Problems', *American Academy of Physical Education Papers*, 20 (1987), pp. 96–108.

Park, Roberta, 'Physiology and Anatomy are Destiny!?: Brains, Bodies and Exercise in Nineteenth Century American Thought', *Journal of Sport History*, 18, 1 (1991), pp. 31–63.

Park, Roberta, 'A Decade of the Body: Researching and Writing About The History of Health, Fitness, Exercise and Sport, 1983–1993', *Journal of Sport History*, 21, 1 (1994), pp. 59–82.

Park, Roberta, '"Mended or Ended?" Football Injuries and the British and American Medical Press, 1870–1910', *The International Journal of the History of Sport*, 18, 2 (2001), pp. 110–33.

Parratt, Catriona, 'From the History of Women in Sport to Women's Sport History: A Research Agenda', in Margaret Costa and Sharon Guthrie (eds), *Women and Sport: Interdisciplinary Perspectives* (Champaign, IL: Human Kinetics, 1994), pp. 5–14.

Parratt, Catriona, Review of Derek Birley's, *Land of Sport and Glory* and *Playing the Game* (Manchester: Manchester University Press, 1995 and 1996), *Journal of Sport History*, 24, 2 (1997), pp. 209–211.

Parratt, Catriona, 'Reflecting on Sport History in the 1990s', *Sport History Review*, 29, 1 (1998), pp. 4–17.

Parratt, Catriona 'Making Leisure Work: Women's Rational Recreation in Late Victorian and Edwardian England', *Journal of Sport History*, 26, 3 (1999), pp. 471–87.

Parratt, Catriona, 'Of Place and Men and Women: Gender and Topophilia in the "Haxey Hood"', *Journal of Sport History*, 27, 2 (2000), pp. 229–45.

Parratt, Catriona, *More Than Mere Amusement: Working-Class Women's Leisure in England, 1750–1914* (Boston, MA: Northeastern University Press, 2001).

Parratt, Catriona, 'Robert W. Malcolmson's *Popular Recreations in English Society, 1700–1850*: An Appreciation', *Journal of Sport History*, 29, 2 (2002), pp. 313–23.

Patrick, Joan, Bathing and Drowning in Late Victorian Manly (BA Honours dissertation, University of Sydney, 1997).

Paxson, Frederick, 'The Rise of Sport', *Mississippi Valley Historical Review*, 4 (1917), pp. 143–68, reprinted in George Sage (ed.), *Sport and American Society: Selected Readings* (Reading, MA: Addison-Wesley, 1974), pp. 80–103.

Peterson, Richard, *Extra Innings: Writing on Baseball* (Urbana, IL: University of Illinois Press, 2001).

Pfister, Gertrude, 'We Love Them and We Hate Them: On the Emotional Involvement and Other Challenges during Biographical Research', in John Bale, Mette Christensen and Gertrude Pfister (eds), *Writing Lives in Sport: Biographies, Life-histories and Methods* (Aarhus: Aarhus University Press, 2004), pp. 131–56.

Phillips, Dennis, *Australian Women at the Olympic Games, 1912–1992* (Sydney: Kangaroo Press, 1992).

Phillips, Jock, 'The Hard Man: Rugby and the Formation of Male Identity in New Zealand', in John Nauright and Tim Chandler (eds), *Making Men: Rugby and Masculine Identity* (London: Frank Cass, 1996), pp. 70–90.

Phillips, Murray, 'Football, Class and War', in John Nauright and Tim Chandler (eds), *Making Men: Rugby and Masculine Identity* (London: Frank Cass, 1996), pp. 158–80.

Phillips, Murray, 'From Suburban Football to International Spectacle: The Commodification of Rugby League in Australia, 1907–1995', *Australian Historical Studies*, 110 (1998), pp. 27–48.

Phillips, Murray, 'Deconstructing Sport History: The Postmodern Challenge', *Journal of Sport History*, 28, 3 (2001), pp. 327–43.

Phillips, Murray, 'A Critical Appraisal of Narrative in Sport History: Reading the Surf Lifesaving Debate', *Journal of Sport History*, 29, 1 (2002), pp. 25–40.

Phillips, Murray, 'Tunnel Vision: The Production of Sport History', in Jan Wright (ed.), *Researching in Sport, Physical and Health Education* (Wollongong: University of Wollongong, 2004), pp. 19–35.

Phillips, Murray (ed.), *Deconstructing Sport History: A Postmodern Analysis* (Albany, NY: State University of New York Press, 2005).

Poliakoff, Michael, *Combat Sports in the Ancient World: Competition, Violence and Culture* (New Haven, CT: Yale University Press, 1987).

Polley, Martin, *Moving the Goalposts: A History of Sport and Society Since 1945* (London: Routledge, 1998).

Pope, S. W., 'Sport Films and Hall of Fame Museums: An Editorial Introduction', *Journal of Sport History*, 23, 3 (1996), pp. 309–12.

Pope S. W. (ed.), 'Roundtable: Ken Burns's *Baseball*', *Journal of Sport History*, 23, 1 (1996), pp. 61–77.

Pope, S. W., *Patriotic Games: Sporting Traditions in the American Imagination, 1876–1926* (New York: Oxford University Press, 1997).

Pope, S. W. (ed.), *The New American Sport History: Recent Approaches and Perspectives* (Urbana, IL: University of Illinois Press, 1997), pp. 1–30.

Possing, Birgitte, 'The Historical Biography: Genre, History and Methodology', in John Bale, Mette Christensen and Gertrude Pfister (eds), *Writing Lives in Sport: Biographies, Life-histories and Methods* (Aarhus: Aarhus University Press, 2004), pp. 17–24.

Rader, Benjamin, 'Modern Sports: In Search of Interpretations', *Journal of Social History*, 13, 2 (1979), pp. 307–21.

Rader, Benjamin, *American Sports: From the Age of Folk Games to the Age of Television* (Englewood Cliffs, NJ: Prentice Hall, 1983).

Rae, Simon, *W. G. Grace: A Life* (London: Faber, 1998).

Redmond, Gerald, *The Sporting Scots of Nineteenth-Century Canada* (Toronto: Associated University Presses, 1982).

Redmond, Gerald, 'Sport History in Academe: Reflections on a Half-Century of Peculiar Progress', *British Journal of Sports History*, 1, 3 (1984), pp. 24–40.

Reeve, Simon, *One Day in September* (New York: Arcade, 2000).

Reid, Louis Arnaud, 'Aesthetics and Education', in H. T. A. Whiting and D. W. Masterson (eds), *Readings in the Aesthetics of Sport* (London: Lepus Books, 1974), pp. 5–20.

Richards, Trevor, *Dancing on Our Bones: New Zealand, South Africa, Rugby and Racism* (Wellington: Bridget Williams Books, 1999).

Riess, Steven, 'Professional Sports as an Avenue of Social Mobility in America: Some Myths and Realities', in Donald Kyle and Gary Stark (eds), *Essays on Sport History and Sport Mythology* (College Station, TX: Texas A & M Press, 1990), pp. 83–117.

Riess, Steven, *City Games: The Evolution of American Urban Society and the Rise of Sports* (Urbana, IL: University of Illinois Press, 1991).

Riess, Steven, *Sport in Industrial America, 1850–1920* (Wheeling, IL: Harlan Davidson, 1995).

Riess, Steven (ed.), *Major Problems in American Sport History: Documents and Essays* (Boston, MA: Houghton Mifflin, 1997).

Rigauer, Bero, 'Marxist Theories', in Jay Coakley and Eric Dunning (eds), *Handbook of Sports Studies* (London: Sage, 2000), pp. 28–47.

Rinehart, Robert, 'Born-Again Sport: Ethics in Biographical Research', in Geneviève Rail (ed.), *Sport and Postmodern Times* (Albany, NY: State University of New York Press, 1998), pp. 33–46.

Riordan, Jim and Arna Krüger (eds), *The International Politics of Sport in the 20th Century* (London, E & FN Spon, 1999).

Ritchie, Andrew, Discussion of methodology in history, ISPHES—Sport History Scholars List, SPORTHIST@PDOMAIN.UWINDSOR.CA, 10 November 2001.

Ritchie, Andrew, 'Seeing the Past as the Present that it once was: A Response to Nancy Struna's "Reframing the Direction of Change in the History of Sport" (*IJHS*, December 2001)', *The International Journal of the History of Sport*, 20, 3 (2003), pp. 128–152.

Ritchie, Ian, 'Sex Tested, Gender Verified: Controlling Female Sexuality in the Age of Containment', *Sport History Review*, 34, 1 (2003), pp. 80–98.

Roberts, Elizabeth, Review of Catriona Parratt, *More than Mere Amusement* (Boston, MA: Northeastern University Press, 2001), *English Historical Review*, 119, 483 (2004), pp. 1078–9.

Roche, Maurice, *Mega-events and Modernity: Olympics and Expos in the Growth of Global Culture* (London: Routledge, 2000).

Rowe, David, 'Saturday Afternoon Theory', *Sporting Traditions*, 4, 1 (1987), pp. 56–66.

Rowe, David and Jim McKay, 'Out of the Shadows: The Critical Sociology of Sport in Australia, 1986 to 1996', *Sociology of Sport Journal*, 14, 4 (1997), pp. 340–61.

Rühl, Joachim, 'Sports Quantification in Tudor and Elizabethan Tournaments', in John Marshall Carter and Arnd Krüger (eds), *Ritual and Record: Sports Records and Quantification in Pre-modern Societies* (New York: Greenwood Press, 1990), pp. 65–86.

Ryan, Greg, *The Making of New Zealand Cricket 1832–1914* (London: Frank Cass, 2004).

Ryle, Gerard and Gary Hughes, 'Breaking China: How Sydney stole the games', *Sydney Morning Herald*, 6 March 1999.

Sage, George, *Power and Ideology in American Sport: A Critical Perspective* (Champaign, IL: Human Kinetics, 1990).

Sammons, Jeffrey, 'A Proportionate and Measured Response to the Provocation That is *Darwin's Athletes*', *Journal of Sport History*, 24, 3 (1997), pp. 378–88.

Sandercock, Leonie and Ian Turner, *Up Where, Cazaly?: The Great Australian Game* (London: Granada, 1982).

Sandiford, Keith, 'The Victorians at Play: Problems in Historiographical Methodology', *Journal of Social History*, 15, 2 (1981), pp. 271–88.

Sansone, David, *Greek Athletics and the Genesis of Sport* (Berkeley, CA: University of California Press, 1988).

Scherman, Tony, 'Sports history: How games tell us who we are', *New York Times*, 28 November 1983.

Schultz, Jaime, ' "A Wager Concerning a Diplomatic Pig": Remembering and Forgetting in the Iowa-Minnesota Football Contests, 1934–1935', *Journal of Sport History*, forthcoming.

Senn, Alfred, *Power, Politics, and the Olympic Games* (Champaign, IL: Human Kinetics, 1999).

Sheridan, Tom, *Report on the Independent Examination for SOCOG* (Sydney Organising Committee for the Olympic Games), 12 March 1999.

Silber, Irwin, *Press Box Red* (Philadelphia, PA: Temple University Press, 2003).

Silverstein, Paul, 'Stadium Politics: Sport, Islam and Amazigh Consciousness in France and North Africa', in Tara Magdalinski and Timothy Chandler (eds), *With God on their Side: Sport in the Service of Religion* (London: Routledge, 2002), pp. 37–55.

Simpson, Clare, 'Respectable Identities: New Zealand Nineteenth-Century "New Women"— On Bicycles!', *The International Journal of the History of Sport*, 18, 2 (2001), pp. 54–77.

Sissons, Ric, *The Players: A Social History of the Professional Cricketer* (Sydney: Pluto Press, 1988).

Smith, Ronald, *Sports and Freedom: The Rise of Big-Time College Athletics* (New York: Oxford University Press, 1988).

Smith, Ronald, Roundtable Discussion: Sport, Nationalism and *Patriotic Games*, paper presented at the North American Society for Sport History Conference, 24 May 1998, University of Windsor.

Smith, Ronald, *Play-by-Play: Radio, Television and Big-Time College Sport* (Baltimore, MD: The Johns Hopkins University Press, 2001).

Smith, Ronald, 'Intercollegiate Athletics/Football History at the Dawn of a New Century', *Journal of Sport History*, 29, 2 (2002), pp. 229–39.

'Sport and Apartheid', *Current Affairs Bulletin* [Australia], November 1970, pp. 188–90.

Stewart, Bob, 'Stoddart on Sport', *Sporting Traditions*, 3, 1 (1986), pp. 82–93.

Stewart, Bob, 'Boom-time Football, 1946–1975', in Rob Hess and Bob Stewart (eds), *More Than a Game: An Unauthorised History of Australian Rules Football* (Melbourne: Melbourne University Press, 1998), pp. 165–99.

Stewart, Bob and Aaron Smith, 'Australian Sport in a Postmodern Age', in J. A. Mangan and John Nauright (eds), *Sport in Australasian Society* (London: Frank Cass, 2000), pp. 278–304.

Stewart, Gordon, 'Tenzing's Two Wrist-Watches: The Conquest of Everest and Late Imperial Culture in Britain 1921–1953, *Past and Present*, 149 (1995), pp. 170–97.

Stewart, Gordon, 'Reply' (to Peter Hansen), *Past and Present*, 157 (1997), pp. 178–90.

Stoddart, Brian, 'Sport, Cultural Imperialism, and Colonial Response to the British Empire', *Comparative Studies in Society and History*, 30, 4 (1988), pp. 649–73.

Stoddart, Brian, 'Sport, Colonialism and Struggle: C. L. R. James and Cricket', in Richard Giulianotti (ed.), *Sport and Modern Social Theorists* (Basingstoke: Palgrave Macmillan, 2004), pp. 111–28.

Struna, Nancy, 'E. P. Thompson's Notion of "Context" and the Writing of Physical Education and Sport History', *Quest*, 38 (1986), pp. 22–32.

Struna, Nancy, ' "Good Wives" and "Gardeners", Spinners and "Fearless Riders": Middle- and Upper-rank Women in the Early American Sporting Culture', in J. A. Mangan and Roberta Park (eds), *From Fair Sex to Feminism: Sport and the Socialization of Women in the Industrial and Post-industrial Eras* (London: Frank Cass, 1987), pp. 235–55.

Struna, Nancy, 'Gender and Sporting Practice in Early America, 1750–1810, *Journal of Sport History*, 18, 1 (1991), pp. 10–30.

Struna, Nancy, *People of Prowess: Sport, Leisure, and Labor in Early Anglo-America* (Urbana, IL: University of Illinois Press, 1996).

Struna, Nancy, 'Historical Research in Physical Activity', in Jerry Thomas and Jack Nelson (eds), *Research Methods in Physical Activity* (Champaign, IL: Human Kinetics, 1996), pp. 251–75.

Struna, Nancy, 'Sport History', in John Massengale and Richard Swanson (eds), *The History of Exercise and Sport Science* (Champaign, IL: Human Kinetics, 1997), pp. 143–79.

Struna, Nancy, 'Social History and Sport', in Jay Coakley and Eric Dunning (eds), *Handbook of Sports Studies* (London: Sage, 2000), pp. 187–203.

Struna, Nancy, 'Reframing the Direction of Change in the History of Sport', *The International Journal of the History of Sport*, 18, 4 (2001), pp. 1–15.

Suits, Bernard, *The Grasshopper: Games, Life and Utopia* (Toronto: University of Toronto Press, 1978).

Sydnor, Synthia, 'A History of Synchronized Swimming', *Journal of Sport History*, 25, 2 (1998), pp. 252–67.

Tatz, Colin, *Obstacle Race: Aborigines in Sport* (Sydney: University of New South Wales Press, 1995).

Tatz, Colin, *A Course of History: Monash Country Club 1931–2001* (Sydney: Allen & Unwin, 2002).

Taylor, Matthew, Review of P. Vasili, *Colouring Over the White Line* (Edinburgh: Mainstream Press, 2000), *Soccer and Society*, 2, 1 (2001), pp. 119–20.

Templeton, Malcolm, *Human Rights and Sporting Contacts: New Zealand Attitudes to Race Relations in South Africa 1921–94* (Auckland: Auckland University Press, 1998).

Thomas de la Peña, Carolyn, 'Dudley Allen Sargent and Gustav Zander: Health Machines and the Energized Male Body', *Research in Philosophy and Technology*, 21 (2002), pp. 9–47.

Thompson, Shona, 'Challenging the Hegemony: New Zealand Women's Opposition to Rugby and the Reproduction of a Capitalist Patriarchy', *International Review for the Sociology of Sport*, 23, 3 (1988), pp. 205–10.

Thompson, Shona, 'The Tour', in Brad Patterson (ed.), *Sport, Society and Culture in New Zealand* (Wellington: Stout Research Centre, 1999), pp. 79–91.

Tomlinson, Alan, 'Good Times, Bad Times and the Politics of Leisure: Working-Class Culture in the 1930s in a Small Northern English Working-Class Community', in Hart Cantelon and Robert Hollands (eds), *Leisure, Sport and Working-Class Cultures: Theory and History* (Toronto: Garamond Press, 1988), pp. 41–64.

Tofel, Richard, 'The "innocuous conspiracy" of baseball's birth: Two long-lost letters show how Doubleday was credited with the game's invention', *Wall Street Journal*, 19 July 2001.

Tosches, Nick, *The Devil and Sonny Liston* (Boston, MA: Little, Brown, 2000).

Tranter, Neil, 'The Social and Occupational Structure of Organized Sport in Central Scotland During the Nineteenth Century', *The International Journal of the History of Sport*, 4, 3 (1987), pp. 301–14.

Tranter, Neil, *Sport, Economy and Society in Britain 1750–1914* (Cambridge: Cambridge University Press, 1998).

Tygiel, Jules, *Baseball's Great Experiment* (New York: Oxford University Press, 1993).

Ungerleider, Steven, *Faust's Gold: Inside the East German Doping Machine* (New York: St Martin's Press, 2001).

Vamplew, Wray, 'Sports Crowd Disorder in Britain, 1870–1914: Causes and Controls', *Journal of Sport History*, 7, 1 (1980), pp. 5–20.

Vamplew, Wray, 'The Economics of a Sports Industry: Scottish Gate-Money Football, 1890–1914', *Economic History Review*, 35, 4 (1982), pp. 549–67.

Vamplew, Wray, *Pay Up and Play the Game: Professional Sport in Britain, 1875–1914* (Cambridge: Cambridge University Press, 1988).

Vamplew, Wray, 'Sport and Industrialization: An Economic Interpretation of the Changes in Popular Sport in Nineteenth-Century England', in J. A. Mangan (ed.), *Pleasure, Profit, Proselytism: British Culture and Sport at Home and Abroad 1700–1914* (London: Frank Cass, 1988), pp. 7–20.

Vamplew, Wray, 'Facts and Artefacts: Sports Historians and Sports Museums', *Journal of Sport History*, 25, 2 (1998), pp. 268–82.

Vasili, Phil, *The First Black Footballer, Arthur Wharton 1865–1930: An Absence of Memory* (London: Frank Cass, 1998).

Vertinsky, Patricia, *The Eternally Wounded Woman: Women, Doctors, and Exercise in the Late Nineteenth Century* (Urbana, IL: University of Illinois Press, 1994).

Vertinsky, Patricia, 'Gender Relations, Women's History and Sport History: A Decade of Changing Enquiry, 1983–1993', *Journal of Sport History*, 21, 1 (1994), pp. 1–24.

Vertinsky, Patricia and Sherry McKay (eds), *Disciplining Bodies in the Gymnasium: Memory, Monument, Modernism* (London: Routledge, 2004).

Vertinsky, Patricia, Sherry McKay and Stephen Petrina, 'No Body/ies in the Gym', in Patricia Vertinsky and Sherry McKay (eds), *Disciplining Bodies in the Gymnasium: Memory, Monument, Modernism* (London: Routledge, 2004), pp. 157–71.

Vincent, Geoffrey and Toby Harfield, 'Repression and Reform: Responses within New Zealand Rugby to the Arrival of the "Northern Game", 1907–8', *New Zealand Journal of History*, 31, 2 (1997), pp. 234–49.

Voigt, David, 'Myths After Baseball: Notes on Myths in Sports', *Quest*, 30 (1978), pp. 46–57.

Walvin, James, 'Sport, Social History and the Historian', *British Journal of Sports History*, 1, 1 (1984), pp. 5–13.

Wamsley, Kevin, 'Cultural Signification and National Ideologies: Rifle-shooting in Late Nineteenth-century Canada', *Social History*, 20, 1 (1995), pp. 63–72.

Wamsley, Kevin (ed.), *Method and Methodology in Sport and Cultural History* (Dubuque, IA: Brown and Benchmark Publishers, 1995).

Wamsley, Kevin, 'Power and Privilege in Historiography: Constructing Percy Page', *Sport History Review*, 28, 2 (1997), pp. 146–55.

Ward, Geoffrey and Ken Burns, *Baseball: An Illustrated History* (New York: Alfred A. Knopf, 1994).

Watterson, John, *College Football: History, Spectacle, Controversy* (Baltimore, MD: The Johns Hopkins University Press, 2000).

Watterson, John, 'Out of Baseball's Shadow: The Paradox of College Football Scholarship', *Journal of Sport History*, 29, 2 (2002), pp. 221–8.

Wenn, Stephen, 'Archival Wanderings: Rubbing Shoulders with History', in Kevin Wamsley (ed.), *Method and Methodology in Sport and Cultural History* (Dubuque, IA: Brown and Benchmark Publishers, 1995), pp. 121–6.

Whannel, Gary, *Media Sport Stars: Masculinities and Moralities* (London: Routledge, 2002).

Whimpress, Bernard, 'The Value of Facts in Sports History', *Sporting Traditions*, 9, 1 (1992), pp. 2–15.

Whimpress, Bernard (ed.), *The Imaginary Grandstand: Identity and Narrative in Australian Sport* (Kent Town: Australian Society for Sports History, 2001).

Whimpress, Bernard, Review of Mike Coleman and Ken Edwards, *Eddie Gilbert: The True Story of an Aboriginal Cricketing Legend* (Sydney: ABC Books, 2002), *Sporting Traditions*, 19, 1 (2002), pp. 91–4.

Wiggins, David, 'Clio and the Black Athlete in America: Myths, Heroes, and Realities', *Quest*, 32, 2 (1980), pp. 217–25.

Wiggins, David, 'Work, Leisure and Sport in America: The British Travelers Image, 1830–1860', *Canadian Journal of History of Sport*, 18, 1 (1982), pp. 28–60.

Wiggins, David, 'Prized Performers, but Frequently Overlooked Students: The Involvement of Black Athletes in Intercollegiate Sports on Predominantly White University Campuses, 1890–1972', *Research Quarterly for Exercise and Sport*, 62, 2 (1991), pp. 164–77.

Wiggins, David, *Glory Bound: Black Athletes in a White America* (Syracuse, NY: Syracuse University Press, 1997).

Wiggins, William, 'Boxing's Sambo Twins: Racial Stereotypes in Jack Johnson and Joe Louis Newspaper Cartoons, 1908 to 1938', *Journal of Sport History*, 15, 3 (1988), pp. 242–54.

Willan, Brian, 'An African in Kimberley: Sol T. Plaatje, 1894–1898', in Shula Marks and Richard Rathbone (eds), *Industrialisation and Social Change in South Africa: African Class Formation, Culture, and Consciousness, 1870–1930* (London: Longman, 1982), pp. 238–58.

Williams, Gareth, 'From Popular Culture to Public Cliché: Image and Identity in Wales, 1890–1914', in J. A. Mangan (ed.), *Pleasure, Profit, Proselytism: British Culture and Sport at Home and Abroad 1700–1915* (London: Frank Cass, 1988), pp. 128–43.

Wilson, Wayne, 'A Bibliometric Analysis of NASSH Literature, 1973–2001: Assessing Innovation, Continuity and Impact', paper presented to the North American Society for Sport History convention, 28 May 2004.

Wilson, Wayne, 'Nawal El Moutawakel', in Karen Christensen, Allen Guttmann and Gertrud Pfister (eds), *International Encyclopedia of Women and Sports*, volume 1 (New York: Macmillan, 2001), pp. 362–3.

Winkler, Karen, 'A lot more than trading baseball cards: Sport history gains a new respectability', *Chronicle of Higher Education*, 5 June 1985.

Womack, Mari, *Sport as Symbol: Images of the Athlete in Art, Literature and Song* (Jefferson, NC: McFarland, 2003).

Young, David, *The Olympic Myth of Greek Amateur Athletics* (Chicago, IL: Ares, 1984).

Young, David, *The Modern Olympics: A Struggle for Revival* (Baltimore, MD: The Johns Hopkins University Press, 1996).

Zakus, Dwight and Synthia Slowikowski, 'Alternative Research Theories and Methodologies for Sport History: From Mills and Carr, Through Hesse, to Nonequilibrium Theory', in Kevin Wamsley (ed.), *Method and Methodology in Sport and Cultural History* (Dubuque, IA: Brown and Benchmark Publishers, 1995), pp. 16–36.

Zang, David, *SportsWars: Athletes in the Age of Aquarius* (Fayetteville, AR: The University of Arkansas Press, 2001).

Zucker, Harvey and Lawrence Babich, *Sports Films: A Complete Reference* (Jefferson, NC: McFarland, 1987).

Index